AF605969

Picturing Mexico:
From the Camera Lucida to Film

For Elaine

Picturing Mexico: From the Camera Lucida to Film

John Fullerton

British Library Cataloguing in Publication Data

Picturing Mexico: From the Camera Lucida to Film

A catalogue entry for this book is available from the British Library

ISBN: 9780 86196 701 8 (Hardback)

Front cover: Detail, Pietro Gualdi, *Vista sudeste del panorama de México* (1841), reproduced by permission of Fondo Reservado, Biblioteca Nacional UNAM.

Rear cover: Decorative motif on front cover, John Lloyd Stephens, *Incident of Travel in Central America, Chiapas, and Yucatan* (twelfth edition, 1852 [1841]), author's collection.

Published by
John Libbey Publishing Ltd, 3 Leicester Road, New Barnet, Herts EN5 5EW, United Kingdom
e-mail: john.libbey@orange.fr; web site: www.johnlibbey.com
Direct orders (UK and Europe): direct.orders@marston.co.uk

Distributed in Asia and North America by **Indiana University Press**, Office of Scholarly Publishing, Herman B Wells Library—350, 1320 E. 10th St., Bloomington, IN 47405, USA. www.iupress.indiana.edu

Printed and bound in China by 1010 Printing International Ltd.

Contents

The Colour Plates are bound between Chapters Two and Three, after page 50

Acknowledgements

The number of people to whom I am indebted is substantial. Some of the most pleasant periods of research were conducted early and late in the project, particularly at the National Library of Scotland and at the Getty Research Institute, where Frances Terpak, Curator of Photographs and Collection Development, and Beth Guynn, Special Collections Cataloger, provided unstinting support when I started out on the project at a time when much of the material I encountered was new to me. With the team of colleagues who work in Special Collections (particularly Kenneth Brown and Charlie Rossow) and Susan M. Allen, chief librarian, periods of research spent in Los Angeles were always energising.

I thank Aurelio de los Reyes for his generous knowledge and hospitality, and for acting as architect of the periods when, as a visiting scholar at the Instituto de Investigaciones Estéticas at Universidad Nacional Autónoma de México, I was able to complete much research in Mexico that otherwise would not have been available to me. In this regard, I am grateful to María Teresa Uriarte Castañeda and Arturo Pascual Soto who, as directors of the Instituto de Investigaciones Estéticas at UNAM, provided support and encouragement at different points during the project. I also owe a deep debt of gratitude to Iván Trujilo Bolio, the former director general of Filmoteca UNAM, and Ángel Martinez Juárez, head of cataloguing, who provided opportunities for me to view films and make frame enlargements. I also received unstinting support from colleagues in the Fototeca UNAM, particularly Pedro Angeles, the coordinator of the Fototeca, and Cecilia Gutiérrez, the curator responsible for the Michaud collection.

In a project that entailed consulting thousands of photographs, considerable periods of study were conducted in Mexican archives where curators always welcomed me with warmth and enthusiasm. Deep gratitude is reserved for Alma del Carmen Vázquez Morales, the head of the Centro de Información Gráfica and her staff at the Archivo General de la Nación, and Jorge Frías Villegos, director of the Central Historical Archive, who arranged for the digitizing of some prints held at the Centro de Información Gráfica on my last research trip to Mexico City. Particular thanks also go to Roberto L. Mayer and Laura Mayer, who provided access to an unparalleled private collection in Mexico, and to Gina Rodriguez and Douglas Nance who shared their knowledge and enthusiasm for Mexican photography and things Mexican with unabashed enthusiasm. Deborah Dorotinsky, at the Instituto de Investigaciones Estéticas UNAM, shared much knowledge and love for photographs and Mexican archaeology, and Pedro Boker provided access to the German-language version of Guillermo Kahlo's *México 1904*. Other institutions and personnel who welcomed me on one or more research trips to Mexico City include Carlos Vidalí Rebolledo, head of the Mapoteca Manuel Orozco y Berra (whose broad taste in music made visits to the collection a delight), Manuel Ramos Medina, director of the Centro de Estudios de Historia de México Condumex, and Teresa Matabuena Peláez, coordinator of historical services in the Biblioteca Francisco Xavier Clavigero at the Universidad Iberoamericana, who provided access to the Spanish-language version of Kahlo's *México 1904*. Jaime Rios, coordinator of the Biblioteca Nacional de México UNAM, and Rosario Rodriguez

Torres at the Iconoteca, Biblioteca Nacional de México UNAM, were also very helpful in providing scans of photographs held in the Fondo Reservado at Biblioteca Nacional de México UNAM.

Other researchers with whom I came into contact who were generous in sharing their knowledge and enthusiasm for things archaeological in Yucatán include Luis Millet Camara, former director of archaeology at Centro INAH Yucatán, and George Bay who, as site director at Kihuic, provided access to an important site that was under investigation during the time-frame of the project. A day spent with the Maya guide, Mario Humberto Margaña Arara, introduced me to little-known archaeological delights in Yucatán, one of the most memorable of experiences spent in the field. I also owe a debt of gratitude to Vetenskapsrådet, Stockholm, and the Department of Media Studies at Stockholm University from whom I received support for periods of research in Mexico, Central America, the United States, and Europe.

Gregor Wolff and Edmund Seifert at the Ibero-Amerikanisches Institut Preussischer Kulturbesitz in Berlin, Susan Snyder, Head, Public Service, David Kessler, Charles Faulhaber, and James Eason provided energetic support for short and intensive periods of study at The Bancroft Library, University of California, Berkeley, as too Christine Barthe at the Musée de l'homme in Paris, Anne Godfroid, curator, at the Documentation Centre of the Musée Royale de l'Armée et d'Histoire Militaire in Brussels, and Susan Palmer at the Sir John Soane's Museum Research Library in London. Other archivists and librarians who gave unreserved support for consulting collections include Claire Welford, rare books superintendent, at Cambridge University Library, Patricia Massé Zendejar, director, Fototeca Nacional del INAH, George Stanley at the National Library of Scotland, who always took delight in finding the most arcane reference, and Sally Pagan and staff at the Centre for Research Collections at the University of Edinburgh. Joanna Brogan and the staff of the National Art Library at the Victoria and Albert Museum, South Kensington, Suzanne Hartley, library services manager and staff in the Special Collections Reading Room at the University of Glasgow, and José de Jesús Hernández at the Biblioteca Justino Fernández in Mexico City provided access to material from which the present study also benefited.

There is also a substantial group of people without whose support and practical advice research trips would never have been realised. Friends abroad include Dorie Baizley and Ed Woll, who gave enormous support to a person who had not been to Los Angeles before the projected started. Jan Olsson and Bart van der Gaag, colleagues in Cinema Studies at Stockholm University, also provided unstinting support, particularly Jan who backed the project without question from the outset. Encouragement could always be anticipated from friends and colleagues in early cinema: Richard Abel, Ramona Curry, Erkki Huhtamo, Gunnar Iversen, Charles Musser, Barry Salt, and Mark Sandberg, who variously provided assistance of an academic or practical nature (sometimes both) at various points during the project.

Friends who supported the project from its inception include Carlos Bustamante, who introduced me to Aurelio de los Reyes. Without Carlos' support, the project would have floundered at an early stage. Former colleagues and friends who also informed the project indirectly include Alan Barnes and John F. X. Berger, to whom I owe a deep debt of gratitude for sharing their love and knowledge of still images, particularly Alan who read drafts of some of the early chapters and provided generous comments. From Alan and John I learnt much, some of which they will recognise in the pages of this book.

Lastly, the muse who supported the project from the outset, who accompanied me on research trips in Mexico, the USA, Central America, and Europe, who withstood sweltering heat in the lowland tropics of Mexico, Guatemala, and Honduras, made notes, often in less than ideal conditions, in archives and libraries in Mexico, and prepared drafts of the Select Bibliography and Index: Elaine King. Without Elaine, this project would not have been possible; thanks to her, it reached completion.

Introduction

The subject of this study is Mexico as represented by visitors to the country from Europe and North America between the late 1830s and 1910, a date often associated with the 'centenary' of Mexican independence; a study of representations of Mexico, in other words, before the revolution. Not only before the revolution, but also before Henry Weston, before Tina Modotti, before Manuel Álvarez Bravo, before Sergei Eisenstein; before, in short, that point in time when a history of the arts and material culture in Mexico coincided with practitioners of Mexican modernism and a history of political and social reform in the 1920s, when Magdalena Carmen Frida Kahlo Calderón was a young woman.[1] Before Frida Kahlo, in other words (but not her father, Guillermo), before Diego Rivera, and before the end of the Porfiriato, when Porfirio Díaz, the ageing president of Mexico, a powerful political figure in Mexico for some forty years, was forced to resign the presidency (together with Vice-President Ramón Corral) in May 1911 and go into exile in Europe. There is, however, also a further sense in which this study is concerned with an anterior state: before the 'birth' of cinema.

André Gaudreault and Philippe Marion have observed that 'a medium does not really impose itself as an autonomous medium ... until it has defined its own way of re-presenting, expressing and communicating the world'. Implicit in such an observation is a recognition that the salient feature that existed before the 'birth' of cinema was that for those 'who came *before* the birth of the cinema ... early cinema was not, in fact, early cinema'. During this phase, film appropriated earlier traditions of stage presentation (magic shows, *féerie*, farce, plays, and other kinds of stage performances), a phase which Gaudreault and Marion characterise as the medium's 'integrating birth', when the new medium integrated the intermedial context that attended its inception without asserting its own identity as a medium.[2] There then followed a second phase, the medium's 'distinguishing birth', a period when the proto-medium became autonomous by negotiating the intermediality inherent in the medium through a form of 'interaction with its own potential'.[3] This stage, Gaudreault and Marion argue, constitutes the medium's second inception, a phase when cinema began to define its 'identity' as a medium.

The antecedents of this second phase, the intermediality evident in certain forms of popular visual culture in the nineteenth century, constitute the concerns of this investigation with regard to picturing Mexico. Analysis aims to demonstrate that many of the formal concerns constituted in cinema as a medium were developed through much of the nineteenth century. In other words, for those who came *before* the 'birth' of cinema, the proto-medium was defined by media practices that had been established and developed in nineteenth-century popular visual culture. This study, therefore, is an investigation of an anterior state before a medium became a medium, an investigation that takes as its object an 'archaeology' of film form, a history of the formal devices which the medium drew on and which, predating cinema, indirectly contributed to its development. An 'archaeology' of film form, not in the sense of recovering a lost or forgotten material past (involving excavation and stratigraphic analysis, the hallmarks of systematic archaeological investigation by the end of the nineteenth century),[4] and not in the sense of examining overlooked, ignored, or occluded technologies and technological devices,[5] but an investigation of stylistic devices and modes which, at a later date, informed the development of film. An 'archaeology' concerned with identifying the material traces of nineteenth-century popular visual culture which cinema later integrated, a process where the pre-history of cinema is read as being palimpsestic, involving stylistic and representational innovations that were 'superimposed' on earlier representational forms. In short, 'cinema' before cinema.

If the above characterises the concern investigated in these pages, what is the nature of the history that will be presented? Primarily one that documents popular visual culture during a period when substantial changes accompanied the introduction and development of a range of media forms in the nineteenth century, from lithographs to photographs, from photographs to the illustrated press and the exhibition of film not only in towns and cities in Mexico, but also in the private home, an arena encapsulated by the Pathé Kok 28mm projector when non-flammable film was introduced for domestic projection. A history which seeks, in other words, to trace Mexico's popular visual culture from the 1830s to the end of the first decade of the twentieth century in a period when the medium had not yet been formed. A history, moreover, that does not seek to chart the period in a linear fashion, documenting the development of a formal concern or a narrational device from one point in time to a later point (if such a historiography could ever be realised); rather, the trajectory of this study is one that centres attention on a series of intersections, a process which traces a lineage that is interrupted yet, over time, demonstrates development in formal terms. In other words, history conceived as a series of nodes or intersections which enable us to compare a representational mode at a given point in time with earlier or later manifestations in a process that demonstrates how innovation in representation superseded earlier modes.

A series of historical intersections provide focus for the study: the 1820s (when, shortly after independence in 1821, Mexico opened its borders to foreign investment and speculation); the 1840s (when Mexico was the object of proto-archaeological investigation); the 1860s, when Mexico, in debt to France, Britain, and Spain, was subject to occupation by the French as Napoleon III (Louis-Napoléon Bonaparte) attempted to make Mexico economically secure by imposing a provisional government and organising a plebiscite to recognise the Austrian archduke, Ferdinand Maximilian of Hapsburg, as Emperor of Mexico;[6] and, finally, the 1890s and turn of the century, when Mexico experienced its first wave of tourists to the country from, in the majority of cases, North America.

The development of tourism and speculation in the economic development of Mexico in the late nineteenth century was significant. In April 1884, the railway between Mexico City and the Rio Grande opened to traffic, introducing a new frontier for trade and development. The following year, the Boston-based company of Raymond and Whitcomb organised its first 'grand excursion' from Boston, touring through the southern states of the United States to Mexico City and back again to Boston. Over the next five years, Raymond and Whitcomb introduced an increasing number of North American tourists to Mexico during winter and spring.[7] En route to Mexico City, visitors were accommodated in luxury vestibuled Pullman cars with a Pullman dining-car where excursionists took all meals.[8] Once the excursionists arrived in Mexico City, they were accommodated at Hotel Iturbide,[9] the pre-eminent hotel in late-nineteenth-century Mexico City. Raymond and Whitcomb's 'grand excursions' were devised for a wealthy elite, some excursionists, such as Mary Elizabeth Blake and Margaret F. Sullivan, members of the first Raymond and Whitcomb excursion, publishing travel accounts that doubtlessly helped fuel the expansion of tourism in Mexico at the end of the century.[10]

By the end of the 1890s, the first wave of tourists had become a veritable flood as other companies began to organise tours on a regular basis with notices of arrivals announced in *The Mexican Herald*, one of two English-language daily newspapers published in Mexico City. On 2 January 1898, for example, the year in which one of the most productive American photographers considered in this study opened a studio in Mexico City, Reau Campbell, manager of an American Tourist Association tour and author of *Campbell's Complete Guide and Descriptive Book of Mexico*,[11] accompanied the first winter tour of the season. Travelling in a Pullman train with dining-car, sleeping-cars, a library car, and an 'open no-top observation car', excursionists were lodged at Hotel Sanz in Mexico City.[12] In the following months, two further companies brought North American tourists to the Mexican capital: the Grafton Excursion (which arrived in Mexico City on 2 February with fifty-seven visitors) and Gates Excursions (which arrived on 2 March with a party of 115 visitors and a second group of fifty-two visitors).[13] The following day, Gates Excursions brought a further 186 visitors to the city ('the largest paid excursion ever brought to Mexico') who lodged at the Hotel del Jardín,[14] and a fourth operator, Ward Excursionists, brought a further thirty-five tourists to Mexico City who arrived on 6 March and were accommodated at the Humboldt Hotel.[15] By the turn of the century, Mexico had become a well-established tourist destination, included in *John L. Stoddard's Lectures* by the well-known North American travel lecturer who had travelled through Mexico in 1890.[16]

Tourist travel to Mexico in the late nineteenth century announces one of the discourses with which this study engages: the picturesque, a movement considered here, in the late eighteenth century, as an expression of the development of a popular visual culture promoted by the writings of William Gilpin, distinct from the aesthetic philosophy developed by Uvedale Price in *An Essay on the Picturesque* (London, 1794) and Richard Payne Knight in *An Analytical Inquiry into the Principles of Taste* (London, 1805). In particular, three formal concerns examined in this study were initiated in the late eighteenth century: the panorama, reverse views, and progression through space, three palimpsestic representational forms that frame the concerns of this investigation.

Chapter One examines the painted panorama, concentrating on a case study of three panoramas devised by Frederick Catherwood in the 1830s before he travelled with John Lloyd Stephens to Mexico and Central America in the early 1840s. Although the painted panorama exhibited in a purpose-built rotunda was never established in Mexico in the nineteenth century, the influence of the panorama in Mexico was pervasive. Associated with this area of artistic production, often regarded as the first mass medium, a more general concern with panoramic views is considered in Chapter Two together with a discussion of the picturesque in Britain towards the end of the eighteenth and early nineteenth centuries. Central to this discussion is a consideration of pictorial composition in the picturesque manner and *repoussoir*, and the articulation of reverse views which were celebrated in many tourist guides published in the late eighteenth century, an aspect that later became central to the development of character-centred narration in classical cinema when the attendant diegetic conception of camera position had become stable.[17] This latter development, however, lies well outside the time-frame of the present study.

The second concern which tourists of the picturesque brought to their tours was a delight in progression through space, a concern which is explored in the third, fourth, and fifth chapters where the discourse associated with the tourist of the picturesque turns to consider proto-archaeological investigation and the way the reader-viewer of mid-nineteenth-century travel accounts modelled space in his or her imagination. Central to this development is the manner in which the written word, formerly (and predominantly) encountered as *spoken* word, began to supervise a new and more intimate relation between reader and text in favour of the individual reader's engaged attention. This concern, initially examined in Chapter Three in a discussion of proto-archaeological investigation in Mexico and Central America before 1840, is examined closely in Chapter Four with regard to the work of John Lloyd Stephens and Frederick Catherwood.

The work of Malcolm Andrews has been central to my consideration of the picturesque as an eighteenth-century movement concerned with landscape aesthetics and its extension, in the nineteenth century, to the metropolitan context, a concern investigated in Chapter Five.[18] In Malcolm Andrews' essay on the 'metropolitan Picturesque', Andrews assessed how the tradition of the picturesque developed in the nineteenth century. He proposed that the term should be retrieved 'from its habitual application to the evolution of landscape and rural life in the late eighteenth century', and identified three ways the tradition developed in the nineteenth century: with regard to architectural design, as an 'aesthetics of poverty', and as a heritage discourse that addressed conservation as a significant concern in the latter part of the nineteenth century. Although it would not be helpful to match these concerns, developed in the context of considering nineteenth-century London, alongside developments in post-independence Mexico, the notion of the metropolitan picturesque is helpful in demonstrating how the metropolitan experience impacted on representational practices in the latter part of the nineteenth century. In this respect, discussion in Chapter Five broadly arises from the metropolitan experience, one which shares elements traditionally associated with the discussion of modernity *per se*. However, the transformation of the picturesque in the context of Mexico from the 1840s in parallel with the metropolitan experience is used to advance our understanding of pictorialism in photography and its engagement with the popular imagination, distinct from the project associated with modernity.

Developing the discussion of three panoramas in Chapter One, I emphasise somatic concerns in examining the painted panorama, a discussion which brings to attention, in Chapter Five, the transformation that attended the photographic image with regard to optical transcription. In this context, insights developed by Martin Kemp are significant in highlighting the transition that attended images in the nineteenth century from media forms that relied on the spectator's unaided eye (such as the painted panorama) to devices such as the camera lucida and the camera obscura that aided depiction by optical means for lithographs and, later, optical transcription in photographs and the cinematograph. Investigating the impact of optical transcription forms a focus for analysis in the latter part of Chapter Five.

In the intervening chapters, discussion centres on 'media convergence', defined in this study as the conjunction of different media on the printed page of nineteenth-century travel accounts, a significant 'platform', I propose, for considering nineteenth-century media convergence. In this regard, the representation of proto-archaeological investigation in the Yucatán peninsula and Central America forms an important arena in which the role of the reader-viewer of engraved (and later photographic) images is considered in Chapter Three and Chapter Four. In this respect, there are significant departures between my use of the term 'media convergence' and that of Henry Jenkins.[19] I propose that the conjunction of image and text in the mid-nineteenth-century travel account provided reader-viewers with a wealth of formal devices with which they interacted with the printed word, including developments in cartography, the drawing of plans and cross-sections, and, importantly, architectural drawing. Whereas, in the Augustan age, the written word was primarily encountered in the form of 'spoken' word (particularly in the forum of the church), one of the major transformations that underpinned reading in the nineteenth century was the development of reading as, essentially, a private activity, when images reproduced in the 'demesne' of the printed page promoted the role of imagination for reader-viewers engaging with the written word alongside engraved (and later, photographic) images. The printed page with text, engravings and, later, photographs thus represents a major arena in the nineteenth century, not only in the transmission of knowledge and affect, but also as a model for discussing the interrelation between images on the printed page and on pages in private photographic albums. In this context, the notion of *mise en page* is employed to discuss the process by which images were organised on the page, the role of succession and sequencing, and the securing of spatial contiguity and narrative development, either in the illustrated press or in private photographic albums. Distinct from the later innovation of photomontage, which often sought a rhetorical effect through juxtaposition (in photomontages by, for example, Aleksandr Rodchenko, Hannah Höch, and Lazlo Moholy-Nagy), *mise en page* posits a process of design which, in the context of the private photographic album, encouraged the non-professional photographer to be creative in the process of organising the album page to construct narrative and spatial progression. One further observation is in order: in Chapter Five, I use the term photographic 'essay'. This term is employed in the context of discussing *mise en page* as applied to a series of photographs that have a common topic or theme. Given that the term is customarily used in discussing the illustrated press in a later period, my use of the term should not be confused with its later employment when photographs are discussed as the primary carriers of narrative and social perspective, as in the case of photographic essays published in the 1930s in a journal such as *Picture Post*. While the two processes are related, in the period with which this study is concerned, the comparative function typical of photomontage is attenuated in the design of a *mise en page*.

The relation of image and printed word is central to discussion in this study, whether that be the relation between a painted panorama and the intepretation that may have been available through spoken commentary or in printed descriptions, or in the illustrated travel accounts discussed in Chapter Four. The relation of image with text helps define the parameters of interpretation that were historically anticipated, and also affords access to the concerns of intentionality, an issue important in interpreting images that are distant in time. Wherever possible, I have indicated where a work has been selected to demonstrate a particular point, but in most cases I have endeavoured to select images on grounds that recognise the context in which the image originally appeared. In such instances, determining the date when copyright was asserted may, on occasion, be a pre-requisite to re-constructing the coherence that obtained in making a series of photographs. In such instances, the date when photographic work was deposited for copyright (from 1883 in the case of Mexico) or the manner in which images were numerically catalogued with a view to sales, have proved helpful in relating what may appear to be autonomous images to a larger body of work, particularly when photographic images are dispersed across an archive.

One primary source of material with which the study makes periodic use is a catalogue of the sale of a private library that belonged to the architect and panoramist, Frederick Catherwood. The sale was conducted in December 1856, two years after Catherwood's death, and provides what I believe to be a reliable indicator of Catherwood's personal interests, even if the date when he may have acquired a particular work is not known. As a litmus of personal interest, the sales catalogue - extensive in its remit - is of particular interest, and has been employed to establish a range of influences that informed the work he carried out with John Lloyd Stephens in the Yucatán peninsula and Central America in the early 1840s.

One subject that is not considered in this study is the interest mid-nineteenth-century balloonists generated in aerial views, best represented, in the case of Mexico, in the publication of *México y sus alrededores* (Mexico City, 1855 and 1856).[20] Such interest represents an important area of investigation, identifying some of the concerns later developed in photographic modernism in the 1920s, particularly in the publication of the celebrated anthology edited by franz roh and jan tschichold, *foto-auge/œil et photo/photo-eye* (Stuttgart, 1929). The interest in aerial views, however, represents a marginal concern compared with the space from which the majority of people viewed the world in the nineteenth century: from a point near ground level. For this reason, in determining the concerns investigated in this study, I decided not to include the topic of aerial views.

I opened the Introduction by citing the work of André Gaudreault and Philippe Marion. Alongside essays such as Tom Gunning's 'Before Documentary', which discusses what Gunning terms the 'view' aesthetic, such writing has proved central to elaborating the point from which this study departs.[21] However, major influences on the project come from a discourse associated with art history, particularly the work of Ann Bermingham and Charlotte Klonk, who have proved central to formulating some of the concerns addressed in Chapter Two, Chapter Four, and Chapter Five. In this respect, my discussion of the contours between topographical image-making in the eighteenth century and photographic work in the nineteenth century is indebted to insights generated by these historians. From a similar background, the work of Martin Kemp has also impacted significantly on my discussion of the emergence of film at the end of the nineteenth century, particularly the departure that optical transcription signalled in the nineteenth century. These historians have constituted what may be termed a 'perspective correction', a welcome stimulus to think outside the boundaries associated with 'early film' at a time when 'early cinema was not in fact early cinema'. From such insights, I trust the present work has benefited.

Chapter One

To Mexico and Central America via Jerusalem, Thebes, and Baalbek: three panoramas after Catherwood

> 'A man that has been all over Greece, at Constantinople, Troy, the pyramids of Egypt, and the deserts of Arabia, talks and looks with a greater air than we little people can do that only crawled about France and Italy.' Joseph Spence.[1]

Towards the end of their 1841–1842 expedition to the Yucatán peninsula, Frederick Catherwood and John Lloyd Stephens arrived at the Maya site of Tulum on the east coast of Yucatán. Having cleared a structure of vegetation and debris, they climbed it to survey the surrounding jungle from an elevated position:

> We had undertaken our long journey to this place in utter uncertainty as to what we should meet with; impediments and difficulties had accumulated upon us, but already we felt indemnified for all our labour. We were amid the wildest scenery we had yet found in Yucatan; and, besides the deep and exciting interest of the ruins themselves, we had around us what we wanted at all the other places, the magnificence of nature. Clearing away the platform in front, we looked over an immense forest; walking around the moulding of the wall, we looked out upon the boundless ocean, and deep in the clear water at the foot of the cliff we saw gliding quietly by a great fish eight or ten feet long.[2]

Like visitors to a nineteenth-century panorama, Catherwood and Stephens were presented with a *coup d'œil*, a wide-ranging prospect view over tropical forest that extended as far as the eye could see, or, after walking round the building, they looked out over a limitless ocean, an experience which Stephens describes as one of superabundance, assailing the mind as much as the eye.[3]

A not dissimilar response awaits the reader when he or she looks at the engraving which served as the Frontispiece to John Lloyd Stephens' *Incidents of Travel in Yucatan* (1843). Arriving at the site of Uxmal in Yucatán near the beginning of their exploration of the peninsula, and having cleared a site overgrown with 'a mass of destroying verdure ... wrapping the city in its suffocating embraces, and burying it from sight',[4] the engraving presents the reader with a view of a large building that stands on a series of platforms rising from the forest floor (1.1). While the Frontispiece represents architectural detail with a degree of accuracy (as Stephens writes, 'it can serve only to give some idea of the general effect; the detail of ornament cannot be shown'),[5] the vantage-point from which the viewer observes the structure confers a mastery of space yet contradicts the topography of the site. Standing on the edge of the lower terrace, visitors can survey the south-east facade of the structure because they are at sufficient distance from the building, but it is not possible to view the building from the elevation depicted in the engraving since a feature that would confer such a position does not exist at the site. In this respect, the view is drawn from an imaginary point in space. The Frontispiece thus acknowledges the tradition of the nineteenth-century panorama and prospect view, in that the engraving provides an elevated view of the structure while maintaining a constant distance of the viewer from the subject, yet depicts a spatial relation that cannot be replicated at the site. The relation of these three concerns – topography, the representation of space, and the spectator – with regard to the painted panorama forms the subject of this chapter, and is developed in respect of Stephens' and Catherwood's work in Central America and the Yucatán peninsula in Chapter Three and Chapter Four.

While we are told that the expeditionary party worked for several weeks to clear the site and expose some of its principal structures, the view with which we are presented – of Maya porters carrying provisions, herding animals, and bearing European and North American members of the party in *cochés* – also stages Stephens' and Catherwood's arrival at the site as a fantasy, since it thematises the moment of their arrival as one where the site had *already* been cleared of trees and debris. Not only does this view thus stage a fantasy (since the view bears little relation to the party's arrival at the site as narrated by Stephens), but, in so doing, confirms a relation between seer and scene which Mary Louise Pratt has characterised as colonial in the trope, the 'monarch-of-all-I-survey'.[6]

While such a characterisation can be advanced, there are other ways of defining the view which the Frontispiece presents, as too the views represented in panoramas after Catherwood. As we will observe, the latter may have promoted quite different responses to that proposed by Pratt, responses which distinguished aesthetic pleasure from the possession of land, a distinction that emphasised an imaginative function rather than the vested interests of land appropriation.[7]

1.1. Frederick Catherwood, engraved by Joseph Napoleon Gimbrede, Frontispiece, John Lloyd Stephens, *Incidents of Travel in Yucatan*, 2 vols. (New York: Harper & Brothers for Henry Bill, 1848 [1843]), I, 18.2 x 79.6 cm. [Reproduced by permission of the National Library of Sweden.]

Before considering these issues, some biographical information is presented as a background to this study. John Lloyd Stephens was born in Shrewsbury, New Jersey, in 1805, and studied at Columbia College and at Tapping Reeve's Law School in Litchfield, Connecticut, before practicing as a lawyer. He travelled in the US before he left the country in the autumn of 1834 to travel in Europe, Egypt, Syria, Asia Minor, and the Holy Land. He returned to the US, via London (where he first came into contact with Frederick Catherwood), in 1836.

Accounts of his travels were published in *Incidents of Travel in Egypt, Arabia Petræa, and the Holy Land* in 1837 and, in the following year, in *Incidents of Travel in Greece, Turkey, Russia and Poland*. In 1839 Stephens was appointed Special Ambassador to Central America by President Martin Van Buren, and sent on a diplomatic mission to the Central American Federation to seek the government of the Federation and scout the possibilities for a railway or canal connection between the Atlantic and Pacific oceans. On this journey, Stephens, travelling with Catherwood, encountered antiquities in Guatemala, Honduras, and Chiapas, a state in present-day Mexico which, at that time, was part of the Central American Federation. Stephens and Catherwood also investigated sites in the Yucatán peninsula.

An account of this expedition, with engravings from drawings by Frederick Catherwood, was published as *Incidents of Travel in Central America, Chiapas, and Yucatan* in 1841. Later that year, Stephens and Catherwood set out on a second expedition specifically to Yucatán where, between autumn 1841 and summer 1842, they documented more than forty Maya sites in the department. An

account of this later expedition was published in 1843 as *Incidents of Travel in Yucatan*.[8]

Frederick Catherwood was born in Hoxton, London, in 1799, and after completing an apprenticeship as an architect, is reputed to have attended the Royal Academy schools where J.W.M. Turner was Professor of Perspective, Henry Fuseli, Professor of Painting, and John Soane, Professor of Architecture.[9] Although Catherwood did not enrol at the Royal Academy schools, he likely attended the public lectures that Soane gave at the Royal Academy of Arts and at the Royal Institution during the period of his apprenticeship, lectures which amounted to over twenty hours and included more than 1000 illustrations.[10] Together with a manuscript copy of Fuseli's *Lectures on Painting* (1801), Robert Morris' *Select Architecture* (1755), and an 1825 edition of Sir William Chambers' *A Treatise on the Decorative Parts of Civil Architecture* (1791), Catherwood's private library attests to the fact that Catherwood acquired, either as an apprentice or at a later date, a number of works that Soane drew on for his lectures between 1817 and 1820.[11] If, therefore, Catherwood was not formally registered as a student at the Royal Academy schools, his library nonetheless reflects the teaching of the schools, an interest also demonstrated by the circle of friends he developed in his late teens and early twenties.

Of particular interest with regard to Catherwood's subsequent career, are the lectures Soane delivered regarding antiquities in Syria, Lebanon, and Egypt. Accompanied with high-quality illustrations prepared by pupils in Soane's architectural office, the archaeological sites of Palmyra and Baalbek were 'sufficient for my present purpose which is to impress the minds of the young students with the utility and necessity of consulting ancient authors'.[12] As we shall observe, one illustration after the work of Robert Wood that Soane used in his lectures at the Royal Academy and at the Royal Institution may have influenced a panorama painting that Catherwood prepared some fifteen years later when he visited the archaeological site of Baalbek. Catherwood's training as an architect also proved beneficial to his career as a panoramist since panoramas, as much buildings as paintings, were exhibited in purpose-built rotundas such as the Panorama, Leicester Square.

After exhibiting at the Royal Academy in 1820, Catherwood travelled to Italy, where he developed a circle of friends that included the future Egyptologists, Joseph Bonomi, Henry Parke, and Joseph John Scoles, two of whom had studied at the Royal Academy schools.[13] In this regard, Catherwood was among the first generation to travel in Europe and the Middle East after the Napoleonic Wars, the conflict having made it impossible, except during the Peace of Amiens (from March 1802 to May 1803), to travel in Europe between 1795 and 1818.[14] In 1823–24 Catherwood visited Greece and Egypt with Parke, Scoles, and Henry Westcar where he met the future eminent Egyptologist, John Gardner Wilkinson.[15] On his return to Malta, Catherwood was introduced by Bonomi to Robert Hay. During the next eight years, Catherwood travelled in Italy, Greece, Egypt, and the Levant, returning periodically to London, before joining Hay's party in September 1832 at Qurna, Egypt, from where he went to the Kharga Oasis with Hay and George Alexander Hoskins.[16] While in Egypt, Catherwood undertook a survey and excavation of the Colossi of Memnon at Thebes, and prepared a large-scale plan of the site. In 1833–34 he visited Sinai, Palestine, and Syria with Bonomi and Francis Arundale, and visited the ruins of Baalbek in Lebanon.[17] On his return to London, Catherwood came into contact with Robert Burford, the proprietor of the Panorama, Leicester Square, who, assisted by Henry Selous, developed Catherwood's drawings as the basis for two large-scale panoramas, the City of Jerusalem and the archaeological sites of Karnak and Thebes, discussed later in this chapter.[18] These panoramas were exhibited at the Panorama, Leicester Square, between 1835 and 1836, by which time, the panorama had existed as a medium of entertainment and education for over forty years.

The patent for 'an entire new Contrivance or Apparatus, called … *La Nature à coup d'œil* [Nature at a glance] for the Purpose of displaying Views of Nature at Large, by Oil-Painting, Fresco, Water-colours, Crayons, or any other Mode of painting or drawing' was registered by the Irish-born miniature and portrait painter, Robert Barker, on 19 June 1787, giving Barker exclusive rights to his invention for a period of fourteen years.[19] The term, 'panorama', a neologism combined from the Greek words *pan* (all) and *horama*

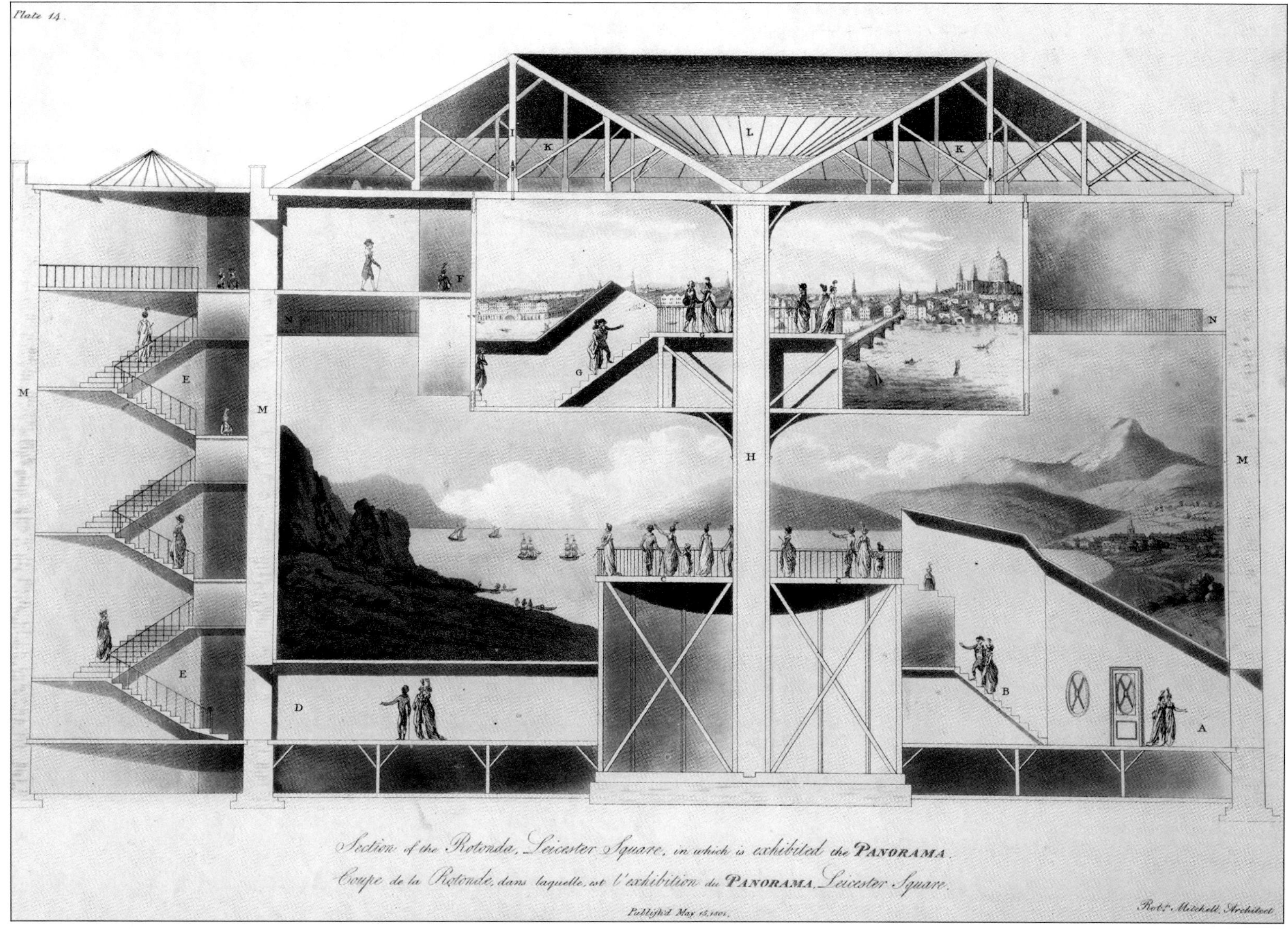

1.2. *Section of the Rotonda in Leicester Square, in which is exhibited the Panorama*, engraving, Robert Mitchell, *Plans, and Views in Perspective, with Descriptions, of Buildings erected in England and Scotland: and also An Essay to elucidate the Grecian, Roman and Gothic Architecture, accompanied with Designs* (London: Printed by Wilson & Co., 1801), Plate 14, platemark 32 x 47 cm., 28.5 x 44.5 cm. (maximum image size). [Courtesy of Erkki Huhtamo Collection Los Angeles.]

(view), rendered as an 'all-embracing view', dates from 1791.[20] A view of Edinburgh from Calton Hill, '[q]uite circular, as an observer sees it, turning round on the Observatory top', was first exhibited by Robert Barker in the Archers' Hall near Holyrood Park, Edinburgh, from 31 January to the beginning of March 1788.[21] The view comprised an extensive prospect of the city from Calton Hill, encompassing Arthur's Seat, Salisbury Crags, and Holyrood Castle (to the south-east), the Old Town, Edinburgh Castle and New Town (to the south and west), the Firth of Forth to the north of the city, extending as far east as the port of Leith and the plain of Prestonpans, before returning the viewer to Calton Hill where the half-completed building of the new observatory and a chimney and roof of the old observatory occupy the extreme foreground set against a view of the large orrery on the top of Calton Hill.[22] The view was subsequently exhibited in the Assembly Rooms in New Town, Edinburgh, from 6 March until 2 June 1788, and was shown for a short time from 27 June, 1788 at the Merchant Hall, Bridgegate, Glasgow.[23] From 14 March 1789, Barker's 'interesting and novel view of the city and castle of Edinburgh' was exhibited at 28 Haymarket, London, before Barker erected a rotunda in his own back garden at 28 Castle Street, Leicester Square, for the presentation of painted panoramas. The earliest panorama presented at this location was a half-circle painting from the roof of the Albion Steam Flour Mills near Blackfriars Bridge, depicting buildings to the north and south of the River Thames with the chimneys and roof of the Albion Mills framing the view in the extreme foreground and locating the spectator, as it were, on the roof of the building.[24] In 1793 Barker leased land on a recently-demolished site between Cranbourn Street and Lisle Street to the north of Leicester-fields, where a purpose-built rotunda, designed by Robert Mitchell, was inaugurated on 25 May 1793.[25] Designed to make observers 'feel as if really on the very spot', the rotunda accommodated two circular panoramas, lit by reflected daylight from above, and viewed from darkened galleries, designated as an 'inclosure' (*sic*) in Barker's patent, at the centre of the rotunda building (1.2). In 1806, John Burford joined the business as a painter at about the time of Robert Barker's death. With the business left to Barker's son, Henry Aston Barker, John Burford initially worked as an assistant to Henry Barker, but in 1817, when the Panorama in the Strand, established in 1803 by Thomas Edward Barker (Henry's older brother) and Ramsay Richard Reinagle, was forced to close, Henry Barker and John Burford acquired equal shares in the business.[26] Henry Barker retired in 1826, selling his interest in the Panorama, Leicester Square, and the Strand Panorama to John Burford and Burford's son, Robert. When John Burford died in 1827, the business passed to Robert, who operated the Strand Panorama until it closed for good in 1831 (when the building was turned into the Strand Theatre) and the Panorama, Leicester Square, until his death in 1861.[27] The Panorama, Leicester Square, finally closed in December 1863, and was sold at auction on 12 November 1864 and, in due course, converted into a Catholic church for London's French community.[28]

Apart from two panoramas exhibited at the Panorama, Leicester Square, in the mid-1830s, developed from sketches by Catherwood, Catherwood also contributed a number of commentaries and sketches to Thomas Hartwell Horne's *Illustrations of the Bible* (1836), which were worked up by, variously, George Balmer, T. C. Dibdin, James Duffield Harding, Samuel Prout, David Roberts, and Clarkson Stanfield, and engraved by Edward and William Finden.[29] Catherwood encountered Stephens for the first time when Stephens, visiting the Panorama, Leicester Square, in 1836, heard Catherwood present a commentary on his work.[30] Later that year, Catherwood moved to New York where, after the devastating fire that ravaged much of the city in the winter of 1835, he established an architectural practice with the English architect, Frederick Diaper, at 94 Greenwich Street.[31] Two years later, Catherwood opened his own panorama rotunda with the bookseller, George W. Jackson, on Broadway at the corner of Prince Street and Mercer Street, near Niblo's Garden.[32] Having come to an arrangement with Robert Burford for importing panoramas to New York, Catherwood exhibited the panorama of Jerusalem in 1838, and in the following year, the panorama of Karnak and Thebes, both of which proved major attractions.[33] In contact again with Stephens, and with a shared interest in travel and the exploration of antiquities, the two men decided to collaborate on a project, setting out for Central America in 1839 and, two years later, the Yucatán peninsula, Catherwood providing drawings for engravings to accompany Stephens' accounts of their expeditions. Back in New York in autumn 1842, Catherwood and Stephens tried unsuccessfully to interest subscribers in a folio edition of chromolithographs from their expeditions, a publication which finally saw the light of day when Catherwood published *Views of Ancient Monuments in Central America Chiapas and Yucatan*, in London, in 1844, the same year that a panorama from sketches he had made ten years earlier of the ruins of Baalbek was exhibited at the Panorama, Leicester Square. This work is also discussed towards the end of this chapter. A founding member of the American Ethnological Society, Catherwood also wrote two articles on antiquities in Tunis which were published in *Transactions of the American Ethnological Society* in 1845.[34] The period, therefore, between the mid-1830s and the mid-1840s represents one in which Catherwood, apprenticed as an architect and architectural draughtsman, and artist-traveller, antiquarian, panoramist, and architect by profession, was able to capitalise on four fields of close personal interest.

Tour writing, 'the very rage of the times', and panoramas

This chapter concentrates on Catherwood's work in the exhibition of panoramas, a medium which, attracting metropolitan and urban audiences, was one of the first mass mediums of the early nineteenth century.[35] As we will observe, a number of concerns in his work as a panoramist informed his work as an illustrator for Stephens. Three panoramas are considered, their stylistic concerns and the sources on which Catherwood drew being the principal considerations of this chapter. In developing this discussion, broad reference is made to other artists who, like Catherwood, independent of private patronage which artists primarily relied on in the eighteenth century, found outlets for their work through engravings published at a time when the market for prints and illustrated travel accounts was expanding. To discuss the work of Catherwood and Stephens in the early 1840s, then, is not only to engage with publications such as *Incidents of Travel in Central America, Chiapas, and Yucatan*, the American sales of which reached 12,000 copies within the first four months of publication,[36] but also to consider some of the debates championed for an informed, general readership through journals published in London, Edinburgh, Dublin, and New York. Two years later, when Stephens had completed *Incidents of Travel in Yucatan*, the success of the account of travels in Central America meant that he was in a position to stipulate terms: the publishers credited Stephens with $5,700 for the expense of preparing Catherwood's plates, and Stephens received royalties of over 20 per cent, a very high rate.[37] Sales of books by Stephens attest to the exceptional interest his work generated.[38]

Interest in learned and professional societies increased in Britain throughout the early nineteenth century. While societies of national scope founded before the 1840s, such as the Linnean Society (founded in 1788), the Geological Society (1807), and the British Association for the Advancement of Science (1831), were primarily offshoots from the Royal Society, the founding of the Royal Institution in 1799, the British Institution in 1805, the opening of William Bullock's private gallery, the Egyptian Hall, in Piccadilly in 1812, the establishment of the Dulwich Picture Gallery in 1817, and the opening of the National Gallery in London in 1824, the latter two providing free entry to the public, helped define an appetite for antiquities and the arts. The British Institution, established 'to form a Public Gallery of the works of British Artists, with a few select specimens of the great schools', with more than 10,000 admissions during its first year of operation, was the earliest public body to demonstrate that considerable interest existed for viewing works of art.[39] The art world in the first quarter of nineteenth-century London also witnessed an explosion of interest in painting and drawing, subsequent to the development of the market for amateur artists, with the introduction of ready-made cakes of watercolour by Thomas and William Reeves in the latter part of the eighteenth century.[40] The growth in the amateur market was further enhanced by Rudolph Ackermann, whose Repository of Arts in the Strand, London, and publication of *Repository of Arts, Literature, Commerce, Manufacturers, Fashions and Politics* presented new opportunities for amateur artists to express themselves, a development that was paralleled by the expansion of career opportunities for artists as drawing-masters.[41] The world in which Catherwood thus worked on his return from the Levant was one quantifiably different to that which existed for a boy brought up in Hoxton at the turn of the nineteenth century.

The British Museum grew rapidly in importance in this period. After the purchase of the Sir William Hamilton collection in 1772 and King George III's gift of his collection of Egyptian antiquities, captured from the French, to the Museum in 1802, a new Department of Antiquities was established in 1807.[42] Two years later, the Charles Townley collection was purchased, and in 1816, the Elgin

Marbles.[43] By 1819, it was recognised that Montagu House, where the Museum was housed, was no longer adequate. The acquisition of the King's Library in 1823 brought matters to a head, though it would be some years before new accommodation was completed for the Museum. Besides national institutions such as the Royal Institute of British Architects (which received its Royal Charter in 1837) and the British Archaeological Association (founded in 1843), a number of associations were also established outside London: in 1839 the Oxford Architectural Society was founded, and in the following year, the Cambridge Antiquarian Society was established, developments which reflected a growing interest in the study of antiquities. Jean-François Champollion's account and table of the Egyptian hieroglyphic alphabet, published in 1822, was followed by Ippolito Rosellini's survey in 1831 which consolidated interest in the study of Egyptian antiquity, the popularity of which was reflected in an exhibition curated by Giovanni Battista Belzoni in 1822 and the publication of John Gardner Wilkinson's six-volume *Manners and Customs of the Ancient Egyptians* in 1837.[44] Behind these developments lay a series of publications from the French expedition in Egypt, particularly Vivant Denon's *Voyage dans la basse et la haute Egypte, pendant les campagnes du Général Bonaparte* (1802, English translation, 1803) and the magnificent, twenty-three-volume *Description de l'Egypte, ou, recueil de observations et des recherches qui ont été faites en Egypte pendant l'éxpédition de l'armée française, publié par les ordres de Sa Majesté l'empereur Napoléon le Grand*, published in Paris between 1809 and 1822. Robert Burford's interest in promoting panoramas of cities and antiquities may thus be seen as part of a wider movement which sought to capitalise on what had become, by the 1830s, an almost insatiable demand for biblical, historical, and antiquarian subjects presented on a grand scale.

Exhibitions that William Bullock organised for the Egyptian Hall – such as Théodore Géricault's *The Raft of the 'Medusa'* (*Le Radeau de la 'Méduse'*), shown to some 40,000 people between June and December 1820,[45] and John Martin's *The Destruction of Pompeii and Herculaneum*, exhibited in a solo exhibition in 1822 – also attest to an emerging metropolitan audience for painting: 'Whatever variety of opinion exists as to the kind and degree of Mr. Martin's genius, the fact of its being of a very high order is placed beyond a doubt, by the extraordinary interest which his pictures excite, not only among the graphically untutored, but by the most cultivated tastes.'[46] For the opening of Martin's solo exhibition in March 1822, *The Destruction of Pompeii and Herculaneum* was accompanied by a 32-page booklet with an etched key,[47] a publication that demonstrates that visitors to Martin's exhibition relied on a printed text to clarify the narrative represented in the painting, a strategy which Martin adopted, at this point in his career, in common with the painted panorama.[48] While the work of John Martin demonstrates that a popular interest existed for paintings with apocalyptic biblical subjects staged against dramatic architecture that displayed 'the geometrical properties of space, magnitude, and number',[49] Catherwood departed from the explicit narrative interest of Martin in favour of incorporating multiple viewing points and depicting antiquities on an even grander scale.

Nowhere is this departure from single-point perspective more evident than in the exhibition of panoramas, where the presentation of spectacle in works reputed to be topographically accurate was the principal concern. In this respect, Catherwood's work as a panoramist observed some of the interest in topographical accuracy which panoramas were understood to inscribe as a mode of representation.[50] Although we shall have cause to qualify this observation, Robert Barker's 1787 patent specified that the goal of his 'contrivance' (which, by the time the patent was approved, had become known as a 'panorama') was to produce 'an entire view of any country or situation, as it appears to an observer turning quite round; to produce which effect, the painter or drawer must fix his station, and delineate correctly and connectedly every object which presents itself to his view as he turns round, concluding his drawing by a connection with where he began'.[51] Such a goal informed a series of sketches made by Thomas Hearne in 1777 on a tour of the Lake District with Sir George Beaumont and Joseph Farington. As recounted by Robert Southey, many years later, Hearne made 'a sketch of the whole circle of this vale [Derwentwater], from a field called Crow Park [near Keswick]', and noted that 'Sir George intended to build a circular banqueting room, and have this painted around the walls. If the execution had not always been procrastinated, here would have been the first panorama. I have seen the sketch, now preserved on a roll more than twenty feet in length.'[52] Although Hearne's painted roll has not survived, a series of six watercolour sketches by Thomas Hearne is extant.[53] The sketches comprise three views of Derwentwater to the south of Crow Park (with Borrowdale valley in the distance), and a further set of three views showing Bassenthwaite Lake and the Skiddaw group of hills to the north of Crow Park, which completes the 360-degree panorama. Hearne's sketches provide an uninterrupted, circular view of a landscape in the Lake District, a region that was rapidly becoming known for work in the picturesque manner, the topographical features of which in Hearne's sketches are recognisable to this day. We will return to this concern in Chapter Two.

In discussing Catherwood's work in panorama painting, I am concerned to demonstrate how his work not only departs, on occasion, from topographical accuracy, but also demonstrates that the viewing of a panorama was explicated by the text and engraved orientation view and key, which, published as a descriptive booklet, was sold for sixpence in addition to the one shilling admission visitors paid to view a panorama.[54] The examination of the relation between image and text in viewing a panorama and, in Chapter Four, in reading the published work of Stephens and Catherwood, thus enables us to identify, in some instances, the interpretations that spectators were expected to make, and allows us to infer the intentions of the artist. More particularly, the textual description also demonstrates, at least in some instances, the order in which spectators were expected to view panoramas after Catherwood. The process of discussing Catherwood's work as a panoramist thus brings into focus one of the methodological procedures adopted in this study: the relation of images to the written word; in this case, the sequence in which spectators were expected to view the panorama as prescribed by the descriptive brochure. Discussion of the descriptive booklet helps us identify how Catherwood's work may not only have been viewed sequentially, but also calls into question some of the viewing protocols that have characterised recent discussion of the viewing of panoramas. In this context, William Galperin, arguing that a panorama may have constituted less a painting in the customary sense than a collection of fragmented sights, has proposed that panoramas were attended by a more heterogeneous public, promoting a more modern form of distracted viewing wherein panoramas increasingly implied 'all things to all people'.[55] Developing this observation, Laurie Garrison has marshalled an impressive range of reviews in her discussion of Robert Burford's panorama, after sketches by Lieutenant William Browne, of the *Panorama of Summer and Winter Views of the Polar Regions as seen during the expedition of Capt James Clark Ross, Kt. F.R.S. in 1848–9* (1850), which demonstrate that diverse interpretations did indeed attend the viewing of panoramas.[56] While there is much that is attractive in Garrison's analysis, my discussion focuses more on the 'somatic' nature of panorama viewing, an argument which arises from a comparative consideration of the three panoramas exhibited in London after drawings by Catherwood. In this respect, the relation between image and text, between the panorama and its illustration and explication in the descriptive booklet, is central to our discussion in this chapter, and is developed in subsquent chapters.

Descriptive booklets associated with the panorama and the opportunity for relating panorama paintings to descriptive texts were, it should be noted, a relatively recent innovation in the turn-of-the-century public sphere, having elements in common with the introduction of guide-books in the late eighteenth century. The term 'guide-book', coined in the early nineteenth century, arose principally with the development of personal travel accounts which, as a literary genre, began to be published in the second half of the eighteenth century.[57] Though travel narratives generally provided accounts of personal incident in the manner of Stephens' publications, they also catered to the needs of travellers by offering recommendations, warnings, and information that ranged from practical advice to potted local history. Such publications became a staple of late-eighteenth-century publishing, John Byng being one of the earliest writers to develop the genre in England, who observed that '[t]our writing is the very rage of the times'.[58] Tours and the associated activity to which the tour gave rise – 'sight-seeing' – entered the English language in the 1830s,[59] at a time when the exotic locations represented in panoramas exploited the interest that existed in a surrogate form of sight-seeing at substantially reduced cost and personal inconvenience to that incurred in the eighteenth-century Grand Tour:

> Panoramas are among the happiest contrivances for saving time and expense in this age of contrivances. What cost a couple of hundred pounds and half a year half a century ago, now costs a shilling and a quarter of an hour. ... Now the affair is settled in a summary manner. The mountain or the sea, the classic vale or the ancient city, is transported to us on the wings of the wind.[60]

Panoramas after sketches by Catherwood

A number of writers have emphasised the large-scale nature of the spectacle presented in panoramas.[61] Drawing on William Wordsworth's *The Prelude* (written 1799–1805), Anne Friedberg has observed that panoramas mimicked what Wordsworth termed the 'absolute presence of reality' to create, as Friedberg puts it, 'an artificial elsewhere for the panorama spectator'.[62] She has also proposed that panoramas brought the country to the city-dweller as much as they transported the past to the present. In addition to *trompe l'œil* and the sensational spatial effects which the commercial panorama provided,[63] Stephan Oettermann has proposed that panoramas represented a multi-perspectival depiction of space, presenting a more 'democratic' representation than that available in single-point perspective,[64] an effect which, he argues, promoted three innovations. First, the spectator's eye was free to roam in all directions, an effect which encouraged artists to create a number of centres of interest in a panorama, rupturing the conventions of single-point perspective.[65] Second, in contrast to private galleries and private collections, panoramas were open to anyone willing to pay the price of admission, a factor which promoted recognizable, realistic locations in favour of the mythological, allegorical, biblical, or historical subjects that were the concerns of painting in the grand style. Such subjects also encouraged a more heterogeneous public to attend the exhibition of panoramas.[66] Third, panoramas contributed to a shift away from an idealisation of nature typical of the grand style towards a greater degree of topographical accuracy.[67] Elevated views, promoting a fixed standpoint and a roving gaze on the part of the spectator, also let the sky dominate the composition of the panorama,[68] a factor which, Ann Bermingham has argued, was enhanced by the large internal scale of panorama paintings. In observing that such compositions imply a manipulation of form while cultivating 'a factual, almost artless look, an appearance of recording the actual features of the view rather than according to the conventional formulas of studio productions', Bermingham qualifies the presumed topographical accuracy which much critical literature has emphasised. Such manipulation also emphasises the vast expanses of space depicted in panoramas which stimulated a sense of the Sublime.[69] While Bermingham notes that panoramas tended to be evenly lit (with shadows depicting dramatic illumination kept to a minimum), Oettermann draws on contemporary discussion in Germany and Switzerland to indicate that panorama painters tended to prefer the times of day (early morning or late afternoon) when sunlight falls more obliquely.[70] In this respect, care was taken to ensure that the orientation of the panorama in the rotunda was consistent with the illumination that prevailed outside the building. What such discussion reveals is that panoramas might mimic reality as far as aerial perspective is concerned,[71] but, in challenging some of the innovations introduced in landscape painting in the early nineteenth century through the manipulation of form, they also departed from the 'inquiry into the laws of nature' that characterised the scientific ambition evident in the work of a 'natural painter' such as John Constable.[72] Panoramas also encouraged a predilection for inclusiveness rather than the selection of salient particulars which academic art theory advocated.[73] Where panoramas, however, acknowledged the centrality of human vision was in the care that was taken to ensure that the illumination depicted in the panorama painting was consistent with the site, a concern that was reinforced by the fact that panoramas were best visited at the time of day represented in the panorama. In this respect, the hanging of the panorama so that daylight reflected on the painted panorama in the rotunda building was consistent with the source of light and time of day depicted in the location, with spectators aligned with the orientation of the location, ensured that the panorama was seen in its most effective manner.[74]

Descriptions for three panoramas after drawings by Frederick Catherwood are considered in this chapter. All three publications comprise an engraved orientation view and key for the panorama accompanied by a textual 'description' which identifies the subjects depicted in the panorama. With the exception of Denise Blake Oleksijczuk's discussion of panoramas before the 1820s, little attention has been given to the engravings that were printed to accompany panoramas (which provide, in most cases, the only record we have of panoramas that have long since been lost), or to the text that was printed in panorama descriptions and the contribution they made to the viewing of a panorama.[75] Importantly, printed booklets not only provided a detailed discussion of the work, but, at least in the case of two of the panoramas after Catherwood, also indicate the sequence in which the work was intended to be viewed when exhibited outside London. In this respect, the *Description* required that the spectator stand at a particular point in the darkened rotunda gallery (termed an 'inclosure' (*sic*) in Barker's 1787 patent) from where the panorama, illuminated by reflected daylight, was to be viewed.[76] The viewing of the nineteenth-century panorama thus shared a practice associated with the viewing of picturesque landscapes in the late eighteenth century from a specific point in space, which point, known as a 'station', was introduced by Thomas West in 1780,[77] and employed by Barker in his 1787 patent for showing 'Views of Nature at Large'.[78] Although we shall consider the term further in Chapter Two, let us, for the moment, examine the panoramas developed after Catherwood through information furnished in their respective *Descriptions*. The three panoramas considered here, in order of their presentation in London, are *View of the City of Jerusalem and the Surrounding Country*, exhibited in the Large Circle at Robert Burford's Panorama, Leicester Square, from 30 March 1835 to February 1836; *View of The Great Temple of Karnak and the Surrounding City of Thebes*, exhibited in the Upper Circle at the same venue from 15 June 1835 to June 1836,[79] and *View of the Ruins of the Temples of Baalbec*, exhibited in the Upper Circle at the Panorama, Leicester Square, from 29 June to 4 December 1844.[80] The panoramas bracket the period from the time Catherwood first met Stephens to the time when, subsequent to their expeditions to Central America and Yucatán, Catherwood published *Views of Ancient Monuments in Central America Chiapas and Yucatan*. The panoramas provide a mode of representation wherein spectators were 'transported by the skills of the panoramic painter into the midst of distant and interesting scenes'.[81] Presented on a monumental scale, Catherwood's panoramas mark a significant departure from the concerns of John Martin where narrative exegesis held the stage. Such concerns are relatively unimportant in panoramas after 1818 where the primary function was to provide spectators with topographical information presented in hyper-real form, guided by the explication available in the printed booklet.[82] As we will observe, the viewing of a panorama benefited considerably from information presented in this manner.

Panorama of Jerusalem

The text of the *Description* of the *View of the City of Jerusalem and the Surrounding Country* ... opens with a characterisation of the terrain encircling the city which is likened to 'a vast amphitheatre, shut in from the rest of the world',[83] a topos which allows the authors of the *Description* to draw a comparison of the city with a passage from the Book of Psalms (Psalm 125: 2): 'As the mountains are round about Jerusalem, so the Lord is round about his people,'[84] as too, we may observe, 'the circumambient world' of the panorama which surrounded the spectator.[85] As simile gives way to less figurative prose, the location from which the panorama was drawn is announced: 'taken from the Terrace of the House of [the] Aga, or Governor, formerly the Palace of Pontius Pilate', a prospect which 'is most comprehensive ... embracing nearly the whole of the important stations mentioned in Scripture', an observation reproduced almost verbatim in the notice published in *The Literary Gazette*.[86] As Catherwood later indicated in a letter to William Henry Bartlett: 'I was at Jerusalem in 1833, in company with my friends, Messrs. Bonomi and Arundale, and a portion of my time was employed in making drawings, from which Burford's panorama was afterwards painted; they were taken from the roof of the governor's house, from whence the best general view of the mosque and its dependencies is obtained.'[87] The introductory comments of the *Description* note that the panorama presents 'a vast assembly of monasteries, mosques, domes, and minarets, &c. which, though they generally resemble each other, are so dissimilar to anything European, that they excite curiosity', an observation which underscores the exoticism that the panorama evoked, a response which *The Literary Gazette* also drew to the attention of its readers, going on to observe that the panorama 'will no doubt attract large classes of spectators, by its important and sacred associations'.[88] Although the *Description* returns to a consideration of the location from which the panorama is organised at the conclusion of the tour (to which we will also return), the spectator proceeds to examine four 'views' of the city from four stations in the rotunda gallery. Just as the panorama was intended, at least in some presentations, to be viewed from four locations in the darkened gallery, each view shifts register as the *Description* draws on sources that provide religious, historical, cultural, or anecdotal information, the latter being most often accompanied with biblical exegesis.[89]

Four descriptive booklets for the panorama of Jerusalem have been consulted. The *Description* printed by William Heriot in Leith in 1837, held at the National Library of Scotland, specifies four 'stations' from which the panorama was to be viewed, locating the spectator, presumably, at the points where Catherwood delivered his commentary for presentations at the Panorama, Leicester Square.[90] For this reason, quotation from the descriptive text considered in this chapter, unless otherwise indicated, is taken from the 1837 Leith edition held at the National Library of Scotland. Two copies of a descriptive booklet for the Jerusalem panorama, printed by Thomas Brettell in Rupert Street, London, are held at Cambridge University Library. The booklets provide a detailed list of seventy-one subjects identified in the panorama, but do not specify the sequence in which the panorama should be viewed, leaving that decision to the spectator in the gallery.[91] Two further booklets (printed by William Heriot in Leith and by M. W. Reid in Edinburgh), held at the University of Glasgow Library, detail, in one instance, the same 'stations' as the copy held at the National Library of Scotland.[92] The copy of the *Description* held at the National Library of Scotland and one of the copies held at the University of Glasgow Library not only provide details of the sequence in which the panorama was be viewed, but relate subjects depicted in the panorama to the spectator's presence in the rotunda gallery. Phrases such as 'on your right', 'considerably to your left', and 'on the right, nearer the spectator', provide a clear indication of the direction in which the viewer in the gallery should look. Such directions guided the spectator in viewing the panorama in the Large Circle at the Panorama, Leicester Square, and helped the spectator orient (and internalise) his or her viewing of scenes from the space of the gallery.

The panorama of Jerusalem, as seen in the engraving to the *Description*, presents a view of the northern part of the city 'from the [t]errace of the House of [the] Aga or Governor, formerly the Palace of Pontius Pilate' in the lower panel, complemented by a view of the southern part of the city in the upper panel (1.3). The terrace which crosses the extreme foreground of the lower panel, presents a group of people ranged across the foreground, set against what appears to be an evenly-lit view of the northern part of the city. The panel includes architectural features that extend from the Gate of Damascus (#43 in the panorama key) to the Minaret, Ben Israel (#68) and the Chapel of the Crown of Thorns (#70). As Bermingham has proposed, the manipulation of the internal scale typical of the nineteenth-century panorama is, in this case, emphasised by the foreground which includes Catherwood sketching under a parasol with Bonomi (#45) seen on the left of the lower panel. The upper panel is dominated by an elevated view of the southern part of the city, a view that shows buildings with strong shadows across the middle ground and foreground, with the city and surrounding landscape in the distance periodically interrupted by buildings on or near the skyline. This section of the panorama presents a view of the city that extends from the Church of St. Pelagia (#1) and the Church of the Ascension (#2) to the Dome of the Temple of the Holy Sepulchre (#39), the minaret of a mosque in the Via Dolorosa (#41), and the Minaret on the Site of Pilate's House (#42). At mid-field, left of centre, the Mosque of Omar (also known as the Dome of the Rock) can be seen with the Mosque of El Aksa (al'Aqsa) to the rear and right of the Mosque of Omar (respectively, #25 and #21). The *Description* notes that the Mosque can be seen '[i]mmediately in front of the spectator, towards the south',[93] thus establishing, at an early point in

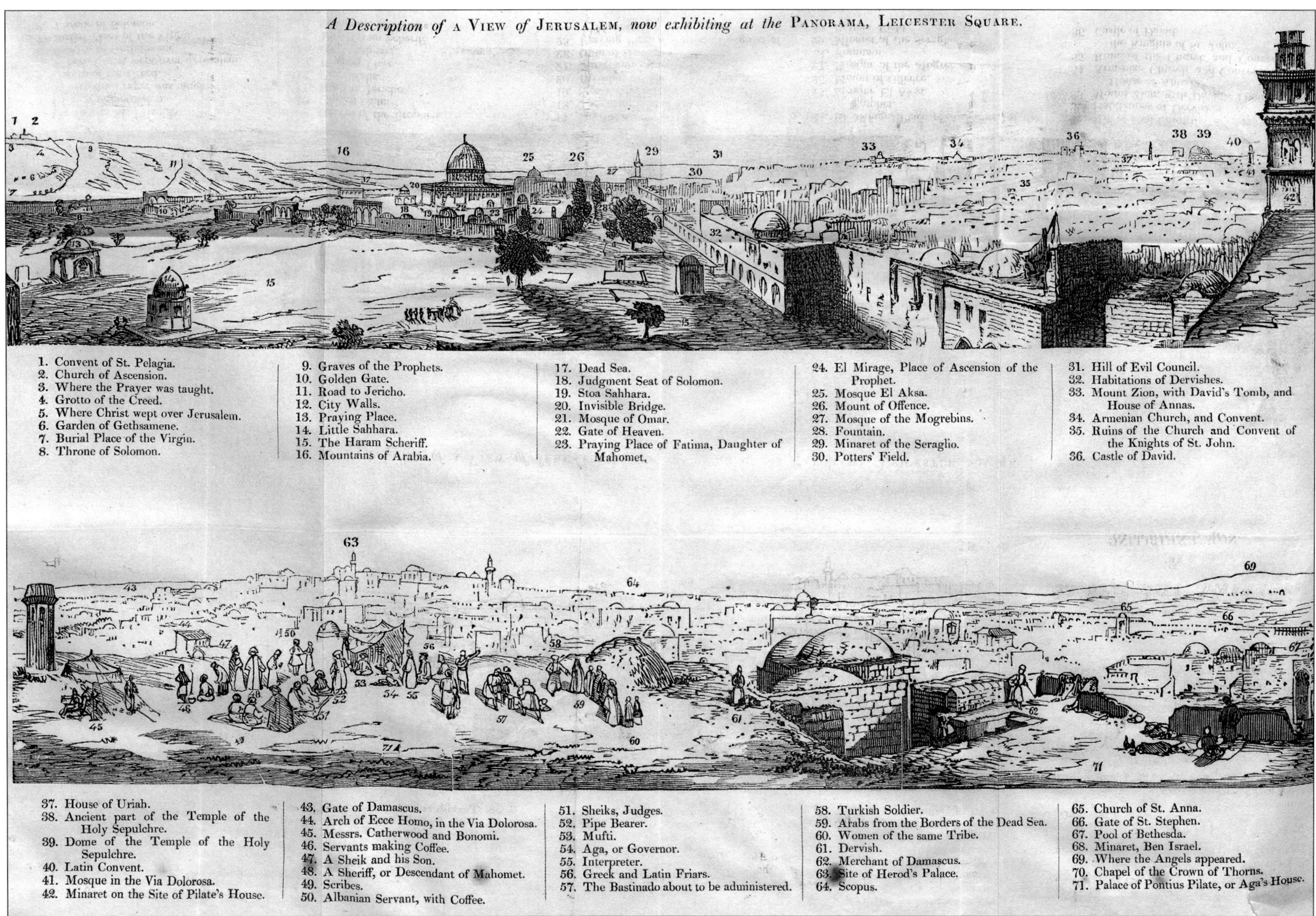

1.3. Orientation view and key, *A Description of a View of Jerusalem, now exhibiting at the Panorama, Leicester Square*, engraving, Robert Burford and (unattributed) Frederick Catherwood, *Description of a View of the City of Jerusalem and the surrounding country, now exhibiting at the Panorama, Leicester Square. Painted by the Proprietor, Robert Burford, from drawings taken in 1834, by Mr. F. Catherwood, Architect* (London: Printed by T. Brettell, 1835), upper panel, 9 x 37.5 cm.; lower panel, 7 x 37.5 cm. [Reproduced by permission of Cambridge University Library.]

the visitor's progression round the panorama, the orientation of the panorama, which helps orient the visitor's spatial relation to the represented scene. Much of the foreground left of the panel is taken up by a large square, the 'Haram Scheriff' (Haram al-Sharif, #15), which, with receding orthogonal lines announced by buildings to the right of the square, define the recessional space of the composition, helping to articulate the scale of the panorama which stretches from the centre of the city as far east as the Dead Sea (#17).[94] Strong shadows, not visible in the lower panel, cast to the right of structures and trees, confirm that the sun is in the south-east quadrant of the sky, thus indicating that the panorama presents a view of Jerusalem in the early morning.

Having established the orientation of the panorama, the point in space from where the panorama was sketched, and the time of day, the *Description* proceeds to a discussion of the buildings and location that can be seen in the left-hand corner of the upper engraved panel of the descriptive booklet (i.e., the south-eastern section of the city). Our attention is drawn to a small mosque 'in the distance ... crowned by a dome ... with a minaret' that was built on the remains of the Church of the Ascension (#2) on the summit of the Mount of Olives.[95] Noting that the building, 'in a state of neglect', is open to both Christians and Muslims, the *Description* informs us, citing Luke 24: 50, that 'in the centre is a portion of bare rock, defended by a low enclosure, which was the scene of our Saviour's last appearance on earth, and ascent to heaven'.[96] The spectator is told that '[t]he print of a foot [of Christ] on the rock is visible, and is much revered' and, moreover, from the direction in which the foot pointed, 'it would appear that the left hand of Jesus was towards Jerusalem, and his face northward'.[97] Not only is the spectator's gaze, in other words, aligned with the topographic orientation of the city, but past action – even the direction in which Christ was facing at a particular moment – can be plotted with regard to the point from which the panorama is viewed.

Information concerning the interior of the mosque, not visible in the panorama, is also brought to our attention: 'The Mosque contains a small niche, for the Turks and Arabs to pray in; and the Greek[s], Armenians, Syrians, and Copts, have altars in the open court.'[98] After drawing attention to a number of other sights in the immediate vicinity of the mosque, the *Description* goes on to indicate the point where, 'a little lower down' according to Luke 11: 2, the Lord's Prayer was taught (#3). The *Description* tells us that 'on your right ... is the Grotto of the Creed [#4] ... where the Apostles are said to have compiled their creed',[99] a spatial relation that is referred once again to the spectator's body. Our orientation as we view the panorama is thus charted in terms of personalised space, which, referencing the human body, establishes our physical relation to the cardinal points of the compass (north, south, east, west). The *Description* goes on to identify the place where Christ turned towards the city and 'wept over Jerusalem' (#5), asking his disciples (Mark 13: 2), '"Seest thou these great buildings?"', and foretelling that '"there shall not be left one stone upon another, that shall not be thrown down."'[100] Although the *Description* returns to consider the present state of Jerusalem in the final part of the booklet, for the moment, citing Luke 22: 44, Christ's agony in the Garden of Gethsemane (#6) is evoked. Whereas the text has, up to this point, relied on biblical sources to present information concerning the city and its sights, the description of the garden of Gethsemane interweaves three sources: extra-textual 'authority', hearsay, and personal account on the part of Catherwood who surveyed Jerusalem for a plan of the old city which he published in 1835 (Plate 1), the same year in which the panorama was first exhibited.[101] The garden, we are told, 'is planted with olive, almond, and fig trees' [*personal observation*]; 'eight of the olive trees are so large [*personal observation*] that they are said to have been there in our Saviour's time [*hearsay*], but that cannot be [*personal observation or deduction from an upcoming extra-textual account*] as Josephus says that Titus cut down all the trees within 100 furlongs of the city; but the olive tree enjoys a sort of immortality, for if the root be left, a new tree shortly springs from it'[*hearsay or personal observation*].[102]

Turning the gaze of the spectator towards the left, a description is provided of a group of six buildings seen from the first station, most of which are located in the extreme right-hand section of the lower engraving in the booklet, although the first location identified in this group of buildings is situated at the extreme left of the upper panel: the burial place of the Virgin Mary (#7) in subterranean chapels near the foot of the Mount of Olives. The *Description* notes that 'considerably to your left is the Church of St. Anna' (#65), a church which 'now in ruins ... occupies the site of the house of St. Anna, the mother of the Virgin Mary ... where the latter was born'.[103] The Marian theme continues with the third structure identified in this group of buildings: the 'Gate of St. Stephen ... also called the Gate of the Virgin Mary' (#66), which is near the location where, according to Acts 7: 58, St. Stephen was stoned. 'On the right, nearer the spectator[,] is the Pool of Bethesda [#67] ... evidently the most ancient work in Jerusalem ... [where] lambs for sacrifice were washed', a location which, the *Description* informs us, 'was supposed to have the power of healing diseases', which belief, confirmed by John 5: 8, relates that this is the location where Christ commanded a man, who had been infirm for thirty-eight years, to 'Rise, take up thy bed and walk'.[104] On the summit of the Mount of Olives (#69), the place where two angels appeared to the apostles after Christ's ascension is indicated (Acts 1: 11) before our attention returns to the foreground of the lower panel (the roof terrace of the House of the Aga or Governor) which, we are told, stands on the ruins of the Palace of Pilate. Steps (the Scala Sancta) leading down from the terrace to the hall of judgement, where the cross was kept, can be seen in the lower right section of the lower panel, presumably close to '62' in the engraving. With the presentation of this information, the description of the first station is completed, and the spectator moves to the second station in the darkened observation gallery to view another section of the panorama.

If a detailed account of the information presented in this part of the *Description* has been provided, this is to demonstrate how our viewing of the panorama is not only guided by the booklet (which orients the spectator's viewing of the panorama in relation to his or her body), but redoubled by the alignment of the panorama with the topography of the location. Not only is the spectator's gaze thus fixed on particular sections of the panorama before moving from one section to another, but a number of locations and historical incidents, some of which are not even depicted in the panorama, are nonetheless recounted. Unlike the paintings of Martin, where biblical narrative was presented in dramatic fashion, here narrative account of past events is provided even when some of the events are not represented. A similar process attends the matter of prophecy where the narration predicts a future for the inhabitants of the city that is defined as one of desolation ('the days shall come upon thee, that thine enemies shall cast a trench about thee ... and shall lay thee even with the ground', Luke 19: 43, 44), a concern to which the *Description* returns in the closing stages of the tour. Prediction of the future identifies narrative circularity (and, indeed, redundancy) as an operation of the *Description* wherein the city's past is alluded to through biblical reference, and its future anticipated in the present-day image of the city as a 'provincial Ottoman town'.[105]

The interweaving of historical reference with biblical account continues throughout the *Description*. Rather than provide a résumé of the information made available to visitors through the descriptive booklet, we will consider three structures that receive particular attention: the Mosque of Omar (#21, upper panel, 'towards the south', discussed in View VI) which is privileged by virtue of the amount of information provided in the booklet;[106] the Armenian Church and Convent (#34, discussed in View VII), and the Temple of the Holy Sepulchre (#39, discussed in View VII). In addition, we also consider a number of locations that afford the opportunity of recounting specific religious traditions: the Golden Gate (#10, towards the south-east); the Invisible Bridge (#20, to the south of the Mosque of Omar); and the Via Dolorosa (#44, towards the north-west section of the lower panel, discussed in View VIII). Rather than concentrate on the Christian associations of the city, the panorama and *Description* privilege cultural and religious diversity to an unusual degree.

Considerable space is given to a discussion of the Mosque of Omar, a building which, before Catherwood visited Jerusalem, no artist, on religious grounds, had been permitted to draw.[107] Here the interest of Catherwood the architectural draughtsman comes to the fore. The *Description* asserts that it is 'the finest piece of Saracenic architecture in existence'.[108] The octagonal structure of the mosque is considered (the four doors that face the cardinal points of the compass are identified), with its roof gently rising towards the 'perpendicular part under the dome, which is covered in coloured tiles, arranged in various elegant devices'. The dome, 'built by Solyman [Süleyman] I. ... spherical, covered with lead, and crowned by a gilt crescent', is contrasted with the blue and white marble below, which the *Description* notes is 'extremely pleasing'.[109] Particular attention is reserved for the walls of the mosque:

> the lower part of the walls is faced with marble, evidently very ancient; it is white, with a slight tinge of blue, and pieces wholly blue are occasionally introduced with good effect; each face is panelled, the sides of the panels forming plain pilasters at the angles; the upper part is faced with small glazed tiles, about eight inches square, of various colours, blue being the prevailing, with passages of the Koran on them, forming a singular and most beautiful mosaic.[110]

The second building to which attention is directed is the Armenian Church and Convent (#34, towards the south-west) which, we are told, occupies the site of the house of the father-in-law of Caiphas. Here, Christ was first incarcerated; here, Peter later denied him, and in this building, the stone which closed Christ's sepulchre was used as an altar. The Gate of David, adjacent to the church, was the place where Christ (Matthew 28: 9) appeared to Mary and Mary Magdalene, and also the place where, according to Acts 12: 2, James, the brother of John, was beheaded by Herod. With a pronounced change of subject, our cicerone informs us that this part of the city is also the cleanest and best part of the city, the convent, having a large garden, being well supplied with every comfort for pilgrims and travellers. While such information might appeal to the prospective visitor or pilgrim, historical incident abounds at this point in the *Description*. On Mount Zion, we are told, the House of Annas (#33, towards the south-west), now used as a mosque, 'is held in great veneration, as it is said to contain the tomb of King David. This was also the ancient church of the Cœnacuium, where our Saviour instituted the Last Supper; the large room on the upper storey, in which it took place' being clearly visible, albeit depicted at a considerable distance from the spectator.[111] The *Description* relates that the Golden Gate (Bab el Derahie, #10, towards the south-east) was not only the gate through which Christ entered the city by ass on Palm Sunday (Matthew 21: 8), but also has 'long been closed up, the Turks having a tradition, that the Christians will enter by it and take the city'.[112] The Invisible Bridge (#20) is identified where Mohammed 'is to sit at the last day, and judge the world' and where 'believers will pass over with the rapidity of lightning, and enter paradise; but from which the infidel will fall into the bottomless pit of hell which is beneath'.[113] If the panorama does not evidence the drama typical of Martin's biblical scenes, Catherwood's panorama is nonetheless saturated with historical detail which, even when not depicted in the panorama, is drawn to the spectator's attention by the *Description*.

Nowhere is the sense of the past more asserted, since the authorities on which the *Description* draws are not identified, than in the last two locations we consider: the Temple of the Holy Sepulchre (#38 and #39 towards the south-west) and the Via Dolorosa (#41, towards the north-west). A detailed chronicle concerning the Temple of the Holy Sepulchre is provided, which is similar, in some respects, to the strategies adopted by eighteenth-century antiquarian writers who often drew on diverse and, by today's standards, unsystematic accounts:

> The tomb of Christ was enclosed by the early Christians forty-six years after the destruction of the city, and was for a long time the most honoured sanctuary of the church; it then became a pagan temple, dedicated to Venus, and remained so until the time of Constantine, whose mother, Helena, erected the temple or church, many portions of which, evidently of the architecture of that age, still exist. Cosroes ravaged this temple 300 years after its erection, when it was very rich in pious offerings, and it was again plundered in 1009. When the Mahomedans reconquered Jerusalem from the crusaders, it was ransomed, and has been permitted to remain in the hands of the Christians, in consideration of the large sum it annually produces. Previous to the year 1695 it was in the undisturbed possession of the Latin Fathers; the Greeks then invaded their privileges, and the most violent commotions have at different times taken place. On the 12th of March 1808, a great portion of the edifice was destroyed by fire, which raged furiously for six hours; it consumed the Armenian chapel, where it commenced, the Greek chapel, the cells of the Franciscans, the chapel of the Virgin, and the great dome, and destroyed many of the fine marble columns and mosaic work of St. Helena; the sepulchre itself was not injured, but the Greeks are accused of pulling down the chapel over it in the confusion; indeed, they have by some been accused of wilfully causing the fire. The present building was commenced immediately, and finished in September, 1810, at the cost of sixteen millions of piasters, wholly defrayed by the Greeks.[114]

A condensed catalogue of events also attends the recounting of Christ's progression along the Via Dolorosa: on this street Christ was mocked and scourged (Matthew 27: 26); on this street Christ, crowned with thorns and dressed in a purple robe, was presented to the Jews by Pilate (John 19: 5); and on this street Christ saluted the Virgin, fainted with carrying the cross, and Simon, from Cyrenia, 'was compelled to bear the cross' for Jesus (Luke 23: 26).[115] Such incidents draw our attention to the torment which, even though not shown in the panorama, nonetheless constitutes a veritable passion play in the *Description* where the stations of the cross, evoked in the mind of a spectator familiar with biblical account, provide a subtext that accompanies the spectator as he or she moves from one station to the next to view the panorama. At its most intense, the spectator's progression round the panorama emulates the procession staged in a passion play. Such coordination of narrative account with the process of viewing would no doubt have signified, at least for some spectators, a strong correlation between the experience of viewing the panorama and the religious events to which the *Description* alludes.

The *Description* closes with a reconsideration of the foreground subject in the lower panel: the roof terrace of the Aga or Governor of Jerusalem where the Aga is 'represented seated under an awning, surrounded by numerous groupes [*sic*] of figures'.[116] Among the figures near the left frame of the lower panel, Catherwood and Joseph Bonomi are identified by the key (#45). Catherwood, seated under a large parasol, is drawing a section of the panorama with a *camera lucida*, an optical instrument which we will consider further in the next chapter.[117] What Catherwood is drawing is what we, at a later time (and much elaborated), view in the panorama, a reciprocity which is figured by the spectator's passage round the exhibit. Even if such recognition might have occurred to only a minority of visitors to the panorama, the correspondence between the panorama and the events described in the *Description* is striking.

Just as the spectator's passage round the panorama thus enacts incidents recounted in the *Description*, so conjuring past events in the spectator's imagination, the staffage on the terrace also shares a degree of similarity with the viewers of the panorama. Although the group of people in the foreground departs significantly from the rustics who would have represented the rural poor in landscape painting contemporary with the panorama, since the group of people assembled in the foreground includes types that would have had a social standing similar to some of the visitors to the panorama (servants, clerics, functionaries, a soldier, a merchant), a commonality between spectators of the panorama and the people represented in the panorama is forged. In this respect, as Oettermann has proposed, panoramas inscribed a more democratic group of individuals than the staffage conventionally represented in landscape painting. The panorama of Jerusalem also embraces diversity consistent with the exoticism associated with contemporary depictions of the orient.[118]

One further sense of alterity in the scene is relayed in the final paragraph of the *Description*:

> Jerusalem from a distance, appears to be a large, well fortified, and splendid city; but within, it presents an extraordinary scene of ruin and wretchedness ... a street nearly half a mile in length, presents a singular scene of desolation, piles of ruins rise on either side in heaps, twenty or thirty feet in height, having the appearance of the remains of some great fire, of which no tradition remains.[119]

Coming after the detailed, multi-cultural perspective of the city, how may we account for what appears to be such a radical change in tone? After providing descriptions of buildings within the Christian, Jewish, Armenian, and Islamic traditions, after recounting historical incident and beliefs associated with the city, and after presenting the viewer with what, in another context, John Britton characterised as 'a *cyclopædia* of *information* – a concentrated history – a focal topography',[120] the response which the *Description* finally acknowledges is an account 'of which no tradition remains'.[121] This observation is similar to one we will encounter when Stephens and Catherwood attempt to come to terms with their expeditions to Central America and Yucatán: the sense that the explorers, along with local Maya communities, lack what Stephens terms a 'traditionary knowledge', information that would help them establish the antiquity and origins of the people whom they have encountered, were such an account available. Irrespective of the histories and subjects represented in the

Jerusalem panorama, what is emphasised in the closing stages of our tour is that the *experience* of history is understood to *outrun* human record *and* the viewer's ability to understand history. The recognition that a knowledge of tradition is not only a pre-requisite for understanding a culture but also fundamental to the process of gaining historical insight at a time when Western culture was still, at base, religious, is a concern to which we will return, one which will lead Stephens and Catherwood to develop a line of reasoning that challenged received opinion in the western hemisphere at the time. As we shall see, the argument that Stephens and Catherwood develop in response to encountering indigenous cultures in Central America and Yucatán is one that flies in the face of tradition since their argument relies on a type of reasoning that has more in common with a modern, secular society than accounts based on the biblical and religious beliefs which underpin the *Description*. In short, although there can be little doubt that Stephens and Catherwood were deists (like most people at the time), the conclusions which Stephens and Catherwood draw from the incidents of travel *they* experience in Central America and Yucatán are ones that challenged received antiquarian account ('traditionary' forms of knowledge *par excellence*) which prevailed as a mode of historical interpretation. What Stephens and Catherwood thus represent, a subtext which can be detected here, is a position which evidences an understanding of history that is typical of a more modern line of inquiry, a perspective which supersedes eighteenth-century antiquarian account, a perspective which we will consider further in Chapter Three and Chapter Four.

Arising from our discussion of the Jerusalem panorama, we should observe the profound correlation that is obtained between viewing the panorama from the rotunda gallery, and processes which orient the spectator's experience with the topography of the location and the time of day delineated in the panorama. In this respect, Catherwood's panorama of Jerusalem marks a considerable departure from the *coup d'œil* of Barker's panoramas – the wide-ranging prospect view with which this chapter opened – towards a more rigorous orientation of the spectator in a 'circumambient world', a concern specified in the notice published in *The Literary Gazette*:

> Immediately in front of the spectator, towards the south, stands boldly prominent ... the beautiful Mosque of Omar ...; towards the west, immediately beneath, commences the Via Dolorosa ...; to the north, is seen the hill Scopo ...; and, towards the east ... the Mount of Olives ... and other holy stations, relieved by patches of cultivation and a few olive trees, closes the view.[122]

The Literary Gazette announces a concern for mapping space in the reader's imagination, a concern to which we will return in the final part of this chapter when the panorama of Baalbek is considered in relation to its *Description*.

Panorama of Karnak and Thebes

The concern with historical reflection, which closed the panorama of Jerusalem, opens the *Description of a View of The Great Temple of Karnak and the Surrounding City of Thebes* with a panegyric:

> THEBES – the renowned capital of the Egyptian monarchy; the ruined, but imperishable city; the great Diospolis, famed by poets and historians; of such prodigious antiquity, that the time of its erection remains enveloped in obscurity, and the date of its destruction is far anterior to the foundation of most other cities – presents one of the most extraordinary, extensive, and interesting ruins extant; the concentrated labour of ages, which neither time nor the frantic rage of the conqueror of Egypt has been able to destroy – an eternal monument of the art and industry of the people, who first civilized the world. It is difficult to describe, and impossible, without inspection, to form an adequate idea of the vast extent, ponderous massiveness, and gigantic appearance of these majestic ruins ... shattered and detached, as if in the very zenith of their beauty, by some mighty convulsion of nature.[123]

The *Description* goes on to quote two declarations which prepare the spectator for viewing the panorama: the first, from a work by Charles Sigisbert Sonnini de Manoncourt (*Travels in Upper and Lower Egypt*, 3 vols., 1799), announces an ecstatic response; the second, from an account by Dominique Vivant Denon (*Travels in Upper and Lower Egypt, in company with several Divisions of the French Army*, 3 vols., 1803), revels in cultural appropriation:

> Sonini [*sic*] describes his sensations, 'as not simple admiration, but as an extacy [*sic*] which suspended his faculties, rendered him immoveable with rapture, and inclined him more than once to prostrate himself in veneration of such monuments – the rearing of which appeared to

> transcend the strength and genius of man.' Denon declares, 'that the whole French army, coming suddenly in sight of the ruins, with one accord stood in amazement, and clapped their hands with delight, as if the end and object of their glorious toil, and the complete conquest of Egypt were accomplished and secured, by taking possession of the splendid remains of the ancient metropolis.'[124]

Following these declarations, the *Description* provides an account of the foundation and early history of Thebes which indicates that the site is 'supposed to have formed part of the kingdom of Misraim, the son of Ham, about one hundred and sixty years after the deluge ...'.[125] The references to Ham and the Deluge indicate a chronology that once again draws on biblical account.

As far as scriptural authority is concerned, by the mid-eighteenth century over seventy biblical chronologies existed concerning the creation and history of the world, with dates for the creation ranging from 5,400 BC to 3,964 BC. Of these, the best known was that of Bishop Ussher, who gave the date of the Creation as 4,004 BC and identified Noah's Flood as occurring in 2,448 BC.[126] Although different theories might stretch or contest these chronologies, the history of the world was one that was generally believed to be circumscribed by scriptural authority which, until biblical accounts began to be challenged towards the end of the eighteenth century, prescribed a very limited and fixed time-frame for prehistory. As we shall see, by the time Stephens and Catherwood were active, such a chronology had not only been called into question, but works in Catherwood's private library, although they included publications of a religious nature (including many sermons), also reveal an interest in geological debate, a discourse which in the late eighteenth century began to call biblical account into question, positing alternative and much extended accounts of the history of the earth.[127] We should observe that in providing a chronology for the panorama, the *Description* locates the history of Karnak and Thebes within biblical tradition, presuming an audience familiar with biblical account which, for the majority of spectators in the 1830s, would have provided an authoritative chronology.

The material presented in the *Description* also draws on two further sources for its chronology: classical accounts and contemporary (or near-contemporary) accounts of exploration in Egypt. Classical writers cited in the *Description* include Strabo, Diodorus Siculus, and Juvenal, and accounts compiled by contemporary writers range from the publications by Sonnini and Denon (both of whom travelled to Egypt as members of Napoleon Bonaparte's expedition in 1798) to works by James Bruce, Giovanni Battista Belzoni, and John Gardner Wilkinson.[128] For a measure of the interest that Belzoni stimulated in Egyptian antiquities in the early 1820s, the exhibition he organised at the Egyptian Hall, which included replicas of two non-contiguous chambers from the tomb of Sety I 'cast in plaster of Paris, from wax impressions taken on the spot', created an unparalleled interest, contributing to the emerging discipline of archaeology in the early nineteenth century.[129]

Apart from the sarcophagus exhibited by Belzoni, the *Description* also refers to 'Bruce's or the Harper's Tomb' at Thebes, a reference to two representations of harpists found by Bruce in the decoration to the tomb of Ramesses III. Bruce observes that:

> These harps, in my opinion, overturn all the accounts hitherto given of the earliest state of music and musical instruments in the east; and are altogether in their form, ornaments, and compass, an incontestible [*sic*] proof, stronger than a thousand Greek quotations, that geometry, drawing, mechanics, and music, were at the greatest perfection when this instrument was made, and that the period, from which we date the invention of these arts, was only the beginning of the æra of their restoration. This was the sentiment of Solomon, a writer who lived at the time when this harp was painted. 'Is there,' says Solomon, 'any thing whereof it may be said, See, this is new! It hath been already of old time which was before us.'[130]

The quotation which closes Bruce's observation echoes a sentiment that Catherwood and Stephens would make some years later when, in melancholic fashion, they reflected on Maya culture, thus demonstrating the degree to which their response to Maya ruins was not only versed in the eighteenth-century tradition of the Picturesque, but also early Romantic literature.[131]

If the melancholic sense of history that pervades the *Description* coincides with a broad understanding of cultural tradition and a shared perspective on the past, the Karnak and Thebes panorama provides a composite view of the subjects seen at the sites. Unlike

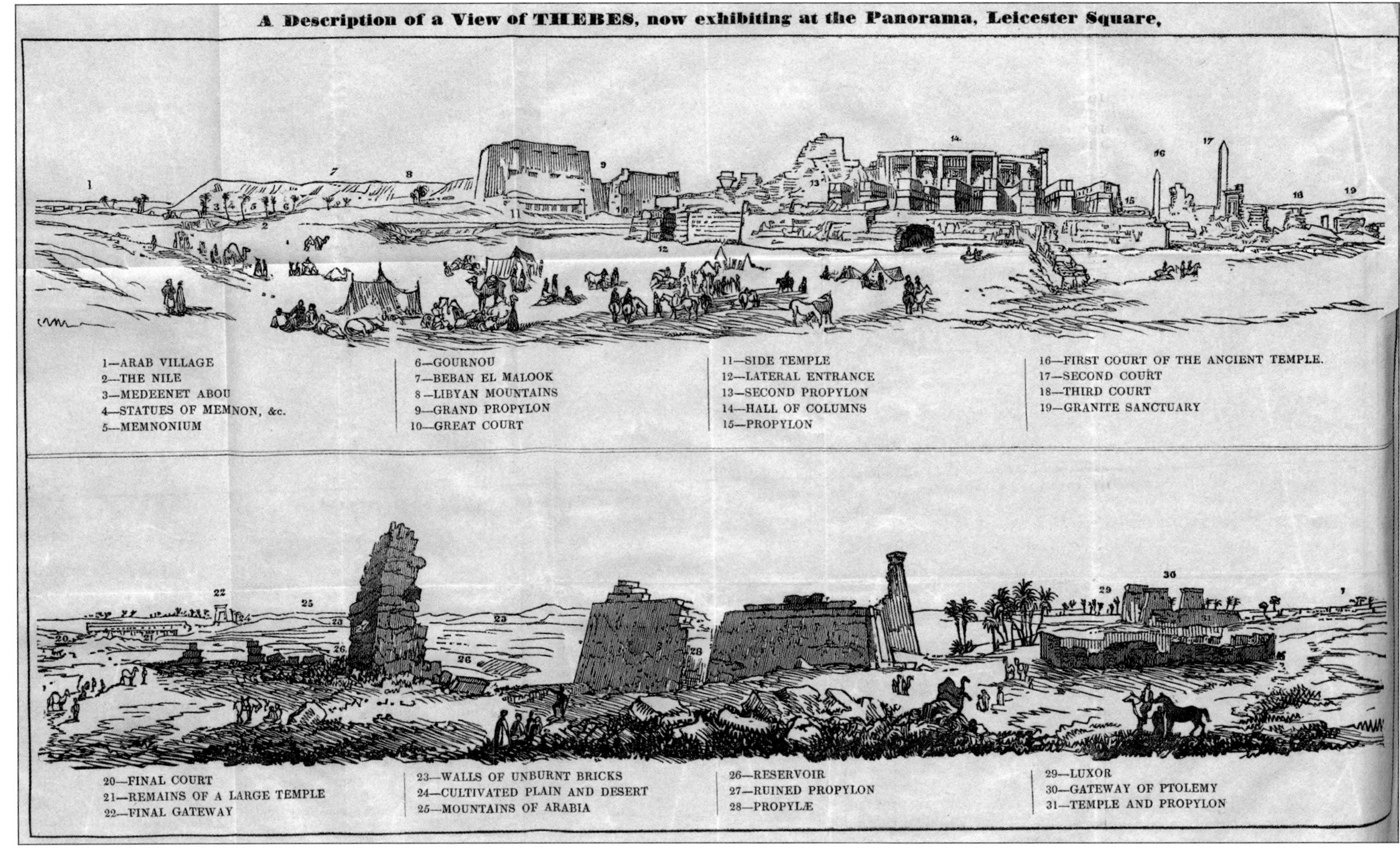

1.4. Orientation view and key, *A Description of a View of Thebes, now exhibiting at the Panorama, Leicester Square*, engraving, Robert Burford and (unattributed) Frederick Catherwood, *Description of a View of The Great Temple of Karnak and the surrounding city of Thebes, now exhibiting at the Panorama, Leicester Square. Painted by the Proprietor, Robert Burford, from drawings taken by Mr. F. Catherwood, Architect, in 1833* (London: Printed by G. Nichols, n.d.), upper panel, 11.7 x 38.8 cm.; lower panel, 10.8 x 38.8 cm. [Reproduced by permission of Cambridge University Library.]

the panorama of Jerusalem, the panorama does not aspire to topographical accuracy (1.4). As the *Description* makes clear, at 'no point can the eye embrace the whole of these extraordinary remains at the same time', a statement echoed by John Lloyd Stephens when he observed that 'the ruins of Thebes … extending on both sides of the river, nowhere burst in one view upon the sight'.[132] In concentrating on the Great Temple of Karnak and the Ramesseum in Thebes, the panorama presents a 'digest' or synthesis of selected structures in the Karnak temple complexes, most notably the northern facade of the Eighth Propylon (#28) in the foreground of the lower panel (which frames a view of Luxor in the distance, towards rear right) and selected structures from Thebes to the west of Karnak which occupy the middle distance of the upper panel.[133] The fact that the Nile, which flows *between* the sites of Karnak and Luxor on the east bank of the river and the site of Thebes to the west of the river, is presented as flowing *behind* the Ramesseum at Thebes (i.e., to the west of the site), indicates the degree to which the panorama presents a major reorientation of archaeological structures relative to the Nile.[134]

The panorama includes a caravan of pilgrims preparing to bed down for the night across the foreground, an activity which indicates that the illumination of the ruins is consistent with the time of day when the 'magic hues of the setting sun' cast shadows on the north facade of the Eighth Propylon at Karnak (#28), even if the orientation of the view is not matched by the shadows cast by structures in front of the Hall of Columns (#14). While the scale of the site militates against topographical accuracy, the panorama nonetheless stages a temporally specific scene, one which promotes affect through aerial perspective and the gradation of colour that softens form in distant objects. This effect is reinforced in the *Description*:

> In the fore-ground, a small caravan of pilgrims, &c., who have just crossed the desert on their way to join the great caravan to Mecca from Cairo, is represented preparing to encamp for the night; the whole illuminated by the magic hues of the setting sun, whose last beams falling on the projecting masses of the temples, where he was worshipped with so much pomp – the obelisks and the white rocks – touching them with the varied and glowing tints of the rainbow – produces a scene of so truly magnificent and extraordinary a character, that the whole world cannot furnish its parallel.[135]

As with the booklets prepared for the Jerusalem panorama as exhibited in Edinburgh and Glasgow, the *Description* of Karnak and Thebes proceeds in an orderly fashion, placing the spectator at four principal stations. Particular sections of the panorama are described in detail before the viewer moves on to consider a further group of subjects. On occasion, the description of a view is interwoven with ethnographic interest, including the fact that local villagers, who offered 'the sale of small antiquities', could be prevailed upon to act as guides for excavators and travellers.[136]

Similar to the discussion of the Mosque of Omar in the Jerusalem panorama, the *Description* provides a detailed description of one structure: the Temple of Karnak.[137] Unlike the Jerusalem panorama, however, the *Description* promotes a sense of awe and reverie as the narrator, following the example of James Bruce, compares the culture of the historical spectator with those of the past:

> From whatever situation this splendid temple of pagan worship is viewed, the effect is striking and wonderful, and cannot fail to impress the intelligent beholder with awe and astonishment. At a little distance, the sublime conception, the noble gateways, the magnificent halls, and towering obelisks, are objects of pleasure and interest; but when, on a nearer approach, the immense masses of the hardest stone become apparent – when the labour necessary to detach these masses from the original rock is considered, the distance they were brought from the quarries, the herculean task of hewing, polishing, and fixing – when the eye contemplates the painting and sculpture, characters of unknown import, symbolical of the mysteries of the worship celebrated therein, or of the great deeds of a race long passed away, the mind is insensibly carried back to the illusions of former ages, and is lost in admiration of a people possessed of the moral and physical means of completing such wonderful undertakings, so far exceeding all modern exertions of man's strength; which, although they may want the powerful classical associations, inseparably connected with Greece or Rome, yet become doubly interesting, when it is remembered that they were raised by the people, to whom those nations were indebted for the arts, sciences, and learning.[138]

The panorama shares a number of strategies with the panorama of Jerusalem: a discussion of architecture; an account which privileges spatial contiguity; the adoption of a variety of registers to promote affect; and a delight in reflecting on ethnographic (and, for the period, exotic) local interest. While the Jerusalem panorama presents a topographically coherent prospect of the city from an elevated position, allowing the spectator a degree of proximity to the people represented on the Aga's roof terrace, the views presented in the panorama of Karnak and Thebes demonstrate selection and synthesis. In this respect, the panorama qualifies the reputed topographical accuracy of the medium, and promotes a more measured response in the spectator, one which echoes the strategy observed in the Frontispiece of *Incidents of Travel in Yucatan*. While the depiction of space may, on the one hand, privilege restraint, the aerial perspective of the panorama, representing the hues of twilight, stages a view which stimulated a visceral response. Such a reaction was commented on in a review published in *The Times* the previous year, when a panorama of the Gulf of Boothia (in the Canadian Arctic) was exhibited at the Panorama, Leicester Square:

> The interest of these scenes fades almost into insignificance before the singular effect produced by the painting of the sky ... perhaps the greatest difficulty which the artist has had to overcome is the representation of the sombre yet clear twilight which pervades this desolate region for so long a period of the year. The effect is beautifully maintained throughout the picture, and imparts to the painting a solemn stillness perfectly in accordance with the awful aspect of the scene.[139]

We may propose that the depiction of twilight at Karnak and Thebes may have promoted a similar response, evoking the Sublime. What is also of interest, if we compare the panorama of the Gulf of Boothia with the panorama of Karnak and Thebes, is that the former not only telescoped space, but also time, since the panorama of the Gulf of Boothia represented events that occurred between 1829 and 1832.[140]

The depiction of twilight raises two issues: first, the issue of illumination in the rotunda; second, the process by which panoramas were painted. An unpublished journal kept by Henry Selous between October 1833 and May 1834 addresses these concerns. Since the journal was written during the period when Catherwood's sketches of Karnak and Thebes and sketches for the panorama of the Gulf of Boothia were being developed for the Panorama, Leicester Square, the journal is of particular interest.[141] It is generally thought that the level of illumination in the panorama rotunda was not strong, a practice that would have departed from the theatre where artificial illumination had been adopted for lighting scenery, at least in London, by the late 1810s. Although Argand lamps had been employed on the stage at the Drury Lane Theatre as early as 1785, where their introduction provoked a 'degree of peculiar satisfaction',[142] Argand lamps and gas lamps were not generally used to light stage scenery until the late 1810s. By the time that Henry Selous worked as a panoramist, gas lamps were regularly used to light stage scenery (rather than illuminate the auditorium and other public spaces), although a singular silence seems to have attended reactions to the introduction of gaslights for stage scenery.[143] It is, therefore, difficult to gauge how theatre-goers responded to the introduction of stage lighting, or what visitors may have thought of the use of daylight in panoramas when compared with artificial lighting in the theatre.

With its innovative arrangement of skylights reflecting daylight onto the interior wall of the rotunda, panoramas made it appear as though light emanated from the panorama itself.[144] The construction of the rotunda relied on the principle of a cone cut in two, with the upper section inverted into the lower so that a skylight running around the lower section of the roof provided reflected light to the lower painting in the rotunda (the Large Circle), while a similar ring around the inverted cone lighted the smaller Upper Circle of the panorama (1.2). A ceiling above the gallery prevented spectators from seeing daylight through the skylights, thus contributing to the illusion that light issued from the painted panorama. Though visitors approached the panorama through a darkened corridor (which let their eyes adjust to the lower light level in the rotunda), the lack of light for viewing a panorama on overcast days remained a problem, particularly during the winter. Selous' journal confirms that a day spent in the 'painting room', the studio where panoramas were prepared, was 'as dull as it was possible to be'.[145] The following month, still working in the studio on the panorama of the Bay of Boothia, Selous observed: 'The wettest day I ever remember[,] one continued torrent of rain the whole day[.] [T]he panorama so dark the [*sic*] we [Burford and Selous] could scarce see to paint[.] [M]anaged to finish four more figures and then left early on account of the badness of the weather.'[146]

The technical expertise for a panorama painter were similar to those demanded of scene-painters in the theatre, and practitioners in each profession received a similar rate of remuneration; in the case of Selous, a weekly salary of £6, often paid in arrears.[147] Scene-painters and panorama-painters were expected to have a knowledge of linear and aerial perspective, and be able 'by fixed geometrical observations, lines bent or inclined, which the spectator ... imagines to be straight ... give the appearance of an extent and distance, existing merely in his own art ... expressing an extent almost infinite'.[148] Artists in each profession used the water-based medium of distemper because it dried quickly, speeding up the time between initial painting and over-painting. In the case of scene-painting, distemper provided a matt finish that countered reflections from artificial lighting; in the case of panorama-painting, a different finish would have likely provoked a rather different response for visitors to the panorama.

As a portrait painter who had trained at the Royal Academy schools,[149] Selous had conflicting opinions of the panorama as a mode of representation. Though he wrote that he was 'still of the opinion that the style of painting ... is capable of great power', he also observed that 'it will require much practise to bring it to any thing like perfection'.[150] Less than a week later, he confided: 'Panorama painting I feel convinced causes a very slovenly and loose style.'[151] Selous usually worked with Robert Burford, yet disapproved of 'the system that B: is pursueing [*sic*] with his son' on the grounds that it was neither 'honourable nor correct'.[152] Four assistants employed, presumably, as pieceworkers sponged in the sky before Selous and Burford painted the more detailed parts of the panorama.[153] In this respect, panorama-painting proceeded in a manner similar to scene-painting in the theatre: painters applied 'local colour … first and when dry … put on the lights and shades and finish[ed] by marking out the detail'.[154]

Work on the panorama of Karnak and Thebes commenced on Wednesday, 19 March 1834, when Selous began the squaring of Catherwood's drawings, a process that translated the single-point perspective of Catherwood's drawings to the requirements of a large, multiple-perspective, curved canvas.[155] After squaring Catherwood's drawings, Selous began to draw in the details of the picture, which he completed a week later.[156] At the beginning of the following week, he 'drew in the model',[157] referring, presumably, to a maquette that Catherwood prepared of one or more structures at Karnak or Thebes. By Wednesday, 2 April, Selous began to paint the sky, a process that was completed the following day, although Selous periodically returned to the sky through much of April.[158] On Friday, 4 April, Selous 'commenced sponging with water colour … amost [*sic*] expediting mode of getting on with the picture' since by the end of the following day, 'the sponging of the picture' had been completed.[159] On Tuesday the following week, Selous began to apply turpentine to the panorama, which process continued, intermittently, until Tuesday, 22 April.[160] The application of Venice turpentine (derived from the Western Larch, *Larix occidentalis*) indicates that panoramas were coated with turpentine to harden and preserve the surface of the canvas, a finish which, like varnish, imparted a lustre to the watercolour paint since panoramas, unlike scene-painting, were not artificially lit and were not, therefore, subject to the same degree of reflection.[161] The painting of the sky recommenced on Wednesday, 23 April, and was completed two days later.[162] The following Monday, without explanation, Selous and Burford 'decided upon giving up Thebes for the present and finishing New York'.[163] In the last entry in the journal, Selous noted that he and Burford anticipated completing the New York panorama 'in about a fortnight'.[164] The journal indicates that the preparation and painting of the panorama continued at a pace, particularly since the surface area of the canvas was approximately 10,000 square feet.[165] Given that spectators in the gallery stood some thirty feet from the panorama canvas, the overall effect would probably have been similar to that of viewing a theatrical scene, except that panoramas, coated with Venice turpentine, would have appeared more refulgent than a theatrical scene. In this respect, we may propose that panoramas promoted a more visceral experience to that offered in the theatre, an aesthetic pleasure which composition could also enhance, as is evident in the last of the three panoramas considered in this chapter.

Panorama of Baalbec

The panorama, *Ruins of the Temples of Baalbec* after Catherwood (1.5), exhibited in the Upper Circle at the Panorama, Leicester Square, from 29 June to 4 December 1844, has greater dynamism than either the panorama of Jerusalem or the panorama of Karnak and Thebes. The city wall that surrounds the northern section of the site inscribes a striking parabola in the right-hand part of the lower engraving printed in the *Description of a View of the Ruins of the Temples of Baalbec*, drawing attention to the off-centre position from which the panorama is depicted.[166] This location, emphasising the scale of the site, was thought to impress the spectator's 'mind with awe', affording 'an awful and instructive lesson on the pride and vanity of man, and the instability of all earthly grandeur'.[167]

Such a response is very different to the work of the Irish scholar and traveller, Robert Wood, who, influenced by architectural engravings of Antoine Desgodetz, visited Baalbek in 1751 with the Italian artist, Giovanni Battista Borra. Borra's drawings in pen and ink and wash served as the basis for engravings in Wood's influential *The Ruins of Balbec, otherwise Heliopolis in Cœlosyria* published in 1757,

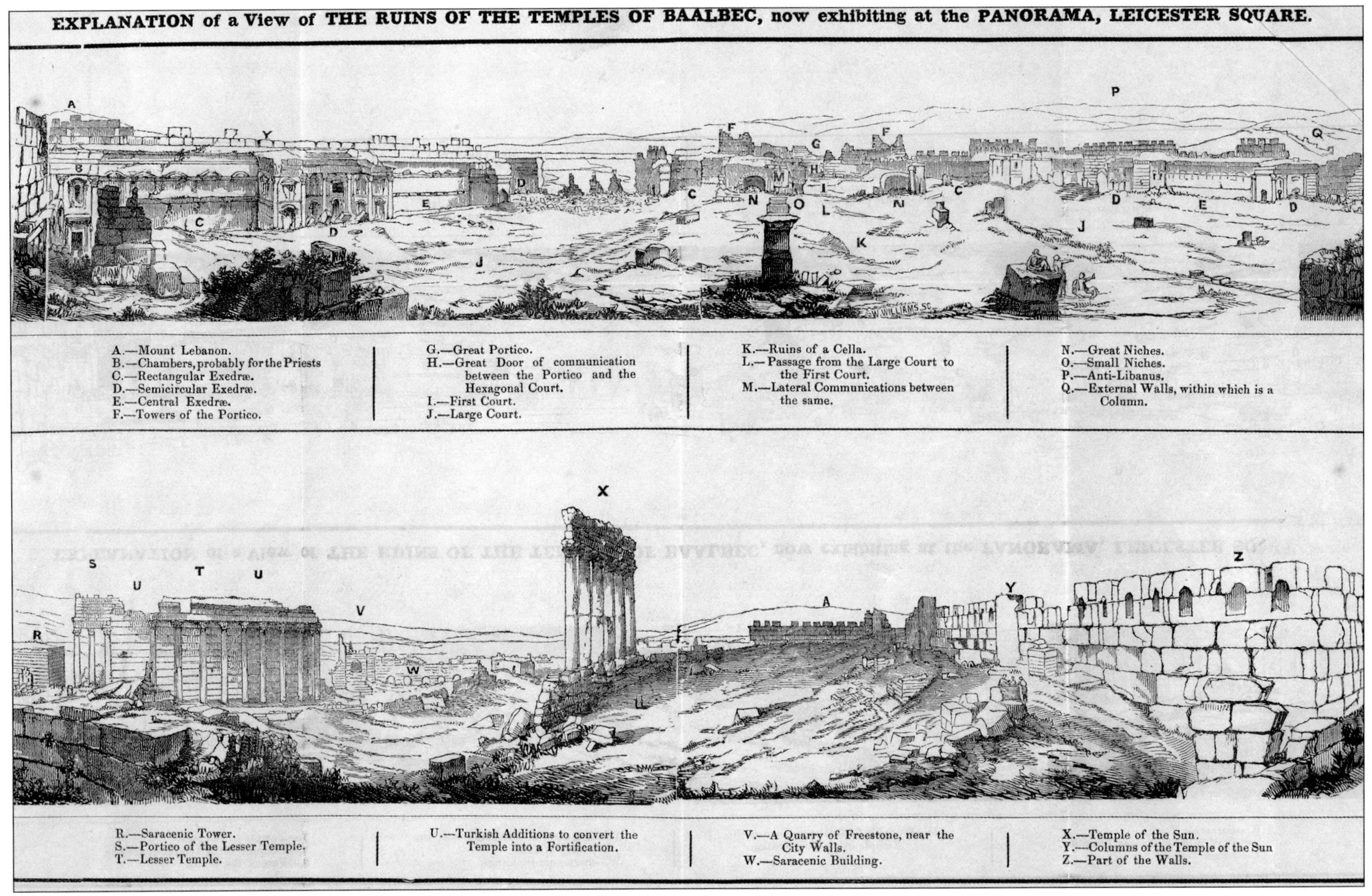

1.5. Orientation view and key, *Explanation of a View of The Ruins of the Temples of Baalbec, now exhibiting at the Panorama, Leicester Square*, engraving, Robert Burford and (unattributed) Frederick Catherwood, *Description of a View of the Ruins of the Temples of Baalbec, Now Exhibiting at the Panorama, Leicester Square. Painted by the Proprietor, Robert Burford, assisted by H.C. Selous, from Drawings taken on the Spot by F. Catherwood, Esq.* (London: Printed by Geo. Nichols, 1844), upper panel, 11.2 x 39.2 cm.; lower panel, 12.8 x 39.2 cm. [Reproduced by permission of the British Library.]

which recorded the site in a suitably 'measured' and 'restored' fashion after the example of Desgodetz.[168] Although Catherwood did not own a copy of Wood, it is clear that he was familiar with Wood since the work is referred to on three occasions in the *Description*. Catherwood notes that at the time when Wood visited the site in 1751, the Temple of the Sun comprised nine columns, 'three of which were probably thrown down by the earthquake of 1756'.[169] It is likely that Catherwood first encountered a view of Baalbek in the series of public lectures John Soane gave at the Royal Academy and at the Royal Institution. A view of the site, looking towards the west, which drew on Wood's *The Ruins of Balbec* (1.6),[170] was shown in the Royal Academy lectures and in the first lecture Soane presented at the Royal Institution on 27 May 1820, a view which Catherwood may have recalled when selecting the point from which he delineated the site.[171] Significantly, Catherwood locates the spectator at a point where, unlike the views presented in Wood and Soane, the courtyard is not symmetrically framed, thus emphasising the 'assemblage of grand and imposing forms which create sensations in the mind better felt than described'.[172] With such a framing of space, the city wall on the north side of the courtyard (1.5, lower panel) dominates Catherwood's panorama, with structures to the east and south appearing on the opposite side of the panorama (1.5, upper panel).[173] While the extreme variation in scale between the north-western part of the panorama and the structures on the far side of the quadrangle make for a dramatic composition, the attention given to architectural detail in the *Description* reads more like an architectural lecture than the discussion that accompanied Catherwood's earlier panoramas. Relatively evenly lit, with short shadows cast on the north facade of the Temple of the Sun ('X', 1.5, lower panel), the panorama of Baalbek indicates that the time of day is late afternoon.

Unlike the panoramas of Jerusalem or Karnak and Thebes, the panorama of Baalbek, as exhibited in London, does not specify the stations from which the panorama was viewed, leaving visitors free to move around the observation gallery of their own accord. Such practice lends support to the observation that the panoramas, as presented in Edinburgh and Glasgow, were usually provided with a spoken commentary in the manner of the panorama of Jerusalem when Catherwood presented a commentary at the Panorama, Leicester Square. Different exhibition practices attended exhibition in London compared with these two cities in Scotland.

Although the form of presentation may have differed, the substance of the panoramas remained the same irrespective of the site of exhibition. The *Description* of the Baalbek panorama opens with three paragraphs that emphasise the Sublime with its depiction, as Soane put it in a lecture at the Royal Institution, of 'melancholy Monuments of the mutability of all sublunary things':[174]

> The mighty ruins of Baalbec, the ancient Heliopolis; rank amongst the most remarkable, most magnificent, and most interesting of the reliques [*sic*] of remote antiquity. Their vastness impresses the mind with awe – and the almost incredible bulk of the material of which they

1.6. 'View of the quadrangular court, in it's [*sic*] present state, as it is seen from the passage between it and the hexagonal court.', engraved by T. Major, Robert Wood, *The Ruins of Balbec, otherwise Heliopolis in Cœlosyria* (London: n.p., 1757), Plate XII, 30 x 69.3 cm. (folded out). [Reproduced by permission of the National Library of Scotland.]

are partly composed, with amazement; whilst the uncertainty of their origin or purpose, gives them a peculiar and striking interest.

The present Panorama, taken from the great quadrangle, in the very centre of the ruins, embraces all the most important and interesting portions. The most prominent object, and the first that commands attention, from its elevated site and imposing appearance, is composed of six lofty columns of peculiar elegance, supporting an entablature; once forming a portion of the peristyle of the great Temple of the Sun; which rising in grandeur and majesty far above the surrounding mass of walls and columns of the other Temples, &c., stands a fit monument on the tomb of former greatness, and is, at first sight, nearly as striking as the ruins of the Acropolis at Athens. A little to the west is a large and more perfect Temple, supposed to be of Roman origin; a proud and stately remnant of architectural magnificence, wrestling with time for existence; ... a scene of frightful desolation, which whilst it presents the most beautiful specimens of human art, ingenuity, and physical strength, at the same time affords an awful and instructive lesson on the pride and vanity of man, and the instability of all early grandeur. ...

The small remnant of the once flourishing town, which lies towards the east, is completely hidden by the immense masses of the ruins; ... Towards the west, the view is bounded by the long range of the mountains of Lebanon, ... and on the east, by the immense chain of the Anti-Libanus, cold, dreary, and severe. ...

The space covered by the ruins of the temples, is at the eastern side of the city – an area of about 900 feet long by 600 feet broad, not however a regular parallelogram, there being offsets at some of the towers; the towers being modern erections, added probably when the place was converted into a fort. ...'[175]

The view, couched in the rhetoric of the Sublime, 'impresses the mind with awe'; it 'commands attention' and, with an 'imposing appearance' and 'grandeur and majesty', conveys 'a scene of frightful desolation' while offering 'an awful and instructive lesson' on pride and vanity. The fact that the Temple of the Sun commands attention by virtue of its elevation confers significance on the Temple and the city wall to the right, and helps designate the spatial relation that obtains between structures specifying their cartographic relation to each other.[176] Unlike the panorama of Jerusalem or the panorama of Karnak and Thebes, the view of Baalbek defines spatial relations by means of compass direction rather than their relation to the body of the spectator, thus signalling a significant departure from the panorama of Jerusalem. Rather than emphasising an all-embracing view ('Nature at a Glance'), the *Description* of Baalbek orients our viewing of the site by means of compass direction. In this respect, the *Description* plots the relation of one structure to another. For example, in the discussion of the Temple of the Sun, we are told that 'On the northern side [of the Temple] built into the modern Saracenic wall, parallel with the six columns to the south, are fourteen pedestals, on four of which are portions of broken shafts.'[177] Although it may take the viewer a little time to identify the four pedestals parallel to the city wall on the extreme right of the lower panel (including three figures standing by the nearest pedestal to the viewer), the *Description* plots space at the same time as the panorama promotes a visceral response from the off-centre position which the spectator is allocated. By delineating Baalbek in this manner, the panorama unites somatic concerns with the concern for cartographic orientation provided in the *Description*, marshalling both in an expression of aesthetic pleasure.

The three panoramas, after sketches by Catherwood, demonstrate the close relation of text and panorama in each *Description* considered here. Two of the panoramas maintain a relatively fixed distance between spectator and panorama, and promote a measured response similar to that observed in the Frontispiece of *Incidents of Travel in Yucatan*. The three panoramas also provide different examples of the relation between topography, representation, and the spectator. The Jerusalem panorama emphasises a 'circumambient world' achieved through representing the 'whole horizon's circuit'; the panorama of Karnak and Thebes, challenging topographical accuracy, displays a synthesis that departs from the topography of the site; and Baalbek, with its off-centre station, promotes a visceral response, probably stronger than that generated in the panorama of Karnak and Thebes where aerial perspective secured affect.[178] In addition to these formal concerns, we have established, depending on the place of exhibition, that spectators viewed panoramas in one of two ways: they were free to move around the gallery of their own accord, or view a panorama according to the protocols of a spoken or printed commentary. We have also observed in the notes that the panorama of Jerusalem was presented as a peristrephic entertainment in Glasgow and re-worked as a moving panorama in Hull;[179]

and we have also established that in the case of exhibition in Scotland, the text for the panorama of Jerusalem departed, on occasion, from that printed for the Panorama, Leicester Square.[180] The formal departure of panorama-painting from scene-painting has also been identified.

While topographical representation, for Henry Fuseli, was deemed, at the beginning of the century, unworthy of artists aspiring to the grand style, by the time Catherwood worked as a panoramist in the mid-1830s and mid-1840s, developments in the painted panorama reflect a significant shift in the status of topographical painting. Commenting in disparaging terms on topography, Fuseli had earlier likened topographical painting to 'map-work':

> the last branch of interesting subjects, that kind of landscape which is entirely occupied with the tame delineation of a given spot; an enumeration of hill and dale, clumps of trees, shrubs, water, meadows, cottages, and houses, what is commonly called Views. These, if not assisted by nature, dictated by taste, or chosen for character, may delight the owner of the spot, perhaps the antiquary or traveller, but to every other eye they are little more than topography. The landscape of Titian, of Mola, of Salvator, of the Poussins, Claude, Rubens, Elzheimer, Rembrandt and Wilson, spurns all relation with this kind of map-work.[181]

A generation later, however, even though Catherwood's panoramas cannot be compared with 'map-work' (since they do not present plans as in the case of some of the panoramas exhibited during the Napoleonic Wars), they nonetheless allude to cartography in two ways. In the case of Jerusalem, we have noted that Catherwood surveyed and published a *Plan of Jerusalem*, a work which will be discussed at greater length in Chapter Two. In the case of Baalbek, we have observed that Catherwood oriented the spectator by specifying the relation of structures to the cardinal points of the compass. We have also seen that the panorama of Baalbek departed from strategies Catherwood employed in his earlier panoramas by emphasising foreground space, a concern represented in a much more marked manner by the chimneys and roofline depicted in Henry Aston Barker's *View of London from the Roof of the Albion Mills*. In comparing Catherwood's work with one of the earliest panoramas, did the panorama of Baalbek represent an anomaly, or was the practice evident in the Baalbek panorama more common at mid-century? Lacking a history of the development of the medium in the second quarter of the nineteenth century, we are not, at present, in a position to answer this question. Yet a discussion of how Catherwood's work developed in the 1840s, and whether his work reflected a more general dynamic in the period is a question we may seek to answer. For now, we may propose that the three panoramas after Catherwood discussed in this chapter demonstrate a range of practice where the relation between topography, representation, and the spectator was one of development, if not transformation. Whether the dynamic that attended historical process may be characterised as one of transformation is a question to which we return in the following chapters.

Chapter Two

The camera lucida, topographical representation, and the picturesque in early-nineteenth-century Britain and Mexico

'In short, if Dr Wollaston, by this invention, have [*sic*] not actually discovered a Royal Road to Drawing, he has at least succeeded in Macadamising the way already known.' Captain Basil Hall, Edinburgh, 2 July 1828.[1]

The camera lucida, referred to in the epigraph for this chapter, was an optical device which Frederick Catherwood used to sketch Jerusalem, Thebes, and Baalbek, and took on the expeditions he made with John Lloyd Stephens to Central America and the Yucatán peninsula. The instrument, patented in December 1806,[2] superseded devices generally used for topographical illustration (such as the camera obscura and the squared landscape frame), demonstrating a growing concern at the turn of the nineteenth century for depicting the world with greater accuracy. This ambition marked a significant departure from the prevailing aesthetic in late-eighteenth-century Britain which, as in the case of the Picturesque, drew on the compositional conventions of neo-classical painting.[3] The aim of this chapter is to trace the understanding that attended the depiction of space from the late eighteenth century to the early nineteenth century, to inform our discussion in Chapter Three and Chapter Four of the conventions that underpinned the picturing of Mexico in the 1830s and 1840s. The chapter opens with a discussion of the innovation that the camera lucida represented, then goes on to consider the development of cartographic representation and topographical illustration in the eighteenth century, practices which informed image-making in Britain and Mexico in the first half of the nineteenth century. As we will observe, some pictorial conventions encountered in the early nineteenth century were introduced in eighteenth-century topographical image-making.

Seeing the world through the camera lucida

The camera lucida, as we have seen in the case of Catherwood, was primarily employed in preparing sketches for drawings, paintings, topographical engravings, and painted panoramas. Characteristics of the instrument are identified in this part of the chapter, and reasons why Catherwood chose this device, in preference to other optical devices, are proposed.[4]

The camera lucida (2.1) was designed, as its inventor, William Hyde Wollaston, stated, 'to facilitate the delineation of objects in true perspective', so that 'any Person may draw in perspective, or may copy or reduce any Print or Drawing'.[5] The patent application granted on 4 December 1806 indicated a number of characteristics which Wollaston compared favourably with the camera obscura, a device that had been available, like the squared landscape frame, for several centuries as a means of tracing views that were subsequently worked up as finished paintings or prints. Like the camera obscura,

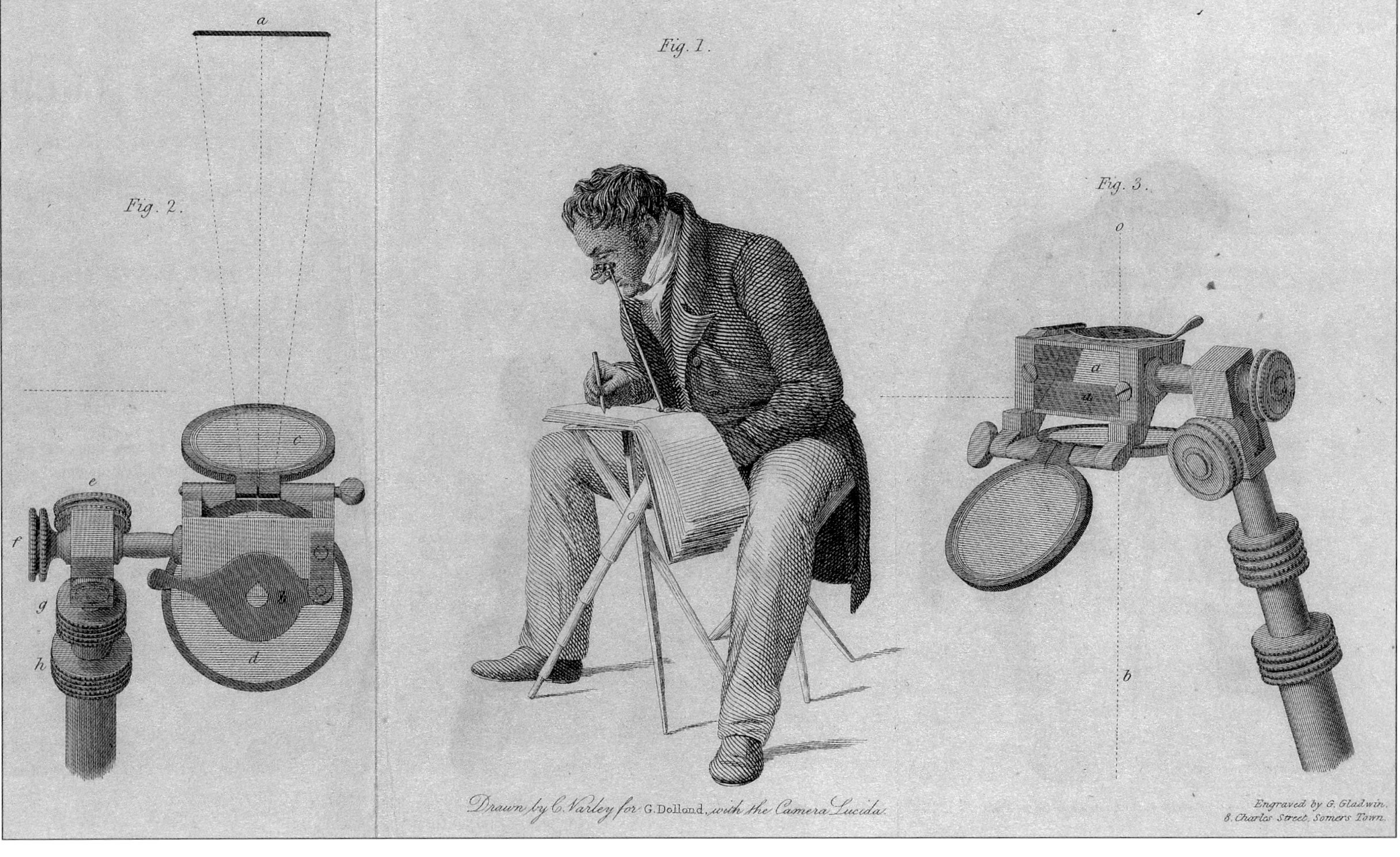

2.1. Cornelius Varley, engraved by George Gladwin, Frontispiece, George Dollond, *Description of the Camera Lucida* (London: George Dollond, n.d. [1830]), 11.9 x 21 cm. (maximum image size). [Courtesy General Collection, Beinecke Rare Book and Manuscript Library, Yale University.]

the camera lucida was thought to represent the world faithfully, a property that demonstrated 'the character of truth which the mechanical accuracy of the Camera Lucida communicates to its work, even in hands but little familiar with the management of the pencil'.[6] In this regard, Basil Hall, a captain in the Royal Navy and Fellow of the Royal Society (of which Wollaston was Secretary), proposed that although the instrument did not guarantee a 'Royal Road to Drawing', it nonetheless represented a significant step in the realisation of such an objective.[7]

According to Wollaston, the camera lucida had several advantages over the camera obscura. The device was 'small and portable'; the prism used in its optical system ensured that objects 'situated near the centre of the view' were not 'more or less distorted', as in the case of the camera obscura; and, given that the field of view in a camera obscura rarely exceeded '30° or at most 35° with distinctness', the camera lucida provided a significantly wider field of view, one which included 'as much as 70° or 80° ... in one view'.[8] Such characteristics would have proved advantageous in drawing architectural structures in the field, or preparing sketches for a panorama. In the case of the panorama, for example, the field of view enabled Catherwood to prepare a panorama of the city of Jerusalem from the 'Spot from whence the panorama was taken' (designated '3' in Plate 1) in no fewer than five or six drawings from the Aga's terrace, two (or possibly three) embracing features to the north of the roof-terrace, and three embracing features to the south.[9] Such a field of view was regarded as optimal, as the instrument-maker, Francis West, observed:

> It has been imagined by many, that if the prism of the Camera-Lucida was made larger, that it would embrace a larger field of view; but this is not the case; the experiment has been tried with them, by the author, of every size, and it has been found that the most desirable one is 11/16 of an inch long.[10]

The field of view of the camera lucida was also wider than the 60° field of view claimed by Cornelius Varley for his Graphic Telescope.[11] Moreover, unlike the camera obscura, the camera lucida did not require a cowl or housing to provide a dark environment in which images could be traced, the virtual image seen in the camera's prism permitting sketches to be made in strong sunlight. For fieldwork in the tropics, this feature would have been particularly attractive.

While some of the claims made by Wollaston for the instrument were exaggerated, Basil Hall relates a number of first-hand accounts of using the instrument which confirm some of the claims made by Wollaston. For Hall, one of the attractions of the device lay in the fact that it enabled 'a person of ordinary diligence to make correct outlines of foreign scenes, to which he might not have leisure, or adequate skill, to do justice in the common way'.[12] The topographical artist and writer, Samuel Prout, corroborated this view when he observed that 'so simple are its parts, and so easy of comprehension, that persons entirely ignorant of drawing, have, in a short time, become capable of producing, with a lead-pencil, outlines of regular and most difficult architectural subjects, that proportions of which are mathematically correct'.[13] While the camera lucida was an aid to drawing, Hall also proposed that the instrument speeded up the process of recording:

> With his Sketch Book in one pocket, [and] the Camera Lucida in the other, ... the amateur may roam where he pleases, possessed of a magical secret for recording the features of Nature with ease and fidelity, however complex that may be, while he is happily exempted from the triple misery of Perspective, Proportion, and Form, – all responsibility respecting these being thus taken off his hands.[14]

Although the ease with which the instrument could be employed has been disputed,[15] one present-day artist who has used a camera lucida confirms that the device imparts speed to the process of depiction:

> [I]t [the camera lucida] is a prism on a stick that creates an illusion of an image of whatever is in front of it on a piece of paper below. This image is not real – it is not actually on the paper, it only seems to be there. When you look through the prism from a single point in space you can see the person or objects in front and the paper below at the same time. If you're using the camera lucida to draw, you can also see your hand and pencil markings on the paper. But only you ... can see these things, no one else can. Because it is portable and can be carried anywhere, the camera lucida is perfect for drawing landscapes. But portraiture is more difficult. You must use it quickly ... A skilled artist could make quick notations, marking the key points of the subject's features. In effect, this is a fast forward of the normal measuring process that takes place in the head of a good draughtsman but which usually takes much longer. After these notations have been made, the hard work begins of observing from life and translating the marks into a more complete form.[16]

For David Hockney, the camera lucida provides a 'shortcut', a point endorsed by Martin Kemp in his correspondence with the artist.[17] Although, therefore, the camera lucida may not have guaranteed a 'Royal Road to Drawing', it nonetheless helped artists plot key reference points, speeding up the process of depiction, so 'Macadamising the way already known'.[18]

Catherwood was not the only artist-draughtsman who employed the device for depicting antiquities. John Sell Cotman, for example, made extensive use of the camera lucida and Varley's Graphic Telescope on his first tour of Normandy in 1817.[19] Francis West noted that the instrument had been 'the means of furnishing us with nearly *all* our best illustrations of foreign scenery; many of the ancient antiquities, too, have been copied in this way, and are familiarly known among artists by the appellation of "Camera-Lucida sketches".'[20] To attain accuracy, much depended on the quality of the prism and the extent to which chromatic aberration

2.2 (facing page). Paul Sandby, *Plan of the Castle of Dumbarton*, c. 1747, pen and wash over graphite, 70.8 x 49.9 cm. [Reproduced by permission of the National Library of Scotland.]

could be avoided since the prism, having no internal surfaces that would lead to the loss of light, brought light waves of different wavelengths into focus at the same point. Wollaston addressed this characteristic when he observed that users:

> conversant with the science of optics will perceive the advantage that may be derived in this instance from prismatic reflection; for when a ray of light has entered a solid piece of glass, and falls from within upon any surface, ... the refractive power of the glass is such as to suffer none of that light to pass out, and the surface becomes in this case the most brilliant reflector that can be employed.[21]

The instrument thus ensured that the reflected image was 'perfectly defined, sharp, and distinct at the edges, and of its natural colour'.[22] In this respect, it had 'two capital advantages – first, its great portability, and secondly, the great perfection of the reflecting surfaces; for these, being internal, absolutely reflect the whole of the light with no loss but what imperfect polishing will occasion'.[23] As the instrument-maker, Cornelius Varley, confirmed:

> The surfaces that reflect light are internal surfaces; consequently they are mathematical planes, having no thickness; on which account this mode of construction is the best, because the action of the eye is to be divided – the upper half looking into the prism, while the lower half looks at the paper, there is no thickness between, and thus the pencil and object may be seen together.[24]

Unlike the camera obscura which taught users 'to see abstractedly', a quality regarded as 'indispensable to the making of a good topographical drawing',[25] the camera lucida announced a new way of registering the visual field. Whereas the camera obscura was predicated on the separation of the observer from the represented scene, the camera lucida inscribed a close relation between the viewing of a scene and the process of depicting it. The camera obscura employed a mirror in conjunction with a lens to project views that were traced; the camera lucida, however, presented a reflected view in the prism, a difference which, as Hockney has observed, constitutes a major distinction:

> The difference between a reflected image from a mirror and a projected image from a mirror is profound. The first has to be related to our bodies – as the body moves so does the reflection. The second, the projected image, has no relation to the body. It is a view which no body saw.[26]

The point Hockney makes is that in employing a mirror, the camera obscura projects a view onto a table, whereas the camera lucida, reflecting the subject in its prism, presents a virtual image, a process in which, as West observed, 'no real image is formed'.[27] The process also responds to bodily movement: if one moves one's body (even slightly) when looking into the prism, the image moves or departs from view, a property that vexed users new to the instrument. Basil Hall acknowledged this problem when he observed that artists often lost 'sight of the object they are drawing, just when they most wish to see it'.[28] In a letter to the instrument-maker, George Dollond, Hall elaborated this point:

> Beginners ought certainly to sketch with the instrument so adjusted, that when the eye is moved from side to side, the object shall not appear to move away from the pencil. When a greater degree of familiarity is acquired with the use of the instrument, this nicety is not absolutely necessary, though it is always pleasant: I endeavour to regulate matters in such a way, as to position, scale, and distance, that there shall be little or no parallax, as this shifting of the object is called.[29]

Rather than presenting a view that was framed 'abstractedly' as a detail, the camera lucida inscribed a more direct relation between the view, the instrument, and the observer since the device presented a shifting perceptual relation to the world where the slightest change in the viewer's position resulted in a change in the view that was to be depicted. Kemp characterises this process as one that requires the viewer to focus differentially so that part of the pupil sees the reflected view through the prism while the other part of the pupil, looking down to the drawing surface, 'sees' the virtual scene on the paper.[30] As Larry J. Schaaf has observed, seeing the world through a camera lucida 'is a very private experience for in reality there is no image projected on the paper. ... The scene is at once vividly bright and ethereal, yet very real.'[31] At the heart, then, of the optical system Catherwood used is a relation to space which is marked by contingency: the sketcher observes a virtual image in the prism rather than a stable, framed, and projected image as in the camera obscura. Seeing the world through the camera lucida thus highlights the contingent relation of viewing to depiction; while the camera lucida could be used to sketch the topography of a site, the subject viewed *in* the prism was perceptually unstable. In short, the camera lucida draws the user's attention to the fact that the activity of *registering* a view was *perceptual* and *fleeting* rather than literal and stable, so drawing to the user's attention that the act of *making* an image with the camera lucida is achieved at the expense of *taking* a view as in the case of the camera obscura. In this respect, the camera lucida marked a significant departure from the mirror and lens system employed in the camera obscura, and, indeed, the lens system of the cinematographic apparatus, an observation that will be examined further in Chapter Five. For now, we may conclude that the camera lucida helped Catherwood prepare sketches quickly and with a degree of ease in the field; it provided a considerably wider field of view than the camera obscura and Varley's Graphic Telescope, and, importantly, could be used in strong sunlight. We may propose that these characteristics, for professional artist-draughtsmen such as Catherwood, outweighed the disadvantages that have been attributed to using the instrument.

Mapping space and topographical illustration in the eighteenth century

Two perspectival systems are used in Catherwood's *Plan of Jerusalem* (Plate 1). The most obvious, a bird's-eye or overhead view, observes the conventions of ichnographic perspective understood as 'a system of parallel rays ... drawn from every angle of the object to the ground plane; or ... a section of the rays made by a plane parallel to the horizon'.[32] The other system is less easily specified, if only because a term did not exist, to my knowledge, to define this practice: we view the hills and gradients from various locations, presenting, as it were, a series of views wherein gradients are angled towards the spectator in a manner closer to that of a prospect view than a bird's-eye view. Rather than presenting an ichnographic plan of the city, a series of partial, prospect views suggest the way the terrain would appear were it viewed from specific locations. In comparison with present-day maps which employ an ichnographic perspective

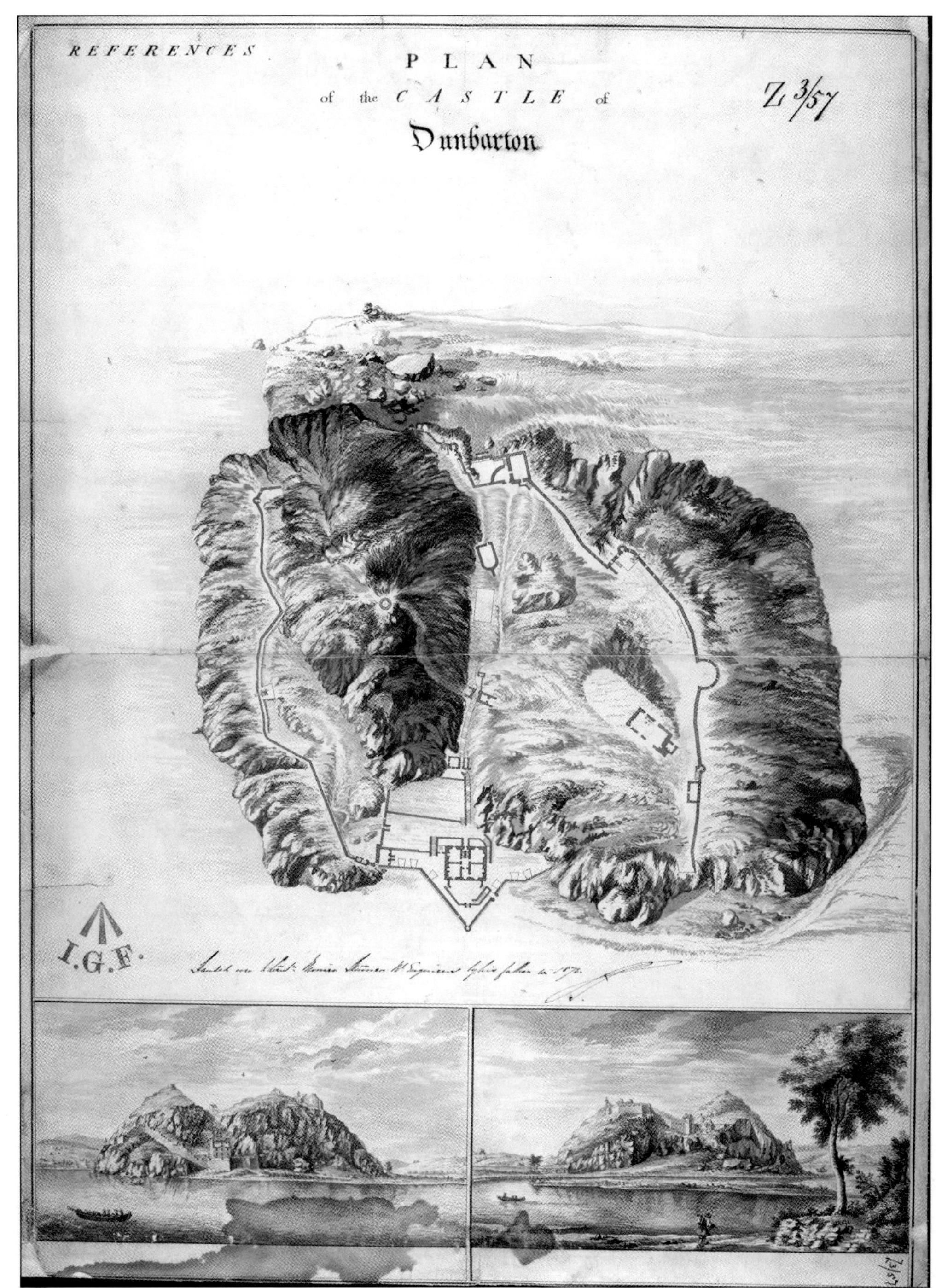

exclusively, Catherwood's *Plan of Jerusalem* employs two perspectival systems: an overhead view and a series of partial prospect views. The latter were derived from mid-eighteenth-century cartography where gradients were represented by means of aligned brush strokes or hatched shading to indicate the direction of slopes, while gradations of tone expressed increases in steepness and height, and serrated lines represented cliff-like features, a procedure that predated the introduction of contour lines in British cartography in the mid-nineteenth century.[33] By the late eighteenth century, this method of depiction had given way to 'hachuring', a process which represented inclines and declivities by means of small strokes drawn in black ink whose density and darkness increased according to the steepness of the terrain.[34] This latter practice (hachuring) was employed by Catherwood in the *Plan of Jerusalem* in addition to an overhead view to represent the plan of the city. For example, in the terrain represented to the east of the city, the hachuring representing the west side of the Valley of Jehosaphat is relatively short in length and closely drawn, indicating that the gradient on the west side of the valley is relatively steep. The gradient on the east side of the valley (rising towards the Mount of Olives) is much less steep since the hachuring is both longer and not as closely drawn until, near the top of the Mount of Olives, the incline is closely drawn and darker, denoting a steep gradient. Similarly, inclines and declivities to the west and south of the city range from closely-drawn, relatively short lines on the south side of Mount Gihon (in the vicinity of the Gate of Bethlehem), which denote a more gentle gradient, to those on the western and southern sides of Mount Sion (closely-drawn, longer lines) which denote a steeply inclined hill. By mid-eighteenth century, this method of representing space had become a convention in British cartography, having been adopted by the artist, Paul Sandby,

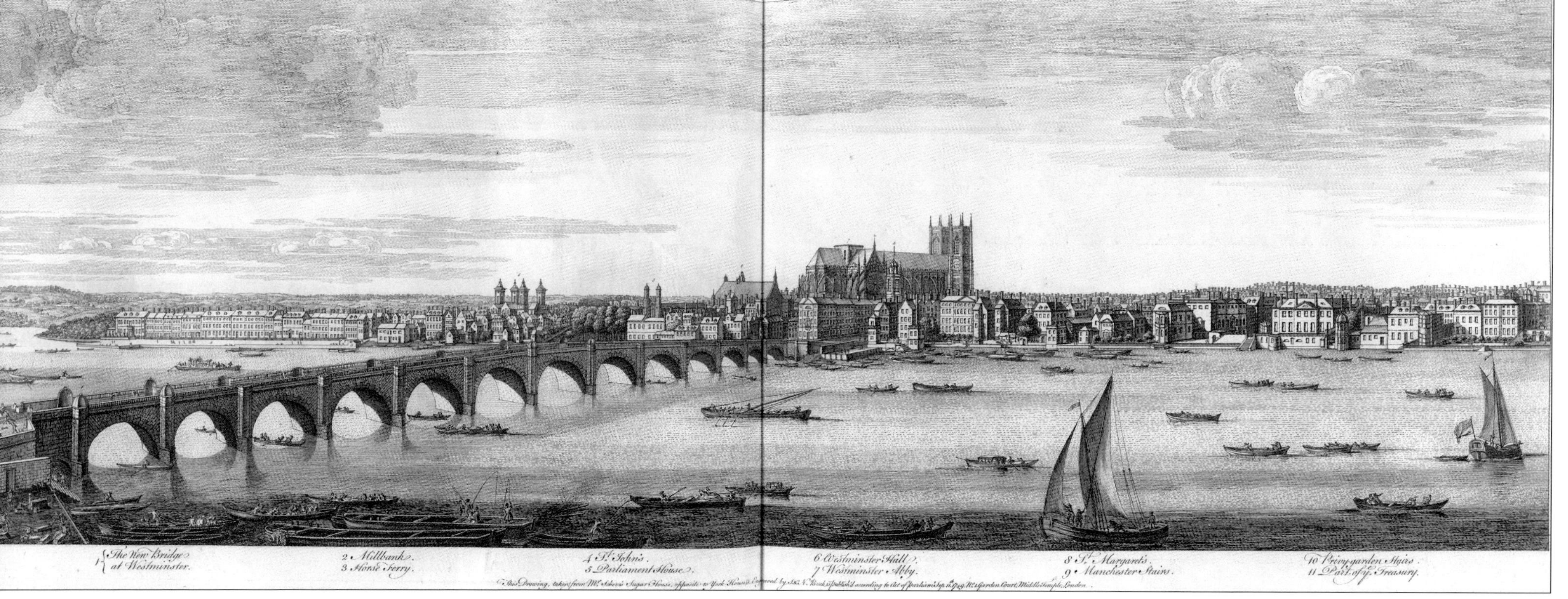

2.3. 'London and Westminster', Samuel and Nathaniel Buck, *Buck's Antiquities*, 3 vols. (London: Printed by D. Bond, 1774), III, Plate 41, 28 x 80 cm. [Reproduced by permission of the National Library of Scotland.]

who, trained in topography and map-making at the Board of Ordnance, was appointed a draughtsman to the Military Survey of North Britain in 1747, the year in which the Ordnance Survey began to map the Highlands and Lowlands of Scotland.[35] Between 1768 and 1796, Sandby was employed as Chief Drawing Master at the Royal Military Academy, Woolwich, where, from 1741, engineers and artillery officers had been trained. Although the Royal Military Academy trained only a minority of officers, Sandby did much to establish the importance of the graphic arts in the production of maps for surveillance and information gathering, and for reconnaissance, route selection, and coastal charting. Instruction in the surveying and drawing of topographical landscapes was designed to help officers understand landscape spatially (to identify prospects and features that could be used as refuges or as vantage points in the landscape) and to help officers form an 'eye to the knowledge of it'.[36] Such elements constituted an essential part of the curriculum at the Royal Military Academy, where classes in 'Landscape and Perspective' were pursued alongside instruction in French, Latin, mathematics, and geography in a curriculum that reflected the gentlemanly aspirations that underwrote the education of officers in the late eighteenth century.[37] The emphasis given to drawing and surveying also demonstrates the extent to which belief in the communicative power of images occupied an increasingly privileged position in the production and circulation of knowledge in the latter part of the eighteenth century, concerns which reflected a more general cultural conviction in the work of artists, surveyors, and travel writers, as well as antiquarians, naturalists, and estate owners.[38]

If we compare the *Plan of Jerusalem* with the plan and topographical views in Sandby's *Plan and View of Dumbarton Castle* (c. 1747), the similarity between Catherwood's plan and the work of Sandby

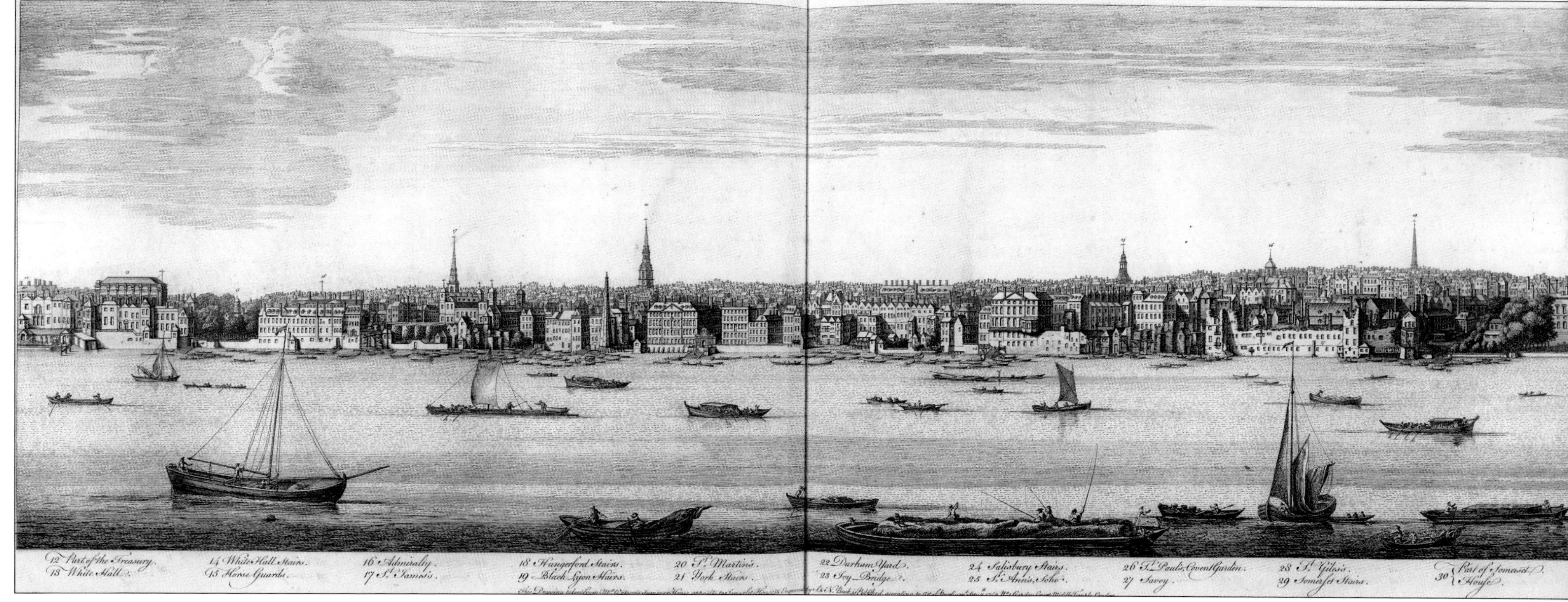

2.4. 'London and Westminster', Samuel and Nathaniel Buck, *Buck's Antiquities*, 3 vols. (London: Printed by D. Bond, 1774), III, Plate 42, 28 x 80 cm. [Reproduced by permission of the National Library of Scotland.]

becomes clear. Sandby's engraving (2.2) consists of two topographical views (seen towards the bottom of the engraving) and an overhead plan of the castle derived from military siege maps.[39] Yet, as we have seen in Catherwood's plan, the hills and inclines appear as if seen from the side *and* from above, presenting thus neither a bird's-eye view of the terrain nor a prospect view but, rather, a combination of the two. Catherwood's plan, in other words, drew on a system of cartographic representation that derived from military sketches made in the field. The conventions Sandby and Catherwood employed were those associated with a *coup d'œil*, a term encountered in Chapter One which, employed in military circles, denoted the ability to take a general view of a position and assess its respective advantages and disadvantages.[40] The term was also employed, as we observed in Chapter One, when Barker patented the panorama, implying that he perceived an analogy between his work and military field sketches, a similarity which is highlighted by the convention of circular orientation plans and keys associated with the exhibition of early panoramas. Not until contours were introduced in British cartography in the mid-nineteenth century was the tension between the two systems of representation – topographical and ichnographic – resolved, when the more symbolic system associated with present-day cartography became a convention in Ordnance Survey maps. Catherwood's *Plan of Jerusalem* – as, too, some of his plans of archaeological sites in Central America and Yucatán, as we will observe in Chapter Four – thus employed two perspectival systems: ichnographic and a hybrid prospect system to show relief.[41]

The concern with depicting relief in turn-of-the-century maps, and the way this process impacted on the viewing of landscape and panoramas in early-nineteenth-century Britain, was advanced by the increase in circulation of Ordnance Survey maps in the early part of

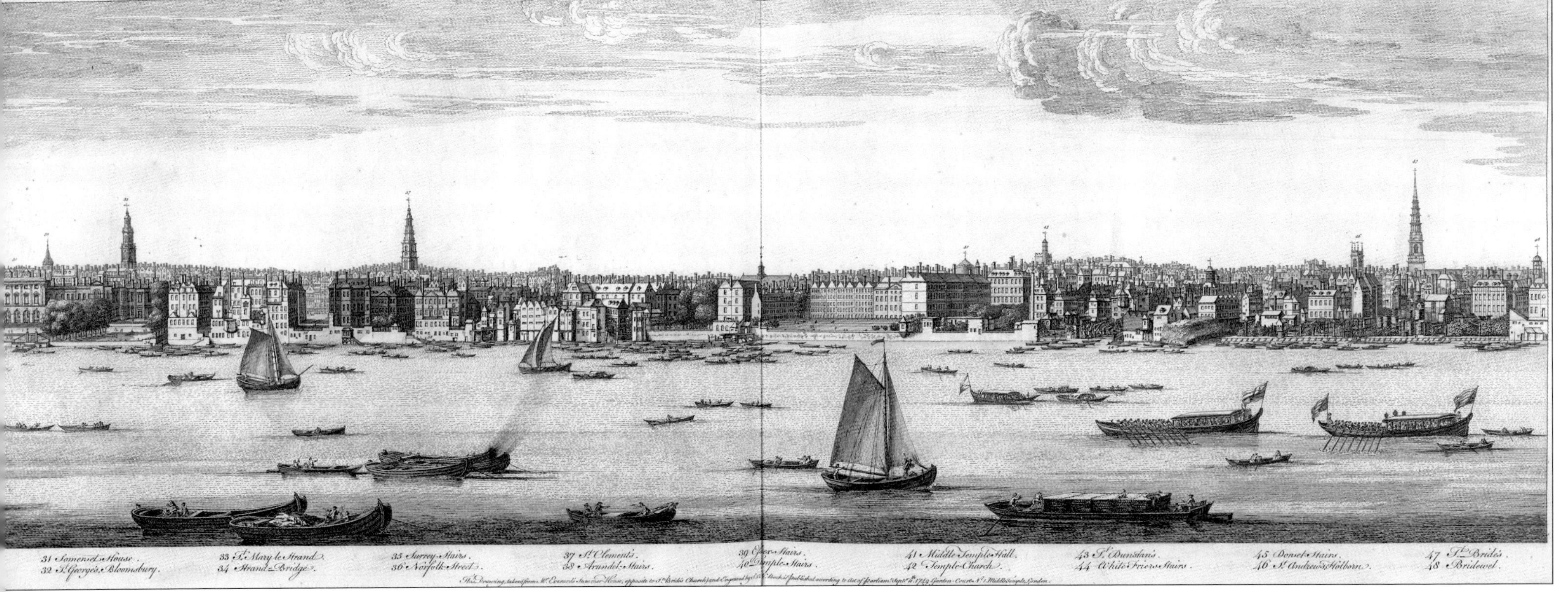

2.5. 'London and Westminster', Samuel and Nathaniel Buck, *Buck's Antiquities*, 3 vols. (London: Printed by D. Bond, 1774), III, Plate 43, 28 x 80 cm. [Reproduced by permission of the National Library of Scotland.]

the century, a development which dates from 1801 when the Ordnance Survey released its first map to the public.[42] In the early 1800s, Ordnance Survey maps cost a prohibitive three guineas, the average weekly wage for one of the engravers of the maps, or twenty days' wages for a lesser craftsman. By the mid-1840s, Ordance Survey maps sold for between three shillings and six shillings, a much reduced sum equivalent to less than two days' wages for a craftsman in the building trade.[43] What Catherwood's *Plan of Jerusalem* points towards is the extent to which, in the period when Catherwood began to exhibit panoramas, virtual travel, inaugurated with the introduction of travel writing in the latter part of the eighteenth century, was accompanied by a growing familiarity with maps on the part of the reading public. Such developments suggest that by the early nineteenth century, the act of viewing a landscape from an elevated position was not only supported by a significant increase in the circulation of maps (with an attendant understanding of their system of representation), but also impacted on the way panoramas were viewed and understood. Convergence between the viewing of landscape in the field and viewing its representation in media such as panoramas and maps can be proposed in a literal sense (arising from the increased circulation of maps) and in a figurative sense, through the pleasure that accrued from comparing representational registers with each other. For example, if a visitor to the panorama of Jerusalem purchased a copy of the panorama booklet and a copy of Catherwood's plan, would the visitor have tried to plot the engraved view in the *Description* against the *Plan*? While we may never know whether visitors to the panorama attempted such a comparison, the relation that maps and panorama engravings initiated has implications for our discussion of Stephens' and Catherwood's investigations in Central America and Yucatán, a concern

2.6. 'London and Westminster', Samuel and Nathaniel Buck, *Buck's Antiquities*, 3 vols. (London: Printed by D. Bond, 1774), III, Plate 44, 28 x 80 cm. [Reproduced by permission of the National Library of Scotland.]

that will be explored in Chapter Three and Chapter Four. For now, suffice it to say that we have seen that Catherwood drew on conventions associated with cartographic practice which, like panoramas, translated a vernacular, local knowledge into a more general condition of cultural and social enlightenment. While such ambitions attended the work of Stephens and Catherwood, we need to establish to what degree the mapping of space in plans and maps shared objectives with the articulation of space in eighteenth-century topographical drawing, since this latter concern closely informed the development of panoramas in the early nineteenth century.

The most extensive (and certainly the most famous) survey of antiquities in Britain in the eighteenth century was undertaken by the typographers and brothers, Samuel and Nathaniel Buck, who, with the publication of *Buck's Antiquities; or Venerable Remains of Above Four Hundred Castles, Monasteries, Palaces, &c., &c. in England and Wales* in 1774, amassed a collection of more than five hundred topographical engravings garnered from investigating 'the mouldering Remains of tottering Ruins' in England and Wales over a thirty-two-year period.[44] In the spirit of eighteenth-century antiquarian investigation, Samuel and Nathaniel Buck undertook to preserve 'what otherwise would have been buried in oblivion, or hid in obscurity', producing a total of 510 engravings.[45]

Many of the plates were initially printed separately, with the owners of the antiquities contributing to the cost of production through subscription. The prints presented a factual transcription of a site, and provided details of ownership and history in the letterpress, a model for topographical illustration through much of the eighteenth century. In striving to present an accurate depiction of a given site, topographical drawings were site specific. Plate 50, for example, a prospect of Scaleby Castle in Cumberland, was described

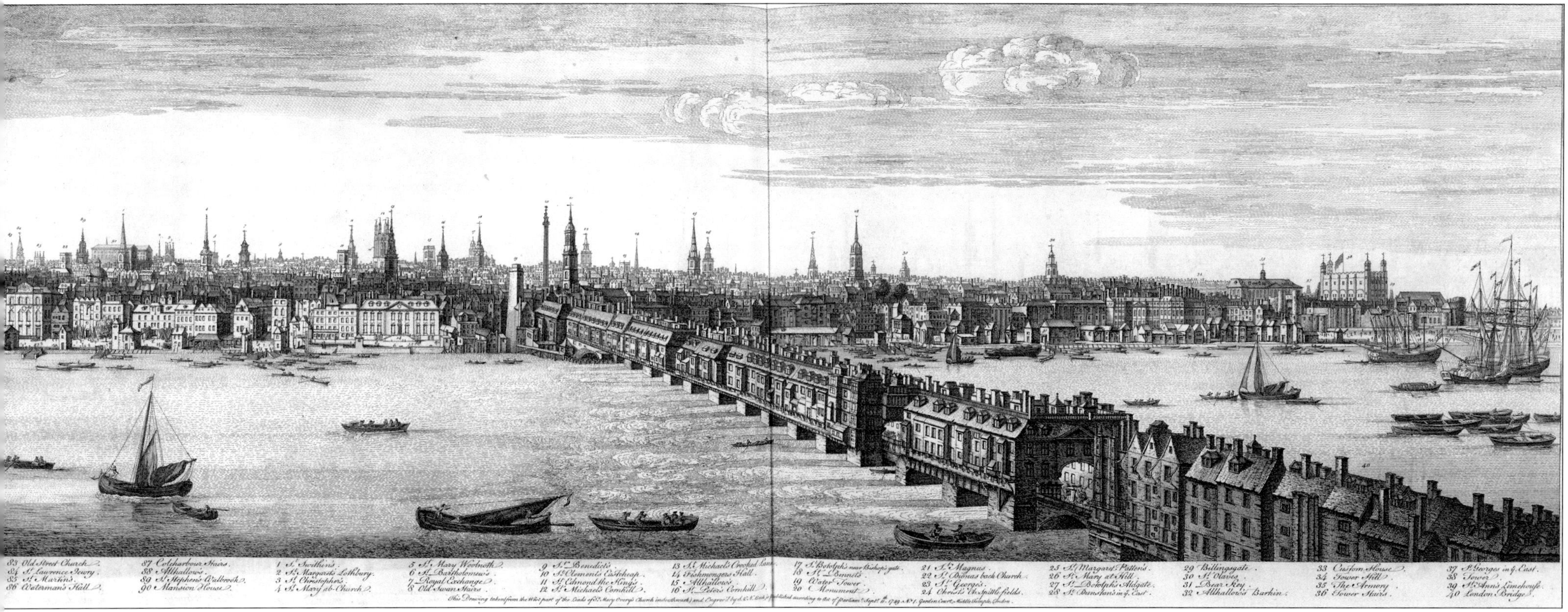

2.7. 'London and Westminster', Samuel and Nathaniel Buck, *Buck's Antiquities*, 3 vols. (London: Printed by D. Bond, 1774), III, Plate 45, 28 x 80 cm. [Reproduced by permission of the National Library of Scotland.]

2.8. 'The North-West View of Lanercost-Priory, in the County of Cumberland', Samuel and Nathaniel Buck, *Buck's Antiquities*, 3 vols. (London: Printed by D. Bond, 1774), I, Plate 44, 14.8 x 35.5 cm. [Reproduced by permission of the National Library of Scotland.]

as 'a place of great antiquity, five miles North of Carlisle, where have been dug up several Roman altars and other antiquities. It has been lately repaired, and is now the residence of a gentleman',[46] the gentleman alluded to in the letterpress being a relation of William Gilpin, the eighteenth-century vicar and writer famous for popularising painting in the picturesque manner, a style important for visitors to Mexico in the period following independence.

A number of sites in *Buck's Antiquities* were represented by two or, occasionally, three plates which, by virtue of the title and orientation of the view, articulated spatial contiguity through adjoining prospect views (between the north and north-east facades, for example), or represented non-contiguous prospects of a site, such as the pairing of north and south facades. The first two volumes comprised, in the main, views of castles and religious foundations; the third volume, prospects of cities and towns. Of the sites included in the three volumes, twenty-three sites were represented by more than one view, with forty-eight prints demonstrating contiguity or non-contiguity.[47] In addition, five plates included in the third volume

2.9. 'The South-East View of Lanercost-Priory, in the County of Cumberland', Samuel and Nathaniel Buck, *Buck's Antiquities*, 3 vols. (London: Printed by D. Bond, 1774), I, Plate 45, 14.7 x 35.5 cm. [Reproduced by permission of the National Library of Scotland.]

presented a continuous, elevated view of the north bank of the River Thames between Westminster Bridge and London Bridge, the letterpress to each plate designating the building on the south bank from which the engravings were drawn.[48] Given that the same distance is maintained between the river and the viewer in all five engravings irrespective of the course of the Thames, and that the viewer is located at the same elevation in all five plates (although the final plate is framed slightly obliquely, since it was drawn from the same location as the penultimate plate in the series), the views inscribe a relation in space similar to that encountered in painted panoramas later in the century (2.3–2.7). Indeed, except for the elevation of the views, the plates inscribe a spatial relation between subject and viewer that is not unlike that encountered in the Frontispiece of *Incidents of Travel in Yucatan* (1.1). Some plates (Plate 233, *The South View of Warkworth Castle, in Northumberland*, for example) identify subjects included in the view by means of a text engraved on the plate; others, such as Plate 28 (*The East View of St. Maws Castle, in the County of Cornwall*), identify subjects by means of a numeral engraved on the plate which refers the viewer to the identification provided in the key below. In this respect, *Buck's Antiquities* anticipates a practice we have observed in the orientation views and keys printed for nineteenth-century panorama *Descriptions*.

The physical relation between a view and the location from which it was made was also identified in the key to some of the plates. In the case of Plate 342 (*The Castle & Town of Scarborough, as they appear a quarter of a mile from the Spaw*), the title specifies the distance between viewer and subject.[49] In the third volume, a further departure was introduced: the location from where a view was drawn was identified by means of a numeral on the plate, which information, elaborated in the key below, specified the location from where a prospect was drawn. Plate 9, for example (*The North-West Prospect of the University, and Town of Cambridge*), indicates that the view was made from 'The Gravil Pitts [*sic*] near Trinity Conduit head from whence this Drawing was taken' (#30 on the respective Plate); Plate 4 (*The East Prospect of Birmingham. In the County of Warwick*) indicates that 'The Station where this Drawing was taken is near the London Road' (identified as #17 on the Plate). A further twenty-two plates identify the location from where the drawing was made which, in three cases, is designated a 'station', the majority being drawn from elevated positions.[50] One pair of engravings, however, is of particular interest: Plates 44 and 45. *The North-West View of Lanercost-Priory* (Plate 44), first printed in 1739, shows the inner arch of the ruined priory gatehouse (2.8) in partial chiaroscuro in the right foreground of the engraving, which frames an oblique view of the priory church in the middle ground of the plate. The following plate bound in the collection presents a view of *The South-East View of Lanercost-Priory* (Plate 45, also printed in 1739) with the inner arch now seen at rear left on the extreme left of the plate (2.9). While the majority of the plates that share a common subject display contiguity in successive plates, in the case of Lanercost Priory, the two plates inscribe a reverse viewpoint: the viewer observes, in Plate 44, the space from which the second plate is depicted. Given that this is the only occasion where such an articulation is inscribed (a relation secured by the title of the two plates which designate that the views depict the north-west and south-east aspects of the priory), this example constitutes a significant departure from the practice adopted in *Buck's Antiquities*. We may propose, therefore, that the prints of Lanercost Priory represent reverse views of the priory, a departure from the articulation of space generally encountered in the collection of views. *Buck's Antiquities* provides an early example of such practice in topographical illustration,[51] one which we will examine more closely in Chapter Four when we turn to discuss Catherwood's work in Mexico and Central America.

Carrying the eye for travellers from the social elite

To demonstrate how images were thought at the turn of the nineteenth century to carry the eye through space, three areas of investigation are discussed: the first considers the analogy that was understood to inform the viewing of panoramas and maps, an early example of what may be termed media 'convergence', a term not employed at the time, of course, but an analogy recognised and commented on in travel accounts by visitors to Mexico in the 1840s. The second – *repoussoir* – considers the compositional principles that were believed to delineate relief, a concern which William Gilpin developed into a quasi-formulaic schema, one which responded to and capitalised on the growth in the market for painting by amateur practitioners.[52] A third concern – an interest in viewpoints that commanded what we may term 'reverse views' and 'reverse-field views' – is also considered in this and subsequent chapters, an interest that arose as travellers, newly sensitised to viewing landscapes that demonstrated picturesque principles, began to travel to little-known corners of Britain in search of novelty. Before turning to Gilpin and the tourist of the picturesque, some of the accounts given by visitors to Mexico regarding their first view of the Valley of Mexico are presented, to demonstrate how analogies between the viewing of landscape and the viewing of panoramas and maps had become a conventionalised trope in the first quarter of the nineteenth century. Writers discussed in this context represented travellers from the social elite; in Chapter Three and Chapter Four, these concerns are investigated in the context of a popular readership for travel accounts.

Frances Calderón de la Barca, who lived in Mexico between December 1839 and January 1842, visited the castle of Chapultepec a few miles to the southwest of Mexico City in December 1839. She commented on the panoramic and map-like view of the city of Mexico that greeted her as she gazed from the terrace of the castle. Her description evokes an Arcadian plain bathed in limpid light typical of the work of Claude Lorrain, the artist who most influenced the development of the Picturesque in eighteenth-century Britain:

> From the terrace that runs round the castle, the view forms the most magnificent panorama that can be imagined. The whole valley of Mexico lies stretched out as in a map; the city itself, with its innumerable churches and convents; the two great aqueducts which cross the plain; the avenues of elms and poplars which lead to the city; the villages, lakes, and plains which surround it. To the north, the magnificent cathedral of Our Lady of Guadalupe – to the south, the villages of San Augustin [*sic*], San Angel, and Tacubaya, which seem embosomed in trees, and look like an immense garden. And if in the plains below there are many uncultivated fields and many buildings falling to ruin, yet with its glorious enclosure of mountains … with its turquoise sky for ever smiling on the scene, the whole landscape, as viewed from this height, is one of nearly unparalleled beauty.[53]

Calderón de la Barca not only compares the landscape of the Valle de México with the viewing of a panorama or map, but she also draws attention to quasi-classical elements represented in the landscape: aqueducts, religious buildings, avenues of trees (including poplars), and buildings falling into ruin encircled by mountains and volcanoes bathed in light from a 'turquoise sky for ever smiling on the scene'. When Calderón de la Barca first viewed the Valle de México on her journey from Puebla to Mexico City, her response was expressed in a similar vein. In 'Letter the Sixth', she drew a comparison between her first view of Mexico City and that of Cortés:

> But at length we arrived at the heights looking down upon the great valley, celebrated in all parts of the world, with its frame-work of everlasting mountains, its snow-crowned volcanoes, great lakes and fertile plains, all surrounding the favoured city of Montezuma, the proudest boast of his conqueror, once of Spain's many diadems the brightest. … The curtains of Time seemed to roll back, and to discover to us the great panorama that burst upon the eyes of Cortes when he first looked down upon the table-land; the whole fertile valley enclosed by its eternal hills and snow-crowned volcanoes – what scenes of wonder and of beauty to burst upon the eyes of these wayfaring men![54]

Calderón de la Barca's response was echoed by Brantz Mayer who, as secretary to the US legation in Mexico between 1841 and 1843, travelling from Puebla to the city of Mexico, also observed the Valle de México from the same range of hills overlooking the valley to the east of the city:

> I feel in some measure bound to make for you a *catalogue* of this valley's features, though I am confident I must fail to describe or paint them.
>
> Conceive yourself placed on a mountain nearly two thousand feet above the valley, and nine thousand above the level of the sea. A sky above you of the most perfect azure, without a cloud, and an atmosphere so transparently pure, and the remotest objects at a distance of many leagues are as distinctly visible as if at hand. The gigantic scale of everything first strikes you – you seem to be looking down on the *world*. No other mountain and valley view has such an assemblage of features, because nowhere else are the mountains at the same time so high, the valley so wide, or filled with such a variety of land and water. The plain beneath is exceedingly level, and for two hundred miles around it extends a barrier of stupendous mountains, most of which have been active volcanoes, and are now covered, some with snow, and some with forests. It is laced with large bodies of water looking more like seas than lakes – it is dotted with innumerable villages and estates and plantations; eminences rise from it which, elsewhere, would be called mountains, yet there, at your feet, they seem but ant-hills on the plain; and now, letting your eye follow the rise of the mountains to the west, (near fifty miles distant,) you look over immediate summits that wall the valley, to another and more distant range – and to range beyond range, with valleys between each, and the whole melts into a vapory distance, blue as the cloudless sky above.
>
> I could have gazed for hours at this little world while the sun and the passing vapor chequered the fields, and sailing off again, left the whole one bright mass of verdure and water … The silence was almost supernatural; one expects to hear the echo of the national strife that filled these plains with discord, yet lingering among the hills. It was a picture of 'still life' inanimate in every feature, save where, on the distant mountain sides, the fire of some poor coal-burner, mingled its blue wreath with the bluer sky, or the tinkle of a bell of a solitary muleteer was heard from among the dark and solemn pines.

> What a theatre for the great drama that has been performed within the limits of this valley![55]

Mayer's response identifies a number of features typical of the painted panorama (an elevated, large-scale view) that demand that the reader, in his or her imagination, 'Conceive yourself placed on a mountain ...'. From this elevation, looking 'down on the *world*', the reader is asked to imagine a bird's-eye view of the valley whose extent is exceptional (having a circumference of some two hundred miles) and imperial since the view, like a colonial subject, is placed 'at your feet'.[56] The view is also couched in a discourse associated with the Picturesque since the clear atmosphere, 'transparently pure' and 'of the most perfect azure', evokes a translucent aerial perspective redolent of the panorama which, as we observed in Chapter One, softens form so that mountains, valleys, and cloudless sky melt 'into a vapory distance'. Such response owes much to the privileged position in which the work of Claude was also held in North America where Claude's ability to represent aerial perspective was regarded highly by a painter such as Thomas Cole.[57]

Mayer describes a 'catalogue of this valley's features', encapsulating what John Britton, writing on Hornor's panorama of London, characterised as a 'cyclopaedia of information ... a focal topography'.[58] The fact that Mayer wanted to catalogue the view in the certain knowledge that he would 'fail to describe or paint' his ambition adequately, is a response that writers on the Picturesque frequently bemoaned. For Mayer, the view 'was a picture of "still life"', 'still' in the sense that he discerned little activity in the valley below, but also because, from his elevated position, the view may have appeared more like a painted panorama than the real world.[59] In this respect, the view suggests 'a theatre for the great drama that has been performed within the limits of this valley!' Mayer not only draws on the discourse of the Picturesque, but perceives a formal correspondence between landscape viewed through an aerial perspective associated with Claude (which lets 'your eye follow the rise of the mountains to the west ... to another and more distant range') and the natural scenery which evokes a stage on which the drama of Mexico's history had recently been played.

The delight in analogy in eighteenth- and early-nineteenth-century literature, particularly that associated with the tradition of the picturesque, has been frequently commented on.[60] William Hickling Prescott, the functionally blind North American historian of Spain and Mexico, envisaged Cortés' and the conquistadors' first view of the Valle de México in similar terms, even though Prescott never travelled to Mexico, and Cortés, of course, would never have seen a painted panorama or encountered the Picturesque:

> They had not advanced far, when, turning an angle of the sierra, they suddenly came on a view which more than compensated the toils of the preceding day. It was the Valley of Mexico, or Tenochtitlan, as more commonly called by the natives; which, with its picturesque assemblage of water, woodland, and cultivated plains, its shining cities and shadowy hills, was spread out like some gay and gorgeous panorama before them. In the highly rarefied atmosphere of these upper vapours, even remote objects have a brilliancy of colouring and a distinctness of outline which seem to annihilate distance. Stretching far away at their feet, were seen noble forests of oak, sycamore, and cedar, and beyond, yellow fields of maize and the towering maguey, intermingled with orchids and blooming gardens ... In the centre of the great basin were beheld the lakes ... and, in the midst, – like some Indian empress with her coronal of pearls, – the fair city of Mexico, with her white towers and pyramidal temples, reposing, as it were, on the bosom of the waters, – the far-famed 'Venice of the Aztecs.'[61]

Like Mayer, Prescott's account of Cortés' first sight of the Valle de México is couched in the discourse of the Picturesque, particularly the panoramic vision of Mexico City set in the bosom of the valley, a metaphor commonly encountered in Augustan literature. William Bullock, arriving on the scene in 1823, compared the natural scenery of the landscape with a map: 'In the afternoon, after a long ascent, a sudden opening gave us a view of the valley of Mexico, with its lakes and bold outlines of volcanic mountains, spread like a map before us', before going on to observe that the descent into the Valley was rapid, animated by an 'extended and ever-varying prospect before us', a phrase which acknowledges the pleasure Bullock experienced in travelling through the landscape.[62] Thus Calderón de la Barca, Mayer, Prescott, and Bullock, visitors to Mexico from Scotland, the USA, and England, variously characterised the sight that greeted their eyes (or, in the case of Prescott, the vision that imagination summoned) in colonialist and picturesque discourses, drawing analogy with panoramas, maps, and stage scenery, and in some instances reflected on the pleasure of being transported physically and metaphorically through the Mexican landscape.

Whether experienced in reality, or displaced in panoramas, maps, or stage scenery, the perception of landscape as a form of natural scenery was a frequent trope. John Britton, writing about Thomas Hornor's panoramic view from the top of St. Paul's Cathedral in the Colosseum, observed that from the four 'stations' assigned the visitor, the Thames and thoroughfares carried the spectator's eye through the city:

> To the East is displayed a succession of objects ... In the immediate fore-ground is St. Paul's School-house; whilst the lines of Cheapside, Cornhill, Leadenhall-street, and White-chapel, carry the eye through the very heart of the city; conducting it to Bow, Stratford, and a fine tract of woodlands in Essex.[63]

Other formulations in Britton's account also acknowledge the importance of the eye: 'Among the objects displayed towards the *North*, the eye recognises Newgate Market, the old College of Physicians, Newgate, ... and the lines of Goswell and St. John's Streets, Pentonville, Islington, and Hoxton'; 'Turning to the right, for the *Southern* view, the eye traces the undulating line of the Surrey hills, in the distance, and the Thames near the fore-ground'; 'The *Western* view unfolds a new and different series of objects. ... This view ... embraces the long lines of thoroughfare, Ludgate-hill, Fleet-street, the Strand, Piccadilly, &c; ... and a long stretch of flat country to Windsor'.[64] Not only did the river and city thoroughfares guide the viewing protocols of the panorama, they also demonstrate that the spectator's powers of suggestion were stimulated to see as far afield as Windsor:

> When it is stated that 'the circle bounding earth and skies,' starting from Windsor Castle and taking to the right, comprehends Harrow, Hampstead, Highgate, Islington, Hackney, Epping Forest, Bow, Plaistow, the Nore, Shooters' Hill, the Beeches on Madam's Court Hill, Sydenham, Norwood, Wimbledon, Richmond, and a thousand intermediate places ... before it returns to the royal residence.[65]

In reality, when the Colosseum opened in 1829, such an extensive view would have been unlikely from the dome of St. Paul's Cathedral, the vantage point where visitors to Hornor's panorama were located, for, as a commentator for *Berliner Kunstblatt* observed, the view from the top of the Cathedral was invariably 'obscured by a veil of haze' from workshops and factories in the city.[66] *The Literary Gazette* informs us that the attraction of the panorama was 'nature ... the stupendous scene itself', presented with 'a scrupulous attention to accuracy' that could only be appreciated from the observation gallery with the aid of a telescope.[67] Through this device, the array of subjects listed in *The Literary Gazette* and in John Britton's *A Brief Account of the Colosseum* were 'distinctly visible, if not with the naked eye, with glasses which are kept in the gallery for the purpose'.[68] Visitors to the panorama, in other words, were attracted to a panoramic view in which subjects in the extreme distance, not observable to the naked eye (either from St. Paul's Cathedral or from the observation galleries in the Colosseum), could supposedly be seen as a depiction with the aid of an optical device.[69] What was seen, therefore, in the extreme distance in Hornor's panorama, in whole or in part, was produced by the telescope itself. Hornor's panorama, in other words, advanced its effect through perception *and* suggestion.

Perhaps the most explicit example of how perception and, in this case, imagination could be borne together is encountered in Wordsworth's *A Guide through the District of the Lakes in the North of England, with A Description of the Scenery, &c. For the use of Tourists and Residents*.[70] Near the opening of the 'Description of the Scenery of the Lakes',[71] Wordsworth imagines the landscape elaborated as a vast panorama viewed from the top of the mountains of Great Gavel or Scawfell:

> ... let us suppose our station to be a cloud hanging midway from the summit of each, and not many yards above their highest elevation; we shall then see stretched at our feet a number of vallies [*sic*], not fewer than eight, diverging from the point, on which we are supposed to stand, like spokes from the nave of a wheel. First, we note, lying to the south-east, the vale of Langdale, which will conduct the eye to the long lake of Winandermere [*sic*], stretched nearly to the sea; or rather to the sands of the vast bay of Morcamb [*sic*], serving here for the rim of this

> imaginary wheel; ... Looking forth again, with an inclination towards the west, we see immediately at our feet the vale of Duddon, in which is no lake, but a copious stream winding among the fields, rocks, and mountains, and terminating its course in the sands of Duddon. ... Next, almost due west, look down into, and along the deep valley of Wastdale, with its little chapel and half a dozen neat dwellings scattered upon a plain of meadow and corn-ground intersected with stone walls apparently innumerable, like a large piece of lawless patch-work, or an array of mathematical figures, such as in the ancient schools of geometry might have been sportively and fantastically traced out upon the sand. ... The vale of Buttermere, with the lake and village of that name, and Crummock-water, beyond, next present themselves. We will follow the main stream, the Coker, through the fertile and beautiful vale of Lorton, till it is lost in the Derwent, below the noble ruins of Cockermouth Castle. Lastly, Borrowdale, of which the vale of Keswick is only a continuation, stretching due north, brings us to a point nearly opposite to the vale of Winandermere [*sic*] with which we began.[72]

Orientation is provided by means of compass direction (four in the above extract) where no fewer than six references are made to the act of viewing or the viewer's eye being conducted through the landscape, a process we have already observed in Brantz Mayer's account of viewing the Valle de México for the first time. Directing the reader's gaze (in his or her imagination) demonstrates the degree to which guide-books and travel literature encouraged readers and tourists to view, imagine, or experience landscape as a form of pleasurable displacement. Panoramas, maps, and imagined, elevated views shared a common feature: they carried the eye through natural scenery, documenting a response that delighted in being transported through the material world. As Gilpin proposed: 'Nature's alphabet consists only of four letters; wood – water – rock – and ground: and yet with these four letters she forms such varied compositions, such infinite combinations, as no language with an alphabet of twenty-four can describe.' Gilpin also acknowledged that poets could speak to 'the *imagination*; and if he deals only in *general ideas*, as all good poets on such subjects will do, every reader will form the phantom according to his *own* conception. But the *painter*, who speaks to the *eye*, has a more difficult work. He cannot deal in *general* terms: he is *obliged* to *particularize* ...'.[73] The ability to particularise the natural landscape yet simultaneously stimulate the imagination, as we have seen in the response of visitors to Mexico, in Hornor's panorama of London, and in Wordsworth's *A Guide through the District of the Lakes in the North of England*, underwrote the ambition of artists and writers in the early nineteenth century, finding its most intense expression in the work of Romantic artists.

Carrying the eye: *repoussoir* and 'continually shifting' scenes

Parallel with panoramas, maps, and guide-books which conducted the eye through virtual worlds, painting in the picturesque manner, as championed and illustrated by William Gilpin, also conducted the eye, following quasi-formulaic principles for depicting the landscape where composition was understood to be an arrangement of planes (foreground, middle ground, and distance) that became progressively lighter in tone towards the horizon. These compositional principles in conjunction with aerial perspective sought to imitate the neo-classical landscape painting of Claude Lorrain whose work (the *beau idéal*) had been collected in Britain for much of the eighteenth century.[74] By the early nineteenth century, for example, over eighty Claudes had been bought by English collectors,[75] and over three hundred works attributed to Gaspard Dughet (also known as Gaspard Poussin, after his now better-known brother-in-law, Nicolas Poussin) had passed through English sale rooms between 1711 and 1759.[76]

The neo-classical tradition was central to the compositional principles of Gilpin, who sought to restrain the viewer's eye to the confines of the picture space, imparting order to the process of depiction and rendering the viewing of a given landscape aesthetically pleasurable:

> Nothing is more delusive, than to suppose, that every view, which pleases in nature, will please in painting. In nature, the pleasure arises from the eye's roaming from one passage to another; and making it's [*sic*] remarks on each. In painting, (as the eye is there confined within certain limits,) it arises from seeing some select spot adorned agreeably to the rules of art.[77]

Although Gilpin did not hold Claude's landscapes in high regard,[78] he nonetheless adopted Claude's planar organisation of the picture to secure the effect of recession by means of relief (*repoussoir*). The latter was achieved by employing framing devices in the foreground of the picture (such as trees, ruins, or mountains) which, it was believed, drew the viewer's eye into the space of the picture.[79] Commenting on the importance of framing and tonal contrast in engravings after Claude, Gilpin observed: 'His *Via sacra* is one of his best prints. The trees and ruins on the left, are beautifully touched; and the whole (though rather formal) would have been pleasing, if the foreground had been in shadow.' Tonal gradation (referred to as 'keeping' in the eighteenth century, a term that continued to have currency until at least the middle of the following century),[80] was employed to simplify and unite neo-classical landscapes, an effect that could also be achieved by employing a Claude glass to intensify views of the landscape framed by the glass. This optical instrument, characterised by Bermingham as 'a distorting device with a built-in picturesque sensibility',[81] was used to compress and transform the view of a given landscape into a more harmonious key. The glass took a variety of forms, the most typical being that used by Thomas Gray which comprised a convex mirror about four inches in diameter bound in a pocket-book carrying case.[82] The convexity of the mirror miniaturised the reflected landscape, gave emphasis to foreground features, and arranged a formally and tonally unified composition. As Gilpin observed: 'in the minute exhibitions of the convex-mirror, composition, forms, and *colours* are brought closer together; and the eye examines the *general* effect, the *forms of the objects*, and the *beauty of the tints* in one complex view'.[83]

Claude glasses with a black backing or tinted blue or grey could suffuse an afternoon scene with moonlight; tinted yellow and used at noon, the Claude glass could transform the scene into a view of a glowing dawn. These harmonising effects earned the Claude glass its name. Ordinarily, such effects were secured by artists present in a location where they might observe scenes over a period of time; with the Claude glass and with little time to spare, tourists could modify the weather and luminosity of a day or season in the space of a few seconds.[84] Using the Claude glass in such fashion promoted a taste for darker tones which, set against the middle distance (to carry the eye into the picture), were employed in many of the less than topographically accurate vignettes that Gilpin included as aquatints of his tours:

> Some apology may perhaps be necessary for the uniformity of one principle, which runs through most of the designs here exhibited; and that is the practice of *throwing the foreground into shade*. Many artists throw their *lights* on the *foreground*; and often, no doubt, with good effect. But, in general, we are perhaps better pleased with a *dark* foreground. It makes a kind of graduating shade, from the eye through the removed parts of the picture; and carries off the distance better than any other contrivance. By throwing the *light* on the *foreground*, this *gradation* is *inverted*.[85]

Just as analogies were perceived between topographical representation, panoramas, and maps, an analogy with theatrical scenography was also drawn in considering landscape as a form of natural scenery, a trope rendered by Stebbing Shaw when he compared a viewpoint on the Piercefield estate in the Wye Valley with a box in the theatre:

> Opposite the cave are bow railings with a seat, which if we may compare the works of nature with those of art, may be called a front box of one of the compleatest [*sic*] theatres in the universe ... Here wants no painted canvas to express its scenery, nature's sweet landscape is quite enough.[86]

Gilpin undertook a tour of the Wye Valley and South Wales (*Cymru*) in the first half of June 1770, and published his account of the tour in the summer of 1783.[87] The publication inaugurated a new type of travel literature and a new form of leisure activity: the picturesque tour. Writing and illustration, the latter providing depictions of a generalised nature that did not necessarily observe topographical accuracy, complemented each other, and gave his work an immediate appeal. As part of Gilpin's tour of the Wye Valley, he travelled through the southern half of Wales, characterising a distant view of the river Towy (*Tywi*, Plate 2) as a natural amphitheatre, a comparison that drew attention to landscape as natural scenery: 'It is a distant view of a grand circular part of the vale of Towy ... surrounded by hills, one behind another; and forming a vast amphitheatre.'[88] The two-day journey down the river Wye (*Gwy*) typified Gilpin's compositional principles (Plate 3),[89] evoking a series of 'continually shifting' scenes of the river:

> The beauty of these scenes arises chiefly from two circumstances – the *lofty banks* of the river, and it's [*sic*] *mazy course*; …
>
> Every view on a river, thus circumstanced, is composed of four grand parts; the *area*, which is the river itself; the *two side-screens*, which are the opposite banks, and mark the perspective; and the *front-screen*, which points out the winding of the river. …
>
> The views on the Wye, tho [*sic*]composed only of these *simple parts*, are yet *infinitely varied*.
>
> They are varied, first, by the *contrast of the screens*. Sometimes one of the side-screens is elevated; sometimes the other; and sometimes the front. Or both the side-screens may be lofty; and the front either high, or low.
>
> Again, they are varied by the *folding of the side-screens over each other*; and hiding more or less of the front. When none of the front is discovered, the folding-side either winds round, like an amphitheatre;* or it becomes a long reach of perspective.
>
> These *simple* variations admit still farther variety from becoming *complex*. One of the sides may be compounded of various parts; while the other remains simple: or both may be compounded; and the front simple: or the front alone may be compounded.[90]

Between 1768 and 1776, Gilpin undertook no fewer than seven tours to various parts of Britain, the tour of the Wye Valley and South Wales being the first such tour of the picturesque.[91] The success of Gilpin's tours and the number of editions through which his work became known helped sensitize a generation of British tourists to the picturesque qualities of the natural landscape. The published tours went through several editions. *Observations on the River Wye*, for example, was initially published in an edition of seven hundred copies in 1783, with fifteen oval landscapes printed as vignettes that combined etching and aquatint prepared by Gilpin's young nephew, William Sawrey Gilpin; a second edition, using aquatint alone, was published in April 1789; a third edition appeared in 1792; and a fourth, pocket-size edition without plates, was published in 1800, the same year in which a fifth edition, with plates from seventeen renewed etchings, was also published.[92] Although the print-run for these editions is, in most cases, not known,[93] changes in the readership for Gilpin are reflected in the publication history of Gilpin's *Observations of the River Wye*, where quotation in Latin in the first edition gave way to loose translation into English in subsequent editions. By the early nineteenth century, Gilpin's publications had not only helped launch a vogue for touring, but contributed to the pleasures that could be derived from viewing landscape as an instance of 'the beauties of the ever shifting scenery'.[94] William Coxe characterised the river Wye as 'serpentine', and went on to observe:

> The effects of these numerous windings are various and striking; the same objects present themselves, are lost and recovered with different accompaniments, and in different points of view: thus the ruins of a castle, hamlets embosomed in trees, the spire of a church bursting from the wood, forges impending over the water, and broken masses of rock fringed with herbage, sometimes are seen on one side, sometimes on the other, and form the fore ground or back ground of a landscape.[95]

By the 1820s, Gilpin's publication, along with other tour-guides, had stimulated tourism in the Wye Valley, leading to the opening of a new road to Tintern Abbey (*Abaty Tyndyrn*) in 1821 and the introduction of steam-boat traffic from Bristol to Chepstow (*Casgwent*) in September 1822. By the following year, 'excursionists' (contemptuously referred to as 'day-trippers') from Bristol and Bath greatly outnumbered the tourists who took the two-day river trip from Ross-on-Wye, in Herefordshire, to Chepstow, completing the journey at much reduced cost.[96] By May 1823, excursionists from Bristol were charged four shillings (cabin), three shillings (mid-ships and fore cabin), two shillings (fore deck), and children under twelve years of age travelled half price, for the trip to Chepstow, from whence they took carriages to visit Piercefield, Tintern Abbey and other tourist 'sights' on the lower reaches of the river Wye.[97] These prices compared favourably with the cost of taking a tour down the Wye Valley: in the 1780s, tourists paid one and a half guineas to sail from Ross to Monmouth (*Trefynwy*), and a similar sum from Monmouth to Chepstow; by the early 1800s, boats carrying twelve tourists from Ross to Chepstow cost £5 12 shillings, and a six-seater cost four guineas.[98] By the 1820s, tourism associated with the viewing of picturesque locations in the Wye Valley had become not only a seasonal diversion for well-to-do tourists, but had become a popular leisure activity for day-trippers.

Carrying the eye: reverse viewpoints and the tourist of the picturesque

Just as guide-books devoted to the Wye provided a new model for tourists keen to indulge their delight in the picturesque tour,[99] the earliest guide-book to the Lake District, *A Guide to the Lakes, in Cumberland, Westmorland, and Lancashire*, written by the Jesuit priest and antiquarian, Thomas West, provided a model for later guide-books.[100] West popularised (and largely institutionalised) the practice of viewing a landscape from a particular point in space which, as in the case of Samuel and Nathaniel Buck and the viewing of panoramas, West termed a 'station'. Viewpoints from which the landscape was best viewed were frequently described in detail, as in the case of the first station that West recommended to tourists visiting Coniston Water: 'A little above the village of *Nibthwaite*, the lake opens in full view. From the rock, on the left of the road, you have a general prospect of the lake upwards. This station is found by observing where you have a hanging rock over the road, on the east, and an ash-tree on the west side of the road.'[101] In the case of Lake Windermere, a viewpoint on the northern side of Belle Isle ('Station III') afforded opportunities to view the southern part of the lake before the tourist turned round to view the northern part of the lake where the view enjoyed in the opposite direction constituted what we would today term a 'reverse field':

> STATION III. From the *north* side of the island the views are more sublime and vast. The lake is here seen both ways. To the south, an expanse of water spreads on both hands, and behind, you see a succession of promontories, with variety of shore, patched with islands, and the whole encircled by an amphitheatre of distant hills, rising in a noble stile. Turning to the north, the view is over a reach of the lake, six miles in length, and above one in breadth, interrupted with scattered islands of different figure and dress; which on a calm day may be seen distinctly reflected from the limpid surface of the water that surrounds them. The environs exhibit all the grandeur of Alpine scenes.[102]

Reverse views, articulated from viewpoints over a considerable distance, were also deemed worthy of the attention of tourists visiting Derwentwater, the most celebrated of the lakes in West's guide-book. No fewer than eight stations were identified on maps drawn by Peter Crosthwaite, whose first map of Derwentwater, published in 1783, continued to be published well into the nineteenth century (2.10).[103] Not only did Derwentwater afford the opportunity of viewing Castle Crag (at the southern end of the lake) from hills to the north of the lake (Crosthwaite's 'first Station', on the right of the map reproduced as 2.10), but from Castle Crag (West's Station IV, 'one Mile South of Grange' to the left of the map), the hills of Skiddaw and Latrigg could be viewed to the north of the lake, thus constituting reverse views, from which point, tourists would turn away from Derwentwater and, in what we would term a 'reverse-field view', look down upon the sublime spectacle of Borrowdale to the south:

> From the top of *Castle-crag* in *Borrowdale* there is a most astonishing view of the lake and vale of *Keswick*, spread out to the north in the most picturesque manner. From the pass of *Borrowdale* is distinctly seen, every bend of the river till it joins the lake; the lake itself, spotted with islands; the most extraordinary line of shore … *Skiddaw*, which rises in the grandest manner, from a verdant base, … closes this prospect in the noblest stile of nature's true sublime. From the summit of this rock [Castle Crag] the views are so singularly great and pleasing, that they ought never to be omitted. …
>
> The view to the south lies in *Borrowdale*. The river is seen winding upward from the lake, through the rugged pass, to where it divides and embraces a triangular vale, completely cut into inclosures of meadow enamelled with the softest verdure, and field waving with fruitful crops. This truly secreted spot is completely surrounded by the most horrid, romantic mountains that are in this region of wonders; and whoever omits this *coup d'oeil* hath probably seen nothing equal to it. …[104]

Once again, we encounter a *coup d'œil*, this time in the context of viewing the sublime landscape of Borrowdale from Castle Crag. West and other writers also delighted in the *frisson* that motion imparted to the viewing the Lakes.[105] In the Addenda to *A Guide to the Lakes*, West quoted from one of the earliest writers to champion the region, Dr. John Brown, a fellow of St. John's College, Cambridge, who, in a letter to Lord Lyttelton, probably written in 1753, and first published, in part, in 1767,[106] remarked on the pleasure that could be derived from viewing the landscape from a boat on Derwentwater:

> So much for what I would call the *permanent* beauties of this astonishing scene. Were I not afraid of being tiresome, I could now dwell as long on its *varying* or *accidental* beauties. I would sail around the lake, anchor

> in every bay, and land you on every promontory and island. I would point out the perpetual change of prospect: the woods, rocks, cliffs, and mountains, by turns vanishing or rising into view: now gaining on the sight, hanging over our heads in their full dimensions, beautifully dreadful; and now by a change of situation, assuming new romantic shapes, retiring and lessening on the eye, and then insensibly losing themselves in an azure mist.[107]

Not only did Dr. Brown know the landscape of the Lakes well (he had been brought up in Cumberland), he had also acted as tutor and drawing-master to William Gilpin in the 1730s and 1740s.[108] Touring the Lakes in 1772, and likely recalling the influence of his childhood drawing-master, Gilpin recounted the experience of approaching Borrowdale, acknowledging the sublime and the thrill that movement through natural scenery imparted:

> The winding of the Derwent was the clue we followed in our passage through these regions of desolation. An aperture between the mountains brought us into another wild recess, where a similar scene opened; diversified from the first only by some new forms, or new position, or varied furniture, of the incumbent mountains.

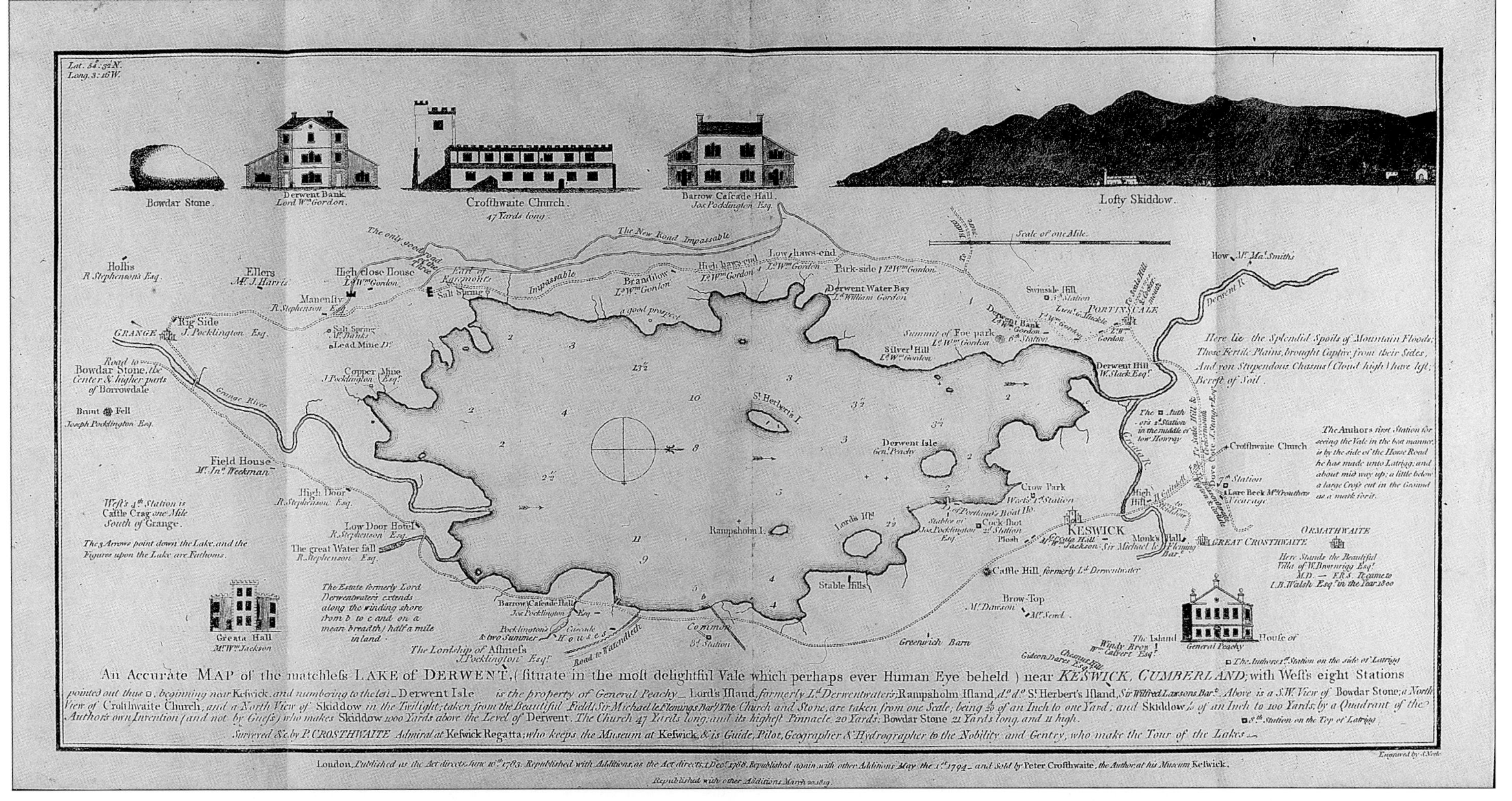

2.10. Peter Crosthwaite, engraved by Samuel John Neele, *An Accurate Map of the Matchless Lake of Derwent* (London, 1819 [1783]), 20.5 x 40.4 cm. [Reproduced by permission of the Wordsworth Trust, Dove Cottage.]

> As we doubled one promontory, another unfolded; and we found ourselves, not in, what appeared at first, a recess of mountains; but in a narrow, winding valley; the scenes of which, by quick transitions, were continually shifting. This valley so replete with hideous grandeur, is known by the name of the straits of Borrodale [*sic*].[109]

By the late eighteenth century, just as the eye of the tourist of the picturesque had become accustomed to observing natural scenery from viewpoints or 'stations', a term shared with topographical views and the recently-introduced panorama, the tourist's eye had also grown used to delighting in the varying prospects that landscape presented, even in the sublime register associated with the 'hideous grandeur' that Gilpin observed on entering Borrowdale. Moreover, the tourist of the picturesque, accustomed to the delight of being transported through 'a continual moving Picture', also appreciated how pictorial relief, achieved through *repoussoir* and the planar organisation of the picture space, could render the landscape picturesque.[110] As Gilpin observed, and many reader-viewers would have concurred, 'picturesque' had indeed become a term 'expressive of that peculiar kind of beauty, which is agreeable in a picture'.[111]

By the early nineteenth century, through touring and viewing landscape, tourists of the picturesque celebrated the delight of being transported through landscape by various means: on private tours, day excursions, or by the virtual means of panoramas, travel accounts, and guide-books. Reader-viewers had become familiar with a range of mediums that offered the pleasure of being physically and metaphorically transported through the landscape. The impact of these developments on antiquarian investigation was to prove significant in the nineteenth century, particularly since reader-viewers and tourists of the picturesque, familiar with the pleasures of reading and viewing illustrated travel accounts, interpreting maps, viewing panoramas, and evaluating compositions in the picturesque manner, came increasingly to have faith in the power of illustration. No longer merely spoken, recited, or declaimed (as in the institution of the church where most people in the Augustan age would have encountered the written word as *spoken* word), by the early nineteenth century, the written word, in concert with illustration, supervised a new and more intimate relation between reader and text, one which closed off the world outside in favour of the individual reader's engaged attention and imagination. A transformation had attended the printed page by the early nineteenth century as the process of reading travel accounts instituted a relation between reader and the *topos* of the printed page which highlighted what we may term 'media convergence'. This private realm was not only defined by reading and viewing illustrated books, panorama booklets, and maps, but was also integral to the process of interpreting plans, elevations, sections, and architectural details which writers and illustrators such as Stephens and Catherwood placed before readers in the 1840s. The conjunction of word and illustration in the private demesne of the printed page provides the focus for discussion in Chapter Three and Chapter Four, where the tourist of the picturesque becomes a 'modern traveller', one who delights in virtual travel, reading texts and viewing images which mid-nineteenth-century travel accounts of Mexico and Central America envision.

Colour Plates

Plate 1 Frederick Catherwood, *Plan of Jerusalem by F. Catherwood. Architect. July 1835*. Published August 1st. 1835, by F. Catherwood, 21, Charles Square, Hoxton. Engraved by S. Bellin, 27 x 21 cm. [Reproduced by permission of the National Archives.]

Plate 2
Francis Jukes, aquatint, William Gilpin, *Observations on the River Wye*, second edition (London: R. Blamire, 1789 [1782]), facing 39, 10.6 x 16.8 cm. (maximum image size). [Reproduced by permission of the National Library of Scotland.]

Plate 3
Francis Jukes, aquatint, William Gilpin, *Observations on the River Wye*, second edition (London: R. Blamire, 1789 [1782]), facing 109, 10.6 x 16.8 cm. (maximum image size). [Reproduced by permission of the National Library of Scotland.]

Plate 4
Jean-Frédéric de Waldeck, engraved by Lemercier, Benard & Cie., *Plate VI, Manière de voyager dans l'Yucatan*, Jean-Frédéric de Waldeck, *Voyage pittoresque et archéologique dans la province d'Yucatan (Amérique centrale), pendant les années 1834 et 1836* (Paris: Bellizard Dufour et Co.; London: J. and W. Boone; Bossange Barthès et Lowell, 1838), 26.2 x 34.8 cm. [Reproduced by permission of Centro de Estudios de Historia de México Condumex.]

Plate 5
Jean-Frédéric de Waldeck, engraved by Beer, Lemercier, Benard & Cie., *Plate XVI, Étude d'une partie du Temple du Soleil*, Jean-Frédéric de Waldeck, *Voyage pittoresque et archéologique dans la province d'Yucatan (Amérique centrale), pendant les années 1834 et 1836* (Paris: Bellizard Dufour et Co.; London: J. and W. Boone; Bossange Barthès et Lowell, 1838), 43.7 x 31.5 cm.
[Reproduced by permission of Centro de Estudios de Historia de México Condumex.]

Plate 6
Frederick Catherwood, engraved by Henry Warren (lithographer), *Plate V. Idol and Altar at Copan*, Frederick Catherwood, *Views of Ancient Monuments in Central America Chiapas and Yucatan* (London: F. Catherwood, 1844), 35.5 x 27.5 cm.
[Reproduced by permission of Cambridge University Library.]

Plate 7 Frederick Catherwood, engraved by William Parrott (lithographer), *Plate IV. Broken Idol at Copan*, Frederick Catherwood, *Views of Ancient Monuments in Central America Chiapas and Yucatan* (London: F. Catherwood, 1844), 28 x 39.8 cm. [Reproduced by permission of Cambridge University Library.]

Plate 8 Frederick Catherwood, engraved by Andrew Picken (lithographer), *Plate VI. General View of Palenque*, Frederick Catherwood, *Views of Ancient Monuments in Central America Chiapas and Yucatan* (London: F. Catherwood, 1844), 29 x 42 cm. [Reproduced by permission of Cambridge University Library.]

Plate 9 Frederick Catherwood, engraved by John Cooke Bourne (lithographer), *Plate VIII. General View of Las Monjas at Uxmal*, Frederick Catherwood, *Views of Ancient Monuments in Central America Chiapas and Yucatan* (London: F. Catherwood, 1844), 26.6 x 37.3 cm. [Reproduced by permission of Cambridge University Library.]

Plate 10 Frederick Catherwood, engraved by Andrew Picken (lithographer), *Plate XIII. General View of Uxmal, taken from the Archway of Las Monjas Looking South*, Frederick Catherwood, *Views of Ancient Monuments in Central America Chiapas and Yucatan* (London: F. Catherwood, 1844), 27.2 x 39.3 cm. [Reproduced by permission of Cambridge University Library.]

Plate 11 Facade, Kuhuic, Yucatán, photographed by the author.

Plate 12 Maya *na*, Santa Elena, Yucatán, photographed by the author.

Plate 13 William Daniell, *Entrance to Fingal's Cave, Staffa*, 1818, hand-coloured aquatint, William Daniell, *A Voyage Round Great Britain, Undertaken in the Summer of the Year 1813*, 8 vols. (London: Longman, Hurst, Rees, Orme, and Brown, and William Daniell, 1814–1825), III, facing 38, 16.4 x 24 cm. [Reproduced by permission of the National Library of Scotland.]

Plate 14 Daniel Thomas Egerton, *Sn Agustin de las Cuevas*, 1839, signed 'D. T. Egerton' and dated bottom left, hand-coloured chromolithograph, D. T. Egerton, *Egerton's Views in Mexico* (London: D. T. Egerton, 1840), 41.6 x 60.3 cm., including mount: 53.3 x 71.3 cm. [Private collection.]

Plate 15 Carl Nebel, engraved by Frédéric (Federico) Miahle (lithographer), *Mexico*[.] *Visto desde el Arsobisbado* [*sic*] *de Tacubaya*, 1836, hand-coloured chromolithograph, Carl Nebel, *Voyage pittoresque et archéologique dans la partie la plus intéressante du Mexique* (Paris: chez M. Moench and chez Paul Renouard, 1836), 23.8 x 34.8 cm. [Reproduced by permission of Cambridge University Library.]

Plate 16 After Nebel, engraved by Pierre-Frédéric Lehnert, *Indios carboneras. Vista General de México Desde Tacubaya*, c. 1849–1852, hand-coloured chromolithograph signed 'F. Lehnert' bottom left, *Álbum pintoresco de la República Mexicana*, 1848–1851, printed by Rose-Joseph Lemercier and Prodhomme, 27.2 x 39.4 cm. [Private collection.]

Plate 17 François Aubert, *Environs de Mexico*, c.1866, albumen print, signed 'Aubert, Mexico' in negative bottom left, 25.8 x 34.3 cm. [Reproduced by permission of Getty Research Institute.]

Plate 18 Plate IV, *Vías de comunicación y movimiento maritimo*, Antonio García Cubas, *Atlas Pintoresco e Histórico de los Estados Unidos Mexicanos por Antonio García Cubas* (Mexico City: Debray Sucesores, 1885), 62.5 x 77 cm. [Reproduced by permission of Mapoteca Manuel Orozco y Berra.]

Plate 19
Ferrocarril Mexicano – Puente del Chiquihuite, inset, bottom right, Plate IV, *Vías de comunicación y movimiento marítimo*, Antonio García Cubas, *Atlas Pintoresco e Histórico de los Estados Unidos Mexicanos por Antonio García Cubas* (Mexico City: Debray Sucesores, 1885), 10 x 12.5 cm.
[Reproduced by permission of Mapoteca Manuel Orozco y Berra.]

Plate 20
Ferrocarril Mexicano – El Infiernillo, inset, lower left, Plate IV, *Vías de comunicación y movimiento marítimo*, Antonio García Cubas, *Atlas Pintoresco e Histórico de los Estados Unidos Mexicanos por Antonio García Cubas* (Mexico City: Debray Sucesores, 1885), 9 x 11.3 cm.
[Reproduced by permission of Mapoteca Manuel Orozco y Berra.]

Plate 21 Casimiro Castro, Plate XVII, *Infiernillo*, engraved by A. Sigogne (lithographer), *Álbum del Ferrocarril Mexicano. Colección de vistas Pintadas del natural por Casimiro Castro* (Mexico City: Víctor Debray y Ca., Editores, 1877), 24 x 35.5 cm., page size 36 x 48.5 cm. [Reproduced by permission of Centro de Estudios de Historia de México Condumex.]

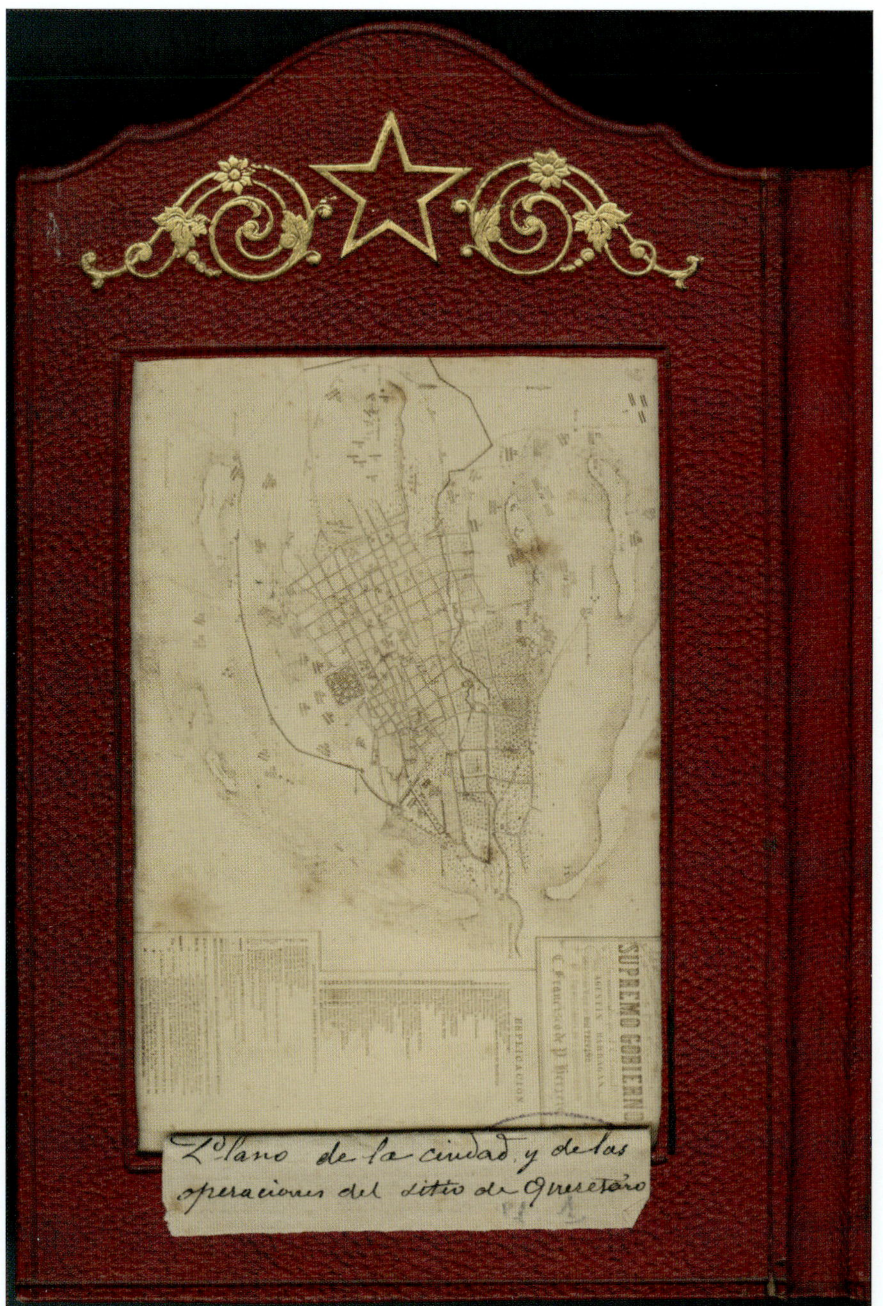

Plate 22 François Aubert, albumen *carte de visite* with titles in ink, *Plano de la ciudad y de las operaciones del sitio de Queretaro*, re-photographed from plan of a military campaign drawn by Francisco de P. Herrera, and *Convento de la* [*Santa*] *Cruz y Capilla del Calvario arrimado en la defensa de Queretaro* mounted in a red leather-bound album of *cartes de visite* with wetstamp on reverse, 'Aubert y Cia Fot.', 1867, each *carte de visite* approx. 6.3 x 10.4 cm. [Reproduced by permission of Collection Musée Royal de l'Armée – Bruxelles, DB-(b)10.340, DB-(b)10.341.]

Plate 23 François Aubert, albumen *carte de visite* with titles in ink, *Lugar en donde fallecieron al Emp^{dor}Maximiliano, Miramon y Mejia* and *Vista de Queretaro*, mounted in a red leather-bound album of *cartes de visite* with wetstamp on reverse, 'Aubert y Cia Fot.', 1867, each *carte de visite* approx. 6.3 x 10.4 cm. [Reproduced by permission of Collection Musée Royal de l'Armée – Bruxelles, DB-(b)10.348, DB-(b)10.349.]

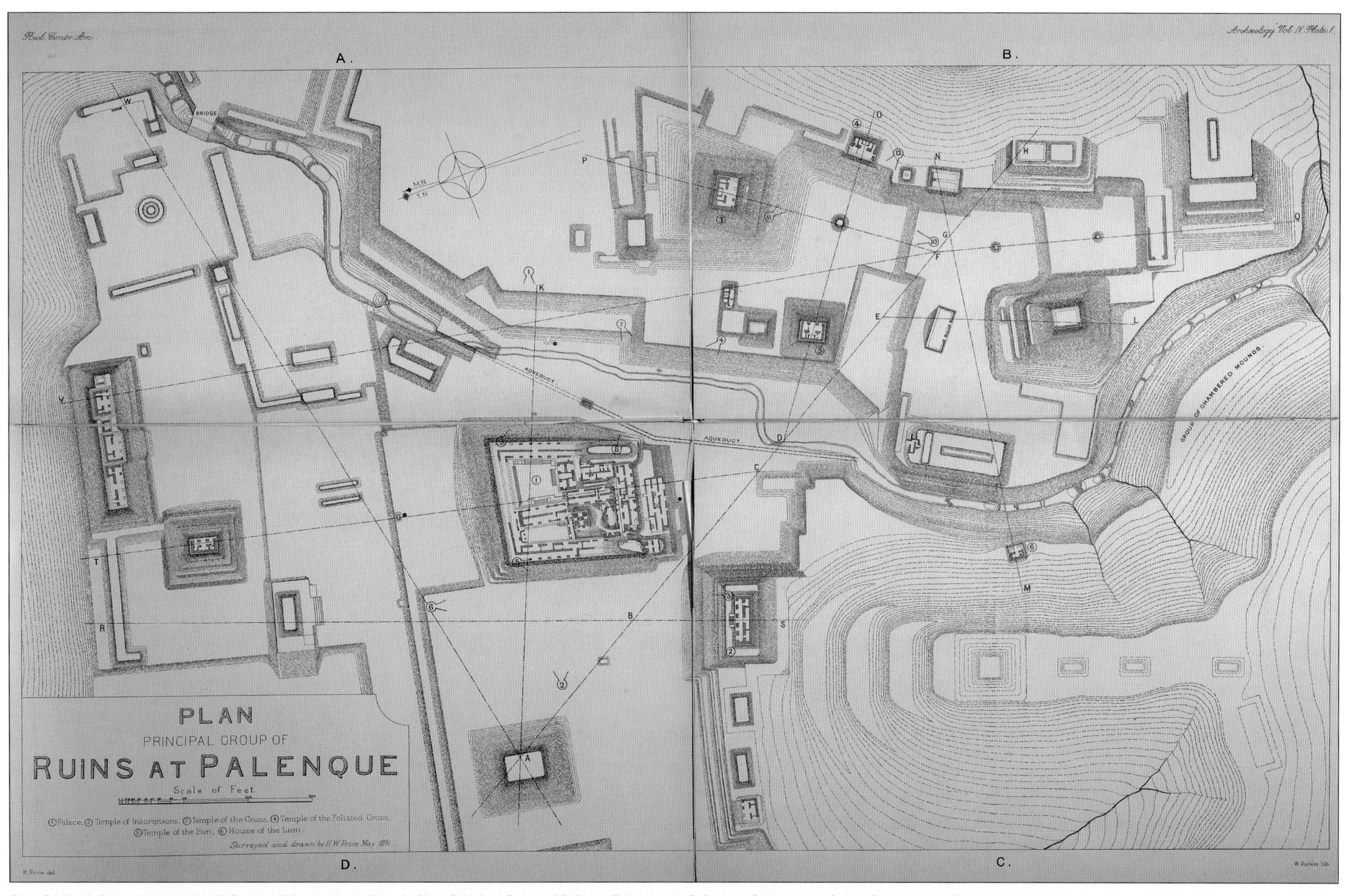

Plate 24 Hugh Price, engraved by W. Purkiss (lithographer), Plate 1, *Plan. Principal Group of Ruins at Palenque*, in F. Ducane Godman and Osbert Salvin (eds.), *Biologia Centrali-Americana; or, Contributions to the Knowledge of the Fauna and Flora of Mexico and Central America*, Vol. LVIII, A. P. Maudslay, *Archaeology*, Vol. IV, Plates (London: R. H. Porter and Dulau & Co., 1896–1899), 52.5 x 87.5 cm.
[Reproduced by permission of Getty Research Institute.]

Plate 25 E. L. [Ernest Louet], *Tepeji-del-Rio Casa Municipal*, albumen print, private album [Views of Mexico during the French Intervention], c. 1864, 16.3 x 21.4 cm., page size 29 x 40.5 cm. [Reproduced by permission of Getty Research Institute.]

Plate 26 E. L. [Ernest Louet], *Tepeji-del-Rio Eglise*, albumen print, private album [Views of Mexico during the French Intervention], c. 1864, 15.9 x 21.3 cm., page size 29 x 40.5 cm. [Reproduced by permission of Getty Research Institute.]

Plate 27 *Mise en page* of four photographic prints on collodion printing-out paper mounted on gilt-edged card, *Mexico 1895 Raymond and Whitcomb*, private album owned by Benjamin F. Freeman, Sommerville, Massachusetts, leaf 50, verso, top left print: 11.1 x 16.3 cm.; top right print: 11.1 x 16.5 cm.; lower left print: 11.1 x 16.4 cm.; lower right print: 11 x 16.2 cm., page size 31 x 39 cm.
[Reproduced by permission of Getty Research Institute.]

Plate 28 Guillermo Kahlo, *Plate 158 La Enseñanza – México D.F. – Vista Interior* (verso), gelatin silver print toned with platinum and gold, 34 x 26.3 cm., page size 35.1 x 27.6 cm. [Reproduced by permission of Getty Research Institute.]

Plate 29 Guillermo Kahlo, *Plate 159 La Enseñanza –México D.F. – Vista Interior* (recto), gelatin silver print toned with platinum and gold, 34 x 26.3 cm., page size 35.1 x 27.6 cm. [Reproduced by permission of Getty Research Institute.]

Plate 30 Guillermo Kahlo, *1. Hauptplatz, Westseite & Kathedrale, S.-N. / 1. Plaza principal (Zócalo), lado de Poniente: Portal de Mercaderes, Empedradillo, Catedral. S. al N.*, gelatin silver print, *Mexico 1904*, private album bound in brown leather with gold embossed lettering, no later than 1904, 25.6 x 66 cm. [Reproduced by permission of Biblioteca Francisco Xavier Clavigero, Universidad Iberoamericana.]

Plate 31 Colour picture postcard view, *Vista General de México*, J. K. 28. México, date-marked 26 September 1907, posted from Mexico City to a private address in Szombathely, Hungary, 9 x 13.9 cm. [Author's collection.]

Plate 32 Antonio García Cubas, engraved by Hipólito Salazar (lithographer), *Carta general de la República Mexicana. Formada en vista de los datos más recientes y exactos que se han reunido con tal objeto, y constan en la noticia presentada al Exmo. Sr. Ministro de Fomento por Antonia García Cubas*, c. 1865 [originally published in *Atlas geográfico, estadístico é hístorico de la República Mexicana formado por Antonio García y Cubas* (Mexico City: Imprenta de José Mariano Fernández de Lara, 1858)], hand-coloured lithograph on paper, 47.5 x 69 cm. [Reproduced by permision of Mapoteca Manuel Orozco y Berra.]

Chapter Three

Investigating antiquities in Central America and Yucatán before the 1840s, and the reception of Stephens and Catherwood

'My object has been, not to produce an illustrated work, but to present the drawings in such an inexpensive form as to place them within reach of the great mass of our reading community.' John Lloyd Stephens.[1]

From tourist of the picturesque to 'The Modern Traveller'

In 1825, four pocket-sized, slim volumes, measuring 15 x 9.5 cm. and bearing the title, *Mexico and Guatimala* [*sic*], were simultaneously published, in soft covers, by James Duncan in London, Oliver and Boyd in Edinburgh, M. Ogle in Glasgow, and R. M. Tims in Dublin. The publication was part of a series, *The Modern Traveller: A Popular Description, Geographical, Historical and Topographical, of the Various Countries of the Globe*, compiled by Josiah Conder.[2] The work on Mexico and Guatemala, totalling 691 pages, included four engravings prepared on steel by Henry Adlard, which were bound at the front of each part, together with a 'Map of Mexico, Engraved for the Modern Traveller' by Sidney Hall. The plates provided, in Part I, a view of the central square in Mexico City, and in Part II and Part III, views of what had become well-known geological and mineralogical sites in Mexico through publications by Alexander von Humboldt.[3] Part III also printed a view of what was reputed to be the largest pyramid in the world on the outskirts of Cholula (*Pyramid of Cholula*), an important pre-Columbian centre near Mexico's second city, Puebla de los Angeles, which had also been brought to international attention by Humboldt.[4] Copies of the publication devoted to Mexico and Guatemala, published in monthly parts at 2/6d (12½p) each, were held in Catherwood's private library when his collection was auctioned in December 1856.[5]

The Modern Traveller represented not only a new type of publication, one which *The Literary Gazette* recommended 'as a fit and valuable present for youth at this season', but also appealed to a new type of reader who sought 'a complete account of a country, as could be derived from the perusal of many large volumes'.[6] The hallmark of the series was that it presented a digest of information from a variety of sources which, individually, would have required a financial outlay far greater than that of *The Modern Traveller*. As the December 1824 issue of *Wesleyan Methodist Magazine* observed:

> The vain, and, as we think, upon the whole, the profitless custom, which of late years has prevailed, of publishing books of travel only in the most expensive form, has excluded a great number of readers from the instruction and gratification which we are afforded by this species of literature. ... Nothing has been exhibited pictorially, with few exceptions, but which might have been represented on a much smaller scale, to equal advantage, and with almost equal finish. The Editor of the work before us, proposes to *cut down* these ponderous tomes, as far as they are accessible, and to exhibit, in a cheap and elegant miniature edition, in monthly Parts, all that is valuable in them, either in the words of the writer, or, where the interest of the narrative will not suffer, in compressed form;[7]

Printed from steel plates innovated in the 1820s in the printing of banknotes, such publications far exceeded the print-runs that could be made from copper plates.[8] When Harper & Brothers in New York and John Murray in London published the work of Stephens and Catherwood in 1841 and 1843, steel engravings were used for plates and vignettes to counter the high production costs that lavishly illustrated antiquarian books customarily entailed.

The publication of *The Modern Traveller* parallels a number of concerns considered in the last two chapters, particularly those relating to the panorama and travel accounts which developed a new market for spectators and readers in the early years of the nineteenth century. As we have seen, Catherwood's panoramas (exhibited in London, Glasgow, and New York during the 1830s) drew on the tradition of the eighteenth-century topographic view, allying interest in panoramas with the expanding market for travel accounts that developed in the late eighteenth and early nineteenth centuries. One of the outcomes of this development was an interest in the picturesque, a concern that has continued to inform the illustration of popular travel accounts, albeit it in very different ways, to the present day. Aspects of how this discourse became influential in mid- and late-nineteenth-century Mexico, following the invention of photography and the introduction of the illustrated press towards the end of the century, are considered in Chapter Five.

The Modern Traveller represented a challenge to traditional antiquarian publications which were expensive to produce. Not only was the format of the series different, its address to the reader also marked a departure, one which privileged information at the expense of speculation. Something of this difference can be instanced by comparing the issues of *The Modern Traveller* devoted to Mexico and Guatemala considered later in this chapter with the publication, in 1838, of Jean-Frédéric de Waldeck's, *Voyage pittoresque et archéologique*, a volume to which Stephens was introduced by John Russell Bartlett, the senior partner of the New York firm of antiquarian booksellers, Bartlett and Welford.[9] The tenor of Waldeck's work can be instanced by two plates in *Voyage pittoresque et archéologique*, a folio that drew on his expedition to the Yucatán peninsula between 1834 and 1836: *Manière de voyager dans l'Yucatan* (Plate 4), which presents a view of the writer being carried in a *coché*, and *Étude d'une partie du Temple du Soleil* (Plate 5), which presents a detail of the Casa de las Monjas at the archaeological site of Uxmal.[10] The first plate presents a scene that depicts ethnographic interest typical of the picturesque as developed in Mexico in the 1830s and 1840s. The scene presents Waldeck who, borne by Maya Yucatecos accompanied by a dragoon, passes comment on the fruit of the tree under which he lies, which Waldeck extols as 'delicious, having a soft flesh with an exquisite taste'.[11] When it comes to discussing the archaeology of the site, not only is Waldeck's skill as an artist and that of his lithographer demonstrated (Waldeck reputedly trained in the studio of the French artist, Joseph Vien),[12] but the emphasis given to a symbolic interpretation of the structure, predicated on associations the central mask evoked for Waldeck, present very different objectives to those of *The Modern Traveller* or the publications of Stephens and Catherwood. While Waldeck's description of the ornamentation is detailed – the central mask of the structure is identified as representing the sun, and the rays of light emanating from the mask are compared with the meridian – it is nonetheless quite fanciful, as Waldeck readily admits when he observes that '[t]o begin to explain this bizarre ensemble, one would need at one's disposition documents which I lack, and to have studied other structures in all their particularities by the same people'.[13] Waldeck concludes by observing the effect of the midday sun on the range:

> The group on this facade in the midday sun offers a grandness that would be difficult to express adequately. The shadows from the cornices and from other projections produce a magical effect, magnifying the contours of the monument to the eye. When confronted with these abandoned temples, I am transported, not without emotion, as I recall my impressions on first seeing them.[14]

Comparison of this structure as depicted by Waldeck with Catherwood's engraving of the complete range, *Uxmal. Eastern Range of Building, Monjas* (3.1), is instructive. Like Waldeck, Catherwood frames the structure perpendicular to the viewer, but, unlike Waldeck, represents it in a more matter-of-fact manner, presenting ornamentation without elaborating the shadows and serpents' heads that animate Waldeck's depiction of the facade:

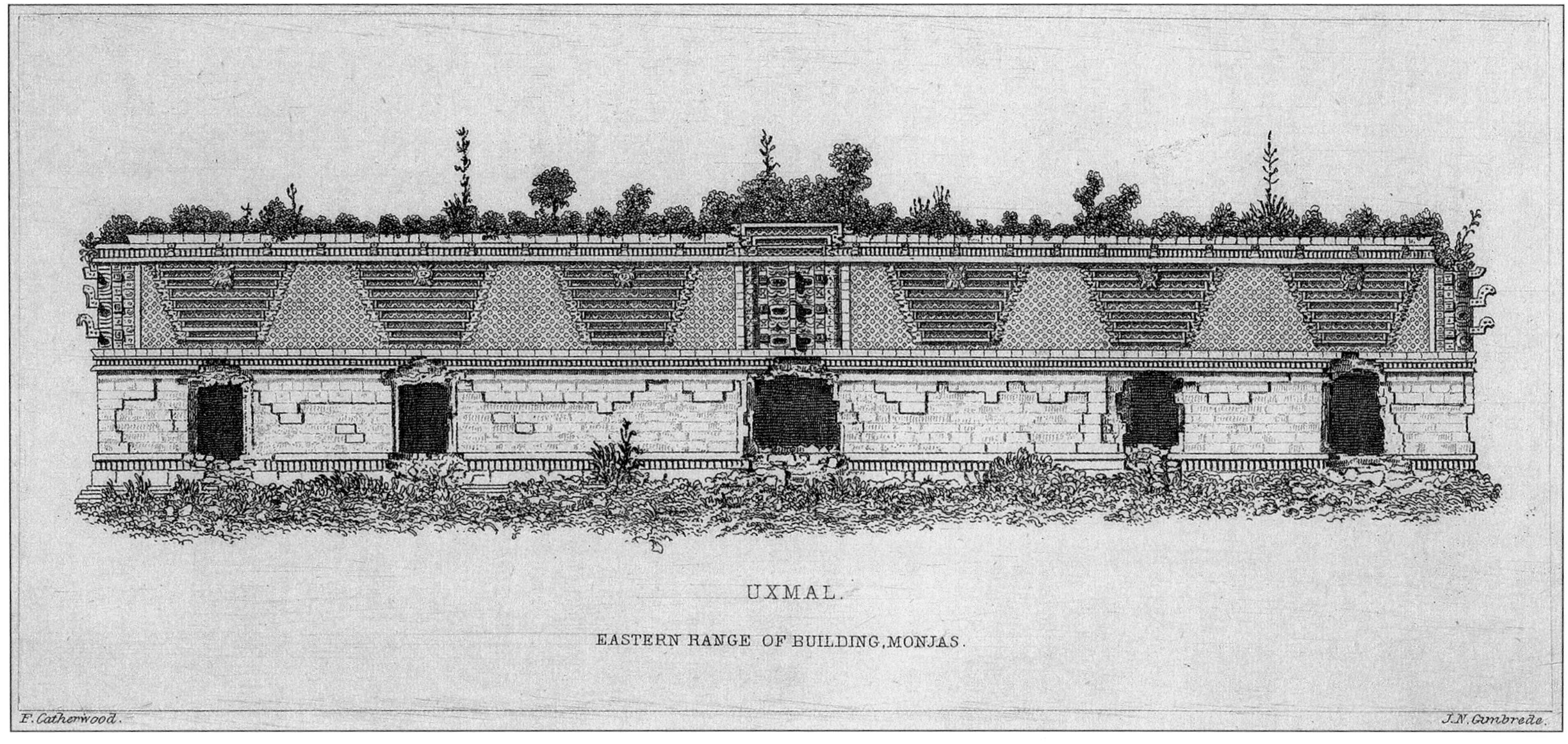

3.1. Frederick Catherwood, engraved by Joseph Napoleon Gimbrede, *Uxmal. Eastern Range of Building, Monjas*, John Lloyd Stephens, *Incidents of Travel in Yucatan*, 2 vols. (New York: Harper & Brothers for Henry Bill, 1848 [1843]), I, facing 306, 8.6 x 19 cm. [Reproduced by permission of the National Library of Sweden.]

> The ornament over the centre doorway is the most important, the most complicated and elaborate, and of that marked and peculiar style which characterizes the highest efforts of these ancient builders. The ornaments over the other doorways are less striking, more simple, and more pleasing. In all of them there is in the centre a masked face with the tongue hanging out, surmounted by an elaborate headdress; between the horizontal bars is a range of diamond-shaped ornaments, in which the remains of red paint are still distinctly visible, and at each end of these bars is a serpent's head, with the mouth wide open.[15]

By including high-quality chromolithographic plates, Waldeck's folio cost a far greater sum than Stephens' and Catherwood's publications, a factor which led a reviewer in *The North American Review* to observe that as late as 1843 only three or four copies of Waldeck had been purchased in the United States.[16] The production cost of Waldeck's work would, however, have been relatively small when compared with the cost of Lord Kingsborough's seven-volume folio set, *Antiquities of Mexico* (1831), which, according to the American traveller and journalist, Benjamin Moore Norman, amounted to an astounding sum ('something like one hundred and fifty thousand [US] dollars') for only fifty copies.[17] Characterised as 'the most costly undertaking ever attempted by a single individual, of a literary kind', and costing, on publication, $400 per volume (with two further volumes published posthumously in 1848), Norman reported that only one set of *Antiquities of Mexico* was held in the United States, at the Pennsylvania Library in Philadelphia.[18] Compared with these publications, *Incidents of Travel in Central America, Chiapas, and Yucatan*, published on 15 June 1841, containing over seventy-five plates and vignettes, and costing five US dollars per two-volume set, was inexpensive.[19]

The investigation of the Maya site of Palenque in Chiapas, a province of Guatemala until Chiapas was ceded to the federated states of Mexico in 1824, constitutes an important case study in the development of interest in Maya culture in the eighteenth and early nineteenth centuries. When news of Palenque began to circulate in the English-speaking world in the 1820s, more than half a century

3.2. *Facing page:* Ignacio Armendáriz, plan of the Palacio, Palenque, engraved by McQueen & Co., Antonio del Río, *Description of the Ruins of an Ancient City, Discovered near Palenque* (London: Henry Berthoud and Suttaby, Evance and Fox, 1822), facing 128, 16.7 x 25.8 cm. [Reproduced by permission of the National Library of Scotland.]

of investigation had been initiated by colonial administrators. Inspection of the ruins was first conducted by relatives of a parish priest from Tumbalá, Antonio de Solís, who had been assigned to the hamlet of Santo Domingo de Palenque around 1746. Some years later, Ramón Ordóñez y Aguiar, a secular priest and influential antiquarian residing in the capital of Chiapas, Ciudad Real de Chiapa (present-day Christóbal de Las Casas), sent two local administrators, Fernando Gómez de Andrade and Esteban Gutiérrez, to investigate the site in 1773.[20] In late 1784, Ramón Ordóñez y Aguiar's brother, José, reported exaggerated claims concerning Palenque to José Estacharía, a magistrate and president of the high court (*Audiencia*) of Guatemala, who dispatched the mayor (*alcalde*) of Santo Domingo de Palenque to the site, where José Antonio Calderón spent three days surveying the ruins and drawing some of the bas-reliefs at the site.[21] With curiosity raised by Calderón's report, Estacharía assigned a second expedition to Palenque, this time under the Italian-born Antonio Bernasconi, the royal architect of Guatemala, who, in 1785, after three months in the field, prepared architectural plans, elevations, cross-sections, and drawings of some of the bas-reliefs.[22] Estachería's conclusions and the reports by Calderón and Bernasconi reached Madrid in March the following year, where they were reviewed by Juan Bautista Muñoz, the Royal Chronicler of the Indies. Muñoz proposed a new expedition, and required that material from Palenque be sent to Spain.[23] Accordingly, José de Gálvez, the minister of the Indies, ordered Estacharía to arrange a third expedition. After some delay, Estacharía assigned further exploration of the site to Antonio del Río, a captain of artillery stationed in the capital of Guatemala. Accompanied by the artist, Ignacio Armendáriz, del Río visited Palenque in May-June 1787, where thirty drawings were prepared for inclusion in the report del Río completed before leaving the site.[24] Del Río's report finally achieved publication in English translation in 1822.[25]

By general agreement the history of how del Río's report came to be published in English is difficult to establish. At some point, Armendáriz's drawings, copied by José Luciano Castañeda, and subsequently printed in collections edited by Kingsborough (1831) and Henri Baradère (1834–1835), were engraved, in the majority of cases, by Waldeck to accompany the publication of del Río's report in 1822. The publication was poorly organised: the thirty plates prepared by Armendáriz were reduced to seventeen in number, and, bound out of sequence, bore little relation to the figure citations in the text.[26] With the exception of a plan of the Palacio (3.2) and a view of a tower in the same complex (a structure unique in Maya architecture), the plates included fifteen bas-reliefs.[27] Del Río's report was accompanied by a long essay by Dr. Paul Félix Cabrera, an Italian lawyer and antiquarian residing in Guatemala City.[28] Rather than unravel how Waldeck's re-working of Castañeda's drawings after Armendáriz came to be printed in London, our task is easier since del Río's text, without illustration, was also published, with minor changes, in *The Modern Traveller*. As this inexpensive edition constituted the version which most readers in Britain would have encountered, my discussion privileges del Río's report as presented in *The Modern Traveller*. Where this version departs from del Río, his report, as published in the English translation of 1822, is provided in the notes.

Two decades after del Río's expedition to Palenque, Charles IV of Spain commissioned Guillermo Dupaix, a retired French captain of dragoons based in Mexico City, to lead three expeditions (in 1805, 1806, and 1807) to survey the ruins of New Spain accompanied by the artist-draughtsman, José Luciano Castañeda.[29] On the last expedition, investigations were conducted at Palenque in January 1808, and Dupaix's reports were published in Kingsborough's *Antiquities of Mexico* and, in French translation, in Baradère's *Antiquités Mexicaines*.[30] In terms of accuracy, Armendáriz's and Castañeda's work at Palenque was superior to that of José Antonio Calderón and Antonio Bernasconi, but, in the case of Castañeda, evidenced considerable licence in his insistence on viewing indigenous architectural structures through pharaonic and classical filters.[31] By the time, therefore, that Stephens wrote *Incidents of Travel in Central America*, investigation at Palenque had been conducted over a considerable period of time and had begun to attract public interest in New York.[32] With the exception of del Río, who Stephens, taking a copy of the 1822 publication with him to Central America, described as his 'guide',[33] most of these investigators were unknown to Stephens and Catherwood when they set out for Central America. Although Stephens consulted Kingsborough's *Antiquities of Mexico* (which he regarded as 'ponderous tomes') and other publications on his return to New York, neither he nor Catherwood were familiar with the account of Dupaix nor Waldeck's *Voyage pittoresque et archéologique* (which was in press) when they set out for Central America.[34]

If Stephens and Catherwood were not familiar with the substantive accounts published in the mid-to-late 1830s, they nonetheless

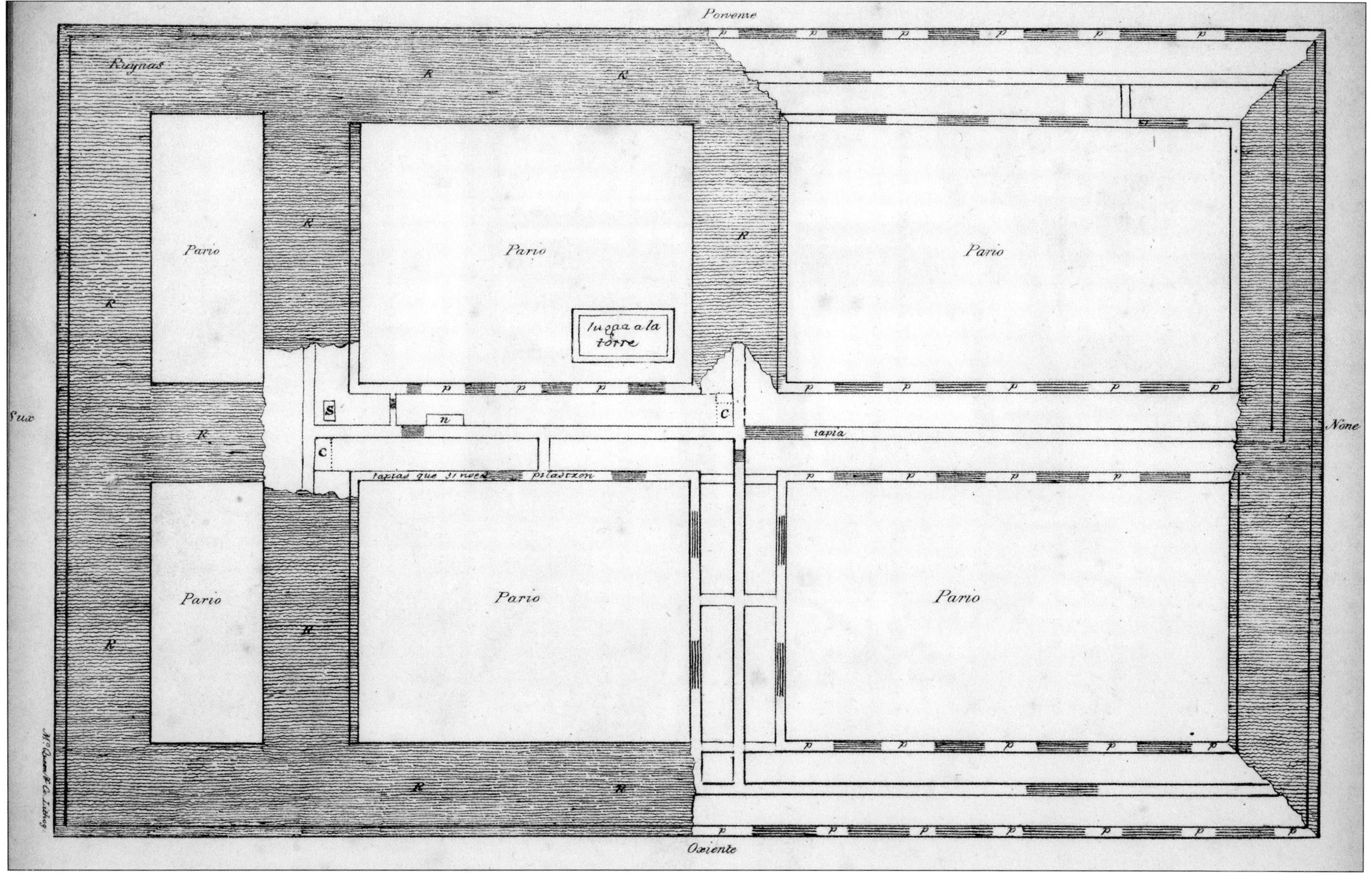

3.3. *Facing page:* Orientation view and key, *Explanation of a View of the City of Mexico, exhibiting in the Panorama, Leicester Square*, engraving, John Burford and Robert Burford and (unattributed) William Bullock, Jr., *Description of a View of the City of Mexico, and surrounding country, now exhibiting at the Panorama, Leicester-Square. Painted by the Proprietors, J. and R. Burford, from drawings taken in the summer of 1823, Brought to this Country, by Mr. W. Bullock* (London: Printed by J. and C. Adlard, 1826), upper panel, 10 x 40.5 cm; lower panel, 10 x 40.5 cm. [Reproduced by permission of Cambridge University Library.]

knew of three sites which they intended to visit when they set out from New York: Copán in Honduras, Tecpán Guatemala (referred to as Tecpan Guatimala by Stephens) in Guatemala, and Palenque in Chiapas.[35] Stephens knew of Copán from the history of Guatemala that Domingo Juarros published between 1808 and 1818 which, translated into English by John Baily, had been published in London in 1823.[36] Stephens informs us that Juarros' account of Copán gave them 'a great inducement to visit the ruins'.[37] Stephens also knew of Copán from articles Juan Galindo published in *The Literary Gazette* in 1835 and in *Archæologia Americana* the following year,[38] and knew of Tecpán Guatemala from Juarros which Stephens declared was 'one of the ruined cities we wished to visit'. Moreover, *The Modern Traveller* also described the site as an 'interesting specimen of ancient art'.[39]

Stephens first heard of the third site they intended to visit – Palenque – from a fellow New Yorker, Noah O. Platt, who 'had gone out to Tobasco [*sic*] as supercargo of a vessel, ascended one of the rivers for logwood, and while his vessel was loading visited the ruins'. His account had given Stephens 'a strong desire to visit them long before the opportunity of doing so presented itself'.[40] With such background reading, it is hardly surprising that when it came to publication, Stephens envisaged a market very different to that of traditional antiquarian account. As Stephens observed: 'My object has been, not to produce an illustrated work, but to present the drawings in such an inexpensive form as to place them within reach of the great mass of our reading community.'[41]

The publication of volumes on Mexico and Guatemala in *The Modern Traveller* coincided with the interest generated in England by two exhibitions devoted to Mexico which, opening at the Egyptian Hall in April 1824, were regarded as having 'done not only what no Englishman, but what no European has done before him'.[42] The exhibitions arising from an expedition William Bullock undertook with his son to Mexico the previous year, displayed a wide range of Mexican artefacts and natural fauna where, in the upper gallery, 'science and curiosity' were 'gratified by a collection of extraordinary ancient Monuments', indigenous deities, stone and pottery figures, codexes (both original and copies), and large-scale plaster casts of statuary which Humboldt had first brought to international attention.[43] In the lower gallery, visitors were presented with a form of 'abridged travel' that 'saved a voyage to Santa [*sic*] Cruz, and a journey from that killing climate, by Jalapa and Puebla, to the grand city of Mexico itself'.[44] Silver ore from the mines belonging to the Count of Regla was also exhibited. Three catalogues were printed, one each for the *Ancient Mexico* and *Modern Mexico* exhibitions of 1824, and one for a combined display of both exhibitions the following year. More than 60,000 people attended the exhibitions, including members of the royal family, the Foreign Secretary, George Canning, and Edward King (Lord Kingsborough) who commissioned Agostino Aglio to make one hundred copies of the *Codex Borturini* as part of the display.[45]

The exhibition of a panorama from drawings by William Bullock Jr., *View of the City of Mexico, and Surrounding Country* (3.3), in the Upper Circle of the Panorama, Leicester Square, also contributed to the growth of interest in Mexico, both in London in the mid-1820s and on the east coast of the United States where the panorama of the City of Mexico was exhibited in 1828 in the Rotunda in New York and in Boston.[46] Like the Frontispiece of *Incidents of Travel in Yucatan*, the panorama was taken from an imaginary point composed, on this occasion, from two station points.[47] The first presents a view of the city (in the upper panel) made from the northwest corner of the tower located on the southwest corner of the cathedral, which represents the southwest to the northeast parts of the city.[48] The second station shows a view of the city from the southeast corner of the tower on the southeast corner of the cathedral overlooking the Segraria, an adjacent religious building whose roof dominates the foreground left of the lower panel. The view shows the northeast to the southern parts of the city.[49] Notwithstanding the fact that the two views were drawn from a similar elevation, the view in the upper panel evidences optical distortion in the depiction of the buildings that border the square to the west of the cathedral. Distortion is less evident in the view drawn from the tower on the southeast corner of the cathedral. We know that Bullock took a camera lucida on his expedition to Mexico.[50] Given that the upper panel evidences optical distortion, William Bullock Jr. may

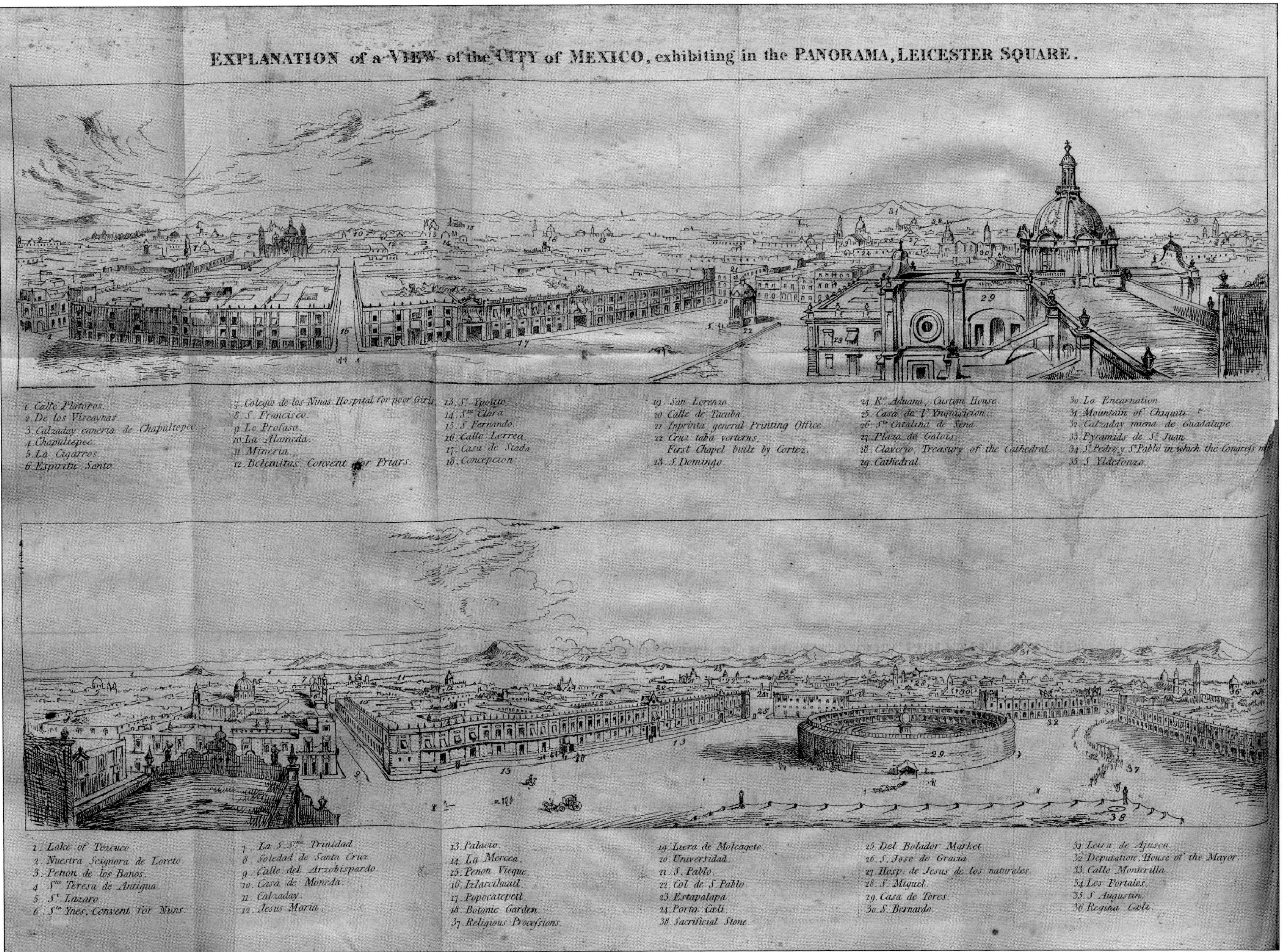
EXPLANATION of a VIEW of the CITY of MEXICO, exhibiting in the PANORAMA, LEICESTER SQUARE.
1. Calle Platoros.
2. De los Viscaynas.
3. Calzaday caneria de Chapultepec.
4. Chapultepec.
5. La Cigarros.
6. Espiritu Santo.
7. Colegio de los Ninas Hospital for poor Girls.
8. S. Francisco.
9. Le Profaso.
10. La Alameda.
11. Mineria.
12. Belemitas Convent for Friars.
13. St. Ypolito.
14. Sta. Clara.
15. S. Fernando.
16. Calle Lerrea.
17. Casa de Stada.
18. Concepcion.
19. San Lorenzo.
20. Calle de Tacuba.
21. Inprinta, general Printing Office.
22. Cruz taba verterus, First Chapel built by Cortez.
23. S. Domingo.
24. Re. Aduana, Custom House.
25. Casa de l' Ynquisicion.
26. Sta. Catalina de Sena.
27. Plaza de Galois.
28. Claverio, Treasury of the Cathedral.
29. Cathedral.
30. La Encarnation.
31. Mountain of Chiquiti.
32. Calzaday mena de Guadalupe.
33. Pyramids de St. Juan.
34. St. Pedro y St. Pablo in which the Congress m
35. S. Yldefonzo.
1. Lake of Tezcuco.
2. Nuestra Seignora de Loreto.
3. Penon de los Banos.
4. Sto. Teresa de Antigua.
5. St. Lazaro.
6. Sta. Ynes, Convent for Nuns.
7. La S. Sma. Trinidad.
8. Soledad de Santa Cruz.
9. Calle del Arzobispardo.
10. Casa de Moneda.
11. Calzaday.
12. Jesus Maria.
13. Palacio.
14. La Mercea.
15. Penon Vieque.
16. Izlaccihuatl.
17. Popocatepetl.
18. Botanic Garden.
37. Religious Procefsions.
19. Liera de Molcagete.
20. Universidad.
21. S. Pablo.
22. Col. de S. Pablo.
23. Estapalapa.
24. Porta Cœli.
38. Sacrificial Stone.
25. Del Bolador Market.
26. S. Jose de Gracia.
27. Hosp. de Jesus de los naturales.
28. S. Miguel.
29. Casa de Tores.
30. S. Bernardo.
31. Leira de Ajusco.
32. Deputation, House of the Mayor.
33. Calle Monterilla.
34. Les Portales.
35. S. Augustin.
36. Regina Cœli.

have employed a convex mirror (or similar device) in conjunction with the camera lucida to make the drawing,[51] which process, compensating for what may have been an obstructed or partial view from the tower, inscribed distortion in the drawing and, presumably, the finished panorama.

The combination of exhibitions in the Egyptian Hall, the panorama of Mexico City, and the publication of Bullock's travel account, *Six Months' Residence and Travels in Mexico*, in summer 1824 stimulated a lively interest in a country whose borders, after Mexico gained independence from Spain in 1821, were open for the first time '[s]ince the period of Charles II', according to *The Literary Gazette*.[52] Interest was so great that the first edition of 1500 copies 'was subscribed ... by the London booksellers on the first day of publication'.[53] The rush to exploit the opportunities that Mexico and the newly-created Central American Federation represented, led *The Literary Gazette* to liken Bullock to a second Hernán Cortés who 'arrived when the flood-gates were opened for the first time during centuries ... [when] our most innovating Countryman was allowed to ransack the superb Capital of Mexico'.[54] Bullock's interventions coincided with the sale of Mexican government bonds post-independence which promised an annual return of eight per cent compared with a return of three per cent or less on the declining rate of British government stocks. Interest in Mexico as an investment opportunity fuelled speculation in joint stock companies that sought to acquire shares in Mexican silver mines, creating a short-lived financial bubble.[55] By the mid-1820s, interest in Mexico and the heady mix that geopolitical change brought about was considerable. As Bullock anticipated, when Britain recognised Mexico's independence in 1825:

> Nothing is now wanting, in my opinion, to re-establish the prosperity of this fine country, but an acknowledgement of its independence by Great Britain. That it is for ever severed from the mother-country I have not the smallest doubt: but in its present state it may yet linger, from the debility to which it is reduced by the revolution, for years, unless cherished by our assistance, with which it would shortly rise and be again in opulence and productiveness – the result of which, to Great Britain, can scarcely be calculated.[56]

In short, by the mid-1820s, Mexico and Central America represented rich pickings for investors, opportunists, and adventurers alike, modern travellers *par excellence*:

> On the 1st of January, 1825, Mr. Canning is stated to have communicated to all the foreign ministers at the English court, that the cabinet of his Britannic Majesty had come to the resolution of acknowledging the independence of the Republics of Mexico and Colombia, and that the commissioners would be sent to those states, charged with full powers to conclude treaties of commerce between them and this country, founded on that recognition. ... This important act of the British Government will not be more conducive to the commercial prosperity of our own country, than to the stability of the Mexican Republic.[57]

The discourse of investigation before Stephens and Catherwood

The opportunities which independence represented for financial speculation set the tone for the opening of the account of Palenque in *The Modern Traveller*, which described a *topos* that would repay investigation:

> Near the village of *San Domingo Palenque* [*sic*] on the borders of Yucatan, are considerable vestiges of an Indian capital, which was accidentally discovered about the middle of the last century, in the midst of a fertile and salubrious tract of country, almost entirely depopulated. These remains, although both their antiquity and architectural beauty have been absurdly magnified, are highly interesting, and merit the attention of future travellers. 'This metropolis,' says Don Domingo Juarros, the historian of Guatimala [*sic*], 'like another Herculaneum, not indeed overwhelmed by the torrent of another Vesuvius, but concealed for ages in the midst of a vast desert, remained unknown until the middle of the eighteenth century, when some Spaniards having penetrated the drear solitude, found themselves, to their great astonishment, within sight of the remains of what had once been a superb city, six leagues in circumference.'[58]

The source, Juarros' *A Statistical and Commercial History of the Kingdom of Guatemala in Spanish America*, announced that Palenque had lain 'concealed for ages'. Similar to the characterisation of Bullock in *The Literary Gazette*, *The Modern Traveller* offered readers, latter-day armchair 'conquistadors', the opportunity of 'discovering' Palenque for themselves. Thereafter, *The Modern Traveller* turned to del Río's report in a more sober fashion.

After the opening passage, *The Modern Traveller* provides a brief account of the clearing of the forest, an account of excavations, and a description of the site drawn from del Río. Compared with Waldeck's account of Uxmal, del Río provides a matter-of-fact description of Palenque. In this regard, attention is given to the orientation of structures and their spatial relation to each other. Measurements are provided, but little indication is given of del Río's response, although conjecture on how the architecture of buildings may have been influenced by non-indigenous cultures is proposed.[59] In privileging a description of the site, del Río's account and *The Modern Traveller* are closer in tone to Stephens than Waldeck. A typical example is the description of what is generally known as the Temple of the Inscriptions:

> On an eminence to the south is another edifice, of about forty yards in height, forming a parallelogram, and resembling the first in the style of its architecture. It has square pillars, an exterior gallery, and a saloon twenty yards long by three and a half broad, embellished with stucco medio-reliefs, representing female figures with children in their arms, all of the natural size: ...[60]

Departures from del Río's 1822 report include the removal of human agency, but variation between the two accounts is not substantial; even technical terms such as 'stucco medio-reliefs' are retained in *The Modern Traveller*. What is significant, however, is that both publications refer to the Temple of the Inscriptions as 'a parallelogram', both employ measurement, and both describe the decoration on the facade of the exterior gallery in terms that draw on classical and European models.[61]

Del Río also considers possible influences on the architecture of Palenque,[62] before proposing that if attention is given to the bas-reliefs:

> we seem to view the idolatry of the Phœnicians, the Greeks, the Romans and other primitive nations most strongly pourtrayed [*sic*]. On this account it may reasonably be conjectured, that some one of these nations pursued their conquests even to this country, where it is probable they only remained long enough to enable the Indian tribes to imitate their ideas and adopt, in a rude and awkward manner, such arts as their invaders thought fit to inculcate.[63]

Unlike del Río, conjecture regarding Old World influence is not included in *The Modern Traveller*. The guide-book neither acknowledges a family resemblance between the architecture of Palenque and that of ancient Egypt (which Juarros proposed),[64] nor suggests that contact with Mediterranean cultures may have influenced the builders of Palenque, a possibility which del Río entertained. Rather, *The Modern Traveller* concludes its discussion of the site with a provocative proposal:

> The province of Chiapa [*sic*] would thus seem to have received its aboriginal population from the same source as the peninsular of Yucatan; and if the language spoken by the Indians should prove to be Maya, (a point which we must look to some future traveller to ascertain,) there will be no room for hesitation in referring to these monuments of ancient civilisation to a race distinct from the Aztec, and bearing more affinity to the Zapotec Indians of Oaxaca.[65]

Unlike Juarros, unlike del Río, and unlike the only notice which del Río's account attracted at the time of publication,[66] *The Modern Traveller* recognised the significance of the architecture of Palenque: that it was distinct from the example of Aztec practice, having more in common with Zapotec culture, and was also distinct from non-indigenous cultures. Such a claim is not encountered again until Stephens and Catherwood visited the region. *The Modern Traveller*, in other words, proposed a bold interpretation of cultural influence, one with which Stephens would have been familiar when he and Catherwood visited the site fifteen years later.

Before turning to Stephens and Catherwood, investigations by Juan Galindo in the early and mid-1830s are briefly considered,[67] and a further party (the Walker-Caddy expedition) to Palenque is also considered, particularly since the party arrived at the site three months before Stephens and Catherwood.[68] Led by Patrick Walker, a colonial administrator in British Honduras (present-day Belize),[69] the investigation was undertaken with Lieutenant John Caddy of the Royal Artillery who had studied at the Royal Military Academy in Woolwich.[70] His background in surveying and drawing reflected a training similar to that which Catherwood received as an architectural apprentice.

Little is known of Galindo's early career other than that he was born in Dublin in 1802 where his English father (of Spanish descent) and Irish mother worked as actors having been engaged for a period in the 1790s with the Theatre Royal, Bath.[71] In 1818 Galindo joined Lord Cochran's Liberationist force and crossed the Atlantic, and may have seen service in South America. By 1827, Galindo had moved to Guatemala where he was employed as secretary and translator at the British consulate.[72] In April 1831 he visited Palenque, from where he corresponded with *The Literary Gazette* and the Société de Géographie in Paris.[73] The publication of Galindo's correspondence to *The Literary Gazette* in October 1831 caused a modest stir.[74] The following year, Galindo wrote a short paper which included discussion of the Palacio at Palenque for the Royal Geographical Society, which was read to the Society in November 1832 and published in its journal in 1834.[75] In May and June 1834, Galindo surveyed and prepared a report on the Honduran site of Copán for the government of Central America before being granted, in August 1834, an extensive tract of land for development by colonisation in Petén, the most northern department of Guatemala.[76]

Typically, Galindo employed a procedure familiar from del Río: he provided a detailed description of structures at a given site. Discussing the site of Palenque in 1831, for example, Galindo provided readers with orientation and the measurement of structures.[77] Unlike his predecessors, however, Galindo observed that 'the architects avoided symmetry, not from ignorance but design', a remark which indicates that he did not automatically assume that Maya antiquities should be compared with European or classical models.[78] He also noted that surviving bas-reliefs at the site evidenced a physiognomy similar to the indigenous people of the region, remarking that 'the Maya language is derived from them'.[79] Such observations were not only insightful, but were known to Stephens and Catherwood when they investigated the site in 1840.

In correspondence to *The Literary Gazette* in March 1834 concerning the Maya site at Copán, Honduras, Galindo drew readers' attention to the fact that the site was occupied at the time of the conquest when the Spanish had been 'so careless of every thing except gain'.[80] After describing the topography of the site, bound by a cliff some thirty metres high caused by erosion from the river on the site's eastern boundary, Galindo relates how he investigated a temple:

> Through a gallery, scarcely 4 feet high and 2½ broad, one can crawl from this square [in the temple complex] through a more elevated part of the temple overhanging the river, and have from the face of the precipice an interesting view.
>
> Among many excavations I have made one at the point where this gallery comes out into the square. I first opened into the entrance of the gallery itself, and digging lower down I broke into a sepulchral vault, whose floor is 12 feet below the level of the square. It is more than 6 feet high, 10 feet long, and 5½ broad, and lies due north and south according to the compass; it has two niches on each side, and both these and the floor of the vault were full of red earthenware dishes and pots. I found more than 50, many of them full of human bones packed with lime; ...[81]

The account mixes details of his activities with their respective outcomes: crawling out of the gallery, Galindo chances upon a precipice overlooking the river from where he sees 'an interesting view'; 'digging lower down I broke into a sepulchral vault'. Action is thus interwoven with details of what Galindo saw or discovered, a process that helped orient the reader's conceptualisation of space, requiring readers to visualise what Galindo saw and, in so doing, emulate his process of deduction. Rather than having spatial relations specified through measurement, orientation, or visual illustration, readers were provided with sufficient information to imagine the site themselves. In short, Galindo's writing rhymed information with visualisation to stimulate a reader's powers of imagination.

A similar process is evident in the accounts that Walker and Caddy wrote of their investigations at Palenque. In the official report, Walker described a hypothetical reader who he guided through the site: 'Passing through the centre of this Portico [of the Palacio] you descend seven steep steps into the first Court Yard ... Crossing the Court Yard you ascend into the opposite Portico ...'.[82] Elsewhere, Walker implicated the reader in the interpretation he offered by employing the first person: '... from the similar habit of the Egyptian race from whom I have ventured to deduce the origin of this place[,] we may conclude that they [the temples] answered the double purpose of habitation for the living and receptacles for the dead', a deduction that was confirmed by evoking the melancholic function that ruins typically represented for tourists of the picturesque: 'the memory of those who once inhabited them has passed away like a sound, offering a marvellous check to proud ambition and shewing [*sic*] the short lived tenure of human glory'.[83]

If Walker reflects on mutability, Caddy's description follows a less sentimental itinerary. Like del Río, Caddy provides a plan of the site,[84] establishes the orientation of structures and their approximate spatial relation to each other, as in the case of the Temple of the Inscriptions:

> Descending the pyramidal base of the Palace from the S.W. corner of it, and continuing in that direction for about 60 yards you come to the base of another structure and ascending about 100 yards up a very steep slope, you come to the walls of the building No. 2 [Temple of the Inscriptions].[85]

Although Caddy refers to hieroglyphs (which neither del Río nor *The Modern Traveller* mention), he, like del Río, employs architectural terms ('pyramidal base', 'apartments', 'corridor'). His plan of the Palace, like del Río's, also presents a symmetry which the Palace does not possess.[86] Like Walker and Galindo, Caddy adopts a first-person account, as when he climbed the tower of the Palace:

> I climbed to the top of this structure and into the upper apartment which is similar to the lower. I imagine from the appearance of the top of the Tower that it has been much higher than it is at present, but how the communication from one story to another took place I cannot say, as it could not be by the stair cases in their present state.[87]

When confronted with bas-reliefs, the interpretation of which was open to conjecture, Caddy interprets gesture and body language in a manner similar to Waldeck at Uxmal, assuming that cultural conventions are universal and that interpretation need not take cultural difference into account.

Although Caddy and Walker had no prior experience of antiquarian investigation, Caddy's training at the Royal Military Academy instilled a procedure for surveying the site. In this respect, the emphasis on surveying and drawing, as we observed in the previous chapter, demonstrates that belief in the communicative power of images occupied a privileged position in the production of knowledge in the late eighteenth and early nineteenth centuries. Caddy's military training, in other words, not only established protocols for investigating the site, even when he had no prior experience of archaeological investigation, but also identifies procedures that Caddy shared with Catherwood. In this regard, Caddy and Catherwood departed from the practice of antiquarian investigators in the previous century many of whom supplied picturesque details of the local population for their readers.[88] A further similarity is that Catherwood and Caddy also presented material to learned societies, engaging in a process of scholarly debate. While Catherwood's contribution in this regard is considered in the next chapter, on returning to England, Caddy presented his work at the Society of Antiquaries in London. As the Minute Book of the Society observed, Caddy's drawings were understood to depart from the practice of an earlier generation of writers and antiquarians such as Waldeck and Kingsborough:

> Captain Caddy exhibited to the Society by the hands of John Britton, Esq., a Series of interesting Drawings of ancient Sculpture, etc., from the Palace, Temple, or Pyramid at Palenque in Yucatan, in Central America. – Having the appearance of great accuracy, and varying as they do from others published by Lord Kingsbury [*sic*] and Mons. Waldeck, they are entitled to particular attention to the English Antiquary.[89]

The investigation of antiquities in Central America and Yucatán in the 1830s thus departed significantly from earlier antiquarian practice. For Galindo and Walker and Caddy, this process sought to stimulate the reader's powers of imagination, a concern shared with Stephens and Catherwood as we will observe in Chapter Four.

The reception of Stephens and Catherwood in the early 1840s

The reception accorded Stephens and Catherwood was immediate and overwhelming. Most reviews of their work asserted that the subject of Mesoamerican archaeology could not 'fail to prove an interesting and welcome antiquarian novelty' and that Stephens' writing was forthright and refreshing.[90] *The North American Review* noted the 'never-flagging vivacity and *bonhomie*' of Stephens' writing in its review of *Incidents of Travel in Central America*. In its review of the subsequent volumes on Yucatán, the journal proposed that:

> People do not go wandering over the world in search of philosophy ... The traveller goes to look for something else, and if he brings not home something else, the 'reading public' soon lets him know that he has gone upon a fool's errand. The adventurous spirit, the quick eye, the facile adaptation of mind and body to changing situations and circumstances, the ready tact, the capacity for good-humored, but shrewd and searching, observation, and the knack of describing what has been seen, or done, or suffered, – these are the stock in trade of the voyager to foreign parts, who would make himself acceptable through the pages of a book; and, if he possess these qualities, he may unceremoniously consign philosophy to the learned halls of colleges and the 'dens' of newspaper editors.
>
> ... In short, we maintain that the business of a traveller is to see and describe; and that, as a general rule, the less he meddles with speculation, the better it is for himself and his readers.[91]

Sensing the popular appeal of Stephens' authorial voice, reviewers in Britain responded in similar vein to their colleagues across the Atlantic. Reviewing *Incidents of Travel in Central America*, *The Athenæum* observed that Stephens' writing was '[c]heerful, manly, observant, graphic', and went on to observe that works by Stephens were 'rich in poetical sympathies, because he never indulges in the rhapsody of "Fine writing"'.[92] A similar point was made in a review of *Incidents of Travel in Central America* in *The Quarterly Review*, where Stephens' descriptive powers were thought 'so simply and so effectively given' that 'we would recommend its study to all the *novel-writing public* as an example how much picturesque power is gained by absence of exaggeration, and ambitions of labouring after point'.[93] Such responses mark the decisive break with antiquarian account and philosophical travel which Stephens' writing represented, and suggest the delight that Stephens' work gave the reading public. *The Monthly Review* characterised Stephens as 'a picturesque penman [who] cannot be surpassed for vivacity, good nature, or taking with ease whatever may chance to offer itself, however rough or out-of-the-way the scene'.[94] Although *The Dublin University Magazine* observed that Stephens' reading on the subject appeared 'to have been far from extensive', this helped him avoid 'idle and baseless conjectures', so making his account of antiquities in Yucatán of 'superior archaeological value to his previous work'.[95]

Probably the most enthusiastic (and certainly the most reflective) assessment of Stephens' contribution to Mesoamerican investigation appeared in *The North American Review*:

> [W]e have thought it to be due to him to point out particularly the ample additions he has made to the existing knowledge on this exceedingly attractive subject. This is its merit, and this is what, in the present little advanced stage of the investigation, is much the most to be desired. The merit of philosophical analysis of, and deduction from, the facts, the work certainly has not; and it must be owned, that it were to be wished the writer had approached his task with better preparation of whatever there is, that may be properly called learning, bearing upon it. It is likely that among the things that fell under his notice, there were some either not recorded, or passed lightly over, which, then would have assumed a different importance in his view, and analogies yet unobserved would have suggested themselves to his mind. But the observations which he has reported are a rich fund for thought, and the minuteness of his descriptions, and their coincidence (to which we have alluded) with those of independent witnesses, as well as their manifest good faith, are conclusive vouchers for their substantial accuracy.[96]

The concern with the accuracy of Stephens' observations was a matter which a number of reviews addressed, particularly when assessing Catherwood's contribution to the projects. Reviewing the Yucatán volumes, *The Monthly Review* observed that 'without the prints from Mr. Catherwood's drawings, the proper effect of the letter-press matter cannot be conveyed',[97] an observation that acknowledged the power that the engravings conferred on Stephens' text. As William H. Prescott opined, Stephens' anecdotal style was to be welcomed not only because it did *not* attempt to make hypotheses or speculate in the manner typical of 'mushrooming, made-up antiquarians', but because it also demonstrated that 'the real value of the work lies in the drawings and the simple descriptions of the ruins'.[98] In similar vein, *The Athenæum* was of the opinion that nowhere would the reader 'find a scene more impressive to the eye or engaging to the fancy',[99] a review which acknowledged that the printed page stimulated the eye as much as the reader's mental engagement. As *Chambers's Edinburgh Journal* remarked:

> As a whole, the work before us, by its *drawings* and details, for the first time *establishes* the truth respecting what many men had come to regard as merely as a fit subject for a newspaper joke – ancient American cities have been regularly resuscitated in these journals, and as regularly consigned to fresh oblivion, once every five years during the last half century.[100]

Quoting (and amending) Stephens, *The Quarterly Review* outlined the process by which the images were made, noting that nothing was added 'to produce effect as pictures':

> 'Our great object,' says Mr. Stephens, 'was to procure true copies, adding nothing to produce effect as pictures. Mr. Catherwood took all the outlines with the camera lucida, and divided his paper into sections, so as to preserve the utmost accuracy of proportion. The plates are, in my opinion, as true copies as can be presented, and except the stone [*sic*] themselves, the reader cannot have better materials for speculation and study.' The illustrations are indeed admirable ...[101]

Elaborating on the accuracy of the engravings, *The Dublin University Magazine* observed that 'the lively descriptions of Mr. Stephens, and the excellent illustrations of his friend, Mr. Catherwood's pencil, ... form a correct idea of the state and character of these remarkable ruins'.[102] *The Edinburgh Review* proposed that the accuracy of Catherwood's illustrations could be verified by comparing Catherwood's work with the drawings made by Caddy, presumably seen in the presentation of his work at the Society of Antiquaries the previous year:

> The accuracy of Mr Catherwood's drawings is vouched by various circumstances. In general character they correspond with the drawings made by Dupaix, (1805–7,) and are evidently copies of the same originals; although Mr Catherwood had not seen Dupaix's work at the time he made them. The mechanical processes by which the drawings of Mr Catherwood were made, and reduced and transferred to the steel or stone from which the illustrations of Mr Stephens' book are printed, were such as to ensure a high degree of accuracy. And, not to waste time by dwelling upon other corroborative circumstances, we have examined a beautiful set of drawings from the ruins of Palenque, by Captain Caddy of the Royal Artillery, who visited them a few weeks before the present travellers; and which correspond so exactly as to leave no doubt on our minds of the perfect fidelity of Mr Catherwood's pencil.[103]

Comparing Catherwood's work with that of Waldeck, *The North American Review* remarked that '[t]he great error of the professional artists ... is to sacrifice fidelity to effect, and it is rare indeed that their efforts present the object in the nakedness of truth'.[104] In comparison with the large-scale lithographs by Waldeck discussed at the opening of this chapter, Catherwood's engravings were deemed to present 'the nakedness of truth'. In reviewing *Incidents of Travel in Yucatan*, *The North American Review* went on to observe that Catherwood's illustrations made the task of describing the ruins largely redundant 'because pages of description would not give an idea so distinct or accurate as a single glance at one of Mr. Catherwood's drawings'.[105] By noting that Catherwood achieved this at 'a single glance', *The North American Review* aligned Catherwood's engravings with a discourse that embraced the prevailing orthodoxy of the day: that panoramic views and topographical images epitomised the *coup d'œil*. By marrying image with text and stimulating the reader's imagination, Stephens and Catherwood established the contours of a fashionable activity, one where picturesque ruins could be inspected by dapper young men armed with appropriate optical devices:

> Hereafter it may become fashionable to visit Copan, and 'eager as lying' to run down to Palenque. Pic-nic [*sic*] parties may be viewed 'seated in the pleasant shade' of those trees which have overgrown the ruins of the former, and nice young men be observed squinting through eye-glasses at the hieroglyphs on the crumbling walls of the latter.[106]

Such a vision implies a tourist of the picturesque intent on close inspection, yet one who also embodies the modern traveller in the guise of the *flâneur*. Just as Stephens sought to place inexpensive drawings 'within reach of the great mass of our reading community', the interest they generated promoted flights of fancy, as the article in *The New York World* demonstrates. This process is examined more closely in Chapter Four.

Chapter Four

Picturing antiquities in Central America and Yucatán in the 1840s: Stephens and Catherwood

'We live in an age whose spirit is to discard phantasms and arrive at truth ...'. John Lloyd Stephens.[1]

At this distance in time it may be difficult to appreciate the degree to which Stephens' accounts of travel in Central America and Yucatán challenged earlier narratives and the conventions of antiquarian writing. Artists such as John Caddy and Frederick Catherwood, as observed in the previous chapter, presented their work publicly. Such opportunities required, at the very least, a forum where investigations could be debated, a facility which did not exist in New York before the American Ethnological Society was established in the winter of 1842.[2] As observed earlier, Stephens had contact with a group of like-minded people in New York, including the historian, William H. Prescott, and the antiquarian booksellers, John R. Bartlett and Charles Welford, who acted as, respectively, Corresponding Secretary and Recording Secretary of the American Ethnological Society. Article I of the Society's Constitution, adopted on 7 December 1844, announced that 'The objects of this Society shall comprise inquiries into the origin, progress, and characteristics of the various races of man', an objective which, at the Society's first meeting, was 'felt to be of daily increasing moment in relation to the commercial and maritime interests of the nation, the missionary enterprise, the study of comparative philology, and many other objects of practical utility'.[3] Founding members of the Society included Stephens, Catherwood, and Brantz Mayer, and Edward Robinson and Henry R. Schoolcraft acted as vice-presidents.[4] Albert Gallatin, President of the Society, prepared an ambitious paper summarising knowledge concerning Mesoamerica which was published in the first volume of the Society's *Transactions*.[5] Running to 352 pages, Gallatin's essay considered indigenous languages, numerical and calendar systems, and Mesoamerican cosmology. The essay also provided a cultural history of Mexico, Yucatán, and Central America, and reflected on the origins of its indigenous population. Corresponding members on whose work Gallatin drew included contacts Stephens had established in Yucatán: Tomás Estanislas Carilla, the cura of Ticul, and Juan Pío Pérez, the *jefe político* of the district of Peto.[6] The first issue of the *Transactions* also published articles by Catherwood on archaeological investigations at Dougga and Bless in Tunisia in the early 1830s.[7] What characterises contributors to the *Transactions* was their readiness to draw on personal observation. This practice typified the approach of Stephens and Catherwood. In February 1844, Catherwood presented a paper at the Royal Institute of British Architects,[8] and two months later, he published a folio of twenty-five chromolithographs in London, printed by Owen Jones, with an introductory essay and map: *Views of Ancient Monuments in Central America Chiapas and Yucatan* (hereafter, *Views of Ancient Monuments*). The work was published in an edition of three hundred copies priced at five guineas, and a small number of hand-coloured sets could be purchased at twelve guineas. Bartlett and Welford took copies for sale at their bookshop in New York.[9]

Three principal interests are addressed in this chapter. The first, developing discussion in the first two chapters, considers the discourse of the picturesque, and the interest in topography and the panorama which Stephens and Catherwood variously demonstrate.[10] Second, consideration is given to the articulation of space in the two principal works on which Stephens and Catherwood collaborated, an analysis which attends to the relation of descriptive text and engravings on the printed page, and proposes that their publications presented a popular example of media convergence in the nineteenth century. In the final part of the chapter, the concern for what Stephens termed 'traditionary knowledge' is briefly discussed.

All-embracing views and picturesque travel in Stephens and Catherwood

In Chapter One we considered the manner in which the tradition of the topographical view was reflected in Catherwood's Frontispiece of the Casa del Gobernador in *Incidents of Travel in Yucatan*. Interest in the panorama, we observed, also informed Stephens' and Catherwood's response to landscape when, towards the end of their second expedition, they viewed the land and sea from the Castillo at Tulum. The delight in panoramic views is evident elsewhere in their work. Exploring the site of Uxmal at the end of their first expedition, Stephens reported that one of the structures (the Casa de las Tortugas) 'stands nearly in the centre of the ruins, and the top commands a view all round of singular but wrecked magnificence'.[11] On their second expedition to Uxmal, Stephens noted that on their earlier visit, he and Catherwood had climbed onto the roof of the Casa de las Tortugas, 'and selected it as a good position from which to make a panoramic sketch of the whole field of ruins'.[12] Although a panoramic view from the building was never published, engravings from other structures at the site, considered below, present extended views of the ruins. The most remarkable panoramic view in which Stephens delighted was encountered on the first expedition. From the crater of the volcano of Cartago in Costa Rica,[13] Stephens commanded a view that embraced the Atlantic and Pacific oceans, and commented on the aerial perspective that the volcano afforded:

> The lofty point on which we stood was perfectly clear, the atmosphere was of transparent purity, and looking beyond the region of desolation, below us, at a distance of perhaps two thousand feet, the whole country was covered with clouds, and the city at the foot of the volcano was visible. By degrees the more distant clouds were lifted, and over the immense bed we saw at the same moment the Atlantic and the Pacific Ocean. This was the grand spectacle we had hoped, but scarcely expected to behold. ... The points at which they were visible were the Gulf of Nicoya and the harbour of San Juan, not directly opposite, but nearly at right angles to each other, so that we saw them without turning the body. In a right line over the tops of the mountains neither was more than twenty miles distant, and from the height at which we stood they seemed almost at our feet. It is the only point in the world which commands a view of the two seas.[14]

Stephens not only revelled in what must have been an extraordinary experience, one which did not even require him to turn his body, but also provided a remarkable *coup d'œil*, imparting intense aesthetic pleasure. Little wonder that Stephens could write that he and Catherwood, 'neither sentimental, nor philosophical, nor moralizing travellers',[15] were moved profoundly in response to the Sublime, understood as the expression of noble or awe-inspiring ideas, a response which painted panoramas also fuelled.

Compared with this experience, most of the other occasions that evoked the discourse of picturesque travel in Stephens' accounts are less grand. In Guatemala, Stephens drew comparison between the valley of the río Motagua with English parkland when, observing cattle grazing on a hillside, he remarked that 'we descended upon a table of rich land, and saw a gate opening into grounds which reminded me of park scenery in England, undulating, and ornamented with trees'.[16] As observed in Chapter Two, European and North American visitors to Mexico remarked on landscapes that suggested natural amphitheatres, a comparison which reminded Stephens of Trenton Falls, New Jersey, when he observed, in similar vein to Gilpin, that 'the mountains closed around us and formed an amphitheatre'.[17] While landscape could inspire a sense of the Sublime for Stephens, a view of the natural landscape also promoted a more conventional response, reminiscent of Gilpin's discussion of side screens, when Stephens and Catherwood approached the town of Panajachel on Lago de Atitlán in Guatemala:

> Our first view of the lake was the most beautiful we had ever seen, but this surpassed it. All the requisites of the grand and beautiful were there; gigantic mountains, a valley of poetic softness, lake, and volcanoes, and from the height on which we stood a waterfall marked a silver line down its sides. A party of Indian men and women were moving in single file

> from the foot of the mountain toward the village, and looked like children. The descent was steep and perpendicular, and, reaching the plain, the view of the mountain-walls was sublime. As we advanced the plain formed a triangle with its base on the lake, the two mountain ranges converged to a point, and communicated by a narrow defile beyond with the village of San Andres.[18]

By the 1840s, the observation of indigenous people performing quotidian chores had also become a convention in written and pictorial discourse: women filling water-jars (*cantaros*) rarely ceased to provide an 'animated picture' or an 'animated spectacle' for tourists of the picturesque.[19] Encountering John Baily, the translator of Juarros and naval officer on half-pay, scouting a route for a ship canal from San Juan on the Pacific coast to the Atlantic,[20] Stephens closed the first volume of *Incidents of Travel in Central America* with an emblematic scene on the shore of Lake Nicaragua:

> In the afternoon, in company with Mr. Bailey [*sic*] and Mr. Wood, I walked down to the lake. At the foot of the street by which we entered, built out into the lake, was an old fort, dismantled, and overgrown with bushes and trees, a relic of the daring Spaniards who first drove the Indians from the lake; probably the very fortress that Cordova built, and in its ruins beautifully picturesque. Under the walls, and within the shade of the fort and trees growing near it, the Indian women of Grenada [*sic*] were washing; garments of every colour were hanging on the bushes to dry and waving in the wind; women were wading out with their water-jars, passing beyond the breakers to obtain it clear of sand; men were swimming, and servants were bringing horses and mules to drink, all together presenting a beautifully animated picture. There were no boats on the water; but about half a dozen piraguas [canoes], the largest of which was forty feet long, and drew three feet of water, were lying on the shore.[21]

The 'animated picture' of *piraguas* on the shore of the lake with women filling their *cantaros*, contrasts sharply with the vision that Stephens entertained when he arrived at a 'station' that Baily had established two years earlier when surveying Nicaragua: 'Looking back, I saw the two great mountain ranges, standing like portals, and could but think what a magnificent spectacle it would be to see a ship, with all its spars and rigging, cross the plain, pass through the great door, and move on to the Pacific.'[22] Fantasising about a ship canal across Central America, Stephens imagined a scene that departed strikingly from the tenor in which the investigation of antiquities on his travels in Central America was written. If discussion demonstrates that Stephens was familiar with the conventions of the picturesque, his response to landscape also demonstrates that all-embracing views spanning the coasts of Costa Rica highlight a quite different response, one more in keeping with the emotional charge of an artist such as Frederic Edwin Church who depicted the volcanic landscape of Ecuador in the mid-to-late 1850s.

Investigators in the first half of the nineteenth century discussed in the last chapter privileged measurement. We know that apart from the camera lucida, Stephens and Catherwood took 'watches, compass, chronometer, thermometer, telescope, &c.' on the expedition to Central America;[23] on their expedition to Yucatán, villagers in Nohcacab responded to Catherwood's drawing materials of tripod, sextant, and compass with suspicion.[24] The instruments Stephens and Catherwood used were typical of the period. When surveying the site of Copán, Stephens informs us:

> Our surveying apparatus was not very extensive. We had a good surveying compass, and the rest consisted in a reel of tape which Mr. C. had used in a survey of the ruins of Thebes and Jerusalem. My part of the business was very scientific. I had to direct the Indians in cutting straight lines through the woods, make Bruno and Frederico stick their hats on poles to mark the stations, and measure up to them.[25]

Two pages of the sale catalogue for Catherwood's library detail the 'philosophical instruments' that were auctioned on the first day of the sale.[26] Although instruments that Catherwood acquired subsequent to expeditions with Stephens were included in the sale, details of surveying instruments such as those employed on the two expeditions are provided: 'two off-set staffs' (item #320), a 'surveying instrument, on iron tripod' (item #321), a quadrant (item #322), and 'a jointed tripod, with drawing board attached' (item #323), possibly the table on which Catherwood would have attached his camera lucida.[27] A surveyor's compass, an instrument closely related to a circumferentor (4.1), two surveying staffs, and a reel of tape were the principal instruments Stephens and Catherwood used to survey archaeological sites such as Copán, where the party spent three days surveying the site.[28] With these instruments, Catherwood mapped sites, plotted structures, and, with his camera lucida, drew structures and sketched sites investigated on the two expeditions.

Interest in measurement *per se* was not particularly new, as del Río and other investigators considered in the last chapter demonstrate. What was new, however, was that measurement was no longer privileged over pictorial imagination, as the tradition of representing the ruins of Rome as *capricci* by the eighteenth-century French artist, Hubert Robert, demonstrates.[29] Historical information and ethnographic digression, concerns favoured by antiquarian investigators, were also to a degree discounted; rather, as Stephens observed: 'I have purposely abstained from all comment.'[30] If one compares the work of Stephens and Catherwood with investigations undertaken by members of the Society of Dilettanti half a century earlier, the transformation of interest is apparent. Eighteenth-century British antiquarian investigators such as James Stuart and Nicholas Revett, providing historical and ethnographic detail in the letterpress that accompanied prints, reflected a concern for the picturesque, as observed in Chapter Three. Such discourse makes a revealing comparison with the *Description* for the panorama of Jerusalem considered in Chapter One. In place of an exclusive concern with measurement and local ethnographic interest, cartography began to be accorded a status equal to that of measurement. The importance of accuracy in depicting archaeological structures and plotting their spatial relation continued to be reflected in the work of Stephens and Catherwood. However, their travel accounts also demonstrate that such concerns impacted on the popular imagination of readers, consolidating an interest in cartography that attended a more scientifically-informed investigation of antiquities. These concerns provide focus for our discussion of Stephens and Catherwood. While their work acknowledges picturesque convention, their publications also attest to the seismic change that informed archaeological investigation in the mid- to late nineteenth century, a period that witnessed the development of archaeology and history as disciplines in their own right, distinct from antiquarian investigation.[31] Four sites investigated on the two expeditions are selected in this chapter to characterise the early development of this transformation.

4.1. Jonathan Sissons (instrument-maker), eighteenth-century circumferentor, photographed by the author.

Copán

On arriving at Copán, the first thing Stephens and Catherwood undertook was a survey of the site. This included a plan of the site (4.2) and a description which identified structures in a key which, as Stephens explained, assisted 'the reader to understand the description'.[32] By the 1840s, the goals of surveying were understood by the general reader, as *The Illustrated London News* demonstrated when it published an article on the surveying of London:

> In every extensive survey, conducted with a due regard to scientific accuracy, it is a matter of the first importance to determine with unerring correctness the relative distances and bearing of the principal or most conspicuous objects within the country or district to be surveyed. To effect this, the first operation is to measure a 'base line' – that is, a straight or right line between two points, varying in length according to the extent of the survey and the facilities afforded by the

> nature of the ground for the measurement. … The base line being measured, the next step is to connect its extremities by means of angles taken with theodolites or other angular instruments, with all the conspicuous objects visible; the relative distances and bearings of which with each other, and with the base, become thus determinable by means of certain well-known trigonometrical formulæ.[33]

The Illustrated London News described the process which Catherwood would have employed in surveying Copán, a process that plotted the position of landmarks relative to each other and their orientation with regard to the plan of the site.[34] Assuming the role of guide, and referencing the site-plan, Stephens introduced the reader to the site at the mid-point of the plan:

> To begin on the right: Near the southwest corner of the river wall and the south wall is a recess … Beyond are the remains of two small pyramidal structures [marked 'Z' on the plan], to the largest of which is attached a wall running along the west bank of the river; this appears to have been one of the principal walls of the city; and between the two pyramids there seems to have been a gateway or principal entrance from the water.

> The south wall runs at right angles to the river, beginning with a range of steps about thirty feet high, and each step about eighteen inches square. At the southeast corner is a massive pyramidal structure one hundred and twenty feet high on the slope. On the right are other remains of terraces and pyramidal buildings; and here also was probably a gateway [to the south of 'E' on the plan], by a passage about twenty

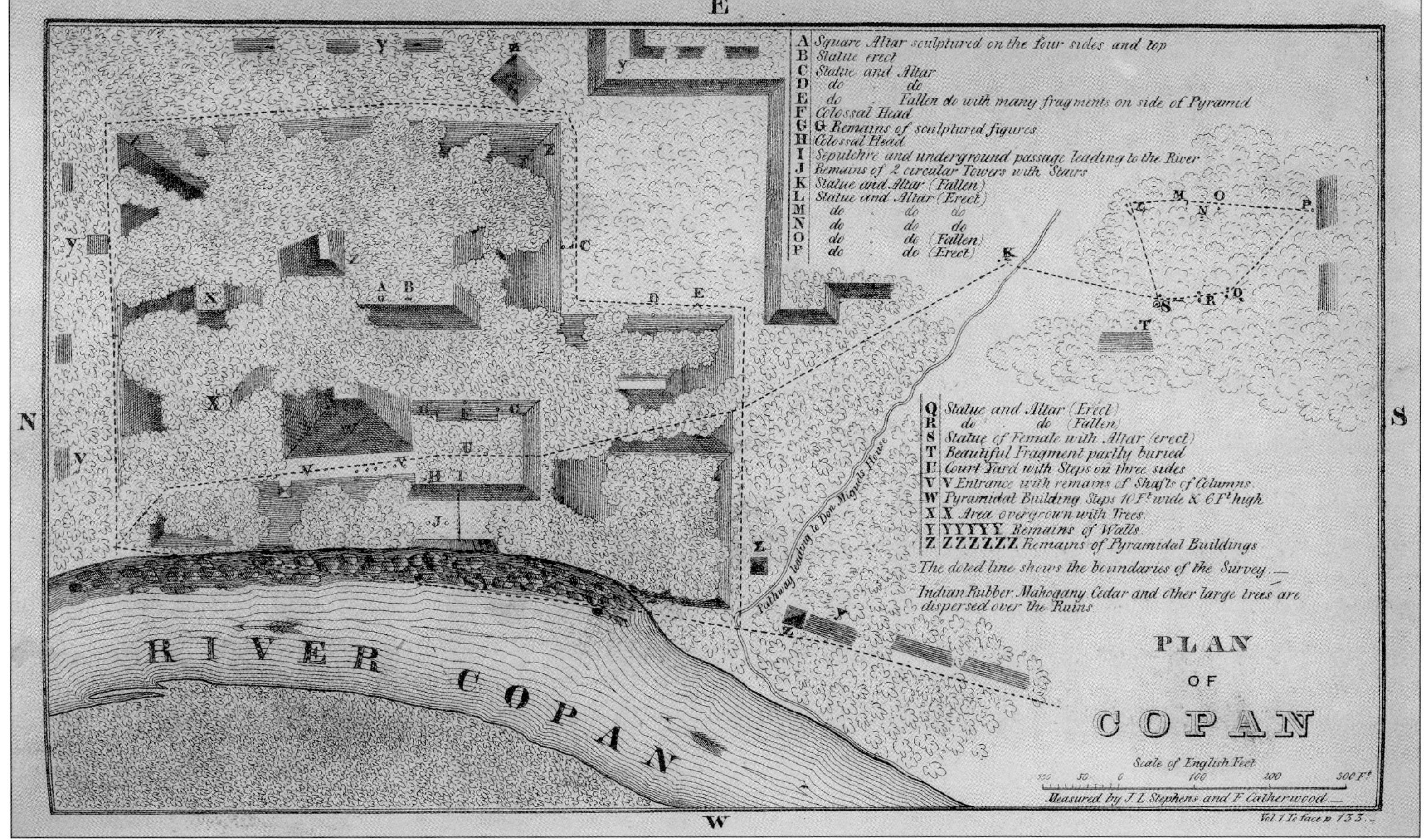

4.2. Frederick Catherwood, engraver unknown, *Plan of Copan Measured by J. L. Stephens and F. Catherwood*, John Lloyd Stephens, *Incidents of Travel in Central America, Chiapas, and Yucatan*, 2 vols. (New York: Harper & Brothers; London: John Murray, 1841), I, facing 133, 11 x 18.2 cm. [Reproduced by permission of Edinburgh University Library, Special Collections, S.B.91(72804)Ste.]

feet wide, into a quadrangular area two hundred and fifty feet square [immediately to the east of 'E' and 'D'], two sides of which are massive pyramids one hundred and twenty feet high on the slope.

At the foot of these structures, and in different parts of the quadrangular area, are numerous remains of sculpture. ...[35]

Although present-day readers may not initially observe the plan's orientation (since, in accordance with the convention of maps in the West, we assume that 'North' lies towards the top of the printed page), once the orientation of the plan has been noted, the letterpress helps the reader negotiate the site with relative ease. Designated structures and monuments act as relays for readers who, interpreting the ichnographic perspective of the plan, are guided around the site by Stephens' commentary. Unlike the conventions for representing steep inclines and lesser gradients considered in Chapter Two, Catherwood adapts hachuring and an ichnographic perspective to imply volume, as discussed in the plan of Jerusalem (Plate 1). This is evident in the case of the pyramidal structure 'W', where three sides of the structure, free of trees and vegetation, imply a projection towards the reader from the plane of the site-plan. Similarly, the area designated 'U' (characterised as a 'Court Yard, with steps on three sides') also denotes a structure that appears to project towards the reader. However, such an interpretation is incorrect since the courtyard, enclosed by terraces on three sides, represents terrain at the same height as the base of 'W'.[36] As Stephens observed: 'The plan was complicated, and, the whole ground being overgrown with trees, difficult to make out. There was no entire pyramid, but, at most, two or three pyramidal sides, and these joined on to terraces or other structures of the same kind.'[37] Stephens' observation may acknowledge the ambivalence observed here.

Having guided the reader through the main structures of the site, Stephens describes the stelae in the upper section of the plan, variously termed 'idols' by Stephens' guide (a term usually employed with quotation marks by Stephens), or referred to, by Stephens, as either a 'stone column', a 'sculptured column', or a 'monument'.[38] The stelae are discussed individually, many of Catherwood's engravings depicting two or more faces so that the reader may infer volume from the juxtaposition of the plates of a particular stela. Drawing the stelae was a particularly difficult process since Catherwood was not only unfamiliar with their iconography, but available light was also often poor: 'The designs were very complicated, and so different from anything Mr. Catherwood had ever seen before as to be perfectly unintelligible. The cutting was in very high relief, and required a strong body of light to bring up the figures; and the foliage was so thick, and the shades so deep, that drawing was impossible.'[39] Nevertheless, a series of detailed engravings of eight stelae was produced. Each stela is described individually by Stephens, the front and back of two stelae, in many instances, being depicted by Catherwood.[40] On three occasions, three faces of a stela are described and illustrated,[41] the description for stela 'P' on the plan (known today as stela D) being typical. Stela 'P':

stands at the foot of a wall rising in steps to the height of thirty or forty feet; originally much higher, but the rest fallen and in ruins. Its face is to the north; its height eleven feet nine inches, the breadth of its sides three feet, and the pedestal is seven feet square. Before it, at a distance of twelve feet, is a colossal altar. It is of good workmanship, and has been painted red, though scarcely any vestige of the paint remains, and the surface is time-worn. The two engravings given opposite represent the front [4.3] and back [4.4] view. The former appears to represent the portrait of a king or hero, perhaps erected into a deity. It is judged to be a portrait, from certain marks of individuality in the features, also observable in most of the others, and its sex is ascertained by the beard, as in the Egyptian monuments, though this has a moustache, which is not found in Egyptian portraits.

The back of this idol, again, presents an entirely different subject, consisting of tablets, each containing two figures oddly grouped together, ill-formed, in some cases with hideous heads, while in others the natural countenance is preserved. The ornaments, diadems, and dresses are interesting, but what these personages are doing or suffering it is impossible to make out. This statue had suffered so much from the action of time and weather, that it was not always easy to make out the characters, the light being in all cases very bad, and coming through irregular openings among the branches of trees.

The stone of which all these altars and statues are made is a soft grit-stone from the quarries before referred to. At the quarries we observed many blocks with hard flint-stones distributed through them, which had been rejected by the workmen after they were quarried out. The back of this monument had contained two. Between the second and third tablets the flint has been picked out, and the sculpture is blurred; the other, in the last row but one from the bottom, remains untouched. An inference from this is, that the sculptor had no instruments with which he could cut so hard a stone, and, consequently, that iron was unknown. We had, of course, directed our searches and inquiries particularly to this point, but did not find any pieces of iron or other metal, nor could we hear of any having ever been

4.3 (left). Frederick Catherwood, engraved by Stephen Henry Gimber, [Stela P, front], John Lloyd Stephens, *Incidents of Travel in Central America, Chiapas, and Yucatan*, 2 vols. (New York: Harper & Brothers; London: John Murray, 1841), I, facing 153, 19 x 11 cm. (maximum image size). [Reproduced by permission of Edinburgh University Library, Special Collections, S.B.91(72804)Ste.]

4.4 (right). Frederick Catherwood, engraved by Henry Jordan, [Stela P, rear], John Lloyd Stephens, *Incidents of Travel in Central America, Chiapas, and Yucatan*, 2 vols. (New York: Harper & Brothers; London: John Murray, 1841), I, facing 153, 18 x 11 cm. (maximum image size). [Reproduced by permission of Edinburgh University Library, Special Collections, S.B.91(72804)Ste.]

found there. Don Miguel had a collection of chay or flint stones, cut in the shape of arrow-heads, which *he* thought, and Don Miguel was no fool, were the instruments employed.[42] They were sufficiently hard to scratch into the stone. Perhaps by men accustomed to the use of them, the whole of these deep relief ornaments might have been scratched, but the chay stones themselves looked as if they had been cut by metal.

4.5. Frederick Catherwood, engraved by Stephen Henry Gimber, [Stela P with altar], John Lloyd Stephens, *Incidents of Travel in Central America, Chiapas, and Yucatan*, 2 vols. (New York: Harper & Brothers; London: John Murray, 1841), I, facing 154, 18.5 x 11.5 cm. (maximum image size). [Reproduced by permission of Edinburgh University Library, Special Collections, S.B.91(72804)Ste.]

The engraving opposite [4.5] represents the altar as it stands before the last monument. It is seven feet square and four feet high, richly sculptured on all its sides. The front represents a death's head. The top is sculptured, and contains grooves, perhaps for the passage of the blood of victims, animal or human, offered in sacrifice. The trees in the engraving give an idea of the forest in which these monuments are buried.[43]

The description instances the methodical way in which Stephens and Catherwood approached the task of documenting the site. Local knowledge and close examination of the site and its immediate surroundings provided Stephens with sufficient information to infer past indigenous practice. Measurement and comparison with other cultures, often drawn from personal observation, also informed the process of interpretation. With evenly-lit stelae occupying most of the height of each plate, set against the forest in the background, the plates served to authenticate Stephens' discussion. In the final plate of stela 'P' (4.5), a detailed view of the altar in front of the stela provides an occasion when the stela is seen against the forest, with headdress, face, chest, and body illuminated by sunlight that falls obliquely on the stela from the right. Whereas the first two plates emphasised the stela, the final plate presents a more dramatic scene, one which, emphasising the location, implies a quite different discourse to that which characterised Stephens' general response to the site, a discourse which Catherwood developed in the chromolithographs he published in *Views of Ancient Monuments*. On the one hand, illustration responded to the concern for depicting the site in a matter-of-fact manner, to provide 'accurate and faithful representations', as in the case of the first two views of the stela;[44] on the other hand, a rather different discourse informed Stephens' response to representing the stela and altar. We return to a consideration of this departure later in the chapter.

Guided by José, a villager from the hacienda estate on which the ruins of Copán stood, Stephens and Catherwood were convinced from the moment they first encountered the monuments that the stelae should be regarded as 'works of art',[45] demonstrating an unknown and independent cultural tradition. Stephens' account also figured an aesthetic response to the site, one which he and Catherwood shared. Stephens proposed, on the one hand, an interpretation of cultural significance which, as R. Tripp Evans and Robert D. Aguirre have argued,[46] enabled Stephens to claim the site as 'American' at a time when the term was evolving as a synonym for the United States, a declaration which denied the proprietary rights of the Central America states, laying bare the region to cultural depredation:

> The sight of this unexpected monument put at rest at once and forever, in our minds, all uncertainty in regard to the character of American antiquities, and gave us the assurance that the objects we were in search of were interesting, not only as the remains of an unknown people, but as works of art, proving, like newly-discovered historical records, that the people who had once occupied the Continent of America were not savages.[47]

On the other hand, Stephens' response was framed in a manner that drew on Picturesque and Romantic discourse, when he commented on the absence of a history of indigenous culture in melancholic fashion:

> The city was desolate. No remnant of this race hangs round the ruins, with traditions handed down from father to son, and from generation to generation. It lay before us like a shattered bark in the midst of the ocean, her masts gone, her name effaced, her crew perished, and none to tell whence she came, to whom she belonged, how long on her voyage, or what caused her destruction; her lost people to be traced only by some fancied resemblance in the construction of the vessel, and, perhaps, never to be known at all. ... All was mystery, dark, impenetrable mystery, and every circumstance increased it.[48]

Stephens also, at times, adopted a discourse associated with sentimental travel when he reflected on 'the moral effect' of the site:

> Of the moral effect of the monuments themselves, standing as they do in the depths of a tropical forest, silent and solemn, strange in design, excellent in sculpture, rich in ornament, different from the works of any other people, their uses and purposes, their whole history so entirely unknown, with hieroglyphics explaining all, but perfectly unintelligible, I shall not pretend to convey any idea. Often the imagination was pained in gazing at them. The tone which pervades the ruins is that of deep solemnity.[49]

The emotional responses which Stephens voices were represented in the five chromolithographs of Copán that Catherwood published in *Views of Ancient Monuments*. In presenting a chromolithograph of stela 'P' (Plate 6), Catherwood drew the stela so that it appeared broader, more stocky, and reduced in height by depicting the stela so that the thighs of the figure coincided with the top of the altar. The shaft of light that lit the stela in *Incidents of Travel in Central America* was replaced in the chromolithograph by a non-naturalistic source seemingly emanating from behind the altar, a source which illuminates the stela from below, creating highlights under the hands, the chin, around the eyes, on the rim of the headdress, and on the headdress itself, accentuating those parts of the bas-relief that stood proud. In short, illumination imparts an unworldly quality to the stela. Relief is achieved in the chromolithograph through tonal contrast and through the organisation of colour towards the rear of the view: a light blue-grey in the upper third of the engraving merges into a predominantly beige-grey colour in the lower part of the chromolithograph, which makes the stela stand out from the steps. White highlights on the altar, on the vegetation at foreground left, and on the tree at foreground right also provide a sense of relief. In short, Catherwood renders stela 'P' in terms which we, after Freud, would characterise as uncanny, stimulating that sense of 'moral effect' and unease which Stephens drew to readers' attention.

The sentimental quality with which Stephens concluded his discussion of Copán is articulated in the second chromolithograph considered here, stela 'O' (known today as stela C):

> At the distance of one hundred and twenty feet north [of 'P'] is the monument marked O, which, unhappily, is fallen and broken [4.6]. In sculpture it is the same with the beautiful half-buried monument before given, and, I repeat it, in workmanship equal to the best remains of Egyptian art. The fallen part was completely bound to the earth by vines and creepers, and before it could be drawn it was necessary to unlace them, and tear the fibres out of the crevices. The paint is very perfect, and has preserved the stone, which makes it more to be regretted that it is broken. The altar is buried, with the top barely visible, which, by excavating, we made out to represent the back of a tortoise.[50]

As depicted in the chromolithograph (Plate 7), the scene presents a violent storm where daylight is much reduced, and the background considerably more detailed than in the engraving reproduced in *Incidents of Travel in Central America*. A pyramidal structure (a *teocallis*), not seen in the 1841 engraving, is observed towards rear centre of the chromolithograph as a flash of lightning renders its depiction more dramatic than the earlier depiction.[51] The lightning also provides the scene with a second source of illumination (in addition to weak sunlight) which picks out, in white, the relief on the fallen monument, casting a shadow over the lower part of the stela and reflections on the water-logged ground across much of the foreground. No such moment or topos is depicted in the 1841 engraving where the stela lies on the ground. Many more trees are visible to the rear left of the scene, and a large flat stone, over which a deer leaps, is absent from the 1841 engraving. A wall behind a tree towards the right of the engraving appears more like an indistinct stela in the chromolithograph. The predominant colours include cream-beige for the stela and foreground subjects, and blue-grey for the clouds and *teocallis* illuminated by the blast of lightning.

In conjunction with the other three views of Copán published in *Views of Ancient Monuments*, Catherwood established a register for depicting the ruins that departed from the measured depiction which previous assessments of Stephens' work have emphasised. Within a short space of time, images such as these began to impact on the popular imagination of mid-nineteenth-century readers. For example, when the figure of Walter Hartright, the drawing-master in Wilkie Collins' epistolary novel, *The Woman in White* (1861), troubles Marian Halcombe in a feverish vision, her vision is described in a manner that evokes Catherwood's illustrations:

4.6. Frederick Catherwood, engraved by Stephen Henry Gimber, [Stela O], John Lloyd Stephens, *Incidents of Travel in Central America, Chiapas, and Yucatan*, 2 vols. (New York: Harper & Brothers; London: John Murray, 1841), I, facing 155, 10 x 19 cm. (maximum image size). [Reproduced by permission of Edinburgh University Library, Special Collections, S.B.91(72804)Ste.]

> The quiet in the house, and the low murmuring hum of summer insects outside the open window, soothed me. My eyes closed of themselves, and I passed gradually into a strange condition, which was not waking – for I knew nothing of what was going on about me, and not sleeping – for I was conscious of my own repose. In this state my fevered mind broke loose from me, while my weary body was at rest, and in a trance, or day-dream of my fancy – I know not what to call it – I saw Walter Hartright. ... He appeared to me as one among many other men, none of whose faces I could plainly discern. They were all lying on the steps of an immense ruined temple. Colossal tropical trees – with rank creepers twining endlessly about their trunks, and hideous stone idols glimmering and grinning at intervals behind leaves and stalk and branches – surrounded the temple and shut out the sky, and threw a dismal shadow over the forlorn band of men on the steps. White exhalations twisted and curled up stealthily from the ground, approached the men in wreaths like smoke, touched them, and stretched them out dead, one by one, in the places where they lay. An agony of pity and fear for Walter loosened my tongue, and I implored him to escape. 'Come back, come back!' I said. 'Remember your promise to *her* and to *me*. Come back to us before the Pestilence reaches you and lays you dead like the rest!'[52]

The sources of Miss Halcombe's dream are diverse. An unsigned article by Henry Morley published in *Household Words* in 1851, a popular weekly journal edited by Charles Dickens, relates:

> from a pillar of broken stone below, the fixed stare of an enormous head encounters us ... We explore farther, and find more and more of these giant stones, elbowed from their places by the growth of trees, some of them buried to the chest in vegetation, staring through the underwood with their blind eyes. ... Who are these gods or heroes buried in the dark recesses of the wood? Who raised their monuments? What Temple, what great city, has existed here? No man can tell. ... These are the ruins of Copan, and tell of a past whose history is effaced.[53]

As a friend of Dickens, as contributor to *Household Words* from early 1852, and a staff writer from 1856, Wilkie Collins would almost certainly have known the article and have been familiar with Stephens' description of the ruins at Copán, particularly Stephens' reference to a 'gigantic head':

> On the left, standing alone, two thirds of the way up the steps, is the gigantic head opposite [4.7]. It is moved a little from its place, and a portion of the ornament on one side has been thrown down some distance by the expansion of the trunk of a large tree, as shown by the drawing. The head is about six feet high, and the style good. Like many of the others, with the great expansion of the eyes it seems intended to inspire awe. ... The whole area is overgrown with trees and encumbered with decayed vegetable matter ...[54]

4.7. Frederick Catherwood, engraved by Stephen Henry Gimber, [Gigantic Head], John Lloyd Stephens, *Incidents of Travel in Central America, Chiapas, and Yucatan*, 2 vols. (New York: Harper & Brothers; London: John Murray, 1841), I, facing 143, 19.5 x 12 cm. (maximum image size). [Reproduced by permission of Edinburgh University Library, Special Collections, S.B.91(72804)Ste.]

An article published in the same journal the previous year refers to *Incidents of Travel in Central America* as 'Stephens's "Central America"', which implies that Stephens' travel account was sufficiently well known that reference could be made to the work in a shortened form.[55] Marion Halcombe's reference to 'stone idols' that glimmer and grin also shares a resemblance with the 'Colossal Head' 'elbowed' from its place 'by the growth of trees' which Henry Morley observed. Such images indicate a popular reputation for Stephens' and Catherwood's work, one fuelled by Catherwood's 1844 chromolithographs which figured the 'moral effect' and 'deep solemnity' that Stephens relates at Copán:

> Of the moral effect of the monuments themselves, standing as they do in the depths of a tropical forest, silent and solemn, strange in design, excellent in sculpture, rich in ornament, different to the works of any other people, their uses and purposes, their whole history so entirely unknown, with hieroglyphics explaining all, but perfectly unintelligible, I shall not pretend to convey any idea. Often the imagination was pained in gazing at them. The tone which pervades the ruins is that of deep solemnity. An imaginative mind might be infected with superstitious feelings.[56]

Catherwood's chromolithographs, in other words, not only framed a response that was widely associated with Central America at mid-century, but also demonstrate the degree to which writing and viewing promoted awe-inspiring fancy (as well as 'truth', to evoke the epigraph for this chapter), responses which, in short, Catherwood's engravings inspired. Although we will briefly return to consider further popular responses Stephens and Catherwood publications inaugurated, for now, let us turn to the second site that prompted extensive discussion in the first expedition to Central America and Yucatán.

Palenque

Palenque presents some of the most complex structures investigated by Stephens and Catherwood.[57] Of the three structures from this site considered here, the first, generally known as the *Palacio* (Palace), constitutes one of the most extensive architectural structures Stephens encountered. An engraving of the *Palacio* provides an initial view (4.8), followed by a ground-plan of the complex:

> A front view of this building is given in the engraving. It does not, however, purport to be given with the same accuracy as the other drawings, the front being in a more ruined condition. It stands on an artificial elevation of an oblong form, forty feet high, three hundred and ten feet in front and rear, and two hundred and sixty feet on each side.[58] This elevation was formerly faced with stone, which has been thrown down by the growth of trees, and its form is hardly distinguishable.
>
> The building stands with its face to the east, and measures two hundred and twenty-eight feet front by one hundred and eighty feet deep. Its height is not more than twenty-five feet, and all around it had a broad projecting cornice of stone. The front contained fourteen doorways, about nine feet wide each, and the intervening piers are between six and seven feet wide. On the left (in approaching the palace) eight of the piers have fallen down, as has also the corner on the right, and the terrace underneath is cumbered with the ruins. But six piers remain entire, and the rest of the front is open.
>
> The engraving opposite represents the ground-plan of the whole [4.9]. The black lines represent walls still standing; the faint lines indicate remains only, but, in general, so clearly marked that there was no difficulty in connecting them together.
>
> The building was constructed of stone, with a mortar of lime and sand, and the whole was covered with stucco and painted ...[59]

After discussing one of the surviving bas-reliefs on the facade of the *Palacio*, Stephens goes on to provide details of the doorways, lintels, and ornamentation on the *Palacio* wall.[60] The reader is provided with a detailed discussion of the complex, one which leads us from the two corridors and main entrance on the east side of the *Palacio* through what is identified on the ground-plan as the Principal Court and the Second Court. This discussion (with interpolation) is provided below. Alongside this account, Stephens also provides insight into the condition of the site as the investigation proceeded:

> The building has two parallel corridors running lengthwise on all four of its sides. In front these corridors are about nine feet wide, and extend the whole length of the building upward of two hundred feet. In the long wall that divides them there is but one door, which is opposite the principal door of entrance, and has a corresponding one on the other side, leading to a courtyard in the rear ['Principal Court']. The floors

4.8. Frederick Catherwood, engraved by John Halpin, *Palace at Palenque*, John Lloyd Stephens, *Incidents of Travel in Central America, Chiapas, and Yucatan*, 2 vols. (New York: Harper & Brothers; London: John Murray, 1841), II, facing 309, 11.3 x 18 cm. [Reproduced by permission of Edinburgh University Library, Special Collections, S.B.91(72804)Ste.]

are of cement, as hard as the best seen in the remains of Roman baths and cisterns. The walls are about ten feet high, plastered, and on each side of the principal entrance ornamented with medallions, of which the borders only remain; these perhaps contained the busts of the royal family. …

From the centre door of this corridor a range of stone steps thirty feet long leads to a rectangular courtyard, eighty feet long by seventy feet broad. On each side of the steps are grim and gigantic figures, carved on stone in basso-relievo, nine or ten feet high, and in a position slightly inclined backward from the end of the steps to the floor of the corridor. The engraving opposite represents this side of the courtyard [4.10], and the one next following shows the figures alone, on a larger scale [4.11]. They are adorned with rich headdresses and necklaces, but their attitude is that of pain and trouble. The design and anatomical proportions of the figures are faulty, but there is a force of expression about them which shows the skill and conceptive power of the artist. When we first took possession of the palace this courtyard was encumbered with trees, so that we could hardly see across it, and it was so filled up with rubbish that we were obliged to make excavations of several feet before these figures could be drawn. …

At the farther side of the courtyard was another flight of stone steps [on the west side of 'Principal Court'], corresponding with those in front, on each side of which are carved figures, and on the flat surface between are single cartouches of hieroglyphics. …

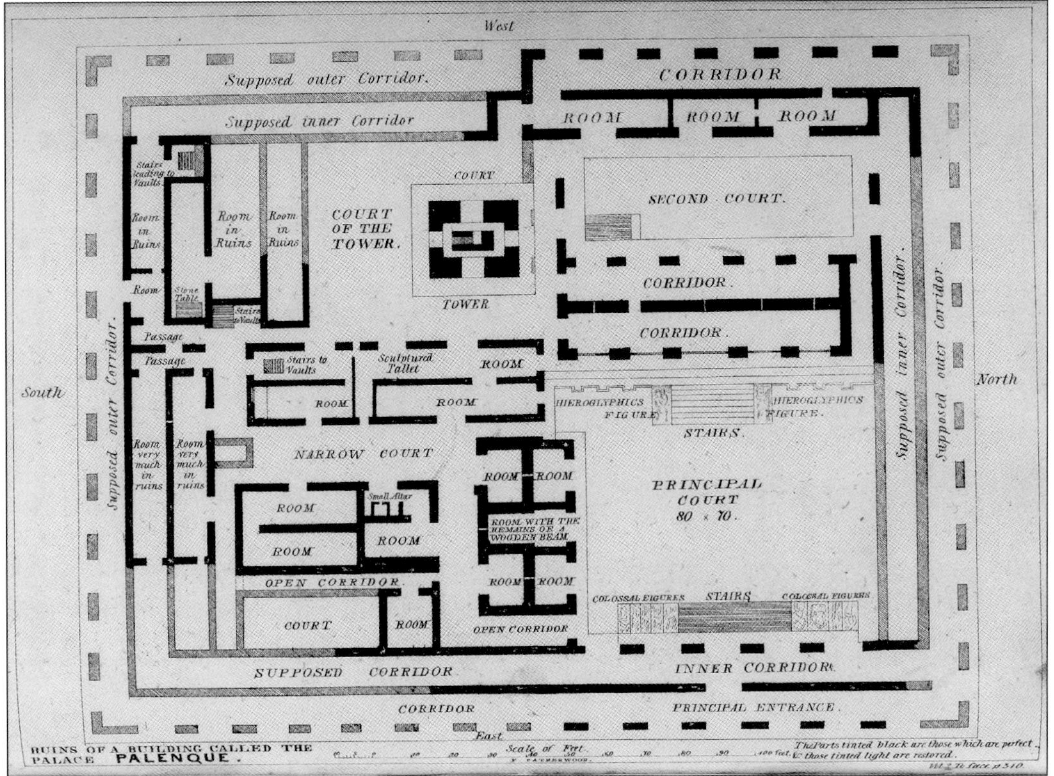

4.9 (upper). Frederick Catherwood, engraver unknown, *Ruins of a Building Called The Palace Palenque*, John Lloyd Stephens, *Incidents of Travel in Central America, Chiapas, and Yucatan*, 2 vols. (New York: Harper & Brothers; London: John Murray, 1841), II, facing 310, 12.5 x 16.7 cm. (including frame, text, and designated cardinal points of the compass). [Reproduced by permission of Edinburgh University Library, Special Collections, S.B.91(72804)Ste.]

4.10 (lower). Frederick Catherwood, engraved by Archibald L. Dick, [East side of Principal Court], John Lloyd Stephens, *Incidents of Travel in Central America, Chiapas, and Yucatan*, 2 vols. (New York: Harper & Brothers; London: John Murray, 1841), II, facing 314, 11.4 x 18.6 cm. [Reproduced by permission of Edinburgh University Library, Special Collections, S.B.91(72804)Ste.]

> The part of the building which forms the rear of the courtyard, communicating with it by the steps, consists of two corridors, the same as the front, paved, plastered, and ornamented with stucco. …
>
> This corridor opened upon a second courtyard ['Second Court'], eighty feet long and but thirty across. The floor of the corridor was ten feet above that of the courtyard, and on the wall underneath were square stones with hieroglyphics sculptured upon them. On the piers were stuccoed figures, but in a ruined condition.
>
> On the other side of the courtyard were two ranges of corridors, which terminated the building in this direction. The first of them is divided into three apartments, with doors opening from the extremities upon the western corridor. All the piers are standing except that of the northwest corner. All are covered with stucco ornaments, and one with hieroglyphics. The rest contain figures in bas-relief …[61]

As Stephens observes, 'the arrangements of the palace are simple and easily understood'.[62] Guided by the description, readers would likely have found the ground-plan for this part of the *Palacio* easy to follow, although the remaining part of the structure (including the Tower and its immediate surroundings, corridors, and apartments) is considerably more complex, as Stephens acknowledges. The account of the *Palacio* concludes with the identification of a room with a small altar leading off the 'Narrow Court' in the southeast part, which leads Stephens, drawing comparison with his own culture, to speculate:

> In our utter ignorance of the habits of the people who had formerly occupied this building, it was impossible to form any conjecture for what uses these different apartments were intended; but if we were right in calling it a palace, the name which the Indians give it, it seems probable that the part surrounding the courtyards was for public and state occasions, and that the rest was occupied as the place of residence of the royal family; this room with the small altar, we may suppose, was what would be called, in our times, a royal chapel.[63]

As in his discussion of Copán, Stephens, on occasion, adopts a sentimental voice which is associated with 'the mournful effect' that a picturesque and romantic sensibility privileged when reflecting on architectural ruins:

> With these helps and the aid of the plan, the reader will be able to find his way through the ruined palace of Palenque; he will form some idea of the profusion of its ornaments, of their unique and striking character,

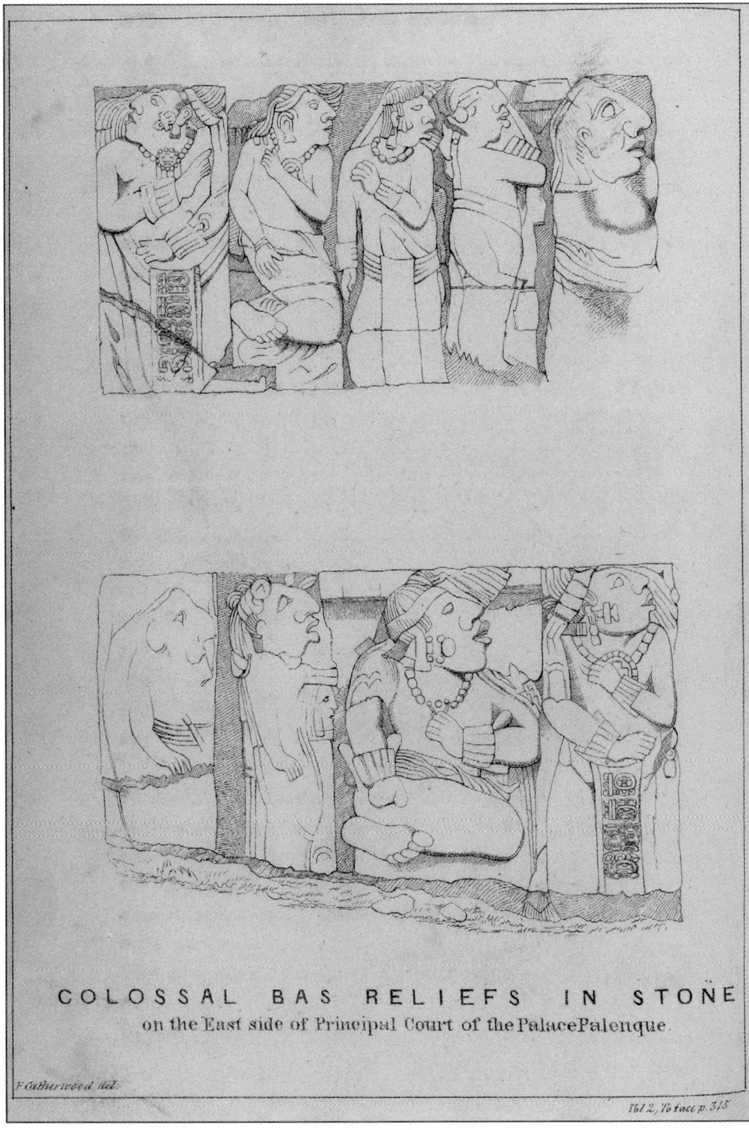

4.11. Frederick Catherwood, engraver unknown, *Colossal Bas Reliefs in Stone on the East side of Principal Court of the Palace Palenque*, John Lloyd Stephens, *Incidents of Travel in Central America, Chiapas, and Yucatan*, 2 vols. (New York: Harper & Brothers; London: John Murray, 1841), II, facing 315, 17.2 x 11.6 cm. (including frame). [Reproduced by permission of Edinburgh University Library, Special Collections, S.B.91(72804)Ste.]

> and of their mournful effect, shrouded by trees; and perhaps with him, as with us, fancy will present it as it was before the hand of ruin had swept over it, perfect in its amplitude and rich decorations, and occupied by the strange people whose portraits and figures now adorn its walls.[64]

Two further structures (the Temple of the Inscriptions and the Temple of the Sun) introduce readers to representational procedures with which they may not have been familiar. In discussing these structures, Stephens and Catherwood adopted a process of illustration where structures were presented 'as restored'. Unlike architectural drawings in the seventeenth and eighteenth centuries, where the drawing of structures was modelled on classical examples (as in the work of Antoine Desgodetz and Robert Wood), 'restoration' for Stephens and Catherwood implied depicting buildings (but not sculpture and stuccoed ornaments) 'as subjects for speculation and comparison with the architecture of other lands and times'.[65] Such a process aspired to represent, 'after a careful examination', how a structure may have looked before it became a ruin.[66] Catherwood therefore represented, on occasion, 'the actual condition of the building, surrounded and overgrown by trees', but, since Stephens did not want to 'give effect to the moral sublimity of the spectacle',[67] an evocation of the picturesque was used primarily for effect, as in the case of the Temple of the Sun discussed below. Stephens reassures us that he 'omitted a series of views, exhibiting the most picturesque and striking subjects that ever presented themselves to the pencil of an artist' in favour of the example architectural drawing provided.[68] Unlike the chromolithographs Catherwood published in 1844, many of the engravings of Palenque employed strategies associated with architectural drawings: ground-plans, elevations, cross-sections, longitudinal cross-sections, and architectural detail, strategies which countered the 'moral sublimity of the spectacle'.

Such a procedure was adopted in discussing the Temple of the Inscriptions. The first engraving of the building presented 'the actual condition of the building, surrounded and overgrown by trees' (4.12). This representation was immediately followed with a plate that depicted the architectural features of the structure: an elevation of the building on the pyramidal structure on which it lay, a longitudinal section of the building, a closer view of the front elevation (so that details of ornamentation could be seen), and a ground-plan of the structure (4.13). To help the reader, Stephens describes the details presented in the plate:

> The engraving opposite [4.13] represents the same building cleared from forest and restored ... In the plate are given the ground-plan (beginning at the bottom), the front elevation, a section showing the

position of tablets within [i.e., two panels of hieroglyphic inscription], and the front elevation on a smaller scale, with the pyramidal structure on which it stands.

The building is seventy-six feet in front and twenty-five feet deep. It has five doors and six piers, all standing. The whole front was richly ornamented in stucco, and the corner piers are covered with hieroglyphics, each of which contains ninety-six squares.[69]

A similar procedure was adopted for the Temple of the Cross followed by a plate printed over two pages that depicted a tablet on an interior wall of the sanctuary. This procedure was also adopted in depicting the Temple of the Sun, and Stephens drew readers' attention to the fact that the structure was presented 'as restored' rather than as the product of 'fancy' or supposition:

The engraving opposite [4.14] represents this building as restored, not from any fancied idea of what it might have been, but from such remains and indications that it was impossible to make anything else of it. It is thirty-eight feet front and twenty-eight feet deep, and has three doors. The end piers are ornamented with hieroglyphics in stucco, two

4.12 (below). Frederick Catherwood, engraved by Alexander Anderson, *Casa No. 1* [Temple of the Inscriptions], John Lloyd Stephens, *Incidents of Travel in Central America, Chiapas, and Yucatan*, 2 vols. (New York: Harper & Brothers; London: John Murray, 1841), II, facing 338, 11.5 x 16.5 cm. (maximum image size). [Reproduced by permission of Edinburgh University Library, Special Collections, S.B.91(72804)Ste.]

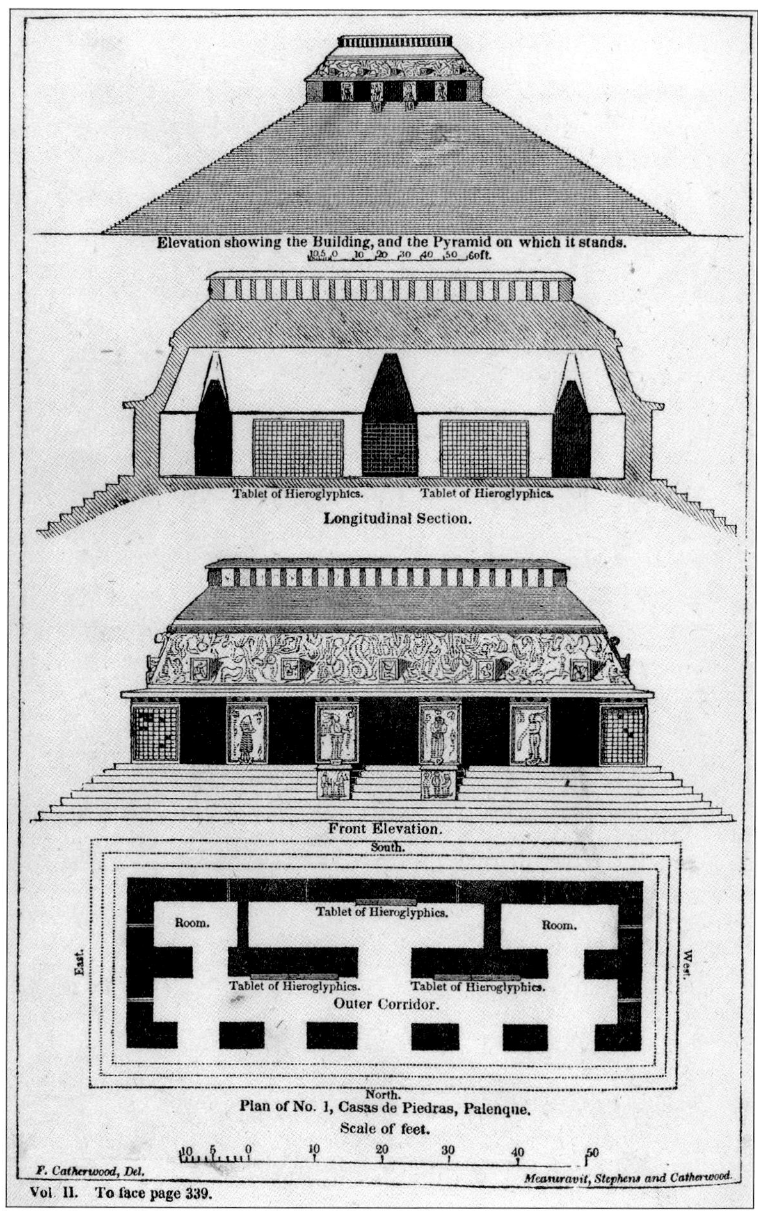

4.13 (above). Frederick Catherwood, engraver unknown, *Elevation, Longitudinal Section, Front Elevation, Plan of No. 1, Casas de Piedras, Palenque, Measured by Stephens and Catherwood* [Temple of the Inscriptions], John Lloyd Stephens, *Incidents of Travel in Central America, Chiapas, and Yucatan*, 2 vols. (New York: Harper & Brothers; London: John Murray, 1841), II, facing 339, 16.4 x 10.2 cm.
[Reproduced by permission of Edinburgh University Library, Special Collections, S.B.91(72804)Ste.]

4.14 (left). Frederick Catherwood, engraver unknown, *Front Elevation, Plan of No. 3, Casas da Piedra, Palenque* [Temple of the Sun], John Lloyd Stephens, *Incidents of Travel in Central America, Chiapas, and Yucatan*, 2 vols. (New York: Harper & Brothers; London: John Murray, 1841), II, facing 350, 17.2 x 10.4 cm. [Reproduced by permission of Edinburgh University Library, Special Collections, S.B.91(72804)Ste.]

large medallions in handsome compartments, and the intermediate ones with bas-reliefs, also in stucco …

The interior, again, is divided into two corridors, about nine feet wide each, and paved with stone. The engraving opposite [4.15] represents the front corridor, with the ceiling rising nearly to a point, and covered at the top with a layer of flat stones. …

The back corridor is divided into three apartments. In the centre, facing the principal door of entrance, is an enclosed chamber similar to that which in the last building we have called an oratory or altar. Its shadow is seen in the engraving. … There were no stuccoed ornaments or paintings, but set in the back wall was a stone tablet covering the whole width of the chamber, nine feet wide and eight feet high.

4.15 (right). Frederick Catherwood, engraved by Lossing, *Casa No. 4* [*sic*], *Front Corridor* [Temple of the Sun], John Lloyd Stephens, *Incidents of Travel in Central America, Chiapas, and Yucatan*, 2 vols. (New York: Harper & Brothers; London: John Murray, 1841), II, facing 351, 15.4 x 10.2 cm. (maximum image size). [Reproduced by permission of Edinburgh University Library, Special Collections, S.B.91(72804)Ste.]

The tablet is given in the frontispiece of this volume [4.16], and I beg to call to it the particular attention of the reader, as the most perfect and most interesting monument in Palenque. Neither Del Rio [*sic*] nor Dupaix has given any drawing of it, and it is now for the first time presented to the public. It is composed of three separate stones, the joints in which are shown by the blurred lines in the engraving. The sculpture is perfect, and the characters and figures stand clear and distinct on the stone.[70]

4.16. Frederick Catherwood, engraved by Archibald L. Dick, Frontispiece, *Tablet on the Back Wall of Altar Casa No. 3* [Temple of the Sun], John Lloyd Stephens, *Incidents of Travel in Central America, Chiapas, and Yucatan*, 2 vols. (New York: Harper & Brothers; London: John Murray, 1841), II, 21.2 x 23.7 cm. (framed image size excluding text outside frame). [Reproduced by permission of Edinburgh University Library, Special Collections, S.B.91(72804)Ste.]

Catherwood presented a ground-plan and detailed elevation of the structure (4.14), with the following plate (4.15) locating the reader in the 'outer corridor' of the sanctuary. Thereafter readers were transported into the inner chamber to view the tablet that constituted the Frontispiece of the second volume of *Incidents of Travel in Central America*.[71] Employing strategies from architectural drawings to organise the progression of the reader through space, Catherwood's illustrations convey the reader through the Temple, and demonstrate the spatial contiguity that the plates successively establish.

Following a detailed discussion of the Frontispiece, Stephens specifies the process of restoration. He recounts how two bas-reliefs (found in the house of two sisters in the village of Santo Domingo de Palenque),[72] that were thought to frame the entrance to the inner sanctuary, were reinstated in the final plate of the Temple in what was believed to be their rightful position. Reserving the expression of sentiment for this 'restoration', Stephens observed:

> We considered the oratorio or altar the most interesting portion of the ruins of Palenque; and in order that the reader may understand it in all its details, the plate opposite is presented [4.17], which shows distinctly all the combinations of doorway, with its broken ornaments, the tablets on each side [from the sisters' house]; and within the doorway is seen the large tablet [Frontispiece] on the back of the inner wall. The reader will form from it some idea of the whole, and of its effect upon the stranger, when, as he climbs up the ruined pyramidal structure, on the threshold of the door this scene presents itself. We could not but regard it as a holy place, dedicated to the gods, and consecrated by the religious observances of a lost and unknown people. Comparatively, the hand of ruin has spared it, and the great tablet, surviving the wreck of elements, stands perfect and entire. Lonely, deserted, and without any worshippers at its shrine, the figures and characters are distinct as when the people who reared it went up to pay their adorations before it. To us it was all a mystery; silent, defying the most scrutinizing gaze and reach of intellect.[73]

Like Copán, a sentimental register informs at least one of the three chromolithographs of Palenque which Catherwood published in *Views of Ancient Monuments*: a general view of the site (Plate 8). Since we learn that from 'the palace no other building [was] visible' and that on the one occasion when Stephens climbed a high mound to view the site, 'no part of the ruined city, not even the palace, could be seen',[74] we may propose that Catherwood's chromolithograph of Palenque presents a comprehensive yet imaginary view of the site.[75] The engraving shows the *Palacio*, on the left, lit by sunlight, dwarfed by a large mound on which the Temple of the Inscriptions stands in sunlight, a mound far higher than is the case in reality. To the right of the Temple, in shade, a further sanctuary is revealed: the Temple of the Fine Relief, a structure containing a bas-relief mutilated by Waldeck.[76] On the far side of the Otolum stream, visible in the mid-field of the engraving, the Temple of the Cross and the Temple of the Sun are seen on high mounds, which again bear little relation to the topography of the site. Towards the rear, an imposing hill shrouded by trees and clouds is seen, a humid condition that often characterises the site. However, not one of these structures could be seen from adjacent structures when Stephens and Catherwood investigated the site, so lost was Palenque amidst the forest.[77] In short,

4.17. Frederick Catherwood, engraved by Archibald L. Dick, *Adoratorio or Altar, Casa No. 3* [Temple of the Sun], John Lloyd Stephens, *Incidents of Travel in Central America, Chiapas, and Yucatan*, 2 vols. (New York: Harper & Brothers; London: John Murray, 1841), II, facing 354, 10.4 x 16.8 cm. (framed image size). [Reproduced by permission of Edinburgh University Library, Special Collections, S.B.91(72804)Ste.]

the view bears sentimental testimony, acting as 'a mournful witness to the world's mutations', a vision of mutability.[78]

The Romantic agony of which Stephens speaks at the close of the investigations at Palenque is forcefully brought to attention elsewhere in his account of the expedition to the Yucatán peninsula in 1841–1842. Whereas the expedition to Central America required Stephens to undertake political duties, on the second expedition to Yucatán, he was free of such responsibilities, a change which was marked by a significant departure: a more intense response to the region's archaeological sites, which identifies Stephens' aesthetic sensibility. On the first expedition, he had been keen to present architectural structures 'as restored'; no such ambition is evident on the second expedition. Although the concern with measurement and accuracy is maintained, a more personal response is also figured in Stephen's writing.

Uxmal

Stephens and Catherwood first encountered the site of Uxmal towards the end of their 1839–1840 expedition to Central America,

4.18. Frederick Catherwood, engraver unknown, Untitled [View from La Casa de las Monjas, Uxmal, Looking South], John Lloyd Stephens, *Incidents of Travel in Yucatan. Illustrated by 120 Engravings*, 2 vols. (New York: Harper & Brothers for Henry Bill, 1848 [1843]), I, facing 305, 11x17.7 cm. [Reproduced by permission of National Library of Sweden.]

when they selected the Casa de las Tortugas as a structure from which a panorama could be sketched.[79] Although other sites encountered during the second expedition presented subjects suitable for a panorama, Uxmal was deemed, on the first expedition, to present 'a scene strange enough for a work of enchantment'.[80] These two concerns, panoramas and enchantment, together with plans, architectural detail, and melancholic reflection characterise Stephens' response to investigating Uxmal.

The Casa de Monjas afforded an opportunity to present a panoramic view. Stephens describes the view from Monjas as if he were writing a description for the Panorama, Leicester Square, or for Catherwood's Panorama in New York, since he guides the reader by

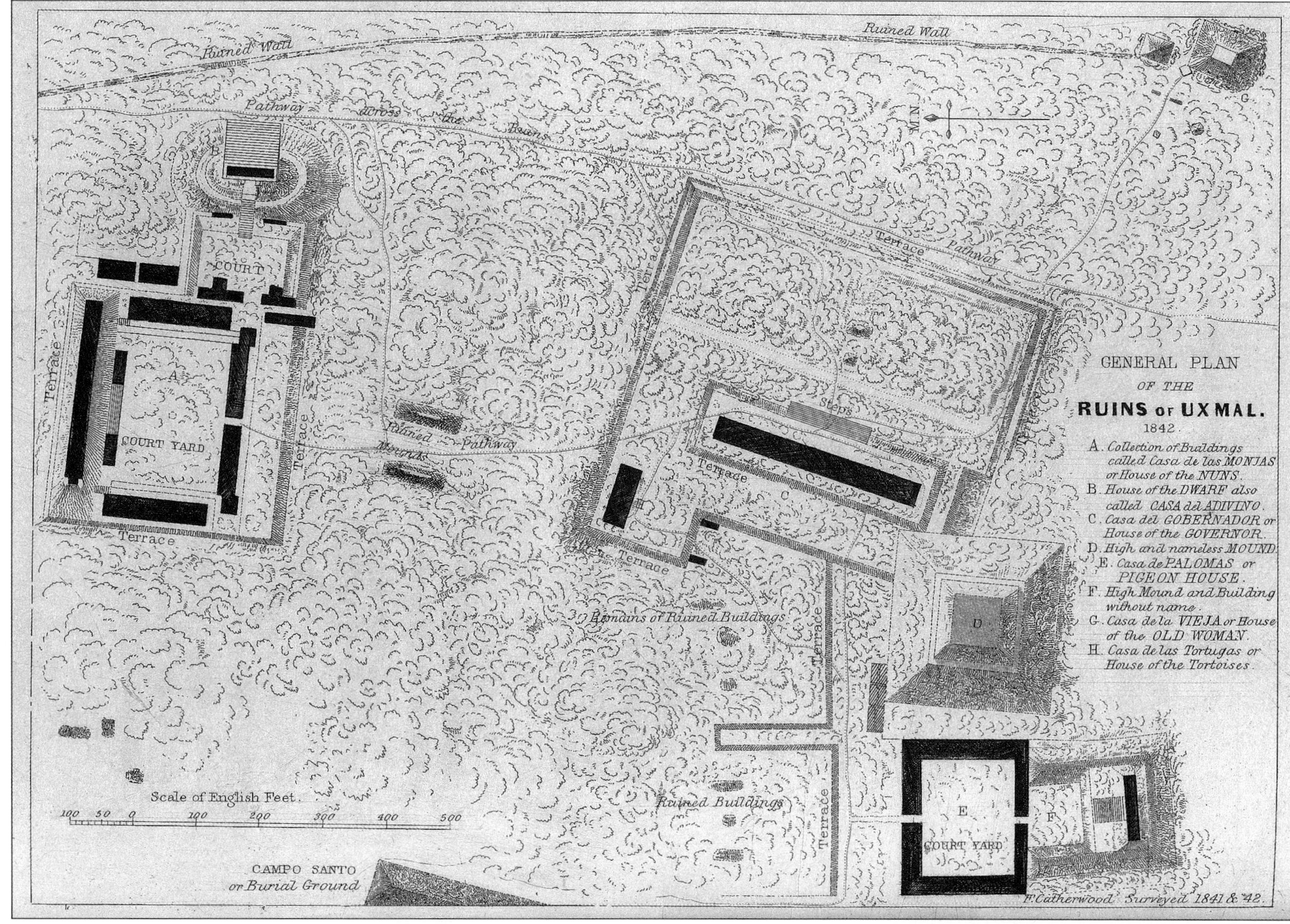

4.19. Frederick Catherwood, engraver unknown, *General Plan of the Ruins of Uxmal. 1842. Surveyed 1841 & 1842*, John Lloyd Stephens, *Incidents of Travel in Yucatan. Illustrated by 120 Engravings*, 2 vols. (New York: Harper & Brothers for Henry Bill, 1848 [1843]), I, facing 165, 13 x 18 cm. [Reproduced by permission of National Library of Sweden.]

4.20. Frederick Catherwood, engraver unknown, Untitled [Ornament over a Doorway, Casa del Gobernador], John Lloyd Stephens, *Incidents of Travel in Yucatan. Illustrated by 120 Engravings*, 2 vols. (New York: Harper & Brothers for Henry Bill, 1848 [1843]), I, 168, 12 x 8.5 cm. (maximum image size). [Reproduced by permission of National Library of Sweden.]

168 INCIDENTS OF TRAVEL.

from it proceed enormous plumes of feathers, dividing at the top, and falling symmetrically on each side, until they touch the ornament on which the feet of the statue rest. Each figure was perhaps the portrait of some cacique, warrior, prophet, or priest, distinguished in the history of this unknown people.

means of bodily orientation to the site:

> From the platform of the steps of this building [Casa de Monjas], looking across the courtyard, a grand view presents itself, embracing all the principal buildings that now tower above the plain, except the House of the Dwarf [to the left of the view]. The engraving opposite represents this view [4.18]. In the foreground is the inner façade of the front range of the Monjas, with a portion of the range on each side of the courtyard. To the left, in the distance, appears the Casa de la Vieja, or of the Old Woman, and, rising grandly above the front of the Monjas, are the House of the Turtles [Casa de las Tortugas], that of the Governor [Casa del Gobernador], and the Casa de Palomas, or the House of the Pigeons.[81]

The position from which Stephens describes the view accords with that in the *General Plan of the Ruins of Uxmal* if the reader were located at the middle of the north facade of the Casa de las Monjas, looking south (4.19).[82] The view includes the southern ends of the ranges on the east and west sides of the complex at the extreme foreground left and foreground right, with the Casa del Adivino visible towards extreme rear left, the Casa de Palomas, towards rear right, the High and nameless Mound ('D' on the *General Plan*) to the left of Palomas, with one further pyramidal structure behind and to the right of 'D'. The Casa del Tortugas and, to its left, the Casa del Gobernador are seen to the left of the pyramidal structures, towards mid-field centre. With a field of view of approximately 80 degrees, the *View from La Casa de las Monjas, Uxmal, Looking South* represents the extended field that the camera lucida could encompass from a single station point, presenting the optimum field of view that could be drawn with the instrument.

The *General Plan* was surveyed in a manner similar to that at Copán, the ranges being 'all taken with the compass, and the distances measured' so that 'the dimensions of the buildings and their distances from each other can be ascertained by means of the scale at the foot of the plate'.[83] The plan provides an ichnographic perspective of the site and, to a limited degree, an *embodied* view since the hachuring on the north and east facades of the principal structures, implies volume as well as denoting gradients. Like the plan of Copán, the *General Plan* models space while providing a bird's-eye view of the site. Topographical orientation is achieved at a stroke if the reader compares the plan with the *View from La Casa de las Monjas*.

In Chapter Two we observed that views of the Valle de México were compared by visitors in the early 1840s with panoramas and

THE ELEPHANTS TRUNK. 171

The engraving opposite represents that part of the ornament immediately above the preceding; it occupies the whole portion of the wall from the top of the head-dress to the cornice along the top of the building. This ornament or combination appears on all parts of the edifice, and throughout the ruins is more frequently seen than any other. In the engraving the centre presents a long, flat, smooth surface. This indicates a projecting ornament, which cannot be exhibited in a front view; but, as seen in profile, consists of a stone projecting from the face of the wall, as shown in the following cut; and the reader

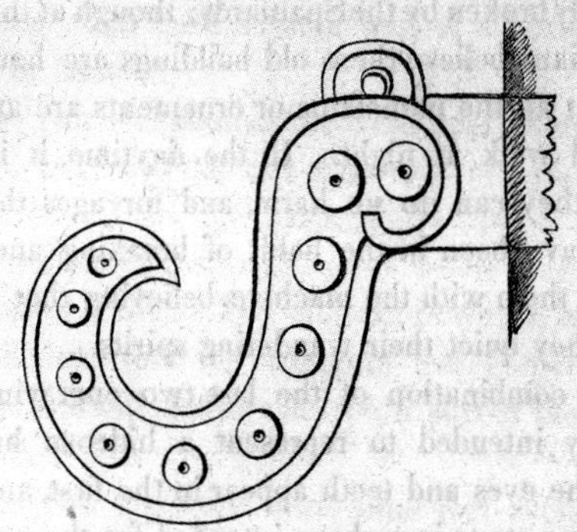

must suppose this stone projecting in order clearly to understand the character of the ornament last presented. It measures one foot seven inches in length from the stem by which it is fixed in the wall to the end of the curve, and resembles somewhat an elephant's

maps. Such analogies were, of course, virtual, since detailed maps were not available to travellers. In the case of Stephens' and Catherwood's exploration of Uxmal, however, such a comparison was more than mere analogy: if the reader compared the *General Plan* with the *View from La Casa de las Monjas*, he or she could plot relations in space against the view of the site. The *View* from Monjas, in other words, confirms the plotting represented in the plan; it provides an heuristic opportunity for readers to exercise their competence in reading a map matched against the terrain presented in the *View*. In short, the process of matching the print against the site-plan provided an object lesson for the reader in conceptualising space wherein one representational system (the ichnographic system of the *General Plan*) confirmed the identification of structures depicted in the *View*. The plan, in other words, helped readers identify structures as if they were in the field, and plot the relation of structures in the plan to the topography of the site. Whereas the plan of Copán provided an opportunity for Stephens to guide the reader *through* the site, at Uxmal readers were encouraged to engage in a process that stimulated the reader's *inferential* activity. In this respect, the *General Plan* of Uxmal with its companion *View* announces a different role for the reader, one which anticipates an imaginative, interactive engagement with the plan.

4.21 (above). Frederick Catherwood, engraved by Strong, Untitled [Ornament on the Casa del Gobernador], John Lloyd Stephens, *Incidents of Travel in Yucatan. Illustrated by 120 Engravings*, 2 vols. (New York: Harper & Brothers for Henry Bill, 1848 [1843]), I, facing 171, 8.2 x 17.1 cm. [Reproduced by permission of National Library of Sweden.]

4.22 (left). Frederick Catherwood, engraver unknown, Untitled [Profile view of Chac motif on Casa del Gobernador], John Lloyd Stephens, *Incidents of Travel in Yucatan. Illustrated by 120 Engravings*, 2 vols. (New York: Harper & Brothers for Henry Bill, 1848 [1843]), I, 171, 5.3 x 6 cm. (maximum image size). [Reproduced by permission of National Library of Sweden.]

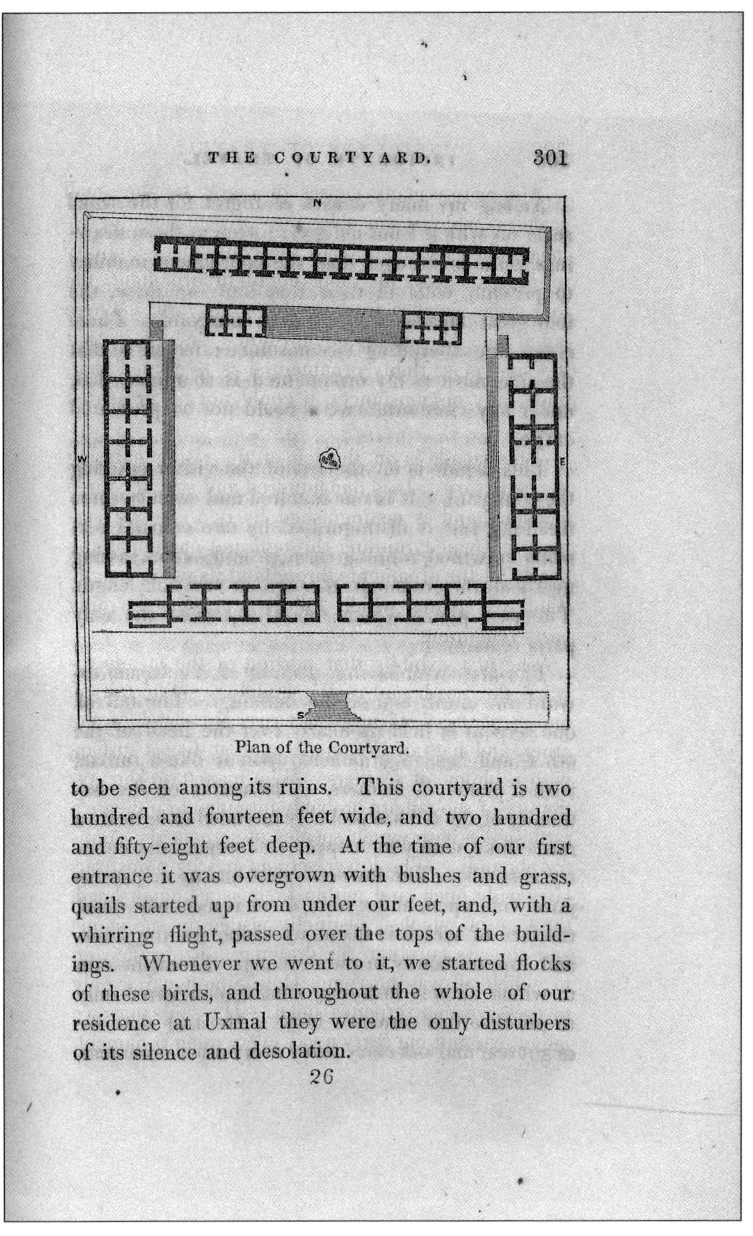
THE COURTYARD. 301

Plan of the Courtyard.

to be seen among its ruins. This courtyard is two hundred and fourteen feet wide, and two hundred and fifty-eight feet deep. At the time of our first entrance it was overgrown with bushes and grass, quails started up from under our feet, and, with a whirring flight, passed over the tops of the buildings. Whenever we went to it, we started flocks of these birds, and throughout the whole of our residence at Uxmal they were the only disturbers of its silence and desolation.

26

4.23. Frederick Catherwood, engraver unknown, *Plan of the Courtyard*, John Lloyd Stephens, *Incidents of Travel in Yucatan. Illustrated by 120 Engravings*, 2 vols. (New York: Harper & Brothers for Henry Bill, 1848 [1843]), I, 301, 9.2 x 8.6 cm. (maximum image size). [Reproduced by permission of National Library of Sweden.]

The sense of volume implied in the *General Plan* also defines some of the details presented in the plates of Uxmal. Two general observations are made. First, no attempt was made on this expedition to present structures 'as restored'. Stephens' intention was, in fact, quite the reverse: 'The edifice is represented as it exists now, without any attempt at restoration.'[84] Second, Stephens observed that ornamental detail on structures at Uxmal could not be represented 'with any effect on the scale adapted to these pages'.[85] In considering the Casa del Gobernador (reproduced as the Frontispiece in the first volume of *Incidents of Travel in Yucatan*, 1.1), details of features in the frieze were provided which, in one case, was defined as 'a figure seated on a kind of throne' with lofty head-dress (4.20).[86] In the other case, a symbolic representation of what is now known to be the figure of Chac (the Maya god of rain) is presented (4.21). The sense of volume was further advanced by depicting the architectural detail not only as it appeared perpendicular to the reader's gaze, an effect enhanced by shadow in the plate of the *Ornament of the Casa del Gobernador*, but also as a profile view. Stephens provided clear indication of the relation that readers should infer from comparing the plate with the profile view:

> The engraving opposite [4.21] represents that part of the ornament immediately above the preceding [4.20]; it occupies the whole portion of the wall from the top of the head-dress to the cornice along the top of the building. This ornament or combination appears on all parts of the edifice, and throughout the ruins is more frequently seen than any other. In the engraving the centre presents a long, flat, smooth surface. This indicates a projecting ornament, which cannot be exhibited in a front view; but, as seen in profile, consists of a stone projecting from the face of the wall, as shown in the following cut [4.22]; and the reader must suppose this stone projecting in order clearly to understand the character of the ornament last presented. It measures one foot seven inches in length from the stem by which it is fixed in the wall to the end of the curve, and resembles somewhat an elephant's trunk, which name has, perhaps not inaptly, been given to it by Waldeck, though it is not probable that as such the sculptor intended it, for the elephant was unknown on the Continent of America.[87]

While Stephens informs us that much of the ornamentation has been broken off,[88] he also describes the ornamentation in terms that help the reader understand the method employed in constructing the frieze, one which utilises a mosaic-like principle typical of decorative features in the Puuc region of Yucatán:

> The combination of the last two engravings [4.21 and 4.22] is probably intended to represent a hideous human face; the eyes and teeth appear

in the first, and the projecting stone is perhaps intended for the nose or snout. It occupies a space in breadth equal to about five feet of the wall. To present the whole façade on the same scale would require an engraving sixty-four times as long as this. The reader will perceive how utterly unprofitable it would be to attempt a verbal description of such a façade, and the lines in the engraving show that, as I remarked in my former account, there is no tablet or single stone representing separately and by itself an entire subject, but every ornament or combination is made up of separate stones, each of which had carved on it part of the subject, and was then set in its place in the wall. Each stone by itself is an unmeaning fractional portion, but, placed by the side of others, makes part of a whole, which without it would be incomplete. Perhaps it may with propriety be called a species of sculptured mosaic; and I have no doubt that all these elements have a symbolical meaning; that each stone is part of a history, allegory, or fable.[89]

The care with which Stephens describes the mosaic of sculpted stones, the indication that if the Chac face were compared with an elephant's trunk, such a comparison would be meaningless to the

4.24. Frederick Catherwood, engraved by Graham, *Portion of Western Building, Monjas. Uxmal*, John Lloyd Stephens, *Incidents of Travel in Yucatan. Illustrated by 120 Engravings*, 2 vols. (New York: Harper & Brothers for Henry Bill, 1848 [1843]), I, facing 302, 11.5 x 18.8 cm.
[Reproduced by permission of National Library of Sweden.]

4.25 (left). Frederick Catherwood, engraved by John Francis Eugene Prud'homme, *South East Angle of Monjas, Uxmal.*, John Lloyd Stephens, *Incidents of Travel in Yucatan. Illustrated by 120 Engravings*, 2 vols. (New York: Harper & Brothers for Henry Bill, 1848 [1843]), I, facing 307, 16.7 x 11 cm. [Reproduced by permission of National Library of Sweden.]

4.26 (right). Frederick Catherwood, engraver unknown, Untitled [Interior of Apartment, Monjas, Uxmal], John Lloyd Stephens, *Incidents of Travel in Yucatan. Illustrated by 120 Engravings*, 2 vols. (New York: Harper & Brothers for Henry Bill, 1848 [1843]), I, facing 308, 17.2 x 10.8 cm. [Reproduced by permission of National Library of Sweden.]

people for whom the facade was sculpted, acknowledge a cultural relativism that is eclipsed in Waldeck's discussion of Uxmal. Such perception, unusual for the period, demonstrates a degree of reflexivity on Stephens' part, an awareness not encountered in other writers of the period with the exception of Galindo.

The other principal structure considered at Uxmal is the Casa de las Monjas. A plan of the ranges and courtyard of the complex is provided (4.23), which shows the eighty-eight 'apartments' that constitute four ranges. Two engravings provide details of decoration on the western range overlooking the interior courtyard. One shows a *Portion of Western Building, Monjas, Uxmal* (4.24), which details a motif involving two intertwined snakes that, at one time, would have decorated the entire western range together with three Chac faces presented over an entrance in the range. The other engraving details decoration on the southeast corner of the building (*South East Angle of Monjas, Uxmal*, 4.25), revealing the Chac motif that decorates the principal entrance and corners of the range seen in its entirety in 3.1. In this instance, the Chac motif is complemented by 'a succession of compartments, alternately plain, and presenting the form of diamond lattice-work'.[90] With the two plates printed on successive pages, the reader is invited to observe the contiguous relation that obtains between the facades, a relation that carries over to the following plate, a view of the interior of the eastern range of Monjas:

> The entrance to this suite is by the centre and principal doorway, and the engraving opposite [4.26] represents the interior. It consists of two parallel chambers, each thirty-three feet long and thirteen feet wide; and at each end of both chambers is a doorway communicating with other chambers nine feet long and thirteen wide. The doorways of all these are ornamented with sculpture, and they are the only ornaments found in the interior of any buildings in Uxmal. The whole suite consists of six rooms; and there is a convenience in the arrangements not unsuited to the habits of what we call civilized life ...[91]

The succession of plates provides an object lesson in matching plates against the plan as the reader matches the plan of the four ranges of the Monjas complex against the eastern range (viewed in its entirety in the plate bound facing page 306), a view of the southeast corner of the eastern range (bound facing page 307), and a partial view of the interior of one of the apartments in the range (bound facing page 308).[92] The sequencing of three engravings as they are encountered on successive leaves invites the reader to infer the spatial relation that obtained in the field.

As earlier, the camera lucida enabled engravings to be made which Stephens regarded as 'the utmost accuracy of proportion and detail'.[93] On this expedition, however, Stephens and Catherwood also took a Daguerreotype camera constructed by the New York instrument-maker, Alexander S. Wolcott.[94] As Stephens observed:

> the results were not sufficiently perfect to suit his [Catherwood's] ideas. At times the projecting cornices and ornaments threw parts of the subject in shade, while others were in broad sunshine; so that, while parts were brought out well, other parts required pencil drawings to supply their defects. They gave a general idea of the character of the buildings, but would not do to put into the hands of the engraver without copying the views on paper, and introducing the defective parts, which would require more labour than that of making at once complete original drawings. He therefore completed everything with his pencil and camera lucida, while Doctor Cabot and myself took up the Daguerreotype; and, in order to ensure the utmost accuracy, the Daguerreotype views were placed with the drawings in the hands of the engravers for their guidance.[95]

In this respect, the Daguerreotyped views made at Uxmal (which have been lost) acted as the handmaid for the engraver in translating Catherwood's drawings to the steel plates.

As at Copán, Stephens and Catherwood delight in the aesthetic pleasure they experienced at Uxmal. Clearing the Casa del Gobernador, Stephens observed that 'The day was overcast, the wind swept mournfully over the desolate city, and since my arrival I had not felt so deeply the solemnity and sublimity of these mysterious ruins.'[96] Investigating the Casa de los Palomas, Stephens observed:

> There was a mournful interest about this great pile of ruins. Entering under the great archway, crossing two noble courtyards, with ruined buildings on each side, and ascending the great staircase to the building on the top, gave a stronger impression of departed greatness than anything else in this desolate city. It commanded a view of every other building, and stood apart in lonely grandeur, seldom disturbed by human footsteps.[97]

The concern with panoramic views is encountered in Catherwood's chromolithographs. Of the eight plates devoted to Uxmal in *Views of Ancient Monuments*, two depict the site from an elevated position that encompass the field of view afforded by the camera lucida. A view of the site looking north from the roof of the Casa del Gobernador (Plate 9), shows a corner of Tortugas at foreground left, the Monjas complex towards rear-field centre, and the Casa del Adivino towards rear right, bathed in afternoon light. A group of indigenous men in the foreground are engaged in clearing the roof of the Casa del Gobernador of vegetation, overseen by Stephens just

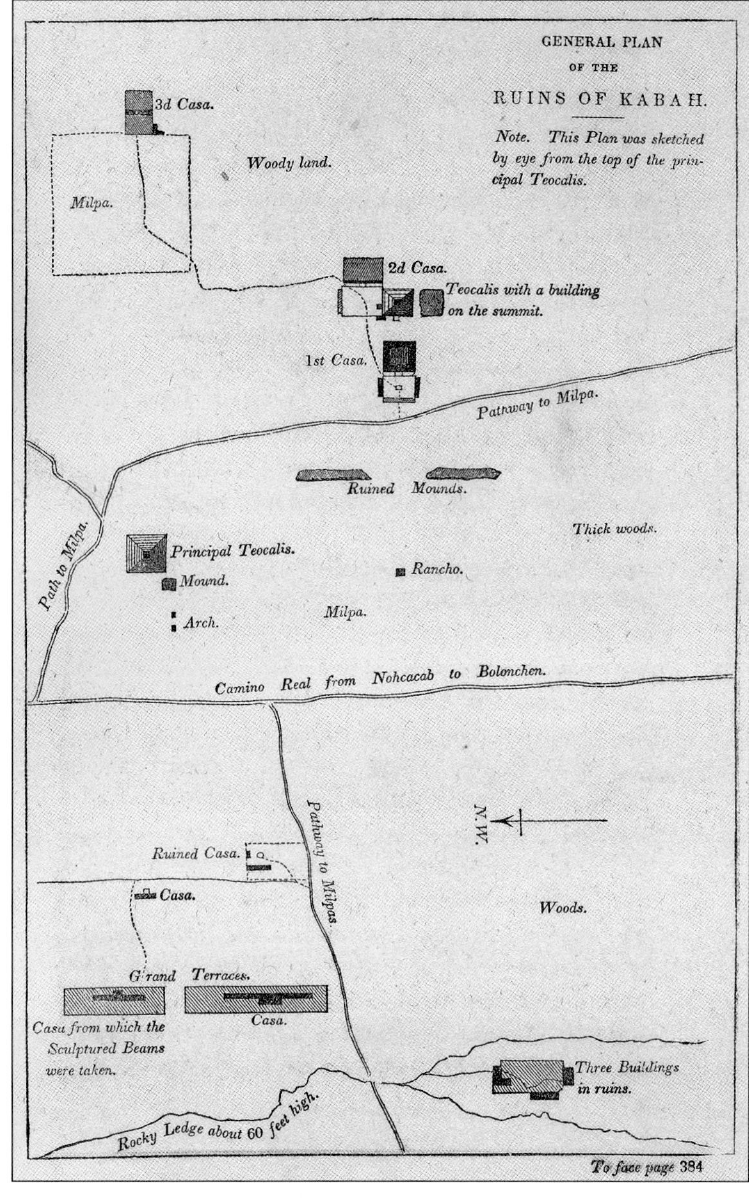

4.27. Frederick Catherwood, engraver unknown, *General Plan of the Ruins of Kabah*, John Lloyd Stephens, *Incidents of Travel in Yucatan. Illustrated by 120 Engravings*, 2 vols. (New York: Harper & Brothers for Henry Bill, 1848 [1843]), I, facing 384, 17.3 x 10.9 cm. [Reproduced by permission of National Library of Sweden.]

right of foreground centre. Sunlight emphasises action in the foreground, picks out the south facade of Tortugas, and warms the Monjas complex and the Casa del Adivino amongst dense vegetation. The other view (Plate 10) shows a reverse view of Plate 9, looking south in early morning light. Viewing the site from the terrace to the south of the Monjas complex, the reader sees the large platform on which Casa del Gobernador (at mid-field left of centre) and Tortugas (at mid-field centre) stand, with the Casa de la Vieja in the distance on the far side of the platform towards rear left. The 'high and nameless Mound' can be seen at right of rear centre on a high terrace, while the Casa de Palomas, with its eight 'Dutch' gable-like structures, and a further *teocallis* (Templo del Sur), rising behind Palomas, are visible towards rear right. In the foreground, a group of indigenous men talk before work commences for the day; behind them and in front of the large platform on which the Casa del Gobernador stands, two smaller mounds covered in dense vegetation are visible.[98] The morning sun picks out foreground interest, adds gentle highlights to structures towards the rear of the view, and provides relief in the depiction of the clouds.

Before turning to a discussion of the last major site considered in this chapter, investigations conducted at two other sites are briefly considered. At Kabah, Catherwood and Stephens did not conduct a comprehensive survey of the site because indigenous workers could not be hired in sufficient number from the village of Nohcacab to clear the site of forest.[99] However, Catherwood was able to draw a plan of the site (4.27), not from measurements taken in the field, but from 'bearings taken with the compass from the top of the great teocalis' with distances 'laid down according to our best judgment with the eye'. As in the case of Copán, Stephens guides the reader through the site:

> On this plan the reader will see a road marked 'Camino Real to Bolonchen,' and on the left a path marked 'Path to Milpa'.[100] Following this path towards the field of ruins, the teocalis is the first object that meets his eye, grand, picturesque, ruined, and covered with trees … towering above every other object on the plain. …
>
> Leaving this mound, again taking the milpa path, and following it to the distance of three or four hundred yards, we reach the foot of a terrace twenty feet high, the edge of which is overgrown with trees; ascending this, we stand on a platform two hundred feet in width by one hundred and forty-two feet deep, and facing us is the building represented in the plate opposite.[101]

4.28 (upper). Frederick Catherwood, engraved by Joseph Napoleon Gimbrede, Untitled [Gateway at Labná], John Lloyd Stephens, *Incidents of Travel in Yucatan. Illustrated by 120 Engravings*, 2 vols. (New York: Harper & Brothers for Henry Bill, 1848 [1843]), II, facing 54, 11 x 17.3 cm. [Reproduced by permission of National Library of Sweden.]

4.29 (lower). Frederick Catherwood, engraved by John A. Rolph, *Interior of Gateway at Labná*, John Lloyd Stephens, *Incidents of Travel in Yucatan. Illustrated by 120 Engravings*, 2 vols. (New York: Harper & Brothers for Henry Bill, 1848 [1843]), II, facing 55, 11.1 x 17.6 cm. [Reproduced by permission of National Library of Sweden.]

The other site is that of Labná investigated between 28 January and 30 January 1842.[102] Two plates depicting a corbelled gateway at Labná – an untitled plate (4.28) and *Interior of Gateway at Labná* (4.29) – are of particular interest since, bound on successive leaves, they establish contiguity between the two views of the gateway, thus constituting a reverse view of the subject.[103]

Chichén Itzá

The last site considered in this chapter is Chichén Itzá.[104] Once again, the reader is provided with a detailed plan of the site (4.30), which supports the itinerary Stephens details as he guides the reader through the site, much abridged in the extracts presented below:

> By referring to the plan the reader will see the position of the hut in which we lived ['K'], and, following the path from our door through the cattle-yard of the hacienda, at the distance of two hundred and fifty yards he will reach the building represented in the plate opposite ['G']. …
>
> Leaving this building, and following the path indicated in the map, at the distance of one hundred and fifty yards westward we reach a modern stone fence, dividing the cattle-field of the hacienda, on the other side of which appears through the trees, between two other buildings, the end façade of a long, majestic pile, called, like one of the principal edifices at Uxmal, the Monjas, or Nuns; it is remarkable for its good state of preservation, and the richness and beauty of its ornaments, as represented in the plate opposite [4.31, the east end of 'H']. The view comprehends the corner of a building on the right, at a short distance, called the Eglesia, or Church. The height of this façade is twenty-five feet, and its width thirty-five. It has two cornices of tasteful and elaborate design. Over the doorway are twenty small cartouches of hieroglyphics in four rows, five in a row, barely indicated in the engraving, and to make room for which the lower cornice is carried up.

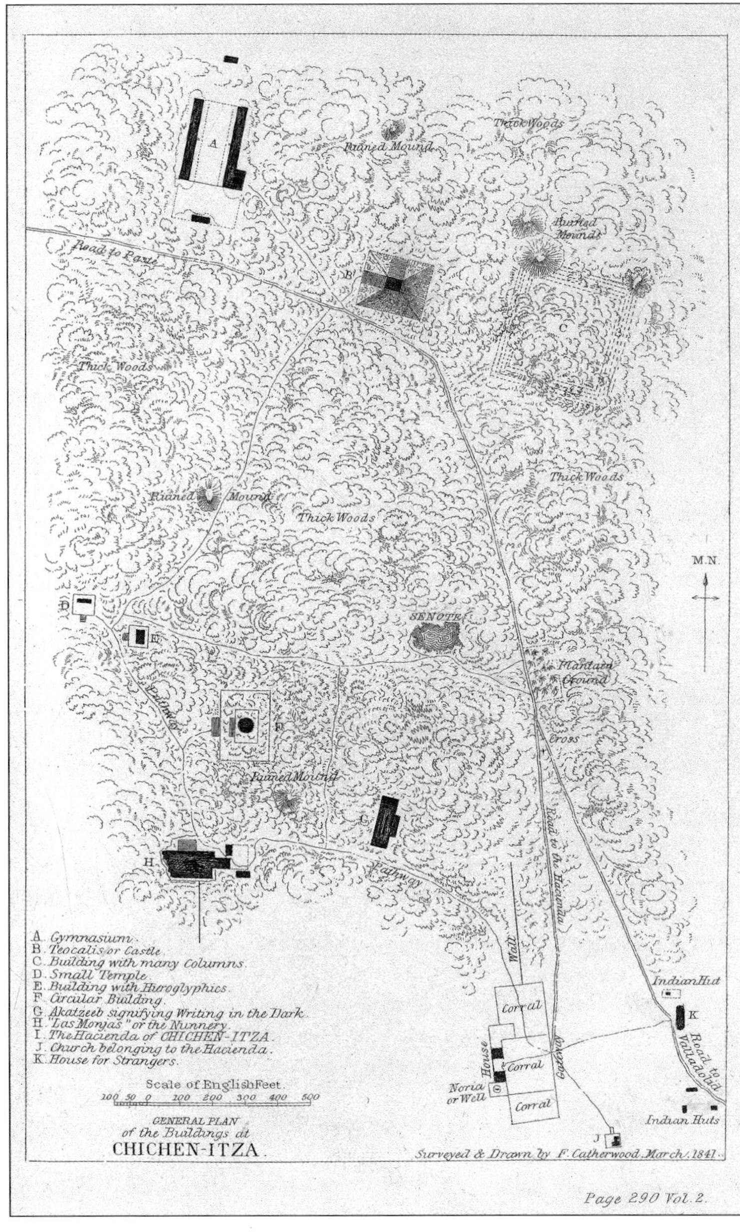

4.30. Frederick Catherwood, engraver unknown, *General Plan of the Buildings at Chichen-Itza. Surveyed & Drawn by F. Catherwood. March. 1841*, John Lloyd Stephens, *Incidents of Travel in Yucatan. Illustrated by 120 Engravings*, 2 vols. (New York: Harper & Brothers for Henry Bill, 1848 [1843]), II, facing 290, 17.9 x 11.2 cm. [Reproduced by permission of National Library of Sweden.]

Over these stand out in a line six bold projecting carved ornaments, like that presented from the House of the Governor at Uxmal, resembling an elephant's trunk, and the upper centre space over the doorway is an irregular circular niche, in which portions of a seated figure, with a head-dress of feathers, still remain. …

The plate opposite [4.32] represents the front of the same building. It is composed of two structures entirely different from each other, one of which forms a sort of wing to the principal edifice, and has at the end the façade before presented [4.31]. …

Descending again to the ground, at the end of the wing stands what is called the Eglesia, or Church, a corner of which was comprehended in a previous view, and the front of which is represented in the plate opposite [4.33]. It is twenty-six feet long, fourteen deep, and thirty-one high, its comparatively great height adding very much to the effect of its appearance. It has three cornices, and the spaces between are richly ornamented. The sculpture is rude but grand. The principal ornament is over the doorway, and on each side are two human figures in a sitting posture, but, unfortunately, much mutilated. The portion of the façade above the second cornice is merely an ornamented wall, like those before mentioned at Zayi [Sayil] and Labnà [Labná].

The whole of this building is in a good state of preservation. The interior consists of a single apartment, once covered with plaster, and along the top of the wall under the arch are seen the traces of a line of medallions or cartouches in plaster, which once contained hieroglyphics. …

Leaving this pile of buildings, and passing on northward from the Monjas, at the distance of four hundred feet we reach the edifice represented in the opposite engraving [4.34], conspicuous among the ruins of Chichen for its picturesque appearance, and unlike any other we had seen, except one at Mayapan much ruined. It is circular in form, and is known by the name of the Caracol, or winding staircase, on account of its interior arrangements. It stands on the upper of two terraces. …[105]

The reader is conducted through the remaining features of the site until, many pages later, Stephens closes his 'brief description of the ruins of Chichen, having presented, with as little detail as possible, all the principal buildings of this ancient city'.[106] The interest in movement through space observed above is a feature which Stephens specifies on a number of occasions, writing in either the first-person singular or first-person plural. At Uxmal, Stephens observed: 'Passing through the arched gateway [at Monjas], we enter a noble courtyard'; on the road to Kabah, Stephens observed: 'Moving on, again, through openings in the trees, we had a glimpse of a great stone edifice, with its front apparently entire', and at Kabah, Stephens observed that 'taking the milpa path, and following it to the distance of three or four hundred yards, we reach the foot of a terrace;

4.31 (upper). Frederick Catherwood, engraved by Joseph Napoleon Gimbrede, *Monjas, Chichen Itza*, John Lloyd Stephens, *Incidents of Travel in Yucatan. Illustrated by 120 Engravings*, 2 vols. (New York: Harper & Brothers for Henry Bill, 1848 [1843]), II, facing 293, 17.7 x 11.2 cm. [Reproduced by permission of National Library of Sweden.]

4.32 (lower). Frederick Catherwood, engraved by Jordan & Halpin, *Casa de las Monjas, Chichen*, John Lloyd Stephens, *Incidents of Travel in Yucatan. Illustrated by 120 Engravings*, 2 vols. (New York: Harper & Brothers for Henry Bill, 1848 [1843]), II, facing 294, 11 x 17.6 cm. [Reproduced by permission of National Library of Sweden.]

MONJAS, CHICHEN ITZA.

CASA DE LAS MONJAS, CHICHEN.

ascending this, we stand on a platform two hundred feet in width by one hundred and fifty-two feet deep, and facing us is the building represented in the plate opposite'.[107] On occasion, Stephens digresses to provide information relating to the history of Chichén Itzá,[108] concerns which demonstrate a similarity between the chronicles that informed Stephens' account and the history which the *Descriptions* of Catherwood's panoramas presented in London and New York. Indeed, the manner in which the reader is conducted through Chichén Itzá would not have seemed strange to readers accustomed to visiting panoramas, where historical and topographical information was presented as visitors toured the panorama. Although the two media were quite different, the pleasures the panorama and travel narratives occasioned share a family resemblance.

Recognition of this similarity help us to identify the extent to which the two media stimulated the imagination of readers and viewers. As we have already seen, *Incidents of Travel in Central America* stimulated the imagination of Wilkie Collins and readers of *The Woman in White*. Other sites produced similar responses. Stephens' discussion of Uxmal stimulated John Abraham Heraud to write *Uxmal: An Antique Love Story*, a story set in Uxmal under Theban domination, where archaeological structures not only bore 'indications of Theban origin and serpent worship', but invited the reader to consult Catherwood's engravings ('to assist his fancy') prior to reading Heraud's 'mythological poem in … dramatic form'.[109] The Maya also featured in an elaborate and celebrated hoax in a tale related by Phineas T. Barnum concerning the Iximaya, an indigenous people who supposedly lived in an unknown city in the Guatemalan forest beyond the department of Petén. Barnum's tale, fuelled by fantasies that Stephens himself had entertained,[110] provoked a series of exhibitions and publications that capitalised on the growth of interest in Central American archaeology to which sensationally-minded audiences thronged in the mid-1850s.[111] Palenque also inspired a lengthy eponymous poem by Charles Lamb, *Palenque, or The Ancient West. A Poem*, which 'made it seem probable that these cities are not of the remote antiquity that had by many been assigned to them'.[112] Although this discussion of the influence that Stephens' and Catherwood's work demonstrated is far from comprehensive, such instances indicate the manner in which Stephens and Catherwood stimulated the popular imagination of readers, contributing to sensational spectacles on both sides of the Atlantic in the decade following the publication of their investigations.

'Traditionary knowledge'

While such tales fired the popular imagination, a serious interest also arose among the community of scholars who were eager to establish the academic credentials of pre-Columbian investigation. As observed at the opening of this chapter, Albert Gallatin, President of the American Ethnological Society, prepared an extensive essay for the *Transactions* of the Society which provided an overview of contemporary learning concerning Mesoamerican culture. Reviewing the investigations undertaken by Stephens and Catherwood, Gallatin proposed that the lacuna of 'traditionary knowledge' (i.e., historical account), which had troubled Stephens, may have arisen in a society where a strong, hierarchical division of labour meant that a knowledge of tradition was exclusively maintained by a religious elite:

4.33 (right). Frederick Catherwood, engraved by John A. Rolph, *Eglesia, Chichen Itza*, John Lloyd Stephens, *Incidents of Travel in Yucatan. Illustrated by 120 Engravings*, 2 vols. (New York: Harper & Brothers for Henry Bill, 1848 [1843]), II, facing 296, 15.5 x 11.3 cm. [Reproduced by permission of National Library of Sweden.]

4.34 (below). Frederick Catherwood, engraved by Alexander Johnson, *Chichen*, John Lloyd Stephens, *Incidents of Travel in Yucatan. Illustrated by 120 Engravings*, 2 vols. (New York: Harper & Brothers for Henry Bill, 1848 [1843]), II, facing 298, 11.2 x 17.4 cm. [Reproduced by permission of National Library of Sweden.]

It proves beyond doubt that, at least during the period which preceded the destruction of their central government and their civil wars, Yucatan was the seat of a numerous and industrious, though perhaps enslaved population. The splendid temples and palaces still standing attest the power of the priests and of the nobles; no trace remains of the huts in which dwelt the mass of the nation.[113]

In the course of *Incidents of Travel in Yucatan*, Stephens summarised the conclusions he reached on the first expedition to Central America:

The conclusion to which I came was, that 'there are not sufficient grounds for belief in the great antiquity that has been ascribed to these ruins;' 'that we are not warranted in going back to any nation of the Old World for the builders of these cities; that they are not the works of people who have passed away, and whose history is lost; but that there are strong reasons to believe them the creation of the same races who inhabited the country at the time of the Spanish conquest, or of some not very distant progenitors'.[114]

During the second expedition, Stephens revised his observations and proposed 'that we cannot go back to any ancient nation of the Old World for the builders of these cities; they are not the works of people who have passed away, and whose history is lost, but of the same great *race* which, changed, miserable, and degraded, still clings around their ruins'.[115] The reformulation was made after Stephens, a lawyer by training, read the title papers for the land on which Uxmal lay. Although the papers consulted by Stephens in Mérida constituted 'truly a formidable pile',[116] they provided him with the evidence that the first formal conveyance of the land on which Uxmal stood was made by colonial administrators on 12 May 1673, at a time when 'one hundred and forty years after the foundation of Merida, the buildings of Uxmal were regarded with reverence by the Indians; that they formed the nucleus of a dispersed and scattered population, and were resorted to for the observance of religious rites at a distance from the eyes of the Spaniards'.[117] Stephens' proposal not only excited the popular imagination, but required that the antiquity which writers had previously ascribed to Mesoamerican culture was ripe for revision, as Lamb opined in the introduction to *Palenque, or The Ancient West. A Poem*. The problem, as Catherwood suggested in his commentary to *Views of Ancient Monuments*, was that 'a desire to theorise [had] preceded a complete and accurate survey of the monuments themselves, from whence the only safe foundations for theory can be derived'.[118] As a man more versed in method than Kingsborough and Waldeck,[119] such an observation led Catherwood to propose that:

the work of Lord Kingsborough (unquestionably the most splendid example of private munificence ever applied to the promotion of antiquarian literature) appears to owe its origin chiefly to the author's conviction in the truth of his favourite hypothesis, – the colonisation of America by the lost tribes of Israel. Other writers have even attributed them to an antediluvian period.[120]

More moderate in his condemnation of Kingsborough and Waldeck than Stephens, Catherwood also observed: 'My own observations have led me to differ from these conclusions, and to consider them as founded on insufficient data.'[121] Unlike earlier writers, Catherwood proposed that excavation would demonstrate that the structures they had investigated had 'been built by cognate races to those who inhabited the country at the time of the conquest', suggesting that:

I do not think we should be safe in ascribing to any of the monuments (which still retain their form) a greater age than from eight hundred to one thousand years; and those which are perfect enough to be delineated, I think it likely are not more than from four to six hundred years old.[122]

Catherwood proposed that the idea that cultures '*derivative*, and always owing to a *transmission* from a cultivated to an unpolished people' lacked philosophical rigour, since it removed 'further back, without explaining the original difficulty of *invention*, which must somewhere have taken place'.[123] Rather, Catherwood proposed:

The results arrived at by Mr. Stephens and myself, after a full and precise comparative survey of the ancient remains, coincide with this opinion, and are briefly: – that they are not of immemorial antiquity, the work of unknown races; but that, as we now see them, they were occupied, and possibly erected, by the Indian tribes in possession of the country at the time of the Spanish conquest, – that they are the production of an indigenous school of art, adapted by the natural circumstances of the country, and to the civil and religious polity then prevailing, – and that they present by very slight and accidental analogies with the works of any people or country in the Old World.[124]

4.35 (below). Frederick Catherwood, engraved by Joseph Napoleon Gimbrede, *Kewick*, John Lloyd Stephens, *Incidents of Travel in Yucatan. Illustrated by 120 Engravings*, 2 vols. (New York: Harper & Brothers for Henry Bill, 1848 [1843]), II, facing 72, 11.2 x 16.8 cm. [Reproduced by permission of National Library of Sweden.]

4.36 (right). Frederick Catherwood, engraved by Alexander Anderson, Untitled [palapa with *na* behind], John Lloyd Stephens, *Incidents of Travel in Yucatan. Illustrated by 120 Engravings*, 2 vols. (New York: Harper & Brothers for Henry Bill, 1848 [1843]), II, 68, 9.5 x 8.5 cm. (maximum image size). [Reproduced by permission of National Library of Sweden.]

Turning to the issue of the lack of 'traditionary knowledge', Catherwood proposed that 'in a country where only the rudest means of transmitting knowledge from one generation to another was employed, it is probable that traditionary facts acquired by experience would be preserved by a sacred caste or tribe of priests, by whom, and for whose use, many of these buildings were undoubtedly erected',[125] an observation supported by Gallatin in his essay in *Transactions of the American Ethnological Society*. In developing this insight, Catherwood drew on Vitruvius to argue that the style of architecture seen in surviving structures may have originated in an indigenous vernacular tradition:

> This original style of house (in use, no doubt, from the earliest period, and still found exclusively in Indian villages, – the walls constructed of bamboo canes, or trunks of trees, placed upright, and bound together by withes, with lattice-work apertures for windows, and an over-hanging, heavily-thatched roof), seems to have been the prototype of much that we find peculiar among the ornamental architecture of the country. If the Vitruvian theory, by which the characteristic forms of the early Grecian temples are traced to the influence of their original timber construction, be correct, a similar inference may fairly be drawn in this instance.[126]

68 INCIDENTS OF TRAVEL.

so wild that even yet we had doubts, and hardly believed that such a path could lead to a village or rancho; but, withal, there was one interesting circumstance. In our desolate and wandering path we had seen in different places, at a distance, and inaccessible, five high mounds, holding aloft the ruins of ancient buildings; and doubtless there were more buried in the woods. At three o'clock we entered a dense forest, and came suddenly upon the casa real of Kewick, standing alone, almost buried among trees, the only habitation of any kind in

Citing Stephens' *Incidents of Travel in Yucatan*, Catherwood proposed that 'reference to the plates in the second volume ... will show more clearly than the most laboured description, the fact that is now stated',[127] going on to indicate that engravings of the sites of Chunhuhu, Kewick (Kuhuic), Sabachtsché, and Sayil demonstrated the point he sought to make. The ornate facade at Kuhuic (4.35), with its column-like, diamond-patterned ornamentation (seen as it appears today in Plate 11),[128] demonstrated the comparison that Catherwood found in Stephens. The illustration that immediately preceded the facade at Kuhuic in *Incidents of Travel in Yucatan*, moreover, showed a palapa in front of a *na*, a traditional Maya house which, with thatched roof over a wall constructed from cane standing on top of a low plinth, 'stood on the platform of an ancient terrace, strewed with the relics of a ruined edifice' (4.36).[129] Whereas the Austrian, Emanuel von Friedrichsthal, presenting Daguerreotypes made in Yucatán to a meeting at the British Museum in December 1841, proposed that, from the sites he had visited, 'three epochs' could be identified,[130] Catherwood, avoiding comparison with the classical orders of Greek architectural ornament, attributed the origin of Maya structures to a vernacular tradition observed in indigenous houses in Yucatán. The vernacular tradition of *na* construction observed by Catherwood has survived to the present-day, and can be seen in villages throughout the Puuc region of the Yucatán peninsula (Plate 12) and in a reconstructed *na*, modelled on traditional Maya design, at the archaeological site of Muyil in the state of Quintana Roo (4.37).[131] Such structures demonstrate the longevity of tradition among the Maya even if Stephens, on occasion, bemoaned the absence of 'traditionary knowledge'.

Interest in the vernacular Maya tradition of *na* construction demonstrates the degree to which Catherwood and Stephens, compared with earlier investigators, acknowledged the importance of indigenous tradition, a concern also brought to attention in *The Modern Traveller*. While it would be difficult to demonstrate direct influence between the popular travel guide of 1825 and the work of Stephens and Catherwood, their publications nonetheless brought a new indigenous culture to popular attention in the United States and Britain and, in translation, elsewhere. They also developed a new type of travel account regarding antiquities, one which required readers to compare engravings with descriptive text, interpret maps, follow plans and architectural drawings, and respond to a range of strategies that stimulated the imagination. This latter concern included the representation of panoramic images on the printed page and the articulation of contiguous views and reverse views. Such processes provided opportunities for readers to be guided in the exploration of space through the sequencing of images, a process that brought to attention matters relating to succession and contiguity. Additionally, readers could attend to measurement and cartographic representation, and infer volume; they could also observe the relation between ichnographic representation and perspective views of the same terrain. Vernacular influence in antiquities, and the depiction of 'restored' and 'unrestored' structures, could also be appreciated, while Catherwood's chromolithographs, drawing on the discourse associated with the Picturesque and the Sublime, provided

4.37. Traditional Maya *na*, reconstruction, Muyil, Quintana Roo, photographed by the author.

pleasures that wealthier readers may have enjoyed. In short, a host of demands that offered readers the opportunity of engaging with a range of practices 'placed within reach of the great mass of our reading public', stimulated fancy, and presented attractions that conferred on readers a means of envisioning a world they would never visit or even imagine other than in the pages of two celebrated travel accounts.

Whether Stephens and Catherwood arrived at 'truth' is, of course, a moot point, but there can be little doubt that in stimulating the imagination of the reading public, their work discarded 'phantasms' in favour of a wealth of roles that would have been new to many readers interacting with the printed page. In this regard, Stephens and Catherwood provide an example of media convergence in popular visual culture at mid-century. As a writer and illustrator team, they stimulated the historical reader's engagement with the printed page and advanced the role of imagination. In so doing, they set in train the convergence of two modes for *picturing* antiquities in Central America and Yucatán.

Chapter Five

Picturing Mexico in lithographs, photographs, and film

'Drawings of buildings, however slight, give clearer and more permanent ideas than can be obtained from the most detailed, correct, and elaborate descriptions; on most occasions drawings of the objects are as much superior even to the best descriptions as models are superior to drawings.' John Soane, 'Lecture II', Royal Academy of Arts.[1]

Near the opening of Jane Austen's *Mansfield Park*, the ten-year old heroine, Fanny Price, is mocked by her older cousins for not being able to 'put the map of Europe together' to finish a jigsaw puzzle.[2] Although we do not know which jigsaw Fanny was trying to complete, it would doubtlessly have been modelled on one of the earliest jigsaws developed for commercial purposes: *Europe Divided into its Kingdoms* (1766), designed by the map-maker and former apprentice to the Royal Geographer, John Spilsbury. In the space of two years, Spilsbury developed a market for jigsaws as a teaching aid to demonstrate how different countries were geographically related to each other. The example of Fanny Price is cited to demonstrate that the ability to visualise the physical relation of one country to another is a knowledge we acquire as our understanding develops of how relatively abstract spaces (such as national borders) may be spatially related. The concern with visualising the interrelation of space in a period when this competence began to be developed by readers of travel accounts, discussed in Chapter Four, is examined further in this chapter, a process which is predicated on the modelling of space in the reader-viewer's imagination.

Models and casts

In the introductory remarks to the second lecture delivered at the Royal Institution, John Soane directed attention to the important role models played in the design process:

> Anxious on all occasions as far as my limited means would permit to assist the young Artists in their Studies[,] I have embraced every opportunity of collecting Models of ancient and Modern Buildings; – Casts from ancient Ornaments, – Marble fragments, – cinerary Urns, and Vases: – these for the advantage of study ... are as necessary to the Students in Architecture as Casts from the Antique Statues are to the Painter and Sculptor ...'[3]

In similar vein, at the Royal Academy, he observed:

> Drawings and prints ... convey certain ideas and make certain impressions ... [l]arge models, faithful to the originals in every respect, not only as to form and construction, but likewise to the various colours of the materials, would produce sensations and impressions of the highest kind, far beyond the powers of description, sensations and impressions which can only be surpassed by the contemplation of the buildings themselves ...'[4]

We may be certain that Soane regarded the study of architectural models and the modelling of space as an important element in the training architects received in matters relating to the expression of form and space, a perception Soane reiterated in the series of popular lectures he delivered at the Royal Institution.[5]

Models and casts were not only important to the training of students in the Academy schools, where, after probationary admission to the Antique school (drawing from the cast collection), students studied in the Living Model school, refining their skills in life-drawing.[6] Models and casts were also prominent in exhibitions, including those devoted to Mexico curated by William Bullock at the Egyptian Hall between 1824 and 1825. Three-dimensional casts of antiquities made in Mexico provided a visceral experience for visitors to the exhibition, where they encountered a three-dimensional 'monstrous figure, and rude, though not ill-proportioned' (5.1) almost equal to what visitors would have encountered *in situ*.[7] In an age when the transportation of large and cumbersome antiquities would have been prohibitively expensive (and almost impossible to organise), public exhibition relied on the presentation of life-size, three-dimensional facsimiles which, like Catherwood's panoramas and illustrations, assumed a central role in the transmission of knowledge and affect.[8]

If life-size casts at the Mexican exhibitions imparted a sense of awe, they were also sensational on two further counts. First, they presented artefacts and produce not previously seen in England; second, as life-size replicas, they provided a simulacrum of the tropics 'at one glance', as a *coup d'œil*:

> But what afford a most perfect notion of Mexico is a series of models, in full size as well as in little, of the fruits and vegetable productions. We never approached any thing so like the idea of a tropical climate as these give at one glance. The doubted *hand* tree, with its fruit resembling the human hand; the gigantic and clustering shapes of the palms, bananas, plaintains, paupaws, avocatas, annonas [*sic*], and hundreds of others whose forms are totally unknown to us, render credible the veriest stories of travellers, and when seen in their true forms and proportions, excite an astonishment which descriptions and pictures cannot create.[9]

5.1. Agostino Aglio, engraved by I. Baker, *View of the Exhibition of Ancient and Modern Mexico*, 1825, 15.8 x 27.5 cm. [Private collection.]

Casts of unknown fruit stimulated strong responses, exceeding those that descriptions and drawings could convey. Casts and models at the Egyptian Hall provided an overwhelming experience, one which, seemingly unmediated, was akin to the experience that awaits present-day visitors to the British Museum seeing the casts of stela 'H' and stela 'A' from Copán for the first time, made by Alfred Percival Maudslay and Lorenzo Giuntini in the late nineteenth century.[10] The point I wish to make is that just as students in the Academy schools learnt to model space from casts and life-drawing, a not unrelated ability was internalised by readers of nineteenth-century travel accounts. In what ways, then, did the nineteenth-century reader-viewer develop the ability to model space through reading and viewing illustrated publications?

In drawing attention to the issue of training in the eighteenth- and nineteenth-century art academy (where drawing from plaster casts and life-drawing were regarded as the epitome of the process by which artists learnt to express form), the relation of drawing to the intaglio process implicit in the range of nineteenth-century media technologies considered in this chapter (casts, lithographs, photographs, and film) requires elaboration. I propose that the historical viewer understood this process as one that relied on the act of making a 'fixed and durable impress',[11] an 'impression', a common trope which expressed a popular understanding in the nineteenth century of how engraved and photographic images shared similar processes of production. I will also characterise the transformation that attended the innovation of what Ann Bermingham terms 'the landscape of sensation', a development which promoted naturalistic observation accompanied by a shift in representational strategies 'attuned to the optical features of a particular scene and their effects on the viewer's perception'.[12] This innovation, Bermingham argues, coincided with a renewed interest in topography and topographical drawing, which informed the development of landscape painting and sketching in the early nineteenth century and also impacted on the painted panorama. Pursuing a similar line of inquiry, Charlotte Klonk has proposed that attention to apparently insignificant details in painting and sketching, evident in work associated with the informal circle of artists that gathered around John Varley and Cornelius Varley (including John Linnell), favoured a meticulous transcribing of natural phenomena rather than observance of the compositional principles typical of the picturesque. Works such as *Ross Market Place, Herefordshire* (1803) by Cornelius Varley (which depicts the topography and architectural detail evident in the location to this day), or John Linnell's *Kensington Gravel Pits* (1812–1813), demonstrate an interest in what would previously have been regarded as insignificant detail, a response to the phenomenal world that reflected a broader shift in the perception of nature.[13] In this regard, the turn to a more naturalistic mode of depiction in the early nineteenth century coincided with a growth of interest in field studies in geology and geological illustration.[14]

The introduction of stratigraphy in geological illustration influenced artists representing the natural landscape. In particular, geological illustration adopted procedures common in architectural drawing: the section, a procedure examined briefly below. Three concerns, therefore, characterise the discussion of nineteenth-century image-making in Mexico in this chapter. First, an examination of how various mediums in the nineteenth century were understood to be created through the act of impression. Second, how the aesthetic of the picturesque gave way to one that placed emphasis on depicting particularised natural landscapes, a strategy which, departing from the compositional principles that had sustained the picturesque, favoured topographical image-making in the early nineteenth century. As an approach to image-making, topographical images continued to be influential for much of the century, particularly after the introduction of photography, a concern that is addressed in examining developments in the picturesque and topographical views in mid-nineteenth-century Mexico. Third, how the reader-viewer inferred three-dimensional space through relating images to the modelling of space in the imagination.

The facsimile and the photographic image

Facsimiles were not only employed in art academies, private cabinets of curiosity, and public exhibitions, they were also closely associated with the process by which images were made in lithographs and photographs. Before the advent of digital imaging, the exhibition of antiquities in facsimile, the printing of lithographs, and the registering of images by photo-chemical means (a process famously characterised by William Henry Fox Talbot as 'the new art of Photogenic Drawing') were variously understood to rely on a process common to engraving and print-making: the making of impressions.[15] The comparison was elaborated in *The Pencil of Nature* (1844), where Talbot characterised the plates of his work as 'impressed by Nature's hand', going on to reflect, 'how charming it would be if it were possible to cause these natural things to imprint themselves durably, and remain fixed upon the paper'.[16]

The process of making casts by means of impression *in situ* was stock-in-trade for artists and antiquarian investigators for much of the nineteenth century.[17] Travelling with Robert Hay and Frederick Catherwood in Egypt in the early1830s, for example, George Alexander Hoskins relates how casts were made to help engravers transfer drawings 'made by the Author with the Camera Lucida' to lithographic stones:

> My servants made me casts in paper of the sculpture on the walls of these two rooms, that is, of all the sculpture in the three large plates, which I now publish. This method of obtaining fac-similes of sculpture in basso relieve, is very successful, and so easy that I had no difficulty in teaching it to my Arabs. I found stiff, unsized, common white paper to be best adapted for the purpose. It should be well damped; and, when applied to sculpture still retaining its colour, not to injure the latter, care should be taken that the side of the paper placed on the figures be dry – that it be not the side which has been sponged. The paper, when applied to the sculpture, should be evenly patted with a napkin folded

rather stiffly; and if any part of the figures or hieroglyphics be in intaglio or elaborately worked, it is better to press the paper over that part with the fingers. Five minutes is quite sufficient time to make a cast of this description: when taken off the wall, it should be laid on the ground or sand to dry. I possess many hundred casts, which my Arabs made for me at Thebes and in the Oasis. Indeed, I very rarely made any drawings of sculpture, without having a cast of the same: and as the latter are now quite as fresh as on the day they were taken, the engraver having not only my drawing, but also these indubitable fac-similes, is enabled to make my plates exactly alike, and quite equal to the original.[18]

Travelling in Spain in spring 1837, Owen Jones, responsible for printing Catherwood's *Views of Ancient Monuments in Central America Chiapas and Yucatan* some years later, observed:

To insure perfect accuracy, an impression of every ornament throughout the palace was taken, either in plaster or with unsized paper, the low relief of the ornaments of the Alhambra rendering them peculiarly susceptible to this process: these casts have been of essential service in preparing the drawings for publication, and having been placed with them in the hands of the engravers, have greatly contributed towards the preservation of that peculiar sentiment which pervades the works of the Arabs.[19]

The making of drawings and casts as preliminary stages in the production of engravings was regarded by some investigators as superior to making daguerreotype views, since moulds could be removed from a given site and used to make multiple copies, a facility not available to the daguerreotype. As Jean-Jacques Ampère, who worked in Egypt in the 1840s, observed:

With a sheet of paper, a glass of water and a brush, in a few minutes one takes the impression of an inscription or a bas-relief; it's a sort of portable printing which makes it possible to make multiple copies of any original that cannot be removed. No inscription, no sketch can equal the mechanical reproduction. The eye and the hand of the copyist can tire or make mistakes; but making squeezes is not liable to distractions or errors. Thanks to it, one carries away the object itself cast accurately and securely. Squeeze-paper and the camera lucida are the two instruments needed to make an exact and easy reproduction of the monuments. The daguerreotype appears to have marvellous claims to speed; in fact, it is rarely easy to use. We are taking one of those instruments with us, however, but I am told that it will not be as useful as it seems it ought to be.[20]

The fear which villagers in Santo Domingo de Palenque expressed when Stephens sought to acquire casts of bas-reliefs from Palenque is borne out by Ampère's observation: casts were not only portable, as a medium, they were also eminently reproducible.

Comparison of pictures and engravings with the photographic image was the subject of comment in discussions concerning the daguerreotype in the popular press. The invention was characterised in an article published in *Gazette de France* and, in English translation, within a week, in the 'Fine Arts' column of *The Literary Gazette*:

The Daguerotype [*sic*].

M. Daguerre has discovered a method to fix the images which are represented at the back of a camera obscura; so that these images are not the temporary reflection of objects, but their fixed and durable impress, which may be removed from the presence of those objects like a picture or an engraving.[21]

The recognition that an impression drawn from a lithographic stone shares an analogy with the image cast on the back of a daguerreotype camera is significant. Common to both processes is an understanding that engraved and photographic images variously utilised a similar means for making an 'impression' in order to fix an image. As Talbot remarked: 'we may receive on paper the fleeting shadow, arrest it there, and in the space of a single minute fix it there so firmly as to be no more capable of change, even if thrown back into the sunbeam from which it derived its origin'.[22] Towards the end of the article, Talbot considered various applications for 'photogenic drawing', and proposed that the fixed image itself could be used to copy an engraving:

... if the picture so obtained is first *preserved* so as to bear sunshine, it may be afterwards itself employed as an object to be copied; and by means of this second process the lights and shadows are brought back to their original disposition. ... I propose to employ this for the purpose more particularly of multiplying at small expense copies of such rare or unique engravings as it would not be worth while to re-engrave, from the limited demand for them.[23]

At the heart, then, of the nineteenth-century representational system of facsimile is a process that was understood to subtend the production of lithographs, photographs, archaeological facsimiles (and, later, film) which pivoted on the making of fixed and enduring impressions. Lithographs, photographs, and the archaeological facsimile, in other words, were understood to capitalise on a process that created a 'fixed and durable impress'.[24] In the case of film, introduced in Mexico during the second half of 1896 by the Lumière agents, Gabriel Veyre and Fernand Bon Bernard, the *cinématographe* was understood primarily as an instrument that shared a lineage with earlier print-making technologies since, in common with photographs, the device created images by means of photo-chemical impression. However, since it was an apparatus that arrested (as much as 'reconstituted') motion through a series of impressions registered by the spectator in rapid succession, the process was regarded as also perceptual, not only tactile as in the case of the other mediums considered here. An article published in *El Mundo Ilustrado*, the leading weekly illustrated magazine in Mexico City, made this distinction clear: 'when the projection of light is interrupted (which lasts a twentieth of a second) ... from the persistence of impressions on the retina, the eye perceives a series of luminous impressions that cause a perfect illusion of bodily movement'.[25] Refuting the uncanny associations that the projection of the apparatus evoked on some occasions, when the *cinématographe* was presented to the press in Mexico City, spectators were seated on either side of the screen, as in the presentation of the device in the Paris reception rooms of the *Revue Générale des Sciences* on 11 July 1895.[26] In this regard, film represented an extension of the notion of impression since it drew attention to the fact that the impression registered by the projection of the film on the retina could also be regarded as a perceptual activity.

Topographical views and the turn to naturalistic observation

In Chapter Four we considered Stephens' investigation of Chichén Itzá. We return to this discussion to consider more closely the process by which reader-viewers may have inferred the spatial relation of two structures at Chichén Itzá: Las Monjas and Iglesia. Our discussion in Chapter Four examined three plates reproduced as 4.31, 4.32, and 4.33, the east and north facades of 'H', and the west facade of the Iglesia situated on the north-east corner of 'H'. Discussing the east facade of 'H' (4.31), Stephens noted that 'The view comprehends the corner of a building on the right [i.e., the Iglesia on the north-east corner of 'H']'. After discussing the north facade of Las Monjas (4.32), he returned to discuss the Iglesia and observed: '... at the end of the wing stands what is called the Eglesia [*sic*], or Church, a corner of which was comprehended in a previous view and the front of which is represented in the plate opposite [4.33]'. The text draws the reader's attention to the proximity of the two buildings with the Iglesia (or at least a part of it) shown in all three plates.[27] Inspecting the sequence of plates, the reader-viewer occupies three positions with regard to the principal structure ('H') and its satellite (the Iglesia): in the first plate, the viewer is located to the east of Monjas looking towards the west; in the second plate, to the north of Monjas looking south, and in the third plate, at the north-east corner of the principal structure (seen on the extreme right of the plate) looking east at the west facade of Iglesia. Although we cannot verify what the historical reader may have inferred (with or without the aid of the site-plan), by drawing attention to the fact that the Iglesia can be seen in all three engravings, Stephens indicates a more complex articulation of a reverse view, one where the relation between 4.31 and 4.33 involves a reverse but parallel field in space. Such an articulation is not common in the early nineteenth century, although one example is of particular interest since it demonstrates a more scientific interest in depicting the natural landscape: William Daniell's, *A Voyage Round Great Britain, Undertaken in the Summer of the Year 1813*.[28]

With advances in scientific inquiry in late-eighteenth-century Britain, the representation of the natural landscape underwent considerable transformation in the early part of the following century. Some examples of the transformation were examined in Chapter One and Chapter Two when we considered the painted panorama, topographical views, and innovations in cartography. Transformations, however, in representational modes in the early nineteenth century also informed developments in depicting the natural landscape with regard to its geology. Whereas cartography, a relatively abstract system of representation, represented space in the horizontal plane, topographical views and geological stratigraphy represented the natural landscape in the vertical plane perpendicular to the viewer.[29] In this regard, stratigraphy represented the landscape in the form of a section, a feature associated with architectural drawing as discussed in the previous chapter.

Some of the earliest studies to employ stratigraphic illustration were drawn by John Clerk of Eldin to accompany the publication of James Hutton's *Theory of the Earth* in 1795, and by William Green to illustrate Thomas Garnett's *Observations on a Tour through the Highlands and Part of the Western Isles of Scotland, particularly Staffa and Icomkill* in 1800.[30] The introduction of stratigraphy in representing the natural landscape impacted broadly on the visual arts in the early nineteenth century. Thomas Webster, for example, an architect by training who had been appointed draughtsman to the Geological Society of London in 1814, contributed to Henry C. Englefield's *A Description of the Principal Picturesque Beauties, Antiquities, and Geological Phenomena, of the Isle of Wight*, transforming what would have been primarily an antiquarian and picturesque account into a work enhanced by geological maps and stratigraphic section, by which means the geology of the landscape was made legible.[31] By the 1810s, readers encountered not only topographic and cartographic representations of the natural landscape, but also its geomorphology by means of stratigraphic section. Such interest informed some of the aquatints William Daniell prepared from his extensive tour of the coast of Britain when he journeyed from Land's End via the west coast of Britain to John O'Groats and back again to Land's End via the east and southern coasts.[32]

By the time Daniell published aquatints of the west coast of Scotland, particularly his study of the island of Staffa, Daniell was familiar with the geological investigations John MacCulloch had undertaken of the island who, as a chemist employed by the Board of Ordnance, had taught chemistry at the Royal Military Academy in Woolwich.[33] Compared with earlier studies of the island,[34] Daniell's aquatints, particularly *Entrance to Fingal's Cave, Staffa* (Plate 13), represented the basalt columns of the cave with considerable accuracy when compared with contemporary publications.[35] The fame of the island was such that when Daniell reprinted aquatints of Staffa in a further publication in 1818, he incorporated 'a summary of the prevailing opinions of the learned respecting this geological curiosity'.[36] Quoting MacCulloch, Daniell went on to make a personal observation concerning the geology of Staffa:

> 'I have indeed been told that a sandstone bed has been seen at low water on the south-western side, but I had not an opportunity of observing it. …
>
> 'The next bed that which is divided into those large columns which form the most conspicuous feature of Staffa, and it varies between thirty to fifty feet in thickness. The upper one appears to be an uniform mass of amorphous basalt, but on a nearer inspection, it is found to consist of small columns laid and entangled in every possible direction, often horizontally, and generally curved. It is this bed which forms the ponderous cap (as it is called) which crowns the summit of the grand *façade*.'
>
> In the succeeding view, entitled ENTRANCE TO FINGAL'S CAVE [Plate 13], these three distinct deposits are observable. The range of perpendicular basalts with their irregular substratum, may be conceived as forming the sides of the cave, of which the roof may be supposed to commence at the junction of the columns with the superincumbent mass.[37]

Daniell's observation implies that a topographical view of Staffa also represented the island's geomorphology.[38] Familiar with the convention of the section, and following Daniell's discussion of MacCulloch, we may propose that some readers would have interpreted the representation of *Entrance to Fingal's Cave, Staffa* as a representational hybrid: a topographical view, on the one hand, yet one which also drew attention to what may be characterised as a stratigraphic 'elevation'. Constituting a topographical view informed by stratigraphic analysis, the aquatint of Staffa demonstrates a scientific turn in image-making in the early nineteenth century.[39] The print also evidences a departure from the conventions that sustained illustration in the picturesque manner. Let us now turn to consider this development with regard to images of Mexico, to ascertain to what degree the picturesque was redefined in the 1830s and 1840s.

The fine arts were in a sorry state in Mexico when Bullock and his son visited the country in 1823. The Academia de San Carlos (the

Academy of Fine Arts, founded in 1781 and granted a royal charter by Carlos IV of Spain two years later), had been modelled on the academies of Rome, Paris, and Madrid, and was the first institution of its kind in Central and South America.[40] After the years of struggle for independence between 1810 and 1821, its revenues had been lost, although the Academia building and its casts remained.[41] According to Bullock, neither student nor director attended the Academia.[42] Of sculptors, there were many, 'as every house has a statue of a saint or Madonna painted and generally superbly dressed', but lithographic engraving was 'unknown in Mexico'.[43] Although a considerable period of time was to pass before the fine arts were set on a firm footing, following reforms in 1843, teaching in the principal areas of the Academia was re-established. Pelegrín Clavé, a Catalonian trained primarily in Italy, was appointed to teach painting and assume the directorship of the Academia in 1846, the same year in which Manuel Vilar (who had studied in Barcelona and Rome) was appointed to teach sculpture.[44] It was not until the 1850s, however, that a school of painting was established in the Academia that defined the nation's history as the principal concern for painting in the academy.[45] In advocating this policy, the political establishment, representing traditionalist or liberal views, played a crucial role. Rafael de Rafael best summarised the position at mid-century, when a policy advocating the representation of a national history began to be promulgated:

> We do not hide from the grave difficulties that face the formation of a school of painting worthy of the name of national; a school that will not be a pale reflection, an imitation (more or less servile, more or less exact, more or less excellent) of schools from other climes. Born yesterday, one can say that our country still has no history; that here, one of the richest sources where the artist and poet can draw inspiration, does not exist among us.[46]

Compared with the styles of painting favoured by the Academia de San Carlos, lithography was more closely associated with popular tradition. The medium was introduced in Mexico in 1826 when the Italian, Claudio Linati de Prévost, visiting the country between February and August, opened a printing business in Mexico City, and published an illustrated, pocket-sized periodical, *El Iris*.[47] Later, in Brussels, Linati published *Costumes civils, militaires et réligieux du Mexique* which, depicting historical personages such as Montezuma (Motecuçoma) and Miguel Hidalgo,[48] established a genre for representing Mexican people (*tipos mexicanos*) that continued as a popular subject in engravings (and, later, photographs) throughout the rest of the century.[49]

Engraving was introduced in the curriculum of the Academia de San Carlos when Ignacio Serrano took up a post responsible for the medium in October 1830, appointing Vincente Montiel as the first draughtsman attached to the lithographic studio.[50] During the next decade, commercial lithographic workshops were established in Mexico City: in 1836 by José Severo Rocha and Carlos Fournier,[51] followed by the printer, José Decaen, in 1838, who worked with the lithographer, Hipólito Salazar. In 1840, Decaen established an enterprise with Agustín Massé, who had come to Mexico from France in 1837, and had worked with Julio Michaud, who had emigrated to Mexico in 1830.[52] Two years later, Decaen sold the business to Ignacio Cumplido. The earliest flowering of lithography in Mexico is generally accorded the publication of *Mosaico Mexicana* by Ignacio Cumplido in 1837,[53] followed by the publication of *Monumentos de Méjico* by the Italian scenographer, Pietro (Pedro) Gualdi. Two traditions were influential in Mexico at mid-century. The first represented a development of the picturesque; the second, a concern for the urban scene and panoramic views. We now turn to consider these developments more closely. We will consider how picturesque and panoramic views changed with regard to image-making in Mexico during the mid-nineteenth century.

Animating the picturesque

Consider an engraving of the village of San Agustín de las Cuevas (5.2), published in John Phillips' *Mexico Illustrated, with Descriptive Letter-press, in English and Spanish* in 1848.[54] The letterpress accompanying the engraving informs us:

> The village of San Agustin [*sic*] de las Cuevas is about four leagues from the city of Mexico, charmingly situated in the midst of handsome villas

5.2. John Phillips, engraved by Day & Son, Plate 18, *San Agustin de las Cuevas*, hand-coloured chromolithograph, John Phillips, *Mexico Illustrated in Twenty-Six Drawings* (London: E. Atchley, Library of Fine Arts, 1848), 24.9 x 37.8 cm. [Reproduced by permission of the National Library of Sweden.]

> and orchards. It is celebrated for the great fête which is held annually at Whitsuntide and attended by every body in Mexico who can by any means provide for the occasion. Most fertile and beautiful as the country is about San Agustin, there lies immediately beyond it a tract of black lava and scoriæ destitute of vegetation, called the Pedregal, extending to the base of the mountain of Ajusco, which forms part of the chain separating the Valley of Mexico from Cuernavaca.[55]

The term, 'scoriae', designates a sharp, clinker-like material formed by the cooling of molten lava distended by the expansion of internal gases. The term, not found in the picturesque, was one which Phillips, appointed Secretary to the board of directors of the Company of Adventurers in the Mines of Real del Monte in January 1840,[56] expected readers to understand. In respect of composition, the view observes the conventions of the picturesque with foreground interest, a generalised middle ground of trees, and side screens comprising the village church in the middle distance and the Calvario towards foreground right. The range of hills and volcanoes on the far side of the Valle de México embosom the valley in a manner typical of the natural amphitheatres which William Gilpin, Frances Calderón de la Barca, and Brantz Mayer admired, as discussed in Chapter Two. The scene, however, also presents a social occasion in the annual calendar of religious festivals, departing from the concerns of the picturesque to provide local colour with an intimation of the exotic. In this regard, we may propose that the tradition of representing the picturesque has mutated, taking on additional inflections in Phillips' engraving.

The attention to detail in the letterpress accompanying Phillips' engraving is reflected in a chromolithograph of the same festival published in 1840 by Daniel Thomas Egerton (Plate 14). Although the aerial perspective of Egerton's work accords with the classical landscape favoured in the picturesque, the letterpress pays equal attention to the social occasion of the festival as celebrations transferred from the village to the Calvario on the hill for dancing before nightfall. We may note that the letterpress, once again, observes an interest in geology, in this case, the range of mountains and the volcano, Iztaccíhuatl, depicted in considerably more detail than in Phillips' engraving:

> The Annual Festival held at this place, about ten miles from the Capital, draws together great numbers of all classes, even from distant places, attracted by the customary amusements of cock-fighting, gambling, and dancing; large sums are betted upon a main of cocks, and the pit is attended, amongst others, by the highest dignitaries of the Church, Ministers of State, and ladies celebrated for their beauty and fashion; in the houses fitted up for gambling, where females are rarely seen, immense stakes change hands upon the turn of a card; and most persons retain some unpleasant reminiscences of 'The Feast of San Agustin' [*sic*]: it lasts three days, and upon each evening – the time represented in the picture – a line of coaches and pedestrians mark the way towards 'El Calvario' (Mount Calvary) outside of the town, where, in the field below, dancing commences, and, accompanied with a band of music, is kept up with great spirit until dusk – the *aristocracy* being mere spectators. In the foreground of the picture two peasants, in their holiday attire, perform the national dance called the '*Jarave*'. The view from this point, looking over verdant fields and groves, at this season thronged with groups of happy faces, is peculiarly animating: the snow-clad mountain in the distance is one of those seen in Plate I. (Iztaccihuatl, *sic*), though now considerably farther off, and viewed on a different side.[57]

The social mix observed by Egerton, typical of the annual carnival, was the subject of comment by Frances Calderón de la Barca on the two occasions she attended the festival. On her first visit in 1840, she noted that ladies, in their elegant costumes, were 'looking forward to a delightful whirl of dancing, cock-fighting, gambling, dining, dressing, and driving about', and observed that 'these three days are excessively amusing, and as all ranks and conditions are mingled, one sees much more variety than at a ball in the city'.[58] Attending the festival the following year, Calderón de la Barca noted that the crowd dancing on El Calvario 'presented the appearance of a bed of butterflies dancing with black ants'.[59] The social mix – '[t]he general *coup d'œil* was exceedingly gay' – was commented on in a manner that acknowledged the carnival atmosphere, quite different to the social distinctions maintained in the city: 'There were people of all classes; *modistes* and carpenters, shop-boys, tailors, hatters, and hosiers, mingled with all the *haut ton* of Mexico. Every shop-boy considered himself entitled to dance with every lady, and no lady considered herself as having a right to refuse him, and then to dance with another person.'[60] Of the gambling in the village square, Calderón de la Barca observed: 'It is a sight, once seen, can never be forgotten. Nothing but the pencil of Hogarth, or the pen of Boz, could do justice to the various groups there assembled. It was a gambling *fête-champêtre*, conducted on the most liberal scale.'[61] Her observations, epitomising the social gulf that existed between city life and country life in the early 1840s, is a concern that would not have been entertained in the picturesque, even though the gulf is disavowed in Egerton's letterpress. Such an image presents a bucolic view of life, a response which the majority of people attending the festival are unlikely to have shared.

In 1836, Carl Nebel, a German architect who travelled in Mexico between 1829 and 1834, published *Voyage pittoresque et archéologique dans la partie la plus intéressante du Mexique par C. Nebel, architecte* in Paris.[62] Nebel states, in the Préface, that it was not his intention to instruct but, rather, to serve the public by way of distraction, since 'in my drawings I have represented the objects with the greatest accuracy, without fancy playing any role'.[63] The emphasis on accuracy designates an interest that departs from the picturesque, even if the title of the work reflects an affiliation with that tradition. The view I select for discussion is one which announces similar concerns to those of Egerton, in this case, a view of the city of Mexico from the outlying village of Tacubaya, overlooking the grounds of the archbishop's palace: *Mexico*[.] *Vista desde el Arsobisbado* [*sic*] *de Tacubaya* (Plate 15).[64] The view encompasses most of the northern half of the Valle de México, composed with a foreground framed by rocks and a large yucca on the right and left, and a tall American century plant (an aloe, *agarve*) at right of foreground centre framing the staffage in the foreground centre. The middle ground, to the rear and right of the gentleman on horseback and the peasant (with a *sarape* over his shoulders) who has removed his hat, reveals the grounds and buildings of the archbishopric. In the distance, towards the left, the Colegio Militar de Chapultepec may be seen beyond which, in the far distance, at the foot of a large hill (the Cerro de Tepeyac), the basilica of Nuestra Señora de Guadalupe and the nearby Capuchin convent can be discerned on the edge of the valley. In front of the basilica (and below Chapultepec), the Molino del Rey can also be discerned. In the distance, in front of a large area of water that fills the far side of the valley (the Lago de Texcoco), the city of Mexico is displayed with the twin towers of the Catedral Metropolitana visible in the distance to the left of the foreground *agarve*. Agricultural land and farms fill the western side of the valley (nearest the viewer), and a tree-lined road leading south (in the direction of San Ángel, beyond the right frame) crosses the valley. Sunlight appears through clouds to the south and east of the city. Before going on to describe specific locations in the valley, Nebel observes: 'It is possible to find a capital situated in a very fertile and picturesque location, but it would be difficult to find one with a character as imposing and as dignified as that which can hold in its breast an area like that of the valley of Mexico'.[65] Here, attention to topographical detail reflects a very different aesthetic to that of the picturesque (even if the scene is once again embosomed in a valley) emphasising the depiction of a particular landscape. In this respect, and contrary to the concerns of the picturesque reflected in the title of the publication, Nebel's depiction of the Valle de México marks a clear shift in representational strategy.

Nebel's view of the Valle de México has, of course, a lineage: Bullock's panoramic view of the valley, made with a camera lucida from a similar location to that later employed by Nebel, was exhibited as a backdrop to the *Exhibition of Modern Mexico: containing a panoramic view of the city* at the Egyptian Hall in 1824 (5.3). A view from the location that Nebel used was also re-worked in *Álbum pintoresco de la República Mexicana* (c. 1849–1852),[66] where the scene was given considerable novelty by including the subject of a *tipos mexicanos* in the foreground which, highlighting the staffage associated with conventional depictions of rural life in landscape painting, omits the tall *agarve* seen in Nebel in favour of an indigenous family of charcoal burners: *Indios carboneros. Vista General de México Desde Tacubaya* (Plate 16).[67] The circulation of images of this location meant that, by the time the French photographer, François Aubert, arrived in Mexico in 1864,[68] he too took a photograph of the valley from an elevated location similar to Nebel, showing a field of *agarve* in the foreground (Plate 17). Although the field of view is restricted in Aubert's albumen print compared with Nebel's engraving, the central features of the composition (the archbishopric, the wall of the estate in the lower part of the print, the cathedral, and the hill on the far side of the city near the thermal baths of Peñon de los Baños) are included in the photograph. Comparison of this print with Nebel's chromolithograph evidences the degree to which a concern for the particular had impinged on the compositional principles associated with the picturesque.

5.3. Agostino Aglio, engraved by Agostino Aglio, *Exhibition of Modern Mexico at the Egyptian-Hall Piccadilly*, 1824, 17 x 28 cm. [Private collection.]

By the time Porfirio Díaz came to power, the notion of the picturesque had undergone substantial redefinition in Mexico.[69] On the one hand, publications drawing on the tradition frequently emphasised a concern for narrative, anecdote, and historical commentary, as demonstrated by the publications of Daniel Thomas Egerton and John Phillips. On the other hand, the positivist concerns espoused during the Porfiriato, which sought to promote the modernisation of the country and strove to emulate a European life-style, also promoted the publication of works that drew on illustration in the picturesque manner, substantially re-working many of the conventions associated with the picturesque. This development may be represented in a series of photographs that Alfred Saint-Ange Briquet took of the railway from Mexico City to the port of Veracruz, inaugurated in 1873. Briquet, who had taught photography at the French military academy in St. Cyr, arrived in Mexico in 1883, when he was contracted by a French shipping firm to photograph Mexican ports. Two years later, he opened a studio in Mexico City, working as a commercial photographer, and photographing a variety of subjects including the Mexican landscape, the cityscape of Mexico City, *tipos mexicanas*, and modern developments in Porfirian Mexico.[70] One of the subjects Briquet photographed was the railway connecting Mexico City with Veracruz, selling a series of albumen prints of bridges built for one of the major engineering projects championed by Díaz in the 1870s.[71]

A typical example of Briquet's work is *Estado de Veracruz – Puentes de Chiquihuite* (5.4), which contrasts two bridges on the Mexico City to Veracruz railway in a visual trope representing 'the old and the new'. The view was transformed when the subject was included as a chromolithograph in Antonio García Cubas' *Atlas pintoresco e histórico de los Estados Unidos de México*, where the bridges were

5.4. Alfred Saint-Ange Briquet, *Estado de Veracruz – Puentes del Chiquihuite*, albumen print, wetstamp 'A. Briquet Phot' bottom left, 1880s, 17.5 x 24.8 cm. [Reproduced by permission of the Getty Research Institute.]

included in an atlas of the communication systems of Mexico: *Vías de comunicación y movimiento marítimo*, published in 1885 (Plate 18), appearing as an inset at bottom right (Plate 19).[72] The addition of a young family with a child in the foreground entering a cottage with a cross on the outside wall, the removal of horses drawing two heavy carriages, seen in the photograph, and the removal of a hut on the far side of the railway constitute substantial changes to the image Briquet photographed, reconfiguring old and familiar forms in place

5.5. Julio Michaud, *El Infiernillo*, vignetted albumen print, blindstamp 'Julio Michaud Mexico', 1880s, 11.2 x 16.8 cm. (maximum image size) mounted on card 20.6 x 23.1 cm. [Reproduced by permission of Fototeca UNAM.]

of the harsh existence that the rural poor experienced in Mexico. Such changes, rendering the image 'picturesque', were in keeping with the elite readership for which *Atlas pintoresco* had been designed: bourgeois consumers rather than bureaucratic consultation. In short, if the publication inspired the imagination, the chromolithographs, as Raymond B. Craib has observed, 'did not move the investor'.[73]

Even more striking a comparison may be made in respect of a bridge photographed by Briquet which, masked, as a vignette like the aquatints that Gilpin used to illustrate his work, were marketed with the blindstamp of Julio Michaud (5.5). The same bridge was the subject of an inset in García Cubas' *Atlas pintoresco e histórico de los Estados Unidos de México* (inset second from bottom left, Plate 20) and in an earlier publication by Casimiro Castro, *Álbum del Ferrocarril Mexicano*,[74] where a steep railway embankment with a Fairlie steam locomotive in the first of a series of gorges known as Infiernillo ('little hell') was rendered as a highly fanciful chromolithograph (Plate 21) for which Antonio García Cubas wrote the following description:

> Before the railway penetrates the gorges of the Infiernillo it passes along the first viaduct of this name, boldly sustained on the fearful slopes of this defile (see Plate XVII). ... and lastly, the whole of this spot, notwithstanding the grandeur of the spectacle, infuse in the mind of the traveller, a sudden fear and terror, at finding himself moving through space, with but a slight defense and like to the eagles, soaring over valleys and forests and crossing ravines and precipices. ... On leaving the tunnel No. 10, the perspective of a deep glade known by the name of 'La Joya' [The Jewel] causes a new and agreeable sensation. 'Not even in Switzerland – says a traveller – have I contemplated any spot more lovely or picturesque than that presented by this portion of the road, called La Joya. On one side of the mountain, which disappears under a mantle of moss and green sward, adorned with thousands of wild flowers, a forest of secular trees, crowns the spot, like to a diadem. On the other side, a dark green valley, watered in its entire length by a meandering rivulet that glides murmuringly over a bed of sand. ... I am certain that no one has ever passed by here without feeling the desire, even for a moment, of fixing their residences, in that spot where every thing breathes peace and happiness.'[75]

The transformation from the gorge as photographed by Briquet to its representation in García Cubas' *Atlas pintoresco* is even more marked if the chromolithograph is compared with the painting to which it alludes: Asher Brown Durand's *Kindred Spirits* (1849), set in the Catskill Mountains, on the rim of the Kaaterskill Falls.[76] In the work by Durand, the painter, Thomas Cole, and the poet, William Cullen Bryant, are, as Barbara Novak has proposed, 'in dialogue not only with each other as kindred spirits, but with each other *through* the equally kindred spirit of nature itself', a process which requires 'not the solitary figure, but two figures in a landscape'.[77] In Durand's painting, the transcendental consonance between artist and nature is a far cry from the historical reality that agrarian communities would have experienced – one of profound dislocation – when land ownership was transferred to the railway company that built and operated the line. This process, wherein property rights and boundaries, traditionally experienced as fluid and ambiguous, were transformed from a social relation into a commodity,[78] highlights the reification of relations that attended the experience of modernisation for the rural poor. Such a process stands in marked opposition to the power that the lithographs were intended to confer on the purchasers of the album. Here, the mastery of space for would-be investors in a modern Mexico meets a historically deracinated other. We may propose, therefore, that the bucolic vision of travel accounts in the picturesque manner underwent a major transformation in Mexico in the second half of the nineteenth century.

Panoramic views and urban scenes

Born in Capri, Pietro Gualdi trained in Modena and at the Accademia di Bella Arti di Brera, Milan (where he studied in the *vedute* tradition) before sailing to Mexico towards the end of 1835 to work as a scenographer for the opera company of Madame Albini. In 1838, when the opera company returned to Italy, Gualdi stayed on in Mexico, working as a painter of the urban landscape.[79] Gualdi painted four large-scale panoramic views of the capital from the tower of the convent church of San Agustín, a location much favoured by artists (and, later, photographers) from which to make panoramic views of the city, before the tower was demolished in 1884 when the convent was converted into the Biblioteca Nacional.[80] In January 1841, Gualdi published an album of the principal monuments of Mexico City, *Monumentos de Méjico*, with a variant edition issued the following year.[81]

Gualdi also published a series of four engravings in 1841 which were developed from the four panoramic paintings: *Vista sudeste del panorama de México* (5.6); *Vista sudoeste del panorama de México* (5.7); *Vista norteoeste del panorama de México* (5.8); and an untitled panoramic view of the northeast of the city (5.9).[82] The engravings are amongst the earliest panoramic views of the city sold in Mexico. A notice for the series first appeared in *Siglo XIX*, drawing subscribers' attention to the fact that the lithographs displayed 'the streets and outskirts of the city, with all its workshops and buildings, copied in the most meticulous detail from life and judged to be equal to what one sees'.[83] Gualdi's views offered local people an opportunity to acquire a series of four, continuous prints of the city. In this regard, the lithographs, each representing a 90° view of the city, presented a verifiable series of views in a manner typical of the camera lucida and the camera obscura.[84] The four engravings were later reworked by Urbano López for publication in *Álbum pintoresco de la República Mexicana*, probably published in Paris, since Gualdi's lithographs were re-engraved by Rose-Joseph Lemercier and Prodhomme in Paris, and sold by Julio Michaud y Thomas in Mexico City from his print workshop.

In the first of Gualdi's panoramic views (5.6), the cloister and convent buildings of San Agustín dominate the foreground of the engraving, with (in sequence from left to right) the Iglesia de Jesús Nazareno, the churches of San José de Gracia and San Miguel Arcángel, and the Convento de San Jerónimo seen to the southeast of the city. The snow-capped volcanoes of Iztaccíhuatl and Popocatépetl are visible in the far distance. The view to the southwest (5.7, in sequence from left to right), presents the Iglesia Regina Coelli, the Colegio de las Vizcainas with, closer to the viewer, just right of centre in the middle ground, the Convento and Oratorio de San Felipe Neri. The church of the Colegio de San Juan de Letrán may also be seen on the edge of the street that runs below the viewer on the extreme right of the engraving. In the distance, on what appears as a small elevation, the Colegio Militar de Chapultepec (later, the Castillo de Chapultepec) may be seen, and to its left, some distance from the city, the village of Tacubaya, nestling among the hills. In the far distance, among the hills on the extreme left of the view, the village of San Ángel may also be discerned. On the western edge of the city, a long aqueduct runs towards the right. In the view to the northwest (5.8, from left to right), the Colegio de Niñas and, just left of centre, the large site of the Convento de San Francisco are seen, with, to the right, on the edge of the city, the tower of the church of San Juan de Dios and the twin towers of the church of Santa Vera Cruz. To the right, the cupola and tower of Nuestra Señora de la Concepción and the Convento Santa Clara may be observed, and the cupola and twin towers of the church of la Profesa towards the right of the view. In front of la Profesa, the tower of the Templo del Espíritu Santo is visible. Finally, in the northeast view of the city (5.9), the Convento de Santo Domingo may be seen on the extreme left, seemingly flanked by the church of Santa Catarina Mártir (on the outskirts of the city) with the church of Nuestra Señora del Carmen to the right. The Catedral Metropolitana and Sagrario occupy the area at left of middle-ground centre. To the right

5.6. Pietro (Pedro) Gualdi, engraved by Pietro Gualdi (lithographer), *Vista sudeste del panorama de México*, *Monumentos de Méjico* (Mexico City: Masse y Decaen, 1841), 34.6 x 51.7 cm. [Reproduced by permission of Fondo Reservado, Biblioteca Nacional UNAM.]

of the cathedral, the cupolas and drums of, first, the Iglesia de Nuestra Señora de Loreto (with two towers), then the church of Santa Teresa la Antigua may be seen, with the pedimented roof of the Cámara de Diputados (Chamber of Deputies) visible on the far side of the Palacio de Gobierno (present-day, Palacio Nacional). The cupola of Santa Iñés (partly obscured) may be seen behind the Cámara de Diputados, and the church of Santisima Trinidad (with a single tower and large cupola) is visible to the right towards the edge of the city. On the right, relatively close to the viewer, the cupola of San Bernardo, behind which, towards the right, on the eastern edge of the city, the twin towers and symmetrical facade of the church of La Soledad de Santa Cruz are visible in the distance. To the left, in the valley beyond the city, and close to a small rise, the thermal baths of Peñon de los Baños can be made out. On the

5.7. Pietro (Pedro) Gualdi, engraved by Pietro Gualdi (lithographer), *Vista sudoeste del panorama de México*, *Monumentos de Méjico* (Mexico City: Masse y Decaen, 1841), 34.6 x 51.8 cm. [Reproduced by permission of Fondo Resrvado, Biblioteca Nacional UNAM.]

extreme right, at the far end of the street that runs beneath the viewer, the pitched roof of the Convento de la Merced is visible.

I observe that the convent and church of Santo Domingo is seemingly 'flanked' by the church of Santa Catarina Mártir. I also observe that the series of engravings has a degree of verisimilitude typical of pictorial transcription. Therein lies a clue since there can be little doubt, given the physical distance between Santo Domingo and Santa Catarina Mártir, that the view is compressed, that it is foreshortened. Familiar with the city and the physical distance between landmarks, the viewer becomes aware that he or she is looking at an optically mediated image of the city which challenges the viewer's haptic experience of the city. The images were doubtlessly secured by means of a camera obscura or similar optical device; what is significant, however, is that the lithograph establishes, as Martin

5.8. Pietro (Pedro) Gualdi, engraved by Pietro Gualdi (lithographer), *Vista norteoeste del panorama de México*, *Monumentos de Méjico* (Mexico City: Masse y Decaen, 1841), 35 x 51.8 cm. [Reproduced by permission of Fondo Reservado, Biblioteca Nacional UNAM.]

Kemp has proposed, that what something '"looks like"' to us is not the same as its optically accurate transcription in an instrument'. As Kemp pointedly observes, the matter is taken 'out of our hands'.[85]

Such an observation brings forcefully to our attention that optical transcription is freighted, that *what* we see optically is different to how we perceive the world by means of human binocular vision. As a corollary, Kemp proposes that what was becoming observable for the nineteenth-century viewer was that no frame of interpretative seeing existed, that the concern with pictorial phenomenalism practiced by Varley and Linnell in the early nineteenth century was subject to a process of transformation. Optical technologies not only transcribed the world, they required that viewers accommodate a new relation to the represented world, a process wherein viewers matched their experience of haptic space against its optical transcription. In short, and contrary to discussion in Chapter One, where I proposed an account of spectatorship that privileged

5.9. Pietro (Pedro) Gualdi, engraved by Pietro Gualdi (lithographer), untitled panoramic view of northeast Mexico City, signed 'Gualdi' bottom left, *Monumentos de Méjico* (Mexico City: Masse y Decaen, 1841), 34.5 x. 51.8 cm. [Reproduced by permission of Fondo Reservado, Biblioteca Nacional UNAM.]

somatic concerns, in this case, where the viewer is familiar with the represented scene, the viewer has to accommodate optical transcription which may, in some cases, challenge his or her experience of haptic space. This transformation need not be particularly significant (certainly not of the order proposed by Jonathan Crary, for example),[86] but accommodation is to some degree necessary as the viewer becomes aware that optical transcription makes its own visual artefact rather than presents things as we perceive them.[87]

The concern with optical transcription can be demonstrated with regard to a particular motif in late-nineteenth-century Mexico, one which marks a transition between what, in the latter part of the century, was regarded in Mexico as 'picturesque', and what was also part of a transition to the 'pictorial', a tendency which Gilpin signalled a century earlier when he observed that the picturesque could be regarded as 'expressive of that peculiar kind of beauty, which is agreeable in a picture'.[88] In 1848, Phillips published a lithograph of

5.10. John Phillips after a drawing by Pietro Gualdi, engraved by Day & Son (lithographer), Plate 14, *Convent of La Merced*, John Phillips, *Mexico Illustrated in Twenty-Six Drawings* (London: E. Atchley, Library of Fine Arts, 1848), 25.7 x 38 cm. [Reproduced by permission of the National Library of Sweden.]

the cloister of the Convento de la Merced in *Mexico Illustrated, with Descriptive Letter-press* (5.10), which animated a lithograph that Gualdi had published in *Monumentos de Méjico* at the beginning of the decade (5.11). Subsequently re-worked, Gualdi's lithograph was also published in *Álbum pintoresco de la República Mexicana*. Comparison of the two earlier engravings is instructive. Phillips moved the roof towards the left of the engraving, to imply, presumably, that the angle of view was slightly different. He also placed three figures on the cloister balconies (considerably larger than the small figure seen on the far balcony in Gualdi), adding an element of local 'colour' to animate the lithograph, concerns which were not important to composition in the picturesque manner.

By the 1880s, composition framed through an arch had itself become a pictorial motif, as may be demonstrated in an engraving in Manuel Rivera Cambas' *México pintoresco, artístico y monumental*, a three-volume study of the history of Mexico and its people, published between 1880 and 1883, which depicted many locations in Mexico that were deemed 'picturesque'. A lithograph of a *calzada* (road) through the arch of an aqueduct provides an example: a view of the Calzada de Guadalupe, which leads to the Santuario de Guadalupe and the Bosque de San Pedro in the state capital of Morelia, where trees frame the view on the far side of the arch of an aqueduct (5.12). Rivera Cambas tells us that the *calzada* terminates with the sanctuary, an area that 'is a favourite location for recreation for many families' which, with the Alameda and the paseo de San Pedro, 'are still the preferred spots for rest and relaxation for the people of Morelia'.[89]

5.11 (above). Pietro (Pedro) Gualdi, engraved by Masse y Decaen (lithographer), *Claustro del convento de N^{a}. S^{r}. de la Merced*, signed 'Gualdi' bottom centre, *Monumentos de Méjico* (Mexico City: Masse y Decaen, 1841), 25.8 x 38.8 cm. [Private collection.]

5.12 (left). Manuel Rivera Cambas, engraved by Casa de Murguia (lithographer), *La Calzada de Guadalupe* [Morelia], *México pintoresco, artístico y monumental*, 3 vols. (Mexico City: Imprenta de la Reforma, 1880–1883), III (1883), facing 444. [Reproduced by permission of Condumex.]

The inclusion of the word 'still' (*todovía*) is telling; it intimates that the repose and tranquillity for which the location is valued is passing into history.

If the composition encapsulates the picturesque for Rivera Cambas, by the early twentieth century, the device of the arch could imply a condition different to that which the location actually signified. Compare the lithographs of Phillips and Gualdi, and the view of Morelia in Rivera Cambas' *México pintoresco* with a composition that evokes the tranquillity associated with religious foundations, but which, in the manner in which the photograph is framed, evokes a rather different response, in this case a photographic view of the Catedral Metropolitana by Hugo Brehme, published in his 1923 photograph album, *México pintoresco*.[90] The view, taken from the neo-colonial balcony of the Casa Municipal (city hall) overlooking the largest square in Mexico City, the Zócalo (5.13), is the first photograph reproduced in the Mexican edition of Brehme's publication: *Plaza de Armas (Zócalo) con la Catedral, (desde el Palacio Municipal).*[91] Not only does the framing of the view evoke the tranquillity we associate with a religious foundation (since the viewer is located on a balcony that recalls images such as the Convento de la Merced), but the framing also indicates that a transformation has taken place; that a principle of composition employed in the late nineteenth century, and regarded as 'picturesque', has become, by the 1920s, a pictorial device expressive of what was deemed 'agreeable in a picture'. A frame from an unidentified actuality film confirms the proposition that the compositional principle had been transformed (5.14). The manner in which the shot in the film fragment is composed not only crops the balusters supporting the balustrade (presumably because the camera could not be placed at sufficient distance to include the complete arch), but also compresses the view, demonstrating that optical transcription does indeed make its own visual artefact.[92] In short, what was deemed, at one point, to convey the 'picturesque' demonstrates that over time, the 'picturesque' is tranformed into a pictorial device.

I conclude this section with a discussion of four panoramic views: two presentations of the city of Mexico and two of the city of Veracruz. The first, a series of panoramic photographic views of the city of Mexico, was taken by Désiré Charnay (Claude-Joseph Le Désiré Charnay), who, brought up in Fleurie in the department of Rhône, France, became fascinated with Mexico as a young man after

5.14. Frame enlargement, [Catedral Metropolitana from Palacio Municipal], unidentified 35mm negative film fragment reversed. [Reproduced by permission of Filmoteca UNAM.]

Plaza de Armas (Zócalo) con la Catedral, (desde el Palacio Municipal) Plaza de Armas (Zócalo) with Cathedral, seen from Palacio Municipal
Plaza (Zócalo) mit Kathedrale, vom Municipal-Palast aus gesehen
México, D. F.

5.13 (right). Hugo Brehme, *Plaza de Armas (Zócalo) con la Catedral, (desde el Palacio Municipal), Plaza de Armas (Zócalo) with Cathedral, seen from Palacio Municipal, México pintoresco* (Mexico City: Hugo Brehme, 1923), 21.5 x 12.8 cm. [Reproduced by permission of Getty Research Institute.]

reading John Lloyd Stephens. He travelled to the USA before going on to Mexico, where he arrived in Veracruz towards the end of November 1857. For the best part of a year, Charnay lived in Mexico City, although he may have travelled to the Yucatán peninsula, Oaxaca, and Chiapas before returning to the capital, where he got to know a number of influential people, including the geographer and historian, Manuel Orozco y Berra, and the publisher, Julio Michaud. During his stay in Mexico City, Charnay prepared an album of twenty-five large-format albumen prints of the city, *Álbum fotográfico mexicano*, with short texts written by Orozco y Berra, which Michaud published in 1860.[93] Contemporary with the series of photographs of the city and its environs, Charnay took a five-plate panoramic view of the city from the tower of San Agustín (5.15), the location used by Gualdi for his series of panoramic lithographs.[94] Duplicating material seen in two of Gualdi's lithographs, Charnay presents the northern part of the city, including (from left to right) the Colegio de Niñas, the convent and church of San Francisco, the churches of la Profesa and Santo Domingo, the Catedral Metropolitana, Santa Teresa la Antigua, the Cámara de Diputados, La Soledad, and the Convento de la Merced. In the far distance, in the foothills to the north of the city, the pilgrimage site of Guadalupe, overlooking the basilica, can be discerned just to the left of centre in the central print of the series. On the extreme right of the last print in the series, the corner of the building from which the panoramic view was taken may be observed, slightly soft in focus. Like a painted panorama (or, indeed, an elevated view of an expansive landscape), the photographic panorama presents a *coup d'œil*, presenting a view of the city over which the viewer looks at his or her leisure, dwelling on features that draw the viewer's attention. In this respect, the viewer establishes an individual itinerary for viewing the photographic panorama even though the landmarks also, doubtlessly, orchestrate the viewing process.

Although prints of this size would have been expensive to buy, smaller and considerably cheaper prints of work by Charnay and other French photographers were sold in Mexico. Petitjean, a French soldier on a tour of duty during the French Intervention in Mexico (1862–1867), purchased reduced copies of Charnay's panoramic view of the city (and work by other photographers) which were included in two private albums compiled by Petitjean, presumably bought as a memento of his service in Mexico (5.16).[95] Some of the prints reflect an interest in the French presence in Mexico (prints of the building occupied by the French legation, for example), but many were also of locations that caught the attention of the soldier. In the top row (upper left), the Fuente del Salto del Agua can be seen, a large public fountain at the end of the aqueduct that brought water to the city from Chapultepec. The Paseo de la Viga (upper centre), a canal that brought produce grown to the south of the city to the city's main market, used also for family recreation; the Casa de Azulejos (upper right, a striking seventeenth-century colonial building with tiles from Puebla on its facade), and views of the Sagraria (lower left), the Palacio Nacional, the Iglesia de Loreto, and the Fuente de la Independencia on the Paseo de la Reforma (towards lower right) can also be seen. These prints are mounted around the panoramic view by Charnay. Assembled as a *mise en page* (a concern discussed later in this chapter), the views present images of a city that was becoming a city of tourist sights. Just as the early-nineteenth-century painted panorama attracted a more democratic audience, Petitjean's album attests to a relatively new recreational activity, one devoted to collecting and organising souvenirs on the pages of personal photographic albums, a market distinct from that for wealthy citizens who purchased large-format albumen prints or a large-scale panoramic view such as the one by Charnay.[96] Given that many of the views are of Puebla and that a *Panorama de la Ville de Puebla* is dated '1865, 66, 67' in a handwritten annotation in the album, it is likely that Petitjean served in Puebla during this period when he would have been stationed either at the Fuerte de Loreto or at the Fuerte de Guadalupe on the Cerro de Guadalupe on what was then the northern periphery of the city.

Compare these panoramic views with a panoramic view of the city of Veracruz presented in a film. Information regarding the film is scant; even the date and title on the 35mm negative copy (*Vista del importante puerto mexicano de Veracruz*, 1912) may not be correct, although a market building, under construction, indicates that the film and the panoramic series of photographic views discussed be-

5.15. Désiré Charnay, [Photographic panorama of Mexico City], 1858, five albumen prints, mounted on canvas, respectively (from left to right), 28.8 x 38.4 cm.; 28.2 x 41.7 cm.; 28.7 x 39 cm.; 29.9 x 37.2 cm.; 29.2 x 39.3 cm, with slight variation depending on trim; overall length: upper edge 199.5 cm; lower edge 198.5 cm. [Reproduced by permission of Mapoteca Manuel Orozco y Berra.]

low, were made at relatively close points in time.[97] Extant footage comprises two shots. The first commences with a view looking out to sea, taken from the top of the lighthouse on the Malecón de Sanidad (Quay of Health, 5.17), the principal jetty on the south side of the port.[98] The *vista* reframes at a fairly constant speed to the left, bringing into view the fortress of San Juan de Ulúa (5.18),[99] then continues to reframe left, as the viewer looks towards the north, before two cargo vessels are observed on the jetty nearest the viewer with cranes and warehouses on the jetty to the north (5.19). Continuing to reframe left, the post and telegraph building is brought into view (in the middle distance, on the left, with the railway station in the middle distance, on the right, 5.20). The reframing continues left with the principal buildings of the port and customs buildings appearing (5.21), before the top of a wall on an exterior balcony of the lighthouse comes into view when a flagpole interrupts the progress of the camera. A cut signals that the camera has been repositioned (5.22), after which, the film reframes left (repeating some of the subjects seen in the earlier part of the *vista*), bringing into view the cathedral and Hotel Diligencias in the middle distance (5.23). Continuing to reframe left (5.24), the naval school (Escuela Naval Militar) is seen (with a small fish market (*pescadería*) visible between the naval school and the uncompleted market) and the Instituto Veracruzana, behind a row of buildings that faces the sea. After a brief pause, the shot continues to reframe to the left, bringing into view the Hospital de San Sebastián (5.25), after which, a defensive bastion, the Baluarte de Santiago, is observed (5.26).[100] Extant footage concludes with the tower of the lighthouse coming once again into view, framing the bastion towards the right frame-line (5.27). Reframing proceeds at an even pace throughout the panoramic *vista*, except for the moment when the flagpole enters the shot; this requires the camera be repositioned when filming is interrupted.

Unlike the photographic panoramic view by Charnay, the film presents a panoramic view of Veracruz in a controlled manner since the process of reframing supervises the speed at which the viewer observes the city. Although a degree of selection is undertaken (particularly for viewers familiar with the location), the film departs significantly from the series of prints Charnay took since the film controls the rate at which the city is exposed to the viewer. This process is very different to the final photographic panoramic view of Veracruz considered below, since the order in which the images are

viewed is, arguably, open to the viewer to determine, the last view of which constituting a variant conclusion to the urban scene. This view of Veracruz was taken in the early summer of 1914 when the US navy occupied the port in an attempt to stop a delivery of German arms to the conservative head of state, Victoriano Huerta. Comprising sixteen black-and-white picture postcard views, each measuring 14 x 9 cm., the panoramic view concludes with a variant seventeenth postcard (5.28), photographed almost a month later.

The photographic panorama of Veracruz was deposited by V. Rivera Melo y Ca., Editores for copyright on 17 May 1914 and 20 May 1914 with the Ministry of Education (Secretaría de Instrucción Pública), as stipulated under the Artistic and Literary Property Law of 1883.[101] The only exception was the variant postcard showing the battleship, USS *New Hampshire*, which was deposited on 9 June 1914 and 18 June 1914.[102] The variant postcard is identical to the last postcard in the series except for the superimposition of the warship. A small sailing boat with one sail, carrying six people, is in an identical position in both postcards (towards the bottom left-hand corner), and the wake of what was probably a small boat can be seen to the right of the cargo ship moored on the far side of the quay in the postcard in which the warship does not appear.[103] The variant postcard is a composite print with a subject that draws attention to optical transcription given the perspective that obtains in all but the variant postcard. First, the warship would have been as large (if not larger) than the cargo ship moored alongside the quay, implying that the view of the warship with which we are presented is foreshortened. Second, the flag flying from the warship's bow may have been painted in since the stars and stripes are prominently displayed and, flying towards frame right, emphasise that the vessel is a US warship. Third, if the vessel was moored (as the title on the postcard indicates), the anchors of the battleship would have been dropped, but the two anchors on the starboard side of the ship have not been dropped (it is difficult to ascertain whether the portside anchors have been dropped or not). Fourth, the bow of the cargo ship has been retouched, as too ripples on the surface of the sea in front of the cargo ship and battleship. The ripples in front of the cargo ship appear as small waves in the variant postcard, and may have been painted in over a change in tone in the card since sunlight at the end of the quay is brighter on the camera side of the quay than in the card with the battleship. This card is also printed in a darker tone, and the rigging

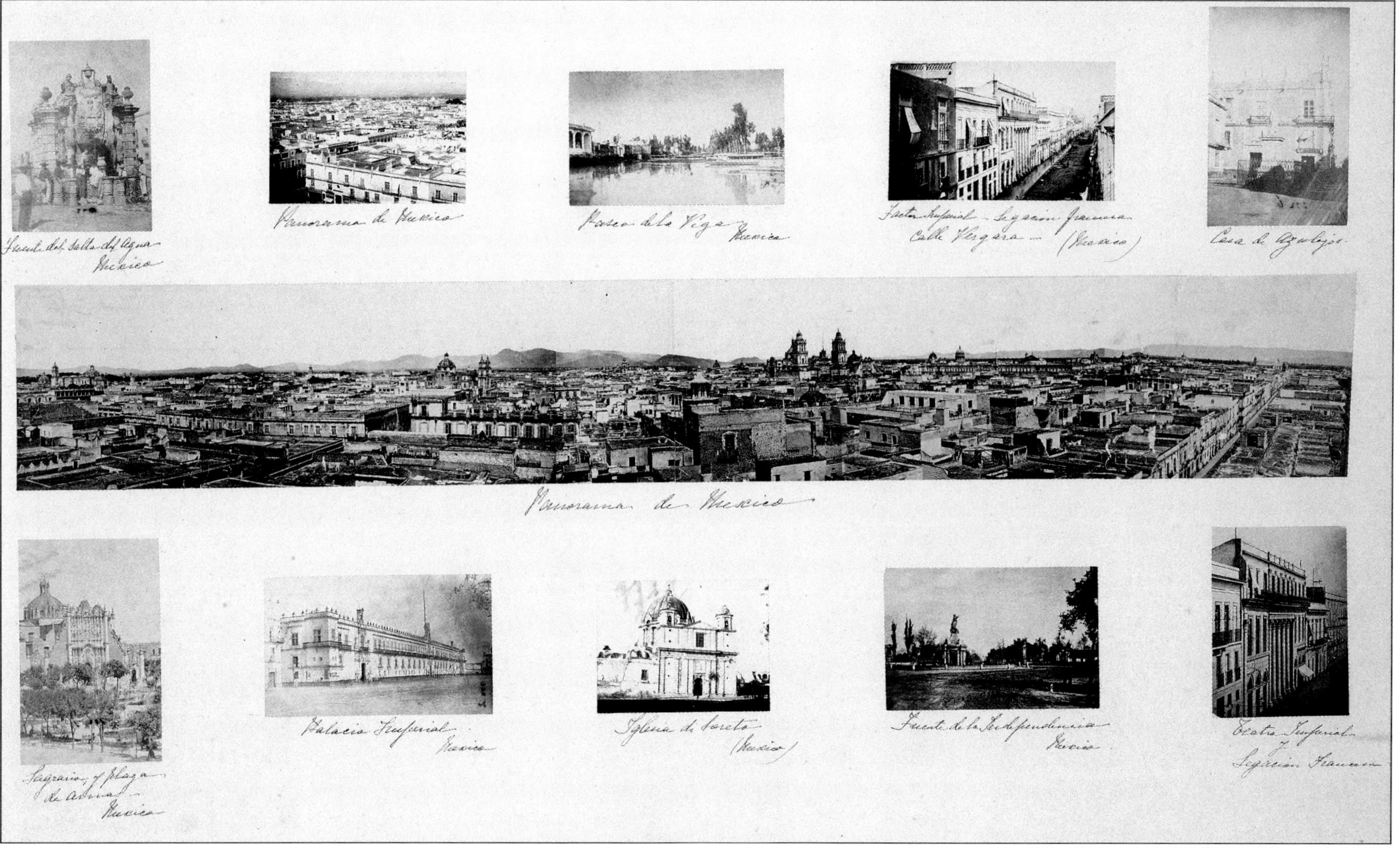

5.16. Désiré Charnay, [Photographic panorama of Mexico City], 1858, reproduced as a reduced format albumen print and titled, in brown ink, *Panorama de Mexico*, mounted as a *mise en page* with ten albumen prints of Mexico City in the first of two private albums titled *Mexique, 1865–1866, 1867* compiled by Petitjean, 1865–1867, with herringbone linen and quarter calf covers; I, leaf 14, 8.5 x 55.2 cm. (comprising two prints 8.5 x 27.5 cm.), page size 47.5 x 62 cm. [Reproduced by permission of Getty Research Institute.]

on the warship may have been accentuated by being drawn in. Lastly, the view of USS *New Hampshire* is taken from a different angle to that seen in the view from the lighthouse, one which makes the stern of the warship appear significantly lower than the vessel's bow. These departures indicate that the variant postcard has been subject to considerable manipulation, and demonstrates, once again, that optical transcription does not necessarily replicate human vision.

While images may 'quote' picturesque or romantic conventions (as in Rivera Cambas' *México pintoresco* or Casimiro Castro's *Álbum del Ferrocarril Mexicano*), the photographic images of Mexico City and Veracruz considered here demonstrate that compositional principles may be transformed by optical transcription and turned into pictorial motifs. The discussion of the panoramic view and urban scene has also highlighted practices that challenged the popularly-held belief (a belief still current today) in the supposed veracity of the photographic image. From a concern with optical transcription to photographic retouching, discussion has demonstrated that images were open to intervention and manipulation, a process that challenged the notion of the photographic image as facsimile or impression. Picturing Mexico, in other words, at the turn of the twentieth century, demonstrates a considerable departure from the aesthetic that attended depiction in the picturesque manner at the turn of the previous century. Practitioners concerned with topographical image-making reflected an interest in a more scientific mode of inquiry to represent knowledge and experience, a process that did not, as observed in the previous chapter, necessarily exclude a concern for affect.

In the last three sections of this chapter, I examine how space was modelled in photographic images in the latter years of the nineteenth century, not only in images taken by professional practitioners, but also by tourists as they organised their experience of visiting Mexico through taking photographs and compiling photographic albums. I also consider how that development was reinforced by the introduction of the illustrated press towards the end of the century, and complemented with the introduction of film. Central to this discussion, I examine how space could be modelled by the viewer in his or her imagination.

'Mapping' space in photographs of Mexico in the latter part of the nineteenth century

On Wednesday, 19 June 1867, Emperor Ferdinand Maximilian (Maximiliano), Archduke of Austria, Emperor of Mexico, and two of his generals (Miguel Miramón and Tomás Mejía) were executed in the early morning by a firing squad on the Cerro de las Campanas to the west of the city of Querétaro. Less than a week later, *The Times* reported in London that Maximilian's life was safe on the grounds that 'Juaréz is afraid to shoot him'.[104] A week later, European newspapers began to carry a rather different story. *L'Indépendance Belge*, for example, reported on 1 July that a dispatch from Vienna brought news that Emperor Maximilian had been shot on 19 June.[105] It took a further three months before one of the more reliable reports concerning the execution was published in *Le Mémorial diplomatique*, on 10 October 1867.[106] The source of the report was given as Maximilian's Hungarian valet, Tudos, whose account, as 'an eyewitness to the scene', was 'corroborated by the account of the priests who helped Maximilian, and the officer in charge of the prison gate',[107] responsible for guarding Maximilian and the generals during their last days in the Convento de Capuchinas after being convicted of treason in a court martial. As Anna Swinbourne has observed, two things are clear from the reports that followed the execution: the act of retelling significantly affected the narrative and, 'for those who were not present, it is impossible to know what happened' on the Cerro de las Campanas on the day of the execution.[108]

If the narrative of events on the Cerro de las Campanas is far from clear, the sequence of events that led to the court martial are relatively clear, and the identity of the photographer responsible for photographing Maximilian immediately after the execution is known: François Aubert.[109] Aubert's albumen prints were circulated in at least two forms. Apart from the production of large-format, albumen prints, Aubert's photographs were also sold as keepsakes which, stamped 'Aubert y Cia Fot.', were sold as a series of albumen *cartes de visite* that represented locations associated with the imprisonment, trial, and execution of Maximilian and the two generals. The album considered here contains twelve *cartes de visite* mounted in a small, red leather-bound concertina album, and included a map re-photographed from a plan of the military campaign conducted by republican forces between 6 March and 15 May 1867.[110] The map, *Plano de la ciudad y de las operaciones del sitio de Queretaro* (Plate 22 and 5.29), drawn by the topographical engineer, Francisco de P. Herrera,[111] shows the positions the troops occupied during the siege of Querétaro before Maximilian surrendered and was taken prisoner. The map also identifies locations associated with Maximilian's trial and imprisonment in the city. With the plan, purchasers of the *cartes de visite* could plot the sequence of events at a time when the chronology concerning the execution itself was impossible to establish with certainty.[112]

Three views are selected for consideration: *Convento de la* [*Santa*] *Cruz y Capilla del Calvario arrimado en la defensa de Queretaro* (Plate 22); *Lugar en donde fallecieron al Emp^dor^ Maximiliano, Miramon y Mejia* (Plate 23); and *Vista de Queretaro* (Plate 23), taken from the Cerro de las Campanas.[113] The first presents a view of the Convento de la Santa Cruz on the eastern edge of the city, Maximilian's former headquarters where he was initially imprisoned (Plate 22). The second print shows three stone markers with improvised crosses that

5.17

5.18

5.19

5.20

5.21

5.22

5.23

5.24

5.27

5.17–5.27. Frame enlargements, *Vista del importante puerto mexicano de Veracruz*, 1912, 35mm negative film reversed. [Reproduced by permission of Filmoteca UNAM.]

5.25

5.26

designate the approximate positions where Maximilian and his generals fell on the Cerro de las Campanas to the west of the city (Plate 23). This *carte de visite* includes Maximilian's insignia placed against a small mound of rubble in the foreground to indicate where, it transpired, Maximilian received the *coup de grâce*.[114] The third print presents a view of Querétaro in the middle distance, taken from the Cerro de las Campanas; the Convento de la Santa Cruz may be discerned, indistinctly, towards frame right (Plate 23).[115] The prints present a series of views where the dramaturgy of events that unfolded in the month between surrender and execution could be plotted by the viewer through matching the *cartes de visite* with the plan. In so doing, the reader-viewer projected an imagined dramaturgy on the sequence of events preceding the execution, adding one further element to the flood of (often contradictory) newspaper reports, eyewitness accounts, signed and anonymous letters, and lithographs concerning the execution that were disseminated in Mexico and Europe through the summer of 1867.[116] Almost five weeks after the execution, *Le Figaro* observed: 'The truth will soon be revealed and verified. Until then, it is the fictional account and not the history of Maximilian's last moments that will be exposed to reading.'[117] In this regard, the album of *cartes de visite* enabled viewers to plot and imagine one further sequence of events in addition to those reported through the summer. As the sequence of events became more clear, viewers could also plot revised accounts.

5.28. [Photographic panorama of the port of Veracruz], May–June 1914, sixteen black-and-white picture postcard views with variant sixteenth postcard view (overleaf), V. Rivera Melo y Ca., Editores, each 14 x 9 cm.

[Reproduced by permission of Archivo General de la Nación.]

5.28. [Photographic panorama of the port of Veracruz], variant of the sixteenth postcard view, 14 x 9 cm. [Reproduced by permission of Archivo General de la Nación.]

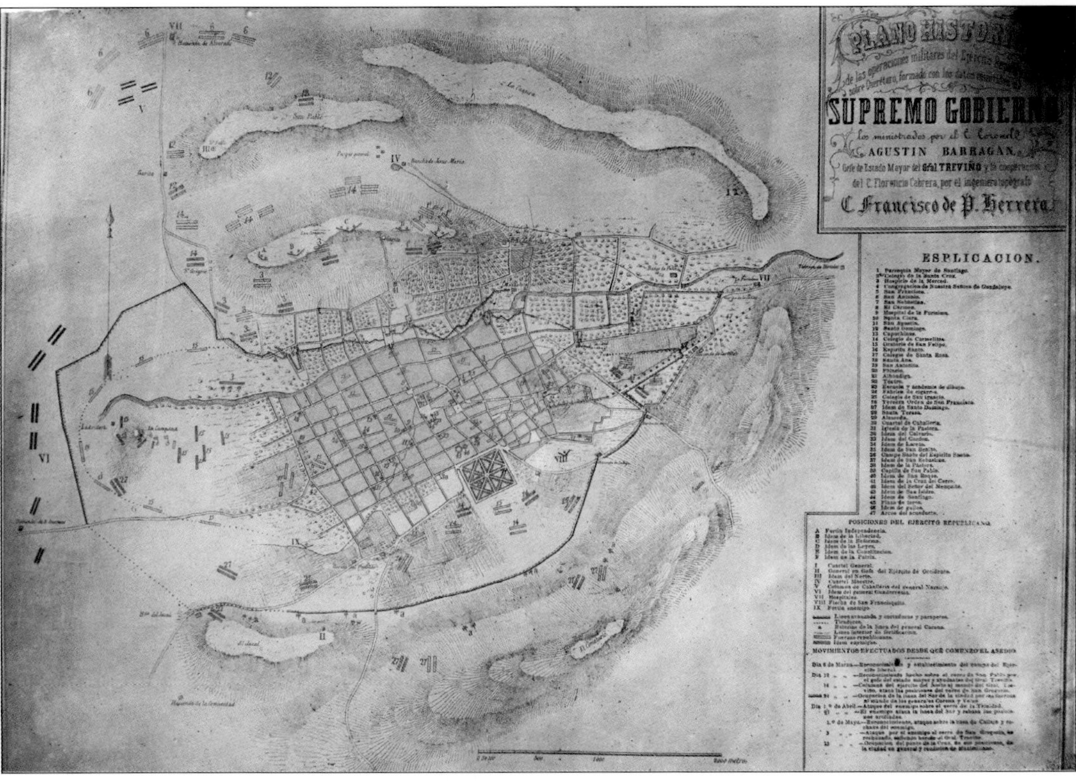

5.29 (right). François Aubert, re-photographed albumen print of a plan of a military campaign drawn by Francisco de P. Herrera, *Plano Historico de las operaciones militares del Ejército Republicano sobre Querétaro*, 1867, 16.5 x 22 cm. [Reproduced by permission of Getty Research Institute.]

Aubert's photographs, in other words, helped the viewer to plot the dramaturgy of recent events by presenting locales where the changing narrative of events could be re-imagined.

Whereas the album of *cartes de visite* demonstrates that interpretation may depend on the historical moment when the reader-viewer engages with a particular work, our second case is very different: the work of Alfred Percival Maudslay, a British archaeologist who conducted investigations at Palenque between 1 February and 12 May 1891.[118] Although only brief discussion, in a study of this length, can be made of the extensive work Maudslay conducted at the site, the tradition in which he worked, photographing Palenque and its architectural details, making moulds, and drawing architectural sections, is readily identified as an elaboration of the concerns for measuring and documenting the site seen earlier in this study.[119]

Unlike Stephens and Catherwood, Maudslay remained at the site for a considerably longer period of time, drawing on a workforce which, on occasion, provided an extensive team of labourers to clear the site.[120] We will recall that when Stephens and Catherwood worked at the site, it was so overgrown with vegetation that they could only discern one structure at any one time. After more than two months clearing the forest that engulfed the site, cleaning facades on buildings, and preparing moulds, Maudslay began to photograph structures, bas-reliefs, and other ornamentation using an 8½ x 6½ inch plate camera.[121] With the site cleared of much of the forest, Maudslay was able to take photographs documenting the site in considerable detail, frequently framing more than one structure in the photographs he took.[122] In this respect, the relation of structures to each other was documented in images for the first time.[123]

The site was surveyed by Hugh Price, using a plane-table and the same principle of triangulation as Frederick Catherwood employed, although doubtlessly using a more sophisticated instrument than Catherwood. Price's survey, *Plan. Principal Group of Ruins*

5.30. Alfred Percival Maudslay, Plate 31, *The Palace. House D, from the West*, gelatin silver print, in F. Ducane Godman and Osbert Salvin (eds.), *Biologia Centrali-Americana; or, Contributions to the Knowledge of the Fauna and Flora of Mexico and Central America*, Vol. LVIII, A. P. Maudslay, *Archaeology*, Vol. IV, Plates (London: R. H. Porter and Dulau & Co., 1896–1899), image size 23.4 x 29.9 cm., page size 33 x 51 cm. [Reproduced by permission of Getty Research Institute.]

at Palenque, is still regarded as one of the most definitive before modern times (Plate 24).[124] The survey commenced on 17 April when Price 'laid out his base lines for the plane-table survey', and, having lost a week due to sickness, was completed on 10 May.[125] With the survey and photographs completed, Palenque as an archaeological site had been rendered legible for the first time. For example, the description of the *Palacio* (identified as 'House D' by Maudslay) was described as something other than a rectangular parallelogram:

> The so-called Palace is in reality a group of buildings, probably temples, originally distinct from one another, but all raised on a common foundation mound. This foundation mound, which may in itself be composite in character, is not in shape a rectangular parallelogram as figured by Waldeck and Stephens, but an irregular oblong, measuring roughly about 340 feet long by 260 feet wide. ... The buildings on top of this mound were raised on secondary foundations and stand at different levels, and are in all probability built at different periods, but the later additions to earlier buildings and the roofing over of passages between them has to some extent welded the whole mass together.[126]

5.31. Alfred Percival Maudslay, Plate 40, *View of the Palace, from the Temple of Inscriptions*, gelatin silver print, in F. Ducane Godman and Osbert Salvin (eds.), *Biologia Centrali-Americana; or, Contributions to the Knowledge of the Fauna and Flora of Mexico and Central America*, Vol. LVIII, A. P. Maudslay, *Archaeology*, Vol. IV, Plates (London: R. H. Porter and Dulau & Co., 1896–1899), image size 23.6 x 30 cm., page size 33 x 51 cm. [Reproduced by permission of Getty Research Institute.]

From the position marked '2' on the site plan, the remains of the northern end of the western exterior facade of the *Palacio* are contrasted with the Temple of the Cross in the middle distance on the right with the forest beyond (*The Palace. House D, from the West*, 5.30).[127] From station '3', the *Palacio* is seen in an elevated view from the Temple of Inscriptions (*View of the Palace, from the Temple of Inscriptions*, 5.31), with the remains of the southern part of the exterior wall of the Palace visible in the middle distance at right of centre.[128] From station '6', the *Palacio* can be seen, from a relatively low camera set-up, towards foreground left, with the Temple of Inscriptions in the middle-ground at right, again with a curtain of trees behind the structure (*The Temple of Inscriptions and the West Side of the Palace, – Looking South*, 5.32).[129]Although the three positions from which the respective structures are viewed do not triangulate space in the manner of a survey, the manner in which the camera is positioned perpendicular to the west facade of 'House D' (5.30) provides a base point from which the spatial relation of 5.31 and 5.32 may be judged to articulate reverse views. In this example,

5.32. Alfred Percival Maudslay, Plate 51, *The Temple of Inscriptions and the West Side of the Palace,– Looking South*, gelatin silver print, in F. Ducane Godman and Osbert Salvin (eds.), *Biologia Centrali-Americana; or, Contributions to the Knowledge of the Fauna and Flora of Mexico and Central America*, Vol. LVIII, A. P. Maudslay, *Archaeology*, Vol. IV, Plates (London: R. H. Porter and Dulau & Co., 1896–1899), image size 21.2 x 30.1 cm., page size 33 x 51 cm. [Reproduced by permission of Getty Research Institute.]

Maudslay's photographs complement Price's survey of the site by documenting overviews of the relation between structures at the site. As with Stephens' and Catherwood's investigations at Palenque, some of the observations Maudslay made concerning the site echo concerns for the melancholy of the location, a response that made a considerable impression on the minds of Maudslay's party, one which, Maudslay observed, 'will never fade': '[t]he beauty of the moonlight nights when we sat smoking and chatting on the western terrace [of the *Palacio*] looking on to the illuminated face of the Temple of Inscriptions and the dark forest behind it will never fade from my memory'.[130] Evoking the picturesque, Maudslay's description provides a counterbalance to the awe that would have prevailed on seeing the site cleared of debris for the first time, a response very different to that which greets visitors today as they approach the manicured landscaped site.

If Maudslay's study of Palenque was more precise in terms of archaeological documentation than earlier investigations, Maudslay also alludes to a sense of romantic displacement, combining scien-

5.33. E. L. [Ernest Louet], *Zacatecas*, albumen print, Plate 26, *Souvenirs de la Campagne du Mexique de 1861 à 1867*, 16.5 x 22.1 cm., page size 33.5 x 49 cm. [Reproduced by permission of Bancroft Library, University of California, Berkeley.]

tific accuracy with affect, a response we observed in Stephens and Catherwood. The concern with using photographic images as a way of charting space also identifies a more popular tradition with regard to the picturing of Mexico in the latter decades of the nineteenth century. We turn to consider work by professional and 'amateur' photographers who charted space before we consider, in the final part of the chapter, the introduction of the illustrated press and film.

Modelling space in photographs of Mexico in the latter part of the nineteenth century

Some of the earliest photographs that evidence a concern for modelling space may be found in the work of a photographer who may also have been the paymaster for the French military during the period of the French intervention, a photographer generally identified as Ernest Louet whose initials ('E. L.') appear in many of the

5.34. E. L. [Ernest Louet], *Zacatecas. Place du Marché. Cathédrale. la Bufa*, albumen print, Plate 27, *Souvenirs de la Campagne du Mexique de 1861 à 1867*, 16.5 x 21.4 cm., page size 33.5 x 49 cm. [Reproduced by permission of Bancroft Library, University of California, Berkeley.]

photographs preserved in two private albums of albumen prints.[131] The albums variously document the French army's campaign as they progressed northwards through Mexico, then south before leaving the country from Veracruz. The albumen prints in each album are titled in the same handwriting.[132] The album held in the Bancroft Library includes four prints taken in Zacatecas, the two prints considered here being mounted on consecutive recto leaves.[133] The first view, inscribed 'Zacatecas', presents a view of one of the main streets of the city, with a partial view of the cathedral and precinct in the middle distance at right of centre (5.33).[134] Buildings with small balconies and a pavement frame a strongly receding view of the street at frame right in the direction of the cathedral, with an arcaded building beyond which crosses the right-hand part of the image and recedes towards frame right; a street lamp on an angled bracket projects into the street from the buildings at frame right, some distance in front of the arcaded building. In front of the cathedral,

5.35. Henry Greenwood Peabody, *120. Tasco with Church of San Sebastian y Santa Prisca, State of Guerrero*, gelatin silver print, Sylvester Baxter, *Spanish Colonial Architecture in Mexico*, The Gómez de Mora Edition (Boston: Art Library Publishing Company, 1902 [1901]), case 9, 18.5 x 23.5 cm., including mount: 26.5 x 32.5 cm. [Reproduced by permission of Fondo Reservado, Biblioteca Nacional UNAM.]

an oblique view of buildings may be seen from foreground left towards the left middle distance. On the building nearest the viewer, 'Espendio de Mescal' may be discerned above the doorway, indicating a liquor store, and a further sign, attached to the side of the building, reads 'Nieve' (sorbet). Sunlight casts shadows from buildings at extreme frame right into the street. Above the arcaded building towards the rear of the print, low hills may be seen; a cobbled street fills the foreground. As the title written below the following print in the album retrospectively indicates, the building beyond the cathedral is the market, 'Zacatecas. Place du Marché. Cathédrale la Bufa' (5.34), the Bufa being a celebrated hill, on top of which a chapel may be seen overlooking the city.[135] This second view constitutes a reverse view of the principal street in Zacatecas.

'E. L.' also took two views of an urban scene in Tepeji-del-Río. In this case, a feature common to the foreground in both prints secures the relation between the two prints. Leaf 20 (recto) presents an obliquely framed view of the single-storey Casa Municipal in Tepeji-del-Río (Plate 25), outside of which a man leans against one of the colonades of the building. On the left, a calvary cross defines the foreground of the composition.[136] The print mounted on the following leaf of the album (leaf 21, recto) reveals the cross now seen in the right foreground with the wall of the Casa Municipal on the extreme right of the print (Plate 26).[137] A low wall crosses the left half of the image marking the wall of a precinct in which a chapel is seen on the far side; the walls of a convent cross the rear of the print. The calvary cross establishes the relation between the two prints as one that articulates a reverse field. Given that the prints are mounted on consecutive leaves, we may propose that the spatial relation between the two prints was one which the viewer may have been expected to observe; alternatively, the relation may have been clarified (and elaborted) when 'E. L.' presented the album to friends or colleagues. This reverse-field view is the earliest example of such an articulation found in photographs researched in this study.

In considering the elaboration of reverse views in photographs of Mexico in the late nineteenth century, two areas of work are considered: photographs by professional photographers and photographs taken by tourists documenting their visit to Mexico in private albums, the latter demonstrating the degree to which the example of professional practive had been internalised by 'amateur' practitioners by the turn of the century. Our first example of work by a professional photographer comprises four consecutive gelatin silver prints taken by Henry Greenwood Peabody which accompanied the publication of Sylvester Baxter's *Spanish Colonial Architecture in Mexico* in

5.36. Henry Greenwood Peabody, *121. Church of San Sebastián y Santa Prisca: Façade*, gelatin silver print, Sylvester Baxter, *Spanish Colonial Architecture in Mexico*, The Gómez de Mora Edition (Boston: Art Library Publishing Company, 1902 [1901]), case 9, 23.5 x 18.5 cm., including mount: 32.5 x 26.5 cm.
[Reproduced by permission of Fondo Reservado, Biblioteca Nacional UNAM.]

5.37. Henry Greenwood Peabody, *122. Church of San Sebastián y Santa Prisca: North Tower*, gelatin silver print, Sylvester Baxter, *Spanish Colonial Architecture in Mexico*, The Gómez de Mora Edition (Boston: Art Library Publishing Company, 1902 [1901]), case 9, 23.5 x 18.5 cm., including mount: 32.5 x 26.5 cm.
[Reproduced by permission of Fondo Reservado, Biblioteca Nacional UNAM.]

1901.[138] Dedicated to the memory of Frederic Edwin Church and Charles Dudley Warner, who had accompanied Church to Mexico in 1887, colonial church architecture was the occasion of a panegyric in Sylvester Baxter's account of colonial architecture which represented 'not only the first, but the most important development of the depictive arts in the New World under European influences':

> Picturesqueness in landscape and architecture is so abounding and so exceedingly varied that it would hardly be possible to say which spot may excel in that quality. But, in the writer's esteem, Tasco – or Taxco as it is less commonly spelled – holds foremost place in the charm of picturesque enchantment. To reach it one must take a horseback journey of twenty miles across wild mountains. Spreading itself over a slope at an altitude of about five thousand feet above the sea, the little city is sheltered from inclement winds by the gigantic precipices of ruddy stone that rise perpendicularly above it, rejoicing in a perfect climate and an air that is tonic and kindly. Extending over the irregular ground, the mass of quaint buildings roofed with red tiles is threaded by a maze of narrow streets. There is not a wheeled vehicle in the city, for the place is inaccessible by such means. The streets are paved with pebbles, laid level from house to house without sidewalks, and are ornamented in mosaic patterns here and there. There is no dust, and the thoroughfares are models of cleanliness. Out of the midst of all the irregularity of ravines, arches, bridges, steps and terraces, rises the great church – the dominant note in a scene that recalls some of those wonderfully picturesque places in Spain.
>
> In such a landscape the florid ornateness of the towers is not excessive in effect. The great dome, decorated with glazed tile in vivid masses of color, – ultramarine, orange, green and white, – seems in the intense sunlight of the place like the blossoming of some gigantic tropical flower, proclaiming in the language of form the immortal words inscribed upon the frieze of the drum: 'Gloria á Dios en las Alturas' – Glory to God on the heights – as the Spanish version renders it most fittingly for this occasion.[139]

A series of four prints of the town of Taxco in the state of Guerrera focus on the church of San Sebastián y Santa Prisca initially seen dominating the skyline. The first print in the series (#120) is accompanied with a text by Baxter on the reverse which draws attention to the 'extraordinarily picturesque' appearance of the town (5.35).[140] The print shows a view looking up towards the west end and southern facade of the church seen towards rearground centre, with the precinct wall below and in front of the south facade of the church.[141] Two towers (with Churrigueresque decoration) and a large cupola at rearground centre are visible. Some adobe buildings with tiled roofs cross the foreground of the composition, and two buildings with exterior wooden balconies may be seen to the left of the church, on the hillside below the church.

The second print in the series (#121), framed perpendicular to the viewer, presents the west end of the church with the two towers cropped just above the belfries in the upper left and upper right parts of the image (5.36). A large, oval, decorative relief on the facade of the church presents a scene of the baptism of Christ, with the figure of John the Baptist standing to the right of Christ, and the figures of God and the Holy Ghost (in the form of a dove) in the upper part of the medallion. The statues of Christ and God may also be observed on, respectively, the left and the right of the clock at the top of the facade, where a statue of Mary, with two putti by her feet, stands with the cupola lantern behind. Two men lean against the wall of the right tower towards the right frame of the print. A view of the tower seen on the left in the second print is the subject of the third photograph, taken on the roof of the church (5.37). The rear of the statues may be seen in the bottom left corner of the print, from where a road leads uphill, visible to the left of the tower. Various adobe buildings, some whitewashed, lead out of town up the hillside behind the tower. A calvary cross may be seen on the hillside, approximagely half-way up the hill near the right frame. The final print in the series (#123) presents a reverse-field view of the drum, cupola, and lantern, photographed from the roof of the church (5.38). The structure occupies the full height of the frame; over the windows of the drum, in polychrome tiles, 'Gloria/a Dios,/en las Alturas,' ('Glory to God on high,') may partially be read below the cupola. The first print in the series establishes a general view of the church, from which the viewer determines the relation of the three succeeding photographs, with the last two photographs establishing a reverse-field view.

The second example of photographs by a professional photographer is a series of views also taken in Taxco in the early twentieth century by C. B. Waite, a photographer who opened a studio in San Francisco, California, in 1889, then worked in El Paso before moving to Mexico City in 1896. After a short period based at calle de Rosales,

5.38. Henry Greenwood Peabody, *123. Tasco with Church of San Sebastián y Santa Prisca: Dome*, gelatin silver print, Sylvester Baxter, *Spanish Colonial Architecture in Mexico*, The Gómez de Mora Edition (Boston: Art Library Publishing Company, 1902 [1901]), case 9, 23.5 x 18.5 cm., including mount: 32.5 x 26.5 cm.
[Reproduced by permission of Fondo Reservado, Biblioteca Nacional UNAM.]

5.39. 'Kodak as you go', strapline for block advertisement, American Photo Supply Co., *Revised Guide and Handbook for Travellers to Mexico City and Vicinity. With Map and Historical Summary* (Mexico City: American Book and Printing Company, 1922), 188.
[Reproduced by permission of Condumex.]

he and his family moved to San Cosme 8 where, on the southern edge of the middle-class district of Santa María la Ribera, Waite opened a photography studio.[142] During the early years of the twentieth century, Waite became the most prolific North American photographer working in Mexico; the views considered here are broadly representative of his work outside the capital at the turn of the century, and were deposited for copyright at the Ministry of Education.[143] On sale to the public, the majority of Waite's photographs were provided with titles and identification numbers, the latter presumably to simplify the purchasing of prints. Wetstamps printed on the reverse identify that the first set of prints were deposited for copyright and sold when his business was based in San Cosme.[144] The second set of prints indicate that by the time Waite sold these views, his studio and business had transferred to San Juan de Letrán 3 and 5, on one of the main streets on the west of the city centre.[145] Given that the prints are numbered sequentially, with the date of copyright known, they constitute a small but coherent body of work rather than individual prints.

Compared with the 1882 commercial directory which listed eleven photographic studios (four located on Plateros – San Francisco (present-day Madero) in the heart of the commercial district),[146] by 1909, when *Terry's Mexico Handbook* was first published, the tourist guide identified four North American photographers working in Mexico City, including Percy S. Cox (who could be reached in the Photo-Engraving Department of *The Mexican Herald*) and C. B. Waite, who sold his photographs and made 'a speciality of developing for travellers' from his studio on San Juan de Letrán.[147] Both Cox and Waite also sold 'artistic souvenirs' through the Sonora News Company store in Mexico City's commercial district, where cyanotypes by Henry Ravell and photographs by Winfield Scott were also sold.[148] By the end of the first decade of the twentieth century, the tourist trade in topographical images and *tipos mexicanos* (photographs of neighbourhood traders and street-vendors) also supported a thriving trade in 'art, antiques, [and] Mexican curios' which, as a block advertisement for Sonora News Company in 1922 proclaimed: 'Antiquarians recognize us as headquarters for unique art objects.'[149] Photographic images, taken or acquired by North American visitors to the country, and complementing the circulation of photographs in the illustrated press at the turn of the century, had become a feature of the tourist and media landscape in Mexico City (5.39).

The sequence of prints of Taxco by Waite commences with two photographs: *1020 Taxco. Guerrero. The First View* (5.40) and *1022 Taxco. Guerrero. View of church and town* (5.41).[150] The first print is an elevated view of the town and surrounding countryside, the foreground of which is defined by trees and scrub in the lower part of the photograph. A road undulates across the lower part of the photograph, 'leading' the eye of the viewer in a manner typical of composition in the picturesque, as discussed in Chapter Two, into the composition, which frames a view of the town and church with a high hill and cliff overlooking the far side of the town. High hills provide a backdrop across much of the view, framing the valley in the foreground and middle distance. The second extant print (5.41) shows the church of San Sebastián y Santa Prisca, taken from an elevated position above the town, possibly from the calvary cross on the hill observed in Baxter. The view is framed by branches in the extreme foreground left and foreground right. A range of hills across the upper part of the photograph recalls the framing of hills in the background of the first view of the town.

In the second series of photographs of Taxco by Waite, deposited at the Ministry of Education in January 1905, the viewer is presented with three consecutive views of a busy open-air market. The sequence comprises *1048 The Market at Taxco Guer. Mex* (5.42), *1049 Sunday Morning in the Plaza. Taxco. Guer. Mexico* (5.43), and *1050 View in the market Taxco, Guer. Mexico* (5.44).[151] The first two prints articulate a reverse view, the street lamp and nearby tree on the far side of the market in 5.42 helping to define spatial contiguity since the same street lamp may be seen in front of the trees towards the right foreground in the second print. The final print in the series presents a detail: a view of the building with four pillars and a balcony seen towards the background in 5.42, now visible at foreground left, with other colonaded buildings in the upper part of the town framing

5.40 (upper). C. B. Waite, *1020 Taxco. Guerrero. The First View*, gelatin silver print, wetstamp on reverse 'San Cosme Vistas', 1901, 12.8 x 20.1 cm. [Reproduced by permission of Archivo General de la Nación.]

5.41 (lower). C. B. Waite, *1022 Taxco. Guerrero. View of church and town*, gelatin silver print, wetstamp on reverse 'San Cosme Vistas', 1901, 12.8 x 20.2 cm. [Reproduced by permission of Archivo General de la Nación.]

the space to the right and rear of the view.[152] Whereas the first sequence of views placed the town in its surrounding landscape, these views articulate space on a much smaller scale, imparting a strong sense of coherence in the location of the Sunday market.

We now turn to consider the issue of articulation with regard to non-professional photographers. Important in this regard is that if a similar sense of spatial contiguity can be demonstrated in non-professional work, we may be certain that the articulation of space observed in the work of Peabody and Waite was one shared by the very different markets for which Peabody and Waite took photographs. If a similar understanding of space can be demonstrated in both cases, then the criteria used to discuss Baxter and Waite were shared by the purchasers of Waite's photographs and 'amateur' photographers. In short, we will have identified how an aesthetic relating to the modelling of space in photographic images was common to professional and non-professional photographers. Two private albums are discussed to demonstrate this proposition.

A private album of 217 collodion prints on printing-out paper documents one of the 1895 tours of Mexico organised by the Raymond and Whitcomb company of Boston.[153] Travelling south from Boston to New Orleans, from where the tour passed through El Paso at the start of a 28-day tour of Mexico, the album documented the visitors' progress on a grand scale.[154] Leaf 50 (recto) in the album of photographs prepared for Benjamin F. Freeman of Sommerville Mass., presents four prints mounted on the same leaf in the album, taken on a boating trip on the Canal de la Viga on the outskirts of Mexico City (Plate 27).[155] The print mounted upper left establishes a view of the canal from the prow of a *trajinera* (a flat-bottomed craft used for transporting fruit and vegetables to the market in Mexico City), seen in soft focus in the lower centre and lower right of the photograph. Ripples in front of the *trajinera* indicate that the boat was in motion when the photograph was taken. The print mounted

5.42 (upper). C. B. Waite, *1048 The Market at Taxco Guer. Mex*, gelatin silver print, wetstamp on reverse 'San Juan No 3', 1905, 12.8 x 17.7 cm.
[Reproduced by permission of Archivo General de la Nación.]

5.43 (lower). C. B. Waite, *1049 Sunday Morning in the Plaza. Taxco. Guer. Mexico*, gelatin silver print, wetstamp on reverse 'San Juan No 3', 1905, 12.8 x 17.7 cm.
[Reproduced by permission of Archivo General de la Nación.]

upper right presents a slightly later view taken from the rear of the *trajinera*. The building seen on the left of the canal is now visible at mid-frame right with the tree at extreme upper frame right, articulating a reverse-field view to the previous print. The print mounted lower left in the album represents a view from the boat (visible once again in soft focus) taken at a later moment than the previous two photographs, and shows the wall, seen initially on the far side of the building, now at mid-frame left. A boat laden with produce approaches; in the distance, a building with a pitched roof and short chimney, and another tall chimney are visible among tall trees. In the print mounted lower right, again taken from the prow of the *trajinera*, the view shows an adobe wall, on the far side of which, the building with a pitched roof and short chimney and the tall chimney are again visible. The features seen from the *trajinera* in this private album articulate moments in the passage of the boat along the canal and, in one case, provide a reverse-field view. Important in this context is that the photo series provides visual cues (soft focus and ripples on the surface of the water) which register the proximity of the viewer to the motion of the *trajinera* as it advances along the canal, so designating that the prints form a series of successive mobilised views.

Given the social background of this visitor to Mexico, it is likely that many of the photographs in Freeman's album were purchased from a professional photographer who may have mounted the prints for Freeman. Alternatively, Freeman may have given instructions, or supervised the mounting of the photographs himself, attending to the sequencing of the prints and their organisation in the album from leaf to leaf. Whichever of these processes obtained, both demonstrate the importance of organising the leaves of the photographic album, and demonstrate the skill with which the *mise en page* of the photographic album was arranged. In other words, the person who assembled the album acted as a *metteur en page*, a person not only responsible for selecting and sequencing the images, but one who decided on the organisation of each leaf and the make-up of the album from leaf to leaf, which process orchestrates the narrative assembled on each leaf and the viewer's progression through the journey undertaken by Freeman.

5.44. C. B. Waite, *1050 View in the market Taxco, Guer. Mexico*, gelatin silver print, wetstamp on reverse 'San Juan No 3', 1905, 12.8 x 17.6 cm. [Reproduced by permission of Archivo General de la Nación.]

One further example: consider the upper six small-format photographs mounted on a leaf of an early twentieth-century private album of small-format prints (5.45).[156] Sequenced from left to right, the first six prints present a trip along a canal towards a colonial building, a well-known landmark and tourist sight in turn-of-the-century Mexico City: the Garita at Santa Anita, a toll house on the Canal de la Viga on the south-eastern approach to the city. The second, third, and fourth prints record the *trajinera* as it approaches the toll house, in front of which a group of men are standing or sitting. Three tourists – a man and two women – stand on a small stone bridge below and to the right of the arch. The fifth print comprises a view of the *trajinera*, now with the male tourist and one of the women in the vessel, as it passes in front of the toll house, photographed from a bank on the far side of the building seen in the previous four prints. The sixth print, taken further along the bank, shows the canal and toll house but the *trajinera* is no longer visible. The sequence of prints presents another series of mobilised views,

5.45. [Canal de la Viga], private album of non-professional views interspersed with prints by C. B. Waite, Alfred Saint-Ange Briquet, and Winfield Scott, leaf 14 (recto), each print 5.7 x 8.3 cm., page size 25 x 33 cm. [Reproduced by permission of Bancroft Library, University of California, Berkeley.]

one which documents moments in the passage of a *trajinera* along the canal before picking up tourists and passing through the toll house in a reverse view as the tourists leave the city. We may propose, therefore, from the evidence of the Freeman album and this 'amateur' album, that reverse views and the sequencing of a series of mobilised views demonstrate a shared modelling of space by professional and non-professional photographers in taking and mounting photographs in photographic albums.

Guillermo Kahlo's work raises the issue of *mise en page* indirectly, and demonstrates a central concern with progression through space.

Born in Pforzheim and brought up in Lichtental near Baden-Baden, Germany, Kahlo moved to Mexico in the late 1890s where he was employed in the accounting department of the German-owned hardware store, Casa Boker, which, at its peak, was regarded as the 'Sears of Mexico'.[157] One of the earliest assignments Kahlo was given, while employed by the company as a clerk, was to document the construction and opening of the new company store, which commenced in 1898 on the site of the former Hotel de la Gran Sociedad. A palace of some 20,000 square feet, Edifico Boker represented a new departure for a hardware business, and met with the acclamation of the Porfirian elite when the store was inaugurated in July 1900.[158] In the next few years, Kahlo completed a number of projects for the Boker family, including the production of a private photographic album, *Mexiko 1904*, of which two privately-owned copies were compiled.[159]

Kahlo initially used a 5 x 7 inch format camera, but at some point in the 1900s, abandoned work in this format in favour of an 11 x 14 inch format camera which enabled him to produce work with considerable depth of field.[160] 'A specialist in "buildings, interior, factories, machinery, etc."', as an advertisement in the 24 February 1901 issue of *El Mundo Ilustrado* announced, Kahlo was commissioned by José Yves Limantour, the finance minister of Mexico, to make a photographic record of property belonging to the federal government, intended to be published in a series of albums that would commemorate the Centennial of Mexican Independence in 1910.[161] The outcome of this project, never published in its intended form, was an inventory of Spanish colonial church architecture in Mexico.[162] Although several secular buildings were included, the photographs show, principally, exterior and interior views of churches, particular attention being given to naves, altars, cupolas, exterior facades, and, occasionally, decorative details and furniture, producing an unrivalled documentation of seventeenth- and eighteenth-century ecclesiastical architecture in Mexico. The prints were grouped by cities and subjects, beginning with Mexico City. Taken with an 11 x 14 inch format camera, the plates were contact printed on dry collodion paper, toned with platinum and gold, mounted on linen to ensure preservation, and hand numbered by Kahlo.[163] Two of the collection of 1314 extant prints held at the Getty Research Institute from this project present interior views of the church of la Ensenañza in Mexico City.[164]

5.46. Guillermo Kahlo, *7. Cinco de Mayo-Str. O.W. links Profesakirche, rechts: Hintergrd: neues Postgebäude / 7. Avenida del Cinco de Mayo, E. al O. (Vista tomada desde la Catedral)*, gelatin silver print, *México 1904*, private album, 26.3 x 33.8 cm., page size 40 x 50.3 cm. [Reproduced by permission of Biblioteca Francisco Xavier Clavigero, Universidad Iberoamericana.]

Two prints, mounted in the second volume, present interior views of la Ensenañza: #158, *Vista Interior* (Plate 28, mounted verso), and #159, *Vista Interior* (Plate 29, mounted recto), numbered in both cases in darker areas on the right side of the respective print. With furniture removed from the nave, the photographs accentuate symmetrical views of the church interior, framed perpendicular to the viewer. Plate 28 presents a view from a position near the altar, looking in the direction of the organ loft and choir, and, through the doors at the far end of the nave, towards another set of doors that admit onto the street outside the church. Plate 29 presents a reciprocal, symmetrically-framed view from under the choir, once again perpendicular to the viewer; the underside decoration of the choir

5.47 (left). Guillermo Kahlo, *8. Aussicht von der Kathedr. Nach Osten. Links: Kuppel der St. Theresenkirche, in der Mitte: Malerakademie, Museum, altes Postgebäude. W.-O. / 8. Calles del Arzobispado, Moneda etc. O. al E.*, gelatin silver print, *México 1904*, private album bound in brown leather with gold embossed lettering, 26.2 x 33.8 cm., page size 40 x 50.3 cm. [Reproduced by permission of Biblioteca Francisco Xavier Clavigero, Universidad Iberoamericana.]

5.48 (right). Guillermo Kahlo, *10. Espiritu Santo-Str. S.-N. (Geschäftshaus Rob. Boker & Co., Span. Kasino, Profesakirche) / 10. Calle del Espiritu Santo, S. al N. (casa de Rob. Boker & Co. – Nuevo Casino Español – Iglesia de la Profesa)*, gelatin silver print, *México 1904*, private album bound in brown leather with gold embossed lettering, 26.2 x 33.8 cm., page size 40 x 50.3 cm. [Reproduced by permission of Biblioteca Francisco Xavier Clavigero, Universidad Iberoamericana.]

frames the upper part of the photograph. Bright sunlight in the vault (seen at its most intense in Plate 28) is balanced by the darker tones of the underside of the choir, which produce a strong contrast between the extreme upper foreground and the brightly-lit interior of the church beyond. In both photographs, the camera is placed at, approximately, the height of an adult Western person, and simulates the view that would obtain if the viewer visited the church.[165] As we have seen in so many of the images examined in this study, composition is organised according to the presumed height of a standing adult; in this respect, composition reflects somatic and cultural conditioning, and exemplifies the understated manner that characterises Kahlo's photographic work.

The second aspect of Kahlo's work considered here relates to the private photographic album, *México 1904*, compiled in a German-language and a Spanish-language version. The albums include a hand-written contents page that designates the subject(s) in each print and details the orientation of each view. Each album comprises fifty prints, twenty-five of Mexico City and twenty-five of Chapultepec (the presidential residence), and includes photographs of the extensive public grounds of Chapultepec.[166] As a latterday cicerone, the albums conduct the viewer on a tour of the city, opening with a panoramic view of the Zócalo and the Catedral Metropolitana seen from the Casa Municipal on the south side of the square (Plate 30).[167] Although there are small variations in how some of the subjects are designated in each album, both provide orientation and a designation of the principal subject(s) in each print. After the opening panorama, four views present buildings in the Zócalo (the Palacio Nacional, the cathedral and Sagraria, and the Casa Municipal including a view of the west side of the Zócalo). Two more prints, from the roof of the cathedral, provide views, respectively, to the west and east of the Zócalo, the view to the west showing the cupola and towers of the church of la Profesa on the left of Cinco de Mayo (5.46), with the edge of the central park marked by trees in the Alameda. The new post office building, under

5.49. Guillermo Kahlo, *15. Stadtpark: Mittlere Querstrasse N.–S. Im Hintergrund Maurischer Kiosk. / 15. Alameda, calzada trasversal del centro, N. al S. (en el fondo Pabellón Morisco)*, gelatin silver print, *México 1904*, private album bound in brown leather with gold embossed lettering, 26.2 x 33.8 cm., page size 40 x 50.3 cm.
[Reproduced by permission of Biblioteca Francisco Xavier Clavigero, Universidad Iberoamericana.]

5.50. Guillermo Kahlo, *19. Statue von Carlos IV & Paseo de la Reforma, N.O. – S.W. Im Hintergrund Statuen von Columbus & Cuauhtemoc. (schnurgerade Verbindungsstr. zwischen Mex. & Chapultepec.) 19. Estatua de Carlos IV y Paseo de la Reforma, N. E. al S. O. Calzada principal y recta entre México y Chapultepec*, gelatin silver print, *México 1904*, private album bound in brown leather with gold embossed lettering, 33.8 x 26.2 cm., page size 40 x 50.3 cm.
[Reproduced by permission of Biblioteca Francisco Xavier Clavigero, Universidad Iberoamericana.]

construction, can be discerned in the distance in front of the Alameda. The other view from the cathedral, overlooking the Sagraria in the extreme foreground (5.47), presents the church of Santa Teresa la Nueva on the left, and one of the streets (Moneda) leading to the eastern part of the city, with the Academia de San Carlos, visible in the middle distance, at the far end of the street, and the old post office towards foreground right.[168] Having presented the central part of the city, the viewer descends to the heart of the commercial district, with prints of the calles de Plateros and San Francisco (present-day Madero) interspersed with a relatively high view that frames Casa Boker at foreground left (5.48), with the recently-opened Spanish Casino and church of la Profesa further along the street.[169] Reaching the west of the city, the viewer traverses the Alameda park from east to west, pausing to look along one of the paths that cross the park which reveals the Pabilion Morisco (5.49) in the north of the park.[170] On reaching the western edge of the Alameda, the tour continues west until the viewer reaches the Paseo de la Reforma, at the head of which, a statue of Carlos IV is seen (5.50).[171] After a detour through the wealthy suburbs west of the city,[172] the viewer is conducted down the Paseo de la Reforma, the most important boulevard developed in the nineteenth century, until the presidential palace of Chapultepec is reached with its public grounds on the south-west periphery of the city. With orientation provided for all the views, the album imparts a strong sense of ordered progression as the viewer is transported through the space of the city. Some of these images were published in the illustrated

EL MUNDO ILUSTRADO

Registrado como artículo de segunda clase, en 3 de Noviembre de 1894.—Impreso en papel de las Fábricas de San Rafael.

Año XIV—Tomo I | México, 3 de Febrero de 1907 | Número 5

Escalera Monumental del Palacio de Correos

Edificio que será solemnemente inaugurado el 5 del actual.

Fot. Kahlo.

EL MUNDO ILUSTRADO

Palacio de Correos.—Escalera. (Fot. Kahlo.)

EL PALACIO DE CORREOS

El mártes próximo, como se había anunciado, tendrá efecto la inauguración solemne del suntuoso Palacio de Correos que mandó construir nuestro Gobierno en la esquina de San Andrés y Santa Isabel, y cuya belleza arquitectónica admiran, con justicia, todos los habitantes de la Metrópoli.

En alguna otra ocasión nos hemos ocupado en describir la nueva casa postal, publicando distintas fotografías de su magnífica fachada y de los departamentos interiores, decorados y amueblados con toda la elegancia que corresponde á la suntuosidad de su construcción.

Ahora reproducimos otras fotografías, dando, además, cuenta á nuestros lectores del programa acordado para el acto inaugural.

Este se verificará á las ocho de la noche, con asistencia del señor Presidente de la República, según la invitación que, firmada por el señor Secretario de Comunicaciones, ha comenzado á circular. El Sr. Ing. D. Gonzalo Garita leerá un informe relativo á la construcción del Palacio y el Sr. Ing. D. Norberto Domínguez, Director General de Correos pronunciará un discurso alusivo á la solemnidad. Entre los demás números del programa figuran una poesía del Sr. Manuel H. San Juan y algunas piezas de música selecta, cuyo desempeño estará á cargo de la Orquesta del Conservatorio.

El señor General Díaz declarará después inaugurado el edificio y, desde ese momento, quedará abierto al público, dando principio todos los empleados á sus respectivas labores.

UNA IMAGEN

En la tarde cálida de junio, el Sol prende en el cielo los románticos jardines crepusculares, los desfallecientes jardines, sembrados de violetas pálidas, de rosas exangües y de grandes lirios sangrientos....

Y desde el cielo, que parece una grande agua azul, inmóvil y profunda, callada y muerta, en donde abren sus corolas cambiantes las ninfeas del crepúsculo, baja á la calle una luz extraña que lo invade todo, que lo penetra todo, y la calle brilla y resplandece inundada por la gran claridad crepuscular.

Son las seis de la tarde. Monótonamente el reloj de la Catedral lo ha dicho en su vieja lengua de bronce. Y á esa hora, de los grandes almacenes huyen los empleados del comercio, las cigarreras salen de sus fábricas, grupos de colegiales atraviesan, deshojando al viento las frescas rosas de sus risas; la calle se llena de vida intensa, se oyen mil voces, se escuchan mil ruidos; el timbre argentino de una bicicleta que cruza, veloz; el áspero estrépito de un coche que pasa, rápido; los vendedores de periódicos que gritan á pleno pulmón. Y entre tanto ruido, tanto bullicio, tanta luz, en el largo crepúsculo de junio, también pasas tú, ¡oh piluelo desarrapado, flacucho, raquítico, enfermizo, con el vestido hecho girones, casi desnudo y con los pies descalzos!....

Yo te veo caminar, indiferente, por la acera llena de luz, entre la muchedumbre apresurada, mirándolo todo, curioseándolo todo, con tus alegres ojillos vivaces, hambriento quizás, friolento tal vez, llevando al extremo de un palo, quien sabe en donde recogido, un andrajo á guisa

Palacio de Correos.—Puerta principal. (Fot. Kahlo.)

5.51 (left). Guillermo Kahlo, 'Escalera Monumental del Palacio de Correos', cover photograph, *El Mundo Ilustrado*, year 14, vol. 1, no. 5, 3 February 1907, page size 39 x 23 cm. [Reproduced by permission of Condumex.]

5.52 (right). Guillermo Kahlo, 'El Palacio de Correos', *El Mundo Ilustrado*, year 14, vol. 1, no. 5, 3 February 1907, unnumbered 10, page size 39 x 23 cm. [Reproduced by permission of Condumex.]

press when *El Mundo Ilustrado* reproduced a number of prints from *México 1904*.[173] Six prints by Kahlo featured the park of Chapultepec, and the series also reproduced views taken in the central part of the city that featured the Colonia Juárez, the Alameda, and Cinco de Mayo in a series titled *México Moderno*.[174] Publication in the magazine indicates that Kahlo's prints achieved relatively wide circulation, particularly in the metropolis.

One of the major commissions Kahlo received in this period was to photograph the new central post office in Mexico City, the Palacio de Correos, designed by the Italian architect, Adamo Boari.[175] Inaugurated on 5 February, *El Mundo Ilustrado* covered the event in issues published on Sunday, 3 February and Sunday, 10 February 1907. Coverage was relatively lavish, opening with a cover photograph by Kahlo that revealed the interior of the building (5.51), with

EL MUNDO ILUSTRADO

Palacio de Correos.—Escalera y corredores. (Fot. Kahlo.)

de bandera, y silbando con todas tus fuerzas nuestro orgulloso himno nacional. Yo te contemplo largo rato, caminar entre los transeuntes, y perderte á lo lejos, hacia el final de la calle luminosa, flameando, lleno de orgullo, tu trofeo de gloria, y ¡oh pilluelo vagabundo! ¡estabas épico!

Y me quedé meditando, llena el alma de profunda tristeza, porque en tí ví la imagen de la patria, ¡oh pilluelo diabólico y perverso, oh pilluelo malévolo y burlón! que hiciste una bandera con un sucio andrajo, y que silbabas el himno nacional, el gran himno, con los labios enfermos, hambrientos y marchitos......

(Venezuela.) ALEJANDRO FERNÁNDEZ GARCÍA,

TEATROS.—Novelli y la Giannini.

Palacio de Correos.—Puerta lateral. (Fot. Kahlo.)

EL MUNDO ILUSTRADO.

EL NUEVO EDIFICIO DE CORREOS

Un detalle del Interior. (Fot. Kahlo.)

5.53 (left). Guillermo Kahlo, 'El Palacio de Correos', *El Mundo Ilustrado*, year 14, vol. 1, no. 5, 3 February 1907, unnumbered 11, page size 39 x 23 cm. [Reproduced by permission of Condumex.]

5.54 (right). Guillermo Kahlo, 'El Nuevo Edificio de Correos. Un detalle del Interior', *El Mundo Ilustrado*, year 14, vol. 1, no. 6, 10 February 1907, unnumbered 11, page size 39 x 23 cm. [Reproduced by permission of Condumex.]

its elaborate stairwell, looking towards the main entrance on San Andrés (present-day Tacuba).[176] A lift-cage may be seen towards the left with a service counter beyond. Defying gravity, the staircase is cantilevered so that its steps rise freely towards the arches that frame the first-floor gallery. A short article, 'El Palacio de Correos', introduces the photographs and informs the reader of the date of inauguration when Porfirio Díaz and other dignitaries, including the Secretary for Communications, will attend the event with an orchestra from the conservatoire (5.52).[177] The photograph, placed above the text, presents a symmetrically-framed view of the stairwell with lifts on either side of the main passage leading to the atrium at the centre of the building. To the left of the text, one of the two main entrances into the building, facing onto the junction of San Andrés and Santa Isabel (present-day Tacuba and Lázaro Cárdenas) may be seen. The following page presents a further view of the stairwell looking down towards the groundfloor, with the bottom of the door

5.55 (left). *Mise en page*, 'El Viaje Presidencial á Yucatan de Chapultepec', *El Tiempo Ilustrado*, year 6, no. 6, 4 February 1906, 100–102, 100, page size 36 x 26.2 cm. [Reproduced by permission of Condumex.]

5.56 (right). *Mise en page*, 'El Viaje Presidencial á Yucatan de Chapultepec', *El Tiempo Ilustrado*, year 6, no. 6, 4 February 1906, 100–102, 101, page size 36 x 26.2 cm. [Reproduced by permission of Condumex.]

of the main entrance on San Andrés visible beneath the first-floor gallery (5.53).[178] This view constitutes a further reverse view to that shown on the previous page (unnumbered, 10) which, in turn, presents a reverse view of the building to that seen in the cover photograph. Below the main photograph, a view presents a side entrance (*puerta latoral*) facing onto Santa Isabel. Many of these views were reprinted in the following issue of the journal when a new photograph of the first- and second-floor galleries, taken from the second-floor balcony looking towards the rear of the building, was also published (5.54).[179]

Kahlo's work at the turn of the century displays a summation of our discussion of photography in turn-of-the-century Mexico:

Entre tanto, el General Díaz pasó á bordo del "Arizona," y después de recorrer algunos de sus departamentos se detuvo sobre cubierta para seguir presenciando las maniobras de la grúa. Terminadas éstas, pasó á sellar las puertas del furgón.

Dichos sellos deberían ser rotos por el mismo Magistrado al llegar á Coatzacoalcos para sacar la carga y pasarla al vapor que debe transportarla á Nueva York.

A la una de la tarde terminó la ceremonia oficial, objeto de nuestro largo viaje, y que tan ansiosamente deseaban presenciar todos los que se interesan por el progreso y engrandecimiento de México.

Después de comer [el Presidente y algunos invitados lo hicieron en sus respectivos trenes, y otros en diversas fondas y restaurants de la población], se procedió á la visita de las obras del puerto, comenzando por el dique seco.

La travesía hasta ese lugar y hasta el extremo Sur del rompe-olas, que se visitó después, se hizo en unas plataformas adornadas, y las cuales fueron remolcadas por una locomotora.

El General Díaz examinó con todo detenimiento y atención los trabajos que se están ejecutando, haciendo varias preguntas á los señores Pearson, Body y Adams, Gerente de la Empresa, que lo acompañaban muy de cerca.

El dique en construcción servirá, como el que hay en Veracruz, para las reparaciones de los buques.

En seguida pasamos á visitar la planta eléctrica, que es amplia y bien dotada, viéndose en ella los grandes dinamos que proporcionan luz y fuerza para las grúas, para las dragas con que se ha trabajado, así como también para las bombas que deberán funcionar en el dique.

Continuóse la expedición hácia el extremo Sur del rompe-olas, punto desde el cual se disfruta de un panorama espléndido: el mar se extiende hasta lo infinito, y á uno y otro lado veían los viajeros los vecinos cerros, coronado el de la derecha por una torrecilla donde está el faro. A poca distancia veían también el malecón y el rompe-olas que por el lado oriental limitan la dársena.

Aquí debemos hacer notar que ese malecón es más ancho y más alto que el de Veracruz y que el rompe-olas está formado, no de blockes de cemento, como en dicho puerto, sino de peñascos gigantescos, que no se explica uno cómo han podido ser llevados hasta allí.

Ya de regreso, la comitiva pudo ver una multitud de barracas, mandadas construir por disposición del Consejo Superior de Salubridad, con el objeto de que en ellas sean sometidos á observación ó cuarentena los chinos y japoneses que desembarquen para venir á trabajar al país.

Estación de San Jerónimo (F. C. N. de T.).

El Sr. Dr. Licéaga hizo otras explicaciones al señor Presidente acerca de ese asunto.

En aquellos momentos hallábanse en las barracas cerca de mil japoneses, que habían llegado en dos buques de esa misma nacionalidad y que se encontraban aún anclados en la bahía.

Dichos inmigrantes saludaron á los visitantes del puerto, y su saludo fué contestado por éstos.

La llegada á la estación se hizo ya casi de noche, y á esa hora comenzó una iluminación general, con luz eléctrica, en la casa del señor Pearson y oficinas de la Compañía.

También el *Arizona* y los buques japoneses á que antes aludimos, se veían iluminados.

El aspecto del puerto, á esa hora, era muy vistoso, y las grúas veíanse á lo lejos como gigantescos esqueletos, destacándose en el fondo del cielo, por donde asomaba una hermosa luna.

El regreso se hizo cerca de las ocho de la noche.

Puente de Tehuantepec (F. C. N. de T.).

IV

Un baile en Tehuantepec.

Estando aún en Salina Cruz, una Comisión de la sociedad de Tehuantepec se acercó al señor Presidente de la República y al señor Gobernador de Oaxaca, para suplicarles se sirvieran aceptar un baile dispuesto en su honor, el cual tendría lugar aquella noche.

Dicha Comisión estaba formada por los señores Manuel Jiménez Ramírez, Arnulfo Piatkowski, Pedro Camacho y Antonio Carbollo, personas prominentes del lugar.

Los dos funcionarios citados contestaron aceptando el obsequio y ofrecieron que asistirían al baile.

Además de éste, las autoridades de Tuxtepec prepararon una serenata en la plaza, la cual comenzó tan pronto como llegaron los viajeros.

La mayor parte de éstos, vestidos de etiqueta, se dirigieron inmediatamente al Colegio de Niñas, cuyo extenso patio fué convertido en vistoso salón, cubierto con una vela blanca de lona, de la cual pendían cintas de colores, que iban á fijarse en los pilares.

El piso estaba alfombrado, y la sillería para la concurrencia se colocó en los corredores.

En diversos estrados, y á los lados del que se preparó para el señor Presidente, veíanse varios grupos de jóvenes tehuanas, ataviadas ricamente con los trajes tradicionales de aquella región. Faldas de finísima seda (una especie de brocado con preciosos bordados de oro), largos collares de onzas de oro y de otras monedas del mismo metal, más pequeñas, anillos y pendientes con brillantes, piedras, brazaletes y pulseras de gran valor, todo formaba una verdadera riqueza en aquellos tocados tan singulares como vistosos.

Los viajeros, al llegar al salón, detuviéronse asombrados para contemplar con ojos de viva curiosidad aquellos grupos de jóvenes tehuanas, las cuales permanecían impasibles, serias, mas no sin cierto aire de candor y sencillez que les sentaba muy bien. De tez morena, de ojos grandes y rasgados, con sus cabelleras negras y brillantes, aquellas beldades tehuanas no podían menos que atraer las miradas y la admiración no sólo de los extranjeros, sino de los mismos mexicanos que las contemplaban.

Por iniciativa del Sr. Godard, los caballeros ofrecieron el brazo á las lindas tehuanas para acompañarlas á escuchar la serenata á la plaza, donde el señor General Díaz se pa-

5.57 (left). *Mise en page*, 'El Viaje Presidencial á Yucatan de Chapultepec', *El Tiempo Ilustrado*, year 6, no. 6, 4 February 1906, 100–102, 102, page size 36 x 26.2 cm. [Reproduced by permission of Condumex.]

5.58 (right). Antonio Carrillo, 'El Viaje Presidencial á Tehuantepec', *El Tiempo Ilustrado*, 3 February 1907, 76–86, 79, page size 36 x 26.2 cm. [Reproduced by permission of Condumex.]

reverse views (in the project documenting colonial architecture), panoramic views, reverse-field views, and progression through space (*Mexico 1904*), and a series of reverse views in Kahlo's photographs of the Palacio de Correos. Such images in private albums and the illustrated press demonstrate that the ground-rules for the articulation of space, which we associate with classical practice and its institutionalisation in film in the late 1910s and early 1920s, had in many ways been established in photographic albums and the Mexican illustrated press at the turn of the century. As discussion has demonstrated, this practice had also been internalised in private photographic albums, a process which indicates that the modelling of space was a practice that 'amateur' and professional photographers (and readers of the illustrated press) had implicitly internalised. It is to the popular illustrated press we finally turn, to assess its relation to film in the early years of the new century.

5.59

5.60

5.61

5.62

f

5.63

5.59–5.63.
Frame enlargements,
Inauguración del tráfico internacional en el istmo de Tehuantepec,
Salvador Toscano, 1907,
35mm viewing copy.
[Reproduced by permission of Filmoteca UNAM.]

Media convergence at the turn of the century and progression through space

In 1906 *El Tiempo Ilustrado* compiled a series of short photographic 'essays' on the occasion when Porfirio Díaz visited Mérida, the state capital of Yucatán, to open a new hospital funded by a federal building project.[180] Since direct travel to Mérida by railway from Mexico City was impossible in the early twentieth century, Díaz travelled to Veracruz by rail from where he took a ship to Progreso, a short distance from Mérida by rail.[181] Six pages of the 4 February 1906 issue of *El Tiempo Ilustrado* were assigned to the visit. Three consecutive pages ostensibly document Díaz's progress from Mexico City to Mérida, which employ a series of photographs of the railway from Mexico City to Veracruz, taken by Briquet in the 1880s, to show 'the principal details of the itinerary that the presidential convoy followed on the rails of the Ferrocarril Mexicano'.[182] Two of these bridges are already familiar to us: Infiernillo and Chiquihuite. Although the photographs give some impression of the terrain through which Díaz travelled, they do not represent his progress which the title of the article leads present-day readers to anticipate. Rather, we are presented with a view of the Castillo de Chapultepec (#1, in the upper left corner of the first *mise en page*, 5.55) and a view of the railway station in Mexico City from which Díaz left for Veracruz (#2). Thereafter, a series of views of bridges on the line to Veracruz are presented: bridges in the Barranca del Infiernillo, photographed by Briquet (#3 and #8); views of the viaduct over the Barranca de Metlac (#4 and #5, an elevated view), again photographed by Briquet; a view of the Puente de Atoyac (#6), photographed by Briquet; and, finally, a view of the station in Córdoba (#7). Although the photographs present the bridges Díaz would have traversed to reach Veracruz, they are not presented in the order in which a passenger would encounter them travelling by train; rather, they present a medley of partially overlapping views (with two printed on the cant), an organisation of the printed page which is repeated in the lay-out for the following page with two photographs cut to simulate roundels.

The second page of the photographic 'essay' presents an inset seemingly photographed by Briquet (#10, 5.56). This view is, in fact, a black and white print of the chromolithograph, based on Briquet's photograph of Chiquihuite, printed in García Cubas' *Atlas pintoresco* in 1885 (Plate 18). According to the text at the bottom of the page, the *mise en page* presents 'the most beautiful details of the route'.[183] The Puente de Metlac is seen once again (#13), with a view of the vessel in which Díaz travelled from Veracruz to Progreso, the *Bravo* (*Brave*), unnumbered, placed immediately below the photograph of Metlac bridge. Views of the outer defences of the harbour at Veracruz are also included (San Juan de Ulúa and Isla de Sacrificios), as too ships in the Mexican fleet. The third and final page of the 'essay' (*La Rada de Progreso*) presents views of the port of Progreso (5.57),[184] the most important in the Yucatán peninsula, and the town's railway station. A panoramic view of Mérida from the east is placed at the bottom of the page, showing the Teatro José Contreras which, in 1906, was under construction.[185] Once again, the photographs are cut and placed on the page so that they appear to be overlapping, as if placed in a scrapbook, and set against an art nouveau-inspired decorative motif. The photographic 'essay' draws on contemporary views of Mérida and Progreso set against well-known photographs of the railway to Veracruz that date back to the 1880s, interweaving photographs and the reproduction of a chromolithograph to create a capriccio of images of mixed origin that evokes Díaz's visit to Mérida. At no point, however, neither in the pages considered here, nor in the other three pages printed in this issue of the magazine, does the reader actually see Díaz travelling to Mérida, or the opening of Hospital O'Horán. In short, the sequence presents images whose purpose bears even less relation to the events they purport to represent than the portfolio of *cartes de visite* considered earlier in the chapter.

Media convergence is also evident in a film and coverage in the illustrated press of the inauguration of a railway by Porfiro Díaz in

— 80 —

[illegible] en unión de sus Ministros y algunos diplomáticos.

A poco regresaron todos al salón y comenzó el baile. En pocos momentos éste adquirió una animación extraordinaria.

Tocáronse varias piezas, entre ellas la famosa «sandunga,» que fué bailada por las tehuanas con la habilidad y gracia especial que sólo ellas poseen.

El General Díaz bailó una danza con la Srita. Ana Urquide, una de las tehuanas más bonitas y mejor ataviadas de las que se veían en el salón. Ese acto de galantería del Presidente, fué muy aplaudido por todos los concurrentes.

Al terminar esa pieza—á eso de las once de la noche—retiróse el Presidente, siendo despedido con nutridos aplausos.

El baile se prolongó hasta las cuatro de la mañana, dejando en todos una impresión deliciosa y un recuerdo imborrable.

Los trenes partieron el día siguiente á las ocho de la mañana.

V

En Rincón Antonio

Se anunció á los viajeros que en esa estación se detendrían los trenes para visitar los grandes talleres de la Empresa Pearson.

Así se hizo, llegando á Rincón Antonio á las once.

Todos los viajeros descendieron de sus respectivos coches, y formando acompañamiento al señor Presidente, se dirigieron á los talleres, en cuya puerta principal leíase con vistosas letras de colores, esta inscripción: «Bienvenida al señor Presidente, por 500 obreros.»

Este número era, efectivamente, el de los que en aquellos momentos trabajaban con toda actividad en los vastos y bien acondicionados salones, donde se hallan instaladas toda clase de máquinas para fabricar piezas de carpintería, herrería, fundición, etc., etc. Todo está movido por electricidad y los obreros trabajan con gran desahogo, pues los techos son altísimos y los operarios pueden moverse y maniobrar con toda comodidad y sin estorbarse unos á otros.

En el taller de carpintería hay sierras mecánicas, tornos y cuanto se necesita para cortar y pulir la madera; en la herrería vénse grandes fraguas, yunques, martillos, entre ellos, uno de 500 libras de peso, que cae á voluntad del operario sobre grandes piezas de fierro al rojo blanco; en la fundición hay hornos y crisoles que á la sazón estaban en plena actividad. En presencia del General Díaz y acompañantes, sacóse uno de estos últimos, y de él se vació en moldes de arcilla, previamente dispuestos, el metal fundido que salía en chorros para modelar diversas piezas de maquinaria. En casi todos los motores y máquinas de los talleres veíanse escritas en letras blancas sobre fondo negro, estas palabras: «Viva México».

Se visitó también la casa redonda, en donde se veían perfectamente alineadas, más de veinte poderosas locomotoras.

Los viajeros pasaron después al salón de dínamos y se pudo ver que todos son de una potencia extraordinaria, suficientes para proveer de luz á la población y para dar movimiento y vida á aquella infinidad de máquinas, repartidas en los vastos talleres.

En todos éstos reinaba un orden admirable; los obreros vestían limpiamente y en su trabajo procedían con una habilidad, tacto y mesura, que llamó la atención de los concurrentes. Era una legión bien disciplinada, y en todos los semblantes leíase la satisfacción que les causaba la visita del Primer Magistrado de la República y de tantos hombres prominentes en la Administración Pública y en la sociedad mexicana.

El General Díaz lo veía todo con interés y fijeza, deteniéndose á contemplar lo que más le llamaba la atención, ya fuese una máquina, ya la habilidad de un obrero. A su lado hallábanse constantemente el señor Pearson, el Director general de los talleres, Ingeniero Galbraith, y el señor Aldasoro, Subsecretario de Fomento, quienes alternativamente le hacían diversas explicaciones.

Como una demostración del agrado con que el General Díaz practicaba aquella visita, diremos que en un momento en que iba á pasar de un punto á otro, con riesgo de ensuciarse su traje con el negro aceite de una máquina, y habiéndoselo advertido un ayudante, exclamó muy contento: —¡Qué importa! y siguió adelante, examinando lo que hallaba á su paso.

Los talleres de Rincón Antonio son como el centro de operaciones de la gran empresa Pearson, y en ellos cifra acaso su mayor satisfacción, porque merced á los trabajos que allí se ejecutan, ha podido dar cima á las grandes obras de Salina Cruz y Coatzacoalcos.

La visita á dichos talleres terminó á la una de la tarde, continuándose el viaje en medio del mayor contento y satisfacción.

El tren presidencial pernoctó en la estación de Almagres, y el número uno avanzó hasta la de Jáltipan, en donde esperaban al señor Presidente las autoridades del lugar y un grupo de señoritas, vestidas con trajes claros. No habiendo llegado el General Díaz, unas y otras regresaron á la población citada, que dista de la estación algo más de dos kilómetros, y á acompañarlas se ofrecieron algunos de los jóvenes viajeros de dicho tren. Ya en la población, improvisóse un baile que duró hasta más de la media noche.

VI

En Coatzacoalcos.

A las ocho en punto de la mañana llegó el tren presidencial á la reja que da entrada al perímetro de la población de Coatzacoalcos. Lo mismo que la de Salina Cruz, hallábase cerrada dicha reja; y ante ella se detuvieron el Presidente de la República, sus Ministros, el Cuerpo Diplomático y demás acompañantes.

El señor Limantour fué invitado por el señor Pearson para cortar el listón tricolor que unía las hojas de la puerta, y con una llave de plata que le fué entregada abrió ésta.

Los viajeros subieron á sus respectivos trenes (pues entretanto habían llegado todos) y se continuó la marcha hácia el puerto. El tramo que hubo de recorrerse desde aquel pun-

El Tren Presidencial llega á Salina Cruz.

Estación de Tehuantepec (F. C. N. de T.).

5.64. Antonio Carrillo, 'El Viaje Presidencial á Tehuantepec', *El Tiempo Ilustrado*, year 7, no. 5, 3 February 1907, 76–86, 80, page size 36 x 26.2 cm. [Reproduced by permission of Condumex.]

5.65

5.66

5.67

5.68

5.69

5.70

5.65–5.70. Frame enlargements, *Inauguración del tráfico internacional en el istmo de Tehuantepec*, Salvador Toscano, 1907, 35mm viewing copy.
[Reproduced by permission of Filmoteca UNAM.]

1907. The railway crossed Mexico at its narrowest point, the isthmus between the Pacific and Atlantic coasts between Salina Cruz and Coatzacoalcos.[186] The inauguration was covered by *El Mundo Ilustrado* and *El Tiempo Ilustrado*,[187] the latter sending Antonio Carrillo to photograph the opening for the magazine. *El Mundo Ilustrado* covered the event in a manner similar to the *mise en page* photographic 'essay' considered earlier when *El Tiempo Ilustrado* 'reported' Díaz's visit to Mérida in 1906 by omission.[188] As with the coverage of Díaz's visit to Mérida, coverage in *El Mundo Ilustrado*, on this occasion, bore little relation to the events it reported, other than the photographs in the *mise en page* comprised views of the two ports.

Coverage by *El Tiempo Ilustrado* was more ambitious. An article provided an account of the railway journey from Mexico City, which left Buenavista station on the morning of Monday, 21 January 1907. Díaz was accompanied by a large presidential party, including ministers from the Treasury, Communications, and Public Education, subsecretaries responsible for Foreign Relations and Development, and governors of the states of Mexico D. F., Oaxaca, and Tamaulipas. Politicians and dignitaries from England, Germany, Japan, Belgium, Russia, El Salvador, Cuba, and Guatemala also travelled with the presidential entourage. The party arrived in Salina Cruz on Wednesday, 23 January, where the president was received with pomp. Having unloaded cargo from the steamship, *Arizona*, the railway was solemnly inaugurated by Díaz sealing a goods train bound for Coatzacoalcos. After a reception and ball that evening, where Díaz danced with a local Tehuana lady, Srita Ana Urquide (*una de las tehuanas más bonitas*),[189] the train set off the next morning for the Atlantic coast where it arrived in Coatzacoalcos the following day. The seals on the train were duly broken by the president and the cargo unloaded, accompanied once again with great ceremony.[190] After this, the presidential party returned to Mexico City.

The article was illustrated with nineteen photographs by Antonio Carrillo, placed in chronological order, with fourteen photographs printed between pages 76 and 81, and a further five photographs between pages 84 and 86. Two additional pages (82–83), comprised a *mise en page* of eight photographs by Carrillo showing some of the events, a group portrait of Tehuana women, and views of the two ports. Two of the events photographed by Carrillo were also shot in a film of the opening of the Tehuantepec railway produced by Salvador Toscano in 1907: *Inauguración del tráfico internacional en el istmo de Tehuantepec*.[191] On page 79 of the article in *El Tiempo Ilustrado*, we are presented with a view of the 'Puente de Tehuantepec', a viaduct crossing the Tehuantepec river (5.58); in the film, after an intertitle (*Tehuantepec*), we view a lateral travelling shot (the thirteenth shot of the film) taken from the same bridge (5.59, 5.60, 5.61, 5.62).[192] Indeed, a shot of press photographers boarding a train on a viaduct – the same viaduct? – is included in Toscano's film (5.63).[193] A photograph of the arrival of Díaz on the presidential train in Salina Cruz ('Le tren presidencial llega á Salina Cruz', 5.64), taken by Carrillo, was shot from a not dissimilar position, although a gate partly blocks the view, to that which Toscano was assigned for the third shot in the film (5.65 and 5.66).[194] In this case, media convergence may be identified between coverage in the popular illustrated press reinforced by coverage in an early actuality film, a term (*actualidad*) that began to be employed in the illustrated press from about this time.[195]

5.71. C. B. Waite, *1429 F. C. Istmo de Tehuantepec. The river from the bridge*, gelatin silver print, wetstamp on reverse 'Waite Vistas' 'San Cosme', 1905, 12.7 x 20.1 cm. [Reproduced by permission of Centro de Información Gráfica, Archivo General de la Nación.]

5.72

5.73

5.74

5.75

5.76

5.77

5.72–5.77. Frame enlargements, *Inauguración del tráfico internacional en el istmo de Tehuantepec*, Salvador Toscano, 1907, 35mm viewing copy.
[Reproduced by permission of Filmoteca UNAM.]

A further comparison may also be made. During the latter part of the film, viewers are presented with a view of local children bathing in the river near Tehuantepec as the camera slowly reframes left, in the seventeenth shot of the film (5.67, 5.68, 5.69, 5.70), before reframing to the right. The river was photographed by Waite three years earlier from a similar position on the river, albeit from a higher point, and includes a view of the railway track that had, by the time Waite travelled to Tehuantepec, been laid: *1429 F. C. Istmo de Tehuantepec. The river from the bridge. Waite. Photo. Copyright. Es propiedad* (5.71).[196] The gelatin silver print and the view in the film identify a common generic interest in taking views of indigenous children, popular as *tipos mexicanos* in still and, by extension, moving images.[197] With regard to this particular location, the film demonstrates a further form of media convergence: one which takes place in the mind of a viewer familiar with Waite's photograph.

The last issue discussed in this chapter relates to mobilised views, a subject discussed by Anne Friedberg and Yuri Tsivian among others.[198] Two views from *Inauguración del tráfico internacional en el istmo de Tehuantepec* were designated a *panorama* and a *panoramic*. The first term was used towards the end of the film when an intertitle (5.72) designates a mobile view taken from the deck of a steamship as it leaves the port of Coatzacoalcos: *Panorama del Puerto Mexicano. desde un Vapor*[.][199] The ship draws away from a pier while the camera reframes slightly left (5.73). After a cut, the vessel sails parallel to the coast in a lateral travelling shot (5.74). Here, the term *panorama* is employed in a manner typical of the period.[200] However, in the second instance, in the fourth shot of the film, how the term functions is less clear. The title, *Panoramic del tren Presidencial*,[201] introduces a view of the presidential train as it approaches the viewer (5.75, 5.76). As the shot runs, the guard leans out of the baggage car to signal that the train is slowing down (5.77). The train passes the viewer (5.78), leaving people free to cross the track, which action closes the shot (5.79). Why is the term *panoramic* employed in this context, a shot which present-day viewers would judge to be a mis-reading of movement in pro-filmic space?

Tsivian has proposed that such a variation in response, between how we interpret movement towards the viewer and how it may have been perceived historically, may arise from a proprioceptive illusion which induces momentary confusion in the viewer's sense of spatial orientation.[202] We are all familiar with this effect when, sitting on a train in a station, a train next to the one in which we are seated draws out of the station, an effect which was doubtlessly induced in a film such as the second *Vue prise d'une plate-forme mobile* filmed at the 1900 Paris Exposition.[203] Tsivian has also proposed that movement such as this displays an interest in kinaesthesia, an effect common in early film, particularly in so-called phantom rides. This reponse may also arise from what Martin Kemp terms a 'vulnerability' which afflicts viewers when placed in a novel situation. Earlier in this chapter, we observed the difference between human binocular vision and optical transcription when we noted that optical instruments make their own visual artefacts rather than show the world in an accurate manner.[204] Kemp proposes that when a new 'visual tool' or optical instrument is introduced, it may not fit neatly into the modes of seeing and representation established in unaided vision.[205] Such a process may account for the use of the term, *panoramic*, in this case, where a view of a train passing viewers unaccustomed to mobile views (and the film-maker who provided titles) may have been interpreted as one

5.78

5.79

5.78–5.79. Frame enlargements, *Inauguración del tráfico internacional en el istmo de Tehuantepec*, Salvador Toscano, 1907, 35mm viewing copy. [Reproduced by permission of Filmoteca UNAM.]

5.80. Guillermo Kahlo, *Mexico Vista panorámica*, black-and-white picture postcard view, 92. Latapí y Bert, 8.9 x 14 cm. [Author's collection.]

involving movement on the viewer's part rather than movement in pro-filmic space. In this event, the shot may have induced momentary confusion in spatial orientation. Alternatively, it may demonstrate that a relatively novel instrument (in this case, the cinematographic camera), with a relatively unfamiliar mode of transcription (travelling views towards the spectator), did not fit easily into the modes of seeing and representation established for unaided vision.[206] If this is how the viewer responded to the shot of the train passing the viewer in *Inauguración del tráfico internacional en el istmo de Tehuantepec*, the shot and its designating intertitle demonstrate an ambivalence that applied historically to the experience of viewing a shot such as this in the film.

Ambivalence regarding how such views are designated in the intertitles of early actuality film also informs the example of still photographic images at the turn of the century. For example, a view we have already considered of a photograph by Kahlo of Avenida Cinco de Mayo from the cathedral (5.46) was also sold as a black-and-white picture postcard view by Latapí y Bert, one of the major suppliers of postcard views in Mexico in the early twentieth century (5.80).[207] The view is designated *Mexico. Vista panorámica*, a term which, in this instance, draws attention to the elevated position from which the photograph was taken. However, a similar view, sold as a colour picture postcard view by J. K., photographed from the same location and at a similar elevation, was designated as *Vista General de México* (Plate 31).[208] With competing claims regarding *panorama* and *panoramic* views at the turn of the century, the confusion of movement observed in Toscano's film may have been typical of a more general terminological ambivalence at the time.[209]

Responses of this kind to the viewing of early actuality films inform the point of departure for the final film considered in this chapter: *Paseo en tranvía por la calle de Brasil en la ciudad de México*, directed by Adriana Elhers and Dolores Elhers, and released in February 1920.[210] Two brief extracts from the film are examined, an example of a 'phantom ride' which demonstrates a delight in kinaesthesia arising from the fact that the film was shot from the back of a tram.[211] Like the camera lucida which, as we observed in Chapter Two, drew attention to the fact that the activity of *registering* a view was *perceptual* and *fleeting* rather than literal and stable, *Paseo en tranvía por la calle de Brasil en la ciudad de México* draws the viewer's attention to a similar relation between the viewer and the optical system of transcription. Rather than viewing a virtual image through a prism, as in the camera lucida, or a stable, framed, and projected image, as in the case of the camera obscura, the film draws attention to the contingent nature of representation, demonstrating that the filmic may be the primary site of representational activity. This observation is proposed not in response to a modernist aesthetic, where the image may be understood to 'bear' the device; rather, the extract demonstrates how an unfamiliar mode of representation did not fit easily into the conventions established in unaided vision in an actuality film released as late as 1920.

The two brief extracts involve the passage of a tram down a street, from the rear of which, the viewer observes the street (5.81). As the viewer is transported along the street, a small *collectivo* bus (no. 5527) approaches the tram in which the viewer is conducted (5.82). The destination of the *collectivo* ('Zócolo via Centenario') as it draws nearer is visible in, respectively, the lower and the upper parts of the

5.81–5.89. Frame enlargements, *Paseo en tranvía por la calle de Brasil en la ciudad de México*, Adriana Elhers and Dolores Elhers, 1920, 35mm viewing copy [Reproduced by permission of Filmoteca UNAM.]

windscreen. The tram in which the viewer is travelling approaches another *collectivo* on the right, on the outside of which, a man stands on the running-board holding onto the *collectivo* (5.83). As the two *collectivos* draw alongside each other, the destination of the second *collectivo* can be read: 'Viga'. A car draws into the road from an unseen road on the left of the shot (5.84). Note the man in the passenger seat of the car entering from the left: his right arm hangs out of the window, he wears a hat and what may be a white collar. As the car draws into the road, it forces *collectivo* 5527 to veer towards the right, which movement, in turn, makes the *collectivo* steer out of view (5.85). The man sitting in the passenger seat with a hat and white collar can still be seen. The viewer travels down the street a short distance before the second brief extract commences. The car that entered the street from the left has no number plate (5.86); the man with the white collar is still visible in the passenger seat, but he now rests his arm on the side of the car. At foreground right, an outstretched arm is visible. As the tram in which the viewer is travelling begins to draw away from the *collectivo* carrying the person with an outstretched arm (5.87), the *collectivo* begins to draw behind the tram carrying the viewer (5.88); the outstretched arm can still be seen, as too, part of the destination of the *collectivo*: 'via Centenario', the *collectivo* seen at the opening of the first extract. As *collectivo* 5527 draws behind the tram (5.89), a car passes on the right of the *collectivo* close to the right frame-line, the vehicle that drew into the road from the side street in the first extract.

What is striking, as the viewer watches the film, are the moving vehicles which come into view only to leave the screen or depart behind something on-screen. In this respect, the film stages an aleatoric performance, a seemingly random on-screen encounter for the viewer, with a series of movements that has no apparent start or conclusion, and certainly little or no order; only a series of incidents that morph from one form to another. In short, much like the virtual image seen through the camera lucida for the nineteenth-century draughtsman, the extract inscribes a relation between viewing and transcription that is fleeting, which, in effect, 'dances' before the viewer. In this respect, the fragment by Adriana and Dolores Elhers instances a new relation between the process of transcription and the process of viewing, one which, as in the case of some of the images examined earlier in this chapter, accentuates the fact that optical transcription created a new way of seeing. On occasion, the medium drew on technological antecedents (engravings, photographic images, lantern projections) that have long been recognised. But in this instance, the medium also demonstrates that the virtual image seen through the camera lucida is closer to the cinematographic image as a projected image than the camera obscura, the instrument which, for so long, has been regarded as the exemplary model for conceptualising the process by which still and moving cameras represented the world by photo-chemical impression. Neither a 'royal road to drawing', as we observed of the camera lucida in Chapter Two, nor Talbot's amateur's preferred route, where drawing's 'royal road' becomes 'the photograph's short cut', as Ann Bermingham has pointedly observed,[212] the cinematographic camera epitomises a form of media convergence in the early twentieth century when viewers, still 'vulnerable' to the cinematographic image as a projected image, delighted in movement as an end in itself. In this respect, the *technology* of the camera obscura may characterise the cinematographic camera as an optical instrument of transcription, yet the *fascination* the device sets in train, when viewing a film such as *Paseo en tranvía*, is more like the virtual image seen through the camera lucida, where fleeting events momentarily converge in the eye of the viewer at the moment of viewing the film. Picturing Mexico, in other words, by means of the camera lucida, and viewing Mexico in moving images may, on such occasions, display an isomorphic relation, an insight that an archaeology of film form brings forcefully to attention.

Epilogue

The comparison between the cinematographic image as a projected image and the image seen through the camera lucida with which Chapter Five closed is, of course, an analogy that would not have been available to the vast majority of people viewing film in the early 1920s. However, as I have shown, the formal concerns investigated in this study (panoramas and panoramic views, reverse views, and progression through space) established a series of material traces upon which popular visual culture drew in the nineteenth century, a reading of the stylistic history of media representations as palimpsestic. The study also demonstrates the extent to which pictorialism was mapped on the picturesque, and how representation was adapted in response to technological innovation.

Long associated with the discussion of modernity as epitomised by Walter Benjamin, the discourse associated with the panorama investigated in the early part of this study establishes what may be regarded as a parallel track for considering the development of popular visual culture in the nineteenth century, highlighting an historical narrative with different interests and emphases that afford new insights. Such a logic characterises the analysis undertaken in this study, central to which has been a concern with how the picturesque gave way to pictorialism, and how those traditions were transformed towards the end of the ninetenth century. In charting this development, attention has been directed at a tradition whose formal concerns passed, in terms of instrumentation, from lithographs to photographs, from photographs to the illustrated press and to early actuality film in a period when 'early cinema was not, in fact, early cinema'. However, that process was also accompanied by a transference from the somatic experience of media (such as the painted panorama viewed from the rotunda gallery) to optically mediated forms expressed, iconically, in the transition from the camera lucida to film as a projected medium, a development marked by a transfer of concern from the human body to the eye. Not yet a modernist discourse associated with the art-historical concept of 'modernism', the trajectory discussed in this study was, nonetheless, profound, not as momentous as the passage from the street to the arcade or from the arcade to the boulevard and the department store, which have defined one way of conceptualising the history of nineteenth-century European and North American culture; nevertheless, a passage from a haptic sensibility to one that also accommodated optical transcription. In short, a passage from the painted panorama to film through the prism of the camera lucida. So, in answer to the question, 'Was there 'cinema' before cinema?', one response includes the formal concerns which sustained popular visual culture in the nineteenth century: the panorama, the panoramic view, reverse views, and progression through space.

This study, however, has also examined a transformation in the practice of reading and viewing images in the nineteenth century. In particular, discussion has demonstrated that the relation between the reader and the *topos* of the printed page stimulated the imagination as much as it provided an understanding of natural wonders and manmade structures as depicted in the insets that border Antonio García Cubas' *Carta general de la República Mexicana* (Plate 32).[1] In the process of engaging with travel accounts, a wealth of new roles were provided for the reader-viewer interacting with the printed page as it embraced site plans, architectural plans, architectural drawings, details, cross-sections, geological cross-section, and engraved views, and, in the second part of the nineteenth century, the continued modelling of space from the organisation of photographic images in series to the design of the *mise en page* in photographic albums and the illustrated press. This process extended the reader-viewer's interaction with media, making non-professional practitioners creators in their own right. In the case of film, distinctions or ambivalence in the historical use of terms are evident (and also, possibly, confusion), indicating that the projected moving image established a new relation for viewers still 'vulnerable' to the cinematographic image who encountered novel forms of optical transcription in films by Salvador Toscano and by Adriana Elhers and Dolores Elhers. Such output marks a significant break with earlier forms of optical transcription.

The contrast between work at the turn of the nineteenth century and work at the beginning of the following century could not be better demonstrated than in a comparison of the Elhers sisters with William Gilpin, who wrote an account of an imaginary journey which takes the reader-viewer on a journey through an imagined landscape. Written and illustrated in the last years of his life, Gilpin's *A Fragment* (an unfinished work, sold at auction in 1802) conducts the reader-viewer on a tour of the fictitious lake Venlis. In the extract quoted below, the first four views, accompanied by four drawings, are described to the reader-viewer, the first in a series of twenty-four sketches that illustrate Gilpin's fictional quest:

> 1. Our first view of the lake displayed an extensive portion of it. On the left, in the 2d. distance arose the promontory, & castle of Bilvers. The island, & castle of Ulmer occupied the middle of the lake. Beyond them appeared the mountains of Ooust ....
> 2. As we moved a little to the left, we had another, and a better view of the promontory of Bilvers. ...
> 3. We had still a nearer view, soon afterwards, of the castle of Bilvers; in which *it* appeared to more advantage, & the promontory lost much of its shape. None but persons used to examine the scenes of nature, can easily conceive what changes in the features of a country a little variation of position occasions. Nobody could have conceived the promontory, as we now saw it, to be the same, which ran out into the lake, in the last view. We saw this landscape to great advantage through the skirts of a grove.
> 4. We had also a different view of the island, and castle of Ulmer, which we had seen at a distance in our first view of the lake. ...[2]

As the scenery unfolds, the reader-viewer is transported through a series of 'continually shifting' scenes, the features of which come more clearly into view as the tour progresses round the lake. Does not this process bring to mind the work of Guillermo Kahlo a century later when, far from charting an imaginary journey, the photographer kindled a similar sense of progression through photographing the 'found' space of Mexico City?

Clearly, the work of Kahlo has a lineage, one which echoes the substantial break in the representational tradition in the West that attended the introduction of the Sublime, after which the eyes of many travellers and spectators were opened to the grandeur of mountain scenery. A major transformation in aesthetic response to the natural landscape characterised the Sublime in the eighteenth century, a concern which Marjorie Hope Nicolson examined in her study, *Mountain Gloom and Mountain Glory*, where she characterised the transformation in sensibility as 'one of the most profound revolutions in thought'.[3] Indebted to the work of John Ruskin, whose *Modern Painters* provided a point of departure for Nicolson, Ruskin provides a fitting note on which to begin to draw this study to a close. Discussing some of his earliest childhood memories, Ruskin recalls the Lake District:

> The first thing which I remember, as an event in life, was being taken by my nurse to the brow of Friar's Crag on Derwentwater; the intense joy, mingled with awe, that I had in looking through the hollows in the mossy roots, over the crag, into the dark lake, has associated itself more or less with all twining roots of trees ever since. ...
>
> [A]lthough there was no definite religious sentiment mingled with it, there was a continual perception of Sanctity in the whole of nature, from the slightest to the vastest; - an instinctive awe, mixed with delight; an indefinable thrill, such as we sometimes imagine to indicate the presence of a disembodied spirit. I could only feel this perfectly when I was alone; and then it would often make me shiver from head to foot with the joy and fear of it ... I cannot in the least *describe* the feeling; but

> I do not think this is my fault, nor that of the English language, for, I am afraid, no feeling *is* describable.[4]

At the beginning of the nineteenth century, Alexander von Humboldt travelled to Mexico. Among the places Humboldt visited was the Pyramid of Cholula which, reputed to be the largest pyramid in the world, was depicted in a plate.[5] Humboldt's discussion of the *teocallis*, in line with a practice informed by the Enlightenment, included detailed measurement, a series of observations concerning the structure, and a discussion of the prospect view from the summit. Humboldt's observations also encompassed the 'traditionary' knowledge which the structure implied for indigenous people in the region:

> The size of the platform of the pyramid of Cholula, on which I made a great number of astronomical observations, is four thousand two hundred square metres. From it the eye ranges over a magnificent prospect, Popocatepetl, Iztaccihuatl, the peak of Orizaba, and the Sierra de Tlascalla, famous for the tempests which gather around its summit. We view at the same time three mountains higher than Mount Blanc, two of which are still burning volcanoes. A small chapel, surrounded with cypress, and dedicated to the Virgin de los Remedios, has succeeded to the temple of the god of the air, or the Mexican Indra. An ecclesiastic of the Indian race celebrates mass every day on the top of this antique monument.
>
> In the time of Cortez, Cholula was considered as a holy city. No where existed a greater number of teocallis, of priests, and religious orders (*tlamacazque*); no spot displayed greater magnificance in the celebration of public worship, or more austerity in its penances and fasts. Since the introduction of christianity among the Indians, the symbols of a new worship have not entirely effaced the remembrance of the old. The people assemble in crowds from distant quarters at the summit of the pyramid, to celebrate the festival of the Virgin. A mysterious dread, a religious awe, fills the soul of the Indian at the sight of this immense pile of bricks, covered with shrubs and perpetual verdure.[6]

Childhood memories and emotional responses, including those variously described by Ruskin and Humboldt, speak of a 'traditionary' knowledge that attests to the noble and awe-inspiring ideas with which the natural world and manmade structures were understood to resonate. Reading and viewing the illustrated works considered in this study, modelling architectonic space in our imagination, and picturing Mexico's history are processes which visitors, virtual or otherwise, have employed to envision the country since the time of Humboldt. That process constitutes a tradition which, in part, this study has sought to delineate, both with and from the camera lucida to film. Not without its own set of contradictions, it is a rich tradition, one which continues to reverberate, informing a transformation in aesthetic expression that characterises the secular world of today and the period with which this investigation has been concerned.

Notes

Notes to the Introduction

1. The classic study of these concerns is Rubén Gallo, *Mexican Modernity: The Avant-Garde and the Technological Revolution* (Cambridge, MA and London: MIT Press, 2005).
2. André Gaudreault and Philippe Marion, 'A medium is always born twice …', trans. Timothy Barnard, Wendy Schubring and Franck Le Gac, *Early Popular Visual Culture*, 3.1 (May 2005): 3–15, 3, 4, emphasis in original.
3. Gaudreault and Marion, 'A medium is always born twice …', 12, 13.
4. Glyn Edmund Daniel, *Cambridge and the Back-Looking Curiosity: An Inaugural Lecture* (Cambridge: Cambridge University Press, 1976), 5; Philippa Levine, *The Amateur and the Professional: Antiquarians, Historians and Archæologists in Victorian England 1838–1886* (Cambridge: Cambridge University Press, 1986), 12, 31, 88.
5. A concern pre-eminently investigated by Erkki Huhtamo with regard to media history and the discursive and material manifestations of culture. See, in particular, Erkki Huhtamo, *Illusions in Motion: Media Archaeology of the Moving Panorama and Related Spectacles* (Cambridge, MA and London: MIT Press, 2013).
6. Far from making Mexico economically secure, the Convention of Miramar, signed by Maximilian and Mexican monarchists in October 1863, tripled Mexico's foreign debt before Maximilian had even set foot in Mexico. The convention pledged Maximilian to pay all expenses incurred by the French troops during their fight for control of the country, 20,000 of whom were to remain in Mexico until the end of 1867.
7. *Raymond's Vacation Excursions: New Orleans, Mexico and California* (Boston: American Printing & Engraving Co., 1890), 3.
8. *Raymond's Vacation Excursions*, 5.
9. *Raymond's Vacation Excursions*, 4, 108.
10. Mary Elizabeth Blake and Margaret F. Sullivan, *Mexico: Picturesque, Political, Progressive* (Boston: Lee & Shepard; New York: Charles T. Dillingham, 1888), note 1, 211; *Raymond's Vacation Excursions*, 147–148.
11. Reau Campbell, *Campbell's Complete Guide and Descriptive Book of Mexico* (Chicago: Poole Bros. Press, 1895).
12. 'American Tourist Association. A Large Party Arrive by Mexican Central', *The Mexican Herald*, 2 January 1898, 1.
13. 'The Grafton Excursion', *The Mexican Herald*, 1 February 1898, 5; 'Gates Excursions', *The Mexican Herald*, 2 March 1898, 5.
14. 'Gates Excursionists. One Hundred and Eight Strong Arrive in Three Sections', *The Mexican Herald*, 3 March 1898, 8.
15. 'Ward Excursionists', *The Mexican Herald*, 8 March 1898, 1.
16. Charles Musser, *The Emergence of Cinema: The American Screen to 1907. History of the American Cinema*, Vol. I (Berkeley, Los Angeles, London: University of California Press, 1990), 39; John L. Stoddard, 'Mexico', *John L. Stoddard's Lectures, illustrated and embellished with views of the world's famous places and people, being the identical discourses delivered during the past eighteen years under the title of The Stoddard Lectures*, 10 vols. (Boston: Balch Brothers Co., 1901 [1898]), VII, 227–336.
17. For discussion of the manner in which early film evidences other concerns, see Elena Dagrada, 'Through the Keyhole: Spectators and Matte Shots in Early Cinema', *iris*, no. 11, 'Early Cinema Audiences / Les spectateurs au début du cinéma' (Spring 1990): 95–106.
18. Malcolm Andrews, *The Search for the Picturesque: Landscape Aesthetics and Tourism in Britain, 1760–1800* (Aldershot: Scolar Press, 1989); Malcolm Andrews, 'The Metropolitan Picturesque', in Stephen Copley and Peter Garside (eds.), *The Politics of the Picturesque: Literature, Landscape and Aesthetics since 1770* (Cambridge: Cambridge University Press, 1994), 282–298.
19. Henry Jenkins, *Convergence Culture: Where Old and New Media Collide* (New York and London: New York University Press, 2006).
20. *México y sus alrededores. Colección de monumentos, trajes y paisajes dibujados al natural y litografiados por los artistas mexicanos C. Castro, J. Campillo, L. Auda y G. Rodriguez* [*Mexico* [*City*] *and its Surroundings: A Collection of Monuments, Dress, and Landscape drawn from life and lithographed by the Mexican artists C. Castro, J. Campillo, L. Auda and G. Rodriguez*] (Mexico City: Establecimiento Litografico de Decaen, Editor, 1855 and 1856). See, in particular, plates drawn and engraved by the lithographer, Casimiro Castro: *La Alameda de México, Tomada en Globo* (Plate 26) and *La Ciudad de México tomada en Globo* (Plate 31). A facsimile edition of this work was published by Editorial del Valle de México, Mexico City, in 1980. For preliminary discussion of aerial views in the context of early actuality film in Mexico, see John Fullerton and Elaine King, 'Local Views and Distant Scenes: Registering Affect in Surviving Mexican Actuality Films of the 1920s', *Film History*, 17.1 (2005): 66–87, 76–78, in particular. For reproduction of Plate 31, see Figure 33, 79.
21. Tom Gunning, 'Before Documentary: Early nonfiction films and the "view" aesthetic', in Daan Hertogs and Nico de Klerk (eds.), *Uncharted Territory: Essays on early nonfiction film* (Amsterdam: Stichting Nederlands Filmmuseum, 1997), 9–24.

Notes to Chapter One

1. Joseph Spence quoted in Bruce Redford, *Dilettanti: The Antic and the Antique in Eighteenth-Century England* (Los Angeles: J. Paul Getty Museum/Getty Research Institute, 2008), 200.

2. John Lloyd Stephens, *Incidents of Travel in Yucatan*, 2 vols. (New York: Harper & Brothers for Henry Bill, 1848 [1843]), II, 389–390.

3. The term, *coup d'œil*, literally translated as 'stroke of the eye', was originally employed by the military at the time of the Napoleonic Wars to denote 'the talent of discerning the military strength and weakness of the land at a glance'. Rachel Hewitt, *Map of a Nation: A Biography of the Ordnance Survey* (London: Granta Books, 2010), 112. A related term, 'prospect view', was also used in discussing topography. Denis Cosgrove has observed that '[b]y the end of the sixteenth century prospect carried the sense of "an extensive or *commanding* sight or view, a view of the landscape as affected by one's position"', going on to note that '[t]he command that it implied was as much social and political as spatial'. Denis Cosgrove, 'Prospect, perspective, and the evolution of the landscape idea', *Transactions, Institute of British Geographers, New Series*, vol. 10 (1985), 45–62, 55–56, emphasis in original. In the early eighteenth century, Joseph Addison spoke of prospect views: '... a spacious Horison [*sic*] is an Image of Liberty, where the Eye has Room to range abroad, to expatiate at large on the Immensity of its Views, and to lose itself amidst the Variety of Objects that offer themselves to its Observation. Such wide and undetermined prospects are as pleasing to the Fancy, as the Speculations of Eternity or Infinitude are to the Understanding'. Joseph Addison, *The Spectator: by Joseph Addison, Richard Steele, et al.*, edited with an introduction and notes by Donald F. Bond, 5 vols. (Oxford: Clarendon Press, 1965), III, 541, quoted in Ann Bermingham, *Learning to Draw: Studies in the Cultural History of a Polite and Useful Art* (New Haven and London: The Paul Mellon Centre for Studies in British Art, Yale University Press, 2000), 91. William Shenstone later observed that he used 'the words landskip [landscape] and prospect, the former as an expressive of home scenes, the later of distant images. Prospects should take in the blue distant hills; but never so remotely, that they be not distinguishable from clouds.' William Shenstone, 'Unconnected Thoughts on Gardening', William Shenstone, *The Works in Verse and Prose of William Shenstone, Esq.*, 3 vols. (London: R. and J. Dodsley, 1764–1769), II [1764], 125–147, 129.

4. Stephens, *Yucatan*, I, 150.

5. Stephens, *Yucatan*, I, 166.

6. Mary Louise Pratt, *Imperial Eyes: Travel Writing and Transculturation* (London and New York: Routledge, 1993), 205–206.

7. Ann Bermingham proposes such a distinction when she observes that in 'place of ownership the touristic pleasure of exploring, viewing, surveying, and comparing' prevailed. Bermingham, *Learning to Draw*, 91. Reflecting on Addison's characterisation of prospect views, Bermingham proposes that '[s]uch a description of a landscape could easily be mapped onto the topographical view with its sweeping horizontality and factual presentation of the landscape's individual features. ... Addison observes that one "often feels a greater satisfaction in the prospect of fields and meadows, than one does in possession".' Bermingham, *Learning to Draw*, 91.

8. Victor Wolfgang von Hagen, *Maya Explorer: John Lloyd Stephens and the Lost Cities of Central America and Yucatán* (Norman: University of Oklahoma Press, 1947), 17–63, *passim*.

9. Victor Wolfgang von Hagen, *Frederick Catherwood Arch^t.* (New York and Oxford: Oxford University Press, 1950), 8, 10–12. Contrary to von Hagen's claim, Catherwood did not enrol as a student in the Royal Academy schools, e-mail communication from Andrew Potter, Royal Academy Library, 20 January 2012, nor does Catherwood's name appear in Sidney C. Hutchison, 'The Royal Academy Schools, 1768–1830', *Walpole Society*, vol. 38 (1962), 123–191. The influence of John Soane's lectures on Catherwood is considered below.

10. David Watkin, *Sir John Soane: Enlightenment Thought and the Royal Academy Lectures. Cambridge Studies in the History of Architecture* (Cambridge: Cambridge University Press, 1996), 396. Soane delivered Lectures I–VI from his first series of lectures (initially delivered in 1809) at the Royal Academy in 1817 (on 20 February, 27 February, 6 March, 13 March, 20 March, and 27 March) and in 1819 (on 18 February, 25 February, 4 March, 11 March, 18 March, and 25 March). In 1820, Lectures VII–IX from the second series of six lectures (first delivered at the Royal Academy in 1815), were delivered in revised form on 24 February, 2 March, and 9 March 1820. Watkin, *Sir John Soane: Enlightenment Thought and the Royal Academy Lectures*, Appendix Five: Susan Palmer, 'Chronology of the delivery of Sir John Soane's Royal Academy Lectures', 731–732, 731. Soane also delivered two lectures at the Royal Institution in 1817 (on Saturday, 7 June and Saturday, 14 June) and four lectures in 1820 (on Saturday, 27 May, Saturday, 3 June, Saturday, 10 June, and Saturday, 17 June), Watkin, *Sir John Soane: Enlightenment Thought and the Royal Academy Lectures*, note 47, 436. Manuscript copies of the Royal Institution lectures, in the hand of Soane, are held in the Research Library, Sir John Soane's Museum, see Soane's Case 157, MSS, 'Lecture the First Royal Institution 7th June 1817' and 'Royal Institution, Lecture the 2^d^ Read on Saturday the 14th June 1817', and Soane Case 158, MS, 'Lectures on Architecture, Royal Institution 1820'.

11. Although we do not know the publication date of Catherwood's copy of Sir Joshua Reynolds' *Discourses on Painting*, we know that Catherwood owned a copy of Robert Wharton's *Essays on Gothic Architecture* (1802), and acquired a copy of the 1848 edition of *Lectures on Painting* by James Barry, John Opie, and Henry Fuseli, works which testify to a continuing interest in the teaching of the Royal Academy throughout Catherwood's career. See *Catalogue of a Portion of the Library of the Late Frederic [sic] Catherwood, Esq. Hon Member of the Royal Institute of British Architects, Author of Views and Monuments in Central America etc. Also a Portion of the Library of an Eminent Surgeon, Retiring from Practice ..., Which will be Sold by Auction by Messrs. Puttick and Simpson, Auctioneers of Literary Property, at their Great Room, 191, Piccadilly, on Monday, December 1st, 1856, and five following days at one o'clock most punctually*, printed sale catalogue, paginated, item #200 (10), item #882 (37), item #1080 (45), item #1202 (50), item #1686 (68).

12. *Sir John Soane: The Royal Academy Lectures*, edited with an Introduction by David Watkin (Cambridge: Cambridge University Press, 2000), 32. Soane, who travelled in France and Italy, never visited Palmyra or Baalbek; for preparing illustrations of these sites in his lectures, Soane relied on two works by Robert Wood, *The Ruins of Palmyra, otherwise Tedmore, in the Desart* (London, 1753) and *The Ruins of Balbec, otherwise Heliopolis in Cœlosyria* (London, 1757). These sites were briefly considered in Lecture I, Lecture III, and Lecture IV (First Series), see *Sir John Soane: The Royal Academy Lectures*, 'Lecture I', 32, 'Lecture III', 76–77,

81, 82, and 'Lecture IV', 90, 92, 94, 96, 99, and were also mentioned in Lecture IX (Second Series, delivered 16 March 1815 and 9 March 1820), Lecture X (delivered 9 March 1815) and Lecture XII (delivered 12 March 1815), see *Sir John Soane: The Royal Academy Lectures*, 200, 228, 236, 237, 264. The sites were also briefly considered in Soane's Royal Institution lectures, see Soane Case 157, MS, 'Lecture the First Royal Institution 7th June 1817', 18, and Soane Case 158, MS, 'Lectures on Architecture, Royal Institution 1820', 25–26, 35–36. Some of the illustrations presented at the Royal Academy were also shown at the Royal Institution. With the exception of the Royal Institution lectures (where I quote from MSS in Soane's hand held at Sir John Soane's Museum), quotations from Soane's lectures in this chapter are from *Sir John Soane: The Royal Academy Lectures* (ed. Watkin).

13. Catherwood exhibited *Buckingham Gate, Adelphi* (catalogue no. 974) at the Royal Academy in 1820. Algernon Graves, *The Royal Academy of Arts: A Complete Dictionary of Contributors and their Work from its Foundation in 1769 to 1904. Compiled with the sanction of the President and Council of The Royal Academy*, 8 vols. (London: Henry Graves and Co. Ltd. and George Bell and Sons, 1905–1906), II, 14. Joseph Bonomi was admitted to the Royal Academy schools on 9 August 1816, and Joseph John Scoles was admitted on 13 January 1820. Hutchison, 'The Royal Academy Schools, 1768–1830', respectively, 168 and 173.

14. William Sandby, *The History of the Royal Academy of Arts from its Foundation in 1768 to the Present Time. With Biographical Notices of all the Members*, 2 vols. (London: Longman, Green, Longman, Roberts & Green, 1862), I, 282. The Peace of Amiens marked the cessation of hostilities between Britain and France in the period between the French Revolutionary Wars (1793–1802) and the Napoleonic Wars (1803–1815).

15. John Madox, *Excursions in the Holy Land, Egypt, Nubia, Syria, &c.*, 2 vols. (London: Richard Bentley, 1834), II, 28. Some sketches, ink drawings, and watercolour paintings of scenes in Egypt by Catherwood, with dates assigned by 'JGW' (John Gardner Wilkinson) between the end of December 1823 and June 1824, on, in some cases, watermarked paper manufactured by J. Whatman, Turkey Mill, Boxley, near Maidstone, Kent, in 1822, are held in the Searight Collection, Prints and Drawings Study Room, Victoria and Albert Museum. For brief discussion of Catherwood's opinion of Sir John Gardner Wilkinson, see Jason Thompson, *Sir Gardner Wilkinson and His Circle* (Austin: University of Texas Press, 1992), 108, 133.

16. Catherwood exhibited *Sketch of a Temple in Nubia* at the Royal Academy in 1828 (catalogue no. 559) and views of a pyramid and of a temple, presumably from Egypt, at the Royal Academy in 1831 (catalogue nos. 615 and 1087). Graves, *The Royal Academy of Arts*, II, 14; George Alexander Hoskins, *Visit to the Great Oasis of the Libyan Desert; With an Account, Ancient and Modern, of the Oasis of Amun, and the Other Oases now under the Dominion of the Pasha of Egypt* (London: Longman, Rees, Orme, Brown, Green, & Longman, 1837), 91; Victor Wolfgang von Hagen, *Frederick Catherwood Archt*., 7–13, *passim*; Warren Royal Dawson and Eric P. Uphill (eds.), *Who was Who in Egyptology*, third revised edition (London: The Egypt Exploration Society, 1995), 86; Peter Arthur Clayton, *The Rediscovery of Ancient Egypt: Artists and Travellers in the 19th Century* (London: Thames and Hudson, 1982), 48. In addition to *Frederick Catherwood Archt*., von Hagen published *F. Catherwood, Architect-Explorer of Two Worlds* (Barre: Barre Publishers, 1968) and two studies of Stephens and Catherwood: *Maya Explorer: John Lloyd Stephens and the Lost Cities of Central America and Yucatán* (Norman: University of Oklahoma Press, 1947) and *Search for the Maya: The Story of Stephens and Catherwood* (New York: Saxon House, 1973). I have drawn primarily on von Hagen with regard to Catherwood's career in the United States.

17. Francis Arundale, *Illustrations of Jerusalem and Mount Sinai; Including the Most Interesting Sites between Grand Cairo and Beirout. From drawings by F. Arundale, Architect* (London: Henry Colburn, Publisher, 1837), 71; William Henry Bartlett, *Walks about the City and Environs of Jerusalem* (London: George Virtue, 1844), where an account of his time in Jerusalem is provided by Catherwood in a letter he wrote to Bartlett. Bartlett, *Walks about the City and Environs of Jerusalem*, 161–178.

18. Henry Courtney Slous, who changed his family name to 'Selous', was admitted to the Royal Academy schools in 1819. Hutchison, 'The Royal Academy Schools, 1768–1830', 172. Selous also developed sketches by Catherwood for the panorama of Baalbek, exhibited at the Panorama, Leicester Square, in 1844, discussed towards the end of this chapter.

19. *The Repertory of Arts and Manufactures: Consisting of Original Communications, Specifications of Patent Inventions, and Selections of Useful Practical Papers from the Transactions of the Philosophical Societies of all Nations, &c. &c.*, Vol. IV (London, 1796), patent no. 1612, 165. Military and maritime traditions provided important source material for panoramas, particularly in the period of the French Revolutionary Wars and Napoleonic Wars, see Denise Blake Oleksijczuk, *The First Panoramas: Visions of British Imperialism* (Minneapolis and London: University of Minnesota Press, 2011). I thank Zoë Druick for bringing this work to my attention.

20. The earliest appearance of the term, 'panorama', in print may be found in *Oracle*, no. 624, 18 May 1791, cited in Erkki Huhtamo, *Illusions in Motion: Media Archaeology of the Moving Panorama and Related Spectacles* (Cambridge, MA and London: MIT Press, 2013), 1 and note 2, 21. The term is transliterated as πανωραμαν in George Richard Corner, *The Panorama: with Memoirs of Its Inventor, Robert Barker, and his son, the late Henry Aston Barker. From the "Art Journal," February, 1857* (London: J. & W. Robins, 1857), 7.

21. *Edinburgh Evening Courant*, 2 February 1788, 1, quoted in Oleksijczuk, *The First Panoramas*, 181, note 35, 26.

22. For illustration, see Ralph Hyde (ed.), *Panoramania! The Art and Entertainment of the 'All-Embracing' View* (London: Trefoil Publications in association with Barbican Art Gallery, 1988), Figure 27, 62–63; Bernard Comment, *The Panorama*, trans. Anne Marie Glasheen (London: Reaktion Books, 1999 [French edition, 1993]), 184–187; Oleksijczuk, *The First Panoramas*, Figure 1.1, facing 160. The *View of Edinburgh and the Surrounding Country from Calton Hill*, twenty-five feet in diameter and painted in tempera on paper pasted on linen, was also sold as a series of six prints or six aquatints, prepared by John Wells after Robert Barker, issued between October 1789 and March 1790. Oleksijczuk, *The First Panoramas*, 27. The view as described here conforms to the order in which the set of aquatints is hung in the collection of the City Art Centre, Edinburgh, Whitson Bequest: the set of aquatints depicts an almost complete 360° panoramic view. For extensive discussion of the view in the context of the Scottish Enlightenment and political relations between Scotland and England in the eighteenth century, see Oleksijczuk, *The First Panoramas*, 23–46. See also Oleksijczuk's discussion of *View of Edinburgh and the Surrounding Country from Calton Hill* when exhibited

in London between 1789 and 1791, Oleksijczuk, *The First Panoramas*, 46–52, 55–56, 65.

23. Oleksijczuk, *The First Panoramas*, 26, note 52, 182,

24. For illustration, see Hyde (ed.), *Panoramania!*, Figure 28, 18–19; Stephan Oettermann, *The Panorama: History of a Mass Medium*, trans. Deborah Lucas Schneider (New York: Zone Books, 1997 [German edition, 1980]), Figure 1.16, 64–65; Oleksijczuk, *The First Panoramas*, Figure 2.1, facing 160.

25. Part of the rotunda of the Panorama, Leicester Square, can be seen in Thomas H. Shepherd, *View of the Entrance to Burford's Panorama, Leicester Square*, 1858, reproduced in Hyde, *Panoramania!*, 26; Oettermann, *The Panorama*, Figure, 2.5, 104; Oleksijczuk, *The First Panoramas*, Figure 1.3, 18.

26. According to William Sandby, Ramsay Richard Reinagle was a 'panoramic painter of considerable ability'. William Sandby, *The History of the Royal Academy of Arts from its Foundation in 1768 to the Present Time. With Biographical Notices of all the Members*, 2 vols. (London: Longman, Green, Longman, Roberts, & Green, 1862), I, 35.

27. Corner, *The Panorama*, 4–6, 11–12; Richard D. Altick, *The Shows of London* (Cambridge, MA and London: The Belknap Press of Harvard University Press, 1978), 129; Ralph Hyde, 'The Early Years', in Hyde (ed.), *Panoramania!*, 57–58, 61; Oettermann, *The Panorama*, 100–101, 103, 111–113, and note 7, 358–359; Comment, *The Panorama*, 23–25, 161. For discussion of the introduction and development of the panorama in the early nineteenth century, see Scott B. Wilcox, 'Unlimiting the Bounds of Painting', in Hyde, *Panoramania!*, 13–44.

28. Hyde (ed.), *Panoramania!*, 61, 78.

29. The full title reads: Thomas Hartwell Horne, *Landscape Illustrations of the Bible, Consisting of Views of the Most Remarkable Places Mentioned in the Old and New Testaments. From original sketches taken on the spot. Engraved by W. and E. Finden. With descriptions by the Rev. Thomas Hartwell Horne, B.D. of St. John's College, Cambridge, author of "An introduction to the study of the Holy Scriptures," Etc.*, 2 vols. (London: John Murray, 1836).

30. Von Hagen, *Frederick Catherwood Archt.*, 42. Although panoramas nurtured the educational objectives of informing and cultivating audiences, Comment has proposed that with the introduction of commentators, a more discursive form of commentary complemented the viewing of panoramas. Comment, *The Panorama*, 117–118. The orientation plan and key for *A View of Edinburgh and the Surrounding Country*, printed in 1805 when the panorama was exhibited in London, informs visitors that 'A Person always attends to explain the Painting'. Oleksijczuk, *The First Panoramas*, Figure 1.4, 31.

31. Von Hagen, *Frederick Catherwood Archt.*, 43.

32. For illustration of Catherwood's Panorama in New York, see Oettermann, *The Panorama*, Figure 6.6, 321. Modelled on Mitchell's design for the Panorama, Leicester Square, the New York rotunda contained two rows of skylights augmented by 'upwards of 200 gas-lights'. Wolfgang von Hagen, Introduction by Aldous Huxley, *F. Catherwood: Architect-Explorer of Two Worlds* (Barre: Barre Publishers, 1967), 35. The New York Panorama was destroyed by fire during the night of 31 July 1842. For further discussion of Catherwood's panorama in New York drawing on von Hagen, see Oettermann, 317, 320–323.

33. Dell Upton, 'Inventing the Metropolis: Civilization and Urbanity in Antebellum New York', in Catherine Hoover Voorsanger and John K. Howat (eds.), *Art and the Empire City: New York, 1825–1861* (New York: The Metropolitan Museum of Art; New Haven and London: Yale University Press, 2000), 3–45, note 224, 38; von Hagen, *Frederick Catherwood Archt.*, 47–51, *passim*. For discussion of the reception of the Jerusalem panorama in New York City, see John Davis, *The Landscape of Belief: Encountering the Holy Land in Nineteenth-Century American Art and Culture. The Princeton Series in Nineteenth-Ventury Art, Culture, and Society* (Princeton: Princeton University Press, 1996), 59–65.

34. Established in New York in 1842, the first meeting of the Society was held on 19 November 1842, *Transactions of the American Ethnological Society*, vol. 1 (1845), x. Catherwood visited two sites in Tunisia in 1832 (at which time Tunisia was a vassal state of Egypt), and presented two papers to the American Ethnological Society, published as Frederick Catherwood, 'Account of the Punico-Libyan Monument at Dugga [*sic*]', and Frederick Catherwood, 'The Remains of an Ancient Structure at Bless, near the site of Ancient Carthage', *Transactions of the American Ethnological Society*, vol. 1 (1845), 475–491. Catherwood presented a further paper, 'Antiquities of Central America', to the Royal Institute of British Architects in February 1844; report published in *The Civil Engineer and Architect's Journal, Scientific and Railway Gazette*, 7 (24 February 1844): 92–94.

35. Drawing on bank account records of Robert Barker and Catherine and Henry Aston Barker held in the archives of Coutts Bank for the period between June 1791 and June 1821, Oleksijczuk estimates that 40,000 spectators a year visited the panorama during the French Revolutionary Wars (1793 to 1802), that annual admissions rose to 60,000 during the Peninsular War (1808–1814), that the number of admissions peaked upward of 200,000 visitors when the panorama of the Battle of Waterloo was exhibited in 1816, and that between 23 June 1793 and 23 June 1820, over one and a half million people visited the Panorama, Leicester Square. Oleksijczuk, *The First Panoramas*, 6. With the price of admission set at one shilling, Oleksijczuk observes that the panorama was a relatively expensive form of entertainment, excluding the poor and many labourers, primarily serving the interests of the middle-to-higher classes. Oleksijczuk, *The First Panoramas*, 162.

36. Review of *Incidents of Travel in Central America, Chiapas, and Yucatan*, *The Quarterly Review* Vol. 69, No. 137 (1842): 52–91, note, 52. The response was so enthusiastic that within three months of publication of the first edition, *Incidents of Travel in Central America, Chiapas, and Yucatan* had reached its tenth edition. John Lloyd Stephens, 'Preface to the Tenth Edition', reprinted in the twelfth edition, *Incidents of Travel in Central America, Chiapas, and Yucatan* (New York: Harper & Brothers, Publishers, 1852), v. The response accorded this work was not exceptional: six editions of Stephens' first travel account, *Incidents of Travel in Egypt, Arabia Petræa, and the Holy Land* (1837), appeared in the first year of publication, for which Stephens received $15,000 in royalties from the publishers, Harper & Brothers, an income that made Stephens financially independent. The work was translated into French and Swedish. Robert Levere Brunhouse, *In Search of the Maya: The First Archaeologists* (Albuquerque: University of New Mexico Press, 1973), 86.

37. The work was translated into six languages. Brunhouse, *In Search of the Maya*, 106.

38. Stephens reputedly received $30,000 from *Incidents of Travel in Yucatan*. Nicholas Trübner (ed.), *Trübner's Bibliographical Guide to American Literature. A Classed List*

of Books Published in the United States of America during the Last Forty Years. With Bibliographical Introduction, Notes, and Alphabetical Index (London: Trübner and Co., 1859), lvi, lxxxvi.

39. 'By-Laws of the British Institution for Promoting the Fine Arts in the United Kingdom, Established the 4th of June, 1805, Under the Patronage of His Majesty, London, 1805', unpaginated, quoted in Peter Fullerton, 'Patronage and Pedagogy: The British Institution in the Early Nineteenth Century', *Art History*, 5.1 (March 1982): 59–72, 66, 64.

40. Thomas and William Reeves were awarded the Greater Silver Palette of the Royal Society of Arts in 1781 for the introduction of cakes of prepared watercolour. Andrew Wilton, *Turner as Draughtsman* (Aldershot and Basingstoke: Ashgate Press, 2006), 25–26. Further factors in the growth of the market for amateur artists included the introduction of 'wove' paper by James Whatman in the eighteenth century, and the introduction of the 'graphite' pencil in the late eighteenth century. Wilton, *Turner as Draughtsman*, 26, 23.

41. For discussion of the development of the amateur art market and the growth of drawing-master as a career opportunity in the early nineteenth century, see Bermingham, *Learning to Draw*, 127–181.

42. Edward Miller, *That Noble Cabinet: A History of the British Museum*. Foreword by Sir John Wolfenden, CBE, Director and Principal Librarian of the British Museum (London: André Deutsch, 1973), 79, 96–97. Although the King's Library was acquired in 1823, it was not transferred to the British Museum until August 1828. Miller, *That Noble Cabinet*, 129, 366.

43. Miller, *That Noble Cabinet*, 97–99, 105–107.

44. Joan Evans, *A History of the Society of Antiquaries* (Oxford: Printed at the University Press by Charles Batey for The Society of Antiquaries, Burlington House, London, 1956), 227–228.

45. Oettermann, *The Panorama*, 131; Michael P. Costeloe, *William Bullock. Connoisseur and Virtuoso of the Egyptian Hall: Piccadilly to Mexico (1773–1849)* (Bristol: HiPLAM, 2008), 109. The painting was exhibited from 10 June 1820 (the date of the preview) until the end of December 1820. Bermingham puts the figure for attendance at the Géricault exhibition as close to 50,000. Bermingham, *Learning to Draw*, 133. *Le Radeau de la 'Méduse'* is in the collection of the Louvre, Paris.

46. 'R. H.' [Robert Hunt], *The Examiner*, 7 April 1822.

47. The exhibition, which ran from 30 March 1822 until the end of July, was accompanied by *A Descriptive Catalogue of The Destruction of Pompeii and Herculaneum; with other Pictures, painted by John Martin, now exhibiting at the Egyptian Hall, Piccadilly. With Two Engravings, explanatory of the principal Pictures* (London: printed by Plummer & Brewis, 1822). Costeloe, *William Bullock*, 122. The *Descriptive Catalogue* was accompanied by two plates: *The Destruction of Pompeii etc.*, an outline etching with subjects numbered 1 to 32, signed 'J. Martin, 1821', and *The Fall of Babylon*, with subjects numbered 1 to 13, unsigned. Thomas Balston, *John Martin 1789–1854: His Life and Works* (London: Gerald Duckworth & Co., 1947), 65–66, note 4, 270. *The Destruction of Pompeii and Herculaneum* (1821, oil on canvas) is in the collection of Tate Britain; a smaller copy of the painting (1826, oil on canvas) is held in the Tabley House Collection (University of Manchester), Knutsford. The painting has recently been restored. Martin Myrone (ed.), *John Martin: Sketches of my Life* (London: Tate Publishing, 2011), note 43, 45.

48. *A Description of the Picture Belshazzar's Feast* (Yale Center for British Art), with reproduction of an etching and key, also accompanied the exhibition of *Beshazzar's Feast* at the British Institution in 1820. Balston, *John Martin 1789–1854*, 260–265; see also the discussion of *Belshazzar's Feast* in Barbara G. Morden, *John Martin: Apocalypse Now!* (Newcastle upon Tyne: Northumbria Press, 2010), 25–26.

49. David Wilkie, letter to Sir George Beaumont, 16 February 1821, on the exhibition of Martin's *Belshazzar's Feast* at the British Institution. Allan Cunningham, *The Life of Sir David Wilkie*, 3 vols. (London: John Murray, 1843), II, 57. It should be observed that Wilkie drew a distinction between the popular appeal of Martin's work and the reception his work was accorded by artists of the day.

50. An explicit example of this ambition can be seen in the series of eight coloured aquatints by Charles Tomkins, Frederick C. Lewis, and G. Lewis, after drawings by Henry Aston Barker, published by Thomas Palser and Henry Aston Barker on 1 January 1813, that depict a view of Constantinople from the Galata Tower to the north of the eastern end of the Golden Horn. The view extends from the Bosphorus (to the east of the Galata Tower) to the upper reaches of the Golden Horn (to the west) and back again to the Bosphorus. The view was exhibited in the Large Circle of the Panorama, Leicester Square, 27 April 1801 – 15 May 1802. For illustration, see Hyde, *Panoramania!*, Figure 46, 72–73; Oleksijczuk, *The First Panoramas*, Figure 4.1, facing 161.

51. From the patent granted Robert Barker, 19 June 1787, reprinted in *Repertory of Arts and Manufactures*, vol. 4 (1796): 165–166. A facsimile of the patent is included in Laurent Mannoni, Donata Pesenti Campagnoni, David Robinson, *Light and Movement: Incunabula of the Motion Picture. 1420–1896 / Luce e movimento. Incunaboli dell'immagine animata, 1420–1896 / Lumière et mouvement. Incunables de l'image animée, 1420–1896* (Pordenone: Le Giornate del Cinema Muto/Cinémathèque française– Musée du Cinéma/Museo Nazionale del Cinema, 1995), 157–158, which includes a short preamble to the patent not printed in *Repertory of Arts and Manufactures* (1796). The patent as reproduced in Mannoni et al includes the occasional departure in wording and punctuation to the patent as printed in *Repertory of Arts and Manufactures*.

52. Robert Southey, Letter to Allan Cunningham, Esq., Keswick, 3 June 1833, *Life and Correspondence of Robert Southey*, edited by Charles Cuthbert Southey, 6 vols. (London: Longman, Brown, Green, and Longmans, 1849–1850), VI, 214–218, 215.

53. Hearne's six pen and ink and watercolour over pencil sketches are held at the Victoria and Albert Museum; for illustration, see David Morris, *Thomas Hearne and his Landscape* (London: Reaktion Books, 1989), Figure 60, 78–79. William Gilpin alludes to this work in *Observations, Relative Chiefly to Picturesque Beauty, Made in the Year 1772; On several Parts of England; particularly the Mountains, and Lakes of Cumberland, and Westmoreland*, 2 vols. (London: R. Blamire, 1786), I, 180.

54. The sum of one shilling rendered in today's terms: 5p. The sale of descriptive booklets was instituted in 1801 with the exhibition of a panorama of Constantinople. Comment, *The Panorama*, 117. Oleksijczuk informs us that descriptive booklets were distributed free of charge between 1801and 1812 when Henry Aston Barker began to sell them for sixpence (in today's terms: 2½p), from which date descriptive booklets are extant for all panoramas. Oleksijczuk, *The First Panoramas*, 15, note 71, 178. Laurie Garrison has proposed that the practice of producing descriptive booklets may have become a convention by

1810. Laurie Garrison, 'Imperial Vision in the Arctic: Fleeting Looks and Pleasurable Distractions in Barker's Panorama and Shelley's *Frankenstein*', *Romanticism and Victorianism on the Net*, no. 51 (November 2008), paragraph 6. The descriptive booklet usually provided information regarding historical background, ethnographic interest, and anecdotal material relating to the subject of a panorama. Wilcox, 'Unlimiting the Bounds of Painting', in Hyde, *Panoramania!*, 36. See also Oettermann, *The Panorama*, 60–63, for further discussion of 'souvenir programmes' and their relation to the publication of small-scale panoramas. I thank Alan Barnes for bringing Laurie Garrison's article to my attention.

55. William H. Galperin, *The Return of the Visible in British Romanticism* (Baltimore and London: Johns Hopkins University Press, 1993), 43. The notion of distracted viewing is developed further in a comparison of Henry Aston Barker's 1819 panorama of the North Coast of Spitzbergen (from a voyage undertaken in 1818), with the account by Captain Robert Walton that frames the epistolary narrative in Mary Shelley's *Frankenstein; or, The Modern Prometheus* (written between June 1816 and May 1817, first published in 1818). Garrison, 'Imperial Vision in the Arctic'.

56. Laurie Garrison, 'Virtual reality and subjective responses: Narrating the search for the Franklin expedition through Robert Burford's panorama', *Early Popular Visual Culture*, 10.1 (February 2012): 7–22, in particular, 17–20.

57. Ian Ousby, *The Englishman's England: Taste, Travel and the Rise of Tourism* (Cambridge: Cambridge University Press, 1990), 12.

58. John Byng, *The Torrington Diaries: Containing the Tours through England and Wales of the Hon. John Byng (Later Fifth Viscount Torrington) between the Years 1781 and 1794*, edited by C. Bruyn Andrews, 4 vols. (London: Eyre and Spottiswoode, 1934–1938), I, 69, quoted in Ousby, *The Englishman's England*, 12.

59. Ousby, *The Englishman's England*, 19.

60. 'The Panorama', *Somerset House Gazette, and Literary Museum: or, weekly miscellany of Fine Arts, Antiquities, and Literary Chit Chat*, No. 36, 12 June 1824, 151–153, 152.

61. For general discussion of the nineteenth-century panorama, see Angela Miller, 'The Panorama, the Cinema, and the Emergence of the Spectacular', *Wide Angle*, 18. 2 (April 1996): 34–69.

62. Anne Friedberg, *Window Shopping: Cinema and the Postmodern* (Berkeley, Los Angeles, Oxford: University of California Press, 1993), 20–22, 21. The quotation from Wordsworth comes from *The Prelude or Growth of a Poet's Mind. An Autobiographical Poem*, in William Wordsworth, *Poetical Works*. Introduction and Notes, edited by Thomas Hutchinson, revised by Ernest de Selincourt (London, New York, Toronto: Oxford University Press, 1936), 'Book Seventh, Residence in London', 495–588, 540, line 233. A similar argument to Friedberg is developed in Comment, *The Panorama*, 136–137. In the context of the argument developed in this chapter, Wordsworth's comparison of the painted panorama with painting in the grand style is apposite: '... and, next, those sights that ape/The absolute presence of reality,/Expressing, as in mirror, sea and land,/And what earth is, and what she has to show./I do not here allude to subtlest craft,/By means refined attaining purest ends,/But imitations, fondly made in plain/Confession of man's weakness and his loves./Whether the Painter, whose ambitious skill/Submits to nothing less than taking in/A whole horizon's circuit, do with power,/Like that of angels or commissioned spirits,/Fix us upon some lofty pinnacle,/ ...', *The Prelude*, Wordsworth, *Poetical Works*, 540–541, lines 232–244.

63. The argument that panoramas promoted a 'sweeping horizontality', one that was 'sensational in the visceral effects it produced', proposed by Bermingham, *Learning to Draw*, 91, 121, is considered in the latter part of this chapter.

64. Oettermann, *The Panorama*, 22.

65. Oettermann, *The Panorama*, 22, 54.

66. Comment, *The Panorama*, 116–117.

67. Oettermann, *The Panorama*, 30–32, 49, 52.

68. Oettermann, *The Panorama*, 30, 51.

69. Ann Bermingham, 'Landscape-O-Rama: The Exhibition Landscape at Somerset House and the Rise of Popular Landscape Entertainments', in David H. Solkin (ed.), *Art on the Line: The Royal Academy Exhibitions at Somerset House 1780–1836* (New Haven and London: Yale University Press for The Paul Mellon Centre for Studies in British Art and The Courtauld Institute Gallery, 2001), 127–144.

70. Bermingham, 'Landscape-O-Rama', 135; Oettermann, *The Panorama*, 52, 55, 57.

71. The concern with aerial perspective is emphasised by Oettermann, *The Panorama*, 57, and Bermingham, 'Landscape-O-Rama', 135, and was emphasised by F. W. Fairholt who observed that 'with the aid of aerial perspective, an almost infinite space and distance can be represented with a degree of illusion quite wonderful'. Entry for 'Panorama' in F[rederick] W[illiam] Fairholt, *A Dictionary of Terms in Art. Edited and Illustrated by F.W. Fairholt, F. S. A. With Five Hundred Engravings on Wood* (London: Strahan & Co., 1854), 324–325, 325.

72. John Constable told his audience in a lecture delivered at the Royal Institution in 1836 that 'Painting is a science, and should be pursued as an inquiry into the laws of nature.' 'Lecture 4th, June 16th' [1836], *Memoirs of the Life of John Constable*, edited by Charles Robert Leslie (London: John Lehman, 1949 [first published in 1843]), 343.

73. Charlotte Klonk, *Science and the Perception of Nature: British Landscape Art in the Late Eighteenth and Early Nineteenth Centuries* (New Haven and London: The Paul Mellon Centre for Studies in British Art, Yale University Press, 1996), 149.

74. For discussion of how panoramas challenged the organisation of space conferred by the frame in painting, and how the maintenance of a pre-determined distance in viewing a panorama departed from the process of viewing a painting, see Comment, *The Panorama*, 97–103, 110–114.

75. The manner in which descriptive booklets, engraved keys, and spoken commentary increasingly constrained interpretation after an initial period of dynamic interaction is central to Oleksijczuk's discussion of panoramas in the period before 1818 when rectangular engraved keys were introduced. Oleksijczuk, *The First Panoramas*, 22, 166, 167, 170. Oleksijczuk identifies five principal types of engraved key employed in the period before 1818: (1) an ichnographic plan designating the central location of the spectator, see Figure 3.1, *View of the Grand Fleet Moored at Spithead* (1793); (2) a circular plan of the observation platform with point of entry designated surrounded by a highly schematic sketch of buildings arranged round the edges of the plan, see Figure 5.1, *View of the City of Bath* (1794); (3) a circular plan of the observation platform designating the four cardinal points of the compass and staircase leading to the obervation platform with a series of profile views of buildings arranged

elliptically round the plan, see Figure 5.7, *View of London From the Roof of the Albion Mills* (1795); (4) a circular plan of the observation platform divided into sections each representing successive moments in the development of a naval battle with sketches of vessels involved in the battle arranged round the edges of the plan, see Figure 5.12, *Lord Bridport's Engagement* (1796); 5) a central circle accompanied by text designating the observation platform surrounded by an anamorphotic view with marked increase in detail and perspectival organisation, see Figure 5.16, *Grand View of La Valetta, the Capital of Malta* (1810). Oleksijczuk, *The First Panoramas*, 68, 128, 140, 150, 157. In its organisation of space, the last type anticipates the disposition of views introduced in 1818, in which tradition Catherwood's engraved keys may be located. For illustration of the earliest engraved rectangular orientation views, see Figure 5.20 (*Outline of the Attach upon Algiers*, 1818), Figure 5.21 (*Explanation of the View of Lausanne and Lake of Geneva*, 1819), and Figure 5.22 (*Explanation of the North Coast of Spitzbergen*, 1819), Oleksijczuk, *The First Panoramas*, 167, 168, 171.

76. The practice of viewing an illuminated painting from a darkened gallery, typical of the panorama, was also adopted by John Martin in his solo exhibition at the Egyptian Hall in 1822.

77. Thomas West, *A Guide to the Lakes, in Cumberland, Westmorland, and Lancashire*, third edition (London: Richardson and Urquhart, 1784 [1780]). A copy of the 1793 edition of this publication was in Catherwood's personal library at the time of his death, *Catalogue of a Portion of the Library of the Late Frederic [sic] Catherwood, Esq.*, item #790 (34). The books in the collection of the unidentified surgeon were auctioned on the first day of the sale, so the books and philosophical instruments listed in the sales catalogue derive, in the main, from Catherwood's collection.

78. See note 19 above. The term 'station' was also used by John Britton in his description of Thomas Hornor's panorama of London at the Colosseum: 'The visitor will better understand the expanded scene before him and the metropolis it represents, by taking four distinct stations in the gallery; and then examine in succession the views towards the North, the East, the South, and the West.' J. B. [John Britton], *A Brief Account of the Colosseum, in the Regent's Park, London: Comprising a Description of the Building; The Panoramic View from the top of St. Paul's Cathedral, The Conservatory, &c. Printed for the Proprietors, and Sold at the Exhibition; and by all Booksellers* (London, 1829), 5.

79. 'Panorama of Jerusalem', *The Literary Gazette; and Journal of the Belles Lettres, Arts, Sciences, &c.*, no. 950, Saturday, 4 April 1835, 218; Hyde, *Panoramania!*, 74. A painting by Charles Halkeston, *Princes Street from the Mound, Edinburgh* (oil on board, 1843, City Art Centre, Edinburgh), which depicts the exterior of a panorama rotunda operated by Peter Marshall and his son, William, the proprietors of Messrs. Marshall, provides a sense of the carnival atmosphere that attended the exhibition of panoramas. An advertisement on the wall of the rotunda next to a menagerie, reads: 'Jerusalem and The[bes]' and 'Battle of Wat[erloo]' (not to be confused, in the first two cases, with panoramas after Catherwood). An elephant, outside the rotunda, carries an advertisement: 'Botanical Gardens, a grand fete tonight, Fireworks at 10'. The painting is reproduced in Hyde, *Panoramania!*, Figure 41, 27, and Comment, *The Panorama*, 150.

80. Scott Barnes Wilcox, *The Panorama and Related Exhibitions in London*, MLitt dissertation, University of Edinburgh, 1976, Appendix C: 'A Chronology of Panoramas Exhibited at the Leicester Square and Strand Panoramas', 254–265, 258, 260.

81. 'Panorama of Jerusalem', *The Literary Gazette*, Saturday, 4 April 1835, 218.

82. Narrative temporality remained important, of course, in panoramas that depicted historical events such as battles. In the case of *Lord Bridport's Engagement* (1796), the circular engraved key represented three moments in a naval battle that were described in the letterpress: 'Plan No. 1. Disposition of the English and French Fleets … on the 23d of June, 1795, at 54 minutes past 5 o'Clock, A. M.'; 'Plan No. 2. Disposition of the Fleets … at ¼ past 7 A. M. on the 23d of June, 1795'; and 'Plan No. 3. Disposition of the Fleets … at 35 minutes past 8 A. M. June the 23d, 1795, and which closed the Engagement'. In the case of *Lord Nelson's Attack of Copenhagen* (1802), a letter Nelson and Bronte wrote to Barker was incorporated in the letterpress on the plan of the circular observation platform which made reference to the timeframe of the panorama: '… making due Allowances of the Positions of many of the Ships, in the Space of One Hour and a Half, which Time I consider the Picture to embrace, I have no Scruple in saying, that I consider it the most correct Picture of any Event I have ever seen …'. Oleksijczuk, *The First Panoramas*, Figure 5.12 and Figure 5.13, 150, 152.

83. Robert Burford and (unattributed) Frederick Catherwood, *Description of a View of The Great Temple of Karnak and the Surrounding City of Thebes; also, The City of Jerusalem, with the Surrounding Country, now exhibiting at the Rotunda, on The Mound, Painted by the Proprietors, From Drawings taken in 1833–34, by Mr F. Catherwood, Architect* (Leith: Printed by William Heriot, Quality Street, 1837), 10.

84. Robert Burford and (unattributed) Catherwood, *Description of a View of The Great Temple of Karnak and the Surrounding City of Thebes; also, The City of Jerusalem, with the Surrounding Country, now exhibiting at the Rotunda, on The Mound, Painted by the Proprietors, From Drawings taken in 1833–34, by Mr F. Catherwood, Architect* (Leith: Printed by William Heriot, Quality Street, 1837), 10. Although authorship of panorama descriptions was generally unattributed, it seems likely that at a time when copyright laws were at an early stage of development, information given in the *Description*, if not authored by Catherwood, would have been provided by him.

85. *The Prelude*, Wordsworth, *Poetical Works*, 'Book Eighth, Retrospect. – Love of Nature leading to Love of Man', 547–555, 548, line 56. The phrase, 'the circumambient world', is a more historically precise concept than the notion of 'immersive view', a formulation adopted by some present-day writers to characterise the experience of viewing panoramas.

86. Robert Burford and (unattributed) Catherwood, *Description of a View of The Great Temple of Karnak and the Surrounding City of Thebes; also, The City of Jerusalem, with the Surrounding Country, now exhibiting at the Rotunda, on The Mound, Painted by the Proprietors, From Drawings taken in 1833–34, by Mr F. Catherwood, Architect* (Leith: Printed by William Heriot, Quality Street, 1837), 10; *The Literary Gazette*, Saturday, 4 April 1835, 218.

87. Bartlett, *Walks about the City and Environs of Jerusalem*, 161–162.

88. Stephan Oettermann's observation that the panorama was a more 'democratic' medium than the audience for easel painting accords with the observation printed in the notice for the Jerusalem panorama in *The Literary Gazette*.

89. For discussion of the manner in which the *Description* for the exhibition of the panorama in New York presented a 'cautionary tale ... [wherein] Catherwood's

audience was asked to extract biblical and moral truths from the evidence strewn about the landscape of the Holy Land', see Davis, *The Landscape of Belief*, 63–64.

90. Robert Burford and (unattributed) Catherwood (hereafter jointly designated as 'Burford', *Jerusalem*), *Description of a View of The Great Temple of Karnak and the Surrounding City of Thebes; also, The City of Jerusalem, with the Surrounding Country, now exhibiting at the Rotunda, on The Mound, Painted by the Proprietors, From Drawings taken in 1833–34, by Mr F. Catherwood, Architect* (Leith: Printed by William Heriot, Quality Street, 1837). The address at which the panorama was exhibited has been amended on the title page to read, in ink: 'Dilettanti Rooms[,] 51 Buçhanan St[.]'. The copy held at the National Library of Scotland, shelfmark APS.2.203.049, lacks the orientation view and key. Unless otherwise indicated, quotation from the *Description* for the panorama of Jerusalem is taken from the copy held at the National Library of Scotland.

91. Robert Burford and (unattributed) Catherwood, *Description of a View of the City of Jerusalem and the surrounding country, now exhibiting at the Panorama, Leicester Square. Painted by the Proprietor, Robert Burford, from drawings taken in 1834, by Mr. F. Catherwood, Architect* (London: Printed by T. Brettell, Rupert Street, Haymarket, 1835). The descriptive booklets of the Jerusalem panorama held at Cambridge University Library are at shelfmark, respectively, 8690.c.2 (item #13) and Pam.5.82.6. The copy shelfmark 8690.c.2 is dated '1835' on the title page; the copy shelfmark Pam.5.82.6 is dated '1836' on the title page. Both booklets contain a reproduction of the panorama engraving; the print, however, in Pam.5.82.6 is less well inked than the print in 8690.c.2. Figure 1.3 reproduces the 1835 copy of the engraving shelfmark 8690.c.2. A copy of the *Description* and engraving for the Karnak and Thebes panorama is also held shelfmark 8690.c.2 (item #25): Robert Burford and (unattributed) Catherwood, *Description of a View of The Great Temple of Karnak and the surrounding city of Thebes, now exhibiting at the Panorama, Leicester Square. Painted by the Proprietor, Robert Burford, from drawings taken by Mr. F. Catherwood , Architect, in 1833* (London: Printed by G. Nichols, Earl's Court, Cranbourn Street, Leicester Square, [n.d.]). Figure 1.4 reproduces the copy of the engraving shelfmark 8690.c.2.

92. Both booklets held at the University of Glasgow Library, shelfmark BG33-h.4, have the same text as the copy held at the National Library of Scotland, although the place of exhibition on the title page ('the Rotunda, on The Mound') has, in one case, been erased and amended to read, in ink: 'Monteith Rooms, Buchanan Street Glasgow'. The other copy held at the University of Glasgow Library bears a different title indicating that the panorama was exhibited as a peristrephic panorama: *Description of the highly interesting peristrephic panorama of the City of Jerusalem, with the surrounding country; and the City of New York, now exhibiting at Monteith Rooms, Buchanan Street, Glasgow. Painted by the proprietors, from Drawings taken in 1834, by Mr. F, CATHERWOOD, Architect, and SIGNOR BONONI. Day Exhibitions precisely at 12 & 2 o'clock, Evening do. at Half past 7 & 9* (Edinburgh: Printed by M. W. Reid, Gabriel's Road, 1837). For consideration of the peristrephic panorama, see Huhtamo, *Illusions in Motion*, 64–91, particularly the account given by Hermann Pückler-Muskau of attending the presentation of a peristrephic panorama in Dublin in August 1828, 69–71. Given that times for presenting the peristrephic panorama are designated, the peristrephic panorama would have offered 'plenty for both the eye and the ear'. Erkki Huhtamo, *The Roll Medium: The Origins and Development of the Moving Panorama until the 1860*, doctoral dissertation, Faculty of Humanities, University of Turku, 2008, 83. Diversity in matters of presentation also attended a copy of Catherwood's panorama which was exhibited as a moving panorama in Hull, see Figure 6.3, James B. Laidlaw, orientation view and key, 'Laidlaw's Panorama of Jerusalem', *Description of a View of the City of Jerusalem and the Surrounding Country, Now Exhibiting at the Panorama in this Town* (Hull: John Hutchinson, 1837) reproduced in Huhtamo, *Illusions in Motion*, 171, and discussion, 170–171.

93. 'VI. View', 'Burford', *Jerusalem*, 11.

94. Much of the description which introduces this view is omitted from the *Description* as sold at the Panorama, Leicester Square: 'Immediately in front of the spectator, towards the south, stands boldly prominent, with most imposing effect, the beautiful mosque of Omar, or El Sahhara, occupying the site of the Temple of Solomon, resembling from its curious style, and variety of gay colours, an immense piece of mosaic work, backed by the rugged summits of stony and unfruitful hills, a portion of the [D]ead [S]ea appearing in the distance, enclosed by lofty and majestic mountains; towards the west, immediately beneath, commences the Via Dolorosa, which may be traced in its ascent through the thickest part of the city.'

95. 'Burford', *Jerusalem*, 10.

96. 'Burford', *Jerusalem*, 10. The account of the resurrection in Luke 24: 50, 51 reads: 'And he led them as far as to Bethany, and he lifted up his hands, and blessed them./And it came to pass while he blessed them, he was parted from them, and carried up into heaven.'

97. 'Burford', *Jerusalem*, 10.

98. 'Burford', *Jerusalem*, 10.

99. 'Burford', *Jerusalem*, 10.

100. 'Burford', *Jerusalem*, 10.

101. Frederick Catherwood, *Plan of Jerusalem by F. Catherwood. Architect. July 1835.* Published August 1st. 1835, by F. Catherwood, 21, Charles Square, Hoxton. Engraved by S. Bellin. The *Plan* identifies 'Spot from whence the panorama was taken' (designated '3' on the *Plan*); the *Plan* is considered further in Chapter Two. The handwritten annotation to the left of the *Plan* reads: '**A** *Real* site of the "Pool of Gihon"[.] The author of the map seems to have placed the "*Pool of Gihon*" in the place best suited to the line of his Map – which has misplaced the Turkish burial ground[.]' Three locations ('28', '29', '30') have been added to the key. Stephens came across the map when he was in Jerusalem in 1836: 'I was fortunate to find a lithographic map made by Mr. Catherwood ... which I found a better guide to all the interesting localities than any other I could procure in Jerusalem.' John Lloyd Stephens, edited with an introduction by Victor Wolfgang von Hagen, *Incidents of Travel in Egypt, Arabia Petræa, and the Holy Land* (Mineola, NY: Dover Publications, Inc., 1996 [1837]), note, 360; Von Hagen, *F. Catherwood: Architect-Explorer*, note, 36. The *Plan* was reproduced in the eighth edition of John Lloyd Stephens' *Incidents of Travel in Egypt, Arabia Petræa, and the Holy Land* and was published, in revised form in an engraving by Henry Adlard, in Albert Barnes, *Notes, Explanatory and Practical on the Gospels: With An Index, a Chronological Table, Table of Weights etc.* (London and Edinburgh: Thomas Nelson, 1847).

102. 'Burford', *Jerusalem*, 10–11.

103. 'Burford', *Jerusalem*, 11.

104. 'Burford', *Jerusalem*, 11.

105. Davis, *The Landscape of Belief*, 59.

106. Because the *Description* of the panorama of Jerusalem was printed in the same booklet as the *Description* of the panorama of Karnak and Thebes, View I of the Jerusalem panorama is numbered as View V, and the three subsequent views (Views II–IV) are numbered as Views VI–VIII.

107. Dressed as an Egyptian officer and carrying a firman that designated Catherwood an engineer in the service of the pasha, Mehemet Ali, Catherwood sketched the Mosque of El-'Aqsá and its precincts with his servant, Süleyman, in November 1833: 'I entered the area [the enclosure of Haram er Shereef] one morning, with an indifferent air, and proceeded to survey, but not too curiously, the many objects of interest it presents. … The success of my first attempt, induced me to make a second visit the following day. I determined to take in my camera lucida, and sit down and make a drawing; a proceeding certain to attract the attention of the most indifferent, and expose me to the dangerous consequences. The cool assurances of my servant, at once befriended and led me on. We entered, and arranging the camera, I quickly sat down to my work, not without some nervousness, as I perceived the Mussulmen, from time to time, mark me with doubtful looks; however, most of them passed on, deceived by my dress and the quiet indifference with which I regarded them. …' Bartlett, *Walks about the City and Environs of Jerusalem*, 162–163.

108. 'Burford', *Jerusalem*, 12.

109. 'Burford', *Jerusalem*, 12.

110. 'Burford', *Jerusalem*, 12.

111. 'Burford', *Jerusalem*, 15.

112. 'Burford', *Jerusalem*, 11.

113. 'Burford', *Jerusalem*, 14.

114. 'Burford', *Jerusalem*, 16.

115. 'Burford', *Jerusalem*, 17.

116. 'Burford', *Jerusalem*, 18. The second significant departure in the *Description* printed for the Panorama, Leicester Square, occurs at this point in the booklet. In place of the phrase quoted in the body text above, the *Description* for the Panorama, Leicester Square, reads: 'The Aga is here represented passing judgment on some Arab robbers, on one for whom the punishment of the bastinado is about to be inflicted', a punishment in which the soles of the feet were beaten with a stick.

117. As John Davis has observed, the inclusion of Catherwood in the panorama likely 'reinforced the message of authenticity, reminding audiences of the proprietor's claims of firsthand experience of the site'. Davis, *The Landscape of Belief*, 63, an aspiration which Comment more generally confirms with regard to panoramas, Comment, *The Panorama*, 129. For encomia, testimonials, and press notices reprinted in a publicity broadside for the exhibition of the panorama in New York City, see Davis, *Landscape of Belief*, 63–65. Charlotte Klonk observes that the strategy of depicting the artist in the represented space not only guarantees the 'authentic' nature of the represented view, but, in providing viewers 'with the impression that they were witnessing a real scene rather than just a painted reproduction of one', inscribed a strategy which implied that each part 'is given equal significance in relation to the observing subject'. Klonk, *Science and the Perception of Nature*, 150.

118. For consideration of the staffage in the foreground of the panorama and its presentation of a 'sampling of contemporary Middle Eastern figures', see Davis, *The Landscape of Belief*, 63.

119. 'Burford', *Jerusalem*, 19–20.

120. The phrase is taken from 'J. B.' [John Britton], *A Brief Account of the Colosseum, in the Regent's Park, London*, 5. Although John Britton is characterising the panorama of London with which Thomas Hornor opened the Colosseum in early 1829, the encyclopaedic ambition of Hornor's panorama is, arguably, replicated in Catherwood's panorama of Jerusalem and the accompanying *Description*.

121. 'Burford', *Jerusalem*, 20. The conclusion in the *Description* departs significantly from the 'cautionary tale' that accompanied the exhibition of the panorama in New York, see Davis, *The Landscape of Belief*, 63–64.

122. 'Panorama of Jerusalem', *The Literary Gazette*, Saturday, 4 April 1835, 218.

123. Robert Burford and, unattributed, Frederick Catherwood (hereafter jointly designated as 'Burford', *Karnak and Thebes*), *Description of a View of The Great Temple of Karnak and the Surrounding City of Thebes; also, The City of Jerusalem, with the Surrounding Country, now exhibiting at the Rotunda, on The Mound, Painted by the Proprietors, From Drawings taken in 1833–34, by Mr F. Catherwood, Architect* (Leith: Printed by William Heriot, Quality Street, 1837), 2, held at the National Library of Scotland. The conqueror referred to in this extract was, of course, Napoleon Bonaparte, whose forces occupied Egypt between 1798 and 1801, ending Ottoman rule since 1517. An undated descriptive booklet of the Karnak and Thebes panorama, printed by G. Nichols, Earl's Court, Cranbourn Street, was sold at the Panorama, Leicester Square. Comparison of the *Description* printed in Leith with the booklet printed by Nichols, held at Cambridge University Library (shelfmark 8690.c.2, item #25), has not been undertaken.

124. 'Burford', *Karnak and Thebes*, 2. The quotations come from, in the first case, C. S. Sonnini de Manoncourt, *Travels in Upper and Lower Egypt: Undertaken by Order of the Old Government of France; by C. S. Sonnini, Engineer in the French Navy, and Member of Several Scientific and Literary Societies. Illustrated with Forty Engravings; Consisting of Portraits, Views, Plans, a Geographical Chart, Antiquities, Plants, Animals, &c. Drawn on the Spot, under the Author's Inspection. Translated from the French by Henry Hunter, D.D.*, 3 vols. (London: Printed for John Stockdale, 1799), III, 234–235. A copy of this work was in Catherwood's private library at the time of his death. *Catalogue of a Portion of the Library of the Late Frederic [sic] Catherwood, Esq.*, item #114 (7). The quotation has been slightly amended in the panorama *Description*, appearing in Sonnini as: 'It was not a simple admiration merely, but an extasy [*sic*] which suspended the use of all my faculties. I remained for some time immovable with rapture, and I felt inclined more than once to prostrate myself in token of veneration before monuments, the rearing of which appeared to transcend the strength and genius of man.' The second quotation comes from Vivant Denon, *Travels in Upper and Lower Egypt, in Company with Several Divisions of the French Army, During the Campaigns of General Bonaparte in that Country; and Published under his Immediate Patronage, by Vivant Denon. Embellished with Numerous Engravings. Translated by Arthur Aikin*, 3 vols. (London: Printed for T.N. Longman and O. Rees, and Richard Phillips, by T. Gillet, 1803), II, 84. Two copies of this work were in Catherwood's private library at the time of his death, *Catalogue of a Portion of the Library of the Late Frederic [sic] Catherwood, Esq.*, item #650 (28) and item #1293 (53). The quotation has been slightly amended in the panorama

Description, appearing in Denon as: '... that the whole army, suddenly and with one accord, stood in amazement at the sight of its scattered ruins, and clapped their hands in delight, as if the end and object of their glorious toils, and the complete conquest of Egypt, were accomplished and secured by taking possession of the splendid remains of this ancient metropolis'.

125. 'Burford', *Karnak and Thebes*, 2.

126. James Ussher, *Annals of the Ancient and New Testaments*, cited in Sam Smiles, *The Image of Antiquity: Ancient Britain and the Romantic Imagination* (New Haven and London: Yale University Press, for The Paul Mellon Centre for Studies in British Art, 1994), 3. Ussher's account, first published in 1650, was included in the Authorised Version of the Bible from 1701.

127. The notion of prehistory and the term, 'prehistoric', was coined in 1851 by Daniel Wilson in *The Archaeology and Prehistoric Annals of Scotland*. Glyn Daniel, *The Idea of Prehistory* (Harmondsworth: Penguin Books, 1971), 9, cited in Smiles, *The Image of Antiquity*, 3.

128. James Bruce, *Travels to Discover the Source of the Nile, In the Years 1768, 1769, 1770, 1771, 1772, and 1773. In five volumes. By James Bruce, of Kinnaird, Esq. F.R.S.* (Edinburgh: Printed by J. Ruthven, for G. G. J. and J. Robinson, London, 1790) and Giovanni Belzoni, *Narrative of the Operations of Recent Discoveries within the Pyramids, Temples, Tombs and Excavations in Egypt and Nubia; and of a Journey to the Coast of the Red Sea, in Search of the Ancient Berenice; and Another to the Oasis of Jupiter Ammon* (London: John Murray, 1820). Born in Padua, Belzoni worked in a travelling circus in Britain and as a strongman at fairs and on the streets of London before travelling to Egypt where, from 1815, he worked for Henry Salt, the British consul-general in Cairo. An alabaster sarcophagus of Sety I, discovered by Belzoni in October 1817, was brought to England and deposited in the British Museum in September 1821. Offered to the Trustees of the Museum for £2,000 in 1824, the purchase was declined, whereupon John Soane bought the sarcophagus from Henry Salt and installed it in the collection of his private home in Lincoln's Inn Fields, London, on 12 May 1824, where it has remained to this day. *A New Description of Sir John Soane's Museum*, eleventh revised edition (London: The Trustees, Sir John Soane's Museum, 2007), 47–48, 100–101; for further discussion of negotiations between Henry Salt and the British Museum over the purchase of the sarcophagus, see Miller, *That Noble Cabinet*, 198–202. John Gardner Wilkinson, regarded as the 'father' of Egyptology, first travelled to Egypt in 1821 where he remained for twelve years before publishing *The Topography of Thebes and General View of Egypt* in 1835, the year in which the panorama of Karnak and Thebes was exhibited in London. Wilkinson's widely-read *Manners and Customs of the Ancient Egyptians*, 6 vols., was published in 1837.

129. *Description of the Egyptian Tomb, discovered by G. Belzoni* (London: John Murray, 1822), 5. The exhibition also included cases of Egyptian curiosities, and models of the 'different halls and passages of the tomb on a scale of one-sixth the size of the original sepulchre', *Description of the Egyptian Tomb*, 13. See also Altick, *The Shows of London*, 244–246, and Costeloe, *William Bullock*, 110–114. Belzoni's exhibition entailed redesigning the interior of the Egyptian Hall in the Egyptian Revival style. Richard G. Carrott, *The Egyptian Revival: Its Sources, Monuments, and Meaning 1808–1858* (Berkeley, Los Angeles, London: University of California Press, 1978), 34–35 and note 69, 45. For further discussion of Belzoni's exhibition at the Egyptian Hall, see Robert D. Aguirre, *Informal Empire: Mexico and Central America in Victorian Culture* (Minneapolis: University of Minnesota Press, 2005), 19–21, where Aguirre argues that cultural display in museums and exhibitions undermined the cultural context in which objects were produced and functioned. For succinct summary of Aguirre's argument regarding the panorama which proposed that the medium visualised 'the logics of imperial geography', see Aguirre, *Informal Empire*, 40–43, 42.

130. Bruce, *Travels to Discover the Source of the Nile*, I, 232–233; the quotation is from Ecclesiastes, 1: 10.

131. For consideration of the Picturesque tour and the sense of melancholy provoked by ruins, particularly those associated with the valley of the River Wye, see Malcolm Andrews, *The Search for the Picturesque: Landscape Aesthetics and Tourism in Britain, 1760–1800* (Aldershot: Scolar Press, 1989), 84–107. See also Wordsworth, *Poetical Works*, 'Poems of the Imagination', XXVI, '*Lines composed a few miles above Tintern Abbey, on revisiting the banks of the Wye during a tour. July 13, 1798.*', 163–165. Given the desert location depicted in the panorama, Shelley's *Ozymandias* (1818, reprinted, 1819) provides comparison with melancholic reflection in the Romantic period: 'I met a traveller from an antique land/Who said: Two vast and trunkless legs of stone/Stand in the desert ... /And on the pedestal these words appear:/'My name is Ozymandias, king of kings: Look on my works, ye Mighty and despair!'/Nothing beside remains. Round the decay/Of that colossal wreck, boundless and bare/The lone and level sands stretch far away.' Percy Bysshe Shelley, 'Ozymandias', Shelley, *Poetical Works*, edited by Thomas Hutchinson, a new edition, corrected by G. M. Matthews (London, New York, Toronto: Oxford University Press, 1970), 550, lines 1–3, 9–15.

132. Respectively, 'Burford', *Karnak and Thebes*, 6, and John Lloyd Stephens, *Incidents of Travel in Central America, Chiapas, and Yucatan*, 2 vols. (New York: Harper & Brothers, Publishers; London: John Murray, 1841), II, 413.

133. For a photograph of the south facade of the Eighth Propylon at Karnak which establishes the topographical orientation of the panorama, see Nigel Strudwick and Helen Strudwick, *Thebes in Egypt: A Guide to the Tombs and Temples of Ancient Luxor* (Ithaca: Cornell University Press, 1999), 54.

134. For a plan of the sites of Karnak, Luxor, and Thebes, see Strudwick and Strudwick, *Thebes in Egypt*, 11.

135. 'Burford', *Karnak and Thebes*, 9.

136. 'Burford', *Karnak and Thebes*, 4.

137. 'Burford', *Karnak and Thebes*, 6: '... the portion that has ... been selected as the principal foreground of this View [from the third station] is the Temple of Karnak, one of the most ancient, extensive, and best preserved, which may be taken as fair illustration of all these monuments of grandeur; for, although, there are no two exactly alike, yet in simplicity of outline, regular disposition of the several parts, and a certain tone of uniformity in the material and workmanship, no striking difference can be discerned. This great temple of the Egyptian Jove is of such vast extent, and composed of such prodigious masses, that it almost suggests the idea of a sculptured mountain; yet such is the beauty and harmony with which its several parts are designed, and the masterly and spirited style in which they are executed, that it stands unique in the whole world. No doubt exists that it is the temple described by Diodorus, as the most wonderful and ancient of the temples of Thebes; and that the ornaments, riches, and workmanship with which it was embellished, correspond with its extent. The area occupied by various buildings connected with it, is at least a mile and a half

in circumference: it is approached in several directions by propylæ, colossal gateways, or moles, in themselves larger than many of the temples; some ornamented with statues of breccia, basalt, or granite, in sitting or erect postures, from twenty to thirty feet in height; others having dromos, with long avenues of sphinxes, and crio-sphinxes, one of which reaches as far as Luxor; the whole being in the best style of Egyptian architecture. This vast group of ruins is covered both within and without by millions of beautifully executed figures, hieroglyphics, and mysterious sculptures – every wall, portico, column, and architrave, with symbolic representations of the divinity, laws, and mysteries of religion; battles on horse and foot, sieges, triumphs, sacrifices, glory in war, and luxury in peace; clearly evincing the military prowess, of the early Egyptians; and eminently calculated to increase the respect, homage, and adoration of those who were admitted into this holy sanctuary.'

138. 'Burford', *Karnak and Thebes*, 9.

139. Review of the panorama of Boothia depicting Captain John Ross's expedition to the Canadian Arctic, published in *The Times*, 14 January 1834 (the day after the private view), quoted in Russell A. Potter, *Arctic Spectacles: The Frozen North in Visual Culture, 1818–1875* (Seattle and London: University of Washington Press, 2007), 69.

140. Potter, *Arctic Spectacles*, 66–67; Garrison, 'Virtual reality and subjective responses', 19. For illustration, see the anamorphotic orientation plan and key published in *Description of a View of the Continent of Boothia, Discovered by Captain Ross, in his Late Expedition to the Polar Region, now Exhibiting at the Panorama, Leicester Square*, reproduced in Potter, *Arctic Spectacles*, Figure 3, 66.

141. Henry Courtney Selous, *Journal kept by a painter while working for R. Burford and the Leicester Square Panorama, 1833 Oct. 29 – 1834 May 10*, manuscript, MSL/1979/5117, pressmark 86.SS.67, National Art Library, Victoria and Albert Museum. The attribution of authorship was proposed by Ralph Hyde and confirmed by Carol Cronquist and David A. Rausch, 'Attribution of a Panorama Painter's Diary', *Notes and Queries*, 41, 3 (September 1994): 348. Selous' journal comprises an untitled bound volume, hand-paginated in pencil in the top right corner, with successive leaves numbered #3–#370, the first two leaves being unnumbered. The last entry in the journal (Saturday, 10 May 1834) is on leaf #255; leaves ##256–370 contain no entries. An additional, unnumbered leaf, is bound between leaves #50 and #51.

142. Unidentified cutting, Drury Lane Theatre press cuttings, January 1785–December 1788, British Library, quoted in Sybil Rosenfeld, *Georgian Scene Painters and Scene Painting* (Cambridge: Cambridge University Press, 1981), 62.

143. Rosenfeld, *Georgian Scene Painters*, 167.

144. For discussion of illumination in the panorama rotunda, see Oettermann, *The Panorama*, 39, 41, 47, 49, 51, 55, 57, *passim*. See also Scott Barnes Wilcox, *The Panorama and Related Exhibitions in London*, MLitt dissertation, University of Edinburgh, 1976, 31, 33, 60, 113, *passim*.

145. Selous, *Journal*, entry, Friday, 22 November 1833, 40. For a pen and wash drawing of the studio used for painting panoramas in the early years, see John Buckler, *Building for Painting the Panoramas near West Square, Southwark*, 1827, reproduced in Hyde (ed.), *Panoramania!*, Figure 31, 65; Oettermann, *The Panorama*, Figure 2.4, 104; Comment, *The Panorama*, 18; Oleksijczuk, *The First Panoramas*, Figure 2.3, 51. The studio was located in West Square, St. George's Fields, Southwark. By the time Selous painted the panoramas from sketches by Catherwood, the studio referred to as the 'painting room' in Selous' *Journal* was located in Rochester Mews, Camden Town. For ground-plans of the panorama premises in Leicester Square and the painting room in Camden Town, see Oleksijczuk, *The First Panoramas*, Figure 3.2, 73.

146. Selous, *Journal*, entry, Monday, 23 December 1833, 90–91; 'the' should read 'that'.

147. See, for example, Selous, *Journal*, entries for Saturday, 15 March 1834, Saturday, 22 March 1834, and Saturday, 23 March 1834, 204, 214, and 223. For comparison with salaries for scene painters working in patent theatres in the late 1810s and 1820s, see Rosenfeld, *Georgian Scene Painters*, 83–84. John Masey Wright, who had worked as a scene painter at Astley's Theatre, was employed earlier by Barker and Burford in the Leicester Square and Strand panoramas, where he received £8 per week. Oettermann, *The Panorama*, 112.

148. Horace Foote, pseud. [John Timbs], *A Companion to the Theatres; and manual of the British Drama*, second edition (London: W. Marsh and A. Miller, 1829), quoted in Rosenfeld, *Georgian Scene Painters*, 84.

149. Selous was admitted to the Royal Academy schools in 1819, note 18 above.

150. Selous, *Journal*, entry for Saturday, 2 November 1833, 12–13.

151. Selous, *Journal*, entry for Thursday, 7 November 1833, 16.

152. Selous, *Journal*, entry for Wednesday, 13 November 1833, 30.

153. Selous, *Journal*, entry for Friday, 29 November 1833, unnumbered leaf bound between 50 and 51.

154. Selous, *Journal*, entry for Saturday, 2 November 1833, 13. The painting of a theatrical scene in the late eighteenth century forms the subject of Michael Angelo Rooker's *A Scene-Painter at Work in his Studio* (watercolour, British Museum), which depicts a scene painter, most likely Rooker himself, working in the scene-painting room of the Theatre Royal, Haymarket, where Rooker was employed from 1779 to 1800. For illustration, see Patrick Conner, *Michael Angelo Rooker (1746–1801)* (London: B. T. Batsford in association with the Victoria & Albert Museum, 1984), Plate V.

155. Selous, *Journal*, entry for Wednesday, 19 March 1834, 210. Selous provides no details of this process, although some of the problems that attended the 'squaring' of drawings when translating them to the curved form of a painted panorama are discussed in Oettermann, *The Panorama*, 54–55, 100: 'noticeable distortions resulted: all the horizontal lines appeared to curve either upward or downward, depending on whether they lay above or below the eye level of the viewer. To eliminate this effect Barker experimented until he found a way to compensate and make the curved sketches appear undistorted to a viewer in the center of the circle.' The entry for 'panorama' in the 1824 edition of *Encyclopædia Britannica* describes this process in the following way: 'In the perspective of the panorama, where the picture consists of the intersection of the cones of rays by a cylinder, these intersections are, in many of the cases, doubly curved curves. When the picture of a straight line, which is neither parallel to the horizon nor to the axis of the cylinder, is drawn on the cylinder of the panorama, the picture of the line is part of an ellipse, because the oblique section of a right cylinder, by a plane passing through the axis, is an ellipse; when the cylinder is developed and unrolled on a plane surface, this ellipse becomes the curve called the sinical curve.' 'Panorama', *Supplement to the Fourth, Fifth, and Sixth Editions of the*

Encyclopædia Britannica (Edinburgh: Archibald Constable and Company; London: Hurst, Robinson, and Company, 1824), VI, 108–109, 108.

156. Selous, entries for, respectively, Saturday, 22 March 1834 and Saturday, 29 March 1834, 213 and 222.

157. Selous, *Journal*, entry for Monday 31 March 1834, 225.

158. Selous, *Journal*, entries for, respectively, Wednesday, 2 April 1834 and Thursday, 3 April 1834, 227, 228.

159. Selous, *Journal*, entries for, respectively, Friday, 4 April 1834 and Saturday, 5 April 1834, 229, 230.

160. Selous, *Journal*, entries for, respectively, Tuesday, 8 April 1834 and Tuesday, 22 April 1834, 233, 248.

161. I thank Alan Barnes for suggesting the advantages that a coating of Venice turpentine may have conferred. An article in *Mechanics' Magazine* proposes that turpentine could also be used for protecting panoramas. F. Maceroni, 'Hints on Hardening and Protecting Stone, Wood, Metal, &. and On the Preservation of Panoramas', *Mechanics' Magazine, Register, Journal and Gazette*, Vol. 24, no. 650, Saturday, 23 January 1836, 309–311.

162. Selous, *Journal*, entries for Wednesday, 2 April, 1834, Wednesday, 23 April 1834, Thursday, 24 April 1834, 227, 248, 249, the last entry including an addition the following day: 'Friday finished the sky'.

163. Selous, *Journal*, entry for Monday, 28 April 1834, 252.

164. Selous, *Journal*, entry for Saturday, 10 May 1834, 255.

165. Scott Barnes Wilcox, *The Panorama and Related Exhibitions in London*, MLitt. Dissertation, University of Edinburgh, 1976, 30. Although Oettermann provides no source of information, he states that the larger of the two panoramas at the Panorama, Leicester Square, was '84 feet 6 inches in diameter' and the canvas '35 feet 9 inches high'. Oettermann, *The Panorama*, Figure 1.11, 58. Robert Mitchell, the architect of the panorama rotunda, states: 'The Rotunda in Leicester Square … forms a circle, including the thickness of the walls, of 90 feet ['diameter', inserted in ink in the copy held at the National Library of Scotland]: the wall from the ground to the roof, with in the building, is 57 feet.' Robert Mitchell, *Plans, and Views in Perspective, with Descriptions, of Buildings erected in England and Scotland: and also An Essay to elucidate the Grecian, Roman and Gothic Architecture, accompanied with Designs* (London: Printed at the Oriental Press by Wilson & Co., 1801), 8, and the letterpress to the key printed for *View of the Grand Fleet Moored at Spithead* (1793) states: 'Diameter of the building ninety feet – Picture painted in oils in four months', Oleksijczuk, *The First Panoramas*, Figure 3.1, 68; see also Oleksijczuk, *The First Panoramas*, 133. Inspection of the present-day site (the location of the church of Notre Dame de France, 5 Leicester Place, rebuilt according to the ground-plan of the Leicester Square rotunda after enemy action in November 1940 destroyed the original building) confirms that the maximum internal diameter of the structure would have been 90 feet.

166. Burford and (unattributed) Frederick Catherwood (hereafter jointly designated as 'Burford', *Baalbec*), *Description of a View of the Ruins of the Temples of Baalbec, Now Exhibiting at the Panorama, Leicester Square. Painted by the Proprietor, Robert Burford, assisted by H. C. Selous, from Drawings taken on the Spot by F. Catherwood, Esq.* (London: Printed by Geo. Nichols, Earl's Court, Leicester Square, 1844), held at the British Library, shelfmark, RB.23.b.5982.

167. 'Burford', *Baalbec*, 3. For monochrome illustration of a 7-sheet watercolour of the panorama of Baalbec by Catherwood, see Hyde, *Panoramania!*, Figure 50, 74–75.

168. For discussion of the work of Robert Wood at Baalbek (Lebanon) and Palmyra (Syria) during his tour of the Levant with Borra, John Bouverie, and James Dawkins, see Redford, *Dilettanti*, 49–51. See also Antoine Desgodetz, *Les Edifices antiques de Rome. Dessinés et mesurés très exactement. Par Antoine Desgodetz Architecte* (Paris: Chez Jean Baptiste Coignard, 1682). Robert Wood was elected to the Society of Dilettanti in 1763, Redford, *Dilettanti*, 204. Although a copy of Wood's *The Ruins of Balbec* was not included in Catherwood's private library, the work of a fellow member of the Society of Dilettanti, Richard Chandler's *Travels in Asia Minor* (2 vols., 1775), was held in Catherwood's library, *Catalogue of a Portion of the Library of the Late Frederic [sic] Catherwood, Esq.*, item #452 (21).

169. 'Burford', *Baalbec*, 12.

170. Robert Wood, *The Ruins of Balbec, otherwise Heliopolis in Cœlosyria* (London, 1757), 21.

171. The watercolour, *Balbec, View of the ruins*, was originally held in Drawer 28, no. 65 in Soane's collection, and was re-catalogued by Susan Palmer as the second illustration in Drawer No 20, Set 1, Sir John Soane's Museum. This illustration was used in Lecture I (Royal Academy, 20 February 1817 and 18 February 1819) and Lecture X (Royal Academy, 9 March 1815), David Watkin, *Sir John Soane: Enlightenment Thought and the Royal Academy Lectures*, 673, 688. A handwritten note on the back of the watercolour records that the illustration was also used in '1st Lect 1820' at the Royal Institution.

172. John Soane, MS, 'Lectures on Architecture, Royal Institution 1820', 'Royal Institution. Lecture the 3d, Read, Saturday the 10th June 1820 – One hour and six Minutes', 35–36, Soane Case 158, Sir John Soane's Museum. The quote is rendered, in Lecture III, Royal Academy (delivered 6 March 1817 and 4 March 1819), as: 'Such an assemblage of grand and imposing forms cannot fail of creating sensations in the mind, easier felt than described.' Watkin (ed.), *Sir John Soane: The Royal Academy Lectures*, 77.

173. Apart from Soane and Wood, other sources cited in the *Description* include the Bible (Second Book of Chronicles and Second Book of Kings), Eusebius, an 'anonymous Greek writer of the age of Constantine', the seventh-century chronicler, John of Antioch, unidentified '[o]riental writers', the sixteenth-century French explorer, André Thevet, and the Swiss, Johann Ludwig (aka John Lewis) Burckhardt, whose *Travels in Syria and the Holy Land* was posthumously published in 1822.

174. John Soane, Soane Case 157, MS, 'Lecture the First Royal Institution 7th June 1817' (revised edition), 18; quotation also in earlier draft, 20.

175. 'Burford', *Baalbec*, 3–4.

176. 'The space covered by the ruins of the temples, is at the eastern side of the city ... These stones, of which there are many, both in the platform and in the wall above, are incredibly large; towards the north are ten, each from 30 to 32 feet in length, by 13 in thickness; on the west, there are in the lowest range eight, the smallest 31, the largest 38 feet in length, and of corresponding thickness …', 'Burford', *Baalbec*, 4.

177. 'Burford', *Baalbec*, 12.

178. The manner in which some early panoramas promoted disorientation for some visitors is discussed by Oleksijczuk, *The First Panoramas*, 11, 13–14; Oleksijczuk proposes that in some cases the popularity of early panoramas may have grown in proportion to their ability to stimulate vicarious pleasure and induce visceral response in the spectator, see Oleksijczuk, *The First Panoramas*, 78, 84–87.

179. See note 92 above.

180. See notes 94 and 116 above.

181. Henry Fuseli, *The Life and Writings of Henry Fuseli, Esq. M.A. R.A. Keeper, and Professor of Painting to the Royal Academy in London; Member of the First Class of the Academy of St. Luke at Rome. The Former written, and the latter edited by John Knowles, F.R.S. Corresponding Member of the Philosophical Society at Rotterdam, His Executor*, 3 vols. (London: Henry Colburn and Richard Bentley, 1831), II, 'Fourth Lecture. Invention. Part II.', 217. A manuscript copy of Fuseli's *Lectures on Painting* (first published in 1810) was included in Catherwood's private library, *Catalogue of a Portion of the Library of the Late Frederic* [*sic*] *Catherwood, Esq.*, item #1686 (68). Catherwood subsequently purchased a copy of Barry, Opie, and Fuseli, *Lectures on Painting by the Royal Academicians Barry, Opie and Fuseli* (1848), *Catalogue of a Portion of the Library of the Late Frederic* [*sic*] *Catherwood, Esq.*, item #882 (37). Although Sir Joshua Reynolds, President of the Royal Academy from its foundation in 1768 until 1792, and mentor to Fuseli, was better disposed towards the topographical concerns of panoramas (Wilcox, 'Unlimiting the Bounds of Painting', in Hyde, *Panoramania!*, 24–25), Reynolds was also of the opinion that: 'instead of endeavouring to amuse mankind with the minute neatness of his imitations, he [the genuine Painter] must endeavour to improve them by the grandeur of his ideas; instead of seeking praise, by deceiving the superficial sense of the spectator, he must strive for fame, by captivating the imagination.' 'A Discourse, delivered to the Students of the Royal Academy, on the Distribution of the Prizes, December 11, 1769, by the President', in Joshua Reynolds, *Seven Discourses delivered in the Royal Academy by the President* (London: T. Cadell, 1778), 65–98, 69.

Notes to Chapter Two

1. Capt. Basil Hall, *Forty Etchings, from Sketches made with the Camera Lucida, in North America, in 1827 and 1828* (Edinburgh: Cadell & Co; London: Simpkin & Marshall and Moon, Boys & Graves, 1829), ii.

2. 'Specification of the Patent granted to William Hyde Wollaston, 4 December 1806', no. 2993, *The Repertory of Arts, Manufactures, and Agriculture*, 10 [Second Series], No. 57, February 1807 (London: J. Wyatt, Repertory Office, 1807), 161–164.

3. For discussion of the transformation in English landscape painting during the eighteenth and early nineteenth centuries, see Ann Bermingham, *Learning to Draw: Studies in the Cultural History of a Polite and Useful Art* (New Haven and London: The Paul Mellon Centre for Studies in British Art, Yale University Press, 2000), 77–126.

4. Other devices employed at the turn of the century included the Royal Delineator, patented by the instrument-maker, William Storer (patent granted 4 March 1778), and the Graphic Telescope patented by Cornelius Varley (patent granted 5 April 1811). Patents for these devices may be found in, respectively, *The Repertory of Arts and Manufactures*, 4 [First Series], 1796, 239–242, and, in facsimile, in Lowell Libson (ed.) *Cornelius Varley: The Art of Observation*, exhibition catalogue (London: Lowell Libson, 2005), Appendix III, 186–191. For illustration of the Royal Delineator, see Martin Kemp, *The Science of Art: Optical Themes in Western Art from Brunelleschi to Seurat* (New Haven and London: Yale University Press, 1990), Figure 376, 190; for illustration of the Graphic Telescope, see Kemp, *The Science of Art*, Figure 403, 202; *Cornelius Varley: The Art of Observation*, plate facing 7. For discussion of the Patent Graphic Telescope and works in which Varley is known to have used the device, see Charlotte Klonk, *Science and the Perception of Nature: British Landscape Art in the Late Eighteenth and Early Nineteenth Centuries* (New Haven and London: The Paul Mellon Centre for Studies in British Art, Yale University Press, 1996), 130–135; for discussion of the Royal Delineator, see Martin Kemp, *Seen | Unseen: Art, Science, and Intuition from Leonardo to the Hubble Telescope* (Oxford: Oxford University Press, 2006), 249–250. I thank Alan Barnes for bringing this latter work to my attention.

5. William Hyde Wollaston, 'Description of the Camera Lucida', *A Journal of Natural Philosophy, Chemistry, and the Arts*, 12 (June 1807): 1–5, 4.

6. Hall, *Forty Etchings, from Sketches made with the Camera Lucida*, i.

7. Hall, *Forty Etchings, from Sketches made with the Camera Lucida*, ii. The figure reproduced as 2.1 was bound as a frontispiece to G[eorge] Dollond, *Description of the Camera Lucida, An Instrument for Drawing in True Perspective, and the Copying, Reducing, or Enlarging Other Drawings. To which is added, by permission, a Letter on the Use of the Camera, by Capt. Basil Hall, R.N., F.R.S.* (London: G. Dollond, n.d. [1830]). The plate, engraved by George Gladwin after a drawing by Cornelius Varley, faces the title page.

8. Wollaston, 'Description of the Camera Lucida', 5. John H. Hammond and Jill Austin question the accuracy of this assertion when they observe that '[t]he 70° angle of view ... is in fact somewhat misleading [since] it may be achieved by a slight rotation of the prism but at the same time the balance of lighting is usually upset'. John H. Hammond and Jill Austin, *The Camera Lucida in Art and Science* (Bristol: IOP, 1987), 79. Notwithstanding Hammond and Austin's observation, the field of view of the camera lucida is considerably wider than that of the camera obscura.

9. From, respectively, an area west of the Gate of Damascus (43) to the Pool of Bethesda (69), and from the Burial Place of the Virgin/Tomb of the Virgin Mary (7) to the area west of the Latin Convent (40), see the panorama of Jerusalem (1.2). By way of comparison, Martin Kemp states that Henry Aston Barker drew eight sketches in 1802 when preparing a study for a panorama of Paris. Kemp, *The Science of Art*, 214.

10. Francis West, *A Description of the Camera-Lucida for Drawing in True Perspective, the Invention of Dr. Wollaston, with Full Directions how to Use and how to Choose a Good Instrument, and the Defects to which Bad Ones are Liable. With the Observations of Captain Basil Hall* (London: Effingham Wilson (Royal Exchange) and Chappell (Pall Mall), 1831), 12.

11. Varley's specification in his patent for the Graphic Telescope, Appendix III, *Cornelius Varley: The Art of Observation*, 186–191, 190.

12. Hall, *Forty Etchings, from Sketches made with the Camera Lucida*, i.

13. Samuel Prout, *Rudiments of Landscape in Progressive Studies. Drawn, and Etched in Imitation of Chalk* (London: R. Ackermann and L. Harrison & J. C. Leigh, 1813), 16.

14. Hall, *Forty Etchings, from Sketches made with the Camera Lucida*, ii.

15. Hammond and Austin cite correspondence in *Mechanics' Magazine* between 1829 and 1830 to demonstrate that the camera lucida may not have been as easy an instrument to use as some writers advocated. Hammond and Austin, *The Camera Lucida in Art and Science*, 86–87. Martin Kemp argues that to use the instrument required considerable determination, relying primarily on the skill of an artist or draughtsman to render scenes effectively and attractively. Kemp, *Seen | Unseen*, 260. As Kemp observes, what something looks like to the human eye is not the same as its optically accurate transcription, a difference which William Henry Fox Talbot encountered when, sketching on his honeymoon in 1833, he found that 'the faithless pencil had only left traces on the paper melancholy to behold', before concluding that the use of the camera lucida required a high level of competence as a draughtsman. William Henry Fox Talbot quoted in Larry J. Schaaf, *Out of the Shadows: Herschel, Talbot and the Invention of Photography* (New Haven and London: Yale University Press, 1992), 35. See also Kemp's discussion of Sir John Herschel's use of the camera lucida in *The Science of Art*, 200–201, and Kemp's discussion of William Henry Fox Talbot in *Seen | Unseen*, 261–265.

16. David Hockney, *Secret Knowledge: Rediscovering the Lost Techniques of the Old Masters*, new and expanded edition (New York: Viking Studio, 2006 [2000]), 28.

17. See e-mail correspondence from Martin Kemp to David Hockney, 7 October 1999, in Hockney, *Secret Knowledge*, 271.

18. Hall, *Forty Etchings, from Sketches made with the Camera Lucida*, ii.

19. Michael Pidgley, 'Cornelius Varley, Cotman, and the Graphic Telescope', *The Burlington Magazine*, vol. 114, no. 836 (November 1972): 781–786, 785; Letter from Mrs. Dawson Turner to her husband, Rouen, 1 July 1818, quoted in 'Introduction', Miklos Rajnai assisted by Marjorie Allthorpe-Guyton, *John Sell Cotman: Drawings of Normandy in Norwich Castle Museum* (Norwich: Norfolk Museums Service, 1975), 5. Cotman had been given a Graphic Telescope by his and Varley's patron, Sir Henry Englefield, an amateur draughtsman, past president of the Society of Arts, and author of *A Description of the Principal Picturesque Beauties, Antiquities, and Geological Phenomena, of the Isle of Wight* (1816).

20. West, *A Description of the Camera-Lucida for Drawing in True Perspective*, 9, where West quotes an editorial in *Mechanics' Magazine*.

21. Wollaston, 'Description of the Camera Lucida', 3.

22. West, *A Description of the Camera-Lucida for Drawing in True Perspective*, 11.

23. Cornelius Varley, *A Treatise on Optical Drawing Instruments by Cornelius Varley, Artist, Member of the Society of Arts, The Microscopical Society, etc; also A Method of Preserving Pictures in Oil and in Water Colours* (London: Horne, Thornwaite, & Wood, 1845), 28.

24. Varley, *A Treatise on Optical Drawing Instruments*, 28.

25. Prout, *Rudiments of Landscape in Progressive Studies*, 16.

26. Hockney, *Secret Knowledge*, 317–318.

27. West, *A Description of the Camera-Lucida for Drawing in True Perspective*, 6.

28. Hall, *Forty Etchings, from Sketches made with the Camera Lucida*, i.

29. [Dollond], *Description of the Camera Lucida*, 8.

30. Kemp, *Seen | Unseen*, 259, 260.

31. Larry J. Schaaf, *Tracings of Light: Sir John Herschel and the Camera Lucida. Drawings in the Graham Nash Collection* (San Francisco: The Friends of Photography, 1989), 12.

32. Richard Brown, *The Principles of Practical Perspective; or, Scenographic Projection: Containing Universal Rules for Delineating Designs on Various Surfaces, and Taking Views from Nature, by the Most Simple and Expeditious Methods. To which are Added, Rules for Shadowing, and the Elements of Painting. The Whole Treated in a Manner Calculated to Render the Science of Perspective and the Art of Drawing Easy of Attainment to Every Capacity. Illustrated with Fifty-one Plates. By Richard Brown, Architect and Professor of Perspective* (London: Samuel Leigh, 1815), 3.

33. For an example of this practice in the mid-eighteenth century, see John Bonehill and Stephen Daniels (eds.), *Paul Sandby (1731–1809): Picturing Britain, A Bicentenary Exhibition*, exhibition catalogue (London: Royal Academy of Arts, 2009), The Board of Ordnance, *A sheet of the fair copy of the Military Survey of the North of Scotland (Culloden Moor)*, c. 1750, 82–83 (in enlarged detail, 84–85).

34. Rachel Hewitt, *Map of a Nation: A Biography of the Ordnance Survey* (London: Granta Books, 2010), 28, 63. For an example of this practice in the first map the Ordnance Survey sold to the public, see William Mudge, *General Survey of England and Wales. An Entirely New & Accurate Survey of the County of Kent*, detail from Sheet 1: Isle of Dogs, Ordnance Survey, 1801, reproduced as Plate O, Hewitt, *Map of a Nation*.

35. Following the Jacobite rising and the Battle of Culloden in 1745, the Board of Ordnance mapped the Scottish Highlands and Lowlands between 1747 and 1755 for the 'Great Map', as the map was known to contemporaries.

36. George Townshend, *Rules and Orders of the Royal Military Academy* (London, 1776), 19, quoted in John Bonehill, Stephen Daniels and Nicholas Alfrey, 'Paul Sandby: Picturing Britain', in Bonehill and Daniels (eds.), *Paul Sandby (1731–1809)*, 12–27, 17.

37. Bonehill, Daniels and Alfrey, 'Paul Sandby: Picturing Britain', in Bonehill and Daniels (eds.), *Paul Sandby (1731–1809)*, 17. By the time of the Napoleonic Wars, five drawing-masters were employed at the Royal Military Academy, Woolwich, and at least one at each of the Royal Military Colleges in Marlow, Sandhurst, and High Wycombe. Bermingham, *Learning to Draw*, 84.

38. John Bonehill, 'Catalogue plates and entries: I Picture-making', in Bonehill and Daniels (eds.), *Paul Sandby (1731–1809)*, 72–119, 74, 93.

39. Bermingham, *Learning to Draw*, 79.

40. For an example, see George Schultz, *A Circular View of the Horizon from the Steeple of the Church of Dieghem, with the Situation of the Incampments of the Army of the Allies*, 1745, in Denise Blake Oleksijczuk, *The First Panoramas: Visions of British Imperialism* (Minneapolis and London: University of Minnesota Press, 2011), Figure 5.6, 139. The drawing presents a military *coup d'œil* of the village of Dieghem and surrounding terrain (in the Low Countries) in bird's-eye perspective, framed as a convex circular projection viewed from an elevated and imaginary point high above the steeple of the village church: the *coup d'œil* shows the encampments of troops of the English and Allies near Brussels during the War of the Austrian Succession. Oleksijczuk, *The First Panoramas*, 137, 138.

41. For further discussion of eighteenth-century mapping techniques and the work of Paul Sandby, see Bermingham, *Learning to Draw*, 79–84; Bonehill, Daniels

and Alfrey, 'Paul Sandby: Picturing Britain', in Bonehill and Daniels (eds.), *Paul Sandby (1731–1809)*, 12–27; and Hewitt, *Map of a Nation*, 189.

42. Hewitt, *Map of a Nation*, 163. The Ordnance Survey first used their name on one of their publications in 1810. Hewitt, *Map of a Nation*, 103.

43. Hewitt, *Map of a Nation*, 166, 296. The sums given here, rendered in today's terms: 3 guineas (£3.15); 3 shillings (15p); 6 shillings (30p).

44. Samuel Buck and Nathaniel Buck (hereafter, 'Buck'), *Buck's Antiquities; or Venerable Remains of Above Four Hundred Castles, Monasteries, Palaces, &c., &c. in England and Wales. With near One Hundred Views of Cities and Chief Towns*, 3 vols. (London: D. Bond, 1774), 'Introduction', I, v.

45. 'Buck', *Buck's Antiquities*, I, v. Ann Bermingham has not found any eighteenth-century drawing manuals that discuss the drawing of topographic views. She has proposed that as topographical illustration was regarded as a form of technical drawing, motivated by concerns that were not primarily aesthetic, topographic drawing was a subject neglected by publishers in Britain. Bermingham, *Learning to Draw*, note 46, 259.

46. 'Buck', *Buck's Antiquities*, 12. The Copyright Act was passed in 1735, forbidding the copying of prints, without permission, for a period of fourteen years from the date of publication, a fine of one shilling being levied on each illegal impression that was found. The rubric, 'published as the Act directs', was included on prints made after the 1735 Act. Ronald Russell, *Guide to British Topographical Prints* (Newton Abbot, London, North Pomfret, VT: David & Charles, 1979), 30.

47. Vol. I: Plates 29 and 30 (*North View of St. Michael's Mount, in the County of Cornwall* and *East View …*); Plates 44 and 45 (*The North-West View of Lanercost-Priory, in the County of Cumberland* and *The South-East View …*); Plates 53 and 54 (*The West View of Bolsover Castle, in the County of Derby* and *The North-East Prospect …*); Plates 126, 127, and 128 (*The West View of Dover-Castle, in the County of Kent, The North View …* and *The North West View …*), the only series in the volume that provides three views, Plate 128 providing a detail of a feature seen in the two previous plates); Plates 138 and 139 (*The North West View of Rochester Castle* and *The South East View …*); Plates 156 and 157 (*The South View of Ashby-de-la-Zouche Castle, in the County of Leicester* and *The North View …*); Plates 158 and 159 (*The East View of Belvoir Castle, in the County of Leicester* and *The South View …*); Plates 165 and 166 (*The South West View of Croyland Abbey near Spalding, in the County of Lincoln* and *The West View …*); Plates 182 and 183 (*The South View of the Tower of London* and *The West View …*). Vol. II: Plates 293 and 294 (*The North-East View of Pevensey-Castle, in the County of Sussex* and The *South-East View …*); Plates 305 and 306 (*The South East View of Warwick Castle* and *The North East View …*); Plates 345 and 346 (*The North View of Beaumaris Castle, in the Isle of Anglesey* and *The South East View …*); Plates 367, 368, and 369 (*The North West View of Caernarvon Castle, The North East View …* and *The South East View …*); Plates 371 and 372 (*The South East View of Conway Castle, in the County of Caernarvon* and *The North East View …*); Plate 380 and 381 (*The West View of Valle Crucis Abbey, in the County of Denbigh* and *The East View …*); Plates 383 and 384 (*The North East View of Denbigh Castle* and *The North View …*). Vol. III: Plates 3 and 4 (*The South West Prospect of Birmingham. In the County of Warwick* and *The East Prospect of Birmingham …*); Plates 6 and 7 (*The North West Prospect of the City of Bristol* and *The South East Prospect …*); Plates 25 and 26 (*The West Prospect of the City of Exeter* and *The South West Prospect …*); Plates 49 and 50 (*The South West Prospect of St. Michael's Mount in Cornwall* and *The South East Prospect …*); Plates 53 and 54 (*The North-East Prospect of the City of Norwich* and *The South-East Prospect …*); Plates 56 and 57 (*The South West Prospect of the University, and City of Oxford* and *The South-East Prospect …*); Plates 65 and 66 (*The North East Prospect of Richmond, in the County of York* and *The South West Prospect …*). Of these plates, only Plates 371 and 372, presenting the northeast view of Conway Castle (in Plate 372) from an almost identical position to that shown in Plate 371, do not present a consistent contiguous relation.

48. Plate 41 was taken *'from Mr. Scheve's Sugar House, opposite to York House'*; Plate 42 *'from Mr. Watson's Summer House, opposite to Somerset House'*; Plate 43 *'from Mr. Everard's Summer-House, opposite to St. Brides Church'*; Plate 44 *'from the West part of the Leads of St. Mary Overy's Church in Southwark*; and Plate 45 *'from the West part of the Leads of St. Mary Overy's Church in Southwark*.

49. Plate 342 (Vol. II) is the only plate in the series that specifies the distance between viewer and subject.

50. Plates in Vol. III that designate the location from which they were drawn include: Plate 14 (*The West Prospect of His Majesty's Dock-Yard at Chatham* – 'Frendsbury Hill'); Plate 17 (*The South-East Prospect of Colchester, in the County of Essex* – 'Clinggoe Hill'); Plate 23 (*The East Prospect of St. Edmunds, Bury, in the County of Suffolk* – 'The top of the Vine Fields'); Plate 33 (*The South-West Prospect of Ipswich, in the County of Suffolk* – 'Stoke Hill'); Plate 36 (*The South-East Prospect of Leeds, in the County of York* – 'Cavalier Hill'); Plate 37 (*The South Prospect of Leicester* – 'The Station near the Turnpike in ye. London Road'); Plate 46 (*The East Prospect of Lynn-Regis, in the County of Norfolk* – 'The road to Norwich'); Plate 47 (*The North-West Prospect of Maidstone, in the County of Kent* – 'Buckland Fields'); Plate 53 (*The North-East Prospect of the City of Norwich* – 'The Hill where this Drawing was taken'); Plate 54 (*The South-East Prospect of the City of Norwich* – 'Mussel Hill'); Plate 57 (*The South-East Prospect of the University, and City of Oxford* – 'between Easley and the Henley Road'); Plate 58 (*The North-West View of Pembroke* – 'near Bush: The Seat of Essex Miyricke Esqr.'); Plate 65 (*The North East Prospect of Richmond, in the County of York* – 'Cling-Wood'); Plate 66 (*The South West Prospect of Richmond, in the County of York* – 'Billy-Bank'); Plate 67 (*The South-East Prospect of Rippon* [*sic*], *in the County of York* – 'Five Oaks, the Hill'); Plate 72 (*The East Prospect of Sheffield, in the County of York* – 'Park Hill'); Plate 74 (*The South Prospect of Stamford, in the County of Lincoln* – 'The Road to Burleigh House'); Plate 75 (*The East View of Swansea, in the County of Glamorgan* – the Plate indicates #11, 'The Station where this Drawing was taken.'); Plate 81 (*The South View of Wrexham, in the County of Denbigh* – 'The Old Tenterfield'); Plate 83 (*The South-East Prospect of York* – 'Lamell Hill'). Plates 4, 57, and 75 use the term 'station' to designate the point from which views were drawn, a term encountered in the context of panoramas in Chapter One, and a term to which we return in this chapter when we consider the tourist of the picturesque.

51. In fine art, this practice had been an established convention since the Renaissance. See Kemp's discussion of Andrea Mantegna, *Oculus in the 'Camera degli Sposi'*, c. 1465–1474, Palazzo Ducale Mantua, Castello de S. Giorgio, Kemp, *Seen | Unseen*, Figure 9, 31.

52. A market which later refashioned the notion of the picturesque, equipping it for a new role in cultural politics, a development which is considered with regard to Mexico in Chapter Five. For discussion of a parallel development in mid-nineteenth-century Britain, see Malcolm Andrews, 'The Metropolitan

Picturesque', in Stephen Copley and Peter Garside (eds.), *The Politics of the Picturesque: Literature, Landscape and Aesthetics since 1770* (Cambridge: Cambridge University Press, 1994), 282–298.

53. 'Letter the Eighth, Mexico [City], 31st.[December 1839]', Frances Calderón de la Barca, *Life in Mexico, during a Residence of Two Years, in that Country. By Madame C- de la B-. With a Preface by W. H. Prescott* (London: Chapman and Hall, 1843), 58. Born in Edinburgh in 1804, Frances Erskine Inglis married Angel Calderón de la Barca in 1838 who had served as head of the Spanish Diplomatic Mission to the United States. Shortly after their marriage, Angel Calderón de la Barca was appointed Isabel II's Minister to Mexico, the first Spanish Envoy to the Republic, and Frances accompanied her husband to Mexico. Frances' letters constitute the basis of *Life in Mexico, during a Residence of Two Years*, published in the same year that Angel Calderón de la Barca returned to Washington as Spanish Minister.

54. 'Letter the Sixth, Mexico [City], 26th. December. [1839]', Frances Calderón de la Barca, *Life in Mexico, during a Residence of Two Years*, 39–40. For further consideration of Frances Calderón de la Barca's response which, drawing on disparities between her diary and its published version, argues that the picturesque tone was disrupted by a note of historical contention linked to Calderón de la Barca's subject position as a cosmopolitan foreign woman, see Nigel Leask, '"The Ghost in Chapultepec": Fanny Calderón de la Barca, William Prescott and Nineteenth-Century Mexican Travel Accounts', in *Voyages and Visions: Towards a Cultural History of Travel*, edited by Jaś Elsner and Joan-Pau Rubiés (London: Reaktion Books, 1999), 184–209, 197–199.

55. 'Letter VII. Last day's ride to Mexico City', Brantz Mayer, *Mexico As It Was and As It Is: by Brantz Mayer, Secretary of the U.S. Legation to that Country in 1841 and 1842. With Numerous Illustrations on Wood, Engraved by Butler* (New York: J. Winchester, New World Press; London and Paris: Wiley and Putnam, 1844), 34–35, emphases in the original.

56. For discussion of the colonialist discourse associated with nineteenth-century European travellers in Central and South America, see Mary Louise Pratt, *Imperial Eyes: Travel Writing and Transculturation* (London and New York: Routledge, 1992), 111–171. For a nuanced discussion of the 'logic' of territorial expansion associated with the struggle for influence in Mexico in the 1830s and 1840s, and an assessment of 'view-taking' as a form of cultural depredation, see Robert D. Aguirre, *Informal Empires: Mexico and Central America in Victorian Culture* (Minneapolis: University of Minnesota Press, 2005), 48–60.

57. For discussion of the influence of Claude on Thomas Cole, see Barbara Novak, *American Painting of the Nineteenth Century: Realism, Idealism and the American Experience*, third edition with a new preface (Oxford and New York: Oxford University Press, 2007 [1980]), 41–58; for discussion of the influence of Claude on Frederic Edwin Church's work in Ecuador at mid-century, see Barbara Novak, *Nature and Culture: American Landscape and Painting, 1825–1875*, third edition with a new preface (Oxford and New York: Oxford University Press, 2007 [1980]), 21, 126, 196–197; for further discussion of the influence of Claude on Frederic Church and Louis Remy Mignot in Ecuador, see Katherine Emma Manthorne, *Tropical Renaissance: North American Artists Exploring Latin America, 1839–1879* (Washington, D.C. and London: Smithsonian Institution Press, 1989), 5–7, 32, 75, 77, 140–144, 148–149. A delight in aerial perspective could also be defined more prosaically: 'the gradation of light and shade on various objects as they recede from the eye; for instance, a house a mile distant would be fainter in light and shade than one a quarter of a mile distant, and so in proportion, until the parts are become imperceptible'. Brown, *The Principles of Practical Perspective*, 2.

58. 'J. B.' [John Britton], *A Brief Account of The Colosseum, in the Regent's Park, London: Comprising a Description of the Building; The Panoramic View from the top of St. Paul's Cathedral, The Conservatory, &c. Printed for the Proprietors, and Sold at the Exhibition; and by all Booksellers* (London, 1829), 5.

59. We should note that elevated viewpoints were generally regarded as unsuitable for composition in the picturesque manner which favoured lower viewpoints that provided a command of the foreground. Malcolm Andrews, *The Search for the Picturesque: Landscape Aesthetics and Tourism in Britain, 1760–1800* (Aldershot: Scolar Press, 1989), 161.

60. For discussion of analogy and metaphor in Augustan literature and its influence on the Picturesque, see Andrews, *The Search for the Picturesque*, 3–23.

61. William H. Prescott, *History of the Conquest of Mexico, with a Preliminary View of the Ancient Mexican Civilization, and the Life of the Conqueror, Hernando Cortes*, new and revised edition with the author's latest corrections and additions, edited by John Foster Kirk, 2 vols. (London: George Routledge and Sons, 1874), I, Book III, Chapter VIII, 437–438.

62. William Bullock, *Six Months' Residence and Travels in Mexico; Containing Remarks on the Present State of New Spain, its Natural Productions, State of Society, Manufactures, Trade, Agriculture, and Antiquities, &c. With Plates and Maps. By W. Bullock, F.L.S. Proprietor of the late London Museum* (London: John Murray, 1824), 119, 120. Bullock was no stranger to panoramas; a panoramic view of Mexico City from the roof of the hotel in which he and his son lodged was described as follows: 'The roofs are all nearly flat, and bricked, and many of them are covered with flowers, affording a pleasant place of resort in a fine evening, as the prospect is delightful, and the air refreshing and uncontaminated by smoke. Owing to this species of ornament, the city, seen from an elevation, presents a far more beautiful appearance than those of Europe, where the red-tiled and deformed roofs, and shapeless stacks and chimnies [*sic*], are the principal features in the prospect. Indeed, no place I ever saw affords so many interesting points for a panoramic view …', Bullock, *Six Months' Residence and Travels in Mexico*, 128–129. Arising from the visit of Bullock and his son to Mexico, William Bullock Jr. sketched a view of the City of Mexico which was exhibited as a panorama in the Upper Circle of the Panorama, Leicester Square, between 12 December 1825 and June 1827. Scott Barnes Wilcox, *The Panorama and Related Exhibitions in London*, MLitt dissertation, University of Edinburgh, 1976, Appendix C: 'A Chronology of Panoramas Exhibited at the Leicester Square and Strand Panoramas', 254–265, 257. Bullock Jr.'s *View of the City of Mexico and Surrounding Country*, drawn with the aid of a camera lucida, is considered in Chapter Three.

63. 'J. B.' [John Britton], *A Brief Account of The Colosseum*, 5.

64. 'J. B.' [John Britton], *A Brief Account of the Colosseum*, variously 5, 6. A similar response to the 'singularity and grandeur' of landscape was observed by William Gilpin when, travelling to Wales, he saw the landscape of the Severn valley from the Cotswolds: 'To the north, we looked up the vale, along the course of the Severn. The town of Cheltenham lay below our feet, at the distance of two or three miles. The vale appeared afterwards confined between Bredon hills, on the right; and those of Malvern on the left. … To the west, we looked toward

Gloucester. ... Beyond Gloucester the eye still pursues the vale into remote distance, till it unite with a range of mountains. Still more to the west arises a distant forest-view composed of the woods of the country uniting with the forest of Dean. ...', William Gilpin, *Observations on the River Wye, and Several Parts of South Wales, &c. relative chiefly to Picturesque Beauty; Made in the Summer of the Year 1770, Second Edition, by William Gilpin, M. A. Prebendary of Salisbury; and Vicar of Boldre in New Forest, near Lymington*, second edition (London: R. Blamire, 1789 [given as 1782 on title-page of first edition]), 8–10. All quotations from Gilpin, *Observations on the River Wye*, are from the second edition (1789).

65. 'The Colosseum', notice of the opening of the panorama on 14 January 1829, 'Fine Arts' column, *The Literary Gazette; and Journal of the Belles Lettres, Arts, Sciences, &c.* No. 626. Saturday, 17 January 1829, 42–43, 42.

66. 'Hornors Riesenpanorama', *Berliner Kunstblatt* (1829), quoted in Stephan Oettermann, *The Panorama: History of a Mass Medium*, trans. Deborah Lucas Schneider (New York: Zone Books, 1997 [German edition, 1980]), 134.

67. 'The Colosseum', *The Literary Gazette*, Saturday, 17 January 1829, 42. Note the analogy drawn, once again, between a natural scene and a panoramic view.

68. 'The Colosseum', *The Literary Gazette*, Saturday, 17 January 1829, 42. For discussion of early telescopes and the manner in which they made visual artefacts rather than showed them in an accurate manner, see Kemp, *Seen | Unseen*, 44–45.

69. The relation of panoramic views, cartography, and optical devices (in this case, a theodolite) may also be instanced by the fact that when, some twenty years later, the Ordnance Survey surveyed London, St. Paul's Cathedral was selected which 'by its position and commanding height, is probably [t]he best station in or about London'. 'Ordnance Survey of London and the Environs', *The Illustrated London News*, vol. 12, no. 322, Saturday, 24 June 1848, 414. Note that the term 'station' was used to designate the location from which the survey was conducted.

70. Quotations are taken from the fifth edition, published in 1835. I thank Alan Barnes who drew this work to my attention. Print-runs of the third, fourth, and fifth editions of Wordsworth's guide are known: 500 copies of the third edition; 1000 copies of the fourth edition; and 1500 copies of the fifth edition. *The Illustrated Wordsworth's Guide to the Lakes*, ed. Peter Bicknell, with a foreword by Alan G. Hill (London: Book Club Associates, 1984), 204, 205.

71. Subtitled, 'Section First. View of the Country as formed by Nature'.

72. *The Illustrated Wordsworth's Guide to the Lakes*, ed. Bicknell, 64–65. Wordsworth's guide first appeared in 1810 when it formed an anonymous introduction to Rev. Joseph Wilkinson, *Select Views in Cumberland, Westmoreland, and Lancashire*, published in twelve monthly parts; the second version of the guide, published as *A Topographical Description of the Country of the Lakes in the North of England* in 1820, was annexed to Wordsworth's *The River Duddon, a Series of Sonnets: and other Poems*; in 1822 Wordsworth published *A Description of the Scenery of the Lakes in the North of England*, a pocket-book edition with a print-run of 500 copies; a fourth, revised edition of *A Description of the Scenery of the Lakes in the North of England* was published in 1823; and a fifth edition, *A Guide through the District of the Lakes in the North of England, with A Description of the Scenery, &c. For the use of Tourists and Residents*, was published in 1835 by Hudson and Nicholson in Kendal, and by Longman & Co., Moxon, and Whittaker & Co. in London. Bicknell, 'Introduction', *The Illustrated Wordsworth's Guide to the Lakes*, 7–30, 16, 21.

73. Gilpin, *Observations on the River Wye* (second edition, 1789), 85, 150; emphases in the original. For discussion of the increasing importance of the imagination as a subjective term in the work of the early Romantics, wherein objects are seen 'not as they are, but as they appear to the mind of the poet', see Andrews, *The Search for the Picturesque*, 70–73; the quote is from Christopher Wordsworth, *Memoirs of William Wordsworth* (1851), II, 477, cited in Andrews, *The Search for the Picturesque*, 71.

74. The formulaic nature of Gilpin's compositions was satirised by Jane Austen in *Northanger Abbey* (completed in 1803) when Catherine Morland, accompanied by General Tilney, admires an elevated view of the city of Bath where she confesses her lack of knowledge regarding the picturesque: '... she confessed and lamented her want of knowledge; declared that she would give any thing in the world to be able to draw; and a lecture on the picturesque immediately followed, in which his [General Tilney] instructions were so clear that she soon began to see beauty in every thing admired by him, and her attention was so earnest, that he became perfectly satisfied of her having a great deal of natural taste. He talked of fore-grounds, distances, and second distances – side-screens and perspectives – light and shades; – and Catherine was so hopeful a scholar, that when they gained the top of Beechen Cliff, she voluntarily rejected the whole city of Bath, as unworthy to make part of a landscape.' Jane Austen, *Northanger Abbey*, edited and with an Introduction and Notes by Marilyn Butler (Harmondsworth: Penguin Books, 1995 [1817, given as 1818 on title-page of first edition]), 106–107.

75. Ann Bermingham has indicated that the schema Gilpin employed for landscape sketching was loosely based on Claude after Richard Earlom's mezzotint reproductions of Claude's sepia drawings, printed by John Boydell, and published in *The Liber Veritatis* (London, 1775). Bermingham, *Learning to Draw*, 96–97; for illustration, see Figure 73, 97.

76. Andrews, *The Search for the Picturesque*, 26.

77. William Gilpin, *Observations, Relative Chiefly to Picturesque Beauty, Made in the Year 1772; On Several Parts of England; particularly the Mountains, and Lakes of Cumberland, and Westmoreland. By William Gilpin, M.A. Prebendary of Salisbury; and Vicar of Boldre, in New-Forest, near Lymington*, 2 vols. (London: R. Blamire, 1786), I, 146. Elsewhere, Gilpin observed: 'when we introduce a scene on canvas – when the eye is to be confined within the frame of a picture, and can no longer range among the varieties of nature; the aids of art become more necessary; and we want the castle, or the abbey, to give consequence to the scene'. Gilpin, *Observations on the River Wye* (second edition, 1789), 25–26.

78. See William Gilpin, *An Essay on Prints. By William Gilpin, M.A. Prebendary of Salisbury; and Vicar of Boldre in New-Forest, Near Lymington*, fifth edition (London: T. Cadell, Jun. and W. Davies, 1802 [1768]), 113.

79. Andrews, *The Search for the Picturesque*, 29. For further discussion of the compositional principles typical of the Picturesque, see Andrews, *The Search for the Picturesque*, 29–36. See also Bermingham, *Learning to Draw*, 93–96 and, regarding the Claude glass, 100–101. For a detailed discussion of Gilpin's theory of the Picturesque, see Carl Paul Barbier, *William Gilpin: His Drawings, Teaching, and Theory of the Picturesque* (Oxford: Clarendon Press, 1963), 98–147.

80. As defined by Gilpin: 'The word implies the different degrees of strength and faintness, which objects receive from nearness, and distance. A nice observance of the gradual fading of light and shade contributes greatly towards the production of a *whole*. Without it, the distant parts, instead of being connected with the objects at hand, appear like foreign objects, without meaning.' Gilpin,

An Essay on Prints, 10–11. The term was defined mid-century as '[a]n attention to the proper subserviency of tone and colour in every part of a picture, so that the general effect is harmonious to the eye. When this is unattended to, a harshness is produced, which gives improper isolation to individual parts, and the picture is said to be *out of keeping*.' F[rederick] W[illiam] Fairholt, *A Dictionary of Terms in Art. Edited and Illustrated by F. W. Fairholt, F. S. A. With Five Hundred Engravings on Wood* (London: Strahan & Co., 1854), 255–256, emphases in original.

81. Bermingham, *Learning to Draw*, 101.

82. For illustration of two examples of the Claude glass, see Andrews, *The Search for the Picturesque*, 68; Kemp, *The Science of Art*, Figure 395, 199.

83. William Gilpin, *Remarks on Forest Scenery, and Other Woodland Views, (Relative Chiefly to Picturesque Beauty) Illustrated by the Scenes of New-Forest in Hampshire*, 3 vols. (London: R. Blamire, 1791), II, 255, emphases in original.

84. Andrews, *The Search for the Picturesque*, 69–70; Arnaud Maillet, *The Claude Glass: Use and Meaning of the Black Mirror in Western Art*, trans. Jeff Fort (New York: Zone Books, 2004), 142.

85. William Gilpin, *Three Essays: On Picturesque Beauty; On Picturesque Travel; and On Sketching Landscape with a Poem, On Landscape Painting. To these are now added Two Essays, giving an Account of the Principles and Modes in which the Author executed his own Drawings. By William Gilpin, M.A. Prebendary of Salisbury; and Vicar of Boldre in New-Forest, near Lymington*, third edition (London: T. Cadell and W. Davies, 1808 [1792]), 175, emphases in original. A variant of these remarks may be seen in a letter Gilpin wrote to William Lock in 1790: 'A dark foreground makes, I think, a kind of pleasing gradation of tint from the eye to the removed parts of the landscape. It carries off the distance better than any other contrivance. By throwing the light on the foreground all this appears to my eye disagreeably inverted. – Besides, the *foreground* is commonly but a mere *appendage*. The middle, & remote distances, (which include the compass of the landscape) make the *scene*; & therefore require most distinction. – In history-painting it is the reverse. The *principal* part of the subject occupies the *foreground*; and the *distance* is the appendage.' William Gilpin, letter to William Lock, 24 February 1790, quoted in Barbier, *William Gilpin*, 122. Regarding tinting and the washing of sketches, see directions from William Gilpin to William Mason (Gilpin's publisher), 25 April 1772, in Barbier, *William Gilpin*, 50–51.

86. Stebbing Shaw, 'A Tour of the West of England in 1788', in J. Pinkerton, *Voyages*, Vol. II (1808), quoted in Julian Mitchell, *The Wye Tour and its Artists* (Little Logoston, Woonton Almeley: Logoston Press, 2010), 79. Laid out in the 1750s by Valentine Morris, the son of a wealthy plantation owner in the Caribbean, Piercefield Park was the height of fashion in the late eighteenth century when tourists visited the estate to enjoy views of the Wye Valley from picturesque viewpoints such as The Alcove, the first viewpoint on the estate constructed around 1750.

87. Although the title-page bears the date of 1782, Gilpin's *Observations on the River Wye*, privately circulated for many years in manuscript form, was first published in 1783. Barbier, *William Gilpin*, 71. The delay in publication arose from difficulty with the aquatint illustrations that accompanied the volume.

88. Gilpin, *Observations on the River Wye* (second edition, 1789), 108, the fourteenth unnumbered aquatint by Francis Jukes, after Gilpin, facing 109.

89. Gilpin, *Observations on the River Wye* (second edition, 1789), the fourth unnumbered aquatint by Francis Jukes, after Gilpin, facing 39. The descriptor 'continually shifting' comes from Gilpin, *Observations, Relative Chiefly to Picturesque Beauty, Made in the Year 1772*, I, 194.

90. Gilpin, *Observations on the River Wye* (second edition, 1789), 17–20, 19, emphases in original. Gilpin glossed the term, 'amphitheatre', in a note, 19: 'The word *amphitheatre*, strictly speaking, is a complete inclosure [*sic*]: but I believe, it is commonly accepted, as here, for any circular piece of architecture, tho [*sic*] it do not wind *entirely* round.'

91. Gilpin toured Kent in 1768; Essex, Suffolk, and Norfolk in 1769; the River Wye and parts of South Wales in 1770; Cumberland and Westmorland (the Lakes) in 1772; North Wales in 1773; the south coast of England in 1774; the west of England in 1775, and the Highlands of Scotland in 1776. Barbier, *William Gilpin*, 41. For further discussion of the Wye Tour, see Andrews, *The Search for the Picturesque*, 85–107.

92. Barbier, *William Gilpin*, 70–71, 79, 82, 83. Gilpin's *A Guide to the Lakes, in Cumberland, Westmorland, and Lancashire* was first published at the end of 1786; a second edition was published in spring 1788 with plates by Francis Jukes; a third edition appeared with aquatints by Samuel Alken in 1792, to which Sawrey Gilpin contributed six signed soft-ground etchings; a further edition was published in 1808. Barbier, *William Gilpin*, 75, 77–78, 81, 83.

93. Since private copies were frequently circulated, and circulating libraries were much in vogue, the number of readers would have been significantly higher than the print-runs.

94. William Coxe, *An Historical Tour in Monmouthshire; Illustrated with Views by Sir R. C. Hoare, Bart. A New Map of the County and other Engravings: by William Coxe, A.M. F.R.S. F.A.S. Rector of Bemberton [sic] and Stourton*, 2 vols. (London: T. Cadell, Jun. and W. Davies, 1801), II, 348. William Coxe, vicar of Bemerton, near Salisbury, made two tours of the Wye Valley with the artist and antiquarian, Sir Richard Colt Hoare, in 1798 and 1799, Hoare having first toured the Wye Valley in 1797. *An Historical Tour in Monmouthshire*, published with illustrations by Hoare, was later printed in an abridged version without illustration as *A Picture of Monmouthshire*, and a further abridged version was published by the Chepstow printer, Samuel Baldwyn Rogers, appearing in 1806. Mitchell, *The Wye Tour*, 30, 150.

95. Coxe, *An Historical Tour in Monmouthshire*, II, 341.

96. A distinction may be drawn here: in eighteenth- and early-nineteenth-century English, a 'tourist' undertook a 'tour' or 'circuit' whereas an 'excursionist' travelled from a particular place and back again on a return ticket, i.e., a 'day-tripper'. For further discussion of the distinction, see Ian Ousby, *The Englishman's England: Taste, Travel and the Rise of Tourism* (Cambridge: Cambridge University Press, 1990), 18.

97. See block advertisement for the Bristol and Chepstow steam packet, *Duke of Beaufort* (named after the landowner on whose land Tintern Abbey stood), reproduced in Mitchell, *The Wye Tour*, 85. Ousby points out that the term 'sight-seeing' entered the English language in the 1830s, 'aptly conveying how the shifting human scenes which had first fascinated eighteenth-century inquirers had been reduced to a static list of objects and monuments', Ousby, *The Englishman's England*, 19. For discussion of the development of Tintern

Abbey as a tourist attraction in the eighteenth century, see Ousby, *The Englishman's England*, 116–129.

98. For details of charges and facilities available to tourists (which generally included a table for drawing and painting (which also served as a dining-table), lockers to hold bottles, sketch-books and guide-books), see Mitchell, *The Wye Tour*, 38–41. The sums given here, rendered in today's terms: 4 shillings (20p); 3 shillings (15p); 2 shillings (10p); one and a half guineas (£1.52½p); £5 12s (£5.60); four guineas (£4.20).

99. Malcolm Andrews and Ian Ousby have observed that the letters which the poet, Thomas Gray, wrote describing his second visit to the Lakes in 1769 (his first visit being made in 1767), published in William Mason's posthumous edition of Gray's works in 1775, helped establish the main stopping-points for a tour of the Lakes. Andrews, *The Search for the Picturesque*, 182; Ousby, *The Englishman's England*, 144. For further discussion of the tour of the Lakes, see Andrews, *The Search for the Picturesque*, 154–195; Ousby, *The Englishman's England*, 143–187.

100. Published in 1778, Thomas West's *A Guide to the Lakes* was revised and enlarged by William Cockin, a Kendal schoolmaster, in 1780, and had gone through seven editions by the end of the century. Andrews, *The Search for the Picturesque*, 158. The third edition of Thomas West, *A Guide to the Lakes, in Cumberland, Westmorland, and Lancashire. By the author of The Antiquities of Furness. The Third Edition, Revised Throughout and Greatly Enlarged* (London: B. Law; Richardson and Urquhart; J. Robson; and Kendal: W. Pennington, 1784 [originally published by Richardson and Urquhart in 1780]) has been consulted.

101. West, *A Guide to the Lakes*, 47, designated 'Station I'. As Kemp has pointed out, the notion that an observer should look from particular 'station points' is urban in nature, being invented as a system of perspectival representation by Filippo Brunelleschi at a time when Florentine society was pioneering new systems for the design of a measured urban environment. See Kemp *Seen* | *Unseen*, 14–19.

102. West, *A Guide to the Lakes*, 62–63, emphasis in original.

103. Peter Crosthwaite, *An Accurate Map of the Matchless Lake of Derwent, Situate in the Most Delightful Vale which perhaps ever Human Eye Beheld & near Keswick, Cumberland, with West's Seven Stations* (1819 [1783]), not completely accurate since, as Andrews observes, Crosthwaite transposed West's First and Second Stations, and marked the Vicarage Station as the Seventh (rather than the Eighth) Station. Andrews, *The Search for the Picturesque*, 179. Crosthwaite's map, reproduced as 2.10, is dated 1819.

104. West, *A Guide to the Lakes*, 93–94, emphases in original.

105. In other words, a mobile spectator experienced new perceptions of the landscape through the act of displacement, becoming aware of a plurality of positions that may be adopted regarding the perception of reality. For an early example in the tradition of Western art, see the discussion of Antonio Correggio, *Ascension of Christ (Vision of St. John on Mount Patmos)*, c. 1520–1522, dome fresco, S. Giovanni Evangelista, Parma, in Kemp, *Seen* | *Unseen*, 32–33, and Figure 12 and Figure 13 (detail), 34, 35. A latterday example may be seen in two panoramas of Constantinople exhibited at the Panorama, Leicester Square: *View of Constantinople from the Tower of Galata* (exhibited in the Large Circle from 21 April 1801 to 15 May 1802) taken from the Galata Tower on the northern side of the Golden Horn near its union with the Bosphorus, and *View of Constantinople from the Tower of Leander* (exhibited in the Upper Circle from 23 November 1801 to 14 May 1803) taken from Kiz Kulesi (also known as the Maiden's Tower) on the Asian side of the Bosphorus near the coast of Üsküdar overlooking the strait leading to the Bosphorus and the entrance to the Golden Horn. For approximately six months, the two panoramas were exhibited simultaneously, the letterpress to the circular orientation plan and key for the *View of Constantinople from the Tower of Leander* stating that the panoramas were 'intended as explanatory of each other'. See Oleksijczuk, *The First Panoramas*, Figure 4.2 and Figure 4.3, 92, 96, and discussion, 89–97. A mobilised view depicted in a panorama may be observed in the circular orientation plan and key for *Two Views of Paris* (1803), the letterpress noting that one view was 'taken between the Pont Neuf, the Louvre, Mint, and Quatre Nations; the Other from a Steam-engine on the River Seine ...'. See Oleksijczuk, *The First Panoramas*, Figure 5.19, 164, and discussion, 163, 165.

106. Andrews, *The Search for the Picturesque*, 159, 177.

107. Addenda. Article I. Dr. Brown's Letter, describing the Vale and Lake of Keswick [Derwentwater], West, *A Guide to the Lakes*, 191–194, 193, emphases in original.

108. Andrews, *The Search for the Picturesque*, 177–178.

109. Gilpin, *Observations, Relative Chiefly to Picturesque Beauty, Made in the Year 1772*, I, 193–194.

110. Not only did Gilpin value motion through landscape, but Thomas Paul Sandby (appointed the first Professor of Architecture at the Royal Academy schools in 1768, and elder brother of Paul Sandby) observed, in his fourth discourse of Lectures: 'The more cultivated the face of the Country, the more cheerful it will appear; and the different hues of Verdure, produced from the Vernal blossoms to the Autumnal Harvest, gives that endless variety, in shape & colour, which every Eye can perceive, but no pen describe: and if the opening occurs between the rising Hills to a Navigable River, or a High Road, at a distance, they will greatly diversify the Landskip, produce a continual moving Picture and increase our delight by constant succession of new and entertaining objects.' Lectures, IV, fols 6–7, first delivered in 1770, quoted in Bonehill, Daniels and Alfrey, 'Paul Sandby: Picturing Britain', in Bonehill and Daniels (eds.), *Paul Sandby (1731–1809): Picturing Britain*, 12–27, 19.

111. Gilpin, *An Essay on Prints*, xii.

Notes to Chapter Three

1. John Lloyd Stephens, *Incidents of Travel in Central America, Chiapas, and Yucatan*, 2 vols. (New York: Harper & Brothers; London: John Murray, 1841), II, 300, hereafter *Incidents of Travel in Central America*.

2. Although Joshua Conder, best known for compiling the *Congregational Hymn Book* (1834), never travelled outside Britain, he published thirty volumes in *The Modern Traveller* series between 1825 and 1829.

3. Respectively, *View of the Great Square at Mexico*; *Volcano of Jorullo*; *Basaltic Rocks & Cascade of Regla*. The full publication details read: Josiah Conder, *The Modern Traveller: A Popular Description, Geographical, Historical and Topographical, of the Various Countries of the Globe. Mexico and Guatimala* [*sic*], 4 vols. (London: James Duncan; Edinburgh: Oliver and Boyd; Glasgow: M. Ogle; Dublin: R. M. Tims,

1825), hereafter, *The Modern Traveller*. Further plates included, Part II: *Indians of Mechoacan* [*sic*], and Part IV: *Suburbs of Guanaxuato,* [*sic*] *(Cala, Mellada & Rayas)*.

4. Alexander von Humboldt, *Vues des Cordillères, et monumens des peuples indigènes de l'Amérique* (Paris: Chez F. Schoell, 1813); in English translation, Alexander von Humboldt, *Researches, Concerning the Institutions & Monuments of the Ancient Inhabitants of America, with Descriptions & Views of some of the most Striking Scenes in the Cordilleras! Written in French by Alexander de Humboldt, & Translated into English by Helen Maria Williams*, 2 vols. (London: Longman, Hurst, Rees Orme & Brown, J. Murray and H. Colburn, 1814). The pyramid of Cholula was reproduced as Plate VII in Humboldt, facing 81. William Bullock, travelling in Mexico in 1823, visited Cholula, and observed that the base of the pyramid was 'more extensive than that of the great pyramid of Egypt'. William Bullock, *Six Months' Residence and Travels in Mexico; Containing Remarks on the Present State of New Spain, its Natural Productions, State of Society, Manufactures, Trade, Agriculture, and Antiquities, &c. With Plates and Maps. By W. Bullock, F.L.S. Proprietor of the late London Museum* (London: John Murray, 1824), 114.

5. *Catalogue of a Portion of the Library of the Late Frederic* [*sic*] *Catherwood, Esq. Hon Member of the Royal Institute of British Architects, Author of Views and Monuments in Central America etc. Also a Portion of the Library of an Eminent Surgeon, Retiring from Practice ..., Which will be Sold by Auction by Messrs. Puttick and Simpson, Auctioneers of Literary Property, at their Great Room, 191, Piccadilly, on Monday, December 1st, 1856, and five following days at one o'clock most punctually*, paginated printed sale catalogue. Item #131 (7) and item #1931 (78) provide, respectively, details of the auction relating to *The Modern Traveller*: item #131 ('Conder (J.) Modern Traveller in Africa, Arabia, Palestine, America, Brazil, and Mexico [including Guatemala], 9 vols. 1830'); item #1931 ('Modern Traveller, 4 vols. 1800', with unspecified countries).

6. *The Literary Gazette*, December 1824, quoted in the press reception for *The Modern Traveller* printed on the inside front cover of *Mexico – Part I*. Printed in London, Edinburgh, Glasgow, Dublin, Paris, Berlin, and St. Petersburg, and with an agent for the USA in London, *The Literary Gazette* was a popular weekly periodical that commanded an international readership.

7. From the press reception quoted on the inside rear cover of *Mexico – Part I*. Emphasis in original.

8. Pigot's *London Directory* for 1822, which mentions the earliest British steel engraver, listed 179 copper engravers, sixteen lithographic printers, and thirty-eight print-sellers working in London. Ronald Russell, *Guide to British Topographical Prints* (Newton Abbot, London, North Pomfret, VT: David & Charles, 1979), 119.

9. Born in Providence, Rhode Island, Bartlett came from an old Massachusetts family who, after graduation, joined the banking house of Cyrus Butler before establishing an antiquarian bookshop with Charles Welford in 1837. Victor Wolfgang von Hagen, *Maya Explorer: John Lloyd Stephens and the Lost Cities of Central America and Yucatán* (Norman: University of Oklahoma Press, 1947), note 4, 70–71. Von Hagen claims that Bartlett introduced Stephens to Waldeck's *Voyage pittoresque et archéologique* before he and Catherwood set out for Central America (*Maya Explorer*, 72–73), a claim which Stephens contradicts, see below. Bartlett may well have introduced Stephens to Waldeck's folio, but this likely occurred *after* Stephens returned to New York from Central America. The full publication details of Waldeck: Jean-Frédéric Waldeck, *Voyage pittoresque et archéologique dans la province d'Yucatan (Amérique centrale), pendant les années 1834 et 1836 par Frédéric de Waldeck, dédié à la mémoire de feu le Vicomte de Kingsborough* (Paris: Bellizard Dufour et Co; London: J. and W. Boone; Bossange Barthès et Lowell, 1838).

10. The plates were printed as, respectively, Plate VI and Plate XVI in Waldeck, *Voyage pittoresque et archéologique*. Waldeck's mode of transport in Plate VI foreshadows the style of mid-nineteenth-century exotic travel exemplified by Flaubert in Egypt who, as evoked by Maxime Du Camp, 'would have preferred to travel stretched out motionless on a divan, watching the landscapes, ruins and cities pass by before him like the canvas of a mechanically-unfolding [moving] panorama'. Roger Cardinal, 'Romantic Travel', in Roy Porter (ed.), *Rewriting the Self: Histories from the Renaissance to the Present* (London: Routledge, 1997), 135–155, 150.

11. Waldeck, *Voyage pittoresque et archéologique*, 93 (*un fruit délicieux, contenant une substance molle d'un goût exquis*). Translations from French are by the author. An example of how Waldeck emphasised the exotic interest of a given location is provided in his portrait of Nicte-tac, a young Lacandon woman bathing in an aqueduct at the site of Palenque, reproduced in Juana Gutiérrez Haces, 'Etnografía y costumbrismo en las imágenes de los viajeros', in *Viajeros europeos del siglo XIX en México*, exhibition catalogue (Mexico City: Fomento Cultural Banamex in collaboration with the Instituto Goethe de México, 1996), 174. Stephens encountered Nicte-tac ('whose portrait Mr. Waldeck had taken to embellish his intended work on Palenque') when he joined a procession at the young woman's funeral in the village of Santo Domingo de Palenque. Stephens observed that the woman's 'sweet face speaking from the grave created an impression which even yet is hardly effaced', Stephens, *Incidents of Travel in Central America*, I, 359–361, 361.

12. R. Tripp Evans, *Romancing the Maya: Mexican Antiquity in the American Imagination 1820–1915* (Austin: University of Texas Press, 2004), 37. Other painters with whom Waldeck may have had contact include Jacques-Louis David and Pierre Proudhon. Howard F. Cline, 'The Apocryphal Early Career of J. F. Waldeck, Pioneer Americanist', *Acta Americana* 5, 4 (1947): 278–300, 290.

13. Waldeck, *Voyage pittoresque et archéologique*, 103. (*Pour parvenir à expliquer cet ensemble bizarre, il faudrait avoir à sa disposition des documents qui me manquent, et avoir étudié dans toutes leurs particularités d'autres édifices de la même nation.*)

14. Waldeck, *Voyage pittoresque et archéologique*, 103. (*L'ensemble de cette façade offre à l'heure de midi un caractère de grandeur dont it serait difficile de donner une idée. Les ombres des corniches et des autres saillies produisent un effet magique et agrandissent à l'œil les lignes du monument. Ce n'est pas sans émotion que je me transporte en idée en face de ces temples abandonnés, et que je me rappelle mes impressions à leur premier aspect.*)

15. John Lloyd Stephens, *Incidents of Travel in Yucatan*, 2 vols. (New York: Harper & Brothers for Henry Bill, 1848 [1843]), I, 306.

16. 'Review of *Incidents of Travel in Yucatan*', *The North American Review*, no. 120, July 1843, 86–108, 90.

17. Norman, B[enjamin] M[oore], *Rambles in Yucatan; or, Notes of Travel through the Peninsula, Including a Visit to the Remarkable Ruins of Chi-chen, Kabah, Zayi, and Uxmal. With Numerous Illustrations*, second edition (New York: J. & H. G. Langley; Philadelphia: Thomas Cowperthwait, & Co.; New Orleans: Norman, Steel, & Co., 1843 [1842]), 198. Nigel Leask, converting Norman's sum into sterling, indicates that the production costs were £30,000. Nigel Leask, *Curiosity and the*

Aesthetics of Travel Writing 1770–1840: 'From an Antique Land' (Oxford: Oxford University Press, 2000), note 21, 305. Norman, who travelled in the Yucatán peninsula between 20 December 1841 and 11 April 1842, opined that Kingsborough's publication 'falls short of its merits'. Norman, *Rambles in Yucatan*, 198. Kingsborough's plates were destroyed after printing; ruined by the cost of publication, Kingsborough died in a debtors' prison in Dublin in 1837.

18. Norman, *Rambles in Yucatan*, 198; Stephens, *Incidents of Travel in Central America*, II, 298. Although no source is provided, von Hagen states that Kingsborough's *Antiquities of Mexico* cost $150 per volume, *Maya Explorer*, 188. Brantz Mayer relates that a copy of Kingsborough was held in the Cabinet of Natural History at the University in Mexico City, and that seventy copies may have been printed. Brantz Mayer, *Mexico As It Was and As It Is: By Brantz Mayer, Secretary of the U.S. Legation to that Country in 1841 and 1842. With Numerous Illustrations on Wood, Engraved by Butler* (New York: J. Winchester, New World Press; London and Paris: Wiley and Putnam, 1844), 91. Mayer also relates that the Cabinet held 'the original drawings of Palenque', referring to Armendáriz's drawings as reworked by Castañeda from Dupaix's investigation of the site in 1808 (see below), a statement confirmed by Stephens in *Incidents of Travel in Central America*, II, 297. William Bullock reported that the Castañeda drawings were earlier in the collection of the Mineria in the city of Mexico. Even though he did not visit Palenque, Bullock observed that 'The drawings of the city of Palenque prove it to have been a magnificent place. The engravings that were taken from them and published in London last year are tolerably correct, as far as they go, but are incomplete. The windows are represented as arched, which is not the case, as the heads are square; but the door is rounded.' Bullock, *Six Months' Residence in Mexico*, 330–331. The work to which Bullock alludes is Antonio del Río, *Description of the Ruins of an Ancient City, Discovered near Palenque, in the Kingdom of Guatemala, in Spanish America: Translated from the Original Manuscript Report of Captain Don Antonio Del Rio: Followed by Teatro Critico Americano; or, a Critical Investigation and Research into the History of the Americans, by Doctor Paul Felix Cabrera, of the City of New Guatemala* (London: Henry Berthoud and Suttaby, Evance and Fox, 1822). For discussion of del Río, see below.

19. David Stuart and George Stuart, *Palenque: Eternal City of the Maya* (London: Thomas & Hudson, 2008), 70; von Hagen, *Frederick Catherwood*, 73.

20. Ramón Ordóñez y Aguiar may have learnt of the ruins from a member of Solís' extended family, Joseph de la Fuente Coronado. Jorge Cañizares-Esguerra, *How to Write the History of the New World: Histories, Epistemologies, and Identities in the Eighteenth-Century Atlantic World* (Stanford: Stanford University Press, 2001), 397–398, note 116, 323. Despite a life-long interest in Palenque, Ordóñez y Aguiar never visited the site, a fact indicative of the epistemological distinction Cañizares-Esguerra draws between European Enlightenment and Baroque historiography which privileged, respectively, 'material evidence over literary sources', see Cañizares-Esguerra, *How to Write the History of the New World*, 343–344, 343.

21. Cañizares-Esguerra, *How to Write the History of the New World*, 323. For details of sketches included in Calderón's report and an example of what would now be regarded as a naïve drawing by Calderón, see Figure 8, Stuart and Stuart, *Palenque*, 37. See also Robert Levere Brunhouse, *In Search of the Maya: The First Archaeologists* (Albuquerque: University of New Mexico Press, 1973), 6–7; Stuart and Stuart, *Palenque*, 36–39.

22. For details of Bernasconi's brief and discussion of the expedition, see Cañizares-Esguerra, *How to Write the History of the New World*, 325–327. Examples of Bernasconi's work are reproduced in Ian Graham, 'A Brief History of Archaeological Exploration', in Peter Schmidt, Mercedes de la Garza, and Enrique Nalda (eds.), *Maya* (Venice: Bompiani-CNCA INAH, 1998), 28–37, 30; in Evans, *Romancing the Maya*, Figure 1.5, 17; and in Stuart and Stuart, *Palenque*, Figure 9A, Figure 9B, and Figure 9C, 38. The reports by Calderón and Bernasconi are held in the Archivo de Indias, Seville. David Drew, *The Lost Chronicles of the Maya Kings* (Berkeley and Los Angeles: University of California Press, 1999), note 23, 420. See also Brunhouse, *In Search of the Maya*, 6–7; Stuart and Stuart, *Palenque*, 37–39. Bernasconi had been engaged to design and build the new capital of Guatemala on neo-classical principles following the 1773 earthquake which devastated the former capital, Antigua Guatemala.

23. The objects sent back to Spain by Antonio del Río are held in the Museo de América, Madrid. Stuart and Stuart, *Palenque*, 40. For a photograph of the objects taken c. 1882, see Stuart and Stuart, *Palenque*, plate I, facing 48.

24. The report, dated 24 June 1787, was published as Antonio del Río, *Description of the Ruins of an Ancient City, Discovered near Palenque*. For discussion of the expedition and damage caused by del Río at the site, see Brunhouse, *In Search of the Maya*, 7–13; Cañizares-Esguerra, *How to Write the History of the New World*, 327–329; Evans, *Romancing the Maya*, 17–22; Stuart and Stuart, *Palenque*, 39–42, 43–48. For discussion of the engravings by Armendáriz, see Stuart and Stuart, *Palenque*, 40–41, 44–45, and for reproduction of some of the engravings, see Stuart and Stuart, *Palenque*, Figure 10A, Figure 10B, Figure 10C, 42, and Figure 12 (upper plate), 44. The engravings by Armendáriz (with del Río's report in Spanish) were first published, in rather indifferent reproduction, in Ricardo Castañeda Paganini, *Las Ruinas de Palenque. Su descubrimiento y primeras exploraciones en el siglo XVIII* (Guatemala City: Ministerio de Educación Pública, 1946), 52–67. Complete sets of drawings by Armendáriz – 'Estampa de Palenque' – are held in the Biblioteca del Palacio Real in Madrid and in the Jay I. Kislak Collection, Library of Congress, Washington, D. C., Stuart and Stuart, *Palenque*, note 18, 250. Armendáriz's first name is usually given as Ricardo, but, on the evidence of having seen his signature, Stuart and Stuart propose that Armendáriz's first name was Ignacio. Stuart and Stuart, *Palenque*, note 19, 250; Brunhouse and Cañizares-Esguerra give Armendáriz's family name as 'Almendáriz'.

25. 'Books published today', *The Literary Gazette*, no. 302, 2 November 1822, 702. Priced at £1–8–0 (£1.40), del Río's report cost a relatively small sum for an antiquarian publication.

26. Stuart and Stuart, *Palenque*, 46–47. Two copies of the publication have been consulted, one at the National Library of Scotland and one at Cambridge University Library; each copy contains seventeen plates. Following Howard F. Cline, most historians propose that a 'Doctor MacQuy' (or, possibly, James MacQueen or James McQueen, the owner of the lithographic firm that printed the plates, who had travelled in the West Indies during the Guatemalan revolution), may have brought the plates to London. Evans, *Romancing the Maya*, note 45, 166; Stuart and Stuart, *Palenque*, note 26, 250. Cline consulted four versions of the 1822 English translation; each version included seventeen plates, but all four had the plates arranged in different order and bound at different places. Cline, 'The Apocryphal Early Career of J. F. Waldeck', note 51, 297. For

further discussion of 'Doctor MacQuy' (also rendered elsewhere as 'Macquy' or 'M'Guy'), see Cline, 'The Apocryphal Early Career of J. F. Waldeck', 298–299.

27. For reproduction of the plate of the tower, see Evans, *Romancing the Maya*, Figure 1.6, 18, and Paganini, *Las Ruinas de Palenque*, Figure 12, 56.

28. The full title of Cabrera's study, written in 1784 according to the 'Prefatory Address' to del Río, reads: *Teatro Critico Americano; or, A Critical Investigation and Research into the History of the Americans*, in del Río, *Description of the Ruins of an Ancient City discovered near Palenque*, 23–128. For discussion of Cabrera's essay, see Brunhouse, *In Search of the Maya*, 13–15 *passim*; for discussion of the debate between Cabrera and Ordóñez y Aguiar regarding the history of Palenque, del Río's report, the Provanza de Votán, and the Popol Vuh, see Cañizares-Esguerra, *How to Write the History of the New World*, 321–322, 329–343.

29. For reproduction of selected engravings after Castañeda, see Stuart and Stuart, *Palenque*, Figure 11, 42, and Figure 12 (lower plate), 44.

30. Dupaix's account was published as *Viajes de Guillermo Dupaix sobre las Antigüedades Mejicanas* in Kingsborough, *Antiquities of Mexico*, Vol. V, and in an abridged English translation (*The Monuments of New Spain*) in Kingsborough, *Antiquities of Mexico*, Vol. VI, Edward King, Lord Kingsborough, *Antiquities of Mexico: Comprising Fac-similes of Ancient Mexican Paintings and Hieroglyphics, preserved in The Royal Libraries of Paris, Berlin, and Dresden; in The Imperial Library of Vienna; in The Vatican Library; in The Borgian Museum at Rome; in The Library of the Institute of Bologna; and in The Bodleian Library at Oxford. Together with The Monuments of New Spain, by M. Dupaix: with their respective scales of measurement and accompanying descriptions. The whole illustrated by many valuable Inedited Manuscripts, by Lord Kingsborough. The Drawings, On Stone, by A[gostino] Aglio*, 7 vols. (London: Robert Havell and Colnaghi, Son, and Co., 1831). Two posthumous volumes of Kingsborough (vols. VIII and IX) were published in London by Henry G. Bohn in 1848. Dupaix's account was subsequently published in French translation in Henri Baradère (ed.), *Antiquités Mexicaines. Relation des trois expéditions du colonel [capitaine] Dupaix, ordonnées en 1807 pour le roi Charles IV, pour la recherche des antiquités du pays, notament celles de Mitla et de Palenque; avec les dessins de Castañeda*, 2 vols. (Paris: Bureau des Antiquités Mexicaines, 1844 [1834–1835]), I. According to Stephens, Baradère cost $800. Stephens, *Incidents of Travel in Central America*, II, 297. Only one copy of Baradère was held in the United States when, in 1840, *The North American Review* published a discussion of antiquities in Mexico, Central America, and South America, a fact which led the writer to observe that the subject of Mesoamerican archaeology was 'a sealed book'. 'Aboriginal Structures', *The North American Review*, Vol. 51, No. 109 (October 1840): 396–433, 397. The final versions of the 127 sheets of drawings which Castañeda completed, including twenty-seven devoted to Palenque, are held in the Biblioteca del Laboratorio de Arte, University of Seville. Stuart and Stuart, *Palenque*, note 22, 250. For further discussion of investigations at Palenque during the colonial period, see Drew, *The Lost Chronicles of the Maya Kings*, 36–54; Cañizares-Esguerra, *How to Write the History of the New World*, 321–345; Evans, *Romancing the Maya*,14–43; Stuart and Stuart, *Palenque*, 35–48, 57–63. For biographical accounts and assessments of archaeological investigations conducted by del Río, Dupaix, Galindo, Waldeck, and Stephens, see Brunhouse, *In Search of the Maya*, 5–112.

31. Evans, *Romancing the Maya*, 26, For reproductions of engravings by Castañeda, see Evans, *Romancing the Maya*, Figure 1.11, 24, Figure 1.14, 28, Figure 1.16, 30, Figure 1.17, 31(for pharaonic and classical influences in representations of the sites of, variously, Tula, Tepeyacan, and Monte Albán), and Figure 1.10, 24, Figure 1.12, 25, Figure 1.13, 27, Figure 1.15, 28, Figure 1.18 (upper plate), 33 (for the sites of, variously, Mitla, Palenque, and San Pablo del Monte).

32. For discussion of the growth of public interest in the site in mid-1830s New York, see Stuart and Stuart, *Palenque*, 61–62.

33. Stephens, *Incidents of Travel in Central America*, II, 305.

34. '[B]efore we set out his [Waldeck's] work on Palenque was announced in Paris'; '[A]t that time we had not seen Dupaix's work', Stephens, *Incidents of Travel in Central America*, II, 298, 305. Elsewhere Stephens states that he travelled to Central America with Waldeck's *Voyage pittoresque et archéologique* in his possession: 'I had this work with me on our last visit', *Incidents of Travel in Yucatan*, I, 176. It is likely that Stephens read Waldeck on his return to New York since Stephens confuses the publication date of Waldeck (1838) with that of Dupaix in Baradère (1834–1835) when he states that Waldeck was published in 1835, *Incidents of Travel in Yucatan*, I, 175. This chronology, however, is contradicted by Victor Wolfgang von Hagen who relates that John R. Bartlett introduced Stephens to Waldeck's *Voyage pittoresque et archéologique* before he departed for Central America. Von Hagen, *Maya Explorer*, 72–73; 'Introduction', John Lloyd Stephens, edited and with an introduction by Victor Wolfgang von Hagen, *Incidents of Travel in Egypt, Arabia Petræa, and the Holy Land* (Mineola: Dover Publications, Inc., 1996 [1970]), xl–xli. Von Hagen's source, John R. Bartlett's private journal held in the John Carter Brown Library, Brown University, has not been consulted.

35. The archaeological site near Tecpán Guatemala is known today as Iximché.

36. The full title of the English translation of Domingo Juarros: *A Statistical and Commercial History of the Kingdom of Guatemala in Spanish America: Containing Important Particulars Relative to its Productions, Manufactures, Customs, &c. &c. &c. With an Account of its Conquest by the Spaniards, and a Narrative of the Principal Events down to the Present Time: From Original Records in the Archives; Actual Observation; and Other Authentic Sources. By Don Domingo Juarros, a Native of New Guatemala. Translated by J. Baily, Lieutenant R. M. Embellished with Two Maps* (London: John Hearne, 1823). John Baily, a British naval officer and engineer, promoted British interests in Central America in the contest between Britain and the United States over territory, resources, and political influence. For further discussion of Baily, see Robert D. Aguirre, *Informal Empire: Mexico and Central America in Victorian Culture* (Minneapolis: University of Minnesota Press, 2005), 76–77.

37. Stephens, *Incidents of Travel in Central America*, I, 132; see also *The Modern Traveller*, IV, 299–300, for a short description of Copán derived from Francisco Antonio de Fuentes y Guzmán as recounted in Juarros, *A Statistical and Commercial History of the Kingdom of Guatemala in Spanish America*. According to Juarros, Fuentes y Guzmán claimed that 'in the year 1700, the Great Circus of Copan, still remained entire. This was a circular space, surrounded by stone pyramids about 6 yards high, and very well constructed; at the bases of these pyramids were figures, both male and female, of very excellent sculpture, which then retained the colours they had been enamelled with; and, what was not less remarkable, the whole of them were habited in the Castilian costume. The same author relates that, at a short distance from the Circus, there was a portal constructed of stone, on the columns of which were the figures of men, likewise represented in Spanish habits, with hose, ruff round the neck, sword, cap, and short cloak. On

entering the gateway there are two fine stone pyramids, moderately large and lofty, from which is suspended a hammock that contains two human figures, one of each sex, clothed in the Indian style. Astonishment is forcibly excited on viewing this structure, because, large as it is, there is no appearance of the component parts being joined together; and, although entirely of stone, and of an enormous weight, it may be put in motion by the slightest impulse of the hand.' Juarros, *A Statistical and Commercial History of the Kingdom of Guatemala in Spanish America*, 56. Stephens summarizes the account of Francisco Antonio de Fuentes y Guzmán as rendered by Juarros (who Stephens refers to as 'Huarros'), and adds dramatically: 'In the middle of this area, elevated above a flight of steps, was the place of sacrifice.' *Incidents of Travel in Central America*, I, 131. For the account on which Juarros drew, see 'Circo Máximo de Copán', Francisco Antonio de Fuentes y Guzmán, *Recordación Florida*, in *Obras Históricas de Francisco Antonio de Fuentes y Guzmán*, edited and with an Introduction by Carmelo Sáenz de Santa María, 3 vols. (Madrid: Atlas, 1969–1972 [1695]), II (1972), *Libro Cuarto, Capítulo XI*, 151–153.

38. Stephens, *Incidents of Travel in Central America*, I, 124, 131–132. Catherwood also states that Galindo had drawn their attention to Copán: 'The first place we attempted to reach was Copan, in the state of Honduras, to which our attention had been drawn by the account of the late Colonel Galindo of the Republic of Central America.' Frederick Catherwood, *Views of Ancient Monuments in Central America Chiapas and Yucatan* (London: F. Catherwood, 1844), 5. The articles referred to by Stephens were Juan Galindo, 'Original Correspondence. Central America. *To the Editor of the Literary Gazette*. Copan, June 18, 1834', published in *The Literary Gazette*, no. 965, 18 July 1835, 456–457, and Juan Galindo, 'The Ruins of Copan, in Central America. Letter from Colonel Galindo. To the Hon. Thomas L. Winthrop, President of the American Antiquarian Society, Boston, Massachusetts. Copan, June 19th, 1835', *Archæologia Americana. Transactions and Collections of the American Antiquarian Society*, 2 (1836), 543–550. Correspondence by Galindo, dated 21 April 1831, from Palenque was sent to the Société de Géographie in Paris, which was published as 'Notions transmises par M. Juan Galindo, officier supérieur de l'Amérique centrale, sur *Palenque* et autres lieux circonvoisins', in Baradère (ed.), *Antiquités Mexicaines*, I, 67–73. Stephens encountered this correspondence on his return from Central America, but does not appear to have known English-language publications by Galindo concerning investigations at Topoxté (Guatemala) and what was probably the site of Yaxchilán (Chiapas), considered briefly below.

39. Stephens, *Incidents of Travel in Central America*, II, 145, 149; *The Modern Traveller*, IV, 270. The account of Tecpán Guatemala by Francisco Antonio de Fuentes y Guzmán as rendered by Juarros: 'To the westward of the city [of Patinamit] there is a little mount that commands it; on this eminence stands a small round building, about 6 feet in height, in the middle of which there is a pedestal formed of a shining substance, resembling glass; but the precise quality of it has not been ascertained. Seated around this building, the judges heard and decided upon the causes brought before them; and here also their sentences were executed. Previous, however, to carrying a sentence into effect, it was necessary to have it confirmed by the oracle: for which purpose, 3 of the judges quitted their seats, and proceeded to a deep ravine, where there was a place of worship, wherein was placed a black transparent stone, of a substance much more valuable than the *chay*; on the surface of this tablet the Deity was supposed to give a representation of the fate that awaited the criminal: if the decision of the judges was approved, the sentence was immediately inflicted; on the contrary, if nothing appeared on the stone, the accused was set at liberty: this oracle was consulted in the affairs of war. The bishop, Francisco Marroquin, having obtained intelligence of this slab, ordered it to be cut square, and consecrated it for the top of the grand altar in the church of Tecpán Guatemala: it is a piece of singular beauty, about half a yard each way.' Juarros, *A Statistical and Commercial History of the Kingdom of Guatemala in Spanish America*, 384. For the source on which Juarros drew, see Francisco Antonio de Fuentes y Guzmán, *Recordación Florida*, in *Obras Históricas de Francisco Antonio de Fuentes y Guzmán*, edited and with an Introduction by Carmelo Sáenz de Santa María, 3 vols. (Madrid: Atlas, 1969–1972 [1695]), I (1969), *Libro Decimoquinto, Capítulo V*, 334–335.

40. Stephens, *Incidents of Travel in Central America*, II, 293. Tabasco, a state bordering the Gulf of Mexico, lies to the north of Chiapas.

41. Stephens, *Incidents of Travel in Central America*, II, 300.

42. 'Some Observations Caused by the recent introduction by Mr. Bullock into England of rare and curious specimens of Mexican Antiquity; intended shortly to be submitted by him to the inspection of the public', *The Classical Journal: for March and June 1824*, Vol. 29, No. 57 (1824): 174–193, 185.

43. 'Sketches of Society, Sights of London, Etc. No. V', *The Literary Gazette*, no. 377, 10 April 1824, 236–237, 237. The exhibition included plaster casts of the Aztec Sacrificial Stone and the Calendar Stone (which had been reproduced as engravings in Humboldt's *Vues de Cordillères* as, respectively, Plate XXI and Plate XXIII), and a large plaster-cast statue of the Aztec goddess of war, Coatlicue. For illustration of the exhibitions, see 5.1 and 5.3, 102 and 110 below.

44. 'Sketches of Society, Sights of London, Etc. No. V', *The Literary Gazette*, no. 377, 10 April 1824, 236–237, 237.

45. Michael P. Costeloe, *William Bullock. Connoisseur and Virtuoso of the Egyptian Hall: Piccadilly to Mexico (1773–1849)* (Bristol: HiPLAM, 2008), 138–143; for further discussion of the exhibitions, particularly the link between cultural inquiry, economic advantage, and laissez-faire capitalism, see Aguirre, *Informal Empire*, 1–11.

46. The panorama of the City of Mexico was exhibited at the Panorama, Leicester Square, between 12 December 1825 and June 1827 (Scott Barnes Wilcox, *The Panorama and Related Exhibitions in London*, MLitt dissertation, University of Edinburgh, 1976, 257), and was subsequently exhibited in New York and in Boston in 1828. *Description of the Panorama of the Superb City of Mexico, and the Surrounding Scenery, Painted on 2700 square feet of Canvas, by Robert Burford, Esq. From Drawings made on the Spot, at the request of the Mexican Government, by Mr. W. Bullock, Jr. Now open for Public Inspection at the Rotunda, New-York. New-York: Printed by E. Conrad, No. 11 Frankfort-St. 1828. Price, one shilling*; *Description of the Panorama of the Superb City of Mexico, and the Surrounding Scenery, Painted on 2700 square feet of Canvas, by Robert Burford, Esq. From Drawings made on the Spot, at the request of the Mexican Government, by Mr. W. Bullock, Jr. Now open for Public Inspection opposite the Atheneum, Pearl Street, Boston. Printed by J. H. Eastburn, No. 60, Congress-St. 1828. Price 12½ cents*. I thank Roberto L. Mayer for generously giving me access to his private collection.

47. The clock which stands between the two towers at the centre of the south facade of the cathedral (represented by the motif of a wall depicted in the extreme lower right corner of the upper panel complemented by a similar motif in the extreme lower left corner of the lower panel) implies spatial contiguity between

the two stations in the orientation views. Contiguity, in this instance, is implied, but, since the panorama was drawn from two different towers, spatial contiguity is illusory.

48. The view in the upper panel ranges from Colegio de las Vizcainas (in the southwest part of the city) to Iglesia San Pedro y San Pablo in the northeast part of the city.

49. The view in the lower panel ranges from Iglesia Nuestra Signora de Loreto (in the northeast part of the city) to Iglesia San Agustín and Iglesia Regina Coelli in the southwest part of the city.

50. Bullock, *Six Months' Residence and Travels in Mexico*, 54.

51. David Hockney has proposed that some artists used a concave mirror to 'collage' various elements together to make a larger painting. David Hockney, *Secret Knowledge: Rediscovering the Lost Techniques of the Old Masters*, new and expanded edition (New York: Viking Studio, 2006 [2000]), 103, 113. On the evidence of Bullock Jr.'s panorama, we may propose that the artist may have used a convex mirror in conjunction with the camera lucida to depict a field of view that was partially obscured.

52. '*Six Months in Mexico*. By William Bullock', *The Literary Gazette*, no. 387, 19 June 1824, 390–392, 390.

53. 'Bullock's Six Months in Mexico', *The Literary Gazette*, no. 389, 3 July 1824, 422–423, 422. Bullock's travel account, published in a print-run double that typical of the period, was quickly translated into French, German, and Dutch; a second English edition appeared in 1825. Aguirre, *Informal Empire*, 2; Costeloe, *William Bullock*, 143.

54. *The Literary Gazette*, 10 January 1824, 25, quoted in Leask, *Curiosity and the Aesthetics of Travel Writing 1770–1840*, 302. The 'flood-gates' not only engulfed Mexico, but also the federated states of Central America after Guatemala gained independence from Spain in 1822 since Guatemala was annexed by Mexico. The following year, Guatemala reasserted its independence, and led the formation of the United Provinces of Central America which included territory in the present-day states of Guatemala, El Salvador, Honduras, Nicaragua, and Costa Rica. Chiapas was ceded to the Mexican federation in 1824.

55. Costeloe, *William Bullock*, 142–143.

56. Bullock, *Six Months' Residence and Travels in Mexico*, 497–498. For further discussion of the opportunities Mexico represented for investors in the immediate post-independence period, see Aguirre, *Informal Empire*, 19–26. The promise of similar advantages in Guatemala spurred the English translation of Juarros' *Compendio de la historia de la ciudad de Guatemala*: 'As Spanish America will probably, in a short time, open a most extensive field for the employment of British capital and British industry, and ultimately prove an inexhaustible source of advantage and commerce; every work, how humble soever its pretensions may be, that, upon good authority, can furnish something in addition to the very slender stock of information we already possess, of any portion of that interesting Country, will, perhaps, be acceptable to the Public.' 'Preface', Juarros, *A Statistical and Commercial History of the Kingdom of Guatemala in Spanish America*, v.

57. *The Modern Traveller*, I, 160. By the end of 1824, the United States 'had already received ministers plenipotentiary from Mexico, Guatimala [*sic*], Colombia, and Buenos Ayres' whilst Britain considered recognising the Argentine Confederation and Chile, *The Modern Traveller*, I, 160.

58. *The Modern Traveller*, IV, 157–158. *The Modern Traveller* draws substantially on Baily's 1823 translation of Juarros in the latter part of the description: 'St. Domingo Palenque a village in the province of Tzendales, on the border of the intendancies of Ciudad Real de Chiapa and Yucatan. It is the head of a curacy; in a wild and salubrious climate, but very thinly inhabited , and now celebrated from having within its jurisdiction the vestiges of a very opulent city, which has been named Ciudad del Palenque; doubtless, formerly the capital of an empire whose history no longer exists. This metropolis, – like another Herculaneum, not indeed overwhelmed by the torrent of another Vesuvius, but concealed for ages in the midst of a vast desert, – remained unknown until the middle of the eighteenth century, when some Spaniards having penetrated the dreary solitude, found themselves, to their great astonishment, within sight of the remains of what once had been a superb city, of six leagues in circumference ...' Juarros, *A Statistical and Commercial History of the Kingdom of Guatemala in Spanish America*, 18–19.

59. Brunhouse emphasises that del Río couched his discussion of the origins of the people who built Palenque in conjectural terms. Brunhouse, *In Search of the Maya*, 12–13.

60. *The Modern Traveller*, IV, 163. The structure was characterised as 'a style of architecture strongly resembling the Gothic', *The Modern Traveller*, IV, 160. The passage quoted here draws closely on del Río (1822): 'I determined on proceeding to one of the buildings, situated on a [*sic*] eminence to the south of about forty yards in height. This edifice forming a parallelogram, resembled the first in its style of architecture, it has square pillars, an exterior gallery, and a saloon twenty yards long by three and a half broad, embellished with a frontispiece on which are described female figures with children in their arms, all of the natural size [i.e., life-size], executed in stucco medio reliefs ...' Del Río, *Description of the Ruins of an Ancient City, Discovered near Palenque*, 16.

61. In discussing Palenque, *The Modern Traveller*, IV, employs the following architectural terms (with page references in parentheses): 'court' (158, 161), 'Gothic' (160), 'pillar(s)' (160, 162, 163, 168),'portico' (160), 'bases or pedestals' (160), 'architrave' (161), 'stucco' (161, 164), 'medallion(s)' (161), 'in the form of a Greek cross' and 'two Greek crosses' (161), 'gallery' (162, 163, 164), 'relievos' (162), 'cupola' (162), 'oratory(ies)' (162, 164, 165), 'apartment(s)' (162), 'bas-relief(s)' (162, 163, 164, 165), 'parallelogram' (163), 'saloon' (163, 164), 'medio-relievos' (163), 'pyramid(s)' and 'pyramidal' (165, 168, 169), 'mosques' (168), 'sepulchral' (168), and 'Cyclopean' (168).

62. 'It might be inferred that this people had some analogy to, and intercourse with the Romans, from a similarity in the choice of situation as well as a subterranean stone aqueduct of great solidity and durability, which passes under the largest building. / I do not take upon myself to assert that these conquerors did actually land in this country; but, there is reasonable ground for hazarding a conjecture that some of the inhabitants of that polished nation did visit these regions; and that, from such intercourse, the natives might have imbibed, during their stay, an idea of the arts, as a reward for their hospitality.' Del Río, *Description of the Ruins of an Ancient City, Discovered near Palenque*, 5.

63. Del Río, *Description of the Ruins of an Ancient City, Discovered near Palenque*, 19.

64. Juarros, *A Statistical and Commercial History of the Kingdom of Guatemala in Spanish America*, 19: 'The hieroglyphics, symbols, and emblems, which have been discovered in the temples, bear so strong a resemblance to those of the Egyptians, as to encourage the supposition that a colony of that nation may have founded the city of Palenque, or Culhuacan', rendered in *The Modern Traveller* as 'The hieroglyphs and emblems found here [Palenque] are represented by the learned historian as bearing so strong a resemblance to those of the Egyptians, that he is strongly inclined to ascribe them to a colony of that nation!', *The Modern Traveller*, IV, 158. Exclamation mark in original. As *The Literary Gazette* ironically observed in its review of del Río and Cabrera: 'If our epitome has explained the original peopling of America to our readers, it will be an unexpected pleasure to us, as we candidly acknowledge that it has not produced that degree of knowledge in our own minds.' *The Literary Gazette*, no. 303, 9 November 1822, 705.

65. *The Modern Traveller*, IV, 168. The state of Oaxaca lies to the west of Chiapas.

66. *The Literary Gazette* observed that the ruins were 'said to resemble Roman Ruins; and the remains of an aqueduct confirms our author in opinion, that the new world was not unknown to these masters of the old', *The Literary Gazette*, no. 303, 9 November 1822, 705.

67. Galindo, as observed earlier (see note 38 above), conducted investigations at Palenque (Chiapas), Topoxté (Guatemala), and Copán (Honduras) at a time when all three states were part of the Central American Federation. In all likelihood, Galindo also visited the ruins of Yaxchilán (known at the time as Menché) on the Mexican bank of the Usumacinta, the river which formed (as it does today) the border between Guatemala and Mexico. Regarding the latter site, Galindo observed that 'Near these falls, and within an extensive cave on the left bank, are some extraordinary and remarkable ruins; and somewhat lower down the stream there is a remarkable monumental stone, with characters.' Juan Galindo, 'Description of the River Usumasinta [*sic*], in Guatemala, communicated by Colonel Don Juan Galindo, of the Central America Service, Corresponding Member of the Royal Geographical Society. Dated Flores, on Lake Peten, 12th March, 1832. Read 26th Nov. 1832', *The Journal of the Royal Geographical Society of London*, 3 (dated 1833; published 1834), 59–64.

68. The Walker-Caddy expedition arrived at the site of Palenque on 5 February 1840, and remained for fourteen days. David M. Pendergast (ed.), *Palenque: The Walker-Caddy Expedition to the Ancient Maya City, 1839–1840* (Norman: University of Oklahoma Press, 1967), 174, 178. Stephens and Catherwood investigated the site between 13 May and 1 June 1840. Stephens, *Incidents of Travel in Central America*, II, 289, 336.

69. In May 1838, Patrick Walker assumed duties as keeper of records and clerk of courts *pro tempore* in British Honduras, before being appointed one of the judges of the supreme court in June. In January the following year, Walker was appointed a member of the general staff of the Prince Regent's Royal Honduras Militia in which he was given the rank of major in February 1839, serving as aide-de-camp to Colonel Alexander MacDonald, the superintendent of the territory. Walker was appointed colonial secretary in mid-1839, a position second in importance to that of Colonel MacDonald. Pendergast (ed.), *Palenque*, 25–28 *passim*.

70. John Caddy enrolled at the Royal Military Academy in Woolwich in 1816, where he trained as an engineer and artillery officer, receiving instruction in the drawing and surveying of landscape. On completing his training, Caddy undertook tours of duty in the West Indies before being posted to the Royal Artillery garrison in British Honduras in December 1838. Pendergast (ed.), *Palenque*, 9–17 *passim*. A prospect view of Belize Town by Caddy, probably drawn with the aid of a camera lucida, is reproduced as Plate 3 in Pendergast (ed.), *Palenque*, ff. 32; a further prospect view of the town of Flores from the shore of Lago Petén Itzá, also probably drawn with the aid of a camera lucida, is reproduced as Plate 4. The whereabouts of these drawings is not known. Caddy's drawings of Palenque survive as black and white photographs, which make it difficult to discuss his work at Palenque in detail. Marshall H. Saville, an archaeologist and member of staff at the Museum of the American Indian, New York, obtained Caddy's plates and a description of the ruins of Palenque from Caddy's granddaughter, Alice Caddy (Mrs. Ben Lucien Burman), and arranged for the plates and paper to be photographed. When nothing came of the plans to publish Caddy's work, the plates and the description of the ruins were returned to the Caddy family, and were destroyed in a warehouse fire in Ottawa, Canada, in 1942. Pendergast (ed.), *Palenque*, x, 200. Brief accounts of the Walker-Caddy expedition are available in Drew, *The Lost Chronicles of the Maya Kings*, 57, 59–60, and Aguirre, *Informal Empire*, 75–76.

71. Ian Graham, 'Juan Galindo, Enthusiast', *Estudios de Cultura Maya*, 3 (1963): 11–35, 12.

72. In the intervening period, Galindo may have worked on his uncle's sugar plantation in Jamaica (who had settled in the West Indies in 1816), and may also have participated in the liberation struggle in Chile. After the Liberals brought the civil war in Central America to a close in April 1829, Galindo obtained naturalization papers from the federal Congress, and established his reputation as a partisan under the patronage of the Honduran president, General Francisco Morazán, and Mariano Gálvez, the Guatemalan chief of state. After fighting for the Central American Federation, which broke up in turmoil and violence towards the end of 1839 (Guatemala, Costa Rica, and Nicaragua banded together against the remnants of the federal government maintained by El Salvador, Quetzaltenango (which had seceded from Guatemala), and occupied Honduras), Galindo was shot in a skirmish in Honduras after defeat at the Hacienda del Potrero in January 1840. Further biographical information relating to Galindo may be found in William J[oyce] Griffith, 'Juan Galindo, Central American chauvinist', *Hispanic American Historical Review* 40, 1 (February 1960): 25–52, 25–28 *passim*; Ian Graham, 'Juan Galindo, Enthusiast', 16–22 *passim*; Brunhouse, *In Search of the Maya*, 32–44 *passim*, 47–49; Drew, *The Lost Chronicles of the Maya Kings*, 50–54 *passim*. For discussion of the disdain for the indigene which Galindo expressed in some publications, see Aguirre, *Informal Empire*, 73, 74.

73. Juan Galindo, 'Original Correspondence. To the Editor, &c. Ruins of Palenque. April 26, 1831', published in *The Literary Gazette*, no. 769, 15 October 1831, 665–666. Correspondence dated 21 April 1831 was also sent to the Société de Géographie, and was published as 'Notions transmises par M. Juan Galindo, officier supérieur de l'Amérique centrale, sur *Palenque* et autres lieux circonvoisins', in Baradère (ed.), *Antiquités Mexicaines*, I, 67–73. Galindo also published a short notice in July 1832 in the French-language newspaper in New York, *Le Courrier des États-Unis*. Graham, 'Juan Galindo, Enthusiast', 22. In subsequent correspondence with *The Literary Gazette*, Galindo observed that at the time he visited Palenque, he had not read del Rió's account. Juan Galindo,

'Original Correspondence. Central America. *To the Editor of the Literary Gazette*, Copan, June 18, 1834', published in *The Literary Gazette*, no. 965, 18 July 1835, 456–457, 456. This article demonstrates the disdain for the indigene that Galindo, on occasion, expressed in his writing.

74. The journal observed that it was indebted to the Governor of Petén 'for this interesting account of a place utterly unknown to European geography and antiquities', an observation that was reiterated in the 'Literary Novelties' column which characterised the department as 'a region so little explored, as hardly be known to the European reader'. Galindo, 'Original Correspondence. To the Editor, &c. Ruins of Palenque. April 26, 1831', published in *The Literary Gazette*, no. 769, 15 October 1831, 665; 'Literary Novelties' column, *The Literary Gazette*, no. 769, 15 October 1831, 670. A week later, these claims had to be corrected: 'We find that we were wrong in stating that this place was utterly unknown to a European geography. It appears that, as far back as 1787, Captain Antonio Del Rio addressed a report to the King of Spain on the existence of these ruins, in the country then designated by the name of Casas de Piedras [*houses of stone*]; and in this report some of the facts are mentioned which are contained in our correspondent's notice, more particularly the very remarkable occurrence of bas-reliefs representing the adoration of the emblem of Christianity, and which are exhibited in Del Rio´s work, subsequently translated and published in this country.' 'Palenque', 'Arts and Sciences' column, *The Literary Gazette*, no. 770, 22 October 1831, 683.

75. Galindo, 'Description of the River Usumasinta [*sic*], in Guatemala', *The Journal of the Royal Geographical Society of London*, 3 (dated 1833; published 1834): 59–64.

76. Graham, 'Juan Galindo, Enthusiast', 18, 19. For an assessment of Galindo's investigations at Copán, see Graham, 'Juan Galindo, Enthusiast', 26–27, 31–32; for a summary of Galindo's unpublished drawings relating to the site, see 'Appendix B: Table of figures accompanying Galindo's report on Copán', Graham, 'Juan Galindo, Enthusiast', 35. Galindo's collection of unpublished papers and drawings held in the Société de Géographie loan, Bibliothèque Nationale, Paris, has not been consulted. For reproduction of Galindo's *Las Ventanas*, a watercolour of the cliff that forms the boundary of the site overlooking the Copán river, see Graham, 'A Brief History of Archaeological Exploration', in Schmidt, de la Garza, and Enrique Nalda (eds.), *Maya*, 31.

77. This procedure was also adopted in describing the Maya site of Topoxté in the department of Petén where a 'tower' was described as: 'forty-five feet high, consisting of five stories, (each receding on all sides two feet,) and having no doors or windows, excepting the upper story: the base is an equilateral rectangle twenty-two yards each way, and a staircase seven yards wide, with steps but four inches high, leads sloping from the west to the top of the Tower; the upper story consisting of three unroofed rooms with low apertures, under which the spectator crawls to enter: though all sounds hollow beneath, yet there is no apparent entrance into the lower stories. I can perceive no similarity between this building and the buildings of Palenque, except that both are of stone; but the stones of which the Tower is constructed are somewhat larger; I should consider it more modern than Palenque, since part of the door-beams and other wood work still remains.' 'XXIII. A short Account of some Antiquities discovered in the District of Peten, in Central America; in a Letter from Lieutenant-Colonel Juan Galindo, Governor of Peten, addressed to Nicholas Carlisle, Esq. F. R. S., Secretary, Read 7th June, 1832. Government House, Flores, October 28, 1831', *Archaeologia: or Miscellaneous Tracts Relating to Antiquity*, 25 (1834): 570–571. The site of Topoxté, on a small island in Laguna Yaxhá, and a 'tower' at the site are considered in 'Notions transmises par M. Juan Galindo', in Baradère (ed.), *Antiquités Mexicaines*, I, 67–73, 68.

78. Galindo, 'Original Correspondence. To the Editor, &c. Ruins of Palenque. April 26, 1831', published in *The Literary Gazette*, no. 769, 15 October 1831, 665, an observation that was also repeated in 'Notions transmises par M. Juan Galindo', in Baradère (ed.), *Antiquités Mexicaines*, I, 67–73, 69 (*On peut bien remarquer que ces architectes évitaient la symétrie, non par ignorance, mais avec préméditation.*) In the course of the article, Galindo reiterates many of the observations he made about Palenque in *The Literary Gazette*: the Palace is considered in 'Notions transmises par M. Juan Galindo', in Baradère (ed.), *Antiquités Mexicaines*, I, 70–71, and the Temple of the Inscriptions and the Temple of the Cross are also considered in 'Notions transmises par M. Juan Galindo', in Baradère (ed.), *Antiquités Mexicaines*, I, 71.

79. Galindo, 'Original Correspondence. To the Editor, &c. Ruins of Palenque. April 26, 1831', published in *The Literary Gazette*, no. 769, 15 October 1831, 666. Language communities amongst the Maya are briefly considered in 'Notions transmises par M. Juan Galindo', in Baradère (ed.), *Antiquités Mexicaines*, I, 72; comparisons between representations of the indigene in the bas-reliefs at Palenque and the present-day indigenous population of the region are also briefly considered in 'Notions transmises par M. Juan Galindo', in Baradère (ed.), *Antiquités Mexicaines* (*La physionomie des figures d'hommes sur les alto-relievos indique qu'ils étaient d'une race non différente des Indiens modernes …*), I, 72.

80. Galindo, 'Original Correspondence. Central America. *To the Editor of the Literary Gazette*, Copan, June 18, 1834', published in *The Literary Gazette*, no. 965, 18 July 1835, 456.

81. Galindo, 'Original Correspondence. Central America. *To the Editor of the Literary Gazette*, Copan, June 18, 1834', published in *The Literary Gazette*, 965, 18 July 1835, 456. In the United States, Galindo's account appeared with minor modification: 'Through a gallery, scarcely four feet high and two and a half broad, one can crawl from this square through a more elevated part of the temple overhanging the river, and have from the face of the precipice an interesting view. / Among many excavations, I have made one at the point where this gallery comes out into the square. I first opened into the entrance of the gallery itself, and digging lower down I broke into a sepulchral vault, the floor of which is twelve feet below the level of the square. It is more than six feet high, ten feet long, and five and a half broad, and lies due north and south, according to the compass, which here varies nine degrees east; it has two niches on each side, and both these and the floor of the vault, were full of red earthenware dishes and pots. I found more than fifty, many of them full of human bones packed with lime; …'. Juan Galindo, 'The Ruins of Copan, in Central America. Letter from Colonel Galindo. To the Hon. Thomas L. Winthrop, President of the American Antiquarian Society, Boston, Massachusetts. Copan, June 19th, 1835', *Archæologia Americana. Transactions and Collections of the American Antiquarian Society*, 2 (1836), 543–550, 547.

82. Pendergast (ed.), *Palenque*, 176. Walker's report of the expedition is held in the Colonial Office, London. Pendergast (ed.), *Palenque*, 208.

83. Pendergast (ed.), *Palenque*, 177. Elsewhere in the report, Walker observes: 'Though little skilled in the science of civil architecture[,] my first but strong

impression regarding these ruins was, that they were of Egypto-Indian origin …', Pendergast (ed.), *Palenque*, 175.

84. Pendergast (ed.), *Palenque*, Plate 10, facing 81.

85. Pendergast (ed.), *Palenque*, 131.

86. Pendergast (ed.), *Palenque*, Plate 13, facing 128. Caddy goes on to observe that part of the building 'is of Saracenic form', and notes that 'it does not appear that the builders were acquainted with the principles of an arch', Pendergast (ed.), *Palenque*, 126. Although the corbelled arch is common in Maya architecture, it is generally accepted that the principle of the cornerstone was not known to the Maya.

87. Pendergast (ed.), *Palenque*, 130.

88. For example, the letterpress for Plate I (*Of a Doric Portico at Athens*) in James Stuart and Nicholas Revett, *The Antiquities of Athens* (1762): 'A View of the Portico in its present State. Through the middle Intercolumniation is seen the Minaret or Steeple of the principal *Moschéa*. It is called by the Turks the *Jawm*, or *Jawmy*, which answers to our Cathedral Church; to these there always belongs a School or College, where those who design to officiate in the *Moschéas*, are instructed in the Mohammedan Ritual, by certain Professors who are held in high Esteem among the Turks, and are called *Mudereeses*, or Lecturers. On the Right Hand is the Church called *tou hagiou Soteros*, or St. Saviour's, which is now deserted and in a ruinous Condition. The Turkish Government makes a great Difficulty of permitting any church to be repaired, and the Greeks are generally obliged to pay very dear for such Permission whenever it is granted. On the Left Hand, in the Wall of the House contiguous to the Portico, and partly in the Light Space, over the Crupper of the more distant Horse's Saddle, is that Jamb of the Door-case, on which is inscribed the Edict of Adrian relating to the Sale of Oils. The Gate out of which a Greek Servant is coming with a Fusil in his Hand, belongs to the House in which Monsieur Etienne Leouson the French Consul lives; who is here introduced sitting between two Gentlemen, one a Turk, and the other a Greek, for the Sake of exhibiting the different Habits of this Country. The Fountain, on the Fore-Ground of the View, was rebuilt at the Expence [*sic*] of the French Consul, and on it are inscribed E. L. the initial Letters of his Name, with the Date of the Year in which it was finished: And although the Characters of Persons are by no Means the Subject of this Book, yet to pass in Silence the disinterested Hospitality with which this Gentleman receives all Strangers, would argue a Want of Sensibility: He is indeed an uncommon Instance of modest Virtue, and universal Benevolence, without Weakness or Ostentation. / 'To erect or repair a public Fountain, is esteemed by the Turks a Work of great Merit; and as the present Volume affords no other Occasion for representing one, the Liberty has been taken of turning this Fountain somewhat from its real Position, so as to give the Reader a View of this Kind of Turkish Fabrick [*sic*]: It stands however exactly on the Spot here assigned to it, and its Form is faithfully represented. The Figures by it are a common Turk, and an ordinary Servant Maid.' James Stuart and Nicholas Revett, *The Antiquities of Athens. Measured and Delineated by James Stuart F.R.S. and F.S.A. and Nicholas Revett. Painters and Architects,* 3 vols. (London: John Haberkorn, 1762–1794), I (1762), 3. For reproduction of the accompanying plate, see James Stuart, 'Gate of Athene Archegetis', Figure 2.25, in Bruce Bedford, *Dilettanti: The Antic and the Antique in Eighteenth-Century England* (Los Angeles: The J. Paul Getty Museum and The Getty Research Institute, 2008), 66.

89. The Minute Book of the Society of Antiquaries, 13 January 1842, quoted in Pendergast (ed.), *Palenque*, 193.

90. 'Central America, Ancient and Modern', *The Dublin University Magazine, A Literary and Political Journal*, Vol. 19, No. 110 (February 1842): 189–200, 189.

91. 'Review of *Incidents of Travel in Central America, Chiapas, and Yucatan*', *The North American Review*, Vol. 53, No. 113 (October 1841): 479–506, 505; 'Review of *Incidents of Travel in Yucatan*', *The North American Review*, no. 120 (July 1843): 86–108, 86–87.

92. Review of *Incidents of Travel in Central America, The Athenaeum Journal of Literature, Science, and the Fine Arts*, 31 July 1841, 574–577, 574.

93. '*Incidents of Travel in Central America, Chiapas, and Yucatan. By John L. Stephens*', *The Quarterly Review* Vol. 69, No. 137 (March 1842): 52–91, 67. Emphasis in original.

94. '*Incidents of Travel in Yucatan*. By John L. Stephens', *The Monthly Review, New and Improved Series*, Vol. 1, No. 4 (April 1843): 542–550, 542. Note: the title page of this issue incorrectly gives the year of publication of the journal as 1842.

95. 'Stephens's Travels in Yucatan', *The Dublin University Magazine, A Literary and Political Journal*. Vol. 22, No. 128 (August 1843): 204–222, respectively 222, 209, 222. The first page of the review is printed as 304. Criticism of Stephens' writing style may be found in *The Edinburgh Review*, where a reviewer opined that Stephens was 'far from precise and clear'. 'Review of *Incidents of Travel in Central America, Chiapas, and Yucatan', The Edinburgh Review or Critical Journal*, Vol. 75, No. 152 (April–July 1842): 397–421, 411. *The Quarterly Review* commented on Stephens' use of neologism, but also observed that his writing was 'correct, clear, and concise, and singularly free from American peculiarities', '*Incidents of Travel in Central America, Chiapas, and Yucatan*. By John L. Stephens', *The Quarterly Review* Vol. 69, No. 137 (March 1842): 52–91, note, 52.

96. 'Review of *Incidents of Travel in Central America, Chiapas, and Yucatan*', *The North American Review*, Vol. 53, No. 113 (October 1841): 479–506, 503.

97. '*Incidents of Travel in Yucatan*. By John L. Stephens', *The Monthly Review, New and Improved Series Vol.* 1, No. 4 (April 1843): 542–550, 547.

98. *The Correspondence of William Hickling Prescott 1833–47*, transcribed and edited by Roger Wolcott (Cambridge, MA, 1925), 239, quoted in Nigel Leask, '"The Ghost in Chapultepec": Fanny Calderón de la Barca, William Prescott and Nineteenth-Century Mexican Travel Accounts', in *Voyages and Visions: Towards a Cultural History of Travel*, edited by Jás Elsner and Joan-Pau Rubiés (London: Reaktion Books, 1999), 189–209, 203.

99. Review of *Incidents of Travel in Central America, The Athenaeum Journal of Literature, Science, and the Fine Arts*, 31 July 1841, 574–577, 576.

100. 'Mr. Stephens [*sic*] New Work – Antiquities of Central America', *Chambers's Edinburgh Journal. New Series*, no. 502, 11 September 1841, 266–267, 267.

101. '*Incidents of Travel in Central America, Chiapas, and Yucatan. By John L. Stephens*', *The Quarterly Review*, Vol. 69, No. 137 (March 1842): 52–91, note, 65–66. The quotation, abridged and amended, is from Stephens, *Incidents of Travel in Central America*, I, 137–138, where the passage reads: 'I will only remark that, from the beginning, our great object and effort was to procure true copies of the originals, adding nothing for effect as pictures. Mr. Catherwood made the outline of all the drawings with the camera lucida, and divided his paper into sections, so as to preserve the utmost accuracy of proportion. The engravings were made with

the same regard to truth, the originals being also in the hands of the engraver; and I consider it proper to mention that a portion of them, of which the frontispiece was one, were sent to London, and executed by engravers on wood whose names stand among the very first in England; yet, though done with exquisite skill, and most effective as pictures, they failed in giving the true character and expression of the originals; and, at some considerable loss both of time and money, were all thrown aside, and re-engraved on steel. Proofs of every plate were given to Mr. Catherwood, who made such corrections as were necessary; and, in my opinion, they are as true copies as can be presented; and, except the stones themselves, the reader cannot have better materials for speculation and study.'

102. 'Central America, Ancient and Modern', *The Dublin University Magazine, A Literary and Political Journal*, Vol. 19, No. 110 (February 1842): 189–200, 193.
103. 'Review of *Incidents of Travel in Central America, Chiapas, and Yucatan*', *The Edinburgh Review, or Critical Journal*, Vol. 75, No. 152 (April–July 1842): 397–421, 400.
104. 'Aboriginal Structures', *The North American Review*, Vol. 51, No. 109 (1840): 396–433, 429.
105. 'Review of *Incidents of Travel in Yucatan*', *The North American Review*, no. 120 (July 1843): 86–108, 88. Regarding the relation between text and image, a rather different opinion was expressed in *Chambers's Edinburgh Journal*: 'Trusting considerably to the plates, Mr Stephens, it unfortunately happens, abstains, for the most part, from long and specific verbal descriptions.' 'Mr. Stephens [*sic*] New Work – Antiquities of Central America', *Chambers's Edinburgh Journal. New Series*, no. 502, 11 September 1841, 266–267, 267.
106. *The New York World*, 4 July 1841, quoted in Stuart and Stuart, *Palenque*, 71.

Notes to Chapter Four

1. John Lloyd Stephens, *Incidents of Travel in Central America, Chiapas, and Yacatan*, 2 vols. (New York: Harper & Brothers; London: John Murray, 1841), II, 456.
2. The first meeting of the Society was held on 19 November 1842. 'Preface', *Transactions of the American Ethnological Society*, vol. 1 (New York: Bartlett & Welford; London: Wiley & Putnam, 1845), ix–x, ix. For related discussion of the early interests of the American Antiquarian Society, founded in Worcester, Massachusetts, in 1812, see R. Tripp Evans, *Romancing the Maya: Mexican Antiquity in the American Imagination 1820–1915* (Austin: University of Texas Press, 2004), 46–48.
3. 'Preface', *Transactions of the American Ethnological Society*, vol. 1, ix.
4. Edward Robinson, regarded as the founder of Palestinian archaeology, was the author of *Researches in Biblical Palestine, Mount Sinai, and Arabia Petræa: A Journal of Travels in the Year 1838*, 3 vols. (London: John Murray, 1841); Henry R. Schoolcraft contributed a short article, 'The Red Hand', to the Appendix in John Lloyd Stephens, *Incidents of Travel in Yucatan*, 2 vols. (New York: Harper & Brothers for Henry Bill, 1848 [1843]), II, 476–478.
5. Albert Gallatin, 'Notes on the Semi-Civilized Nations of Mexico, Yucatan, and Central America', *Transactions of the American Ethnological Society*, vol. 1 (1845), 1–352.
6. Juan Pío Pérez contributed an article, 'Ancient Chronology of Yucatan; or, a true exposition of the method used by the Indians for computing time' and 'An Almanac, adjusted according to the chronological calculation of the ancient Indians of Yucatan, for the years 1841 and 1842' to the Appendix in Stephens, *Incidents of Travel in Yucatan*, I, 434–448, 448–459; a commentary to 'A Manuscript written in the Maya language, treating of the principal epochs of the history of the peninsula of Yucatan before the Conquest' was also published in the Appendix, *Incidents of Travel in Yucatan*, II, 465–469.
7. Frederick Catherwood, 'Account of the Punico-Libyan Monument at Dugga [*sic*]', and Frederick Catherwood, 'The Remains of an Ancient Structure at Bless, in the southern part of the Regency of Tunis. (Visited in May, 1832.)', *Transactions of the American Ethnological Society*, vol. 1 (1845), 475–488, 489–491.
8. 'Antiquities of Central America', presented to the Royal Institute of British Architects, 19 February 1844. A report of the meeting, chaired by Thomas Leverton Donaldson, the founder and Vice-President of Royal Institute of British Architects, was published in London, New York, and Paris in 'Proceedings of Scientific Societies. Royal Institute of British Architects', *The Civil Engineer and Architect's Journal, Scientific and Railway Gazette*, 7 (24 February 1844): 92–94. The early part of the paper presents some of the material published in Frederick Catherwood, *Views of Ancient Monuments in Central America Chiapas and Yucatan* (London: F. Catherwood, 1844) including a discussion of the Maya corbelled arch, and a summary of questions posed by members and Catherwood's responses. The extent to which the terms *scientific* and *scientific societies* were, in 1844, a relatively recent coinage may be gauged from a review of Mary Somerville's *On the Connexion of the Physical Sciences*, which comments on the lack of an appropriate collective noun to designate investigators of the material world: 'A curious illustration of this result may be observed in the want of any name by which we can designate students of the knowledge of the material world collectively. We are informed that this difficulty was felt very oppressive by the members of the British Association for the Advancement of Science, at their meetings at York, Oxford, and Cambridge, in the last three summers. There was no general term by which these gentlemen could describe themselves with reference to their pursuits. *Philosophers* was felt too wide and too lofty a term, and was very properly forbidden them by Mr. Coleridge, both in his capacity of philologer and metaphysician; *savans* was rather assuming, besides being French instead of English; some ingenious gentleman proposed that, by analogy with *artist*, they might form *scientist*, and added that there could be no scruple in making free with this termination when we have such words as *socialist*, *economist*, and *atheist* – but this was not generally palatable; others attempted to translate the term by which members of similar associations in Germany have described themselves, but it was not easy to discover an English equivalent for *natur-forscher*[*sic*].' 'Mrs. Somerville, "On the Connexion of the Physical Sciences"', *The Quarterly Review* 51 (1834): 54–68, 59. A copy of Somerville's *On the Connexion of the Physical Sciences* was held in Catherwood's private library, see *Catalogue of a Portion of the Library of the Late Frederic* [*sic*] *Catherwood, Esq. Hon Member of the Royal Institute of British Architects, Author of Views and Monuments in Central America etc. Also a Portion of the Library of an Eminent Surgeon, Retiring from Practice ..., Which will be Sold by Auction by Messrs. Puttick and Simpson, Auctioneers of Literary Property, at their Great Room, 191, Piccadilly, on Monday, December 1st, 1856, and five following days at one o'clock most punctually*, paginated printed sale catalogue, item #840 (36).

9. For discussion of the project, initially envisaged as a work to be called *The American Antiquities*, containing between 100 and 120 engravings with contributions from Gallatin, John Gardner Wilkinson (an Honorary Member of the American Ethnological Society), Alexander von Humboldt, William H. Prescott, and Stephens, see the announcements printed in the *Boston Semi-Weekly Advertiser*, 10 May 1843 and 3 June 1843, reproduced in Victor Wolfgang von Hagen, *Frederick Catherwood Arch^t.* (New York and Oxford: Oxford University Press, 1950), note 10 and note 11, 158–159. Rendered in today's terms, 5 guineas was the equivalent of £5–5–0 (£5.25) and 12 guineas was the equivalent of £12–12–0 (£12.60).

10. Catherwood's library contained three works closely associated with the Picturesque and picturesque tourism when the library was auctioned in December 1856: Thomas West, *A Guide to the Lakes, in Cumberland, Westmorland, and Lancashire* (in an edition published in 1793); William Shenstone, *The Works in Verse and Prose, of William Shenstone, Esq; Most of which were never before printed*, 2 vols. (London: R. and J. Dodsley, 1764); *The Works in Verse and Prose, of William Shenstone, Esq; Vol. III. Containing Letters to Particular Friends, from the Year 1739 to 1763* (London: J. Dodsley, 1769); and Virgil's *Eclogues* (in an unspecified Latin and English edition published in 1810). *Catalogue of a Portion of the Library of the Late Frederic [sic] Catherwood, Esq. Hon Member of the Royal Institute of British Architects, Author of Views and Monuments in Central America etc. Also a Portion of the Library of an Eminent Surgeon, Retiring from Practice ..., Which will be Sold by Auction by Messrs. Puttick and Simpson, Auctioneers of Literary Property, at their Great Room, 191, Piccadilly, on Monday, December 1st, 1856, and five following days at one o'clock most punctually*, paginated printed sale catalogue, respectively, item #790 (34), item #1109 (46), item #1792 (73).

11. Stephens, *Incidents of Travel in Central America*, II, 426.

12. Stephens, *Incidents of Travel in Yucatan*, I, 185.

13. On a clear day, the Pacific and Atlantic oceans may be seen from the top of Volcán Irazú, the volcano which Stephens refers to as Cartago.

14. Stephens, *Incidents of Travel in Central America*, I, 365–366.

15. Stephens, *Incidents of Travel in Central America*, II, 235.

16. Stephens, *Incidents of Travel in Central America*, I, 188. Elsewhere in the valley of the río Motagua, Stephens observes that 'A few cattle were wandering wild over the great expanse, but without imparting that domestic aspect which in other countries attends the presence of cattle.' Stephens, *Incidents of Travel in Central America*, I, 57.

17. Stephens, *Incidents of Travel in Central America*, I, 349. Elsewhere, Stephens observed 'the hollow of an amphitheatre of mountains' that encircled the village of El Puente, and noted that Antigua Guatemala, the former capital, stood 'in a delightful valley, shut in by mountains and hills'. Stephens, *Incidents of Travel in Central America*, I, respectively, 187, 265.

18. Stephens, *Incidents of Travel in Central America*, II, 158.

19. Respectively, Stephens, *Incidents of Travel in Central America*, I, 424, and Stephens, *Incidents of Travel in Central America*, II, 16.

20. About which Stephens would have read in *The Modern Traveller* which stated that there was 'no room for doubt, that the line of communication by its great lakes is by far the most feasible and advantageous'. *The Modern Traveller*, IV, 307; 'I had read and examined all that had been published on this subject in England or this country.' Stephens, *Incidents of Travel in Central America*, I, 400. Details of Baily's survey, and a discussion of the implications and estimate of the cost of the project were given in Stephens, *Incidents of Travel in Central America*, I, 407–414.

21. Stephens, *Incidents of Travel in Central America*, I, 424.

22. Stephens, *Incidents of Travel in Central America*, I, 403.

23. Stephens, *Incidents of Travel in Central America*, I, 89. Stephens notes that at some point early in the expedition, a quadrant 'had become bent, and, like the barometer, was useless'. Stephens, *Incidents of Travel in Central America*, I, 132.

24. Stephens, *Incidents of Travel in Yucatan*, I, 373.

25. Stephens, *Incidents of Travel in Central America*, I, 130.

26. 'Philosophical instruments', a term used in the eighteenth and first half of the nineteenth centuries to designate instruments that were designed to examine phenomena experimentally, rather than through naturalistic observation, distinct also from instruments designed for the study of exact sciences, such as mathematics, astronomy, and surveying.

27. See *Catalogue of a Portion of the Library of the Late Frederic [sic] Catherwood, Esq. Hon Member of the Royal Institute of British Architects, Author of Views and Monuments in Central America etc. Also a Portion of the Library of an Eminent Surgeon, Retiring from Practice ..., Which will be Sold by Auction by Messrs. Puttick and Simpson, Auctioneers of Literary Property, at their Great Room, 191, Piccadilly, on Monday, December 1st, 1856, and five following days at one o'clock most punctually*, printed sale catalogue, paginated, 15. Other instruments listed in the catalogue included a 'costly 6 inch transit theodolite, by Troughton and Simms', a theodolite made by R. Adie, Liverpool, a Gunter's chain, assorted levels, a camera obscura, a photographic portrait camera and tripod, a stereoscope, a telescope, a solar microscope, and various drawing instruments, *Catalogue of a portion of the library of the late Frederic [sic] Catherwood, Esq.*, 15–16. Details of Catherwood's camera lucida are not available in the sale catalogue.

28. Stephens, *Incidents of Travel in Central America*, I, 130. The circumferentor was a precision instrument used for measuring angles in the horizontal plane on the level; how the circumferantor was used is discussed below.

29. For examples, see Hubert Robert ('Robert des Ruines'), *Architectural Caprice with Bridge and Triumphal Arch* (c. 1768) and *Architectural Capriccio with Obelisk* (1768), The Bowes Museum, Barnard Castle, or *Grand Monument voûté avec femmes et enfants* (c. 1780), Musée Jacquemart-André, Paris.

30. Stephens, *Incidents of Travel in Central America*, I, 158.

31. For discussion of this development in Victorian England, see Philippa Levine, *The Amateur and the Professional: Antiquarians, Historians, and Archaeologists in Victorian England, 1838–1886* (Cambridge: Cambridge University Press, 1986).

32. Stephens, *Incidents of Travel in Central America*, I, 133. We should note that orientations for 'South' and 'North' are designated, respectively, at the top and at the bottom of the *Plan of Copan*, with the orientation for 'West' forming the binding edge of the *Plan of Copan*. This orientation is incorrect since the river and cliff form the eastern boundary of the site. The northern part of the site is presented in the upper half of the *Plan of Copan*; the southern part is presented in the lower half of the *Plan of Copan*. Stephens and Catherwood reached Copán, Honduras, on 16 November 1839, and worked at the site between 18 November and 2 December when Stephens left for Guatemala City. Catherwood remained at the site 'for at least a month', before travelling to Quiriguá (Guatemala), where

he drew further stelae. Stephens, *Incidents of Travel in Central America*, I, 95, 117, 148–149, 161. Stephens and Catherwood were reunited in Guatemala City on 25 December 1839. Stephens, *Incidents of Travel in Central America*, I, 298.

33. *The Builder*, quoted in 'Ordnance Survey of London and the Environs', *The Illustrated London News*, vol. 12, no. 322, 24 June 1848, 414.

34. For further discussion of triangulation (known earlier as 'trigonometrical surveying'), see Rachel Hewitt, *Map of a Nation: A Biography of the Ordnance Survey* (London: Granta Books, 2010), 15–16, 22–23.

35. Stephens, *Incidents of Travel in Central America*, I, 134.

36. The courtyard is known today as Patio Oriental or Patio de los Jaguares. Stephens speculated that the courtyard may have been the location of the circus of Fuentes as recounted by Juarros. Although Stephens and Catherwood found the sepulchral vault which Galindo excavated in 1834 (in the vicinity of 'J', according to Stephens), they did not locate the stone hammock mentioned by Fuentes, which had been their 'great inducement to visit these ruins'. Stephens, *Incidents of Travel in Central America*, I, 142–143, 144. Structure 'W' is generally known today as Estructura 16.

37. Stephens, *Incidents of Travel in Central America*, I, 139. Confusion in reading three-dimensional space in the plan of Copán is not raised in reviews of *Incidents of Travel in Central America*, although *The North American Review* opined that the maps of Central America included in the work were 'defective', going on to observe that the 'map of the interior of the peninsular is almost a *tabula rasa*'. 'Aboriginal Structures', *The North American Review*, Vol. 51, No. 109 (1840), 396–433, 421; *The North American Review* also observed that Stephens' publishers 'should by all means have afforded him a better map; a thing which it is not even now too late to do, and which, from the great popularity of the work, they can now better than ever afford'. 'Review of *Incidents of Travel in Central America, Chiapas, and Yucatan*', *The North American Review*, Vol. 53, No. 113 (1841): 479–506, 506.

38. For an example of a passage that employs all three terms by Stephens and the term 'idol' by his guide, see Stephens, *Incidents of Travel in Central America*, I, 102. The terms 'idol' and 'monument' (and their corresponding plural forms) are usually employed by Stephens in referring to stelae at Copán, the former usually accompanied with quotation marks; 'statue' and 'sculptor' are each employed on two occasions. Stephens, *Incidents of Travel in Central America*, I, respectively, 152, 157, 152, 154. The term 'sculpture' is employed on four occasions. Stephens, *Incidents of Travel in Central America*, I, 152, 154, 155, 159.

39. Stephens, *Incidents of Travel in Central America*, I, 117–118.

40. Identified as stelae 'S' and 'Q' by Stephens (generally known today as, respectively, stelae H and F).

41. Identified as stelae 'P', 'N', and 'L' by Stephens (generally known today as stelae D(?), 4, and A).

42. Don Miguel was a sub-tenant on the Copán estate in whose thatched hut Stephens and Catherwood stayed while investigating the site. For a description of the hut and living conditions, see Stephens, *Incidents of Travel in Central America*, I, 109–110.

43. Stephens, *Incidents of Travel in Central America*, I, 153–154. Emphasis in original.

44. Stephens, *Incidents of Travel in Central America*, I, 158.

45. Stephens, *Incidents of Travel in Central America*, I, 102.

46. Stephens, *Incidents of Travel in Central America*, I, 115–116. For discussion of Stephens' 'nationalist agenda' in the context of the Monroe Doctrine, regional hegemony, and Stephens' attempts to purchase sites in Central America and Yucatán to establish 'a national museum of American antiquities', see Evans, *Romancing the Maya*, 54–59, 67, 71–73, 76; for discussion of Stephens and the nineteenth-century cultural depredation of Central America by British institutions, see Robert D. Aguirre, *Informal Empire: Mexico and Central America in Victorian Culture* (Minneapolis: University of Minnesota Press, 2005), 61–101.

47. Stephens, *Incidents of Travel in Central America*, I, 102.

48. Stephens, *Incidents of Travel in Central America*, I, 105.

49. Stephens, *Incidents of Travel in Central America*, I, 158.

50. Stephens, *Incidents of Travel in Central America*, I, 155.

51. *Teocallis*, aka *teocalis*: a four-sided truncated pyramid-like structure, constructed from terraces, usually surmounted by a temple.

52. 'The Second Epoch, The Story continued by Marian Halcombe, VI, June 18th, 1850', Wilkie Collins, *The Woman in White* (Harmondsworth: Penguin Books, 1994 [1861]), 238–258, 244. The novel was first published in serialised form in *All the Year Round*, 1859–1860. We should not overlook the fact that Collins, brought up in artistic circles, was given his first name after his father's friend and fellow artist, David Wilkie, and toured the Wye Valley as a child in 1834. Julian Mitchell, *The Wye Tour and its Artists* (Little Logaston, Woonton Almeley: Logaston Press, 2010), 90.

53. [Henry Morley], 'Our Phantom Ship. Central America', *Household Words*, vol. 2, no. 48, 22 February 1851, 516–522, 518. For further discussion of the influence of Copán on Wilkie Collins, see Richard Collins, 'The Ruins of Copán in "The Woman in White": Wilkie Collins and John Stephens' *Incidents of Travel in Central America, Chiapas and Yucatan*', *Wilkie Collins Society Journal*, New Series, 2 (1999): 5–17.

54. Stephens, *Incidents of Travel in Central America*, I, 143. The 'Colossal Head', designated 'F' in the site-plan, is located in what is known today as Patio Oriental or Patio de los Jaguares.

55. [William Weir and W. H. Wills], 'Short Cuts Across the Globe', *Household Words*, vol. 1, no. 3, 13 April 1850, 65–68, 66. Priced at tuppence (2d) an issue, Dickens targeted the journal at a broad readership, although most readers appear to have been middle class.

56. Stephens, *Incidents of Travel in Central America*, I, 158–159.

57. Stephens and Catherwood conducted investigations at Palenque between 13 May and 1 June 1840. Stephens, *Incidents of Travel in Central America*, II, 289, 336.

58. Contrary to these dimensions and the ground-plan reproduced below, the Palace complex is not rectangular. A more accurate ground-plan will be found in Guillermo Bernal Romero, Martha Cuevas García, Arnoldo González Crux, *Palenque, Chiapas, Mexico: Archaeological Zone and Site Museum* (Mexico City: Editorial Raíces/Instituto Nacional de Antropología e Historia, 2000), 22–23. One of the most accurate plans of the site was surveyed by Hugh W. Price in May 1891 on an expedition to Palenque with Alfred Percival Maudslay. Price's plan, *Principal Group of Ruins at Palenque*, is discussed in Chapter Five.

59. Stephens, *Incidents of Travel in Central America*, II, 309–310.

60. On the evidence of having seen wooden lintels made of sapote-wood at the site of Ocosingo, Stephens proposed that the lintels at Palenque were also

constructed from a hard wood which, in the intervening period between construction and the arrival of the party at Palenque, had eroded. Stephens *Incidents of Travel in Central America*, II, 312–313.

61. Stephens, *Incidents of Travel in Central America*, II, 313–316.

62. Stephens, *Incidents of Travel in Central America*, II, 317.

63. Stephens, *Incidents of Travel in Central America*, II, 319–320.

64. Stephens, *Incidents of Travel in Central America*, II, 320.

65. Stephens, *Incidents of Travel in Central America*, II, 338. For examples of work by Desgodetz, see *Les Edifices antiques de Rome* (Paris, 1682), reproduced as Figure 2.2, Figure 2.3, and Figure 2.4 in Bruce Redford, *Dilettanti: The Antic and the Antique in Eighteenth-Century England* (Los Angeles: J. Paul Getty Museum and The Getty Research Institute, 2008), 47.

66. Stephens, *Incidents of Travel in Central America*, II, 338.

67. Stephens, *Incidents of Travel in Central America*, II, 338.

68. Stephens, *Incidents of Travel in Central America*, II, 338.

69. Stephens, *Incidents of Travel in Central America*, II, 339.

70. Stephens, *Incidents of Travel in Central America*, II, 350–351.

71. The tablet reproduced as the Frontispiece for the second volume of *Incidents of Travel in Central America* was also adopted as a motif in the design for the front board of the first edition, and is reproduced as a motif on the back of this book.

72. Stephens tried to acquire the reliefs by exchanging them for engravings of the same subjects from his copy of del Río, or giving the sisters drawings by Catherwood. Stephens, *Incidents of Travel in Central America*, II, 352–353. The two women are described, elsewhere, as 'a widow lady and a single sister'. Stephens, *Incidents of Travel in Central America*, II, 363.

73. Stephens, *Incidents of Travel in Central America*, II, 353. The bas-reliefs, it transpires, came from the Temple of the Cross and not the Temple of the Sun, thus the 'restoration' drawn by Catherwood proved to be erroneous. David Stuart and George Stuart, *Palenque: Eternal City of the Maya* (London: Thomas & Hudson, 2008), 69.

74. Stephens, *Incidents of Travel in Central America*, II, 337, 321.

75. In their exploration of the site, the party employed a guide who had acted in the same capacity for Waldeck and Walker and Caddy. Stephens, *Incidents of Travel in Central America*, II, 304.

76. Stuart and Stuart, *Palenque*, 57, 77. Waldeck drew the relief before partly destroying it; for a photograph of the relief as it appeared in 1942, see Stuart and Stuart, *Palenque*, Figure 15B, 59.

77. In *Views of Ancient Monuments*, Catherwoods observes: 'It is due to the reader to state, that this general view of Palenque is composed of separate sketches of each Casa, or Building, and from the ground-plan each is made to occupy its respective position. No other method could be adopted, as the large size of the trees and dense nature of the forest, precluded any idea of making a clearing sufficient to embrace all in one view. The clearing is, therefore, not real, but imaginary.' Catherwood, *Views of Ancient Monuments*, 14.

78. Stephens, *Incidents of Travel in Central America*, II, 357.

79. Stephens, *Incidents of Travel in Yucatan*, I, 185.

80. Stephens, *Incidents of Travel in Central America*, II, 421. Members of the second expedition remained at Uxmal, on land belonging to the hacienda (one of a number of estates owned by Simon Peon) between 15 November 1841 and 1 January 1842. Stephens, *Incidents of Travel in Yucatan*, I, 150, 327. Members of the party were occasionally away from the site, mainly for reasons of ill health; Stephens appears to have been away from the site between 18 November and 13 December 1841. Stephens first encountered Simon Peon at a hotel frequented by Spanish-Americans in Fulton Street, New York. Stephens, *Incidents on Travel in Central America*, II, 397.

81. Stephens, *Incidents of Travel in Yucatan*, I, 305.

82. The modern reader assumes that 'North' is represented towards the top of the plate, whereas the *General Plan of the Ruins of Uxmal* indicates that Magnetic North is represented towards the bottom of the plate. On this occasion, unlike the *Plan of Copan*, the orientation of the *General Plan of the Ruins of Uxmal* is correct.

83. Stephens, *Incidents of Travel in Yucatan*, I, 165–166.

84. Stephens, *Incidents of Travel in Yucatan*, I, 166; Stephens refers here to engravings of the Casa del Gobernador.

85. Stephens, *Incidents of Travel in Yucatan*, I, 167. As indicated in Chapter One, Stephens observed that 'Large as the engraving is, it [the Frontispiece] can serve only to give some idea of the general effect; the detail of ornament cannot be shown.' Stephens, *Incidents of Travel in Yucatan*, I, 166. On two further occasions Stephens expressed concern that Catherwood's engravings were printed on too small a scale to show detail or suggest effect. Stephens, *Incidents of Travel in Yucatan*, I, 302 (with regard to the Casa de las Monjas), 319 (with regard to the Casa de Palomas). Describing the Casa del Adivino, Stephens observed that no idea of the structure 'could be given in any but a large engraving'. Stephens, *Incidents of Travel in Yucatan*, I, 314.

86. Stephens, *Incidents of Travel in Yucatan*, I, 167.

87. Stephens, *Incidents of Travel in Yucatan*, I, 171–172.

88. '… the Indians have been in the habit of breaking and disfiguring them with the machete, believing that by so doing they quiet their wandering spirits'. Stephens, *Incidents of Travel in Yucatan*, I, 172.

89. Stephens, *Incidents of Travel in Yucatan*, I, 172–173. This example displays an extravagance of style seen also in the Chenes tradition of decoration in, for example, the elaboratedly-sculpted entrances at the site of Chicanná in the Río Bec region (Structure II, in particular) and at the site of Hochob in the state of Campeche.

90. Stephens, *Incidents of Travel in Yucatan*, I, 307.

91. Stephens, *Incidents of Travel in Yucatan*, I, 307–308.

92. The apartment, constructed with a corbelled ceiling, demonstrates the architectural principle used by the Maya in place of the keystone in constructing arches. Although Stephens does not comment on this aspect of construction on this occasion, the principle of the corbelled arch is considered elsewhere by Stephens, in particular, in the Appendix, 'System adopted by the ancient builders of Yucatan in covering their rooms with stone roofs'. Stephens, *Incidents of Travel in Yucatan*, I, 429–434. The plan of the Monjas complex was printed on page 301, and two plates with details of decoration on the west range were bound facing pages 302 and 303.

93. Stephens, *Incidents of Travel in Yucatan*, I, 174–175.

94. Rosa Casanova and Olivier Debroise, *Sobre la superficie bruñida de un espejo. Fotógrafos del siglo XIX* (Mexico City: Fondo de Cultura Económica, 1989), 25. Baron Emanuel von Friedrichsthal, the First Secretary of the Austrian legation in Mexico, took Daguerreotypes of archaeological structures at Aké, Chichén Itzá, and Uxmal on his expedition to Yucatán in 1840. According to Stephens, Friedrichsthal was the first person to draw European and North American attention to the site of Chichén Itzá. Stephens, *Incidents of Travel in Yucatan*, II, 184; elsewhere, Stephens remarks that 'Chichen was the only place we heard of in Merida, and the only place we knew with certainty before we embarked for Yucatan'. Stephens, *Incidents of Travel in Yucatan*, I, 233. Louis Prélier, the first person to bring the Daguerreotype to Mexico, daguerreotyped the port of Veracruz in December 1839, and the Zócalo and the Catedral Metropolitana in Mexico City in late January 1840. Peter E. Palmquist and Thomas R. Kailbourn, *Pioneer Photographers of the Far West: A Biographical Dictionary, 1840–1865* (Stanford: Stanford University Press, 2000), 5. Frances Calderón de la Barca took Daguerreotypes of the Castillo de Chapultepec on her trip to Mexico, see 'Letter the Twenty-Ninth, 21st [November 1840]', Frances Calderón de la Barca, *Life in Mexico, during a Residence of Two Years, in that Country. By Madame C- de la B-. With a Preface by W. H. Prescott* (London: Chapman and Hall, 1843), 233.

95. Stephens, *Incidents of Travel in Yucatan*, I, 175. Dr. Samuel Cabot, the third non-indigenous member of Stephens' party, travelled to Yucatán to collect ornithological specimens.

96. Stephens, *Incidents of Travel in Yucatan*, I, 254.

97. Stephens, *Incidents of Travel in Yucatan*, I, 319–320.

98. The mounds, representing a ball-court, appear much larger than they are in reality.

99. Stephens' party investigated Kabah between 8 January and 11 January 1842. Stephens, *Incidents of Travel in Yucatan*, I, 368, 414.

100. *Milpa*: a Maya term denoting land cleared annually by burning for the cultivation of maize (sweet corn).

101. Stephens, *Incidents of Travel in Yucatan*, I, 384, 387. Plate XV is designated '1st Casa', and the two routes designated on the *General Plan of the Ruins of Kabah* are, respectively, 'Camino Real from Nohcacab to Bolonchen' and 'Path to Milpa/Pathway to Milpa'. For discussion of the arch at Kabah, see Evans, *Romancing the Maya*, 64–66 and Figure 2.9, 65; for discussion of the removal of a carved, sapote-wood lintel from Kabah, see Evans, *Romancing the Maya*, 73, 75, and Figure 2.11, 74.

102. Stephens, *Incidents of Travel in Yucatan*, II, 49, 66.

103. The plates are bound facing pages 54 and 55. Although Stephens does not comment on the two views in this manner, he recounts a reverse-field view in El Salvador when, looking back at the terrain he had just traversed, he turned round to look towards a village he was approaching: 'Continuing another league through the same rich country, we rose upon a table of land, from which, looking back, we saw an immense plain, wooded, and extending to the shore, and beyond, the boundless waters of the Pacific. Before us, at the extreme end of a long street, was the church of Izalco, standing out in strong relief against the base of the volcano, which at that moment, with a loud report like the rolling of thunder, threw in the air a column of black smoke and ashes, lighted by a single flash of flame.' Stephens, *Incidents of Travel in Central America*, I, 326.

104. The party, accommodated in a palapa on the hacienda of Chichén Itzá, undertook a preliminary survey of the site on 14 March and remained at the site until 29 March 1842. Stephens, *Incidents of Travel in Yucatan*, II, 282, 325.

105. Stephens, *Incidents of Travel in Yucatan*, II, 291-298.

106. Stephens, *Incidents of Travel in Yucatan*, II, 318.

107. Stephens, *Incidents of Travel in Yucatan*, I, respectively, 300, 370, 387.

108. Earlier in the account, the conquest of the Itzá was provided by Stephens, drawing, variously, on Antonio de Herrera y Tordesillas, Juan de Villagutierra Sotomayor, and Diego López de Cogolludo, whose *Historia de Yucatán* (Madrid, 1668) Stephens carried with him to Yucatán. A copy of Antonio de Herrera y Tordesillas' *Descriptions* [*sic*] *des Indes Occidentales* (1622) and a copy of Antonio de Solís' *Historia de la Conquista de Mexico* (*sic*, 1704) were held in the private library of Catherwood when it was auctioned in December 1856. *Catalogue of a Portion of the Library of the Late Frederic* [*sic*] *Catherwood, Esq. Hon Member of the Royal Institute of British Architects, Author of Views and Monuments in Central America etc. Also a Portion of the Library of an Eminent Surgeon, Retiring from Practice ..., Which will be Sold by Auction by Messrs. Puttick and Simpson, Auctioneers of Literary Property, at their Great Room, 191, Piccadilly, on Monday, December 1st, 1856, and five following days at one o'clock most punctually*, paginated printed sale catalogue, respectively, item #1734 (70), item #1742 (71).

109. John Abraham Heraud, *Uxmal: An Antique Love Story; Macée de Léodepart: An Historical Romance* (London: Simpkin, Marshall & Co., 1877), B2.

110. A folk narrative, as told by villagers from Chajul, was recounted to Stephens by the padre of Santa Cruz del Quiché, and formed the basis of a fantasy on the part of Stephens: 'the thing that roused us was the assertion by the padre that, four days on the road to Mexico, on the other side of the great sierra, was a living city, large and populous, occupied by Indians, precisely in the same state as before the discovery of America. He had heard it many years before at the village of Chajul, and was told by the villagers that from the topmost ridge of the sierra, from which, at a height of ten or twelve thousand feet, he looked over an immense plain extending to Yucatan and the Gulf of Mexico, and saw at a great distance a large city spread over a great space, and with turrets white and glittering in the sun. The traditionary account of the Indians of Chajul is, that no white man has ever reached this city; that the inhabitants speak the Maya language, are aware that a race of strangers has conquered the whole country around, and murder any white man who attempts to enter their territory.' Stephens, *Incidents of Travel in Central America*, II, 195–196.

111. Published as *Memoir of an Eventful Expedition in Central America; Resulting in the Discovery of the Idolatrous City of Iximaya, in an unexplored region; and the possession of two Remarkable Aztec Children, Descendants and Specimens of the Sacerdotal Caste (now nearly extinct) of the Ancient Aztec Founders of the Ruined Temples of that Country; Described by John L. Stevens* [*sic*]*, Esq., and other Travellers. Translated from the Spanish by Pedro Velasquez, of San Salvador*. For further discussion, see Evans, *Romancing the Maya*, 68, 85–87; for an insightful discussion of the publication in the context of mid-nineteenth-century popular culture, scientific culture, and Victorian racial discourse, see Aguirre, *Informal Empire*, 103–131. See, in particular, Figure 22, 114, and Figure 23, 115, which present parodic illustrations of Catherwood's work at Copán and Palenque. Several extant versions of this work, published

in New York and London between 1850 and 1853, are known to exist; the copy consulted at the Getty Research Institute has a variant title: *Illustrated Memoir of an Eventful Expedition into Central America Resulting in the Discovery of the Idolatrous City of Iximaya, in an unexplored region; and the possession of two Remarkable Aztec Children, Maximo [sic], (the Man), & Bartola, (the Girl), Descendants and Specimens of the Sacerdotal Cast, (now nearly extinct), of the Ancient Aztec Founders of the Ruined Temples of that Country; Described by John L. Stevens [sic], Esq., and other Travellers. Translated from the Spanish by Pedro Velasquez, of San Salvador* (n.d.). The name of a publisher (real or imagined) is not provided in either edition.

112. Untitled introduction, Charles Lamb, *Palenque, or The Ancient West. A Poem* (London: Saunders and Otley, 1849), v.

113. Albert Gallatin, 'Notes on the Semi-Civilized Nations of Mexico, Yucatan, and Central America', *Transactions of the American Ethnological Society*, vol. 1 (1845), 1–352, 174.

114. Stephens, *Incidents of Travel in Yucatan*, I, 94–95.

115. Stephens, *Incidents of Travel in Yucatan*, I, 284, emphasis in original.

116. Stephens, *Incidents of Travel in Yucatan*, I, 322.

117. Stephens, *Incidents of Travel in Yucatan*, I, 324.

118. Catherwood, *Views of Ancient Monuments*, 8.

119. Catherwood's article on Dougga, published in the *Transactions of the American Ethnological Society* (1845), cites Polybius as a model for evaluating material evidence, demonstrating 'the utility and necessity of consulting ancient authors', which recommendation, as we saw in Chapter One, was made in lectures by John Soane.

120. Catherwood, *Views of Ancient Monuments*, 8. The reference to the lost tribes of Israel alludes to colonial historiography which proposed that the biblical patriarch, Jacob, and his twelve sons colonised the New World, a belief that underwrote the series of thirteen portraits commissioned for the New World from the Spanish painter, Francisco de Zurbarán, twelve of which are held in the collection of Auckland Castle, Bishop Auckland. The reference to an 'antediluvian period' alludes to arguments advanced by Waldeck.

121. Catherwood, *Views of Ancient Monuments*, 8.

122. Catherwood, *Views of Ancient Monuments*, 8.

123. Catherwood, *Views of Ancient Monuments*, 9.

124. Catherwood, *Views of Ancient Monuments*, 9.

125. Catherwood, *Views of Ancient Monuments*, 9.

126. Catherwood, *Views of Ancient Monuments*, 9–10. Although Vitruvius was not included in the sale of Catherwood's private library in 1856, an edition, translated by Joseph Gwilt and published in 1826, may have been known to Catherwood, where Vitruvius (c. 90 – c. 20 BC) discussed the construction of early dwellings: 'The first attempt was the mere erection of a few spars united together with twigs and covered with mud. Others built their walls of dried lumps of turf, connected these together by means of timbers laid across horizontally, and covered the erections with reeds and boughs, for the purpose of sheltering themselves from the inclemency of the seasons. … We are certain that buildings were thus originally constructed, from the present practice of uncivilized nations …'. Marcus Vitruvius Pollio, *The Architecture of Marcus Vitruvius Pollio, in Ten Books. Translated from the Latin by Joseph Gwilt, fellow of the Society of Antiquaries of London* (London: Priestley and Weale, 1826), Book the Second, Chapter 1, *Of the Origin of Building*, 37–41, 38. Such practice bears comparison with the traditional method of constructing the Maya *na*, see below.

127. Catherwood, *Views of Ancient Monuments*, 10.

128. I thank Luis Millet Camara, (former) Director, Centro INAH Yucatán, Dr. George Bay, Site Director, Kuhuic, and Mario Humberto Margaña Arara, Maya guide, for their help in arranging a visit to Kuhuic.

129. Stephens, *Incidents of Travel in Yucatan*, II, 69; the figure is printed on the preceding page. Maya builders often incorporated a row of small drum pillars ('colonnettes') as an ornamented plinth at the bottom of a facade. The plinth is not visible in the figure reproduced in Stephens.

130. 'Three different epochs of art may be distinguished in these structures; and they bear undoubted traces of identity of origin with the remains of Palenque.' 'Ancient Ruins in Central America', report on the presentation of Emanuel von Friedrichsthal's paper at the British Museum, 18 December 1841. The report mentions that 'twenty-five or thirty daguerreotypes of the ruins, plans of three towns … and a portfolio of drawings of the details of buildings, statues, and columns' were shown during the presentation at the British Museum. 'Ancient Ruins in Central America', *Chambers's Edinburgh Journal*, New Series, Number 517, 25 December 1841, 390–391, 391.

131. The site is also known as 'Chunyaxché'; the present-day Maya *na* (Plate 12) was photographed in the village of Santa Elena, Yucatán, with the permission of the owners.

Notes to Chapter Five

1. John Soane, 'Lecture II', David Watkin, *Sir John Soane: Enlightenment Thought and the Royal Academy Lectures. Cambridge Studies in the History of Architecture* (Cambridge: Cambridge University Press, 1996), 500–514, 500. Spelling has been modernised and capitalisation removed from the original manuscript volumes of Soane's Royal Academy lectures, written for Soane by pupils in his architectural practice. Watkin, *Sir John Soane*, 489. Soane delivered Lecture II, from his first series of lectures (initially delivered in 1809), at the Royal Academy on 27 February 1817 and on 25 February 1819. Watkin, *Sir John Soane*, Appendix Five: Susan Palmer, 'Chronology of the delivery of Sir John Soane's Royal Academy Lectures', 731–732, 731. For dates when Soane lectured at the Royal Institution, see Notes to Chapter One, #10, 166 above.

2. Jane Austen, *Mansfield Park*, edited by James Kingsley, with an Introduction and Notes by Jane Stabler (Oxford: Oxford University Press, 2003 [1814; second edition, 1816]), 15.

3. John Soane, Soane Case 157, MS, 'Royal Institution, Lecture the Second', Saturday, 14 June 1817, 20**–20*** (asterisks denote matter inserted on consecutive leaves bound following leaf 20), Research Library, Sir John Soane's Museum. The quotation reproduces the original manuscript folio volume written by Soane, and includes punctation and capitalisation as in the MS. The MS of the first lecture in 1817 notes that approximately 800 persons, including women (who were excluded from lectures at the Royal Academy), attended the lecture at the Royal Institution.

4. John Soane, 'Lecture XII', first delivered at the Royal Academy, 12 March 1815, in Watkin, *Sir John Soane*, 651–667, 661. This was the only time Soane delivered the lecture himself; the lecture was subsequently read by Henry Howard on 21 March 1833 and 12 February 1835. Watkin, *Sir John Soane*, Appendix Five: Susan Palmer, 'Chronology of the delivery of Sir John Soane's Royal Academy Lectures', 731–732, 732.

5. Soane occasionally illustrated his lectures at the Royal Academy with models brought from his extensive collection in Lincoln's Inn Fields. Watkin, *Sir John Soane*, 407. For an illustration of a model used by Soane, see the perspective view of the Tomb of Horatii and Curiatti in the Via Appia, Albano, Italy, after a model by Peter Turnerelli, reproduced in Watkin, *Sir John Soane*, Figure 31, ff. 300. Founded in 1799, the Royal Institution became known for its series of popular lectures on music, architecture, painting, and the fine arts, as well as geology, chemistry, and natural history. For further discussion of the training of architects at the Royal Academy, see Neil Bingham, 'Architecture at the Royal Academy Schools, 1768–1836', in Neil Bingham (ed.), *The Education of the Architect. Proceedings of the 22nd Annual Symposium of the Society of Architectural Historians of Great Britain* (London: Art Workers' Guild, 1993), 5–14.

6. Watkin, *Sir John Soane*, 429; Holger Hoock, *The King's Artists: The Royal Academy of Arts and the Politics of British Culture 1760–1840* (Oxford: Oxford University Press, 2003), 55, 56–57. Study was complemented by instruction in anatomy and perspective, lectures on painting and architecture, and, from 1810, lectures on sculpture. For work depicting students studying in the Royal Academy schools, see Edward Francis Burney, *The Antique School at New Somerset House* (c. 1779), and Thomas Rowlandson and Augustus Pugin, *Drawing from the Life at the Royal Academy, Somerset House* (1808), reproduced as, respectively, Figure 1.10 and Figure 1.8 in Hoock, *The King's Artists*, 45, and facing 43. Students of architecture were admitted to the Antique school; Hoock indicates that approximately 15 per cent of student admissions between 1769 and 1820 were in this discipline. Hoock, *The King's Artists*, 53.

7. 'Travels and Acquisitions in Mexico; By Mr. Bullock: second Paper', 'Arts and Sciences' column, *The Literary Gazette, and Journal of Belles Lettres, Arts, Sciences, &c.*, No. 364, Saturday, 10 January 1824, 25–26, 25, the second of two notices concerning the exhibition at the Egyptian Hall. Three large, life-size facsimiles were exhibited from casts made in Mexico City by Bullock and his son, William Bullock, Jr.: the Calendar Stone; the Sacrifical Stone; and Coatlicue, the Aztec goddess of war, referred to as 'Teoyamiqui' by Bullock, illustrated on the left in 5.1. William Bullock, *Six Months' Residence and Travels in Mexico; Containing Remarks on the Present State of New Spain, its Natural Productions, State of Society, Manufactures, Trade, Agriculture, and Antiquities, &c. With Plates and Maps. By W. Bullock, F.L.S. Proprietor of the late London Museum* (London: John Murray, 1824), 327, 336, 342, 375–377. For further discussion of the exhibition, see Robert D. Aguirre, *Informal Empire: Mexico and Central America in Victorian Culture* (Minneapolis: University of Minnesota Press, 2005), 1–11, and Michael P. Costeloe, *William Bullock. Connoisseur and Virtuoso of the Egyptian Hall: Piccadilly to Mexico (1773–1849)* (Bristol: HiPLAM, 2008), 138–143. For discussion of the sale of exhibits at auction after the exhibition closed in September 1825, see Costeloe, 151–155. Bullock's facsimile of the Aztec Calendar Stone, one of the few casts exhibited at the Egyptian Hall whose whereabouts are known today, is held in storage at the National Museum of Scotland, Edinburgh. Costeloe, *William Bullock*, note 62, 152.

8. We should not overlook the fact that cultural depredation was a significant by-product of this process, as Robert D. Aguirre has argued. The making of casts, for example, caused considerable disquiet among indigenous communities. Attempts by John Lloyd Stephens to transport casts from Palenque to New York in the 1840s provoked villagers in Santo Domingo de Palenque to write to Charles Russell, the United States consul to Mexico at Isla del Carmen, to complain that the local community should benefit from the casts whose value was estimated at between 'four or five thousand [US] dollars'. The villagers argued that casts 'may serve to mould after them as many copies as may be wished, and in this manner they may supply the world with these precious things without a six cents' piece expense. ... Indeed, if this treasure is ours, and by right belongs to our town, why should it not be benefited by it?' Appendix, letter dated 15 October 1840, John Lloyd Stephens, *Incidents of Travel in Central America, Chiapas, and Yucatan*, 2 vols. (New York: Harper & Brothers; London: John Murray, 1841), II, 470–471. For further discussion of the issue of cultural depredation with regard to archaeological investigation in Mexico in the nineteenth century, see R. Tripp Evans, *Romancing the Maya: Mexican Antiquity in the American Imagination 1820–1915* (Austin: University of Texas Press, 2004), 55–57; Aguirre, *Informal Empire*, 61–101; for discussion of the related concept of visual expropriation, see Aguirre, *Informal Empire*, 58–59, and Tom Gunning, '"The Whole World within Reach": Travel Images without Borders', in Roland Cosandey and François Albera (eds.), *Cinéma sans frontiers 1896–1918 / Images Across Borders* (Lausanne: Editions Payot Lausanne; Québec: Nuit Blanche Editeur, 1995), 21–36.

9. 'Mr. Bullock's Travels and Acquisitions in Mexico', 'Arts and Sciences' column, *The Literary Gazette*, No. 363, Saturday, 3 January 1824, 8–9, 9, the first of two notices concerning the exhibition at the Egyptian Hall.

10. Respectively designated as stela 'P' and stela 'L' in Stephens, *Incidents of Travel in Central America*, see Ian Graham, *Alfred Maudslay and the Maya: A Biography* (London: British Museum Press, 2002), 135–141, *passim*. Maudslay and Giuntini were assisted by two Guatemalan brothers, José Domingo López and Gorgonio López in making casts at Copán. The López brothers and José Domingo López's son, Caralampio, later assisted Maudslay in the making of moulds at Palenque. Graham, *Alfred Maudslay and the Maya*, 174.

11. The phrase, discussed below, comes from *The Literary Gazette*, No. 1147, Saturday, 12 January 1839, 28.

12. Ann Bermingham, *Learning to Draw: Studies in the Cultural History of a Polite and Useful Art* (New Haven and London: The Paul Mellon Centre for Studies in British Art, Yale University Press, 2000), 120–126, 120.

13. Held, respectively, at the Victoria and Albert Museum and Tate Britain. For reproduction of these works, see Charlotte Klonk, *Science and the Perception of Nature: British Landscape in the Late Eighteenth and Early Nineteenth Centuries* (New Haven and London: The Paul Mellon Centre for Studies in British Art, Yale University Press, 1996), Figure 71, 108, and Figure 93, 131; Steven Parissien (ed.), *Turner and Constable Sketching from Nature: Works from the Tate Collection*, exhibition catalogue (London: Tate Publishing, 2013), Figure 1, 9. For further discussion of work by John Varley, Cornelius Varley, and John Linnell, see Klonk, *Science and the Perception of Nature*, in particular, 105–111, 130–135, 142.

14. Klonk, *Science and the Perception of Nature*, 99.

15. The term 'Photogenic Drawing' was employed by Talbot in William Henry Fox Talbot, *The Pencil of Nature* (London: Longman, Brown, Green, & Longmans, 1844), n.p., and adopted by Theodore Henry Adolphus Fielding in his entry for 'Photography' in T. H. Fielding, *The Art of Engraving, With the Various Modes of Operation, Under the Following Different Divisions: Etching. Soft-Ground Etching. Line Engraving. Chalk and Stipple. Aquatint. Mezzotint. Lithography. Wood Engraving. Medallic Engraving. Electrography. And Photography. Illustrated with Ten Specimens of the Different Styles of Engraving* (London: M. A. Nattali, 1844 [1841]), 101–109.

16. Talbot, *The Pencil of Nature*, 'Introductory Remarks' (n.p.) and 'Brief Historical Sketch of the Invention of the Art' (n.p.).

17. Stephens informs us that Frederick Catherwood, 'in pursuance of his artistical studies had perforce made castings with his own hands' in Athens when the city was besieged by the Turks during the Greek Revolution. Stephens, *Incidents of Travel in Central America*, II, 364.

18. George Alexander Hoskins, *Visit to the Great Oasis of the Libyan Desert; With an Account, Ancient and Modern, of the Oasis of Amun, and the Other Oases now under the Dominion of the Pasha of Egypt. By G. A. Hoskins, Esq. Author of "Travels in Ethiopia." With a Map, and Twenty Plates Illustrating the Temples, Scenery, etc., From Drawings Finished on the Spot by the Author* (London: Longman, Rees, Orme, Brown, Green, & Longman, 1837), 8, 109–110.

19. 'Advertisement', Jules Goury and Owen Jones, *Plans, Elevations, Sections and Details of the Alhambra: From Drawings Taken on the Spot in 1834 by the Late M. Jules Goury and in 1834 and 1837 by Owen Jones, Arch*[t]*. With a Complete Translation of the Arabic Inscriptions, and an Historical Notice of the Kings of Granada, from the Conquest of that City by the Arabs to the Expulsion of the Moors, by Mr. Pasqual de Gayangos*, 2 vols. (London: Owen Jones, 1842–1845), I (1842).

20. Jean-Jacques Ampère, *Voyage en Égypte et en Nubie* (Paris: Lévy, 1868), 2–3, quoted in Derek Gregory, 'Emperor of the Gaze: Photographic Practices and Productions of Space in Egypt, 1839–1914', in Joan M. Schwartz and James R. Ryan (eds.), *Picturing Place: Photography and the Geographical Imagination* (London and New York: I. B. Tauris, 2003), 196–225, note 16, 330–331. Gregory renders the French term, *estampage*, as 'squeeze'.

21. 'The Daguerotype' [*sic*],*The Literary Gazette*, No. 1147, Saturday, 12 January 1839, 28. The article by H. Gaucheraud was first published in *Gazette de France*, Sunday, 6 January 1839. The importance of being able to fix images produced in this manner was emphasised by Talbot in 'Some Account of the Art of Photogenic Drawing', where Talbot writes that he had already discovered a method 'of *fixing* the image in such a manner that it is no more liable to injury or destruction'. H. F. Talbot, 'Some Account of the Art of Photogenic Drawing', *The London and Edinburgh Philosophical Magazine and Journal of Science*, vol. 14, no. 87 (March 1839): 196–208, 198. Emphasis in original. Talbot's article was originally presented as a paper ('Some Account of the Art of Photogenic Drawing, or the process by which natural objects may be made to delineate themselves without the aid of the artist's pencil') read before the Royal Society on 31 January 1839.

22. Talbot, 'Some Account of the Art of Photogenic Drawing', section 4, 'On the Art of fixing a Shadow', 201.

23. Talbot, 'Some Account of the Art of Photogenic Drawing', 207–208. Emphasis in original.

24. In this context, we should note that Maudslay was of the opinion that, for serious work, photographs should always be supplemented by the examination of casts. Robert Levere Brunhouse, *Pursuit of the Ancient Maya: Some Archaeologists of Yesteryear* (Albuquerque: University of New Mexico Press,1975), 42.

25. 'La novedad del día en México. – El Cinematógrafo Lumière', *El Mundo Ilustrado*, year 3, vol. 2, no. 8, Sunday, 23 August 1896, 118–119, 118. ([*D*]*urante este intervalo se interrumpe la proyección de rayos luminosos, y mediante la persistencia de las impresiones en la retina, que dura un vigésimo de segundo, el ojo percibe una serie de impresiones luminosas, que le causan la perfecta ilusión de cuerpos en movimiento*.) Translation from Spanish by the author unless otherwise indicated.

26. Auguste and Louis Lumière, *Letters*, edited and annotated by Jacques Rittaud-Hutinet with the collaboration of Yvelise Dentzer, trans. Pierre Hodgson (London and Boston: Faber and Faber, 1995 [French edition, 1994]), note 1, 22. For further discussion of the reception of the *cinématographe* in Mexico, see John Fullerton, 'Creating an audience for the *cinématographe*: two Lumière agents in Mexico, 1896', *Film History*, 20.1 (2008): 95–114, in particular, 100–101. Probably the most famous instance of the uncanny being evoked by cinematographic projection is Maxim Gorky's review of the *cinématographe* when it was presented at the Nizhni-Novgorod Fair in July 1896. See 'I. M. Pacatus' [pseud.], 'Beglye zametki. Sinematograf Lyum'era', *Nizhegorodskii listok*, 4 July 1896, trans. Leda Swan, in Jay Leyda, *Kino: A History of the Russian and Soviet Film. A study of the development of Russian cinema, from 1896 to the present* (London: George Allen & Unwin, 1960), Appendix 2, 407–409; an extract from the review is also available in Richard Taylor (editor and trans.) with Ian Christie (co-editor with an Introduction), *The Film Factory: Russian and Soviet Cinema in Documents 1896–1939* (London: Routledge and Kegan Paul, 1988), 25–26.

27. In 4.31, the corner of the Iglesia is seen on the right of the plate; in 4.32, two walls of the Iglesia can be seen on the left of the principal structure; and 4.33 presents the west facade of Iglesia with the corner of Las Monjas on the extreme right. The plates are bound in sequence, facing 293, 294, and 296.

28. William Daniell [and Richard Ayton], *A Voyage Round Great Britain, Undertaken in the Summer of the Year 1813, and Commencing from the Land's-End, Cornwall, by Richard Ayton. With a Series of Views, Illustrative of the Character and Prominent Features of the Coast, Drawn and Engraved by William Daniell, A.R.A.*, 8 vols. (London: Longman, Hurst, Rees, Orme, and Brown, and William Daniell, 1814–1825), respectively, Vol. I (1814), Vol. II (1815), Vol. III (1818), Vol. IV (1820), Vol. V (1821), Vol. VI (1822), Vol. VII (1824), Vol. VIII (1825). Richard Ayton contributed the letterpress for the first two volumes (1814–1815); thereafter, authorship passed to William Daniell. A landmark in English topographical books published in the early 1800s, *A Voyage Round Great Britain* contained 308 hand-coloured plates engraved in aquatint with more than 800 pages of descriptive text. The articulation to which I allude occurs between three consecutive plates: *Exterior of Fingal's Cave, Staffa*; *Entrance to Fingal's Cave, Staffa*; and *In Fingals* [*sic*] *Cave*. Daniell, *A Voyage Round Great Britain*, facing 37, facing 38, and facing 40.

29. For discussion of stratigraphy in eighteenth-century archaeological investigation, see Alain Schnapp, *The Discovery of the Past: The Origins of Archaeology* (London: British Museum Press, 1996 [French edition, 1993]), 275–316.

30. For illustrations by John Clerk of Eldin, see Dennis R. Dean, *James Hutton and the History of Geology* (Ithaca and London: Cornell University Press, 1992), Figure

4, facing 16 (Arthur's Seat and Salisbury Crags, Edinburgh, c. 1785); Figure 10, facing 62 ('Section of a bank of mineral strata in the River near Jedburgh', 1787, reproduced as Plate III in Hutton); Figure 11, facing 65 ('Alpine schistus appearing as discovered in Jedd River by Jedburgh', detail of a panoramic section of the Jedburgh unconformity, 1787(?)), first published in James Hutton, *Theory of the Earth, with Proofs and Illustrations*, 2 vols. (Edinburgh: Printed for Messrs. Cadell, Junior, and Davies, London; Edinburgh: William Creech, 1795). A third volume of *Theory of the Earth*, comprising previously unpublished notes edited by Archibald Geikie, was published by The Geological Society of London, in 1899. John Clerk of Eldin studied under Paul Sandby in Edinburgh in the 1740s. Klonk, *Science and the Perception of Nature*, 78. For discussion of vulcanist and neptunist accounts in geological discourse at the turn of the century with particular regard to Hutton, see Dean, *James Hutton and the History of Geology*, 93–94, 96–97; Klonk, *Science and the Perception of Nature*, 76–80.

31. Webster included a 'Geological Map of the Isle of Wight and the adjacent part of Hamphsire and Dorsetshire' in which the following strata were identified in a key: 'Strata above the Chalk'; 'Chalk, Chalk marl'; 'Green sandstone'; 'Blue marl'; 'Ferruginous sand'; 'Purbeck limestone'; 'Portland Oolite'; 'Kimmeridge Strata'; 'Other Beds below the Portland'. Thomas Webster, 'Explanation of the Plate', Henry C. Englefield, *A Description of the Principal Picturesque Beauties, Antiquities, and Geological Phenomena, of the Isle of Wight. By Sir Henry C. Englefield, Bar[t]. With Additional Observations of the Strata of the Island, and their Continuation in the Adjacent Parts of Dorsetshire. By Thomas Webster, Esq. Illustrated by Maps and Numerous Engravings by W. and G. Cooke, From Original Drawings by Sir H. Englefield and T. Webster* (London: printed by William Bulmer and Co. for Payne and Foss, 1816), xxvii. For illustration, see David Gainster, Sarah McCarthy, Bernard Nurse (eds.), *Making History: Antiquaries in Britain 1707–2007*, exhibition catalogue (London: Royal Academy of Arts and Society of Antiquaries of London, 2007), 190–191. Thomas Webster, who had been associated with John Varley and Cornelius Varley in the early nineteenth century, should not to be confused with the Victorian genre painter of the same name.

32. Aquatint is an intaglio process in which the outline of the image is first etched or engraved on the copper plate and then dusted with rosin and heated so that the rosin adheres to it. When the plate is bitten, the acid eats around the grains of rosin. If, at this point, the plate were inked and printed, it would print as uniformly toned. Through a process of stopping-out and re-biting, the tones can be varied: the more the plate is bitten, the deeper the pits made by the acid become, which areas, when printed, appear darker. Bermingham, *Learning to Draw*, note 61, 259. Aquatint was first developed in France. In Britain, P. P. Burdett is credited with the earliest aquatint in England (1771); John Clerk of Eldin tried to copy the process in 1775, the same year in which Paul Sandby issued his first series of Welsh views which demonstrated that he had mastered the medium. Carl Paul Barbier, *William Gilpin: His Drawings, Teaching, and Theory of the Picturesque* (Oxford: Clarendon Press, 1963), 67.

33. John MacCulloch, 'On Staffa', *Transactions of the Geological Society* [*of London*], vol. 2 (1814), 501–509, 501. MacCulloch was appointed geologist to the Trigonometrical Survey in 1814 and served as Vice-President of the Geological Society of London before serving as President between 1816 and 1818.

34. For reproduction of engravings of Fingal's Cave in Thomas Pennant, *A Tour in Scotland, and Voyage to the Hebrides*, 2 vols. (London, 1774–1776), and Barthélemi Faujas de Saint-Fond, *Voyage en Angleterre, en Écosse, et aux Hébrides*, 2 vols. (Paris, 1797, English translation, London, 1799), see Klonk, *Science and the Perception of Nature*, Figure 46 and Figure 47, 75; for reproduction of engravings of the entrance to Fingal's Cave and the island of Staffa in John MacCulloch, *A Description of the Western Isles*, 3 vols. (Edinburgh, 1819), see Klonk, *Science and the Perception of Nature*, Figure 54 and Figure 55, 84.

35. The aquatint reproduced in this study is from a copy of Daniell, *A Voyage Round Great Britain*, III (1818), held at the National Library of Scotland, shelfmark FB.1.169. Between 1784 and 1794, William Daniell toured India with his uncle, where he is known to have used a camera obscura. Daniell may also have used the device (or similar instrument) for some of his drawings in *A Voyage Round Great Britain*. Klonk, *Science and the Perception of Nature*, 131.

36. William Daniell, *Illustrations of the Island of Staffa in a Series of Views. Accompanied by Topographical and Geological Descriptions* (London: Longman, Hurst, Rees, Orme, and Brown; William Daniel, 1818), 1.

37. Daniell, *Illustrations of the Island of Staffa in a Series of Views*, 3–4. The quotation from MacCulloch was first published in John MacCulloch, 'On Staffa', 503. For further discussion of Daniell's aquatints of Staffa, particularly his use of colour and the distribution of light and shade, see Klonk, *Science and the Perception of Nature*, 67–68, 80, 85, 87.

38. The stratigraphy of Staffa and its relation to that of the neighbouring islands of Iona, Mull, and what McCulloch refers to as the Treshanish Islands (i.e., the Treshnish islands of Bac Mor, Lunga, and Fladda), is discussed by MacCulloch: 'If we cast our eyes on the map ... we shall perceive that it [Staffa] is embayed in large sinuosity, formed in the island of Mull, and nearly enclosed on the opposite side of Iona, and the Treshanish Islands. ... It is to the former then, that we must look for the origin of the rolled stones which cover Staffa.' MacCulloch, 'On Staffa', 507.

39. The conjunction of such interests is demonstrated by Catherwood's library which contained the following geological studies published before 1845: W. Mullinger Higgins, *The Book of Geology: Being an Elementary Treatise on that Science* (London, 1842); Andrew Ure, *New System of Geology in which the Great Revolutions of the Earth and Animated Nature are Reconciled at Once to Modern Science and Sacred History* (London, 1829); G. Poulett Scrope, *Considerations on Volcanoes, the Probable Causes of their Phenomena, the Laws which Determine their March, and the Disposition of their Products, and their Connexion with the Present State and Past History of the Globe; Leading to the Establishment of A New Theory of the Earth* (London, 1825); Claude Nicholas Ordinaire, trans. R. C. Dallas, *Natural History of Volcanoes* (London, 1801); Thomas Allan of Edinburgh, *Mineralogical Nomenclature Alphabetically Arranged: With Synoptic Tables of the Chemical Analyses of Minerals* (Edinburgh, 1814). *Catalogue of a Portion of the Library of the Late Frederic* [*sic*] *Catherwood, Esq. Hon Member of the Royal Institute of British Architects, Author of Views and Monuments in Central America etc. Also a Portion of the Library of an Eminent Surgeon, Retiring from Practice ..., Which will be Sold by Auction by Messrs. Puttick and Simpson, Auctioneers of Literary Property, at their Great Room, 191, Piccadilly, on Monday, December 1st, 1856, and five following days at one o'clock most punctually*, printed sale catalogue, paginated, item #409 (19), item #507 (23), item #810 (35), item #1176 (49), item #1288 (53). Unspecified works in the sale catalogue included eleven volumes 'on mineralogy and geology', item #1982 (80), and unspecified plates and maps published in the first two volumes of *Transactions of the Geological Society of London* (1811–1814), item #1002 (42).

40. Stacie G. Widdifield, *The Embodiment of the National in Late Nineteenth-Century Mexican Painting* (Tucson: University of Arizona Press, 1996), 14–15. Established as a School of Engraving by Carlos III of Spain, the Academy was originally housed in the Casa de Moneda (Royal Mint).

41. Bullock, *Six Months' Residence and Travels in Mexico*, 163.

42. '[N]ot one landscape nor architectural painter remains … and the only few artists are those who copy religious subjects for the churches, and some who attempt portraits, but they are deplorably bad', Bullock, *Six Months' Residence and Travels in Mexico*, 164.

43. Bullock, *Six Months' Residence and Travels in Mexico*, 167.

44. Other appointments made in the 1850s included J. James Baggally (engraving, appointed 1853), Eugenio Landesio (landscape painting, appointed 1855), and Javier Cavallari (architecture, appointed 1856). Widdifield, *The Embodiment of the National in Late Nineteenth-Century Mexican Painting*, 18, note 12, 169.

45. For an overview of the period to 1867, see Widdifield, *The Embodiment of the National in Late Nineteenth-Century Mexican Painting*, 14–31.

46. Rafael de Rafael, 'Tercera exposición de la Academia Nacional de San Carlos de México', *El Espectador de México*, a series of articles published between 4 January 1851 and 11 October 1851, with the article titled, 'Escuela Mexicana de pintura', appearing in the issue dated 5 June 1851; reprinted in Ida Rodríguez Prampolini, *La crítica de arte en México en el siglo XIX*, 3 vols. (Mexico City: Instituto de Investigaciones Estéticas, Universidad Nacional Autónoma de México, second edition, 1997 [1964]), I, 218–284; 'Escuela Mexicana de pintura', 245–252, 245–246. Translation modified by the author. (*No se nos ocultan las graves dificultades que se oponen a la formación de una escuela de pintura que merezca el nombre de nacional; una escuela que no venga a ser un pálido reflejo, una imitación más o menos servile, más o menos exacts, más o menos excelente, de escuelas de otras climas. Nacido ayer, puede decirse que nuestro país aún no tiene historia; y he acquí que una de las más ricas fuentes donde el artista y el poeta beben sus inspiraciones, no existe entre nosotros.*) For a study of José María Velasco, the international exemplar of a national school of landscape painting in the second half of the nineteenth century and early twentieth century, see María Elena Altamirano Piolle, trans. Antonio Castro, 'José María Velasco: Landscapes of Light, Horizons of the Modern Era', in *National Homage: José María Velasco (1840–1912)*, 2 vols. (Mexico City: Museo Nacional de Arte, 1993), I and II, 35–515. See also 'Landscapes and Identities: Mexico, 1850–1900', in Jorge Cañizares-Esguerra, *Nature, Empire, and Nation: Explorations of the History of Science in the Iberian World* (Stanford: Stanford University Press, 2006), 129–168. For a study of the promotion of Mexico at international expositions in the nineteenth and early twentieth centuries and Velasco's contribution to this project, see Mauricio Tenorio-Trillo, *Mexico at the World's Fairs: Crafting a Modern Nation* (Berkeley, Los Angeles, London: University of California Press, 1996), in particular, 55–58, 64–124.

47. Jean Charlot, *Mexican Art and the Academy of San Carlos, 1785–1915*. Foreword by Elizabeth Wilder Weismann (Austin: University of Texas Press, 1961), 72, 74–75; José N. Iturriaga de la Fuente, *Litografía y grabado en el México de siglo XIX* (Mexico City: Cálamo Currente, 1993), 14–15; Arturo Aguilar Ochoa, 'Nota introductoria', *Álbum pintoresco de la República Mexicana*, facsimile edition (Mexico City: Centro de Estudios de Historia de México Condumex, 2000 [c. 1849–1852]), 13. Charlot has proposed that Linati probably left Mexico for political reasons after advocating an independent general staff for the army as a check to political influence. Charlot, *Mexican Art and the Academy of San Carlos*, 74–75. For further discussion of Linati and reproduction of two early examples of *tipos mexicanos*, see Megali M. Carrera, *Traveling from New Spain to Mexico: Mapping Practices of Nineteenth-Century Mexico* (Durham, NC, and London: Duke University Press, 2011), 87–89, Figure 28, 88, and Figure 29, 89.

48. Claudio Linati, *Costumes civils, militaires et réligieux du Mexique; dessinés d'après nature par C. Linati* (Brussels: C. Sattanino, imprimés à la Lithographie Royal de Jobard, 1828). Miguel Hidalgo y Costilla, the parish priest of Dolores in the state of Guanajuato, sparked the independence movement with his famous *grito* (call for independence) on 16 September 1810.

49. This genre of popular visual culture is often associated with the literary genre dealing with local customs, *costumbrismo*.

50. Iturriaga de la Fuente, *Litografía y grabado en el México de siglo XIX*, 15; Charlot, *Mexican Art and the Academy of San Carlos*, 72.

51. Carrera, *Traveling from New Spain to Mexico*, 124.

52. Iturriaga de la Fuente, *Litografía y grabado en el México de siglo XIX*, 16; Aguilar Ochoa, 'Nota introductoria', *Álbum pintoresco de la República Mexicana*, 15–16; Rosa Casanova and Adriana Konzevik, with foreword by Olivier Debroise, trans. Deborah Nagao, *Mexico, A Photographic History: A Selective Catalogue of the Fototeca Nacional of the INAH* [Instituto Nacional de Antropología e Historia] (Mexico City: Instituto Nacional de Antropología e Historia / CONACULTA [Consejo Nacional para la Cultura y las Artes] / Editorial RM, 2007), 154.

53. Aguilar Ochoa, 'Nota introductoria', *Álbum pintoresco de la República Mexicana*, 13.

54. John Phillips, *Mexico Illustrated, with Descriptive Letter-press, in English and Spanish* (London: E. Atchley, Library of Fine Arts, 1848). Phillips prepared the letterpress for *Mexico Illustrated*, and Phillips and Alfred Rider (who arrived in Mexico in May 1844) were variously responsible for the lithographs engraved by Day & Son in London. The work of Carl Nebel and Pietro Gualdi had considerable influence on the twenty-six hand-coloured chromolithographs included in *Mexico Illustrated*; the chromolithograph, *San Agustín de las Cuevas*, is attributed to Phillips. Roberto L. Mayer, 'Phillips, Rider y su álbum *Mexico Illustrated: ¿Quiénes fueron los autores de los dibujos originales?*', *Anales del Instituto de Investigaciones Estéticas*, vol. 22, no. 76 (Spring 2000), 291–306, 292, 302, 306.

55. Phillips, *Mexico Illustrated*, unpaginated letterpress to plate 17, *San Agustin* [*sic*] *de las Cuevas*.

56. Mayer, 'Phillips, Rider y su álbum *Mexico Illustrated*', 291. From the late 1820s, a series of studies concerning the mineral wealth of Mexico was published, the model being established by Henry George Ward, *Mexico in 1827. By H. G. Ward. His Majesty's Chargé d'Affaires in that Country during the years 1825, 1826, and part of 1827* (London: Henry Colburn, 1828). The following year, Elizabeth Emily Ward, his wife, published engravings after drawings she made in Henry George Ward, *Six Views of the Most Important Towns and Mining Districts upon the Table Land of Mexico. Drawn by Mrs. H. G. Ward, and Engraved by Mr. Pye. With a statistical account of each* (London: Henry Colburn, 1829).

57. *San Agustin* [*sic*] *de las Cuevas, at the time of the 'Fiesta'*, letterpress, Daniel Thomas Egerton, *Egerton's Views in Mexico; Being a Series of Twelve Coloured Plates, Executed by Himself from his Original Drawings, Accompanied with a short Description* (London: D. T. Egerton, 1840). Emphasis in original. The chromolithograph is signed by

Egerton and dated 1839. Between 1824 and 1829, Egerton exhibited paintings at the Society of British Artists, before visiting Mexico in 1830. In 1835, he travelled to the USA and on his return to London, exhibited paintings of Mexico at the Society of British Artists. Twelve of these subjects were reproduced as hand-coloured chromolithographs in *Egerton's Views in Mexico*, with descriptions by Egerton. Egerton returned to Mexico, moving to the outlying village of Tacubaya where, in April 1842, he and his partner, Agnes Edwards, were murdered. Martin Kiek, 'Prologo, Egerton en México', *Egerton en México 1830–1842*, n.p., facsimile edition (Mexico City: Edicion Privada de Cartón y Papel de México, 1976), copy no. 0427 consulted, Fondo Reservado, Biblioteca Nacional UNAM. The village of San Agustín de las Cuevas, better known today as Tlalpan, constitutes a distinct suburban community to the south of Mexico City, where an annual festival is still held at Easter. I thank Roberto L. Mayer who generously gave me access to *Egerton's Views in Mexico* in his private collection.

58. 'Letter the Twenty-First', 15 June [1840], Frances Calderón de la Barca, *Life in Mexico, during a Residence of Two Years, in that Country. By Madame C- de la B-. With a Preface by W. H. Prescott* (London: Chapman and Hall, 1843), 164, 168.

59. 'Letter the Forty-First', 10 June [1841], Calderón de la Barca, *Life in Mexico, during a Residence of Two Years*, 306.

60. 'Letter the Forty-First', 10 June [1841], Calderón de la Barca, *Life in Mexico, during a Residence of Two Years*, 305, 307.

61. 'Letter the Forty-First', 10 June [1841], Calderón de la Barca, *Life in Mexico, during a Residence of Two Years*, 307.

62. With fifty engravings (twenty of which were hand coloured), the publication was printed in Paris by chez M. Moench and chez Paul Renouard. An edition (in Spanish) was subsequently published in Mexico City in 1840.

63. Carl Nebel, 'Préface', *Voyage pittoresque et archéologique dans la partie la plus intéressante du Mexique par C. Nebel, architecte* (Paris: chez M. Moench and chez Paul Renouard, 1836), n.p. (*[D]ans mes dessins, j'ai représente les objets consciencieusement et avec la plus grande exactitude, sans que la fantasie y ait eu aucune part.*) Translation from French by the author.

64. *Mexico [City.] View from the Archbishopric of Tacubaya*. The chromolithograph was prepared by Frédéric (Federico) Miahle.

65. Nebel, *Voyage pittoresque et archéologique*, n.p. (*Il peut se trouver dans le monde des capitales situées dans des parages plus fertiles et plus pittoresques; mais il sera difficile de trouver une contrée d'un caractère plus grandiose et plus digne de posséder dans son sein le chef-lieu d'un empire que la vallée de Mexico.*)

66. *Álbum pintoresco de la Repúblic Mexicana* (Mexico City: Julio Michaud y Thomas, n.d. [c. 1849–1852]), a publication which reworked engravings by Gualdi and Nebel, and included, in three instances, work by Pedro Irigoyen, Herculano Méndez, and James Walker. I thank Roberto L. Mayer who generously gave me access to *Álbum pintoresco de la República Mexicana* in his private collection.

67. *Indian charcoal burners. General view of Mexico [City] from Tacubaya*. The chromolithograph was prepared by Pierre-Frédéric Lehnert. Arturo Aguilar Ochoa has proposed that, despite the reference to Julio Michaud y Thomas on the title-page (who sold the publication in Mexico City), the album was printed in Paris by Rose-Joseph Lemercier and Prodhomme. Aguilar Ochoa, 'Nota introductoria', *Álbum pintoresco de la República Mexicana*, 12.

68. Aubert, born in Lyon in 1829, where he studied painting, arrived in Mexico with the imperial court of Emperor Maximilian (Maximiliano). Aubert set up business at 2ª Calle de San Francisco 7 (present-day Madero), one of the principal streets of Mexico City, in a studio that had been previously occupied by a French photographer, Amiel, known as a photographer of *cartes de visite*. At least two other photographers were associated with Aubert y Compañía: Julio de Maria de Campo (possibly of Spanish origin) and a photographer named Torres. Aubert was appointed court photographer in August 1866, and was primarily responsible for documenting the French presence in Mexico, producing portraits of important political and social figures, ladies of the court, chamberlains, and aides-de-camp. After the French withdrawal from Mexico in 1867, Aubert set up a photographic practice in Algeria. Arturo Aguilar Ochoa, 'Fotorreporteros viajeros en México', *Alquimia*, 2.5 (1999): 7–15, 8; Olivier Debroise, *Mexican Suite: A History of Photography in Mexico*, trans. (and revised in collaboration with the author) Stella de Sá Rego (Austin: University of Texas Press, 2001 [Spanish-language edition, 1994]), 168–169.

69. Porfirio Díaz was head of state between 1876 and 1911 (when Díaz abdicated) except for the period between 1880 and 1884 when Manuel González held the presidency.

70. Debroise, *Mexican Suite*, 79.

71. Briquet may have been commissioned by the railway company to take photographs. Casanova and Konzevik, *Mexico, A Photographic History*, 139. In the latter part of the century, Briquet's photographs were sold in Mexico City by Claudio Pellandini, constructor of the Pasaje Ignacio Zaragoza in Puebla. Rosa Casanova, 'De vistas y retratos: la construcción de un repertorio fotográfico en México, 1839–1890', in Rosa Casanova, Alberto del Castillo Troncoso, Rebeca Monroy Nasr, Alfonso Morales, coordinated by Emma Cecilia García Krinsky, *Imaginarios y fotografía en México 1839–1970* (Barcelona, Madrid, Mexico City: Lunwerg Editores / CONACULTA [Consejo Nacional para la Cultura y las Artes] INAH [Instituto Nacional de Antropología e Historia] Sistema Nacional de Fototecas, 2005), 2–23, note 83, 23.

72. Mexico City: Debray Sucesores, 1886.

73. Raymond B. Craib, *Cartographic Mexico: A History of State Fixations and Fugitive Landscapes* (Durham, NC and London: Duke University Press, 2004), 183. For further consideration of the opportunity Mexico represented for foreign investment, immigration, and the role García Cubas' *Atlas pintoresco* played in such a project, see Carrera, *Traveling from New Spain to Mexico*, 211, 213, 219–220, 224–225.

74. The date of publication, printed in gilt on the front of the embossed binding of the book, is given as 1878; the publication date of 1877 is generally assigned to the work.

75. Casimiro Castro and Antonio García Cubas, *Álbum del Ferrocarril Mexicano. Colección de vistas Pintadas del natural por Casimiro Castro* (Mexico City: Víctor Debray y Ca., 1877), 41–42. The text by García Cubas was printed in Spanish and English, translated by George P. Henderson (quoted here unmodified); the chromolithographs were prepared by A. Sigogne and Casimiro Castro. (*Antes de internarse la vía en las gargantas del Infiernillo, recorre el primer viaducto de estre nombre, atrevidamente sustentado en la horrenda cuesta de un desfiladero (véase la lámina XVII). ... en fin, todo aquel conjunto, á pesar de la grandiosidad del espectáculo, infunde en el ánima del viajero el mayor pavor y sobresalto al mirarse, como las águilas, recorriendo el*

espacio, en virtud de un leve apoye, remontándose sobre los valles y las selves, y salvano barrancas y precipicios. ... Al salir del túnel 10, la perpsectiva de una hondonada conocida con el nombre de la 'Joya' causa una nueva y agradable sensacion. „Ni en Suiza he contemplado, dice un viajero, un sitio más bello y pintoresco que el que presenta esta porción del camino que se llama la Joya. A un lado de la montaña, que desaparece bajo un manto de musgo y de césped bordado de mil flores silvestres, corónola á manera de diademna una selva de árboles seculares. Al otre lado un valle verde oscuro, atravesado en toda su longitud por un apacible riachuelo que corre murmurando sobre un lecho de arena. ... Seguro estoy que nadie ha pasado por allí sin desear, siquiera por un momento, vivir en aquel lugar, en donde todo respira paz y felicidad.") A watercolour by Castro of the same subject (*Túnel No. 10 Infiernillo*, 1874) is reproduced in *Casimiro Castro y su taller*, exhibition catalogue (Mexico City: Fomento Cultural Banamex, 1996), facing 89.

76. For reproduction of the painting, see Barbara Novak, *Nature and Culture: American Landscape and Painting, 1825–1875,* revised edition with a new preface (Oxford and New York: Oxford University Press, 2007 [originally published 1980, revised with an extended preface, 1995]), Plate 4. The painting is held at the Crystal Bridges Museum of American Art, Bentonville, Arkansas, Walton Family Foundation.

77. Novak, *Nature and Culture*, 12.

78. An argument made in Craib, *Cartographic Mexico*, 65, 123. For discussion of malpractice in land surveying in the state of Veracruz, see Craib, *Cartographic Mexico*, 98–123, particularly 116–123.

79. Rosa Casanova, 'Entre academias y escenografias: el itinerario de Gualdi en Italia', in *El Escenario urbano de Pedro Gualdi 1808–1857*, exhibition catalogue (Mexico City: Instituto de Bellas Artes and Museo Nacional de Arte, 1997), 19–31, 22–31, *passim*; Aguilar Ochoa, 'Nota introductoria', *Álbum pintoresco de la República Mexicana*, 21–22. Gualdi also worked as a painter in mansions of the Mexican aristocracy.

80. Two of Gualdi's panoramic paintings (*Vista panorámica noroeste del centro de México*, 1842, oil on canvas, and *Vista panorámica suroeste del centro de México*, 1842, oil on canvas) are held in Museo Franz Mayer; a third painting in the series is in a private collection; the whereabouts of the fourth painting is not known. Roberto L. Mayer, 'Los dos álbumes de Pedro Gualdi', *Anales del Instituto de Investigaciones Estéticas*, 69 (1996), 81–89, 85.

81. A notice for subscription was published in the periodical, *El Zurriago*, in November 1839. Printed by Massé and Decaen, the first edition was published on 9 January 1841. Arturo Aguilar, 'Pedro Gualdi, pintor de perspectiva en México', in *El Escenario urbano de Pedro Gualdi 1808–1857*, 33–67, 42. For discussion of variations between the two editions, see Mayer, 'Los dos álbumes de Pedro Gualdi', *Anales del Instituto de Investigaciones Estéticas*, 81–89.

82. Respectively, *Southeast view of the panorama of Mexico* [*City*]; *Southwest view of the panorama of Mexico* [*City*]; *Northwest view of the panorama of Mexico* [*City*].

83. 'Panorama de México', *Siglo XIX*, 5 September 1842, 4, quoted in Aguilar, 'Pedro Gualdi, pintor de perspectiva en México', 52. (*... el calle y los contornos de la ciudad con todas sus fábricas y edificios, copiados del natural con la más exacta proligidad* [*sic*] *como puede juzgarlo cualquiera que lo vea.*)

84. The four lithographs considered here are included in an unbound portfolio of engravings, *Monumentos de Méjico* (printed by Massé y Decaen, 1841), held in Reservado Fondo, Biblioteca Nacional UNAM, shelfmark R917.2521F GUA.m. The panoramic view of the northeast part of the city is signed 'Gualdi'.

85. Martin Kemp, *Seen | Unseen: Art, Science, and Intuition from Leonardo to the Hubble Telescope* (Oxford: Oxford University Press, 2006), 241–332, 260.

86. Jonathan Crary, *Techniques of the Observer: On Vision and Modernity in the Nineteenth Century* (Cambridge, MA and London: MIT Press, 1990).

87. Kemp, *Seen | Unseen*, 44–45.

88. William Gilpin, *An Essay on Prints. By William Gilpin, M.A. Prebendary of Salisbury; and Vicar of Boldre in New-Forest, Near Lymington*, fifth edition (London: T. Cadell, Jun. and W. Davies, 1802 [1768]), xii.

89. Manuel Rivera Cambas, *México pintoresco, artístico y monumental. Vistas, descripción, anécdotas y episodios de los lugars más notables de la capital y de los estados, aun de las poblaciónes cortas, pero de importancia geográfica ó histórica. Obra ilustrada con gran número de hermosas litografías, representando las iglesias, plazas y calles principales, fuentes ... todo cuanto puede señalar el grado de nuestro adelanto y el aspecto físico, moral é intelectual de la República. Las descripciones contienen datos cientificos, históricos y estadísticos*, 3 vols. (Mexico City: Imprenta de la Reforma, 1880–1883), III (1883), 444. The lithograph faces 444. (*... el sitio favorito y lugar de recreo de muchas familias ... son todovía los preferidos sitios para solaz y recreo de los habitantes de Morelia.*)

90. Born in Eisenach, Turingia, Germany, in 1882, Brehme studied photography in Erfurt, the capital of Turingia, before travelling to Africa. He returned to Germany and opened a photography studio, but also spent some months in Veracruz in 1906. After a brief trip back to Germany, he returned to Mexico City with his wife, Augusta Carolina Hartmann, in 1910, and opened a photographic studio at 27 Avenida Cinco de Mayo. The following year he joined the Agencia Fotográfica Mexicana, founded by Augustín Casasola, photographing the Revolution. In December 1923, Brehme published his most famous album of photographs from his early years in Mexico: *México pintoresco* (Mexico City: Hugo Brehme, 1923). The album was subsequently published as *Picturesque Mexico: The Country, the People and the Architecture* by Brentano's in New York (1925) and as *Mexiko. Baukunst, Landschaft, Volksleben aufnahmen von Hugo Brehme, mit ein Einleitung von Walther Staub* (Berlin: Verlag Ernst Wasmuth, 1925). Brehme introduced the 'pictorialist' style to Mexico in using filters, toners, gum bichromate prints, and platinum prints. Debroise, *Mexican Suite*, 59–60, 62; Dennis Brehme, 'Hugo Brehme. Una vida entre la tradición y la modernidad', in Michael Nungesser (ed.), exhibition catalogue, *1882 Hugo Brehme 1954, fotograf. Mexiko zwischen Revolution und Romantik / Fotógrafo. México entre revolución y romanticismo* (Berlin: Ibero-Amerikanisches Institut Preussischer Kulturbesitz; Verlag Willmuth Arenhövel, 2004), 12–27, 13; José Antonio Rodríguez, 'Hugo Brehme. La construcción de un imaginario nacionalista', in Nungesser (ed.), *1882 Hugo Brehme 1954, fotograf*, 28–43, 29.

91. *Plaza of Armas (Zócalo) with Cathedral, seen from Palacio Municipal*. With 197 plates reproduced in the Mexican edition of *México pintoresco* and 256 plates reproduced in the German edition, there are singificant differences between the Spanish-, German-, and English-language editions. For example, the plate, *Plaza de Armas (Zócalo) con la Catedral, (desde el Palacio Municipal)*, is not reproduced in the German edition. The Casa Municipal was remodelled in the early twentieth century when the building was provided with two extra floors, a balcony (from which Brehme's photograph was taken), and two belvederes. For photographs of the building in the nineteenth and twentieth centuries, see Guillermo Tovar

de Teresa, Introductory texts by Enrique Krauze and José Iturriaga, *The City of Palaces: Chronicle of a Lost Heritage*, 2 vols. (Mexico City: Vuelta, 1990), I, unnumbered plate, 46, unnumbered plate, 47.

92. The view reproduced in 5.14 was taken from one of the two belvederes added to the Casa Municipal in the early twentieth century.

93. Keith F. Davis, *Désiré Charnay, Expeditionary Photographer* (Albuquerque: University of New Mexico Press, 1981), 165; Debroise, *Mexican Suite*, 88–89, 108–109. Rosa Casanova has proposed that Charnay took the photographs in 1858. Rosa Casanova, 'Las fotografías se vuelven historia: algunos usos entre 1865 y 1910', in *La Fabricación del Estado, 1864–1910*, exhibition catalogue for the exhibition, *Los pinceles de la Historia. La fabricación del Estado, 1864–1910*, co-ordinated by Esther Aceredo and Fausto Ramirez (Mexico City: CONACULTA [Consejo Nacional para la Cultura y las Artes], Instituto Nacional de Belles Artes, and Instituto de Investigaciones Estéticas, UNAM, 2003), 214–241, 222 and note 45, 238. At the end of September 1859, Charnay set out on a further expedition to investigate antiquities at Mitla (in the state of Oaxaca) and in the states of Chiapas, Yucatán, and Campeche, publishing an account of his travels in 1863. Although the chronology of his travels in Mexico is difficult to establish, Charnay published an account on his return to France in February 1861: Désiré Charnay, *Le Mexique, 1858–1861. Souvenirs et impressions de voyage* (Paris: E. Dentu, Éditeur, 1863). Charnay also published a series of large-format albumen prints relating to investigations in Mitla, Palenque, Izamal, Chichén Itzá, and Uxmal: Désiré Charnay, *Cités et ruines américaines: Mitla, Palenqué, Izamal, Chichen-Itza, Uxmal recueillies et photographiées par Désiré Charnay avec un texte par M. Viollet-le-Duc Architecte du Gouvernement suivi du voyage et des documents de l'auteur. Ouvrage dédié à S.M. L'Empereur Napoléon III et publié sous le patronage de sa majesté.* (Paris: Gide Éditeur, A. Morel et Ce, 1863).

94. The five prints held at Mapoteca Manuel Orozco y Berra, Mexico City, reproduced here, measure, respectively, from left to right: 28.2 x 38.4 cm.; 28.2 x 41.7 cm.; 28.7 x 39 cm.; 29.9 x 37.2 cm.; and 29.2 x 39.3 cm. The total length of the prints varies between 199.5 cm. (at the upper edge) and 198.5 cm. (at the lower edge). Four, slightly larger prints (not mounted as a panoramic view), respectively, 33.5 x 44cm., 33.5 x 44.3 cm., 33.9 x 44.5 cm., and 33.5 x 44.6 cm., are held at Musée de l'homme/Musée du quai Branly, Paris. The photographic panorama was published as an engraving by W. Thomas in *The Illustrated London News*, vol. 42, no. 1184, 17 January 1863, 64–65. The first two photographs (from the left) were printed at the bottom of the double-page illustration whilst the third and fourth photographs were reproduced at the top of the page. The final photograph (far right) was not reproduced.

95. The panoramic series of photographs is placed on leaf 14 of the first volume of photographs, *Mexique 1865–1866* and *1867*, held in the collection of the Getty Research Institute. Volume II includes an albumen print by Aubert, identified by Petitjean as *Mexico – Vue pris de Tacubaya* (leaf 3, 22.5 x 34.5 cm.), reproduced as Plate 17 in this study.

96. Petitjean's albums include a 5-print panorama of Puebla (*Panorama de la Ville de Puebla – (1865, 66, 67)*) in the first volume (leaf 3), and a 2-print panorama of the Zócalo in Mexico City (*Palais et Place de México*) in the second volume (leaf 7). Other single prints, designated *panoramas* (i.e., elevated views, taken, in many cases, from churches in Puebla such as Templo de San José and Iglesia de la Compañia) are included in the two volumes. A single-print, *Parte del panorama de Mexico*, signed 'Phot. Pestel' (II, leaf 14), shows a view of Mexico City towards the east, photographed from the mirador of the Colegio de Minería, with a cupola and tower of Templo de Betlemitas in the foreground. For reproduction of this photograph, see Tovar de Teresa, *The City of Palaces*, I, 28.

97. *View of the important Mexican port of Veracruz*. There is no entry for a film with this title in Moisés Viñas, *Índice general del cine mexicano* (Mexico City: CONACULTA [Consejo Nacional para la Cultura y las Artes] / IMCINE [Instituto Mexicano de Cinematografía], 2005). This extensive catalogue of film details two *vista panorámica* of Mexico City (filmed by Salvador Toscano in 1905 and 1906) and various *vistas* of the cities of Guanajuato, Ciudad Juárez, Mexico City, León, and Orizaba. Viñas, *Índice general del cine mexicano*, 540–541. Entries under 'Veracruz' and 'puerto' do not match the title of the footage considered here.

98. The view was taken, like the panorama comprising sixteen picture postcard views considered below, from the top of a relatively new lighthouse rather than the nineteenth-century lighthouse, Faro Benito Juárez, which, located in a former convent, had been used earlier for taking panoramic views of the city. Many of the buildings seen in the panorama were of recent construction: the post and telegraph building was completed in 1902, the customs house completed in 1910, and the lighthouse from which the film was shot began operation in 1910.

99. Built primarily between 1552 and 1779, the central part, the Fuerte San José, was a notorious prison during the Porfiriato.

100. From the sixteenth century until the nineteenth century, Veracruz was surrounded by a defensive wall that included nine bastions (*baluarte*); the Baluarte de Santiago is the only fort to survive to the present-day.

101. Photographs at the Ministry of Education (in the Fondo de la Propiedad Artística y Literaria) were later transferred to the Archivo General de la Nación where, today, they are held in the Centro de Información Gráfica. Casanova and Konzevik, *Mexico, A Photographic History*, 172. The titles on the cards read: #1 *Las postales de esta colección forman la vista general del puerto de Vera-cruz, colocando de izquierda a derecha desde el 1 al 16* ('The postcards in this collection form a general view of the port of Veracruz, arranged from left to right, from 1 to 16'); #2 *Hospital de S. Sebastián Veracruz*; #3 *Instituto Veracruzano. Veracruz*; #4 *Escuela Naval Militar. Veracruz*; #5 *Calle Arista y Pescadería. Veracruz* (street names); #6 *Mercado en construcción. Veracruz* ('Market under construction'); #7 *Calle de Landero y Cos. Veracruz* (street names); #8 *Hotel "Diligencias" Veracruz*; #9 *Cobertizos de la Aduana. Veracruz* ('Customs sheds'); #10 *Entrada al Malecón de Sanidad Veracruz Veracruz* ('Entrance to the Quay of Health'); #11 *Cobertizos de piedra de la Aduana. Veracruz* ('Stone customs sheds'); #12 *Entrada al muelle Fiscal. Veracruz* ('Entrance to Fiscal Quay'); #13 *Estación "Terminal." Veracruz* ('Station "Terminus"'); #14 *Malecón "Porfirio Diaz." Veracruz* ('"Porfirio Díaz" Quay'); #15 *Bodegas de la Terminal. Veracruz* ('Terminal warehouses'); #16 Terminación del Muelle Fiscal. Veracruz. ('End of Fiscal Quay'); variant #16: *El Acorazado Am. "New Hampshire*[.*"*] *Anclado en el Muelle Fiscal Veracruz* ('The battleship USS "New Hamphsire" anchored at Fiscal Quay').

102. USS *New Hampshire* sailed into the port of Veracruz on 15 April 1914, to support the US occupation of the city, and sailed north on 21 June 1914.

103. The moored vessel extends from postcard #13 to postcard #16.

104. American correspondent, 'The United States', *The Times*, 25 June 1867, 6, quoted in Jasper Ridley, *Maximilian and Juárez* (London: Constable, 1993), 276, and cited in John Elderfield, *Manet and the Execution of Maximilian* (New York: The Museum of Modern Art, 2006), 183. Benito Juaréz, a Zapotec lawyer brought up in the state of Oaxaca, led the republican forces that assumed power after the French withdrew from Mexico. Juárez entered Mexico City on 15 July 1867, almost one month after Maximilian had been executed.

105. Elderfield, *Manet and the Execution of Maximilian*, 183.

106. 'Mexique', *Le Mémorial diplomatique*, 10 October 1867, 1122, in Elderfield, *Manet and the Execution of Maximilian*, 191. For other extracts, in English translation, from contemporary newspaper reports, see Anna Swinbourne, 'Newspaper excerpts', Elderfield, *Manet and the Execution of Maximilian*, 182–191.

107. 'Mexique', *Le Mémorial diplomatique*, 10 October 1867, 1122, quoted in Elderfield, *Manet and the Execution of Maximilian*, 191.

108. Elderfield, *Manet and the Execution of Maximilian*, 182.

109. Other French photographers working in Mexico – Auguste (Agustín) Peraire and Adrián Codiglia – also took images of some of the execution victims and their clothing. Codiglia, for example, made a composite print of the firing squad photographed by Aubert before the execution. With the print cut into two sections (and one soldier removed from the image), members of the firing squad were placed on the Cerro de las Companas (previously photographed by Aubert) in an image that included three larger figures onto which the victims' heads, of varying size, were placed before the composite image was re-photographed. The composite print demonstrates a narrative logic that bears little relation to historical record at a time when invention was rife. For illustration, see the glass plate negative, reproduced as a positive print, in Elderfield, *Manet and the Execution of Maximilian*, Figure 37, 90, and the photograph and albumen *carte de visite* (both photographed by Aubert) reproduced in Figure 38 and Figure 39, 90.

110. The re-photographed map by Aubert is the first print contained in the album of *cartes de visite* held at Musée Royal de l'Armée et d'Histoire Militaire, Brussels. The hand-written tags that identify the subject of each photograph appear to be original.

111. *Plan of the city and of operations conducted in Querétaro*. Note the hachuring that represents terrain in the military plan. Figure 5.29, a reproduction of a large-format albumen print of the plan, is printed so that the reader can see more clearly the hachuring and the locations identified in the military plan.

112. Unlike the sequence of action identified in some of the early painted panoramas of British naval engagements considered in Chapter One.

113. Respectively, *The Convent of the [Holy] Cross and the Chapel of Calvario acquired in the defence of Querétaro*; *Place where the Emperor Maximilian, Miramón, and Mejía were executed*; *View of Querétaro*.

114. For discussion of newspaper reports and the narrativisation of historical events, see Elderfield, *Manet and the Execution of Maximilian*, 69–73, 81, 84–93, 121–125, 131–135.

115. The other *cartes de visite* in the album comprise the following views: the exterior of the Convento de Santa Cruz; a bridge and ruined buildings in the San Sebastián neighbourhood of Querétaro; a view of the Cerro de las Campanas; the exterior of the Convento de las Capuchinas (where Maximilian, Miramón, and Mejía were imprisoned); a photograph of a painting of Maximilian's cell; the exterior of the Gran Teatro de Iturbide (where the court martial was held); a view of Querétaro from Casa blanca; and a view of the Emperor's residence in Mexico City, Castillo de Chapultepec.

116. For reproduction of three lithographs depicting the execution, see Elderfield, *Manet and the Execution of Maximilian*, Figure 99, Figure 100, and Figure 101, 182–183. An advertisement for photographs taken in Querétaro, offered for sale at Fotografía de Aubert y Compañía, first appeared in *El Siglo XIX*, 4 September 1867, 3. Arturo Aguilar Ochoa, *La fotografía durante el imperio de Maximiliano* (Mexico City: Universidad Nacional Autónoma de México, Instituto de Investigaciones Estéticas, 2001), 46.

117. 'Courrier politique: Paris, 22 Juillet', *Le Figaro*, 23 July 1867, 3, quoted in Elderfield, *Manet and the Execution of Maximilian*, 187.

118. Educated at Trinity Hall, Cambridge, Maudslay studied Natural Sciences for his first degree which included chemistry, mineralogy, geology, botany, and comparative anatomy (including zoology); physics was not included in the Natural Sciences Tripos at Cambridge until 1870. Graham, *Alfred Maudslay and the Maya*, 25.

119. Maudslay also undertook extensive investigations in Honduras, Guatemala, and Yucatán. A comparable example of an early study of a specific site is represented in E. A. E. Mühlenpfordt's study of Mitla in the state of Oaxaca, *Die Paläste der Zapotecos zu Mitla nebst andern Alterthümern welche im Freistaate Oajaca, Mejico, aufgefunden worden, 1830–1831*, facsimile edition edited with an Introduction by Juan A. Ortega y Medina and Jesús Monjarás Ruiz, *Los Palacios de los Zapotecos en Mitla* (Mexico City: Universidad Nacional Autónoma de México, 1984).

120. Members of the party included a British volunteer, Hugh Price, a young Frenchman, Louis (Ludovico) Chambon ('on a tour through Mexico'), and Gorgonio López and José Domingo López with his son, Caralampio, from Guatemala, who arrived by horse on 20 February. In the main, the workforce numbered only a few labourers from the local villages of Santo Domingo de Palenque and Las Playas de Catasajá, supplemented by villagers from Tumbalá. On rare occasions, Maudslay hired as many as fifty labourers through the *jefe político* of El Salto, Amada Salozorgo (two days' journey from Palenque), or the state governor of Chiapas, resident in San Cristobál de las Casas (seven days' journey from the site). On some days, no labourers worked at the site at all. A. P. Maudslay, 'Ruins of Palenque. Personal Narrative', in F. Ducane Godman and Osbert Salvin (eds.), *Biologia Centrali-Americana; or, Contributions to the Knowledge of the Fauna and Flora of Mexico and Central America. Archaeology. By A. P. Maudslay*, 5 vols. (London: R. H. Porter and Dulau & Co., 1889–1902), Vols. LV–LIX, LIX, 1–6, 3–4, hereafter referred to as Maudslay, *Archaeology*, followed by the page reference to the text volume that accompanies the four volumes of plates devoted to Palenque. A travel account by Chambon was published in Paris in 1893: *Un Gascon au Mexique*.

121. Maudslay, *Archaeology*, LIX, 5; Graham mentions that Maudslay's 10 x 8 format camera was accidentally delayed in New York by his agents, but reached Maudslay at some point, although no date is provided. Graham, *Alfred Maudslay and the Maya*, 175. For discussion of the funding of *Biologia Centrali-Americana*, a work which was as expensive an undertaking as Lord Kingsborough's *Antiquities of Mexico*, see Graham, *Alfred Maudslay and the Maya*, 220–234.

122. For discussion of the clearing of the site, see Maudslay, *Archaeology*, LIX, 4–5, 6.

123. The difficulty that such an undertaking entailed should not be underestimated. Teobert Maler, a contemporary of Maudslay's, investigating sites in the Yucatán peninsula, provides details of the times of day when it was best to photograph structures at the site of Hochob in the state of Campeche. See, for example, Maler's account of taking images at the site on 12 May 1887, in Teobert Maler (ed. Hanns J. Prem), *Península Yucatán. Monumenta Americana herausgegeben vom Ibero-Amerikanischen Institut, Preussischer Kulturbesitz* (Berlin: Gebr. Mann Verlag, 1997), 'Hochob', 106–109, 109.

124. Commenting generally on Maudslay's work, Brunhouse opines that 'attention to detail made the publication a model of archaeological reporting and a standard reference work on the subject for years to come'. Brunhouse, *Pursuit of the Ancient Maya*, 41.

125. Maudslay, *Archaeology*, LIX, 6; Graham, *Alfred Maudslay and the Maya*, 17; Graham states that the survey commenced on 18 April 1891.

126. Maudslay, 'Detailed Description of the Principal Structures. The Palace', *Archaeology*, LIX, 11–26, 11.

127. Plate 31, Maudslay, *Archaeology*, LVIII.

128. Plate 40, Maudslay, *Archaeology*, LVIII.

129. Plate 51, Maudslay, *Archaeology*, LVIII.

130. Maudslay, *Archaeology*, LIX, 6. Before providing a detailed description of each structure at Palenque, Maudslay provided a short summary of earlier investigations at the site ('Principal Notices and Descriptions of the Ruins') and a topographical description ('General Description of the Site'), Maudslay, *Archaeology*, LIX, respectively, 7–8, 8–11.

131. One album containing fifty-one prints is held at the Bancroft Library, University of California, Berkeley; the other album containing forty-two prints is held at the Getty Research Institute, Los Angeles, many of the prints being numbered on the left side of the photograph and/or initialed on the right side of the photograph. Prints are mounted on recto leaves only in each album.

132. The album held at University of California, Berkeley, documents the following progression through Mexico according to the sequence in which the prints are mounted in the album: Veracruz, Orizaba, Puebla, Mexico City, Guadalupe, San Juan del Río, Tepeji-del-Río, San Juan de Los Lagos, Querétaro, Aguascalientes, León, Zacatecas, Sombrerete, Guadalajara, Durango, Maravatio, La Noria (state of Durango), Nazas (Durango), Salinas, Allende (state of Chihuahua), Le Parral, Tepíc, San Francisco (on the road from San Juan del Río to Mexico City), San Miguelito (on the road from Mexico City to Querétaro), and Dolores Hidalgo. The album held at the Getty Research Institute documents the following progression through Mexico according to the sequence in which the prints are mounted in the album: Guadalupe, Aguascalientes, Lagos, León, Dolores Hidalgo, Celaya, Querétaro, San Juan del Río, Arroyo-Zarco, La Cañada (north of Tepeji-del-Río), Tepeji-del-Río, an unnamed hacienda near Acambaro, Chapultepec, Guadalupe, Mexico City, Puebla, Orizaba, and Veracruz. In some cases, prints are duplicated in the two albums

133. The four prints are mounted on consecutive leaves 25–28. Prints #77 and #80, considered here, are mounted on consecutive leaves recto 26 and recto, 27; the two prints not considered here, #81, 'L'Aqueduc', and #76, 'Panorama de la ville pris de Cerro de la Cruz verde', are mounted on, respectively, 25, recto, and 28, recto.

134. The number '77' is visible towards lower frame left, inscribed in the doorway of a bar, and the initials 'E.L.' are inscribed towards lower frame right, over the pavement.

135. '80' is inscribed at lower left; 'E.L.' (very feint) is inscribed in the lower right corner of the print.

136. '36' is inscribed in the lower left; 'E.L.', with the number '64' inscribed beneath, is visible in the lower right corner of the print.

137. 'E.L.' is inscribed on the base of the calvary, an unnumbered print.

138. Sylvester Baxter, *Spanish Colonial Architecture in Mexico, With Photographic Plates by Henry Greenwood Peabody and Plans by Bertram Grosvenor Goodhue* (Boston: J. B. Millet, 1902 [1901]), Introduction, xi. The copy consulted in Fondo Reservado, Biblioteca Nacional UNAM, Mexico City, is a limited edition, the Gómez de Mora edition of Baxter's study, published in Boston by Art Library Publishing Company and J. B. Millet in 1902. The work was first published in Boston by J. B. Millet in 1901. The limited edition comprises a volume of text with 150 prints bound in eight accompanying cases: the prints reproduced here are from copy #41 of the 1902 limited edition.

139. 'The Splendid Church of Tasco', Baxter, *Spanish Colonial Architecture in Mexico*, 196–200, 197–198.

140. The text reads: 'In the extraordinarily picturesque old mining town of Tasco [*sic*], remote among the mountains of Guerrero, is the most splendid example of a church to be seen in all Mexico. This church was erected at the expense of the multi-millionaire, José de la Borda, a mining magnate. It was completed in 1757, and the amount expended upon its construction, decoration and furnishing is set as high as eight million dollars.'

141. In Mexico, churches do not observe the orientation evident in churches in Britain where the chancel and altar generally face east. In the case of the church in Taxco, the church is aligned on a west-east axis, unlike, for example, the north-south alignment of the Catedral Metropolitana in Mexico City.

142. Charles Burlingame Waite remained in Mexico City until approximately 1913, when, after the murder of his brother in 1912 and the violence of the *Decena Trágica* (at the end of which, Francisco Madero and José María Pino Suárez, former president and vice-president, were assassinated outside the state penitentiary), Waite left Mexico for Los Angeles, California. Francisco Montellano, *C. B. Waite, Fotógrafo. Una mirada diversa sobre el México de principios del siglo XX* (Mexico City: Editorial Grijalbo / CONACULTA [Consejo Nacional para la Cultura y las Artes], 1994), 25; Debroise, *Mexican Suite*, 82; Casanova and Konzevik, *Mexico, A Photographic History*, 172, 174.

143. The first two photographs considered here were deposited on 14 August 1901; a subsequent set of photographs of Taxco was deposited on 26 January 1905; two further photographs in the series were deposited on 26 December 1906 and 30 July 1907.

144. The prints include a wetstamp on the back of the photographs: 'San Cosme Vistas'. Santa María la Ribera, a neighbourhood developed in the 1880s and 1890s, was primarily inhabited by skilled workers, small merchants, and professionals.

145. The prints include a wetstamp on the back of the photographs: 'San Juan No 3'.

146. Ireneo Paz and Manuel Tornel, *Nueva Guía de México. En inglés, francés y castellano con toda clase de instrucciones y noticias para viajeros y hombres de negocios* (Mexico City: Imprenta de Ireneo Paz, 1882), 821. For comparison, the 1882 commercial directory lists seven lithographic businesses in the centre of Mexico City and twenty-two jewellery shops, thirteen of which were located on Plateros – San Francisco (present-day Madero), Paz and Tornel, *Nueva Guía de México*, 826, 824.

147. T. Philip Terry, *Terry's Mexico Handbook for Travellers* (Mexico City: Sonora News Company, Publishers; Boston: Houghton Mifflin Co., 1909), xxxi.

148. Born in Michigan, Scott arrived in Mexico in 1895 and settled in Siloa, Guanajuato. In his first years in Mexico, he worked as a photographer for the Ferrocarril Central Mexicano, before moving to Ocotlán, on the shores of Lake Chapala, in 1900, in which year, Scott began to collaborate with C. B. Waite; in later years, he travelled back and forth between Mexico and California, leaving Mexico for good in 1924. Casanova and Konzevik, *Mexico, A Photographic History*, 174. Percy S. Cox deposited photographs at the Ministry of Education in 1907 and 1908; Winfield Scott in 1909; the French photographer, Félix Miret, deposited a series of black-and-white picture postcard views of Mexico City and nearby towns and cities (Cuernavaca, Querétaro, and Texcoco) at the Ministry of Education between 22 August 1907 and 8 February 1908.

149. *Revised Guide and Handbook for Travellers to Mexico City and Vicinity. With Map and Historical Summary* (Mexico City: American Book and Printing Company, 1922), 193.

150. Gelatin silver prints of both views were deposited for copyright at the Ministry of Education on 14 August 1901, with a wetstamp on the reverse of each print: 'San Cosme Vistas'. Print #1021, the intervening print in the photographic series, is not held in the collection at the Archivo General de la Nación.

151. Gelatin silver prints of all three views were deposited for copyright at the Ministry of Education on 26 January 1905, with a wetstamp on the reverse of each print: 'San Juan No 3'.

152. Although it is not evident from Waite's prints, the market-square was located immediately west of the church of San Sebastián y Santa Prisca. The buildings seen in Waite's photographs of the market, some of which face onto the present-day square, lie just west of the market-square.

153. Raymond and Whitcomb began organising winter and spring tours of Mexico in 1885 for wealthy North American tourists who travelled from Boston through the southern states of the USA to Mexico and back. Travelling in luxury in Pullman carriages (which provided overnight accommodation en route) and Pullman dining-car, the first of the 'Two Grand Excursions of 82 Days through the Southern States, Mexico, and California', in the sixth season of operation, departed from Boston on Monday, 13 January 1890, and returned to Boston on Friday, 4 April. The second 82-day tour departed from Boston on Monday, 10 February 1890, and returned to Boston on Friday, 2 May. *Raymond's Vacation Excursions: New Orleans, Mexico and California* (Boston: American Printing & Engraving Co., 1890), 1, 3. These tours were complemented by 'Two Grand Excursions of 47 Days through the Southern States and Mexico', the first departing from Boston on Monday, 3 March 1890 (returning to Boston on Friday, 18 April), the second departing from Boston on Monday, 10 March 1890, and returning on Friday, 25 April. *Raymond's Vacation Excursions*, 157. The 82-day tours covered a distance totalling 12,236 miles; the 47-day tours covered a distance of 6,448 miles between Boston and the tour of Mexico, returning as far as El Paso, *Raymond's Vacation Excursions*, respectively, 119, 181. The 47-day tours included the same itinerary in Mexico as the 82-day tours except for two cities (Guadalajara and Puebla) which were visited in reverse order. The 82-day tour cost $700; the 47-day tour cost $475, *Raymond's Vacation Excursions*, respectively, 2, 157. For an additional $116, the 82-day tour could be extended to include an excursion to Yellowstone National Park, *Raymond's Vacation Excursions*, 2.

154. The tour travelled through Torreón, Zacatecas, Aguascalientes, León, Silao, Guanajuato, Guadalajara, Querétaro, with a ten-day stay in Mexico City (where tourists visited Guadalupe, the presidential summer retreat of Chapultepec, and Toluca on day excursions), Orizaba, and Córdova, before returning to the USA via Tlaxcala, Puebla, Cholula, and Mexico City before reaching Chihuahua and Ciudad Juárez. The photographic album prepared for Benjamin F. Freeman of Sommerville Mass. follows the order of the tour through the United States but thereafter departs from the itinerary, although all of the major cities visited on the tour are included in the album.

155. Two series of prints shot from the rear of a moving tram in Guanajuato also appear in Freeman's album. Each print has an identification number, presumably to simplify the process of ordering prints.

156. The owner of the album is unknown. Non-professional prints are interspersed on some leaves with prints purchased from professional photographers who worked in Mexico City, primarily Alfred Saint-Ange Briquet and C. B. Waite. One print by Winfield Scott is included in the album, which indicates that the album was compiled no earlier than 1909, the only year in which Scott deposited prints at the Ministry of Education.

157. Kahlo's father, a Hungarian jeweller who had emigrated to Germany, also sold cameras and photographic supplies. After his second marriage to the daughter of a Oaxacan studio photographer, Guillermo Kahlo was able to establish a portrait studio on the top floors of the jewellery shop, Joyería La Perla, Mexico City. Debroise, *Mexican Suite*, 109.

158. The building stands on the corner of Isabel la Católica and 16 de Septiembre, although much of the original space of the building is now occupied by Sanborns, a department store. Part of the original business is still conducted from Casa Boker in 16 de Septiembre, which houses the Boker family archive. For reproduction of some of the photographs Kahlo took shortly before the store was opened, including the store's sumptuous main marble staircase, see Jürgen Buchenau, *Tools of Progress: A German Merchant Family in Mexico City, 1865 – Present* (Albuquerque: University of New Mexico Press, 2004), Figure 4 and Figure 5, 57, and Figure 6, 58; and Gaby Franger and Rainer Huhle, *Fridas Vater: Der Fotograf Guillermo Kahlo. Von Pforzheim bis Mexiko* (Munich: Schirmer/Mosel, 2005), Plates 21–30, 108–120, in particular Plate 25, 114–115, '"Casa Boker". 2 Juli 1900'.

159. One album, in Spanish, is held at the Biblioteca Francisco Xavier Clavigero, Universidad Iberoamericana; the other, in German, is held at the archives of Casa Boker.

160. Alfonso Morales and Servando Aréchiga, 'Domus Dei, Porta-Cœli', in *Guillermo Kahlo. Fotógrafico oficial de monumentos*, with articles by Jorge Alberto Manrique,

Alfonso Morales, Servando Aréchiga (Mexico City: Fototeca del INAH [Instituto Nacional de Antropología e Historia] / Casa de las Imágenes, 1992), 21–35, 21.

161. Casanova and Konzevik, *Mexico, A Photographic History*, 184.

162. 179 prints were later published in Dr. Atl, *Iglesias de Mexico*, 6 vols. (Mexico City: Publicaciones de la Secretaría de Hacienda, 1924–1927), printed by Talleres de la Editorial 'Cultura'.

163. Morales and Aréchiga, 'Domus Dei, Porta-Cœli', in *Guillermo Kahlo. Fotógrafico oficial de monumentos*, 32.

164. The prints discussed here were published along with other photographs of the church in 'El Templo de la Enseñanza', *El Mundo Ilustrado*, year 8, no. 10, 4 March 1906, n.p. (10–11), and 'Joyas del Arte Cristiano', *El Mundo Ilustrado*, year 8, no. 11, 11 March 1906, n.p. (13, 15); the view from under the choir was also subsequently published, in a cropped print with considerably less contrast (with Kahlo's identification number also removed), in Dr. Atl, *Iglesias de México*, III (1925), *Tipos Ultra-Barrocos Valle de México*, 53. La Ensenañza is the popular name by which the church of La Nuestra Señora del Pilar is known.

165. I state 'Western' because many indigenous people in Mexico (and elsewhere in Central and South America) are considerably less tall.

166. I thank Pedro Boker Trauwitz for generously providing access to the German-language version of the photographic album held in the collection of Casa Boker.

167. *1. Hauptplatz, Westseite & Kathedrale, S.-N. / 1. Plaza principal (Zócalo), lado de Poniente: Portal de Mercaderes, Empedradillo, Catedral. S. al N. (1 Principal Square (Zócalo), west side and Cathedral, South-North.*) Translation from German by the author.

168. Respectively, *7. Cinco de Mayo-Str. O.W. links Profesakirche, rechts: Hintergrd: neues Postgebäude / 7. Avenida del Cinco de Mayo, E. al O. (Vista tomada desde la Catedral)* and *8. Aussicht von der Kathedr. Nach Osten. Links: Kuppel der St. Theresenkirche, in der Mitte: Malerakademie, Museum, altes Postgebäude. W.-O. / 8. Calles del Arzobispado, Moneda etc. O. al E.* (*7. Avenida 5 de Mayo, east-west, with la Profesa on the left and and on the right, in the background, the new post office building. 8. View from the cathedral towards the east. On the left, the cupola of Santa Teresa la Nueva, in the middle distance, the art academy, museum and old post office building, west-east*).

169. Casa Boker was designed by the New York architectural firm, DeLemos and Cordes, who later designed Macy's in New York City. Buchenau, *Tools of Progress*, 55. *10. Espiritu Santo-Str. S.-N. (Geschäftshaus Rob. Boker & Co., Span. Kasino, Profesakirche) / 10. Calle del Espiritu Santo, S. al N. (casa de Rob. Boker & Co. – Nuevo Casino Español – Iglesia de la Profesa)* (*10. Calle del Espíritu Santo (employer's establishment, Boker & Co., the Spanish Casino, and the church of la Profesa*).

170. *15. Stadtpark: Mittlere Querstrasse N.–S. Im Hintergrund Maurischer Kiosk. / 15. Alameda, calzada trasversal del centro, N. al S. (en el fondo Pabellón Morisco)* (*15. Alameda park with a cross-path, north-south. In the background, the Moorish Pavilion*). Also known as *Kiosko Morisco*, the pavilion was designed by the engineer, José Ramon Ibarrola, for the New Orleans international exposition held between December 1884 and May 1885, the pavilion being installed in the Alameda after the world's fair. In September 1910, the pavilion was transferred to the Alameda in Santa María la Ribera, where it stands today. Tenorio-Trillo, *Mexico at the World's Fair*, 41.

171. *19. Statue von Carlos IV & Paseo de la Reforma, N.O. – S.W. Im Hintergrund Statuen von Columbus & Cuauhtemoc. (schnurgerade Verbindungsstr. zwischen Mex. & Chapultepec.) 19. Estatua de Carlos IV y Paseo de la Reforma, N. E. al S. O. Calzada principal y recta entre México y Chapultepec* (*19. Statue of Carlos IV and the Paseo de la Reforma, northeast-southwest. In the background, the statues of Columbus & Cuauhtemoc / Principal avenue running straight from Mexico City to Chapultepec*). Popularly known as *El Caballito*, the bronze statue, designed by the architect and sculptor, Manuel Tolsá, was originally installed in the Plaza Mayor (Zócalo) before being transferred to the courtyard of the University in 1834. The statue was subsequently moved to the Paseo de la Reforma in 1852 and, later, moved to its present location outside the Museo Nacional de Arte.

172. Including the calles de Berlin, Bruselas, Londres, and Dinamarca in Colonía Juárez, regarded at the time as the smartest residential district of the city.

173. In the issues published in May and June, and in early December 1905. *El Mundo Ilustrado* was originally established as *El Mundo* in 1894, with publication offices in Mexico City and Puebla. The first issue of the illustrated magazine was published on Sunday, 14 October 1894, priced at 20 centavos an issue and, from 1900, published under the title of *El Mundo Ilustrado*, included 12 unnumbered pages per issue with a page size of 39 x 29 cm. This format continued until July 1908 when the magazine began to be printed on finer paper with 32 pages per issue and a page size of 27.5 x 20 cm., priced at 35 centavos (in Mexico City) and 50 centavos (outside the capital). Issues of the magazine occasionally included two pages devoted to fashion (*Páginas de Modo*) which were later expanded to four pages, placed at the end of the issue. The magazine published articles to tie in with religious festivals and processions, portraits of society ladies, and social dignitaries and politicans. The magazine also published a regular photo series, *México Moderno*, and, on occasion, *México Antiguo*. The magazine was published until the end of December 1909, although cheaper issues (printed on inferior paper, and priced at 25 centavos and 30 centavos outside the capital) were published between 3 October 1909 and the end of the year. The run of the periodical at Condumex has been consulted until the end of 1909.

174. *Glorieta Central de la Colonia Juárez*, *Edificios de la Colonia Juárez*, *Las Calles del Cinco de Mayo*, *Avenida Juárez*, *Fuente de Neptuno en la Alameda*, *Una glorieta de la Alameda*, and *La Avenida del Cinco de Mayo* in, respectively, *El Mundo Ilustrado*, year 8, vol. 1, no. 20, 14 May 1905, 5; vol. 1, no. 22, 28 May 1905, 12; vol. 1, no. 22, 28 May 1905, 13; vol. 1, no. 24, 11 June 1905, 13; vol. 1, no. 25, 18 June 1905, 16; vol. 1, no. 26, 25 June 1905, 8, and year 8, vol. 2, no. 23, 3 December 1905, 15. Unlike other journals published in Mexico, *El Mundo Ilustrado* was published in two volumes per year, issues published between 1 January and 30 June constituting volume 1, and issues published between 1 July and 31 December constituting volume 2 in any given year of publication.

175. Michael Johns, *The City of Mexico in the Age of Díaz* (Austin: University of Texas Press, 1997), 22.

176. Cover, *El Mundo Ilustrado*, year 14, vol. 1, no. 5, 3 February 1907.

177. 'El Palacio de Correos', *El Mundo Ilustrado*, year 14, vol. 1, no. 5, 3 February 1907, n.p. (10).

178. 'El Palacio de Correos', *El Mundo Ilustrado*, year 14, vol. 1, no. 5, 3 February 1907, n.p. (11).

179. 'El Nuevo Edificio de Correos', *El Mundo Ilustrado*, year 14, vol. 1, no. 6, 10 February 1907, n.p. (11).

180. 'El Viaje Presidencial a Yucatan de Chapultepec', *El Tiempo Ilustrado*, year 6, no. 6, 4 February 1906, 100–102. Established as *El Tiempo Literaria Ilustrado. Semanario de Literatura, Historia, Bellas Artes, Variedades, etc.* in December 1900, the magazine was published each Monday under a series of titles (including *Semanario Ilustrado* and *Semanario Literario Ilustrado*) until 1904, when the magazine began to be published each Sunday as *El Tiempo Ilustrado*. Priced at 50 centavos (in Mexico City) and 75 centravos (outside the capital), the page size of the magazine remained constant at 36 x 26.2 cm. During the course of 1901, photographers whose work was published included C. B. Waite (in considerable volume), Manuel Ramos, José María Lupercio, Guillermo Kahlo, Agustín Casasola, and, in later years, Percy S. Cox and Winfield Scott. The run of the periodical at Condumex has been consulted through to the end of 1911.

181. Travel in this part of Mexico was not easy in the early twentieth century. For example, *Terry's Mexico Handbood for Travellers*, published in 1909, states: 'The present method of reaching *Palenque* is to travel by a steamship of the *Compañia Mexicana de Navegación, S.A.* from *Vera Cruz* (3 sailings a month) or from *Coatzacoalcos* to the town of *Frontera*, state of *Tabasco*. ... Sailing dates on application to the head office of the company at *Vera Cruz*. The *Bushnell Steamship Line* operates boats on the *Usumacinta River* ... [but] [t]he journey is usually impracticable except in the dry season, which begins in Feb. and ends in May. While the heat in the forest is almost suffocating, it is preferable to the discomfort produced by the torrential rains – when the rivers overflow their banks, the trails are submerged, mosquitoes and ticks make life a burden, and the Indians refuse to enter the forest.' T. Philip Terry, *Terry's Mexico Handbook for Travellers by T. Philip Terry with two maps and twenty-five plans* (Mexico City: Sonora News Company, Publishers; Boston: Houghton Mifflin Co., 1909), 566.

182. 'El Viaje Presidencial a Yucatan de Chapultepec', 102. The other two photographic 'essays', both titled 'Mérida', were published in the same issue of *El Tiempo Ilustrado*, 108–109, and 112 (... *los principales detalles del itinerario que seguirá el convoy presidencial sobre la vía del Ferrocarril Mexicano*.)

183. *Grupo de los más harmosos detalles del camino.*

184. *The road from Progreso.*

185. Construction of the theatre began in 1900, but, forced to stop in 1902, building was not resumed until 1906. The theatre was inaugurated in December 1908. The shell of the building, with a large dome and the structure to support the roof, can be discerned in the photograph; the towers of Mérida cathedral may be seen to the left of the theatre.

186. The latter port was also known at the time as Puerto México.

187. In, respectively, 'Las grandes obras de Tehuantepec', double-page illustration, *El Mundo Ilustrado*, year 14, vol. 1, no. 4, 27 January 1907, n.p. (8–9), and 'El Viaje Presidencial á Tehuantepec', *El Tiempo Ilustrado*, year 7, no. 5, 3 February 1907, 76–86.

188. The magazine used topographical photographs which had previously appeared in the magazine: four photographs by Eden von Duben (including an elevated panoramic view of the bay of Salina Cruz), one photograph by Waite (of steamships unloading cargo in Coatzacoalcos), and a general view of the harbour photographed by Cox and Carmichael.

189. '[*O*]*ne of the most beautiful tehuana ladies*'.

190. 'El Viaje Presidencial á Tehuantepec', 76, 78–80, *passim*.

191. The film was shot by Toscano and/or Antonio Ocañas who began an association with Toscano in 1907. Ángel Miquel, *Acercamientos al cine silente mexicano* (Cuernavaca: Universidad Autónoma del Estado de Morelos, 2005), 36. The opening of the railway was also the subject of three lost films shot in 1907: *14 vistas tomadas en la vía del ferrocarril de Tehuantepec* (Enrique Echániz Brust and Jorge Alcalde); *Inauguración del interoceánico* (Fernando S. Orozco); and *Inauguración del tráfico internacional por el istmo de Tehuantepec* (Hermanos Alva, 1907). Viñas, *Índice general del cine mexicano*, 101, 253. The shot numbers designated in the discussion of Toscano's film are based on a 35mm viewing copy held at Filmoteca UNAM.

192. Miquel designates this shot as '*Panorámica de Tehuantepec*' in Ángel Miquel, *Salvador Toscano* (Guadalajara, Puebla, Veracruz, Mexico City: Universidad de Guadalajara, Gobierno del Estado de Puebla, Universidad Veracruzana, Universidad Nacional Autónoma de México, 1997), 41–42, 109–110; Miquel, *Acercamientos al cine silente mexicano*, 132. Other shots designated in this manner by Miquel, irrespective of the intertitles which announce the shots, include: *Vista panorámica de Salina Cruz*; *Panorámica del tren presidencial*; *Panorámica de Tehuantepec*; *Panorámica de Rincón Antonio*; and *Panorámica de Puerto México*. Miquel, *Salvador Toscano*, 109–110; Miquel, *Acercamientos al cine silente mexicano*, 132.

193. The shot appears as the last shot in the 35mm viewing copy held at Filmoteca UNAM; a DVD of the film, produced by Filmoteca UNAM, places this shot as the eighteenth shot of the film.

194. *El Señor Presidente abre la reja* (The President opens the gate [literally: railings]).

195. In 1908, the term 'Fotografias de Actualidad' began to be occasionally used for what appear, in the main, to be unposed scenes of everyday life. See, for example: *El Mundo Ilustrado*, year 15, vol. 1, no. 18, 3 May 1908, unnumbered (16): 'Desembarque de Marinos de la Escuadra Blanca en San Diego, (Cal). – (Fot. Fitch)' and 'Playa de San Diego (Cal.) á llegada de la Escuadra. (Fot. Fitch)' which, in the first photograph, is a very high view of marines disembarking; the second photograph presents a very high view of a beach at San Diego with a few people bathing on the beach. Both photographs have the text, 'Fotografias de Actualidad', placed above the image. We should not overlook the fact that in his earliest exhibitions, Toscano included lantern projections which he continued to use, periodically, throughout the first decade of the twentieth century, although no lantern slides appear to have been used in the exhibition of *Inauguración del tráfico internacional en el istmo de Tehuantepec*. For details of the subjects of lantern projections Toscano is known to have produced or used, see Miquel, *Acercamientos al cine silente mexicano*, 112–113; for details of presentations where Toscano used lantern projections exclusively, see Miquel, *Acercamientos al cine silente mexicano*, 114–115; for details of presentations where Toscano exhibited film in combination with lantern projections, see Miquel, *Acercamientos al cine silente mexicano*, 115–125.

196. A gelatin silver print was deposited for copyright at the Ministry of Education on 18 February 1905, with two wetstamps on the reverse of the print: 'Waite Vistas' and 'San Cosme'.

197. Images of the indigenous people of Tehuantepec include a view of people leaving church after mass with women dressed in regional costume, and views of,

primarily, women and children in the market. The view of people leaving church likely comprises stock footage since decoration outside the church indicates that the shot was filmed on Palm Sunday.

198. Anne Friedberg, *Window Shopping: Cinema and the Postmodern* (Berkeley, Los Angeles, Oxford: University of California Press, 1993), 29–38, 81–94; Yuri Tsivian (ed. Richard Taylor), *Early Cinema in Russia and its Cultural Reception*, trans. Alan Bodger, with a foreword by Tom Gunning (London and New York: Routledge, 1994 [Russian edition, 1991]), 201–213; Anne Friedberg, '*Trottoir roulant*: the cinema and new mobilities of spectatorship', in John Fullerton and Jan Olsson (eds.), *Allegories of Communication: Intermedial concerns from cinema to the digital* (Rome: John Libbey Publishing – CIC, 2004), 263–276; John Fullerton and Elaine King, 'Local Views, Distant Scenes: Registering Affect in Surviving Mexican Actuality Films of the 1920s', *Film History*, 17.1 (2005): 66–87.

199. *Panorama of the Port of Mexico* [Coatzacoalcos] *from a steamship*[.]

200. Lateral travelling shots designate what would have been regarded as one type of *panorama* in early actuality film, for example, the well-known *Panorama du Grand Canal pris d'un bateau*, Alexandre Promio, Venice, 1896, Lumière catalogue number 295, although the travelling shot in this instance is relatively obliquely framed. Other examples of travelling shots include the earlier *Panorama pris d'un bateau*, Constant Girel, Cologne, 1896, Lumière catalogue number 227, and *Panorama de l'arrivée en gare de Perrache pris du train*, unknown operator, Lyon, 1896, Lumière catalogue number 130. For discussion and illustration of *Panorama pris d'un bateau*, see Martin Loiperdinger, '227. Panorama pris d'un bateau', in *Film & Schokolade: Stollwercks Geschäfte mit lebenden Bildern. KINtop Schriften 4* (Frankfurt am Main and Basel: Stroemfeld/Roter Stern, 1999), 212–213.

201. *Panorama of the Presidential train.*

202. Tsivian, *Early Cinema in Russia and its Cultural Reception*, 202.

203. *Vue prise d'une plate-forme mobile,* II, unknown operator, Paris, 1900, Lumière catalogue number 1156.

204. Kemp, *Seen | Unseen*, 44.

205. Kemp, *Seen | Unseen*, 45.

206. Other novel optical effects which we find easy to accommodate today but which, historically, were perceived, in a very different light include the famous *Arrivée d'un train à La Ciotat*, Louis Lumière, France, summer 1897, Lumière catalogue number 653. For discussion of this film and responses of the historical viewer, see Martin Loiperdinger, 'Lumière's *Arrival of the Train*: Cinema's Founding Myth', *The Moving Image: The Journal of the Association of Moving Image Archivists* (Spring 2004): 89–118.

207. Ruhland & Alschier were commissioned in 1897 to produce illustrated postcards of Catedral Metropolitana and the Castillo de Chapultepec, but it appears that the cards were samples and did not achieve distribution. The earliest locally manufactured postcards that achieved circulation date back to 1900, when Ruhland & Ahlschier started to publish postcards in Mexico City. Latapí y Bert, a partnership of Eugenio Latapí and Enrique Bert, followed shortly; other companies that published postcards in Mexico in the 1900s included J.G. and I.G. Hatton, J. Granar, K.K., La Joyita, and Iturbide Curio Store. Isabel Fernández Tejedo, trans. Traducciones MB, *Memories of Mexico. Mexican Postcards, 1882–1930* (Mexico City: Banco Nacional de Obras y Servicios Públicas, 1994), 22, 37, 39.

208. The card published by Latapí y Bert is unused; the card published by J. K. is date-marked 26 September 1907 (the same year in which Toscano's film was produced), and was posted from Mexico to a private address in Szombathely, Hungary. In conformity with the Union Postale Universelle, the greeting was written on the recto (image) side of the card, although by 1907, this regulation was in the process of being modified. Fernández Tejedo, *Memories of Mexico*, 31–32.

209. For example, the terms 'panorama' and 'panoramic view' were variously employed by James H. White when filming at the 1900 Paris Exposition for the Edison Manufacturing Company. *Palace of Electricity* (aka *Circular Panoramic View of the Champs de Mars, [no. 1]*) involves an extended circular view (although not a complete turn of 360°); *Panorama of Eiffel Tower* (aka *Eiffel Tower, no. 1* and *Panoramic View of the Eiffel Tower Taken from the Outside*) uses a vertical tilt up and down of the camera, and *Scene from the Elevator Ascending Eiffel Tower* (aka *Scene from the Eiffel Tower, Ascending and Descending* and *Panoramic View from the Eiffel Tower, Ascending and Descending*) was shot from the elevator as the camera ascended the Eiffel Tower. Charles Musser, *Edison Motion Pictures, 1890–1900: An Annotated Filmography* (Pordenone: Le Giornate del Cinema Muto; Washington, D. C.: Smithsonian Institution Press, 1997), entries 841, 842, 844, 606–607.

210. Aurelio de los Reyes García-Rojas, 'Last Years of the Porfiriato – The Cinema Discovers Mexico, Mexico Discovers the Cinema', programme notes to the 'Messico: la rivoluzione filmata / Mexico: Records of Revolution', in *Le Giornate del cinema muto, Catalogo / Catalogue* (Pordenone: Le Giornate del Cinema Muto, 2013), 89–104, 93. Until recently, extant footage was known as *1925 Nuestra Ciudad*, the title at the head of the 35mm viewing fragment held at Filmoteca UNAM.

211. Other considerably earlier films that demonstrate a similar delight in motion include *Départ de Jérusalem en chemin de fer (Panorama)*, Alexandre Promio, Jerusalem, 1897, Lumière catalogue number 408, and *Le Village de Namo: panorama pris d'une chaise à porteurs*, Gabriel Veyre, Namo, French Indochina [Vietnam], 1900, Lumière catalogue number 1296.

212. Ann Bermingham, *Learning to Draw: Studies in the Cultural History of a Polite and Useful Art* (New Haven and London: The Paul Mellon Centre for Studies in British Art, Yale University Press, 2000), 241.

Notes to the Epilogue

1. In the inset on the left of the title, eight natural features, discussed by Alexander von Humboldt in *Vues des Cordillères*, are depicted: the Organos de Actopan; the volcano, Iztaccíhuatl; the Cofre de Perote; the volcano, Popocatépetl; the Montañas de Jacal; the volcano, Orizava [Orizaba]; and the Cascada de Regla. In the inset on the right of the title, four archaeological sites are depicted: Palenque, after Catherwood's 'Front Corridor of the Palace Palenque', in John Lloyd Stephens, *Incidents of Travel in Central America, Chiapas, and Yucatan*, 2 vols. (New York: Harper & Brothers; London: John Murray, 1841), II, facing 313;

Papantla (also known as El Tajín), after 'La Pirámide de Papantla (Llamado el Tajin.)', in Carl Nebel, *Voyage pittoresque et archéologique dans la partie la plus intéressante du Mexique* (Paris: chez M. Moench and chez Paul Renouard, 1836); the site of Monte Albán, south-west of Oaxaca, identified as 'Mitla'; and Uxmal, after Catherwood's 'Portion of La Casa de Las Monjas Uxmal', in Frederick Catherwood, *Views of Ancient Monuments in Central America Chiapas and Yucatan* (London: F. Catherwood, 1844).

2. 'William Gilpin: *A Fragment*', reproduced as Appendix B, Carl Paul Barbier, *William Gilpin: His Drawings, Teaching, and Theory of the Picturesque* (Oxford: Clarendon Press, 1963), 177–180, 177–178, emphasis in original. Gilpin's sketches illustrating the manuscript of *A Fragment* are reproduced as Plates 13–16 in Barbier, *William Gilpin*.

3. Marjorie Hope Nicolson, *Mountain Gloom and Mountain Glory: The Development of the Aesthetics of the Infinite* (Ithaca: Cornell University Press, 1959), 3.

4. John Ruskin, 'The Moral of Landscape', *Modern Painters*, second edition in complete form, 5 vols. (Orpington and London: George Allen, 1892 [1843-1860]), III, Containing Part IV, Chapter XVII, *Of Many Things*, 286–314, 295–296, 297–298, emphases in original.

5. Alexander von Humboldt, *Researches Concerning the Institutions & Monuments of the Ancient Inhabitants of America with Descriptions & Views of some of the most Striking Scenes in the Cordilleras! Written in French by Alexander von Humboldt, & Translated into English by Helen Maria Williams*, 2 vols. (London: Longman, Hurst, Rees, Orme & Brown, J. Murray & H. Colburn, 1814 [French edition, 1810–1813]), Plate VII, *A View of the Pyramid of Cholula, near Mexico*, facing 81. For reproduction of Plate VII, see Laura Dassow Walls, *The Passage to Cosmos: Alexander von Humboldt and the Shaping of America* (Chicago and London: University of Chicago Press, 2009), Figure 5, 89.

6. Humboldt, 'Pyramid of Cholula', *Researches Concerning the Institutions & Monuments of the Ancient Inhabitants of America*, 81–104, 97–98.

Select Bibliography

Aguilar, Arturo, 'Pedro Gualdi, pintor de perspectiva en México', in *El Escenario urbano de Pedro Gualdi 1808–1857*, exhibition catalogue (Mexico City: Instituto de Bellas Artes and Museo Nacional de Arte, 1997), 33–67. *See also* [José] Arturo Aguilar Ochoa.

Aguilar Ochoa, Arturo, 'Nota introductoria', *Álbum pintoresco de la República Mexicana*, facsimile edition (Mexico City: Centro de Estudios de Historia de México Condumex, 2000 [c. 1849–1852]). *See also* [José] Arturo Aguilar.

Aguilar Ochoa, Arturo, *La fotografía durante el imperio de Maximiliano* (Mexico City: Universidad Nacional Autónoma de México, Instituto de Investigaciones Estéticas, 2001). *See also* [José] Arturo Aguilar.

Aguirre, Robert D., *Informal Empire: Mexico and Central America in Victorian Culture* (Minneapolis: University of Minnesota Press, 2005).

Álbum pintoresco de la República Mexicano (Mexico City: Julio Michaud y Thomas, n.d. [c. 1849–1852]).

Altamirano Piolle, María Elena, trans. Antonio Castro, 'José María Velasco: Landscapes of Light, Horizons of the Modern Era', in *National Homage: José María Velasco (1840–1912)*, 2 vols. (Mexico City: Museo Nacional de Arte, 1993), I and II, 35–515.

Altick, Richard D., *The Shows of London* (Cambridge, MA and London: The Belknap Press of Harvard University Press, 1978).

Andrews, Malcolm, 'The Metropolitan Picturesque', in Stephen Copley and Peter Garside (eds.), *The Politics of the Picturesque: Literature, Landscape and Aesthetics since 1770* (Cambridge: Cambridge University Press, 1994), 282–298.

Andrews, Malcolm, *The Search for the Picturesque: Landscape Aesthetics and Tourism in Britain, 1760–1800* (Aldershot: Scolar Press, 1989).

Arundale, Francis, *Illustrations of Jerusalem and Mount Sinai; Including the Most Interesting Sites between Grand Cairo and Beirout. From drawings by F. Arundale, Architect. With a Descriptive Account of his Tour and Residence in those Remarkable Countries* (London: Henry Colburn, 1837).

Aubert, Michelle and Jean-Claude Seguin (eds.), *La Production cinématographique des Frères Lumière* (Paris: Centre National de la Cinématographie, La Bibliothèque du Film, La Librairie du Premier Siècle, Editions Mémoires de cinéma, 1996).

Austen, Jane, *Mansfield Park*, edited by James Kingsley, with an Introduction and Notes by Jane Stabler (Oxford: Oxford University Press, 2003 [1814; second edition, 1816]).

Austen, Jane, *Northanger Abbey*, edited and with an Introduction and Notes by Marilyn Butler (Harmondsworth: Penguin Books, 1995 [1817, given as 1818 on title-page of first edition]).

Balston, Thomas, *John Martin 1789–1854: His Life and Works* (London: Gerald Duckworth & Co., 1947).

Baradère, Henri (ed.), *Antiquités Mexicaines. Relation des trois expéditions du colonel [capitaine] Dupaix, ordonnées en 1807 pour le roi Charles IV, pour la recherche des antiquités du pays, notament celles de Mitla et de Palenque; avec les dessins de Castañeda*, 2 vols. (Paris: Bureau des Antiquités Mexicaines, 1844 [1834–1835]).

Barbier, Carl Paul, *William Gilpin: His Drawings, Teaching, and Theory of the Picturesque* (Oxford: Clarendon Press, 1963).

[Barnum, Phineas T.], *Illustrated Memoir of an Eventful Expedition into Central America Resulting in the Discovery of the Idolatrous City of Iximaya, in an unexplored region; and the possession of two Remarkable Aztec Children, Maximo [sic], (the Man), & Bartola, (the Girl), Descendants and Specimens of the Sacerdotal Cast, (now nearly extinct), of the Ancient Aztec Founders of the Ruined Temples of that Country; Described by John L. Stevens [sic], Esq., and other Travellers. Translated from the Spanish by Pedro Velasquez, of San Salvador* [New York, 1850].

[Barnum, Phineas T.], *Memoir of an Eventful Expedition in Central America; Resulting in the Discovery of the Idolatrous City of Iximaya, in an unexplored region; and the possession of two Remarkable Aztec Children, Descendants and Specimens of the Sacerdotal Caste (now nearly extinct) of the Ancient Aztec Founders of the Ruined Temples of that Country; Described by John L. Stevens [sic], Esq., and other Travellers. Translated from the Spanish by Pedro Velasquez, of San Salvador* (n.d.).

Bartlett, William Henry, *Walks about the City and Environs of Jerusalem* (London: George Virtue, 1844).

Baxter, Sylvester, *Spanish Colonial Architecture in Mexico, With Photographic Plates by Henry Greenwood Peabody and Plans by Bertram Grosvenor Goodhue* (Boston: J. B. Millet, 1902 [1901]).

Belzoni, Giovanni, *Description of the Egyptian Tomb, discovered by G. Belzoni* (London: John Murray, 1822).

Belzoni, Giovanni, *Narrative of the Operations of Recent Discoveries within the Pyramids, Temples, Tombs and Excavations in Egypt and Nubia; and of a Journey to the Coast of the Red Sea, in Search of the Ancient Berenice; and Another to the Oasis of Jupiter Ammon* (London: John Murray, 1820).

Bermingham, Ann, 'Landscape-O-Rama: The Exhibition Landscape at Somerset House and the Rise of Popular Landscape Entertainments', in David H. Solkin (ed.), *Art on the Line: The Royal Academy Exhibitions at Somerset House 1780–1836* (New Haven and London: Yale University Press for The Paul Mellon Centre for Studies in British Art and The Courtauld Institute Gallery, 2001), 127–144.

Bermingham, Ann, *Learning to Draw: Studies in the Cultural History of a Polite and Useful Art* (New Haven and London: The Paul Mellon Centre for Studies in British Art, Yale University Press, 2000).

Bicknell, Peter (ed.) with a foreword by Alan G. Hill, *The Illustrated Wordsworth's Guide to the Lakes* (London: Book Club Associates, 1984).

Bingham, Neil, 'Architecture at the Royal Academy Schools, 1768–1836', in Neil Bingham (ed.), *The Education of the Architect. Proceedings of the 22nd Annual Symposium of the Society of Architectural Historians of Great Britain* (London: Art Workers' Guild, 1993), 5–14.

Blake, Mary Elizabeth and Margaret F. Sullivan, *Mexico: Picturesque, Political, Progressive* (Boston: Lee & Shepard; New York: Charles T. Dillingham, 1888).

Bonehill, John and Stephen Daniels (eds.), *Paul Sandby (1731–1809): Picturing Britain, A Bicentenary Exhibition*, exhibition catalogue (London: Royal Academy of Arts, 2009).

Brehme, Dennis, 'Hugo Brehme. Una vida entre la tradición y la modernidad', in Michael Nungesser (ed.), *1882 Hugo Brehme 1954, fotograf. Mexiko zwischen Revolution und Romantik / Fotógrafo. México entre revolución y romanticismo*, exhibition catalogue (Berlin: Ibero-Amerikanisches Institut Preussischer Kulturbesitz; Verlag Willmuth Arenhövel, 2004), 12–27.

Brehme, Hugo, *México pintoresco* (Mexico City: Hugo Brehme, 1923).

Brown, Richard, *The Principles of Practical Perspective; or, Scenographic Projection: Containing Universal Rules for Delineating Designs on Various Surfaces, and Taking Views from Nature, by the Most Simple and Expeditious Methods. To which are Added, Rules for Shadowing, and the Elements of Painting. The Whole Treated in a Manner Calculated to Render the Science of Perspective and the Art of Drawing Easy of Attainment to Every Capacity. Illustrated with Fifty-one Plates. By Richard Brown, Architect and Professor of Perspective* (London: Samuel Leigh, 1815).

Bruce, James, *Travels to Discover the Source of the Nile, In the Years 1768, 1769, 1770, 1771, 1772, and 1773. In five volumes. By James Bruce, of Kinnaird, Esq. F.R.S.* (Edinburgh: Printed by J. Ruthven, for G. G. J. and J. Robinson, London, 1790).

Brunhouse, Robert Levere, *In Search of the Maya: The First Archaeologists* (Albuquerque: University of New Mexico Press, 1973).

Brunhouse, Robert Levere, *Pursuit of the Ancient Maya: Some Archaeologists of Yesteryear* (Albuquerque: University of New Mexico Press, 1975).

Buchenau, Jürgen, *Tools of Progress: A German Merchant Family in Mexico City, 1865 - Present* (Albuquerque: University of New Mexico Press, 2004).

Buck, Samuel and Nathaniel Buck, *Buck's Antiquities; or Venerable Remains of Above Four Hundred Castles, Monasteries, Palaces, &c., &c. in England and Wales. With near One Hundred Views of Cities and Chief Towns*, 3 vols. (London: D. Bond, 1774).

Bullock, William, *Six Months' Residence and Travels in Mexico; Containing Remarks on the Present State of New Spain, its Natural Productions, State of Society, Manufactures, Trade, Agriculture, and Antiquities, &c. With Plates and Maps. By W. Bullock, F.L.S. Proprietor of the late London Museum* (London: John Murray, 1824).

Burford, John and Robert Burford and (unattributed) William Bullock, Jr., *Description of a View of the City of Mexico, and surrounding country, now exhibiting at the Panorama, Leicester-Square. Painted by the Proprietors, J. and R. Burford, from drawings taken in the summer of 1823, Brought to this Country, by Mr. W. Bullock* (London: J. and C. Adlard, 1826).

Burford, Robert and (unattributed) Frederick Catherwood, *Description of a View of the City of Jerusalem and the surrounding country, now exhibiting at the Panorama, Leicester Square. Painted by the Proprietor, Robert Burford, from drawings taken in 1834, by Mr. F. Catherwood, Architect* (London: Printed by T. Brettell, 1835).

Burford, Robert and (unattributed) Frederick Catherwood, *Description of a View of The Great Temple of Karnak and the surrounding city of Thebes, now exhibiting at the Panorama, Leicester Square. Painted by the Proprietor, Robert Burford, from drawings taken by Mr. F. Catherwood , Architect, in 1833* (London: Printed by G. Nichols [n.d.]).

Burford, Robert and (unattributed) Frederick Catherwood, *Description of a View of The Great Temple of Karnak and the Surrounding City of Thebes; also, The City of Jerusalem, with the Surrounding Country, now exhibiting at the Rotunda, on The Mound, Painted by the Proprietors, From Drawings taken in 1833–34, by Mr F. Catherwood, Architect* (Leith: Printed by William Heriot, 1837).

Burford, Robert and (unattributed) Frederick Catherwood, *Description of a View of the Ruins of the Temples of Baalbec, Now Exhibiting at the Panorama, Leicester Square. Painted by the Proprietor, Robert Burford, assisted by H. C. Selous, from Drawings taken on the Spot by F. Catherwood, Esq.* (London: Printed by Geo. Nichols, 1844).

Burford, Robert, *Description of the Panorama of the Superb City of Mexico, and the Surrounding Scenery, Painted on 2700 square feet of Canvas, by Robert Burford, Esq. From Drawings made on the Spot, at the request of the Mexican Government, by Mr. W. Bullock, Jr. Now open for Public Inspection at the Rotunda, New-York* (New York: Printed by E. Conrad, 1828).

Cabrera, Paul Félix, *Teatro Critico Americano*, *see* Antonio del Río.

Calderón de la Barca, Frances, *Life in Mexico, during a Residence of Two Years, in that Country. By Madame C- de la B-. With a Preface by W. H. Prescott* (London: Chapman and Hall, 1843).

Campbell, Reau, *Campbell's Complete Guide and Descriptive Book of Mexico* (Chicago: Poole Bros. Press, 1895).

Cañizares-Esguerra, Jorge, *How to Write the History of the New World: Histories, Epistemologies, and Identities in the Eighteenth-Century Atlantic World* (Stanford: Stanford University Press, 2001).

Cañizares-Esguerra, Jorge, *Nature, Empire, and Nation: Explorations of the History of Science in the Iberian World* (Stanford: Stanford University Press, 2006).

Cardinal, Roger, 'Romantic Travel', in Roy Porter (ed.), *Rewriting the Self: Histories from the Renaissance to the Present* (London: Routledge, 1997), 135–155.

Carrera, Megali M., *Traveling from New Spain to Mexico: Mapping Practices of Nineteenth-Century Mexico* (Durham, NC, and London: Duke University Press, 2011).

Carrott, Richard G., *The Egyptian Revival: Its Sources, Monuments, and Meaning 1808–1858* (Berkeley, Los Angeles, London: University of California Press, 1978).

Casanova, Rosa, 'De vistas y retratos: la construcción de un repertorio fotográfico en México, 1839–1890', in Rosa Casanova, Alberto del Castillo Troncoso, Rebeca Monroy Nasr, Alfonso Morales, coordinated by Emma Cecilia García Krinsky, *Imaginarios y fotografía en México 1839–1970* (Barcelona, Madrid, Mexico City: Lunwerg Editores / CONACULTA / INAH / Sistema Nacional de Fototecas, 2005), 2–23.

Casanova, Rosa, 'Entre academias y escenografías: el itinerario de Gualdi en Italia', in *El Escenario urbano de Pedro Gualdi 1808–1857*, exhibition catalogue (Mexico City: Instituto de Bellas Artes and Museo Nacional de Arte, 1997), 19–31.

Casanova, Rosa, 'Las fotografías se vuelven historia: algunos usos entre 1865 y 1910', in *La Fabricación del Estado, 1864–1910*, exhibition catalogue for the exhibition *Los pinceles de la Historia. La fabricación del Estado, 1864–1910*, co-ordinated by Esther Aceredo and Fausto Ramirez (Mexico City: CONACULTA, Instituto Nacional de Belles Artes, and Instituto de Investigaciones Estéticas, UNAM, 2003), 214–241.

Casanova, Rosa and Adriana Konzevik, with foreword by Olivier Debroise, trans. Deborah Nagao, *Mexico, A Photographic History: A Selective Catalogue of the Fototeca Nacional of the INAH* (Mexico City: INAH / CONACULTA / Editorial RM, 2007).

Casanova, Rosa and Olivier Debroise, *Sobre la superficie bruñida de un espejo. Fotógrafos del siglo XIX* (Mexico City: Fondo de Cultura Económica, 1989).

Castañeda Paganini, Ricardo, *Las Ruinas de Palenque. Su descubrimiento y primeras exploraciones en el siglo XVIII* (Guatemala City: Ministerio de Educación Pública, 1946).

Castro, Casimiro and Antonio García Cubas, *Álbum del Ferrocarril Mexicano. Colección de vistas Pintadas del natural por Casimiro Castro* (Mexico City: Víctor Debray y Ca., 1877).

Catalogue of a Portion of the Library of the Late Frederic [sic] Catherwood, Esq. Hon Member of the Royal Institute of British Architects, Author of Views and Monuments in Central America etc. Also a Portion of the Library of an Eminent Surgeon, Retiring from Practice ..., Which will be Sold by Auction by Messrs. Puttick and Simpson, Auctioneers of Literary Property, at their Great Room, 191, Piccadilly, on Monday, December 1st, 1856, and five following days at one o'clock most punctually, paginated printed sale catalogue, n.d.

Catherwood, Frederick, 'Account of the Punico-Libyan Monument at Dugga [*sic*]', *Transactions of the American Ethnological Society*, vol. 1 (1845), 478–488.

Catherwood, Frederick, 'Antiquities of Central America', report on a paper delivered by Frederick Catherwood to the Royal Institute of British Architects, 19 February 1844 (in the chair, Thomas Leverton Donaldson), 'Proceedings of Scientific Societies. Royal Institute of British Architects', *The Civil Engineer and Architect's Journal, Scientific and Railway Gazette*, 7 (24 February 1844): 92–94.

Catherwood, Frederick, *Plan of Jerusalem by F. Catherwood. Architect. July 1835* (London: F. Catherwood, 1835).

Catherwood, Frederick, 'The remains of an ancient structure at Bless, near the site of Ancient Carthage', *Transactions of the American Ethnological Society*, vol. 1 (1845), 489–491.

Catherwood, Frederick, *Views of Ancient Monuments in Central America Chiapas and Yucatan* (London: F. Catherwood, 1844).

Charlot, Jean, *Mexican Art and the Academy of San Carlos, 1785–1915*. Foreword by Elizabeth Wilder Weismann (Austin: University of Texas Press, 1961).

Charnay, Désiré, *Cités et ruines américaines: Mitla, Palenqué, Izamal, Chichen-Itza, Uxmal recueillies et photographiées par Désiré Charnay avec un texte par M. Viollet-le-Duc Architecte du Gouvernement suivi du voyage et des documents de l'auteur. Ouvrage dédié à S.M. L'Empereur Napoléon III et publié sous le patronage de sa majesté.* (Paris: Gide Éditeur, A. Morel et Ce, 1863).

Charnay, Désiré, *Le Mexique, 1858–1861. Souvenirs et impressions de voyage* (Paris: E. Dentu, Éditeur, 1863).

Charnay, Désiré, 'Panorama of the City of Mexico – From Photographs by M. Edouard [*sic*] Charnay', *The Illustrated London News*, vol. 42, no. 1184, 17 January 1863, 64–65.

Clayton, Peter Arthur, *The Rediscovery of Ancient Egypt: Artists and Travellers in the 19th Century* (London: Thames and Hudson, 1982).

Cline, Howard F., 'The Apocryphal Early Career of J. F. Waldeck, Pioneer Americanist', *Acta Americana* 5, 4 (1947): 278–300.

Collins, Richard, 'The Ruins of Copán in "The Woman in White": Wilkie Collins and John Stephens' *Incidents of Travel in Central America, Chiapas and Yucatan*', *Wilkie Collins Society Journal*, New Series, 2 (1999): 5–17.

Collins, Wilkie, *The Woman in White* (Harmondsworth: Penguin Books, 1994 [1861]).

Comment, Bernard, *The Panorama*, trans. Anne-Marie Glasheen (London: Reaktion Books, 1999 [French edition, 1993]).

Conder, Josiah, *The Modern Traveller: A Popular Description, Geographical, Historical and Topographical, of the Various Countries of the Globe. Mexico and Guatimala* [*sic*], 4 vols. (London: James Duncan; Edinburgh: Oliver and Boyd; Glasgow: M. Ogle; Dublin: R. M. Tims, 1825).

Corner, George Richard, *The Panorama: with Memoirs of Its Inventor, Robert Barker, and his son, the late Henry Aston Barker. From the "Art Journal," February, 1857* (London: J. & W. Robins, 1857).

Cosgrove, Denis, 'Prospect, perspective, and the evolution of the landscape idea', *Transactions, Institute of British Geographers, New Series*, vol. 10 (1985), 45–62.

Costeloe, Michael P., *William Bullock. Connoisseur and Virtuoso of the Egyptian Hall: Piccadilly to Mexico (1773–1849)* (Bristol: HiPLAM, 2008).

Coxe, William, *An Historical Tour in Monmouthshire; Illustrated with Views by Sir R. C. Hoare, Bart. A New Map of the County and other Engravings: by William Coxe, A.M. F.R.S. F.A.S. Rector of Bemberton* [*sic*] *and Stourton*, 2 vols. (London: T. Cadell, Jun. and W. Davies, 1801).

Craib, Raymond B., *Cartographic Mexico: A History of State Fixations and Fugitive Landscapes* (Durham, NC and London: Duke University Press, 2004).

Crary, Jonathan, *Techniques of the Observer: On Vision and Modernity in the Nineteenth Century* (Cambridge, MA and London: MIT Press, 1990).

Crosthwaite, Peter, *An Accurate Map of the Matchless Lake of Derwent, Situate in the Most Delightful Vale which perhaps ever Human Eye Beheld & near Keswick, Cumberland, with West's Seven Stations* (1819 [1783]).

Cunningham, Allan, *The Life of Sir David Wilkie*, 3 vols. (London: John Murray, 1843).

Dagrada, Elena, 'Through the Keyhole: Spectators and Matte Shots in Early Cinema', *iris*, no. 11, 'Early Cinema Audiences / Les spectateurs au début du cinéma' (Spring 1990): 95–106.

Daniel, Glyn Edmund, *Cambridge and the Back-Looking Curiosity: An Inaugural Lecture* (Cambridge: Cambridge University Press, 1976).

Daniell, William [and Richard Ayton], *A Voyage Round Great Britain, Undertaken in the Summer of the Year 1813, and Commencing from the Land's-End, Cornwall, by Richard Ayton. With a Series of Views, Illustrative of the Character and Prominent Features of the Coast, Drawn and Engraved by William Daniell, A.R.A.*, 8 vols. (London: Longman, Hurst, Rees, Orme, and Brown, and William Daniell, 1814–1825).

Daniell, William, *Illustrations of the Island of Staffa in a Series of Views. Accompanied by Topographical and Geological Descriptions* (London: Longman, Hurst, Rees, Orme, and Brown; William Daniel, 1818).

Davis, John, *The Landscape of Belief: Encountering the Holy Land in Nineteenth-Century American Art and Culture. The Princeton Series in Nineteenth-Century Art, Culture, and Society* (Princeton: Princeton University Press, 1996).

Davis, Keith F., *Désiré Charnay, Expeditionary Photographer* (Albuquerque: University of New Mexico Press, 1981).

Dawson, Warren Royal and Eric P. Uphill (eds.), *Who was Who in Egyptology*, third revised edition (London: The Egypt Exploration Society, 1995).

De los Reyes García-Rojas, Aurelio 'Last Years of the Porfiriato - The Cinema Discovers Mexico, Mexico Discovers the Cinema', programme notes to the 'Messico: la rivoluzione filmata / Mexico: Records of Revolution', in *Le Giornate del Cinema Muto, Catalogo / Catalogue* (Pordenone: Le Giornate del Cinema Muto, 2013), 89–104.

Dean, Dennis R., *James Hutton and the History of Geology* (Ithaca and London: Cornell University Press, 1992).

Debroise, Olivier, *Mexican Suite: A History of Photography in Mexico*, trans. (and revised in collaboration with the author) Stella de Sá Rego (Austin: University of Texas Press, 2001 [Spanish-language edition, 1994]).

Del Río, Antonio, *Description of the Ruins of an Ancient City, Discovered near Palenque, in the Kingdom of Guatemala, in Spanish America: Translated from the Original Manuscript Report of Captain Don Antonio Del Rio: Followed by Teatro Critico Americano; or, a Critical Investigation and Research into the History of the Americans, by Doctor Paul Felix Cabrera, of the City of New Guatemala* (London: Henry Berthoud and Suttaby, Evance and Fox, 1822).

Denon, Dominique Vivant, *Travels in Upper and Lower Egypt, in Company with Several Divisions of the French Army, During the Campaigns of General Bonaparte in that Country; and Published under his Immediate Patronage, by Vivant Denon. Embellished with Numerous Engravings. Translated by Arthur Aikin*, 3 vols. (London: Printed for T. N. Longman and O. Rees, and Richard Phillips, by T. Gillet, 1803).

Description of the highly interesting peristrephic panorama of the City of Jerusalem, with the surrounding country; and the City of New York, now exhibiting at Monteith Rooms, Buchanan Street, Glasgow. Painted by the proprietors, from Drawings taken in 1834, by Mr. F. CATHERWOOD, Architect, and SIGNOR BONONI. Day Exhibitions precisely at 12 & 2 o'clock, Evening do. at Half past 7 & 9 (Edinburgh: Printed by M. W. Reid, 1837).

Desgodetz, Antoine, *Les Edifices antiques de Rome. Dessinés et mesurés très exactement. Par Antoine Desgodetz Architecte* (Paris: Jean Baptiste Coignard, 1682).

Dollond, G[eorge], *Description of the Camera Lucida, An Instrument for Drawing in True Perspective, and the Copying, Reducing, or Enlarging Other Drawings. To which is added, by permission, a Letter on the Use of the Camera, by Capt. Basil Hall, R.N., F.R.S.* (London: G. Dollond, n.d. [1830]).

Dr. Atl [Gerardo Murillo Cornado], *Iglesias de Mexico*, 6 vols. (Mexico City: Publicaciones de la Secretaría de Hacienda, 1924–1927).

Drew, David, *The Lost Chronicles of the Maya Kings* (Berkeley and Los Angeles: University of California Press, 1999).

Egerton, Daniel Thomas, *Egerton's Views in Mexico; Being a Series of Twelve Coloured Plates, Executed by Himself from his Original Drawings, Accompanied with a short Description* (London: D. T. Egerton, 1840).

Elderfield, John, *Manet and the Execution of Maximilian* (New York: The Museum of Modern Art, 2006).

Englefield, Henry C., *A Description of the Principal Picturesque Beauties, Antiquities, and Geological Phenomena, of the Isle of Wight. By Sir Henry C. Englefield, Bar[t]. With Additional Observations of the Strata of the Island, and their Continuation in the Adjacent Parts of Dorsetshire. By Thomas Webster, Esq. Illustrated by Maps and Numerous Engravings by W. and G. Cooke, From Original Drawings by Sir H. Englefield and T. Webster* (London: printed by William Bulmer and Co. for Payne and Foss, 1816).

Evans, Joan, *A History of the Society of Antiquaries* (Oxford: Printed at the University Press by Charles Batey for The Society of Antiquaries, Burlington House, London, 1956).

Evans, R. Tripp, *Romancing the Maya: Mexican Antiquity in the American Imagination 1820–1915* (Austin: University of Texas Press, 2004).

Fairholt, F[rederick] W[illiam], *A Dictionary of Terms in Art. Edited and Illustrated by F. W. Fairholt, F. S. A. With Five Hundred Engravings on Wood* (London: Strahan & Co., 1854).

Fernández Tejedo, Isabel, trans. Traducciones MB, *Memories of Mexico. Mexican Postcards, 1882–1930* (Mexico City: Banco Nacional de Obras y Servicios Públicas, 1994).

Fielding, Theodore Henry Adolphus, *The Art of Engraving, With the Various Modes of Operation, Under the Following Different Divisions: Etching. Soft-Ground Etching. Line Engraving. Chalk and Stipple. Aquatint. Mezzotint. Lithography. Wood Engraving. Medallic Engraving. Electrography. And Photography. Illustrated with Ten Specimens of the Different Styles of Engraving* (London: M. A. Nattali, 1844 [1841]).

Franger, Gaby and Rainer Huhle, *Fridas Vater: Der Fotograf Guillermo Kahlo. Von Pforzheim bis Mexiko* (Munich: Schirmer/Mosel, 2005).

Friedberg, Anne, '*Trottoir roulant*: the cinema and new mobilities of spectatorship', in John Fullerton and Jan Olsson (eds.), *Allegories of Communication: Intermedial concerns from cinema to the digital* (Rome: John Libbey Publishing - CIC, 2004), 263–276.

Friedberg, Anne, *Window Shopping: Cinema and the Postmodern* (Berkeley, Los Angeles, Oxford: University of California Press, 1993).

Fullerton, John, 'Creating an audience for the *cinématographe*: two Lumière agents in Mexico, 1896', *Film History*, 20.1 (2008): 95–114.

Fullerton, John and Elaine King, 'Local Views, Distant Scenes: Registering Affect in Surviving Mexican Actuality Films of the 1920s', *Film History*, 17.1 (2005): 66–87.

Fullerton, Peter, 'Patronage and Pedagogy: The British Institution in the Early Nineteenth Century', *Art History*, 5.1 (March 1982): 59–72.

Fuseli, Henry, *The Life and Writings of Henry Fuseli, Esq. M.A. R.A. Keeper, and Professor of Painting to the Royal Academy in London; Member of the First Class of the Academy of St. Luke at Rome. The Former written, and the latter edited by John Knowles, F.R.S. Corresponding Member of the Philosophical Society at Rotterdam, His Executor*, 3 vols. (London: Henry Colburn and Richard Bentley, 1831).

Gainster, David, Sarah McCarthy, Bernard Nurse (eds.), *Making History: Antiquities in Britain 1707–2007*, exhibition catalogue (London: Royal Academy of Arts and the Society of Antiquaries of London, 2007).

Galindo, Juan, 'Description of the River Usumasinta [*sic*], in Guatemala, communicated by Colonel Don Juan Galindo of the Central American Service, Corresponding Member of the Royal Geographical Society. Dated Flores, on Lake Peten, 12th March, 1832. Read 26th Nov. 1832', *The Journal of the Royal Geographical Society of London. Volume the third. 1833* (London: John Murray, 1834), 59–64.

Galindo, Juan, 'Original Correspondence. Central America. *To the Editor of the Literary Gazette*, Copan, June 18, 1834', *The Literary Gazette; and Journal of the Belles Lettres, Arts, Sciences, &c.*, no. 965, 18 July 1835, 456.

Galindo, Juan, 'Original Correspondence. To the Editor, &c. Ruins of Palenque. April 26, 1831', *The Literary Gazette; and Journal of the Belles Lettres, Arts, Sciences, &c.*, no. 769, 15 October 1831, 665–666.

Galindo, Juan, 'The Ruins of Copan, in Central America. Letter from Colonel Galindo. To the Hon. Thomas L. Winthrop, President of the American Antiquarian Society, Boston, Massachusetts. Copan, June 19th, 1835', *Archæologia Americana. Transactions and Collections of the American Antiquarian Society*, 2 (1836), 543–550.

Gallatin, Albert, 'Notes on the Semi-Civilized Nations of Mexico, Yucatan, and Central America', *Transactions of the American Ethnological Society*, vol. 1 (1845), 1–352.

Gallo, Rubén, *Mexican Modernity: The Avant-Garde and the Technological Revolution* (Cambridge, MA and London: MIT Press, 2005).

Galperin, William H., *The Return of the Visible in British Romanticism* (Baltimore and London: Johns Hopkins University Press, 1993).

Garrison, Laurie, 'Imperial Vision in the Arctic: Fleeting Looks and Pleasurable Distractions in Barker's Panorama and Shelley's *Frankenstein*', *Romanticism and Victorianism on the Net*, no. 51 (November 2008).

Garrison, Laurie, 'Virtual reality and subjective responses: Narrating the search for the Franklin expedition through Robert Burford's panorama', *Early Popular Visual Culture*, 10.1 (February 2012): 7–22.

Gaudreault, André and Philippe Marion, 'A medium is always born twice …', trans. Timothy Barnard, Wendy Schubring and Franck Le Gac, *Early Popular Visual Culture*, 3.1 (May 2005): 3–15.

Gilpin, William, *An Essay on Prints. By William Gilpin, M.A. Prebendary of Salisbury; and Vicar of Boldre in New-Forest, Near Lymington*, fifth edition (London: T. Cadell, Jun. and W. Davies, 1802 [1768]).

Gilpin, William, *Observations on the River Wye, and Several Parts of South Wales, &c. relative chiefly to Picturesque Beauty; Made in the Summer of the Year 1770, Second Edition, by William Gilpin, M. A. Prebendary of Salisbury; and Vicar of Boldre in New Forest, near Lymington*, second edition (London: R. Blamire, 1789 [given as 1782 on title-page of first edition]).

Gilpin, William, *Observations, Relative Chiefly to Picturesque Beauty, Made in the Year 1772; On Several Parts of England; particularly the Mountains, and Lakes of Cumberland, and Westmoreland. By William Gilpin, M.A. Prebendary of Salisbury; and Vicar of Boldre, in New-Forest, near Lymington*, 2 vols. (London: R. Blamire, 1786).

Gilpin, William, *Remarks on Forest Scenery, and Other Woodland Views, (Relative Chiefly to Picturesque Beauty) Illustrated by the Scenes of New-Forest in Hampshire*, 3 vols. (London: R. Blamire, 1791).

Gilpin, William, *Three Essays: On Picturesque Beauty; On Picturesque Travel; and On Sketching Landscape with a Poem, On Landscape Painting. To these are now added Two Essays, giving an Account of the Principles and Modes in which the Author executed his own Drawings. By William Gilpin, M.A. Prebendary of Salisbury; and Vicar of Boldre in New-Forest, near Lymington*, third edition (London: T. Cadell and W. Davies, 1808 [1792]).

Goury, Jules and Owen Jones, *Plans, Elevations, Sections and Details of the Alhambra: From Drawings Taken on the Spot in 1834 by the Late M. Jules Goury and in 1834 and 1837 by Owen Jones, Arch^t. With a Complete Translation of the Arabic Inscriptions, and an Historical Notice of the Kings of Granada, from the Conquest of that City by the Arabs to the Expulsion of the Moors, by Mr. Pasqual de Gayangos*, 2 vols. (London: Owen Jones, 1842–1845).

Graham, Ian, *Alfred Maudslay and the Maya: A Biography* (London: British Museum Press, 2002).

Graham, Ian, 'Juan Galindo, Enthusiast', *Estudios de Cultura Maya*, 3 (1963): 11–35.

Graves, Algernon, *The Royal Academy of Arts: A Complete Dictionary of Contributors and their Work from its Foundation in 1769 to 1904. Compiled with the sanction of the President and Council of The Royal Academy*, 8 vols. (London: Henry Graves and Co. Ltd. and George Bell and Sons, 1905–1906).

Gregory, Derek, 'Emperor of the Gaze: Photographic Practices and Productions of Space in Egypt, 1839–1914', in Joan M. Schwartz and James R. Ryan (eds.), *Picturing Place: Photography and the Geographical Imagination* (London and New York: I. B. Tauris, 2003), 196–225.

Griffith, William J[oyce], 'Juan Galindo, Central American chauvinist', *Hispanic American Historical Review* 40, 1 (February 1960): 25–52.

Gunning, Tom, '"The Whole World within Reach": Travel Images without Borders', in Roland Cosandey and François Albera (eds.), *Cinéma sans frontiers 1896–1918 / Images Across Borders* (Lausanne: Editions Payot Lausanne; Québec: Nuit Blanche Editeur, 1995), 21–36.

Gunning, Tom, 'Before Documentary: Early nonfiction films and the "view" aesthetic', in Daan Hertogs and Nico de Klerk (eds.), *Uncharted Territory: Essays on early nonfiction film* (Amsterdam: Stichting Nederlands Filmmuseum, 1997), 9–24.

Gutiérrez Haces, Juana, 'Etnografía y costumbrismo en las imágenes de los viajeros', in *Viajeros europeos del siglo XIX en México*, exhibition catalogue (Mexico City: Fomento Cultural Banamex in collaboration with the Instituto Goethe de México, 1996).

H. Gaucheraud, 'The Daguerotype' [*sic*], *The Literary Gazette, and Journal of Belles Lettres, Arts, Sciences, &c.*, No. 1147, Saturday, 12 January 1839, 28.

Hagen, Victor Wolfgang von, *Frederick Catherwood Arch^t.* (New York and Oxford: Oxford University Press, 1950).

Hagen, Victor Wolfgang von, *Maya Explorer: John Lloyd Stephens and the Lost Cities of Central America and Yucatán* (Norman: University of Oklahoma Press, 1947).

Hagen, Victor Wolfgang von, *Search for the Maya: The Story of Stephens and Catherwood* (New York: Saxon House, 1973).

Hall, Capt. Basil, *Forty Etchings, from Sketches made with the Camera Lucida, in North America, in 1827 and 1828* (Edinburgh: Cadell & Co; London: Simpkin & Marshall and Moon, Boys & Graves, 1829).

Hammond, John H. and Jill Austin, *The Camera Lucida in Art and Science* (Bristol: IOP, 1987).

Heraud, John Abraham, *Uxmal: An Antique Love Story; Macée de Léodepart: An Historical Romance* (London: Simpkin, Marshall & Co., 1877).

Hewitt, Rachel, *Map of a Nation: A Biography of the Ordnance Survey* (London: Granta Books, 2010).

Hockney, David, *Secret Knowledge: Rediscovering the Lost Techniques of the Old Masters*, new and expanded edition (New York: Viking Studio, 2006 [2000]).

Hoock, Holger, *The King's Artists: The Royal Academy of Arts and the Politics of British Culture 1760–1840* (Oxford: Clarendon Press, 2003).

Horne, Thomas Hartwell, *Landscape Illustrations of the Bible, Consisting of Views of the Most Remarkable Places Mentioned in the Old and New Testaments. From original sketches taken on the spot. Engraved by W. and E. Finden. With descriptions by the Rev. Thomas Hartwell Horne, B.D. of St. John's College, Cambridge, author of "An introduction to the study of the Holy Scriptures," Etc.*, 2 vols. (London: John Murray, 1836).

Hoskins, George Alexander, *Visit to the Great Oasis of the Libyan Desert; With an Account, Ancient and Modern, of the Oasis of Amun, and the Other Oases now under the Dominion of the Pasha of Egypt. By G. A. Hoskins, Esq. Author of "Travels in Ethiopia." With a Map, and Twenty Plates Illustrating the Temples, Scenery, etc., From Drawings Finished on the Spot by the Author* (London: Longman, Rees, Orme, Brown, Green, & Longman, 1837).

Huhtamo, Erkki, *Illusions in Motion: Media Archaeology of the Moving Panorama and Related Spectacles* (Cambridge, MA and London: MIT Press, 2013).

Huhtamo, Erkki, *The Roll Medium: The Origins and Development of the Moving Panorama until the 1860*, doctoral dissertation, Faculty of Humanities, University of Turku, 2008.

Humboldt, Alexander von, *Researches, Concerning the Institutions & Monuments of the Ancient Inhabitants of America, with Descriptions & Views of some of the most Striking Scenes in the Cordilleras! Written in French by Alexander de Humboldt, & Translated into English by*

Helen Maria Williams, 2 vols. (London: Longman, Hurst, Rees Orme & Brown, J. Murray and H. Colburn, 1814).

Humboldt, Alexander von, *Vues des Cordillères, et monumens des peuples indigènes de l'Amérique* (Paris: Chez F. Schoell, 1813).

Hutchison, Sidney C., 'The Royal Academy Schools, 1768–1830', *Walpole Society*, vol. 38 (1962), 123–191.

Hutton, James, *Theory of the Earth, with Proofs and Illustrations*, 2 vols. (Edinburgh: Printed for Messrs. Cadell, Junior, and Davies, London; Edinburgh: William Creech, 1795).

Hyde, Ralph (ed.), *Panoramania! The Art and Entertainment of the 'All-Embracing' View* (London: Trefoil Publications in association with Barbican Art Gallery, 1988).

Iturriaga de la Fuente, José N., *Litografía y grabado en el México de siglo XIX* (Mexico City: Cálamo Currente, 1993).

J. B. [John Britton], *A Brief Account of the Colosseum, in the Regent's Park, London: Comprising a Description of the Building; The Panoramic View from the top of St. Paul's Cathedral, The Conservatory, &c. Printed for the Proprietors, and Sold at the Exhibition; and by all Booksellers* (London, 1829).

Jenkins, Henry, *Convergence Culture: Where Old and New Media Collide* (New York and London: New York University Press, 2006).

Johns, Michael, *The City of Mexico in the Age of Díaz* (Austin: University of Texas Press, 1997).

Juarros, Domingo, *A Statistical and Commercial History of the Kingdom of Guatemala in Spanish America: Containing Important Particulars Relative to its Productions, Manufactures, Customs, &c. &c. &c. With an Account of its Conquest by the Spaniards, and a Narrative of the Principal Events down to the Present Time: From Original Records in the Archives; Actual Observation; and Other Authentic Sources. By Don Domingo Juarros, a Native of New Guatemala. Translated by J. Baily, Lieutenant R. M. Embellished with Two Maps* (London: John Hearne, 1823).

Kemp, Martin, *Seen | Unseen: Art, Science, and Intuition from Leonardo to the Hubble Telescope* (Oxford: Oxford University Press, 2006).

Kemp, Martin, *The Science of Art: Optical Themes in Western Art from Brunelleschi to Seurat* (New Haven and London: Yale University Press, 1990).

Kiek, Martin, 'Prologo, Egerton en México', *Egerton en México 1830–1842*, facsimile edition (Mexico City: Edicion Privada de Cartón y Papel de México, 1976), n.p.

Kingsborough, Edward King, Lord, *Antiquities of Mexico: Comprising Fac-similes of Ancient Mexican Paintings and Hieroglyphics, preserved in The Royal Libraries of Paris, Berlin, and Dresden; in The Imperial Library of Vienna; in The Vatican Library; in The Borgian Museum at Rome; in The Library of the Institute of Bologna; and in The Bodleian Library at Oxford. Together with The Monuments of New Spain, by M. Dupaix: with their respective scales of measurement and accompanying descriptions. The whole illustrated by many valuable Inedited Manuscripts, by Lord Kingsborough. The Drawings, On Stone, by A[gostino] Aglio*, 7 vols. (London: Robert Havell and Colnaghi, Son, and Co., 1831), vol. VIII and vol. IX published posthumously (1848).

Klonk, Charlotte, *Science and the Perception of Nature: British Landscape Art in the Late Eighteenth and Early Nineteenth Centuries* (New Haven and London: The Paul Mellon Centre for Studies in British Art, Yale University Press, 1996).

Lamb, Charles, *Palenque, or The Ancient West. A Poem* (London: Saunders and Otley, 1849).

Leask, Nigel, '"The Ghost in Chapultepec": Fanny Calderón de la Barca, William Prescott and Nineteenth-Century Mexican Travel Accounts', in *Voyages and Visions: Towards a Cultural History of Travel*, edited by Jás Elsner and Joan-Pau Rubiés (London: Reaktion Books, 1999), 184–209.

Leask, Nigel, *Curiosity and the Aesthetics of Travel Writing 1770–1840: 'From an Antique Land'* (Oxford: Oxford University Press, 2000).

Leslie, Charles Robert (ed.), *Memoirs of the Life of John Constable* (London: John Lehman, 1949 [1843]).

Levine, Philippa, *The Amateur and the Professional: Antiquarians, Historians, and Archaeologists in Victorian England, 1838–1886* (Cambridge: Cambridge University Press, 1986).

Libson, Lowell (ed.), *Cornelius Varley: The Art of Observation*, exhibition catalogue (London: Lowell Libson, 2005).

Linati, Claudio, *Costumes civils, militaires et réligieux du Mexique; dessinés d'après nature par C. Linati* (Brussels: C. Sattanino, imprimés à la Lithographie Royal de Jobard, 1828).

Loiperdinger, Martin, *Film & Schokolade: Stollwercks Geschäfte mit lebenden Bildern. KINtop Schriften 4* (Frankfurt am Main and Basel: Stroemfeld/Roter Stern, 1999).

Loiperdinger, Martin, 'Lumière's *Arrival of the Train*: Cinema's Founding Myth', *The Moving Image: The Journal of the Association of Moving Image Archivists* (Spring 2004): 89–118.

Lumière, Auguste and Louis, *Letters*, edited and annotated by Jacques Rittaud-Hutinet with the collaboration of Yvelise Dentzer, trans. Pierre Hodgson (London and Boston: Faber and Faber, 1995 [French Edition, 1994]).

MacCulloch, John, 'On Staffa', *Transactions of the Geological Society [of London]*, vol. 2 (1814), 501–509.

Maceroni, F., 'Hints on Hardening and Protecting Stone, Wood, Metal, &. and On the Preservation of Panoramas', *Mechanics' Magazine, Register, Journal and Gazette*, Vol. 24, no. 650, Saturday, 23 January 1836, 309–311.

Madox, John, *Excursions in the Holy Land, Egypt, Nubia, Syria, &c. Including a Visit to the Unfrequented District of Haouran*, 2 vols. (London: Richard Bentley, 1834).

Maillet, Arnaud, *The Claude Glass: Use and Meaning of the Black Mirror in Western Art*, trans. Jeff Fort (New York: Zone Books, 2004).

Maler, Teobert (ed. Hanns J. Prem), *Península Yucatán. Monumenta Americana herausgegeben vom Ibero-Amerikanischen Institut, Preussischer Kulturbesitz* (Berlin: Gebr. Mann Verlag, 1997).

Mannoni, Laurent, Donata Pesenti Campagnoni, David Robinson, *Light and Movement: Incunabula of the Motion Picture. 1420–1896 / Luce e movimento. Incunaboli dell'immagine animata, 1420–1896 / Lumière et mouvement. Incunables de l'image animée, 1420–1896* (Pordenone: Le Giornate del Cinema Muto/Cinémathèque française-Musée du Cinéma/Museo Nazionale del Cinema, 1995).

Manthorne, Katherine Emma, *Tropical Renaissance: North American Artists Exploring Latin America, 1839–1879* (Washington, D.C. and London: Smithsonian Institution Press, 1989).

Maudslay, A. P., 'Ruins of Palenque. Personal Narrative', in F. Ducane Godman and Osbert Salvin (eds.), *Biologia Centrali-Americana; or, Contributions to the Knowledge of the Fauna and Flora of Mexico and Central America. Archaeology. By A. P. Maudslay*, 5 vols. (London: R. H. Porter and Dulau & Co., 1889–1902), Vols. LV-LIX.

Mayer, Brantz, *Mexico As It Was and As It Is: by Brantz Mayer, Secretary of the U.S. Legation to that Country in 1841 and 1842. With Numerous Illustrations on Wood, Engraved by Butler*

(New York: J. Winchester, New World Press; London and Paris: Wiley and Putnam, 1844).

Mayer, Roberto L., 'Los dos álbumes de Pedro Gualdi', *Anales del Instituto de Investigaciones Estéticas*, 69 (1996), 81–89.

Mayer, Roberto L., 'Phillips, Rider y su álbum *Mexico Illustrated: ¿Quiénes fueron los autores de los dibujos originales?*', *Anales del Instituto de Investigaciones Estéticas*, vol. 22, no. 76 (Spring 2000), 291–306.

México y sus alrededores. Colección de monumentos, trajes y paisajes dibujados al natural y litografiados por los artistas mexicanos C. Castro, J. Campillo, L. Auda y G. Rodriguez, with essays by Márcos Arroniz, José M. Roa Bárcena, José T. de Cuellar, Francisco Gonzalez Bocanegra, José M. Gonzalez, Hilarion Frías y Soto, Luis G. Ortiz, Manuel Payno, Anselmo de la Portilla, Vicente Segura Argüelles, Francisco Zarco, Niceto de Zamacois (Mexico City: Establecimiento Litografico de Decaen, Editor, 1855 and 1856).

Miller, Angela, 'The Panorama, the Cinema, and the Emergence of the Spectacular', *Wide Angle*, 18. 2 (April 1996): 34–69.

Miller, Edward, *That Noble Cabinet: A History of the British Museum* (London: André Deutsch, 1973).

Miquel, Ángel, *Acercamientos al cine silente mexicano* (Cuernavaca: Universidad Autónoma del Estado de Morelos, 2005).

Miquel, Ángel, *Salvador Toscano* (Guadalajara, Puebla, Veracruz, Mexico City: Universidad de Guadalajara, Gobierno del Estado de Puebla, Universidad Veracruzana, Universidad Nacional Autónoma de México, 1997).

Mitchell, Julian, *The Wye Tour and its Artists* (Little Logaston, Woonton Almeley: Logaston Press, 2010).

Mitchell, Robert, *Plans, and Views in Perspective, with Descriptions, of Buildings erected in England and Scotland: and also An Essay to elucidate the Grecian, Roman and Gothic Architecture, accompanied with Designs* (London: Printed at the Oriental Press by Wilson & Co., 1801).

Montellano, Francisco, *C. B. Waite, Fotógrafo. Una mirada diversa sobre el México de principios del siglo XX* (Mexico City: Editorial Grijalbo / CONACULTA, 1994).

Morales, Alfonso and Servando Aréchiga, 'Domus Dei, Porta-Cœli', in *Guillermo Kahlo. Fotógrafico oficial de monumentos*, with articles by Jorge Alberto Manrique, Alfonso Morales, Servando Aréchiga (Mexico City: Fototeca del INAH / Casa de las Imágenes, 1992), 21–35.

Morris, David, *Thomas Hearne and his Landscape* (London: Reaktion Books, 1989).

Mühlenpfordt, E. A. E., *Die Paläste der Zapotecos zu Mitla nebst andern Alterthümern welche im Freistaate Oajaca, Mejico, aufgefunden worden, 1830–1831*, facsimile edition edited with an Introduction by Juan A. Ortega y Medina and Jesús Monjarás Ruiz, *Los Palacios de los Zapotecos en Mitla* (Mexico City: Universidad Nacional Autónoma de México, 1984).

Musser, Charles, *Edison Motion Pictures, 1890–1900: An Annotated Filmography* (Pordenone: Le Giornate del Cinema Muto; Washington, D.C.: Smithsonian Institution Press, 1997).

Musser, Charles, *The Emergence of Cinema: The American Screen to 1907. History of the American Cinema*, Vol. I (Berkeley, Los Angeles, London: University of California Press, 1990).

Nebel, Carl, *Voyage pittoresque et archéologique dans la partie la plus intéressante du Mexique par C. Nebel, architecte* (Paris: chez M. Moench and chez Paul Renouard, 1836).

Nicolson, Marjorie Hope, *Mountain Gloom and Mountain Glory: The Development of the Aesthetics of the Infinite* (Ithaca: Cornell University Press, 1959).

Norman, B[enjamin] M[oore], *Rambles in Yucatan; or, Notes of Travel through the Peninsula, Including a Visit to the Remarkable Ruins of Chi-chen, Kabah, Zayi, and Uxmal. With Numerous Illustrations*, second edition (New York: J. & H. G. Langley; Philadelphia: Thomas Cowperthwait, & Co.; New Orleans: Norman, Steel, & Co., 1843 [1842]).

Novak, Barbara, *American Painting of the Nineteenth Century: Realism, Idealism and the American Experience*, third edition with a new preface (Oxford and New York: Oxford University Press, 2007 [1980]).

Novak, Barbara, *Nature and Culture: American Landscape and Painting, 1825–1875*, third edition with a new preface (Oxford and New York: Oxford University Press, 2007 [1980]).

Nungesser, Michael (ed.), *1882 Hugo Brehme 1954, fotograf. Mexiko zwischen Revolution und Romantik / Fotógrafo. México entre revolución y romanticismo*, exhibition catalogue (Berlin: Ibero-Amerikanisches Institut Preussischer Kulturbesitz; Verlag Willmuth Arenhövel, 2004).

Oettermann, Stephan, *The Panorama: History of a Mass Medium*, trans. Deborah Lucas Schneider (New York: Zone Books, 1997 [German edition, 1980]).

Oleksijczuk, Denise Blake, *The First Panoramas: Visions of British Imperialism* (Minneapolis and London: University of Minnesota Press, 2011).

Ousby, Ian, *The Englishman's England: Taste, Travel and the Rise of Tourism* (Cambridge: Cambridge University Press, 1990).

Pacatus, I. M. [pseud. Maxim Gorky], 'Beglye zametki. Sinematograf Lyum'era', *Nizhegorodskii listok*, 4 July 1896, trans. Leda Swan, in Jay Leyda, *Kino: A History of the Russian and Soviet Film. A study of the development of Russian cinema, from 1896 to the present* (London: George Allen & Unwin, 1960), Appendix 2, 407–409.

Palmer, Susan, 'Chronology of the delivery of Sir John Soane's Royal Academy Lectures', in David Watkin, *Sir John Soane: Enlightenment Thought and the Royal Academy Lectures. Cambridge Studies in the History of Architecture* (Cambridge: Cambridge University Press, 1996), Appendix 5, 731–732.

Palmquist, Peter E. and Thomas R. Kailbourn, *Pioneer Photographers of the Far West: A Biographical Dictionary, 1840–1865* (Stanford: Stanford University Press, 2000).

Parissien, Steven (ed.), *Turner and Constable Sketching from Nature: Works from the Tate Collection*, exhibition catalogue (London: Tate Publishing, 2013).

Paz, Ireneo and Manuel Tornel, *Nueva Guía de México. En inglés, francés y castellano con toda clase de instrucciones y noticias para viajeros y hombres de negocios* (Mexico City: Imprenta de Ireneo Paz, 1882).

Pendergast, David M. (ed.), *Palenque: The Walker-Caddy Expedition to the Ancient Maya City, 1839–1840* (Norman: University of Oklahoma Press, 1967).

Phillips, John, *Mexico Illustrated, with Descriptive Letter-press, in English and Spanish* (London: E. Atchley, Library of Fine Arts, 1848).

Pidgley, Michael, 'Cornelius Varley, Cotman, and the Graphic Telescope', *The Burlington Magazine*, vol. 114, no. 836 (November 1972): 781–786.

Pío Pérez, Juan, 'A Manuscript written in the Maya language, treating of the principal epochs of the history of the peninsula of Yucatan before the Conquest', in Stephens, *Incidents of Travel in Yucatan*, 2 vols. (New York: Harper & Brothers for Henry Bill, 1848 [1843]), II, Appendix, 465–469.

Pío Pérez, Juan, 'An Almanac, adjusted according to the chronological calculation of the ancient Indians of Yucatan, for the years 1841 and 1842', in Stephens, *Incidents of Travel in Yucatan*, 2 vols. (New York: Harper & Brothers for Henry Bill, 1848 [1843]), I, Appendix, 448–459.

Pío Pérez, Juan, 'Ancient Chronology of Yucatan; or, a true exposition of the method used by the Indians for computing time', in Stephens, *Incidents of Travel in Yucatan*, 2 vols. (New York: Harper & Brothers for Henry Bill, 1848 [1843]), I, Appendix, 434–448.

Potter, Russell A., *Arctic Spectacles: The Frozen North in Visual Culture, 1818–1875* (Seattle and London: University of Washington Press, 2007).

Pratt, Mary Louise, *Imperial Eyes: Travel Writing and Transculturation* (London and New York: Routledge, 1992).

Prescott, William H., *History of the Conquest of Mexico, with a Preliminary View of the Ancient Mexican Civilization, and the Life of the Conqueror, Hernando Cortes*, new and revised edition with the author's latest corrections and additions, edited by John Foster Kirk, 2 vols. (London: George Routledge and Sons, 1874).

Prout, Samuel, *Rudiments of Landscape in Progressive Studies. Drawn, and Etched in Imitation of Chalk* (London: R. Ackermann and L. Harrison & J. C. Leigh, 1813).

Rafael, Rafael de, 'Escuela Mexicana de pintura' [5 June 1851] in 'Tercera exposición de la Academia Nacional de San Carlos de México', *El Espectador de México*, 4 January 1851 - 11 October 1851; reprinted in Ida Rodríguez Prampolini, *La crítica de arte en México en el siglo XIX*, 3 vols. (Mexico City: Instituto de Investigaciones Estéticas, Universidad Nacional Autónoma de México, second edition, 1997 [1964]), I, 218–284; 'Escuela Mexicana de pintura', 245–252.

Rajnai, Miklos assisted by Marjorie Allthorpe-Guyton, *John Sell Cotman: Drawings of Normandy in Norwich Castle Museum* (Norwich: Norfolk Museums Service, 1975).

Raymond's Vacation Excursions: New Orleans, Mexico and California (Boston: American Printing & Engraving Co., 1890).

Redford, Bruce, *Dilettanti: The Antic and the Antique in Eighteenth-Century England* (Los Angeles: J. Paul Getty Museum/Getty Research Institute, 2008).

Revised Guide and Handbook for Travellers to Mexico City and Vicinity. With Map and Historical Summary (Mexico City: American Book and Printing Company, 1922).

Reynolds, Joshua, *Seven Discourses delivered in the Royal Academy by the President* (London: T. Cadell, 1778).

Rivera Cambas, Manuel, *México pintoresco, artístico y monumental. Vistas, descripción, anécdotas y episodios de los lugars más notables de la capital y de los estados, aun de las poblaciónes cortas, pero de importancia geográfica ó histórica. Obra ilustrada con gran número de hermosas litografías, representando las iglesias, plazas y calles principales, fuentes … todo cuanto puede señalar el grado de nuestro adelanto y el aspecto físico, moral é intelectual de la República. Las descripciones contienen datos científicos, históricos y estadísticos*, 3 vols. (Mexico City: Imprenta de la Reforma, 1880–1883).

Robinson, Edward, *Researches in Biblical Palestine, Mount Sinai, and Arabia Petræa: A Journal of Travels in the Year 1838*, 3 vols. (London: John Murray, 1841).

Rodríguez, José Antonio, 'Hugo Brehme. La construcción de un imaginario nacionalista', in Michael Nungesser (ed.), *1882 Hugo Brehme 1954, fotograf. Mexiko zwischen Revolution und Romantik / Fotógrafo. México entre revolución y romanticismo* (Berlin: Ibero-Amerikanisches Institut Preussischer Kulturbesitz; Verlag Willmuth Arenhövel, 2004), 28–43.

Rosenfeld, Sybil, *Georgian Scene Painters and Scene Painting* (Cambridge: Cambridge University Press, 1981).

Ruskin, John, 'The Moral of Landscape', *Modern Painters*, second edition in complete form, 5 vols. (Orpington and London: George Allen, 1892 [1843–1860]), III, 286–314.

Russell, Ronald, *Guide to British Topographical Prints* (Newton Abbot, London, North Pomfret, VT: David & Charles, 1979).

Sandby, William, *The History of the Royal Academy of Arts from its Foundation in 1768 to the Present Time. With Biographical Notes of all the Members*, 2 vols. (London: Longman, Green, Longman, Roberts & Green, 1862).

Schaaf, Larry J., *Out of the Shadows: Herschel, Talbot and the Invention of Photography* (New Haven and London: Yale University Press, 1992).

Schaaf, Larry J., *Tracings of Light: Sir John Herschel and the Camera Lucida. Drawings in the Graham Nash Collection* (San Francisco: The Friends of Photography, 1989).

Schnapp, Alain, *The Discovery of the Past: The Origins of Archaeology* (London: British Museum Press, 1996 [French edition, 1993]).

Schoolcraft, Henry R., 'The Red Hand', in John Lloyd Stephens, *Incidents of Travel in Yucatan*, 2 vols. (New York: Harper & Brothers for Henry Bill, 1848 [1843]), II, Appendix, 476–478.

Selous, Henry Courtney, *Journal kept by a painter while working for R. Burford and the Leicester Square Panorama, 1833 Oct. 29 - 1834 May 10*, manuscript, MSL/1979/5117, pressmark 86.SS.67, National Art Library, Victoria and Albert Museum.

Shenstone, William, *The Works in Verse and Prose, of William Shenstone, Esq; Most of which were never before printed*, 2 vols. (London: R. and J. Dodsley, 1764).

Shenstone, William, *The Works in Verse and Prose, of William Shenstone, Esq; Vol. III. Containing Letters to Particular Friends, from the Year 1739 to 1763*, vol. 3 (London: J. Dodsley, 1769).

Smiles, Sam, *The Image of Antiquity: Ancient Britain and the Romantic Imagination* (New Haven and London: Yale University Press, for The Paul Mellon Centre for Studies in British Art, 1994).

Soane, John, MS, 'Lecture the First Royal Institution 7th June 1817', Soane Case 157, Research Library, Sir John Soane's Museum.

Soane, John, MS, 'Lectures on Architecture, Royal Institution 1820', 'Royal Institution. Lecture the 3d, Read, Saturday the 10th June 1820 - One hour and six Minutes', Soane Case 158, Research Library, Sir John Soane's Museum.

Sonnini de Manoncourt, C. S. [Charles-Nicolas-Sigisbert], *Travels in Upper and Lower Egypt: Undertaken by Order of the Old Government of France; by C. S. Sonnini, Engineer in the French Navy, and Member of Several Scientific and Literary Societies. Illustrated with Forty Engravings; Consisting of Portraits, Views, Plans, a Geographical Chart, Antiquities, Plants, Animals, &c. Drawn on the Spot, under the Author's Inspection. Translated from the French by Henry Hunter, D.D.*, 3 vols. (London: Printed for John Stockdale, 1799).

Southey, Robert, *Life and Correspondence of Robert Southey*, edited by Charles Cuthbert Southey, 6 vols. (London: Longman, Brown, Green, and Longmans, 1849–1850).

Stephens, John Lloyd, *Incidents of Travel in Central America, Chiapas, and Yucatan*, 2 vols. (New York: Harper & Brothers; London: John Murray, 1841).

Stephens, John Lloyd, edited and with an Introduction by Victor Wolfgang von Hagen, *Incidents of Travel in Egypt, Arabia Petræa, and the Holy Land* (Mineola, NY: Dover Publications, Inc., 1996 [1837]).

Stephens, John Lloyd, *Incidents of Travel in Yucatan*, 2 vols. (New York: Harper & Brothers for Henry Bill, 1848 [1843]).

Stoddard, John L., 'Mexico', *John L. Stoddard's Lectures, illustrated and embellished with views of the world's famous places and people, being the identical discourses delivered during the past eighteen years under the title of The Stoddard Lectures*, 10 vols. (Boston: Balch Brothers Co., 1901 [1898]), VII, 227–336.

Strudwick, Nigel and Helen Strudwick, *Thebes in Egypt: A Guide to the Tombs and Temples of Ancient Luxor* (Ithaca: Cornell University Press, 1999).

Stuart, David and George Stuart, *Palenque: Eternal City of the Maya* (London: Thames & Hudson, 2008).

Stuart, James and Nicholas Revett, *The Antiquities of Athens. Measured and Delineated by James Stuart F.R.S. and F.S.A. and Nicholas Revett. Painters and Architects,* 3 vols. (London: John Haberkorn, 1762–1794).

Talbot, H. F. [William Henry Fox], 'Some Account of the Art of Photogenic Drawing', *The London and Edinburgh Philosophical Magazine and Journal of Science*, vol. 14, no. 87 (March 1839): 196–208.

Talbot, William Henry Fox, *The Pencil of Nature* (London: Longman, Brown, Green, & Longmans, 1844).

Taylor, Richard and Ian Christie (eds.), *The Film Factory: Russian and Soviet Cinema in Documents 1896–1939* (London: Routledge and Kegan Paul, 1988).

Tenorio-Trillo, Mauricio, *Mexico at the World's Fairs: Crafting a Modern Nation* (Berkeley, Los Angeles, London: University of California Press, 1996).

Terry, T. Philip, *Terry's Mexico Handbook for Travellers by T. Philip Terry with two maps and twenty-five plans* (Mexico City: Sonora News Company, Publishers; Boston: Houghton Mifflin Co., 1909).

The Repertory of Arts and Manufactures: Consisting of Original Communications, Specifications of Patent Inventions, and Selections of Useful Practical Papers from the Transactions of the Philosophical Societies of all Nations, &c. &c., Vol. IV (London, Printed for the Proprietors,1796).

The Repertory of Arts, Manufactures, and Agriculture. Consisting of Original Communications, Specifications of Patent Inventions, Practical and Interesting Papers, Selected from Philosophical Transactions and Scientific Journals of all Nations. Monthly Intelligence Relating to the Useful Arts, Proceedings of Learned Societies, and Notices of all Patents Granted for Inventions. 10 [Second Series], No. 57, February 1807 (London: J. Wyatt, Repertory Office, 1807).

Thompson, Jason, *Sir Gardner Wilkinson and His Circle* (Austin: University of Texas Press, 1992).

Tovar de Teresa, Guillermo, Introductory texts by Enrique Krauze and José Iturriaga, *The City of Palaces: Chronicle of a Lost Heritage*, 2 vols. (Mexico City: Vuelta, 1990).

Transactions of the American Ethnological Society, vol. 1 (New York: Bartlett & Welford; London: Wiley & Putnam, 1845).

Trübner , Nicholas (ed.), *Trübner's Bibliographical Guide to American Literature. A Classed List of Books Published in the United States of America during the Last Forty Years. With Bibliographical Introduction, Notes, and Alphabetical Index* (London: Trübner and Co., 1859).

Tsivian, Yuri (ed. Richard Taylor), *Early Cinema in Russia and its Cultural Reception*, trans. Alan Bodger, with a foreword by Tom Gunning (London and New York: Routledge, 1994 [Russian edition, 1991]).

Upton, Dell, 'Inventing the Metropolis: Civilization and Urbanity in Antebellum New York', in Catherine Hoover Voorsanger and John K. Howat (eds.), *Art and the Empire City: New York, 1825–1861* (New York: The Metropolitan Museum of Art; New Haven and London: Yale University Press, 2000), 3–45.

Varley, Cornelius, *A Treatise on Optical Drawing Instruments by Cornelius Varley, Artist, Member of the Society of Arts, The Microscopical Society, etc; also A Method of Preserving Pictures in Oil and in Water Colours* (London: Horne, Thornwaite, & Wood, 1845).

Velásquez, Pedro (pseud.), *see* Phineas T. Barnum.

Viñas, Moisés, *Índice general del cine mexicano* (Mexico City: CONACULTA/IMCINE, 2005).

Vitruvius Pollio, Marcus, *The Architecture of Marcus Vitruvius Pollio, in Ten Books. Translated from the Latin by Joseph Gwilt, fellow of the Society of Antiquaries of London* (London: Priestley and Weale, 1826).

Waldeck, Jean-Frédéric, Comte de, *Voyage pittoresque et archéologique dans la province d'Yucatan (Amérique centrale), pendant les années 1834 et 1836 par Frédéric de Waldeck, dédié à la mémoire de feu le Vicomte de Kingsborough* (Paris: Bellizard Dufour et C°; London: J. and W. Boone; Bossange Barthès et Lowell, 1838).

Walls, Laura Dassow, *The Passage to Cosmos: Alexander von Humboldt and the Shaping of America* (Chicago and London: University of Chicago Press, 2009).

Ward, Elizabeth Emily, *Six Views of the Most Important Towns and Mining Districts upon the Table Land of Mexico. Drawn by Mrs. H. G. Ward, and Engraved by Mr. Pye. With a statistical account of each* (London: Henry Colburn, 1829).

Ward, Henry George, *Mexico in 1827. By H. G. Ward. His Majesty's Chargé d'Affaires in that Country during the years 1825, 1826, and part of 1827* (London: Henry Colburn, 1828).

Watkin, David, *Sir John Soane: Enlightenment Thought and the Royal Academy Lectures. Cambridge Studies in the History of Architecture* (Cambridge: Cambridge University Press, 1996).

West, Francis, *A Description of the Camera-Lucida for Drawing in True Perspective, the Invention of Dr. Wollaston, with Full Directions how to Use and how to Choose a Good Instrument, and the Defects to which Bad Ones are Liable. With the Observations of Captain Basil Hall* (London: Effingham Wilson (Royal Exchange) and Chappell (Pall Mall), 1831).

West, Thomas, *A Guide to the Lakes, in Cumberland, Westmorland, and Lancashire. By the author of The Antiquities of Furness. The Third Edition, Revised Throughout and Greatly Enlarged* (London: B. Law; Richardson and Urquhart; J. Robson; and Kendal: W. Pennington, 1784 [originally published by Richardson and Urquhart in 1780].

Widdifield, Stacie G., *The Embodiment of the National in Late Nineteenth-Century Mexican Painting* (Tucson: University of Arizona Press, 1996).

Wilcox, Scott B., 'Unlimiting the Bounds of Painting', in Hyde, *Panoramania! The Art and Entertainment of the 'All-Embracing' View* (London: Trefoil Publications in association with Barbican Art Gallery, 1988), 13–44.

Wilcox, Scott Barnes, *The Panorama and Related Exhibitions in London*, MLitt dissertation, University of Edinburgh, 1976.

Wilton, Andrew, *Turner as Draughtsman* (Aldershot and Basingstoke: Ashgate Press, 2006).

Wollaston, William Hyde, 'Description of the Camera Lucida', *A Journal of Natural Philosophy, Chemistry, and the Arts*, 12 (June 1807): 1–5.

Wood, Robert, *The Ruins of Balbec, otherwise Heliopolis in Cœlosyria* (London, 1757).

Wood, Robert, *The Ruins of Palmyra, otherwise Tedmore, in the Desart* (London, 1753).

Wordsworth, William, *Poetical Works.* Introduction and Notes, edited by Thomas Hutchinson, revised by Ernest de Selincourt (London, New York, Toronto: Oxford University Press, 1936).

Anonymous Articles, Notices, and Reviews

'Aboriginal Structures', *The North American Review*, Vol. 51, No. 109 (1840): 396–433.

'American Tourist Association. A Large Party Arrive by Mexican Central', *The Mexican Herald*, 2 January 1898, 1.

'Ancient Ruins in Central America', *Chambers's Edinburgh Journal*, New Series, Number 517, 25 December 1841, 390–391.

'Books published today', *The Literary Gazette; and Journal of the Belles Lettres, Arts, Sciences, &c.*no. 302, 2 November 1822, 702.

'Bullock's Six Months in Mexico', *The Literary Gazette; and Journal of the Belles Lettres, Arts, Sciences, &c.*, no. 389, 3 July 1824, 422–423.

'Central America, Ancient and Modern', *The Dublin University Magazine, A Literary and Political Journal*, Vol. 19, No. 110 (February 1842): 189–200.

'Description of the Ruins of an Ancient City discovered near Palenque, Kingdom of Guatemala, in America: from the Original Report of Captain Don Antonio del Rio: followed by a Critical Investigation into the History of the Americas, by Doctor Paul F. Cabrera', *The Literary Gazette; and Journal of the Belles Lettres, Arts, Sciences, &c.*, no. 303, 9 November 1822, 705.

'El Nuevo Edificio de Correos', *El Mundo Illustrado*, year 14, vol. 1, no. 6, 10 February 1907, n.p. (11).

'El Palacio de Correos', *El Mundo Illustrado*, year 14, vol. 1, no. 5, 3 February 1907, n.p. (10–11).

'El Templo de la Enseñanza', *El Mundo Ilustrado*, year 8, no. 10, 4 March 1906, n.p. (10–11).

'El Viaje Presidencial á Tehuantepec', *El Tiempo Ilustrado*, year 7, no. 5, 3 February 1907, 76–86.

'El Viaje Presidencial á Yucatan de Chapultepec', *El Tiempo Ilustrado*, year 6, no. 6, 4 February 1906, 100–102.

'Gates Excursionists. One Hundred and Eight Strong Arrive in Three Sections', *The Mexican Herald*, 3 March 1898, 8.

'Gates Excursions', *The Mexican Herald*, 2 March 1898, 5.

'*Incidents of Travel in Central America, Chiapas, and Yucatan*. By John L. Stephens', *The Quarterly Review* Vol. 69, No. 137 (March 1842): 52–91.

'*Incidents of Travel in Yucatan*. By John L. Stephens', *The Monthly Review, New and Improved Series*, Vol. 1, No. 4 (April 1843): 542–550.

'*Incidents of Travel in Yucatan*', *The North American Review*, no. 120 (July 1843): 86–108.

'Joyas del Arte Cristiano', *El Mundo Ilustrado*, year 8, no. 11, 11 March 1906, n.p. (13, 15).

'La novedad del día en México. - El Cinematógrafo Lumière', *El Mundo Ilustrado*, year 3, vol. 2, no. 8, Sunday, 23 August 1896, 118–119.

'Las grandes obras de Tehuantepec', *El Mundo Ilustrado*, year 14, vol. 1, no. 4, 27 January 1907, n.p. (8–9).

[Morley, Henry], 'Our Phantom Ship. Central America', *Household Words*, vol. 2, no. 48, 22 February 1851, 516–522.

'Mr. Bullock's Travels and Acquisitions in Mexico', 'Arts and Sciences' column, *The Literary Gazette, and Journal of Belles Lettres, Arts, Sciences, &c.*, No. 363, Saturday, 3 January 1824, 8–9.

'Mr. Stephens [*sic*] New Work - Antiquities of Central America', *Chambers's Edinburgh Journal. New Series*, no. 502, 11 September 1841, 266–267.

'Mrs. Somerville, "On the Connexion of the Physical Sciences"', *The Quarterly Review* 51 (1834): 54–68.

'Ordnance Survey of London and the Environs', *The Illustrated London News*, vol. 12, no. 322, Saturday, 24 June 1848, 414.

'Palenque', 'Arts and Sciences' column, *The Literary Gazette; and Journal of the Belles Lettres, Arts, Sciences, &c.*, no. 770, 22 October 1831, 683.

'Panorama of Jerusalem', *The Literary Gazette; and Journal of the Belles Lettres, Arts, Sciences, &c.*, no. 950, Saturday, 4 April 1835, 218.

'Panorama', *Supplement to the Fouth, Fifth and Sixth Editions of the Encyclopædia Britannica* (Edinburgh: Archibald Constable and Company; London: Hurst, Robinson, and Company, 1824), VI, 108–109.

[Review], *Incidents of Travel in Central America, Chiapas, and Yucatan, The Athenaeum Journal of Literature, Science, and the Fine Arts for the year 1841*, no. 718, 31 July 1841, 574–577.

'Review of *Incidents of Travel in Central America, Chiapas, and Yucatan*', *The North American Review*, Vol. 53, No. 113 (October 1841): 479–506.

'Review of *Incidents of Travel in Central America, Chiapas, and Yucatan*', *The Edinburgh Review or Critical Journal*, Vol. 75, No. 152 (April-July 1842): 397–421.

'Six Months in Mexico. By William Bullock', *The Literary Gazette; and Journal of the Belles Lettres, Arts, Sciences, &c.*, no. 387, 19 June 1824, 390–392.

'Sketches of Society, Sights of London, Etc. No. V', *The Literary Gazette; and Journal of the Belles Lettres, Arts, Sciences, &c.*, no. 377, 10 April 1824, 236–237.

'Some Observations Caused by the recent introduction by Mr. Bullock into England of rare and curious specimens of Mexican Antiquity; intended shortly to be submitted by him to the inspection of the public', *The Classical Journal: for March and June 1824*, Vol. 29, No. 57 (1824): 174–193.

'Stephens's Travels in Yucatan', *The Dublin University Magazine, A Literary and Political Journal*, Vol. 22, No. 128 (August 1843): 204–222.

'The Colosseum', 'Fine Arts' column, *The Literary Gazette; and Journal of the Belles Lettres, Arts, Sciences, &c.* No. 626. Saturday, 17 January 1829, 42–43.

'The Grafton Excursion', *The Mexican Herald*, 1 February 1898, 5.

'The Panorama', *Somerset House Gazette, and Literary Museum: or, weekly miscellany of Fine Arts, and Literary Chit Chat,* No. 36, 12 June 1824, 151–153.

'Travels and Acquisitions in Mexico; By Mr. Bullock: second Paper', 'Arts and Sciences' column, *The Literary Gazette, and Journal of Belles Lettres, Arts, Sciences, &c.*, No. 364, Saturday, 10 January 1824, 25–26.

'Ward Excursionists', *The Mexican Herald*, 8 March 1898, 1.

[Weir, William and W. H. Wills], 'Short Cuts Across the Globe', *Household Words*, vol. 1, no. 3, 13 April 1850, 65–68.

Illustrations

Colour Plates

Figures

Index